Claudia
Galetti

REAL ESTATE LAW

Second Edition

FRANK GIBSON
The Ohio State University

JAMES KARP
Syracuse University

ELLIOT KLAYMAN
The Ohio State University

Longman Financial Services Publishing, Inc.
a subsidiary of Longman Financial Services Institute

While a great deal of care has been taken to provide accurate and current information, the ideas, suggestions, general principles and conclusions presented in this text are subject to local, state and federal laws and regulations, court cases and any revisions of same. The reader thus is urged to consult legal counsel regarding any points of law—this publication should not be used as a substitute for competent legal advice.

© 1987, 1983 by Longman Group USA Inc.

Published by Real Estate Education Company/Chicago,
a Longman Group USA company

87 88 89   10 9 8 7 6 5 4 3 2

Sr. Acquisitions Editor: Richard Hagle
Acquisitions Editor: Paul Revenko-Jones
Sponsoring Editor: Jeny Sejdinaj
Copyeditor: Chris Benton
Cover/Interior Design: Robert L. Cooley
Production Coordinator: Susan Gilbert
Illustrations: Billy Fisher

Library of Congress Cataloging-in-Publication Data

Gibson, Frank F.
  Real estate law.

  Includes index.
  1. Real property—United States.   I. Karp, James.
II. Klayman, Elliot I.   III. Title.
KF570.G5 1987   346.7304'3   86-26204
ISBN 0-88462-614-8   347.30643

Contents

Preface

This text was written primarily for men and women preparing for or leading a career in some phase of the real estate business. The material is general in nature and focuses primarily upon the substantive body of real estate law, although principles and teaching materials necessary for applied skills are highlighted. We indicate instances where substantial differences exist in state law or in the use of a term. We are hopeful that instructors will emphasize specific rules and usage of local law, yet at the same time we believe that educated real estate professionals should be familiar with the existing variations in the law.

In recent years, modern technology has provided educators with many ingenious and effective teaching aids. As professional educators, however, we are convinced that from a viewpoint of economy, usefulness and practicality the textbook continues to be the most effective method of supplementing classroom instruction. In spite of this, while working on this text, we often questioned the wisdom of adding another book to a field where a number of excellent works already exist. Our justification is a shared belief that the pedagogical format employed will help educators teach and students learn real estate law most efficiently.

Because the fundamental principles of real estate law developed in a society in which economic and social conditions differed from those that exist today, these principles are difficult for most people to grasp. Additionally, real estate law—because of land's historic importance as a source of wealth—is replete with terms that are hardly household words today. Law, like many subjects, has its own, some might say, peculiar vocabulary. These characteristics often foster in the uninitiated a lack of confidence and a negative attitude toward the subject matter.

In order to overcome these obstacles to understanding, we have integrated definitions of terms and short explanations of principles with the textual material. Following each definition, we provide a more detailed explanation of the term or principle, relating it to other terms and principles and to real estate law in general. In addition, we frequently relate the term or principle to the work of the real estate professional by providing illustrations.

The illustrations are called Case Briefs or Case Examples. The Case Briefs are abstracts of actual cases. (In some instances we have created a hypothetical situation that illustrates a point of law that came out of the case cited because the actual case was not relevant in total.) The Case Examples are hypothetical, although a few are modifications of actual cases. Case Examples are used because in some instances no actual case was found that clearly illustrated the point that we were trying to stress.

To increase the usefulness of the text we have added new features to this second edition. The *glossary* provides the reader convenient access to the terms introduced in the text. The *Alphabetical Index of Cases* allows for quick reference to particular cases. The *Subject Index of Cases* refers readers to cases relating to a particular area of study.

Although the sequence of the chapters seems logical to us, it is not the only logical order. For the classroom the chapters can probably be used effectively in several different ways and adapted to student needs.

Each of us received help from many people, and for this we thank them. We would like to acknowledge the following reviewers for their helpful suggestions and recommendations on several drafts of the manuscript: Agu J. Ananaba, Jr., Norfolk State University; Floyd M. Baird, J.D., First National Bank and Trust Company of Tulsa; John Ballou, Moraine Valley Community College; Leo Kearney O'Drudy, Jr., University of Virginia; Albert M. Suguitan, GRI, Southern Illinois University; Nancy Daggett White, Mississippi County Community College. Thanks are also extended to Donald Boren, Christian Day, Gordon Gulitz, Dugald Hudson, Glen Laughlin, Henry Mallue and Nancy Melia for their contributions to the first edition of this text. The end-of-chapter summaries were originally written by Eleanor McConnell. Professor Gibson wishes especially to thank Ms. Barb Gladman, who typed his portion of the manuscript in spite of his continued refusal to dot his *i*s. We want additionally to extend special appreciation to the following law students: Timothy K. Williams and Wendy Siegelbaum for their capable research assistance, as well as Sarah Jane Wilson and M. Michael Smith, who proofread portions of the manuscript.

Frank F. Gibson, J.D., M.A.
Associate Director of the Center for Real Estate Education and Research; Professor of Business Law in the College of Administrative Science, Faculty of Finance, The Ohio State University

James P. Karp, J.D.
Professor and Chairman of the Department of Law and Public Policy, The School of Management, Syracuse University

Elliot I. Klayman, J.D., L.L.M.
Associate Professor of Business Law in the College of Administrative Science, Faculty of Finance, The Ohio State University

1
Introduction to Law and Legal Systems

LAW AND THE REAL ESTATE BUSINESS

Many aspects of the real estate business are closely associated with law. In fact, only the world of finance may be more closely controlled by law. Almost any professional activity of a broker, salesperson, appraiser or investor involves certain legal restrictions. For this reason, people employed to do these jobs, as well as people employed to do many other jobs in real estate, have a genuine need to know about the law and legal systems. The more extensive their knowledge, the more effectively will they be able to do their jobs.

Real estate professionals deal not only with lawyers but also with recording clerks, building inspectors, tax officials, zoning board employees and personnel from state and federal housing agencies. All of these people have specialized functions in the legal system. Understanding what they do and some of the responsibilities of their jobs increases the real estate professional's ability to work effectively with them. Many private individuals with whom salespeople and brokers come in contact also have specialized knowledge of the law; loan officers and appraisers are examples. Real estate professionals who have similar knowledge will be able to work more effectively with other specialists and improve their professional image at the same time.

Legal knowledge is especially important to people who sell real estate. They are involved in the real estate transaction at a critical point as far as legal input is concerned. Clients and customers will of-

1

ten question them about legal matters or the advisability of consulting an attorney. Although sales personnel should never give legal advice, a knowledge of law will help them develop an awareness of situations in which a lawyer should be consulted. Because legal knowledge is considered so important, some states require salespeople and brokers engaged in selling real estate to complete a formal course in real estate law.

Although this book is devoted to a study of real estate law, to some extent that designation is misleading. Real estate law cannot really be separated from other types of law. A famous jurist once said, "Law is a seamless web"; nevertheless, because of the complexity of law, people who want to understand it often consider it in small segments. The boundaries of these segments are never exact, nor is there general agreement on what each segment includes. So, initially, the reader must realize that, although much of what is said about real estate law applies to law in general, some strands of the "seamless web" are more important to the real estate business than others. This book deals primarily with these strands.

Most of this book discusses specific rules important to real estate people. In this first chapter, however, the book takes a broader look at law and the legal system. This chapter attempts to clarify the law by looking at some of its functions, where it is found and the structure in which it operates.

WHAT DOES LAW DO?

Defining law has been a challenge to thoughtful men and women throughout the ages. Although numerous definitions have been proposed, no single one is satisfactory. Each civilization, each age, each segment of society has different ideas about what law is. This fact is readily understandable; ideas about the law reflect the way people think about such things as religion, ethics, economics and morality. Some people contend that nothing can be law unless it is also moral. Others argue that law is merely the command of the sovereign or that law is anything the courts will enforce as law.

In the absence of general agreement of what law is, one way to understand it better is not to define it but to look at some of the things it does. Law is one of a number of institutions that people have developed to solve some of the difficult problems that arise out of societal life. Although other institutions direct their resources to the same difficult questions, in the Western world legal solutions generally provide the ultimate answer.

Consider, for example, a dispute between a brother and a sister over ownership of certain property. Ordinarily the dispute will be solved in consultation with other members of the family. If the dispute is really serious, perhaps neighbors, the church or even an employer will become involved. If the dispute remains unsettled, however, eventually the parties will take their problems to a court. What then are some of the major purposes of law and the legal system?

Provides Order

Order is a need fundamental to every society. Without order no society can survive. Where there is chaos, men and women must spend inordinate amounts of their time protecting themselves, their families and their possessions. This leaves them with little time to obtain from a hostile natural world those items that are necessary for enjoyable, productive lives. The first task of law then is to provide conditions that are conducive to an orderly society so that people can devote their time to winning their livelihoods and trying to live fulfilling lives.

Settles Disputes

Order is difficult to maintain. To maintain order, parties that have a dispute must reasonably expect that it can be settled. In addition, for resolution of the dispute to be satisfactory, the parties must be confident that their controversy will be settled fairly and within a reasonable time. The legal system provides a forum for settling many disputes between individuals. Local, state and federal courts as well as administrative tribunals offer the facilities and supervise the processes that resolve many problems. The courts also indirectly support individuals who use means such as mediation and arbitration to settle problems.

If public facilities were not available, the parties in many instances would resort to self-help. Threats and eventually violence would be involved in the resolution of disputes. Both of these would lead to retaliation and the consequent disruption of society.

Protects Expectations

The kind of order that is necessary for a society to function effectively extends beyond the elimination of violence and strife. People need the assurance of reliability in their dealings with others. In the modern world, planning is vital in almost everything that we do. Unless we can depend upon promises and commitments that are made to us, our efforts to plan are futile. Law protects reasonable expectations of the future. The legal system provides compensation if anticipations based upon promises are not met. Protection of expectations is especially necessary to the real estate business. The legal relationships and objectives of leases, land contracts, insurance policies, listing agreements and employment all depend upon the protection of expectations.

Prevents Exploitation

One of the significant contributions that law can make is to prevent exploitation. Many laws that are important to real estate people have this as their primary purpose. Laws allowing a remedy for victims of false advertising, fraud and misrepresentation are among those that prevent the exploitation of one individual by another. In a democracy, laws also prevent the exploitation of an individual by government. An illustration would be those constitutional provisions that require the government to provide just compensation when it takes private property. Although the state does have the right of eminent domain (to be discussed later in the book), this right cannot be exercised unless the individual's property is to be used for public purpose. In addition, an owner who feels that the compensation offered by the state is insufficient has a right to a judicial determination of a fair price.

Ensures Equality

Justice is an integral part of what we have come to call "the good life"—an ordered society. Although the concept of justice differs from one society to another, the promotion of justice is usually considered a major responsibility of law. In the United States, one significant contribution that law makes in promoting justice is to ensure that equality of treatment exists for all Americans. In a democracy, government should not permit different treatment of people because of their race, nationality, religion or sex. A number of laws important to the daily work of real estate personnel are intended to ensure equal treatment for all people.

SOURCES OF LAW

The answer to many legal questions comes from life's experiences. As a person learns in school, on the job or through daily living, laws important to that person become part of his or her knowledge of the manner in which things operate. Sometimes legal questions arise that are not answerable from experience. How does one find the answers to these questions? To what source does the student, the real estate professional, the lawyer or the judge turn to find out what the law is?

One of the prevailing myths about law is that all laws are found in nicely indexed, officially published volumes of statutes enacted by a legislative body. According to this belief, all a person has to do to answer a legal question is to locate the correct page in the right book, and the law will be there in clear black letters. Unfortunately, few legal questions are answered this simply.

In order to answer a legal question involving real estate, a person might have to examine one source or a number of different sources. Sometimes an answer will be found in a state constitution or the federal Constitution. Most often, however, people find the answer to real estate law questions in court opinions, often referred to as *precedents*, in statutes and in the regulations of administrative agencies. The different sources of law are discussed in the paragraphs that follow.

Constitutions

A basic source of law, constitutions provide the framework within which the federal and state governments must operate. Ordinarily one does not associate real estate law with constitutional problems, but at least two functions of constitutions are important to the real estate business. First, the U.S. Constitution allocates power between the states and the federal government. Because the states generally have retained power over local matters, most real estate law is state law. On the other hand, inasmuch as the states have given the federal government power to regulate businesses affecting interstate commerce, numerous federal statutes apply to the real estate business. At present, many people in the field are concerned with the application to real estate of federal statutes such as the Sherman and Clayton Acts. Bankruptcy statutes and consumer protection laws like "Truth-in-Lending," the Real Estate Settlement Procedures Act and environmental protection legislation are other examples of federal law that apply to real estate.

A second function of constitutions—both state and federal—is the protection of individual rights, including private property. Constitutional provisions require that the law be applied equally to all; in addition, they prohibit government from depriving a person of life, liberty or property without due process. This means that an individual's property can be taken by government only under limited circumstances. But the protection accorded the individual is far from absolute. Both the power of eminent domain and the police power allow government to acquire private property.

Precedent

A published opinion of an appellate court that serves as authority for determining a legal question in a later case with similar facts.

A distinctive feature of the law of English-speaking countries is its reliance upon cases decided by appellate courts as a source of law. Reports of these cases are published in opinions, which provide the answers to many legal questions.

CASE EXAMPLE

Clayborne and his adult daughter lived in a house that Clayborne owned. At the request of the daughter, Dexter painted the house. Clayborne did not authorize the work, but he knew that it was being done and raised no objection. Clayborne refused to pay Dexter, arguing that he had not contracted to have the house painted.

Dexter asked his attorney if Clayborne was legally liable to pay him. The attorney told Dexter that in their state several published appellate court decisions had established that, when a home-owner allows work to be done on his home by a person who would ordinarily expect to be paid, a duty to pay exists. The attorney stated that, based on these *precedents*, it was advisable for Dexter to bring a suit to collect the reasonable value of the work that he had done.

In the legal system of English-speaking countries, judges are obligated to follow principles established by prior cases (precedent). This obligation is ingrained in our system. The extent to which a court is governed by precedent is difficult to assess. Although the practice of following precedent is not a legal duty, it is definitely more than a tradition. A judge who failed to follow precedent would not be convicted of a crime, but he or she ordinarily would be reversed and in extreme cases censured or possibly impeached. People trained in our system generally consider reliance upon precedent an effective and fair way to reach a decision, and the concept is fundamental to American law.

The obligation to follow precedent is limited by a number of factors. A court need not follow precedent established in another state, although in reaching decisions courts sometimes consider precedent from other states when their own state has no case law on the subject. Lower courts are bound to follow decisions rendered by higher courts of their state. Again, failure to do so may result merely in the lower court's decision being reversed. The highest appellate court in a state can overrule its own precedent. Although this occurs on occasion, most state appellate courts overrule reluctantly because they believe that certainty is a desirable characteristic of law. The reluctance to overrule is often seen in private areas such as real estate law, for certainty is deemed very important where property rights are involved. A court will overrule a prior decision when the rule of law was applied incorrectly in the first place or when the rule is not considered applicable because of a change in circumstances.

Courts and attorneys frequently avoid the effect of a previous case by distinguishing it from the case under consideration. A case is distinguished when a significant factual difference can be pointed out between the two situations. For example, assume that, in defending Clayborne in a suit brought by Dexter, Clayborne's attorney asks the court to dismiss the case, because she has found the published decision of a case with like facts where the appellate court held that the homeowner was not required to pay. Dexter's attorney argues that in that case the homeowner was on vacation and did not know that the work was being done. As Clayborne knew that his house was being painted, the two cases are different and can be distinguished. If the court agrees that the two cases are significantly different, *i.e.*, can be distinguished, it will decide that the earlier decision is not precedent and therefore not controlling in deciding the case before it.

Law that evolves from published opinions of appellate courts or precedent is often called *judge-made law* or *decisional law*. In England, reliance upon previous decisions and upon custom and tradition created a law that was common to the entire country. Therefore, the law based upon prior opinions is often referred to as *common law*. Sometimes people have difficulty accepting the idea that in these opinions statutes are not involved in any manner. In fact, often no statute exists that can be used to settle the dispute.

A modern example of judge-made law is found in those appellate decisions that impose responsibility upon builders of defective homes. Before World War II, the builder of a defective home had little legal responsibility for injury or property damage once the home was sold. The buyer was required to make his or her own inspection of the premises. On the basis of this inspection, the buyer accepted responsibility for all defects, relieving the builder of responsibility for any defective construction. The courts were applying the ancient doctrine of *caveat emptor*—"let the buyer beware."

During the 1950s and the 1960s, courts began to recognize the unfairness of this rule. They began to allow buyers of new homes to recover for personal injury and property damage resulting from defective construction. In numerous states, this modification of the law from *caveat emptor* to *caveat venditor* ("let the seller beware") was accomplished without legislation. As one state court commented:

> If at one time . . . the rule of caveat emptor had application to the sale of a new house by a vendor-builder, that time is now past. The decisions and legal writings herein referred to afford numerous examples and situations illustrating the harshness and injustice of the rule when applied to the sale of a new house by a builder-vendor. . . . Obviously, the ordinary purchaser is not in a position to ascertain when there is a defect in a chimney flue, or vent of a heating apparatus, or whether the plumbing work covered by a concrete slab foundation is faulty. . . .
>
> The caveat emptor rule as applied to new houses is an anachronism patently out of harmony with modern home buying practices. It does a disservice not only to the ordinary

prudent purchaser but to the industry itself by lending encouragement to the unscrupulous, fly-by-night operator and purveyor of shoddy work. *Humber v. Morton*, 426 S.W.2d 554 (Tex. 1968).

Statutory Law

Law enacted by local and state legislative bodies and by Congress.

The Role of Statutes

Although for many years the opinions of courts were the chief source of real estate law in English-speaking countries and for the legal system generally, during the past 100 years statutes have gradually assumed this role. Among the numerous reasons for this trend to statutory law are these: statutes are more comprehensive; statutes can modify the law more rapidly; statutes can treat an entire problem rather than just a part and statutes are usually more understandable than cases.

During the past 75 years, statutes have been used to bring greater uniformity to state law. Economic expansion after the Civil War has been characterized by the growth of regional and national markets. States, however, have often adopted different laws to solve common problems occurring in these markets. This practice has increased the cost of doing business and caused confusion and uncertainty.

Uniform Laws

In 1890, the National Conference of Commissioners on Uniform State Law was established to alleviate this problem. The commission is charged with determining what uniform laws are necessary, drafting a uniform statute and trying to get states to adopt it. More than 100 uniform laws have been recommended, although few have been adopted by all or even a majority of the states.

The commission's most conspicuous success has been the Uniform Commercial Code. This statute has been adopted in all of the states. In some instances it applies to transactions involving real property. This limited application will be discussed more fully later in the book.

The commission has recently proposed a number of laws that deal with real estate. These include a uniform condominium act, a uniform residential landlord-tenant act, a uniform simplification of land transfers act and a uniform eminent domain code. As of 1986, however, the impact of these uniform laws on real estate has been minimal.

Court Interpretation of Statutes

Despite the growing importance of statutes as a source of law, court opinions continue to play a significant role in determining what the law is. Many statutes are broadly written. Often their meaning is not clear until they have been interpreted by a court. It is probably safe to say that, in a majority of instances, a lawyer looking for the answer to a legal question will first check for an appropriate statute and then review relevant court opinions interpreting that statute.

Codification of Appellate Judge-made Law

Another reason that court opinion continues to be important is that statutes often are merely a codification of the cases dealing with a particular legal problem. When a legislative body codifies the law, it adopts a statute that reflects the decisional law. For example, when the courts in some states decided that the act of selling real property implied a warranty of fitness for habitation, the state legislature passed statutes mirroring the court's decisions.

Administrative Rules and Regulations

In our dynamic, complex society, much of the work of government is done by administrative agencies. Both Congress and state legislatures create administrative agencies as part of legislation that aims to cure some social ill. The agency is empowered to enforce and implement the goals of the legislation. A substantial number of administrative agencies significantly influence the real estate business. Among such federal agencies are the Department of Housing and Urban Development, the Environmental Protection Agency and the Federal Home Loan Bank Board. State administrative agencies also have a far-reaching influence on the real estate business. They are the source of rules pertaining to such matters as licensing and disciplining real estate sales personnel, zoning, safeguarding the environment, and landlord and tenant rights.

Administrative agencies perform several functions. They are authorized to settle disputes and, in doing so, act like courts; this is called *administrative adjudication*. The procedures used in administrative adjudication are generally much less formal than those used by the courts, making reaching a settlement less time-consuming and costly. Another benefit of administrative adjudication is that the agency personnel resolving the dispute are experts in the subject area of the dispute and can therefore resolve the case more effectively than is sometimes possible in a court.

Many agencies also have the power to make rules and regulations that have the force of law. In this respect they act like legislatures. An agency's authority to make rules and regulations is granted in the legislation that created the agency. If the rule or regulation issued by the agency is constitutional, proper procedures have been followed and the agency has not exceeded the power and authority granted to it by the legislature, the rule or regulation is immune from modification or invalidation by the courts.

COURT STRUCTURE

People in the real estate business sometimes become involved in litigation, so it is helpful for them to know something about the structure of the system that applies the law.

Trial and Appellate Courts

Two types of courts are fundamental to the operation of the legal system. They are trial and appellate courts.

Trial Courts

The function of a trial court is to determine the facts and to apply the relevant law to these facts. A jury usually makes the factual determination, but in some cases the parties are not entitled to a jury, or they waive this right. Disputed facts are then decided by the judge. Whether a judge or jury makes the factual determination, findings are based upon evidence. In most instances evidence is the oral testimony of witnesses who are questioned by attorneys for the parties.

The testimony of most witnesses is valuable because the witness has personal knowledge of the facts. One important type of witness often does not have personal knowledge of the situation, but does have expertise related to a disputed fact. This person is the expert witness. The testimony of the expert witness is not permitted until the trial court judge is convinced that the witness is qualified. When qualified, the expert witness answers a hypothetical question that covers technical aspects of a disputed fact. Real estate brokers and appraisers often testify as expert witnesses in cases involving disputed land values.

Appellate Courts

If either party thinks that a legal error has been made by the trial court judge, the party may ask a higher court to review the case. This procedure is called an *appeal*, and the court hearing the case is an appellate court. The function of the appellate court is quite different from that of the trial court. This court is not concerned with deciding disputed facts; rather, it corrects legal mistakes. For this reason there is no jury in an appellate court, and the judges do not listen to the testimony of witnesses. They read briefs in which the parties explain what they believe the law to be, and they may hear oral arguments presented by attorneys. Later the judges decide which party is correct. One of the judges will then write an opinion presenting the views of the majority. If the court finds that an error has been made, the opinion will order the lower court to correct its mistake. These opinions are the judge-made law as explained earlier.

Federal and State Courts

A first step in understanding the American legal structure is to recognize that the federal government and each of the states have their own system of trial and appellate courts. Each of the systems—state and federal—in most instances is the final authority within its own jurisdiction. One exception to this principle is that federal courts do have authority over state courts in questions involving the U.S. Constitution.

Jurisdiction of State Courts

The authority of state courts is extensive. It includes cases involving violations of the state's criminal statute as well as statutes that involve matters as diverse as divorce, education, public health and social welfare. Most contract cases and those involving personal injuries are also heard in state courts. In fact, state courts have jurisdiction over all matters except those the Constitution or Congress has given exclusively to the federal courts or has denied to the states.

Jurisdiction of Federal Courts

The jurisdiction of federal courts is limited to that given to them by the Constitution and the federal statutes that create them. As a result federal courts hear only cases that involve the Constitution, treaties between the U.S. and a foreign nation, federal statutes, and citizens of different states.

The power of federal courts to hear cases that arise under the Constitution, treaties and federal statutes is called *federal question* jurisdiction. Most federal question matters involve the application or interpretation of one of the many federal statutes, such as the Environmental Protection Act, the Civil Rights Act or the Internal Revenue Code.

The power of federal courts to hear cases involving citizens of different states is called *diversity jurisdiction*. Diversity jurisdiction exists because when the Constitution was adopted many people believed that a citizen of one state would not get a fair trial if sued in another state. Consequently, those who drafted the Constitution included in it a provision extending federal judicial power to disputes between citizens of different states. Because diversity jurisdiction places a substantial burden on the federal courts as they are often applying state law, Congress has limited the diversity jurisdiction of these courts to cases in which the dispute involves more than $10,000.

CASE EXAMPLE

Able was a resident of New Hampshire and Baker a resident of New York. The two entered into a contract in which Baker agreed to purchase a large resort hotel in New Hampshire from Able. Baker breached the contract, and Able sued her in the New Hampshire courts for $25,000 damages. Baker may transfer the case to the federal district court since the parties are residents of different states and the amount in controversy exceeds $10,000.

Most real estate litigation is brought in state courts because the dispute does not involve a federal statute or U.S. Constitutional question, and the parties are usually residents of the same state. In addition, most real estate legal disputes concern land located within the state, and there is no basis whatsoever for a federal court's taking jurisdiction.

State Court System

As there are 51 independent court systems operating within the United States, understanding the structure of American courts might seem an impossible task. The task is, however, simplified by the existence of a pattern common to both the federal and the 50 state systems. This structure can be visualized as a pyramid with two or sometimes three levels.

State Trial Courts

Trial courts are at the base of the structural pyramid. Trial courts can be classified into three broad groups. This classification is based upon the court's power to hear a case, which is termed its *jurisdiction*.

Courts of General Jurisdiction.   Each state usually has a trial court of general jurisdiction. In some states these are called *superior courts*. Other states call them *county courts, district courts, circuit courts* or *courts of common pleas*. These courts have the power to hear a wide variety of civil and criminal cases. Ordinarily, there are no limits on the court's monetary jurisdiction, and the court has the power to grant extraordinary remedies, such as the injunction and specific performance. An injunction is an order forbidding a person to do a particular act. Conversely, an order for specific performance commands that a particular act be performed.

In a number of states these courts hear appeals from administrative agencies and courts of limited jurisdiction (see Figure 1.1).

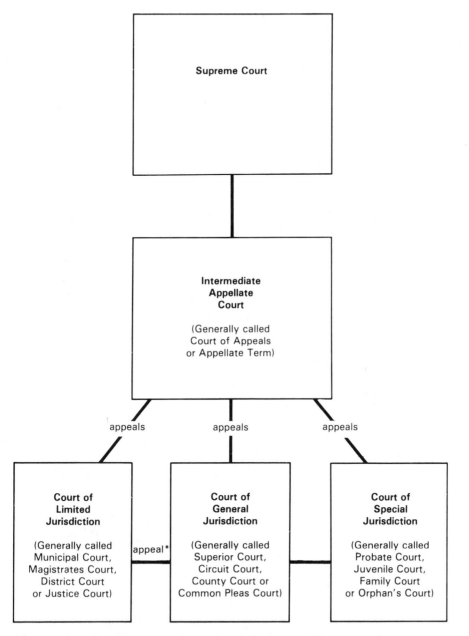

* In a number of states, courts of general jurisdiction consider appeals from courts of limited jurisdiction.

Figure 1.1: A typical state judicial system

Trial by jury is available for most cases. The court generally has state-wide jurisdiction but is organized on a district basis. These courts are generally considered the cornerstones of judicial administration.

Courts of Limited Jurisdiction.   Many of the more populous states have created trial courts that are limited to hearing cases in which the damages are less than a certain amount, fixed by statute. Depending upon the state, this amount ranges from a few hundred to thousands of dollars. These courts also generally have criminal jurisdiction over cases involving petty crimes and misdemeanors. *Municipal courts* is a common name for these courts. Other states call them *justice courts, magistrates courts* or *district courts.*

Generalizations about courts of limited jurisdiction are difficult to make. Their authority differs widely from state to state. In metropolitan areas their monetary jurisdiction is sometimes extensive, and the courts are manned by full-time judges with large staffs. In some rural areas these courts hear only the most trivial cases and may be presided over by part-time judges with no legal training. Courts of limited jurisdiction are important to the legal system because they take some of the pressures off the courts of general jurisdiction.

Courts of Special Jurisdiction.   Either because of tradition or because of the peculiar needs of judicial administration, in many states special courts have been established to resolve a wide variety of disputes. Traffic offenses are one type of case often tried in a court of special jurisdiction. Traffic cases are generally tried in a special court or a special division of a trial court as so many traffic offenses are processed that they would clog the regular judicial machinery.

Juvenile and domestic relations cases are also heard by a special court. These courts provide privacy and informal procedures that are effective in dealing with juvenile and family matters.

Numerous states also have separate probate courts. These courts exercise jurisdiction over the administration of decedents' estates. When a real estate broker or sales associate is involved in a transaction that has to do with a decedent's real property, the broker or sales associate often has to deal with a probate court. In some states, probate courts have jurisdiction in guardianship, adoption, and competency proceedings.

Intermediate Appellate Courts

About half the states have, by constitution or statute, established an intermediate level of appellate courts. The purpose of these courts is to lighten the burden of the state's supreme court. Some intermediate appellate courts have limited powers to act as trial courts. Usually this involves the power to issue extraordinary writs. However, the primary function of these courts is to provide appellate review. Although the extent of appellate jurisdiction is generally broad, some states place limits on the appeals that can be heard, possibly on the type of case or the maximum monetary amount. An intermediate appellate court might be permitted to hear civil appeals or civil appeals only in cases wherein the amount in controversy is under $30,000.

Supreme Court

At the apex of a state's judicial system is the state supreme court, which in most states hears appeals in all civil and criminal matters. This jurisdiction is often concurrent with that of the intermediate appellate court. Because of the extensiveness of the review process and the large number of appeals, most states allow their court of last resort to accept for review only cases that the justices or judges consider important. Appeals as a matter of right may, however, often be taken in important cases, such as those that involve constitutionality of a state or federal statute or the death penalty.

Federal Court System

U.S. District Courts

The U.S. District Courts are the trial courts of the federal system. The United States is divided into 94 districts, each with a single district court. Almost all federal cases are initiated in these courts as they have the power to hear all types of federal cases except those assigned by Congress to special courts such as the tax court.

U.S. Courts of Appeal

The federal intermediate appellate courts are called *U.S. Courts of Appeal.* In 1985 the United States was divided into 12 geographic areas called *circuits,* with a court of appeals for each. These courts hear appeals from the federal district courts that are included in their circuit. They also hear appeals from administrative agencies. They do not have the power to act as trial courts.

U.S. Supreme Court

The United States Supreme Court is the final appellate court in the federal system. Most of the cases the Supreme Court reviews come from the U.S. Courts of Appeal and from the state supreme courts. The Supreme Court may review state supreme court decisions involving the federal Constitution or a federal statute.

In certain cases the Supreme Court must hear an appeal. One example is a case in which a U.S. Court of Appeals has held a state statute unconstitutional. Another is when a lower federal court has held a federal statute unconstitutional and the United States is a party. In most cases the party seeking review must first ask the Supreme Court to hear the case by petitioning for a writ of certiorari. This is a writ in which a superior court orders an inferior court to supply a record of a particular case. The Supreme Court denies most petitions for certiorari as it does not consider the case important enough to hear. Denial of certiorari does not mean that the petitioner has been denied an appeal. All of these cases have been heard by at least one appellate court and sometimes more.

SUMMARY

People employed in the real estate field have a genuine need to know about the law and the legal systems that regulate the profession. In fact, licensing requirements in some states include a course in real estate law.

The laws of any society reflect the way its leaders think about basic social and moral questions. In Western society the functions of law are to provide order, to settle disputes between parties, to protect citizens' expectations about the actions of others, to prevent exploitation by means of force or fraud and to ensure equality of all persons under the law.

Law has several sources: published appellate court opinions or precedents, laws or statutes, and rules and regulations issued by regulatory agencies, as well as the provisions of the federal and various state constitutions. Judges have a fundamental obligation to follow precedent. The body of law that has evolved as appellate judges base their written decisions on precedent is called *common law*.

Much law today results from appellate courts' interpretations of statutes. These interpretations become precedent, which establishes the meaning of the statute. In the past half century, administrative agencies have become an increasingly important source of law as they are empowered to make rules and regulations.

The court system, consisting of several types and levels of courts, is established to settle disputes or apply penalties when laws are broken. In trial courts, judges or jury panels decide the facts based on evidence and apply the relevant law. If either party feels that a legal error has been made, he or she may appeal to a higher court, called an *appellate court*. Cases here are decided not by juries but by judges who hear the arguments presented by both sides. Most real estate disputes are decided at the state level in trial courts.

REVIEW AND DISCUSSION QUESTIONS

1. Name the courts in your state having (a) general jurisdiction, (b) limited jurisdiction and (c) final jurisdiction.
2. (a) Define the doctrine of precedent. (b) Indicate limitations on the use of precedent.

3. During the past 50 years, statutory law has gradually replaced judge-made or decisional law. Explain the reasons for this.

CASE PROBLEMS

1. Sorensen, a licensed real estate broker, entered into a listing agreement with Schomas. Sorensen located a buyer who submitted a purchase offer. Schomas refused to accept the offer or to pay Sorensen the commission that was clearly owed. Enraged, Sorensen threatened to "take the case to the United States Supreme Court, if necessary." Explain why Sorensen probably would be unable to do this.

2. Taylor was involved in litigation involving a real estate problem. Taylor's friend Bennett testified in Taylor's behalf at the trial. Bennett's testimony was critical to the outcome of the case. Taylor lost the case and decided to appeal. When Taylor informed Bennett of his intention to appeal, Bennett told him that he could not testify a second time as the experience had drained him emotionally. Taylor told Bennett that it would not be necessary for him to testify again. Explain why.

3. Stanley Beck purchased a remote farm to which he moved with his family. After living there for a time, Beck became disturbed because his children had a long walk to the school bus. The walk was especially dangerous during the winter, because there were no sidewalks and the road was often icy. Beck asked an attorney whether the purchase could be rescinded on the grounds of fraud. Beck contended that the seller, knowing Beck had school-age children, should have informed him that the walk to the bus stop could be dangerous in winter.

   The attorney told Beck that, in their state, silence could not be the basis for fraud unless the seller, knowing of a hidden defect in the property that could cause injury, failed to disclose it. The attorney stated that there was no precedent for the proposition that a long walk on an icy road to a school bus is a hidden defect that a seller is bound to reveal. Explain what the attorney meant by *precedent* and why the fact that no precedent existed was significant.

4. The City of Lubbock, Texas, under the Texas Urban Renewal Act, designated a particular area for slum clearance. The land was to be cleared and sold for private development. The sales would be subject to restrictions to prevent the future growth of slums. Johnson owned property within the designated area. Although his structures met all requirements of the city's building code, they were to be demolished along with substandard buildings. What arguments might Johnson raise against the

condemnation? Would he be successful? *Davis v. City of Lub-bock, 326 S.W.2d 699 (Tex. 1959).*

5. Ed Freeman, who lives in Michigan, enters into an agreement to construct a building for Bartley Bros. Inc., a New York corporation. The contract price is $250,000. The building is to be built on land owned by Bartley Bros. in Pennsylvania. The agreement was signed in Freeman's office in Michigan. Freeman defaults, and Bartley Bros. sues in federal court. Does the federal court have jurisdiction? Support your answer.

2

Land and Related Concerns

LAND

**A commodity limited in supply that, along with
elements associated with it (water and minerals), is both
an essential agent in production and a desirable
consumer good.**

Until recently the idea that people could exist for any length of time
apart from land was inconceivable. Even today, when the idea of human beings living out their lives on islands in space is a possibility accepted by serious scientists, human destiny remains linked with land.
Whenever humans have survived, they have taken their living directly
or indirectly from the land. Because land and people have always been
inseparable, the ways in which land has been viewed are as diverse as
the world's communities.

Much of the conflict between the American Indians and Europeans who settled this hemisphere resulted from attitudes toward
land. The Indians regarded land differently than did the Europeans
who settled North and South America after 1500. Land, to the Indians, was a resource possessed by the tribe. It was not subject to individual ownership. Some native groups in Africa, Australia and South
America hold similar views today. In western Europe during the late
Middle Ages the idea of community ownership in some lands existed,
but by the time major colonization occurred in North America, the
concept of individual property rights prevailed. Most settlers who
came to this country after 1700 wanted to own their own land. Although themes other than individual ownership can be discerned in

the way Americans regard land, a majority, especially those living in the United States, continue to consider it a commodity to be owned individually.

A number of factors account for this view. Probably the most important is historic. Our pioneer ancestors were individualistic in economic matters. The men and women who wrested the land from the great forests of the East and from the prairies of the West were acquiring wealth for themselves and their families. They saw land, like any commodity, as something that could be bought and sold or passed on to their children. These people also believed in personal freedom. They regarded private ownership of land as a bulwark against both the intrusion of the state and the inquisitiveness of their neighbors. Finally, traditional economic theory in the Western world includes land as an important factor of production. Although land—like labor and capital—is not productive on its own, a price has to be paid for it because it is both necessary and scarce. Land is an important good that, with labor and capital, can be put to work to provide profit for the owner.

Real Estate

Land and its improvements; mines, minerals and quarries under the land; air and water rights associated with land; and other rights and privileges related to land.

Although it is a commonly used term, the meaning of *real estate* varies from place to place and from situation to situation. For example, in a number of states, leases are not considered real estate. In some states the duration of the lease determines whether the tenant's interest is real estate; in other states it does not. In addition, *real estate* sometimes has more than one statutory definition within a single state, some definitions being broader than others. It is difficult to give *real estate* one definition, because the sense in which it is used in everyday speech does not always correspond to its specific legal meaning.

In some contexts the terms *real estate* and *land* are used interchangeably; however, the meaning of *real estate* is generally broader than the meaning of *land*. Real estate includes not only land but also improvements on the land, such as a house, a barn and other structures. Many rights and privileges associated with land are considered to be real estate as well. For example, if one has a right of way from his or her own land across the land of a neighbor to reach a road, that right-of-way is real estate and can be sold or transferred as such in many instances. Water rights, mines, minerals and quarries are also considered real estate for most purposes.

Real property is a term lawyers and judges often use as a synonym for *real estate*. This chapter discusses real estate, or real property, principles in greater detail.

Land as a Natural Resource

Although the view of land as a commodity has been dominant in the United States, this is but one view of land. A contrasting view of land as a social resource that must be preserved for future generations has gained increasing acceptance in recent years. As a result of this trend, vast areas of our nation have been set aside as a public domain, and governments at all levels have adopted legislation to control land use for the benefit of society. Land has become the subject of a large body of law as our nation tries to cope with the problems involved with its use and disposition.

As traditionally defined by courts and commentators, land encompasses the surface of the earth, everything above that surface and all that is below. Land has been described as an inverted pyramid extending upward indefinitely into space and downward to the center of the earth. Many items such as water, minerals, oil and gas can be separated from the land. Because these things are both scarce and desirable, they, along with space, are often severed and treated as independent commodities. The result has been that detailed laws regulating their use have developed throughout the United States. These laws differ from place to place as they reflect the needs of people in a particular area.

WATER

Water is an element essential to human survival. Without water, land is of little value. Consequently, lands adjacent to water or having water readily available are usually more valuable than other lands. Because of water's importance, disputes sometimes develop between property owners attempting to take advantage of this valuable resource. Efforts to solve these disputes have led to an extensive law of water rights.

Whatever the legal system, several factors appear to have a major influence on water rights law. The most significant is water's scarcity or abundance. The influence of this condition is clearly evident in American law. Another important factor is the type of economy prevailing in the area. Climate and technology are also significant in determining rights of individuals to water. Water rights law in the United States has been involved mainly with problems involving surface water, primarily because of technological inability to use underground water effectively. More recently, however, legal questions have also arisen concerning water that flows underground and water that percolates, or rises to the surface of the earth.

Surface Water

Water upon the surface of the earth in flowing streams and lakes.

Lakes and streams that are the subject of water rights can be navigable or nonnavigable. A navigable body of water is one that has the capacity to be useful for commerce or travel. The U.S. Constitution allocates power to Congress to regulate navigable waters, but until Congress acts, the states also may regulate. Although Congress frequently has taken actions that involve navigable waters, it has not, except in limited instances, restricted the rights of owners of land along these waterways. As Congress has not asserted all its powers over navigable waters, the power of the state over waters within its jurisdiction is paramount, just as it is for nonnavigable waters.

Riparian Lands

Riparian lands are those that border on a stream or watercourse. Riparian lands extend away from the stream, including the stream's drainage area or watershed, although all of the drainage area is not necessarily riparian land. The riparian area of the watershed is only that portion under ownership of a person whose property fronts on the waterway. A landowner's property might be in the watershed of a stream, but the landowner is not a riparian owner unless his or her property fronts on the stream.

Littoral Lands

Littoral lands are those that border on an ocean, a sea, or a lake. In some states *littoral* applies only to lands that border on a tidal body such as an ocean or a sea. Other states use the term to describe lands that border on lakes as well. In many states the term is not used at all: *riparian* is used to designate lands bordering on lakes, oceans and seas as well as those bordering on flowing streams.

In general, the rights of owners of littoral lands are the same as those of the owners of riparian lands. These rights are discussed in the paragraphs that follow. However, at least one difference exists between riparian owners and littoral owners. Littoral owners do not own the land to the water. They own only to the line to which the high tide rises. This is called the *high-water mark*. From the high-water mark to the water (the *low-water mark*), the property is owned by the state. Therefore, the states have the power to control and regulate from the high-water mark to the low-water mark.

Surface Water Rights Theories

At present, two distinct theories of surface water rights exist in the United States. They are *riparianism* and *prior appropriation*. The riparian rights doctrine is the foundation of water rights law in most of the eastern United States. All states east of the Mississippi follow this theory to some extent, although the theory has been greatly modified by statute in Mississippi. Riparian rights are also the basis of water rights law in a number of states west of the Mississippi. Generally, these states, such as Minnesota, Arkansas and Louisiana, have an abundance of water.

Prior appropriation is the basis of water rights law in the more arid regions of the western United States. A number of the western states, however, use both doctrines. This is generally the case in those large states that are arid in certain sections but have sufficient water in others, such as California, Washington, Oregon, Texas and Oklahoma.

Riparianism (Riparian Rights)

Water rights doctrine based upon the idea that all owners of riparian lands are entitled to share equally in the use of water.

Riparianism has two basic principles. First, ownership of the land bordering on water establishes a right to use the water equally. This right cannot be lost by disuse, but it is clearly limited to use, not ownership.

• CASE BRIEF •

Kerley owned land on the upper end of a lake. The upper and lower ends of the lake were connected by a narrow neck of water about 18 inches deep. Wolfe, who owned the land on both sides of this passage, erected a fence to prevent rowboats and other small craft from passing through. Kerley, claiming that he was a riparian owner, brought an action to have the fence removed. The court ordered Wolfe to remove the fence as it interfered with the rightful use of the lake by other riparian owners. *Kerley v. Wolfe, 349 Mich. 350, 84 N.W.2d 748 (1957).*

Second, as the abutting land owner has no proprietary right in the water itself, any control over flowing water is lost once it passes the riparian tract. Conflicts concerning right of use that sometimes arise between upstream and downstream owners have generally been solved in one of two ways: natural flow doctrine or reasonable use doctrine.

Natural Flow.   The riparian rights principle that each riparian owner possesses the right to the ordinary flow of water along his or her land undiminished in quantity and unimpaired in quality is called the *natural flow doctrine.* In a natural flow jurisdiction a downstream or lower riparian owner can limit the use of water by the upper riparian owner if the upper riparian owner interferes with the stream's natural flow. This doctrine developed in England at a time when the English economy was primarily agrarian. Rainfall was abundant, and even extensive use of water by farm owners did not ordinarily decrease the natural flow of the stream. In the United States the natural flow principle was adopted in eastern states with abundant rainfall when they were primarily agrarian. The natural flow principle, however, is not conducive to effective use of water in an industrialized economy. Thus, in most states the principle is greatly modified by legislation and judicial decision. It is doubtful that the original principle exists in pure form anywhere in the United States today.

Reasonable Use.   The riparian rights principle that allows a riparian owner to make reasonable use of the water that flows by his or her land is called the *reasonable use doctrine*. The doctrine of reasonable use dominates water rights law in the riparian states. It permits the riparian owner to make any use of water that does not unreasonably harm a lower riparian owner. The upper owner thus may reduce the natural flow of the stream as long as this does not unreasonably injure the lower owner. The test of reasonable use turns on the circumstances of each case. Many factors are considered, including the intended use, its extent, its duration, and the necessity for it. Other factors that courts consider are the needs of other riparian owners, climate conditions, the nature of the stream and the customs of the area.

The doctrine of reasonable use thus does not concern itself with impairment of the natural flow or quality of the water but allows full use of the water in any beneficial manner, provided it does not unreasonably interfere with the beneficial use by others. In some states the riparian owner's beneficial use of water is restricted to riparian lands; others permit the use on or off the land if this does not cause damage to other riparian owners.

Most jurisdictions following the reasonable use doctrine have established a hierarchy of uses as a means of determining reasonable use. Domestic uses have priority over agricultural uses, and agricultural uses have priority over industrial and commercial uses.

• CASE BRIEF •

Deetz and Carter owned land along the Cold Creek. The creek followed a natural course through the Carter ranch down to the Deetz property. Cold Creek, although small, had a steady year-round flow, and the Deetz family obtained all its domestic supply of water from it. Carter diverted water from the creek for irrigation and livestock. This action so lowered the level of the creek that the Deetz family could not use the water for domestic purposes. An appellate court affirmed a decree restricting Carter's agricultural use of the water to permit Deetz's domestic use. *Deetz v. Carter, 232 Cal. App. 2d 851, 43 Cal. Rpr. 321 (1965).*

Riparian rights are subordinate to navigation and to regulation by the federal government. Where the public has access to navigable streams or lakes, most states permit the use of these waters without obstruction or restriction by abutting landowners.

Prior Appropriation
A water rights doctrine giving primary rights to the first users of water.

The doctrine of riparianism is not suited to the conditions in the arid states of the West, especially where irrigation is necessary. In these states the principle of prior appropriation developed. In general, a system of prior appropriation creates a superior right in the person who is the first to use a body of water for economic purposes.

Prior appropriation was originally based upon custom and necessity and eventually became a part of the positive law. Today, prior appropriation is recognized in either the constitutions or statutes of all the western states. Several of these states have rejected riparian rights completely. Colorado was the leader in this move, and absolute rejection of riparianism is referred to as the *Colorado doctrine.* California and other states with areas of abundant water combine riparian rights with prior appropriation principles.

• CASE BRIEF •

Hunter was the first settler in a valley in Washington. A sizable creek flowed through the valley, but Hunter's land was not on the creek. Sogle settled in the valley shortly after Hunter. In 1882, the two began construction of an irrigation ditch from the creek to Sogle's land. Later the ditch was to be extended to Hunter's land, but the two had a dispute and the ditch was not extended.

In 1883, Hunter began to construct his own ditch. This ditch was finally completed in 1885. In litigation during the 1920s involving conflicting claims to water rights from the creek, the court held that owners with title through Sogle had superior rights to those holding title through Hunter. The court also held that Hunter's claim commenced from 1883, when he started his own ditch. It ruled that the time of diversion relates back to the beginning of work when the work has been pursued with reasonable diligence. *Hunter Land Co. v. Laungenour, 140 Wash. 558, 250 P. 41 (1926).*

The right of prior appropriation is limited to the extent that the water can be used beneficially. However, once an appropriator has established priority, the right to have water exists except for changes that are the result of natural causes. Like the riparian system, prior appropriation does not create title but merely invests a right to use the water.

In addition to the doctrine of prior appropriation, water rights law in the western states is characterized by a system of administrative controls. Although procedures vary appreciably, permits are basic to the administration of these controls. Permits to appropriate water are granted by a state agency after a hearing based upon the application and permit approval. The permits make up part of a public record and set forth the water rights of the holder.

The foundation of the system of prior appropriation is the beneficial use of water. In order to obtain a permit, intent to apply the water to a beneficial use must be established.

• CASE BRIEF •

Lake Shore Duck Club (Lake Shore) obtained a permit to divert all water from Dix Creek. The water was to be used to improve the habitat for wildfowl on public lands. The club constructed the necessary dams and ditches to divert the water from the creek. The Lake View Duck Club (Lake View), which had been using water from the creek for many years, continued to do so. Lake View contended that the permit received by Lake Shore was invalid because the use of the water was not beneficial.

Lake Shore sued to quiet its title to the water, and Lake View moved to dismiss. The trial and appellate courts held for Lake View. Both courts agreed that a beneficial use must inure to the exclusive benefit of the appropriator and be subject to that person's complete dominion and control. Diverting water onto public lands to aid in the propagation of wildlife did not meet this requirement. *Lake Shore Duck Club v. Lake View Duck Club, 50 Utah 76, 166 P. 309 (1917).*

Generally, "beneficial use" is construed liberally, and ordinarily one beneficial use is not preferred over others. There may, however, be constitutional or statutory guidelines for determining preferential uses. Where such guidelines exist, domestic use is invariably preferred. A change of beneficial use is permissible but cannot be used as an excuse for enlarging an appropriation.

In addition to beneficial use, the applicant for a permit must

- Establish that the water is subject to appropriation;
- Show that it can be taken without injury to others;
- Actually divert water by means of an artificial structure;
- Apply the water to a beneficial use within a reasonable time.

A fifth requirement, that of notice, is sometimes imposed by statute. Often the user is required to post signs at the point of diversion, stating the amount of water to be diverted, its destination and general route, the means of diversion and its intended use. In the absence of a statute, notice is not indispensable, yet local custom sometimes has the force of a statute.

Subterranean Water

Subterranean water is an important resource in many areas of the United States. In recent years litigation involving subterranean water has increased. One reason is that methods for obtaining it have improved. Another is that population has expanded in many areas of the country that lack adequate supplies of surface water. This has led to increased dependence on subterranean waters in these areas. Subterranean water is divided into two classes: percolating waters and underground streams.

Percolating Waters

Water that passes through the ground, not flowing in a clearly defined underground stream or supplied by streams flowing on the surface.

Percolating waters may be rainwater infiltrating the soil or water from a stream that has seeped or oozed from the streambed and is no longer part of the flow. Percolating waters include underground lakes, artesian basins and veins and rivulets that flow in a course not discoverable from the surface without excavation.

Percolating waters are involved in more legal disputes than underground streams are. The reason is that underground streams are difficult to identify as such, and courts in many states presume that the water is percolating unless it can be shown to flow in a clearly defined channel.

In the traditional English common law of subterranean water rights, percolating waters belong absolutely to the owner of the land in which they are found. This traditional English rule is followed in many areas of the United States. Where this common law rule is followed, the landowner may deal with percolating water without regard to the manner in which his or her actions affect others. For example, the landowner may divert the percolating waters completely to the detriment of adjoining landowners. Conversely, if an owner does something on his or her property that inhibits the drainage of percolating waters, he or she is not responsible for damage caused to neighbors by the backup.

Because of injustices resulting from the application of the common law rule, a number of states courts and legislatures have modified it. The most common modification is the substitution of a rule based on reasonable use. This rule has been recognized in states as diverse as Florida, Minnesota, New Jersey and Washington.

Reasonable Use Rule.   According to this rule, each owner of land has the right to use the percolating waters to fulfill the reasonable needs and necessities of the land.

• CASE BRIEF •

The City of Shawnee purchased 20 acres of land about eight miles from the city. It drilled 12 wells on the tract and transported the water in pipelines to the city. This action caused wells on farms to dry up, and the residents sought an injunction. The trial court refused to grant the injunction. Upon appeal relief was granted, the appellate court stating "the rule of reasonable use is that each landowner is restricted to a reasonable . . . use of his own property, in view of the similar rights of others." *Canada v. City of Shawnee, 179 Okla. 53, 64 P.2d 694 (1937).*

Reasonable use does not prevent the proper use of percolating waters by landowners in manufacturing, agriculture or irrigation. The landowner is immune from liability to the extent that the use of the water was reasonably necessary in connection with the use or improvement of the land. The reasonable use rule does prohibit, as the previous case illustrates, the withdrawal of percolating waters for distribution or sale for uses not connected with property ownership or sale for uses not connected with the property ownership if this use damages neighboring owners.

Correlative Rights Doctrine.   California courts have rejected both the common law and reasonable use rules as these apply to percolating waters. Instead these courts have adopted a doctrine that requires landowners to share percolating waters in proportion to their ownership of the surface area. A property owner may not extract more than his or her share even if the water is being used beneficially on the land. This *correlative rights doctrine*, as it is known, is similar to that applied by some states to the extraction of oil and gas. However, because the correlative rights doctrine is hard to apply, it has not been accepted outside of California.

Underground Streams
Subterranean waters that flow in a clearly defined channel discoverable from the earth's surface.

Water rights in subterranean streams are relatively less important than those involving percolating waters, for the two reasons previously mentioned. First, establishing that an underground stream exists is difficult. The person asserting that water is flowing in an underground stream must establish from the surface the direction and course of the stream and that the stream has a definite bed, bank and current. Excavation to prove this is not permitted. Second, the courts in most cases presume that subterranean water is percolating water.

Legal disputes involving underground streams are ordinarily solved by applying the surface water law of the jurisdiction. If the state applies riparian rights to surface water problems, riparian rights will be applied to underground streams. When prior appropriation is the rule for surface water, it will be applied to underground streams as well.

MINERAL RIGHTS

The right to extract minerals from under the land, which may be legally assigned to or owned by someone other than the surface owner.

The common law envisioned the surface owner's rights as extending upward indefinitely into the sky and downward to the center of the earth. Until the industrial revolution, this definition was adequate to solve most legal questions. Except for a limited number of metals such as gold and silver, minerals were not of great concern to society. Consequently, problems involving subsurface rights were rare. The industrial and technological revolutions changed this situation. The demand expended for many minerals found below the surface. This led to an increase in the value of these minerals and the subsurface in which they are found.

Early industrialization depended upon coal as a source of energy. Metals such as iron, copper, tin and lead also contributed to commercial growth. Technological developments of the 20th century have further increased dependence upon these and other minerals as well as gas and oil. As these resources become more valuable, real property law adapted to provide solutions for legal problems created by their increased use.

Land was recognized as a commodity that could be divided horizontally for the purposes of ownership. One person could own the surface while others had rights in the subsurface. An owner could grant the right to extract minerals, lease land with the right to take minerals or convey title to the subsurface in which valuable resources were located. American law clearly allows a surface estate and one or more subsurface estates to be carved separately out of a single tract and held in entirely separate ownership.

• CASE BRIEF •

McCoy had title to 18 acres of vacant land. Unknown to him, the Pacific Coast Coal Co. had recorded mineral rights in the land. A statute provided that a person having a color of title to vacant land who pays taxes for seven successive years becomes the legal owner. When McCoy discovered the existence of the mineral rights, he claimed that because he had paid taxes for seven years, he had title to the subsurface as well as the surface. The court disagreed, holding that payment of taxes on land does not constitute payment of taxes on mineral rights that have been separated from the land. *McCoy v. Lourie, 42 Wash. 2d 24, 253 P.2d 415 (1953).*

Mineral rights may be acquired in four different ways: by (1) mineral deed, (2) mineral reservation, (3) mineral lease and (4) mineral rights option.

A *mineral deed* is similar to the deed, discussed in Chapter 7, used to transfer title to surface estates. Although the mineral deed transfers only title to mineral rights, the law relating to the two has many of the same features. The person acquiring mineral rights by deed ordinarily acquires absolute title just as one would who acquired a surface estate. The deed grants in express terms a mineral estate, describing the size and kinds of mineral acquired. The deed or other document conveying the mineral rights should also grant all rights necessary to conduct a mining operation. These would include rights related to access, development, processing and transportation.

Absolute title to mineral rights is also often acquired by a *mineral reservation* in a deed. In this situation the owner, upon disposing of the surface, retains the mineral rights. In each instance, the grant or the reservation, the owner of the mineral rights has an interest that can be conveyed without regard to surface ownership.

Mineral rights are often acquired by *mineral lease*. The lessee obtains an exclusive right to carry out mining operations and title to the ore. Unlike the absolute sale of mineral rights, the lessor usually retains a present or future right in the mineral estate. In a lease arrangement the owner of the property is compensated by royalty payments. These payments are based on a fixed percentage of the value of extracted minerals. A mineral lease should contain provisions setting forth the duration of the lease, renewal rights of the lessee, any rights to suspend lease provisions and responsibilities of the lessee relative to the surface condition of the property.

An option is a contract used in many real estate transactions (see Chapter 19). The contract is between a landowner and another, who is said to be the holder of the option. The contract gives the holder a designated period of time to buy or lease a specified parcel of land. During this time the landowner agrees not to sell or lease the property to anyone but the holder.

A *mineral rights option* provides the holder, usually a mining company, with the right to explore the property for the presence of minerals. The agreement establishes a period of time within which the exploration must take place. Before the period ends, the mining company must decide whether to lease or purchase the land at the price stated in the option.

OWNERSHIP OF OIL AND GAS

American courts have not been consistent in their treatment of the nature of the landowner's interest in oil and gas under the surface. Some courts have attempted to solve legal disputes involving oil and gas ownership by applying principles developed in cases involving ownership and mining of solid minerals. The theory that evolved is known as the *ownership theory.* Other courts recognized that oil and gas migrate under the ground from high-pressure to low-pressure areas. These courts applied rules similar to those applied to questions involving the ownership of wild animals and migratory birds. This theory is called the *nonownership theory.* The two theories are discussed below.

Ownership Theory

The theory under which oil and gas are minerals and are therefore as subject to absolute ownership as coal or any other solid mineral.

"Absolute" is the key to this theory. In fact, the term *absolute* is often used in place of *ownership.* The ownership theory is not applicable logically to gas and oil because they are migratory within the earth. However, many states apparently have adopted this theory. In addition to Texas (see the following Case Brief), states following this principle include Arkansas, Colorado, Kansas, Pennsylvania, Tennessee and West Virginia.

• CASE BRIEF •

S.R. Hill executed a lease of oil and gas rights to Mid-Kansas Oil and Gas Co. The county assessed a tax against the company based on the lease. At the time, no oil or gas had been taken from the ground. The company argued that it could not be taxed, because oil and gas in place cannot be owned. This argument was based on the premise that, until oil or gas is brought to the surface, owners of adjacent land may lawfully appropriate the oil or gas.

The question of tax liability was decided in favor of the county. The court stated: "[G]as and oil in place are minerals and realty, subject to ownership, severance, and sale while embedded in the sands or rocks beneath the earth's surface, in like manner and to the same extent as coal or any other mineral." *Stephens County vs. Mid-Kansas Oil and Gas Co., 113 Tex. 160, 254 S.W. 290 (1923).*

Under the ownership theory, the landowner may sever oil and gas by deed just as he or she would sever solid minerals or a portion of the surface itself. The person who acquires the oil or gas gets the same property rights that are acquired when buying a lot on the surface.

Nonownership Theory

The theory that oil and gas are not the subject of ownership because of their migratory nature.

Under this theory, the landowner has no ownership of oil and gas in place. Each landowner has an exclusive right to drill on the land and becomes the owner when the oil is brought to the surface. The right can be transferred by sale or otherwise. Although the right to search for oil and gas is an interest in land, it is not real property. Some states by statute attribute to this interest many rules applying to real property. Ohio, Louisiana, New York, Alabama, Indiana and Kentucky are among the states in which courts generally adhere to the nonownership theory.

• CASE BRIEF •

In 1914, the Oil Fuel Co. acquired oil and gas rights in a tract of land. Although the conveyance to them was a deed in form, the company recorded it in the register for leases. This was the manner in which oil and gas rights were generally recorded. In 1949, Back acquired title to the land by deed. He had no knowledge of the 1914 conveyance of oil and gas rights. When he learned of this, he claimed the company had lost its rights because it should have recorded the instrument as a deed.

The Ohio court rejected Back's claim. The court stated that a conveyance of oil and gas rights was a license and properly recorded as a lease. An oil and gas conveyance did not give the grantee any rights in oil and gas in the ground. Oil and gas in place is not owned until taken. *Back v. Ohio Fuel Gas Co., 160 Ohio St. 2d 81, 113 N.E.2d 865 (1953).*

Although the nature of oil and gas ownership differs under these two theories, many significant aspects of oil and gas law are the same under both. For example, although drilling near the boundary line of one's land in most states is not an illegal interference with the rights of owners of adjoining land, a slanted well that goes under the surface of another's land is a trespass. Under both theories, government has the power to regulate operating and production practices, waste is not permitted and no driller may unreasonably injure the reservoir. Additionally, the important *rule of capture* is recognized under both.

Rule of Capture

The rule that states that the owner of the surface has the right to appropriate all oil and gas from wells on his or her land, including oil and gas that have migrated from the land of another.

Whether a jurisdiction recognizes the ownership or the nonownership theory, as oil and gas migrate under the ground, the person whose wells produce the oil and gas owns it. This principle is applied in jurisdictions accepting the ownership doctrine even though oil brought to the surface does not always originate beneath the land of the driller. Similarly, ownership of oil and gas that migrate away from the surface owner's lands is lost. The rule of capture is a logical approach to ownership of oil and gas. It is impossible to distinguish oil that has seeped from under the land of another from that originally under the surface on which the well is located.

• CASE BRIEF •

Hastings owned 165 acres of land in northern Ohio. The Ohio Oil Co. owned oil and gas rights in several large parcels of land partially surrounding Hastings's acreage. Although the company had ample space to locate wells elsewhere, it drilled several wells at 400-foot intervals 25 feet from the Hastings property line. Hastings sought an injunction prohibiting the company from operating oil wells at any point within 200 feet of Hastings's farm. He argued that much of the oil produced from the company's wells percolated from under his land. Ohio courts refused to grant the injunction, thus recognizing the rule of capture. *Kelley v. The Ohio Oil Co., 57 Ohio St. 317 (1897).*

The rule of capture allows each landowner to appropriate oil and gas produced by all wells on his or her property. Early cases even permitted the wasteful disposal of whatever these wells produced. In some states an operator may increase flow from wells by pumping, although this practice draws oil from adjoining land. The only protection available to a neighbor is to drill and pump on his or her own land.

State Statutes

During the past 25 years, court opinions and statutes in a number of states have extended the rights of all landowners to share in a common source of oil and gas. Waste is prohibited, and each landowner is permitted a reasonable opportunity to obtain a just and equitable share of the oil or gas in the pool. This is known as the doctrine of *correlative rights.* The gas under the ground may go wherever it will, but an operator may not draw off gas from a neighbor's land in a manner that will unnecessarily deplete a common pool.

A few states have adopted legislation defining the amount of land that must surround a well or requiring a specific distance between wells. These are known as *spacing statutes*. Their purpose is to prevent waste and to give each surface owner an opportunity to take from the common pool.

Other states attempt to control production so that each owner has a reasonable opportunity to recover a fair share of the oil and gas under his or her tract by pooling or prorating the allowable production of oil. Extensive regulation by the state is a fact of life where oil is involved.

AIR RIGHTS

Until recently, the traditional theory that whoever owns the soil owns to the heavens was sufficient to solve most disputes involving invasion of airspace. Airspace problems, which usually concerned overhanging branches, bushes or eaves, were important to the parties but of little significance to society. With the advent of the airplane as a major means of transportation, courts and legislative bodies had to reconsider the old concept of absolute control of airspace. The early English rule that airspace was an appurtenance to land, giving absolute and exclusive right to the owner "to the highest heavens," was repudiated. In general, the courts recognize that the public interest in efficient transportation outweighs any theoretical trespass in airspace. As long as air flight does not interfere with the owner's right to the effective use of the space above his land, airplanes passing through this space are not trespassing. In brief, a landowner's exclusive domain extends at least to a height that makes it possible for the land to be used in a reasonable manner. To this extent the owner of the surface has absolute ownership of the space above his or her land.

Recently some important developments in real estate have been possible because the ownership of airspace may be separated from ownership of the surface. As population has expanded, investors have turned to space above land to satisfy both commercial and residential needs. When an individual purchases a high-rise condominium, that person is acquiring title to airspace. In metropolitan areas such as New York City and Chicago, railroads owning downtown property have separately conveyed airspace above the tracks to be used for commercial buildings. The purchaser acquires that space above the area needed by the railroad for its trains and a surface easement sufficient to support construction and facilities.

SUMMARY

Land is a limited commodity that is fundamental to human survival. Throughout much of history, land was considered a resource of the tribe or social group, to be cultivated for the general good. By the time North America was opened for colonization, individual property rights prevailed. Now land was viewed as wealth—a major factor of production to be controlled according to the prevailing economic and political theory of the nation in which it lies.

Real estate, or real property, is defined differently according to the situation and the place and usually includes more than land. Improvements and rights and privileges associated with land are also considered real estate.

Of growing significance to environmentalists is the view of land as a social resource to be preserved for future use. This view currently influences the passage of laws affecting land use and development. Large areas have been set aside for public use. Land has become the topic of a large body of environmental law.

The value of land is increased by its closeness to water or by the presence of mineral deposits underneath it. Extensive law serves to resolve disputes and regulate usage when water or mineral rights are at issue.

Water rights law, which pertains mainly to surface water, falls into two categories: riparianism and prior appropriation. Under riparian rights, generally, all users of adjacent water have equal rights to it. Riparian principles apply generally in states where water is abundant, such as in the East and a few western states. Where water is scarce, prior appropriation, granting water rights to the first users, generally prevails. Central to the doctrine of prior appropriation is the beneficial use of scarce water.

Mineral rights in the land have increased in importance as technology has developed. These rights may be acquired by deed, by reservation, by lease or by option.

Oil and gas rights differ from mineral rights in that these underground substances may migrate from one person's property to another. Just as water rights theory varies, so do these property theories vary from one state to another.

Air rights have also been affected by recent change in the laws regarding their use, by changes in building practices as population expands and by demands for more efficient transportation.

REVIEW AND DISCUSSION QUESTIONS

1. Outline those arguments supporting individual ownership of land. Evaluate these arguments.
2. Compare the riparian doctrines of reasonable use and natural flow. What limitations exist upon reasonable use? From a public policy viewpoint, which doctrine is most valuable? Why?
3. (a) List the four methods of acquiring mineral rights. (b) What are the major legal differences among them?

CASE PROBLEMS

1. Richards and Schneider owned adjoining land. Richards drilled several oil wells on his property very close to the boundary between the two parcels. When Richards began to pump substantial quantities of oil from these wells, Schneider sought an injunction. At the hearing Schneider's witnesses, all expert geologists, testified that most of the oil came from under Schneider's land. (a) In a state that had no correlative rights legislation, would Schneider's injunction be granted? (b) Would your answer differ if the state's oil and gas law were based upon ownership theory? Discuss.

2. Gilliam owned an airplane that he used for crop dusting. While he was flying over Shrock's property to reach a field that was to be sprayed, crop dust was released. Although it was not clear *how* this occurred, Gilliam clearly was not negligent. At the time the dust was released, Gilliam was flying at a safe altitude. Shrock sued for damages as the poison dust destroyed valuable nursery stock. Would Shrock be successful? Discuss.

3. In 1968 Coffin purchased land along St. Vrain Creek. He built a dam and used water from the creek to irrigate his farm. Several years prior to Coffin's purchase, the Left Hand Ditch Co. had constructed a ditch diverting water from St. Vrain creek to James Creek and then to Left Hand Creek, where it irrigated land adjacent to that stream. None of this land was adjacent to St. Vrain Creek. When a drought struck, the Left Hand Ditch Co. tore out a portion of Coffin's dam, which was impeding the flow of water to land irrigated by Left Hand Creek. Coffin sought damages and an injunction. Although this was a prior appropriation jurisdiction, he argued that he had a better right to the water because his land was adjacent to St. Vrain's Creek. (a) Explain prior appropriation. (b) Discuss the validity of Coffin's argument. See *Coffin v. Left Hand Ditch Co.*, 6 Colo. 443 (1882).

4. Rodney Pape owned a farm that had two major springs feeding into Racoon Creek. This creek was a major tributary of the Licking River. The river flowed through a state park near a second farm owned by Pape. This farm was not on the river. During a period of severe drought, Pape entered the state park and attempted to draw water from the river. When stopped, he argued that he had a right to do so, as his farm on Racoon Creek was in the watershed of the Licking River. Is he correct? Support your answer.

5. The Delaware River has its headwaters in New York. At one point in its flow, the river serves as the boundary between Pennsylvania and New Jersey. In 1929 New York began to di-

vert water from the river to meet the increasing public need in the area for water. New Jersey and Pennsylvania objected to this. In 1931 and again in 1952, as a result of litigation, the three states entered into an agreement allowing New York to draw a set amount of water from the river each year. As a result, owners of riparian lands situated in Pennsylvania sought damages. They were able to prove that the diminished flow of water adjacent to their lands was detrimental to the temperature, flow, state and quality of the water. This reduced the value of their land. A lower court allowed these damages. Was the lower court correct? Support your answer. *Badgley v. City of New York*, 606 F.2d 358 (2d Cir., 1979).

3
Property and Related Concerns

PROPERTY

Legal rights that an individual possesses with respect to a thing; rights that are themselves of economic value.

In traditional legal usage, *property* generally refers to an aggregate or "bundle" of rights that people have in tangible items. People often refer to the items—the automobile, guitar or home—as their property; from a legal point of view, however, the items themselves are not significant. What is important are the rights the person has in these items. These rights include the right to use the item, sell it or even destroy it if the person wishes. In his famous *Commentaries on the Law of England*, Blackstone describes property as an "absolute right, inherent in every Englishman . . . which consists in the free use, enjoyment, and disposal of all his acquisitions, without any control or diminution, save only by the laws of the land." Today, the term *ownership* is often used as a synonym for *property*.

The concept of property is readily understood when related to something tangible like an automobile or land. A person can, however, own something that is related only indirectly to a tangible item. An example would be a lease. The tenant of a commercial building has a right to occupy space. This right is valuable because of the building's existence, but the right itself is intangible. Property also is used to refer to rights that people possess independent of anything tangible. Contracts, trademarks, copyrights and patents are examples. They are all property as they establish rights that the owner can enjoy, sell, give away or deny to others.

The existence of property depends upon government. State and federal laws provide guarantees and protections creating and maintaining the "bundle of rights" that the legal system refers to as property. For example, in our society property exists in land because numerous laws allow individuals to do certain things with land such as sell it, dispose of it to one's heirs or exclude others from it. On the other hand, although one's right to vote is important, it is not property. The state provides no aggregate of rights related to a person's right to vote. All that the individual can do is vote or refrain from voting. Whether or not something is a property right has important constitutional implications because the Bill of Rights prohibits government from taking property without due process of law. Thus, in taking property government must follow legal procedures that safeguard the owner's rights, the property must be taken for public use, and the owner must be compensated adequately. These limitations are discussed in Chapter 8.

Property is a dynamic concept that is continually being reshaped to meet new economic and social needs. In the United States today, appreciable legislation and case law are developing that modify traditional property rights or at least reevaluate them in relation to civil rights. Many good examples can be found in cases and legislation protecting fundamental interests of minorities.

• CASE BRIEF •

Shelly, a black man, purchased real estate from Fitzgerald. The sale violated a recorded restriction upon which former owners of this parcel and a number of other owners had agreed. This restriction prohibited occupancy by "any person not of the Caucasian race." Kramer and others who owned real property subject to the restriction sued to restrain Shelly from taking possession and to divest him of title. When the Missouri courts granted the relief requested, the United States Supreme Court reversed. The court held that state courts are prohibited by the equal protection clause of the Constitution from enforcing a private agreement denying a person because of his race the right to own real property. *Shelly v. Kramer, 334 U.S. 1 (1948).*

Although one clearly visible trend in the law is to limit property rights when weighed against civil rights, in other areas property rights have been expanded. In a number of cases, plaintiffs have contended that they have a property interest in their employment or in the facilities necessary to practice a chosen profession and even in their status and reputation. At present the movement of the law in this direction is slow, but the trend is discernible.

• CASE BRIEF •

Roth was hired as an assistant professor at a state university for a term of one year. His contract was not renewed by the university, and he was given no reason for this action. Roth brought an action against the university, arguing that the due process clause of the Constitution, which prohibits government from taking property without due process, required the university to give him reasons for its decision. Since no reasons were given, he contended, the university was taking his property unfairly. The United States Supreme Court ruled against him on the grounds that the terms of his employment accorded him no property interest in employment beyond one year. *Board of Regents v. Roth, 408 U.S. 564 (1972).*

Real Property Rights

Ownership or proprietary rights in land and anything permanently affixed to land.

Legal institutions reflect dominant economic, political and social values. Laws and the legal system sustain the existing order and are used to attain objectives that society considers important. Throughout the history of England and the United States, land and law have been closely interwoven. In both countries, as well as in most other nations of the Western world, land has been an important form of wealth. In addition, for many hundreds of years in England not only was land the major source of wealth, but the possession of land, even particular tracts of land, determined an individual's social position. Possession or ownership of land also had important political connotations in both England and the United States. For many years in England and in most of the United States, only landowners were permitted to vote.

One result of the historic importance of land is a distinction in the law of English-speaking countries between it and other forms of wealth. Because of land's economic significance, the early common law provided extensive protection to landowners. A landowner ousted from possession could immediately bring an action to recover the land (called an *action in ejectment*). In contrast, the right of an owner of personal property against one who wrongfully took that property was limited to a lawsuit for money (called *damages*). Legal actions like ejectment that protect the rights of owners in their land were known as *real actions*, and that is the reason land is called *real property* or *real estate*. The lawsuit for money of a person who lost control of something of economic value other than land, usually a movable item, was known as a *personal action* because the items involved were personal property. In modern law, as will be discussed later, the distinction between real and personal property continues to be recognized in many areas.

Personal property generally is characterized as being movable. Historically, the items of personal property of importance were tangible things such as cattle, farm equipment and the tools of a person's trade. Today, many intangible forms of wealth exist. An example would be a franchise. These intangible rights are also personal property. Over the centuries these forms of personal property have expanded, and personal property has become more equivalent to real property as wealth. One result has been a narrowing of the legal distinctions between the two, but differences continue to exist and to influence American law.

Real and Personal Property: Legal Problems

The fact that real and personal property continue to be treated differently in the law of English-speaking countries causes many problems. For example, a deed, the written document establishing ownership of real estate, conveys only real property, separate from personal property. This sometimes results in confusion when a home or business is sold. The potential buyer of a home, an apartment for investment, a factory or a farm examines the premises from a functional, not a legal, viewpoint. If the real estate is a residence, the buyer is thinking about a place to live, not about the distinction between real and personal property. Items such as the stove, refrigerator, storm windows and perhaps a bar are functionally related to the reason for the purchase. The buyer understandably considers these items integral parts of the building. At the same time the seller, perhaps having purchased the items separately, often thinks of them as independent of the structure. If the law considers these articles part of the real estate, they pass to the buyer by deed unless specifically excluded by agreement. If the items are deemed personalty and hence not part of the real estate, they are not covered by the deed, and the buyer does not get them.

CASE EXAMPLE

David, by deed, conveyed land to Bessie. A hay barn was located on the land. The barn contained equipment for unloading hay. The equipment consisted of a track, hangers to support the track, a carrier, a hay harpoon, two pulleys and rope. The hangers were bolted to the rafters, and the track was attached to the hangers. David removed the equipment. Bessie demanded that he return it, claiming that it was real estate as it was a part of the barn. Although a court would find for Bessie if David refused to return the equipment, the problem could have been avoided if

David and Bessie had agreed in the contract how the equipment was to be treated.

The distinction between real and personal property is also significant in real estate financing. A debt secured by a mortgage is secured only by the real estate. Personal property is not part of the security. For example, if a bank takes back a mortgage on a motel as security for a debt, the furniture that is integral to successful operation of the business is not covered. Of course, the furniture could also be used as security if designated as such by a separate security agreement.

CASE EXAMPLE

National Bank lent funds to a small manufacturing company and took back a mortgage on realty owned by the company. On the premises was a 2,000-gallon tank set on concrete blocks. The tank was used to store gas and was connected to a garage by lines that ran above ground. The bank was forced to foreclose because the debt was not paid. Both the bank and the company claimed the tank. If the court held the tank to be part of the real estate, the tank could be sold at the foreclosure sale.

Whether an item is real or personal property also raises important insurance, tax and inheritance questions. Sometimes state statutes help provide answers to these questions, but most continue to be settled by case law. Contracts and mortgages should make clear what property the parties intend to be personal property and what they intend to be real property.

Fixtures (Real Property)

Separately identifiable items that were once personal property but that have become real property generally through annexation to land or buildings.

Chandeliers, carpeting, electric hot water heaters and shrubbery are common examples of fixtures associated with residential real estate. All these items are personal property while part of the seller's inventory, but when annexed to land or buildings they are generally considered part of the real estate. On a farm, items such as cattle stanchions, water pumps and fencing would ordinarily be fixtures. Many items associated with industrial or commercial real estate are also classified as fixtures. How would you classify the mirror behind the bar in your favorite restaurant or the overhead track for moving heavy material in a factory? Both could be readily detached without harm to the building, and they appear movable as is personal property, but they, too, are probably fixtures.

The chief test in determining whether an item is a fixture is the intention of the party who attached it to the real estate. Intention will, however, be determined by the manner in which the one who affixed the item acted, not by his or her secret intention.

• CASE BRIEF •

Los Angeles County included in its real estate tax assessment of Allstate's regional office building the value of computer equipment located in it. The equipment was housed in a room that took up approximately three percent of the total building space. The room had been specially modified to house the equipment. The computer weighed more than 16 tons, but it consisted of a number of separate parts. Extensive heavy cables connected the components to their own 220-volt power source and to each other. The units were movable, but moving them was inconvenient and required extensive advance planning.

Allstate protested the assessment on grounds that the computer equipment was not a fixture. The trial court found for the county. The court ruled the equipment a fixture because it was essential to Allstate's business, the company intended the system to be permanent and the company regarded it as part of the realty.

Upon appeal, the appellate court reversed. It stated that items do not become fixtures merely because they are essential to the operation of the business. Similarly, the fact that the components of the system could not be disconnected without advance planning did not indicate an intent to annex. According to the court, there were two key factors. First, the system could be removed from the realty without damage to itself or to the realty. Second, the evidence showed that Allstate acted in a manner indicating that ownership of the computer equipment was unrelated to ownership of the realty. *Allstate Ins. Co. v. County of Los Angeles, 161 Cal. App. 3d 877 (1985).*

In the previous case, the appellate court held that the computer equipment was not a fixture because Allstate clearly acted in a manner indicating that it did not intend to annex the items to the realty. In the absence of clear proof of a party's intention, the courts consider several factors in deciding whether or not an article is a fixture. Among them are the following:

- character and use of the item;
- how securely the item is affixed to the realty;
- relationship between the party who affixed the article and other claimants to it.

Many problems arise in identifying fixtures because infinite variations in facts complicate legal analysis. For parties involved in a real estate transaction, the most effective way to prevent these problems is for them to agree in writing as to whether particular items are to be treated as personalty or real property (fixtures).

Trade Fixtures

Items annexed to land or buildings by a tenant to be used in the tenant's trade or business.

We have seen that items of personal property, annexed to realty with the intention that the item become part of the realty, are fixtures. *Fixtures are real estate* and usually may not be removed or treated separately unless the parties agree. It is clear, however, that a business firm leasing real estate would be seriously hampered if this rule applied to items needed to operate a plant or shop effectively. Therefore, the legal system differentiates between fixtures and trade fixtures, the latter being personalty attached to real estate in order to carry on a trade or business. A tenant may generally remove trade fixtures. Agricultural fixtures have been treated in a similar manner. In order to remove a trade or agricultural fixture, the tenant must restore the premise to its original condition and remove the trade fixture before the lease terminates.

Allowing tenants to remove trade fixtures has social benefits. It encourages both the use of land and efficiency in business. Tenants are more likely to invest in new and improved equipment if they can remove these items after they have been attached to the realty. Statutes in a number of states establish tenants' rights to remove trade fixtures.

Although the law allows tenants to remove trade fixtures at the end of a lease even if the lease doesn't mention this point, parties to a commercial lease should include provisions that express their agreement as to how trade fixtures will be treated when the lease ends. They might agree that the tenant shall not remove items that ordinarily would be trade fixtures. On the other hand, a lease provision stating the tenant's right to remove those items added to carry out the business or trade shows the intention of the parties and lessens possibilities for disagreement and litigation as to whether or not the items may be removed.

Growing Crops

Traditionally, courts classified growing crops in two categories. An annual crop that was the product of human effort was referred to as *fructus industriales*. This classification included crops such as wheat, corn, oats, cotton and rice. Crops that were produced on perennial roots such as trees, bushes and vines were categorized as *fructus naturales*. Fructus naturales were crops such as citrus fruits, apples, berries and grapes. As a general rule, fructus industriales were considered personal property and fructus naturales real property.

Today, in most states, for most purposes the classification of fructus naturales has been broadened considerably. In general, it includes any crop that owes its value to human care and labor. Thus, fruit and berry crops as well as crops like hay are classified as fructus industriales. In a limited number of states the courts consider the produce of perennial roots fructus industriales, although the trees, vines and bushes that produce the crop are fructus naturales.

Although these classifications continue to be of importance when a dispute arises involving growing crops, modern courts consider a number of other factors when determining whether a crop is realty or personalty.

One significant factor in some states is the maturity of the crop. The more mature the crop, the more likely courts are to consider it personal property. In addition to maturity, courts often consider factors such as the relationship of the parties, their intentions and the type of transaction. Many present-day legal problems involving growing crops are solved by statutes, which individual states have adopted because of the uncertainty of the case law.

One of the most significant of these statutes is the Uniform Commercial Code (UCC), which has been adopted by all states. Article 2 of the UCC deals with the sale of goods. "Goods" under the UCC are always personal property. Furthermore, the UCC defines growing crops as goods whether they are grown on annual or perennial roots. This definition eliminates the traditional legal distinction between fructus industriales and fructus naturales, at least for UCC purposes. The UCC also states that growing crops become goods if they can be removed without harm at the time buyer and seller contract for their sale even if they are part of the real estate at the time. Thus, Christmas trees and sod grown on the land become personal property before severance if they are identified as the subject of a contract.

Although statutes such as the UCC bring some certainty to the law, the real estate practitioner should realize that the most effective method of preventing controversy is to have the parties agree how the crops are to be treated. This agreement should then be included in the lease, deed, purchase offer or other written documentation that covers the transaction.

SECURED TRANSACTIONS

A transaction in which the parties agree that personal property or fixtures will secure a loan or the purchase of an item on credit.

Lenders use various types of personal property to secure repayment of loans. Sellers, too, often retain an interest in goods being sold on credit to ensure payment of the purchase price. Secured transactions of this nature are very important to the economy of the United States. They range from relatively minor purchases by consumers of appliances and television sets to extensive financing of inventory and equipment by business firms. These secured transactions frequently involve real estate, inasmuch as fixtures are often used as collateral, or security for the loan. Common examples would be air-conditioning equipment and industrial machinery. Even after these are installed in a building, the credit seller may retain a security interest until the purchase price is paid.

The law pertaining to secured transactions is found in Article 9 of the UCC. Article 9 applies to all personal property and fixture security interests created by agreement. For Article 9 to protect a creditor effectively, both attachment and perfection must occur.

Attachment

The process by which a secured party acquires a security interest in collateral.

A security interest is not effective between the parties until it has attached to the collateral. Three events must take place for a security interest to attach. Although these events usually occur in the following order, no particular order is required. The security interest attaches when the last event occurs.

- The debtor and secured party (creditor) agree that a security interest attaches.
- The secured party (creditor) gives value to the debtor.
- The debtor has or acquires rights in the collateral.

In most secured transactions, the agreement must be in writing; however, if the secured party retains possession of the security, an oral agreement is sufficient. The written agreement is known as a *security agreement*. The UCC defines a security agreement as "an agreement which creates or provides for a security interest." In those situations in which the secured party retains possession of the security, the transaction is known as a *pledge*.

Ordinarily a security agreement is initiated when the secured party supplies a standard form that is to be completed by the borrower or buyer. This form is usually labeled "Security Agreement," but other terms such as "Conditional Sales Contract" are also used. Whatever the form is called, if it includes the necessary information, a security agreement exists under the UCC.

Perfection

The process by which the secured party establishes priority in the collateral over claims of third parties.

The purpose of perfection is to notify third parties of the existence of a security agreement. Under general legal principles, when a third party knows of or has available information as to the existence of a security interest, the third party's rights are subordinate to that security interest. Two principal methods for perfecting a security interest under the UCC are *public filing* of a notice that such an interest exists and *possession* of the collateral by the secured party. The latter is usually not applicable where fixtures are involved because the debtor almost always is in possession of the real property to which the fixture is attached. Although public filing may be accomplished by recording the signed security agreement, a form containing information from the agreement is used more frequently. This form is called a *financing statement.*

State law must be checked to determine the proper place for filing a financing statement for most items, but the UCC specifically states that to properly perfect a security interest in a fixture, the secured party must file in the office where real estate mortgages are recorded. This *fixture filing* must contain the name of the real property owner and the address of the property.

Sometimes there is a question as to whether an item is a fixture. In this event, the secured party should file twice. The second filing should be made as state law directs for items other than fixtures.

Fixture Filing

A section of the UCC that allows a security interest in goods (personal property) that later become fixtures.

With few exceptions, a security agreement that has been perfected by recording a financing statement provides the secured creditor with priority over claims of third parties. This sometimes results in problems where fixtures are involved. Conflict can occur between the mortgage lender who has a security interest in the real property and a second party who has a security interest in a fixture located on the same real property.

CASE EXAMPLE

Fran's Pizza needed a new oven. One was purchased on credit from Only Oven, Inc., which had Fran sign a security agreement. The oven was installed in the pizza parlor, which was owned by Fran but heavily mortgaged to the Bank of Durango. Despite the new oven, Fran's business was unsuccessful, and she became bankrupt. Only Oven tried to remove the oven, but the bank argued that it was a fixture and should be sold as a part of the building.

In the past, the law relating to security interests in fixtures varied from state to state. Initial efforts through the UCC to deal with the problem created by conflicting interests between a real property lender and a person whose security is a fixture were not very successful. A number of states did not accept the UCC's provisions; in others, real estate lenders objected, since the UCC appeared to favor the fixture security interest. In the early 1970s, the UCC was amended to reduce these objections. By 1981 a majority of states had adopted the amendments.

Under the current provisions of the UCC, Only Oven would have priority over the Bank of Durango if it had properly perfected its security interest. Proper perfection requires fixture filing before the goods become fixtures or within ten days thereafter. The ten-day grace period given to the secured party applies only against prior recorded interests in the real estate. A fixture filing has priority against subsequent interests as of the date of filing. If the Bank of Durango had advanced funds after the manufacturer had installed the oven, Only Oven would not enjoy a priority unless its security interest were already perfected by a fixture filing.

Fixture security interests are subject to an exception when a construction mortgage is involved.

CASE EXAMPLE

Claude Real Estate is building an office on land that it owns. The construction is being financed by Central Bank, which has agreed to advance funds as the work progresses. The bank has recorded a construction mortgage. Claude purchases plumbing fixtures from Little John, which perfects a security interest by properly recording a fixture filing statement. Soon after the building is completed, Claude fails, and Little John attempts to remove the fixtures. Central Bank objects, claiming a prior interest on the basis of its construction mortgage.

In this situation, Little John would not be able to remove the plumbing fixtures. The UCC expressly gives priority to a *construction* mortgage recorded before the filing of a fixture security interest. In addition, the UCC provides that no fixture security interest exists in ordinary building materials, such as bricks and lumber, once they are incorporated into a structure, for obvious reasons.

MOBILE HOMES

A transportable structure built on a chassis and designed for year-round living, usually set up on a permanent foundation and connected to utilities.

The UCC offers a solution to problems that arise when lenders use as security p_rsonal property that can readily become a fixture. However, in those areas dealing with property whose classification as real or personal is not clear, problems abound. One kind of property the courts find difficult to classify as real or personal is the mobile home.

A substantial percentage of housing in the United States consists of mobile homes. Census figures for 1980 indicate that nearly four million mobile homes are used as dwellings. As the average number of occupants is 2.8, between 11 and 12 million people live in dwellings of this type.

The unique quality of locomotion of mobile homes has made it difficult for courts to decide whether to classify them as real or personal property. This has caused legal controversy, especially regarding taxation. Owners argue that mobile homes are not real estate and thus cannot be taxed as real estate. On the other hand, taxing authorities contend that mobile homes use local services supported by real estate taxation and therefore should contribute to the cost of these services.

Taxation of Mobile Homes

When used on the highways, the mobile home is subject to all highway rules and regulations as well as vehicular license fees. However, revenue from these sources is limited as most mobile homes are intended as permanent or semipermanent housing, and highway usage is generally confined to towing between sites.

States have adopted a number of taxing devices to ensure that mobile home owners carry their fair share of the cost of government. States that have effective personal property taxes treat mobile homes as personal property and collect taxes on the same basis as for other personal property. A number of states exact a license fee or excise tax in lieu of the personal property tax. Some states that do not have personal property taxes assess and tax mobile homes as real property. If a question arises between the owner and the taxing authority as to whether a mobile home has lost its primary mobility, the answer is determined in a manner similar to that used to identify a fixture. The intention of the owner is used as the major test.

Real estate personnel concerned with questions involving mobile home taxations should carefully check applicable state statutes. Laws in this area differ substantially from state to state.

SUMMARY

The term *property* generally refers to various rights a person has in a tangible item—a building, car or other possession—but it can also refer to something intangible, such as a lease or even the right to use a trademark. Possession of this "bundle of rights" depends on the laws a government creates and maintains for the benefit of citizens. A major development changing the laws regarding the use and sale of property is found in civil rights legislation.

Historically, personal property in general is differentiated from real property—land and buildings a person owns—because of the economic significance attached to land. Personal property is characterized as being movable, although in today's usage some personal property, such as a franchise, is intangible. Real estate professionals need to be aware of the distinction between the two kinds of property so that contracts and other legal documents will be written properly.

The legal distinction becomes important when courts determine whether an item attached to land or buildings becomes real property. If so, the item (such as built-in shelving or certain kitchen appliances) is characterized as a *fixture* and must not be removed upon sale of the realty. A number of states have established tenants' rights to remove *trade fixtures* upon termination of a commercial lease. Even so, parties to a commercial lease should agree in writing on the terms at the outset in order to reduce possibilities of litigation.

Often a purchaser of business fixtures uses the fixtures themselves as collateral to secure a loan for their payment. The Uniform Commercial Code, Article 9, provides legal protection for both buyer and seller in this type of secured transaction, when the two legal requirements of attachment and perfection are met. In the attachment process, three events occur: both parties consent in writing to the arrangement, value must be given by the secured party and the debtor must have rights in the collateral. In perfection, the secured party establishes priority in the collateral over other debtors through an official recording of the transaction. The UCC requires that all documents be both written and filed, as a mortgage agreement would be.

In some areas the distinction between realty and personal property is not so clear. One example is mobile homes, which, although similar in many ways to realty, are still considered movable.

REVIEW AND DISCUSSION QUESTIONS

1. Explain the statement "During the past half-century the traditional legal concept of property has both expanded and contracted."
2. Define a trade fixture and explain how the law relating to trade

fixtures differs from the law relating to fixtures generally.

3. What legal problems might arise because American law distinguishes between real and personal property?

4. Explain the difference between attachment and perfection of a security interest.

5. Discuss the factors courts consider when attempting to determine if an item is a fixture.

CASE PROBLEMS

1. Stephens purchased a steel grain-drying bin from B. C. Manufacturing and executed a conditional sales contract and a financing statement. The financing statement was filed in the county clerk's office but not in the office of the registrar for deeds. The bin was placed on a concrete base on property owned by Newman Grove Grain Company. This property was later mortgaged to Battle Creek Bank. The mortgage was foreclosed, and Tillotson purchased at the foreclosure sale. B. C. Manufacturing sued for the value of the bin. Would B. C. Manufacturing be successful? Discuss. *Tillotson v. Stephens,* 195 Neb. 104, 237 N.W.2d 108 (1975).

2. Holsopple obtained a building permit for construction of a single-family dwelling. Zoning regulations prohibited use of mobile homes in the area. The structure in question consisted of three units. The main unit, about 12 by 70 feet, was mounted on a metal frame with three axles. Each axle had two wheels. The main unit was pulled by a truck to the site, where two smaller units were bolted to it. The entire structure was mounted on a concrete foundation. The wheels were removed and stored under the structure; the frames and axles remained attached. The basic assembly of the three units took two men working 19 hours each. Was the unit a mobile home or single-family dwelling? Discuss. *Bowman v. Holsopple,* 155 Ind. App. 272, 292 N.E.2d 274 (Ct. App. 1973).

3. Stanley King purchased an old Victorian residence from its owner, Helen Floyd. After King took possession of the home he discovered that Floyd had taken drapes that had been tailored to fit an odd-sized window, a window air conditioner and an antique bathtub. The tub had been replaced by a new tub of excellent quality. The contract of sale signed by both parties did not mention any of these items. Is King entitled to recover damages? Support your answer.

4. Thatcher was interested in buying a business. She finally located a gift shop and agreed to buy it. The business was located in a building that Thatcher leased for three years. In order to

increase the shop's business, she purchased several new display cases. These were attached to the floor. The business was successful; however, the landlord notified Thatcher that the lease would not be renewed. Does Thatcher have the right to remove the display cases? Support your answer.

4
Estates in Land

ALLODIUM

Land owned absolutely; the holder owes no obligation to a superior.

Interests in land existing in the United States today are the result of two different systems of ownership. For several centuries, both systems existed side by side in Europe. One of these systems was *feudalism*, in which everyone holding land except the sovereign owed rents or services to a superior. In the *allodial* system, on the other hand, all land was owned absolutely. The holder had no obligation to pay rents or services to another.

Absolute ownership was the basis of Roman real property law. After the collapse of the Roman Empire, feudalism gradually became dominant in most of Europe except in some sections where the Roman influence persisted. In many of these areas the Roman idea of absolute ownership continued as the basis for holding land. Land was held without obligation to superiors. The owner had an absolute title with few limitations or restrictions on rights to use or dispose of it.

Today, the allodial concept of ownership is the distinguishing feature of real property ownership in the United States. Private ownership of land is free and absolute, subject only to governmental and voluntary private restrictions.

FEUDALISM

An economic and social system that dominated European life between A.D. 1000 and 1350, based primarily upon obligations owed to a superior in return for the right to occupy land.

The fall of the Roman Empire brought to western Europe a long period

55

of intense disruption. Law and order, established and maintained by the military might and organizational genius of Rome, collapsed. The chaos that resulted for about 500 years led to extensive disintegration of organized society. In order to survive, the people of western Europe turned to local leaders for protection of family and wealth.

Since most wealth consisted of land, which was also necessary for survival, people in a particular locality would join together and turn their land over to a local leader who, in exchange, would guarantee them protection and grant them rights in the land for a period of time. This practice, which proved relatively effective, spread throughout most of Europe over a period of several generations.

Local leaders who protected small groups of people often allied themselves to a stronger protector by a similar process. As a result, the interests of many people were sometimes united through a single piece of land. Frequently, several intermediaries existed between the person at the top and the actual occupant of the land.

In this system land was not owned in the sense that we think of ownership today. A person holding land was spoken of as being "seised" of the land. As a tenant, the occupant owed certain services that arose because he had possession, but the overlord also enjoyed rights arising out of the same parcel. In many instances this immediate overlord owed duties and services to another based upon his rights in the land.

The conquest of the Angles and Saxons by the Normans in 1066 brought a relatively advanced and sophisticated form of feudalism to England. The Norman dukes who became kings in England faced serious problems in a hostile environment. Their supply lines were long, they were opposed by most of the population and many of their followers were more interested in returning to Normandy than remaining in England. To consolidate his power and to induce his followers to remain in England, William the Conqueror, the first of the Norman dukes to serve as an English king, imported a modified form of the continental system of feudalism to England.

Tenure

The fundamental principal of feudalism; all land was held on the condition that certain duties and services be performed for a superior.

William declared all English lands forfeited to him because of the failure of the Angle and Saxon lords to recognize him as the rightful king. As supreme lord of all English land, he parceled it out as fiefs to his Norman followers and those Angles and Saxons who would swear allegiance to him. Those who acquired fiefs from the king, however, were not given absolute ownership. They held the land as tenants but were required, in return, to perform services for the king or their respective overlords.

Tenants who held land in *military tenure,* or *knight service,* agreed to furnish military service. Those who held in *socage tenure* were required to furnish supplies. Still others furnished personal service to the king in a type of tenure known as *serjeanty.* Finally, certain religious orders were given land as tenants for which religious support was required. Although all land was held eventually by the king, vassals to whom extensive grants of land were given allocated portions of their lands in a similar manner. The result was a system of landholding based upon tenancy very similar in many aspects to the system that existed on the Continent. In England, however, all land rights were derived from the Crown, then in the person of William the Conqueror.

In addition to the specific duties owed by the tenant, the relationship created other valuable rights for the lord. For example, if a tenant died with his heirs underage, the lord had the right to guardianship, which entitled him to all profits from the estate until the heir became of age. The lord also had the right to arrange a marriage for the heir. If the heir rejected his choice, the estate was subject to a substantial penalty. If a tenant died without heirs, his land *escheated*—that is, was returned to the lord's possession. The lord also had the right to collect contributions from tenants to defray the costs of knighting his oldest son, to provide a dowry for his oldest daughter and to ransom himself if he were taken prisoner.

Many of these valuable rights were greatly reduced in value in the early stages of feudalism as tenants generally were permitted to create subtenancies of their holdings.

CASE EXAMPLE

Sir John holds two parcels of land in knight service of Lord Lacy. Sir John transfers one of these parcels to his brother Sir James to hold at a rent of 10 bushels of wheat per year. Sir John is killed in a crusade, leaving an infant heir. Lord Lacy, instead of being entitled to possession of all the lands held by Sir John as guardian of the infant, is entitled only to ten bushels of wheat from the lands transferred to Sir James.

Faced with losses of this nature, the powerful lords in England forced through Parliament the Statute of Quia Emptores.

Statute of Quia Emptores
Landmark English statute that affirmed the right of the tenant to sell land but required the new owner to perform all feudal duties connected with the land.

This statute affirmed the right of free men to sell their tenancies while assuring the lord that the new tenant held directly of the same lord and by the same services. The statute, along with changes in economic and political conditions that resulted in the gradual substitution of monetary payments for the feudal services, eventually led to the termination of the tenure system of landholding in England. The last vestiges of this system were finally abolished by statute in the 1920s.

Tenure in the United States

In the eastern part of the United States, some of the early colonial grants were based upon tenure. The proprietor held his land directly from the king. The small monetary payment required as a token of this relationship was called a *quitrent.* When the proprietor of a colony granted smaller tracts to individual settlers, each owed a quitrent by an extension of the feudal theory. These quitrents were very often ignored because of the ready availability of land on the frontier. In Massachusetts, Rhode Island and Connecticut, the tenurial system never existed; land there was held allodially. After the Revolution quitrents were abolished, and the notion prevailed that a person who owned land had an absolute title limited only by the state.

Vestiges of feudalism and tenure are retained in American real property law. One example is the law of *escheat*, in which the state is paramount, with land reverting to it if a person dies without heirs. Probably more important is the English concept of estates in land, for our legal system continues to recognize the idea that separate divisible interests can exist simultaneously in the same piece of land.

ESTATE

The extent and character of a person's rights and interests in land; to be an estate, the person's interest must be one that is (or may become) possessory.

The feudal notion of tenure is the foundation of the doctrine of estates in land. This doctrine has substantially influenced the rights that individuals may have in real property. The term *estate* as used in this context has a restrictive and technical meaning. It should not be confused with more common usage—that is, as a synonym for all of a person's assets.

In the system of tenure as it developed in England, land was separated from interests that might exist in it. Because land was one thing and interests in it another, several people could possess interests or estates in the same piece of land. This idea continues to be a feature of the law of English-speaking countries. Although a complete estate in land may exist at the present moment, it can be divided into various slices in such a way that each slice is regarded as existing now.

CASE EXAMPLE

Lansing Thomas owns a large farm. He directs by will that, upon his death, the property pass to Beverly Lane, his only daughter, for life and then to her oldest son. When Lansing dies, two estates exist in the land simultaneously.

Lansing's daughter Beverly has a *life estate*. This is a possessory estate because she is entitled to the rents and profits from the farm for her life. Beverly's oldest son has a *future estate*. Upon his mother's death he is entitled to the farm, but he can claim nothing in possession until she dies.

Although the nature, quality and extent of their interests often differ, each holder of an estate invariably has a present or future right of possession. Sometimes this right may be deferred until a future time, or it might even be conditional, but it is currently recognized by the courts. During his mother's life, the son in the example above does not have a right to occupy the land or profit from it. He does, however, possess an interest or estate that would be recognized in American courts as it was in the English. Further, he has rights to prevent *waste* of the property by the life tenant.

As there are many possible interests in land, estates have numerous dimensions. Several classifications of estates have developed reflecting these differences. This chapter distinguishes between two types of estates characterized by the duration of the owner's right to possession: freehold and nonfreehold estates. Nonfreehold estates are discussed in full in Chapter 25. Defeasible estates, those concerned primarily with the quality of the owner's interest, and future estates are discussed in this chapter along with other types of freehold estates. A later chapter deals with estates from the viewpoint of the number and relationship of owners.

FREEHOLD ESTATE

An estate of uncertain duration.

Numerous freehold interests exist in land. Although they all have in common uncertainty as to their termination, other rights of the owners differ. The holders of most freehold estates may pass their interests along to their heirs. These are generally called *freehold estates of inheritance*. The most usual is the *fee simple* or *fee simple absolute*. Life estates are also freehold estates since their duration is uncertain. Life estates, however, are not estates of inheritance because they terminate upon the owner's death.

Some estates are created for a fixed period of time. The principal estates of this nature are the estate or tenancy for years and the tenancy from period to period. At common law, these nonfreehold estates were distinguished from freehold estates. For many purposes, they were treated as personal, not real, property. The holder of a non-freehold estate did not have the same status or legal rights as the holder of a freehold estate. Tenancies at will and tenancies at sufferance are other estates less than a freehold.

Fee Simple or Fee Simple Absolute

The most extensive interest in land that a holder might possess; one that is potentially indefinite in duration.

Most land in the United States is held in fee simple. A fee simple is a freehold and, in addition, the most extensive estate known to the law. The holder of a fee simple title possesses all rights commonly associated with property or ownership. Possession is one of these rights. Subject to limitations by the state, the owner may sell the estate or give it away during his or her lifetime; the owner may direct the disposition of the estate by will; if the owner dies without a will, the fee will be disposed of according to the laws of the jurisdiction in which the fee is located. Creditors may levy against the estate, or the owner may use it as security. The holder of a fee may voluntarily limit uses to which it may be put or carve out lesser estates from it. Use limitations will be recognized by the courts if they do not violate public policy. Although the term has its roots in feudal times, in most respects the holder of a *fee simple* has the rights of allodial ownership.

Except in cases of conveyances to institutions such as corporations or government, the common law required the grantor to use specific words to create a fee simple. The words *and his heirs* continue in common use today, although in most states any words that indicate an intention to create a fee simple are sufficient. Thus, the granting clause in a deed will generally state "to [grantee] and his heirs" or "to [grantee] and his heirs forever." In some parts of the country, this estate is referred to simply as a *fee*.

Defeasible Fee

A fee simple that terminates upon the happening of some future stated event.

The holder of a fee simple or lesser estate has the right to create other estates in the land, which may be limited in several ways. Although this factor has complicated property law of English-speaking countries, it has also provided variety in the uses to which real property may be put. A grantor, by using the defeasible fee, is often able to benefit society and, at the same time, protect interests he or she considers important. The two types of defeasible fees next discussed have been used for self-serving, narrow-minded purposes, but they also have been used for benevolent purposes in a manner benefiting the entire community. In this context, it is important to remember that, until a defeasible fee terminates because the stated condition has occurred, the interests of the owner are the same as those possessed by the owner of a fee simple absolute.

CASE EXAMPLE

Mrs. Zahn, who is an environmentalist, owns a large tract of land in Wisconsin on which she desires to establish a wildlife sanctuary. She proposes to do this by giving the land to the National Wildlife Society. Although the directors of the society have agreed to administer and maintain the sanctuary, Mrs. Zahn fears that, as time passes and the land becomes more valuable, her original intent might be forgotten.

The law provides a number of methods for Mrs. Zahn to accomplish her objective and ensure that her intentions are honored. One of these would be to limit the future use of the land by imposing conditions in the deed. This task can be accomplished in two ways.

Fee Simple Determinable.   This is a fee simple that automatically terminates when a stated condition is fulfilled.

If the granting clause in the deed to the wildlife society states, "to the National Wildlife Society and its successors and assigns so long as the property is used as a wildlife preserve," a fee simple determinable would be created. The estate thus created is also known as a *base* or *qualified fee*. The fee is indefinite in duration as it is a fee simple, but the grantee's interest terminates automatically and reverts back to the grantor if the condition is fulfilled.

Fee Simple Subject to Condition Subsequent.   This is a fee simple that may be terminated by the grantor or the grantor's successor when a stated condition is fulfilled. This estate is very similar to a determinable fee. The major difference is that termination is not automatic. The estate continues when the stated condition is fulfilled unless the grantor or the grantor's successors take steps to terminate it. The grantor or successor is said to have a *power of termination.* Our environmentalist might create an estate of this nature by stating in the deed: "to the National Wildlife Society and its successors and assigns forever on condition that the land is used as a wildlife preserve, but if the land is used for any other purposes, Mrs. Zahn and her heirs shall have a right of entry and repossession."

Fee Tail

An estate that was restricted by its creator to direct descendants.

The concept of estates in land provided English and American lawyers with appreciable flexibility to arrange property rights in land for their clients. A person who possessed a fee simple estate could carve out lesser interests in the land as well as control the disposition of the land well into the future. For example, if the owner of a fee simple made a grant to "A and the heirs of his body" and A had a son, the estate would pass to the son upon A's death. If A did not have children, the estate would revert to the grantor to descend as directed by him or to his heirs if the original grantor were dead.

CASE EXAMPLE

Sir Phillip, who has two sons, Francis and Dumont, possesses a fee simple in Blackacre. Sir Phillip wishes to keep Blackacre in his family, so he grants Blackacre to his oldest son: "Francis and the heirs of his body, but if Francis dies without issue, to Dumont and the heirs of his body." As long as Francis has direct descendants, they would be entitled to the estate. If Francis's line were to terminate, Dumont's line would have the estate.

By creating this type of estate, Sir Phillip has been able to keep the land in his family. He has been able also to prevent both Francis and Dumont or their lineal descendants from squandering his interest and leaving nothing for the next generation.

Estates of this type were referred to as *estates in fee tail*. Many variations were possible. The grant might be to "A and the male heirs of his body" or "the female heirs of his body." As these and other limitations were used primarily to perpetuate the English landed aristocracy, they have been accepted in American law only to a very limited degree. The basic idea of allowing the owner of land to restrict its use by limitations on the estate granted does, however, have a place in modern American law.

Future Estate (Future Interest)

An interest in land that may become possessory in the future.

The common law accepted the idea that several estates of different duration could exist in land at the same time. Our legal system continues to recognize this concept. Only one of these interests is possessory, but because of the estate concept the party in possession does not necessarily have all interests associated with ownership. If A, the holder of a fee simple, grants a life estate to B, B's interest terminates with death and something obviously is left over. As A has a fee simple, A's estate, from which the grant to B was carved, is infinite in duration. If A's grant to B said nothing about what was left after B's death, A and his heirs have a future interest. This is an interest that entitles them to possession at that time in the future when B dies.

This particular type of future interest is called a *reversion*, as the residue reverts back to *A* or his heirs.

Suppose, however, that *A*'s deed is worded "to *B* for life remainder to *C* and her heirs"; then *C* has a future interest. Although *C* has no present right to possession, her future interest is probably more valuable than *B*'s life estate, for upon the death of *B*, *C* or her heirs acquire a fee simple absolute. *C*'s interest is called a *remainder*. As *C*'s interest is not subject to any condition except *B*'s death, the remainder is said to be *vested*.

In addition to the reversion and the remainder, other future interests also exist. An example is the previously mentioned fee simple determinable. In creating this estate, the holder does not make an absolute grant of his or her entire interest. When the condition limiting the grant is fulfilled, the interest of the party in possession automatically terminates. The grantor and his or her heirs thus have a possibility of regaining possession at some time in the future. This future interest is called a *possibility of reverter*.

The creation of a fee simple subject to a condition subsequent also creates a future interest. This future interest is referred to as a *right of reentry* or a *power of termination*. When the possessory estate terminates because the condition is fulfilled, the holder of the right of reentry may get the land by filing suit.

Current Status of the Future Interest

The acceptance of the concept of possessory estates in land followed by a future interest lends flexibility to the disposition of real property; in many instances, however, future interests exist because a grantor wishes to limit the free transferability of land. Often the creator of the estate wishes to control the use of the land not only during his or her lifetime but after death as well. Conditional and defeasible fees have been used in the past for this purpose and continue to be used today.

The right of reentry and the possibility of reverter cause especially serious problems. The fees that give rise to these interests are created to last forever and often do last for many years. As a result, the right of reentry and the possibility of reverter are merely expectant interests with almost no present economic value. Often the current possessors of these interests are remote descendants of the original creator. Frequently they are unaware that another interest exists. When a title search reveals the existence of these interests, a person attempting to clear the title is presented with a difficult, if not insoluble, problem arising from the fact that often it is impossible to contact many of the parties who might retain an interest in the land because of the future interest.

A small but growing number of states have attempted to solve this problem through legislation. This legislation often places limitations on the time a future interest can last. Another type of legislation places limitations on the time during which a future interest can be enforced. Other states have adopted legislation that ensures a person who has an unbroken chain of title extending over a given number of years a fee simple free of future interests.

Life Estate

An estate of limited duration measured by a life or lives.

Granting an estate to an individual for life has been a common practice in the United States. A life estate typically is measured by the life of the owner, but it may be measured by the life of some other person. If the holder of a fee simple absolute makes a grant "to A for life," A has an estate that terminates with his or her death. If the grant were "to A for the life of B," A's estate would terminate upon the death of B. This type of life estate is called an estate *pur autre vie*. In modern practice, estates *pur autre vie* are seldom created.

Rights and Duties of Life Tenants

The holder of a life estate, usually called the *life tenant*, has an ownership interest in the land. This interest can be sold, mortgaged or leased, but it is not very valuable. Any interest a buyer, mortgagee or lessee acquires ends with the death of the life tenant. Life tenants are entitled to rents and profits from the property while their tenancy lasts, but they may not use the property in a manner that will permanently reduce its market value. If they do so, the owner of the estate that follows may bring an action against them for *waste*.

Life tenants must make ordinary repairs to the property. They are responsible for annual property taxes but for only a proportionate share of special assessments for sewers, sidewalks and other permanent improvements. As a general rule, the life tenant is required to pay the interest on a mortgage but not the principal. The life tenant's obligations generally are limited to the extent the property provides income or profits.

• CASE BRIEF •

Upon his death in 1920, H.B. Stout gave Addie, his wife, a life estate in three rental properties with remainder to his daughter, Olive. The properties rented well until 1929. From 1929 until her death in 1933, Addie had difficulty in renting them. The rental income barely paid the taxes, and few repairs were made. Upon Addie's death, Olive filed a claim for waste against the estate. The court held her claim valid because income from the property over the 13-year period was sufficient to keep it in repair. *In re Stout's Estate, 151 Or. 411, 50 P.2d 768 (1935).*

Life estates frequently cause legal problems. In many cases, these problems involve the relationship between the life tenant and the holders of the estate to be enjoyed upon the termination of the life estate.

• CASE BRIEF •

Bridges owned a life interest in realty upon which there was a building worth $10,000. She insured the building, using her own funds. The building was destroyed by a hurricane and the proceeds of the policy paid to Bridges. The court approved a petition by the owner of the remainder that Bridges be ordered to rebuild or hold the insurance proceeds for the remainderman with interest going to Bridges for life. *Crisp Lumber Co. v. Bridges, 187 Ga. 484, 200 S.E. 777 (1939).*

In modern practice, the use of the life estate in the disposition of real property is gradually being replaced by use of the trust. Lawyers have found that the trust provides a more effective and flexible method of disposing of wealth. A trustee can be given legal title to land to hold for the life of a beneficiary. Proceeds from the land are paid to the beneficiary. Upon the death of the beneficiary, the land or proceeds from the sale of the land are distributed as the creator of the trust has directed. The trustee can also be given additional authority such as power of sale, which would permit disposal of the property if a profitable opportunity arises. Trusts will be discussed in greater detail in a later chapter.

Despite the potential legal problems, the life estate concept has been used in some states to provide security for one spouse upon the death of another. The law grants the surviving spouse a life interest in the real property of the deceased. Life estates of this nature are called *legal life estates*.

Legal Life Estates

At common law several types of life estates in land were created as a result of marriage. A primary objective of these estates was to provide support for the wife upon the death of her husband, but a husband also had a life interest in the wife's real property upon her death. In some states features of these marital life estates continue as important elements of real property law. A considerable number of states, however, have abolished them and substituted a statutory plan to provide for the widow and widower. These plans provide that the surviving spouse be entitled to choose what is called an *elective share*.

Elective share. These statutory plans allow the surviving spouse a specified share of the decedent's net estate. The surviving spouse can elect to take this share if not provided for in the will or if the provi-

sions of the will are deemed by the surviving spouse to be less beneficial than the elective share provided for by statute. The decedent's net
estate consists of real and personal property minus funeral and administration expenses, family allowances and debts. Under the Uniform
Probate Code, which has been adopted in 16 states, the elective share
is one-third. Many other states also allow a right to elect one-third,
and some states allow one-half. Statutes providing the spouse with a
right to elect almost always contain provisions that prevent a married
person from deliberately disposing of property during his or her life to
defeat the right of the surviving spouse to the elective share.

Dower. *Life estate of a widow in one-third of any real property to
which her husband had legal title during marriage.* For many generations, dower was an important right that a widow acquired in her husband's real property upon his death. This right minimally entitled her
to a one-third interest in his lands for life. The widow was entitled to
dower as well as any gifts made in the husband's will, unless the will
clearly stated that the gifts were in lieu of dower. If it was clear that
the bequests were in lieu of dower, the widow had to elect one or the
other.

   While the husband was alive, the wife's right, which did not
materialize unless the husband died before she did, was protected
against both the husband's acts and claims of his creditors arising after the marriage. The wife's interest, which was called *inchoate dower,* was a potential estate. She acquired a legal estate only if she survived her husband.

CASE EXAMPLE

Mary and Ed were secretly married in 1974. At that time, Ed
owned a large office building. In order to modernize the building, in 1976 Ed borrowed a substantial amount of money and
gave a mortgage to secure the loan. As a result of depressed
economic conditions, Ed could not meet payments on the loan,
and the mortgage was foreclosed. Any purchaser at the foreclosure sale would be subject to Mary's inchoate right of dower.

In order for dower to be allowed, the parties must have been legally
married at the time of the husband's death. Consequently, in most
states the right to dower is terminated by divorce, although some
states allow dower if divorce is the result of the husband's fault. A
wife can ordinarily release her inchoate right of dower by joining in
any conveyance of the husband's real property. In the event a husband mortgages his property, the wife will release her inchoate right
of dower if she signs the mortgage, but dower is restored upon payment of the debt.

Curtesy. *A common law estate that provided a husband with a life* *interest in all his wife's real property as soon as a child was born of the marriage.* English common law provided a husband with extensive rights in his wife's real property. While both were alive, he was entitled to the rents and profits as well as the use and enjoyment of any real estate that she owned. In addition, upon birth of a living child, he acquired a life estate in her lands that survived her death. This was the legal life estate of curtesy.

Although common law curtesy and dower had some similarities, they also differed extensively. First, for the husband to acquire curtesy, a living child had to be born of the marriage. The wife's dower interest did not depend upon the birth of a child. Secondly, the life estate the husband acquired by curtesy was in all the real estate owned by the wife, not just in one-third, the interest the wife acquired by dower. Finally, unlike dower, curtesy was a present, not just a potential, estate. This meant that the husband could encumber or sell his interest.

The extensive control over the wife's property that the common law afforded to the husband is no longer law in either the United States or England, but variations of common law curtesy exist to a limited extent in a number of American jurisdictions. These are generally the states that continue to recognize dower. In states where a modified form of curtesy exists, the principal change has been to remove any distinction between it and dower. In the many jurisdictions that have abolished both dower and curtesy, protection for the surviving husband or wife is provided by statute. These statutes ordinarily allow the surviving spouse either to elect a share, generally a one-third interest for life, in both the decendent's real and personal property or to take the interest given by the will.

Homestead Exemption Laws

Laws that (1) exempt the family from a forced sale of its home by certain classes of creditors; (2) may prevent an owner from selling or mortgaging the home without consent of the spouse; and (3) allow the designated family homestead to be used for the family's benefit after the head of the family dies.

CASE EXAMPLE

Cecil Statham, a single man without dependents, recorded a declaration of homestead on real estate that was his home. Shortly thereafter he filed a voluntary petition in bankruptcy and was adjudicated a bankrupt. He claimed the real estate was exempt from creditors under that state's homestead laws. The referee in bankruptcy denied Statham's claim on the grounds that Statham was not head of a family.

Homestead laws, which have been adopted in most states, provide for heads of families some exemptions from creditors' claims. A family is defined in various ways, but most courts take a very liberal approach. They consider that a family exists when two or more persons reside together with one having a legal or moral obligation to support the others. A common and certainly more restrictive definition used in some states limits the family to a currently married husband and wife or a widow or widower still living in the homestead. Some states have extended the exemption to single, unmarried persons.

In spite of the fact that the statutes grant exemptions in favor of the head of the family, they are intended primarily to protect dependents. The exemption rests upon an expression of public policy. A legislature adopting a homestead exemption statute indicates it believes that a person's obligation to support dependents is at least as important as payment of debts. The expressed objective of homestead statutes in most states is to secure a family home beyond the reach of financial misfortune.

In addition to requiring that the owner have a family, most state homestead laws require that the exempt real estate be the permanent residence of the family. Several states also require the owner to formally declare a particular piece of real estate as a homestead.

Exempt property usually includes a lot and improvements up to a stated dollar or acreage amount. Some states use a combination of acreage and dollars. The dollar amounts vary widely. They range from a few thousand dollars to much higher amounts. Five to ten thousand dollars is a common dollar limitation. In rural areas, exempt acreage is frequently 160 acres; urban area exemptions are one-third to one-half acre. As a general rule, if the value or extent of the homestead exceeds the exemptions, creditors may force a sale of part of the property. The debtor retains the amount of the exemption.

CASE EXAMPLE

Richard Rainey owned and occupied a 250-acre farm. He incurred a number of debts that he was unable to pay. When his creditors obtained judgments against him and attempted to sell the farm, Rainey claimed his homestead exemption. State law limited the exemption to 160 acres, and the court ordered 90 acres sold and the proceeds applied to pay Rainey's debts. As was customary, the unsold portion included the residence.

Although the homestead exemption provides some protection to a debtor and his/her family, the exemption does not protect the debtor against all claims. The following claims are often given priority by state law:

- an existing mortgage or deed of trust;
- a mortgage or deed of trust given to secure purchase of a residence;
- real property taxes and assessments;
- mechanics' liens;
- debts incurred before the homestead was acquired.

The homestead exemption is probably an anachronism in today's economy. Most exemption statutes were enacted at a time when the American economy was primarily agricultural. The statutes protected the farmer and his family and helped to ensure that food would be available to the nation. Today, many families live in apartments or rented homes. Homestead exemptions provide them with limited protection. In addition, many of the homestead exemptions are set at such low levels that the debtor's equity often exceeds them. The result is a forced sale and loss of the home. The owner does get the amount of the exemption in cash, but usually this amount is small and not sufficient to purchase a new home.

Homestead Property Tax Exemption.   A number of states also use the term *homestead exemption* for statutes that afford property tax relief to older people of limited income and to people with limited income who are permanently and totally disabled. These statutes provide for a reduction of the taxable value of a person's residence if the person has reached a certain age—usually 65—or if a person is totally disabled. In both instances, for a person to qualify for benefits that person's income must not exceed an amount specified by statute. This amount usually is quite low.

SUMMARY

Two systems have shaped real property ownership in the United States: the allodial system and the feudal system. The primary feature of modern real estate practice, however, is the allodial concept that private ownership of realty is free and absolute, subject only to governmental and voluntary restrictions. The feudal system, on the other hand, granted only the right to occupy land owned by a superior.

The continental version of feudalism was brought to England in the 11th century by William the Conqueror, a powerful king who parceled out land and granted tenure to those local lords who would swear allegiance to him. Tenants were required to provide soldiers and arms, supplies or other service to the king and the lords. Social and political pressures over the centuries brought an end to feudalism.

Nevertheless, some modern land policies have been carried over from that time. For example, the concept of estates in land has its roots in the feudal notion of tenure. Several types of ownership or estates in land exist: fee simple absolute, fee tail, fee simple determinable, fee simple subject to condition subsequent and future estates. All these forms have different legal statuses.

Future estates and many of the conditional forms of ownership have been used by the creators of estates to limit the free transferability of an estate. But they often make it impossible for a new owner to gain clear title. Some states have adopted legislation to remedy this problem.

Another form of ownership is the life estate, granted for the life of the owner or some other person. After death of the life tenant, the person(s) named as remainderman takes possession. Legal problems frequently result from this relationship.

The legal life estate is a form that has arisen from the desire to protect the surviving spouse in a marriage. Life interests related to marriage are dower, the wife's interest and curtesy, the surviving husband's interest. Both have roots in the British common law.

Modern law is changing in response to social changes. Most states have some form of homestead law to provide some exemption from creditors' claims for heads of families where the property is a principal residence. Even the homestead exemption may be out of date, however, since many family residences are now rented and exemption amounts are small.

REVIEW AND DISCUSSION QUESTIONS

1. (a) What is the chief characteristic of an *estate*? (b) Explain how the concept of estates has influenced the development of real estate law.
2. Distinguish between a freehold estate and a nonfreehold estate. Give an example of each.
3. Explain the difference between a *fee simple subject to condition subsequent* and a *fee simple determinable*.
4. Explain the difference between the *homestead right* and *dower*.

CASE PROBLEMS

1. In 1904 John F. McElveen conveyed to the trustees of Central Common Free School a tract of one acre. The deed contained the following provision:

Provided, always nevertheless notwithstanding, that in case it should so happen at any time that a free common school shall not be maintained on the described premises for a period of three consecutive years, then the said premises shall be considered abandoned and revert back to John F. McElveen.

Describe the interest of John F. McElveen in the one-acre tract. Does he have a right to sell his interest? Discuss.

2. Ann Shelf was married to Brian Shelf in a state that recognized common law dower. During the marriage Brian leased land for 99 years for the purpose of erecting an office building. Brian also took title to a large farm, which he sold several years later. Neither of those transactions was known to Ann until Brian's death. Discuss her interest, if any, in the two properties.

3. In 1928 Isaac Bennett executed a deed to his son, John Bell Bennett. The instrument contained this language: "...do grant, bargain and sell unto said John Bell Bennett, Jr., his heirs and assigns, all of the following...." The deed also contained the following statement: "It is part of the consideration of this deed that John Bell Bennett cannot sell this property during his lifetime and at his death it is to be divided equally among his children." (a) If John Bennett is survived by his wife Belle and his son, John Bennett, Jr., on what grounds might the son argue that he possessed a fee simple title? (b) Indicate any weakness in this argument. *Bennett v. Humphreys*, 159 Kan. 434, 155 P.2d 431 (1945).

4. In 1965 Maricopa Country executed two quitclaim deeds to the City of Tempe. The deeds contained the following provision:

Subject to the restriction that the...real property shall be operated and maintained solely for park, recreation, public accommodation, and convenience purposes.

No words creating a right of reentry or indicating a reversionary interest in the county were used.

The city leased the land to Baseball Facilities, Inc. (BFI). In 1973 BFI applied for a sales tax permit to conduct activities such as a music festival and evangelical meetings on the land. None of these uses was prohibited by the lease. The city, however, denied the permit on grounds that the use for these purposes would create a right in Maricopa Country to recover the property. The city argued that the provision in the deeds created a defeasible fee. Was the city correct? Discuss. *City of Tempe v. Baseball Facilities, Inc.*, 23 Ariz. App. 557, 534 P.2d 1056 (Ct. App. 1975).

5. Melody Davis purchased a farm from Boyd Bishop, who was very ill. After Melody and her son Don moved into the farmhouse, Don discovered an old deed that conveyed the farm to "Boyd Bishop and his heirs forever." As Bishop had several children, Don was concerned that the children might as heirs have

a claim to the farm when Bishop died. Explain to Don what these words mean.

6. Ronald Guard was married to Loretta Guard in a state that had abolished dower and curtesy. The state had, however, adopted the Uniform Probate Code. Loretta was a successful investor in real estate. She owned several multifamily buildings appraised at $500,000. In addition, she held securities valued at $100,000. When Ronald and Loretta quarreled, she destroyed her will, under which he had been left her entire estate. What claim, if any, might Ronald have against Loretta's estate if she dies before he does?

5
Co-Ownership

CO-OWNERSHIP

A form of ownership in which two or more persons have undivided interests in the same property.

Rights and interests in real estate may be divided in various ways, and a number of different interests often exist simultaneously in the same parcel. A common division of interests is horizontal in relationship to space. Chapter 2 indicated that one person might own the surface while others owned the minerals below or the airspace above the surface. Rights and interests are sometimes divided over time. For example, a life estate might be followed by a remainder in fee. Both estates are valuable, but the owner of the life estate has a present possessory interest. Simultaneously, the owner of the remainder in fee has a present interest, but the right to possession will not materialize until the life estate terminates in the future. A third division of rights exists when several people own undivided interests in a parcel of land at the same time. Generally, in this type of ownership each person is entitled to a specific fraction of the parcel but also shares with the others a single right to possession and profits from the land. This is generally referred to as *concurrent ownership* or *co-ownership.*

Co-ownership was important to the common law, and the various concurrent estates that developed at common law remain important today. A number of legal problems are associated with these common law concurrent estates. Many of these problems are reduced or eliminated if multiple owners use a partnership, corporation or trust to hold title to the property. As a result these devices are becoming increasingly important in real estate holdings and to a degree are replacing the common law forms of multiple ownership. This chapter discusses the traditional concurrent estates: joint tenancy, tenancy in common, tenancy by the entirety and tenancy in partnership. State laws regarding community property are considered briefly. Some modern alternatives for multiple owners when investing in real estate are also presented.

JOINT TENANCY

A form of co-ownership significant in that the entire estate passes to the survivor upon the death of the other joint tenant or tenants.

The principal feature of the joint tenancy is the *right of survivorship.* Upon the death of one of the co-owners, that person's interest passes automatically to surviving joint owners.

CASE EXAMPLE

Tom Casicollo conveys Blackacre in fee simple to his wife Helen and son Tony "as joint tenants." Helen dies. Tony becomes the sole owner of the fee. As this is a joint tenancy, upon Helen's death her interest in Blackacre does not become part of her inheritance estate, but automatically becomes Tony's property.

Joint tenancy with the right of survivorship is an additional example of the manner in which law tends to reflect existing economic and social conditions. During the feudal period, when English property law was developing, ownership of an estate by a single individual facilitated the lord's collection of the dues and services to which he was entitled. As a result, when a deed or will created rights in co-owners, the common law courts presumed that a joint tenancy was intended unless some other form of co-ownership was clearly indicated. Thus, in an earlier time, if Tom had not stated that Helen and Tony were to hold as joint tenants, the law would have presumed that they held in this manner. The survivor possessed the entire fee. The estate was in the possession of one owner, and the overlord had only to deal with a single individual.

Additional forms of co-ownership developed during the feudal period, and, after feudalism ended, the joint tenancy with its right of survivorship continued to meet the needs of English society. Throughout the 17th and 18th centuries, the wealth and power of the English aristocracy was based upon large landholdings. Land was a principal source of political power, the chief source of wealth and the basis of social status. If the landholding became fragmented because of too much division of property among multiple owners or through inheritance, the power of the English upper class would have been diluted. Because joint tenancy helped to prevent this dilution of power, it continued to be the dominant form of co-ownership and the form assumed by the courts to have been selected when the grantor's intention was not clear.

Although joint tenancy played a role in colonial American real property law, it was never as important in this country as it was in England. The reason for this was the marked difference in social and economic conditions between the two countries.

As forms of wealth other than land have become important, joint tenancy gradually has been replaced by other types of co-ownership. Most of these developed because they were more readily adapted to modern society's need for the free transferability of property.

Rights of Joint Tenants

Each co-owner who holds as a joint tenant has an equal right to possession of the entire property. This is referred to as an *undivided interest*. Although a joint tenant may not exclude other joint tenants from possession, strangely enough the law considers occupancy by one as occupancy by all. In the above example, if Tony Casicollo occupied Blackacre as a residence without his mother's objection, he would not be responsible to her for a proportionate share of the rent; neither would he be required to share income with her if Blackacre were a farm or commercial real estate. Helen Casicollo has the same rights, however; hence if each tenant is to benefit, all must agree to share the proceeds of the property. Where agreement cannot be reached, the tenancy must be terminated.

Severance of Joint Tenancy

A number of different methods exist to sever or terminate a joint tenancy. Traditionally, for a joint tenancy to be created or to continue, four "unities" are required. First, the *unity of possession* requires that each have an undivided right to possession. Second, the *unity of interest* requires that each receive a similar estate. For example, one joint tenant cannot hold as a life tenant while the other holds in fee simple. Finally, they have to take at the same time (*unity of time*) and from the same instrument (*unity of title*). If any of these unities terminates, the joint tenancy also ends. The new form of ownership is tenancy in common, a form in which the right of survivorship does not exist.

CASE EXAMPLE

Elaine and Jean O'Brien hold land as joint tenants. Elaine sells her interest to Renaldo Romano. This act terminates the joint tenancy since Romano's interest was not created at the same time or from the same instrument. Jean O'Brien and Romano now hold as tenants in common.

In some states a joint tenancy is destroyed if one of the owners mortgages his or her interest or agrees to sell by land contract. A lease by one joint tenant, however, does not terminate the tenancy. Joint tenancies may also be terminated involuntarily. One example would be if the interest of a joint tenancy is sold to satisfy a debt. The purchaser at the sale becomes a *tenant in common* with the remaining co-owners.

Statutes in some states prohibit the creation of a joint tenancy with the right of survivorship. In most states, however, it is still possible to create a joint tenancy with the right of survivorship, but the instrument creating the interest must clearly indicate that this is the grantor's intention.

CASE EXAMPLE

Don Hickey grants Blackacre to his children, Jane and Don, Jr., as "joint tenants." Nothing is said in the deed about the right of survivorship. Upon the death of Jane or Don, Jr., the property becomes part of the decedent's inheritable estate. If Don had said as "joint tenants with the right of survivorship," a joint tenancy would have been created.

In the states that require the grantor to *express* the intention to include the right of survivorship for it to exist, failure to express it in the language creating an estate in two or more persons results in a tenancy in common.

TENANCY IN COMMON

A form of concurrent ownership in which each owner possesses an undivided right to the entire parcel of land, with each owner's rights similar to those possessed by a sole owner.

In the United States today, the tenancy in common is probably the most frequently occurring form of concurrent ownership. Although tenancy in common developed contemporaneously at common law with joint tenancy, the joint tenancy was for centuries the favored form of multiple ownership. This is no longer true. Many states have abolished the joint tenancy. In those that have retained it, a tenancy in common is implied unless a joint tenancy is clearly indicated by the instrument creating the concurrent estate.

• CASE BRIEF •

By a provision in his will, Patrick Cross gave all his property to his sons, Thomas and William, "share and share alike, or to the survivor of them." William died before Thomas, and Thomas's heirs claimed the property, arguing that their father was a joint tenant with the right of survivorship. The court held that William and Thomas were tenants in common, not joint tenants; as a result, the share of each, upon death, became part of his separate estate. *Cross v. Cross, 324 Mass. 186, 85 N.E.2d 325 (1949).*

Rights of Tenants in Common

Like joint tenants, each tenant in common has an undivided right to possession of the entire parcel. Normally, a tenant in common will not be responsible to the co-owners for any benefits obtained through exclusive occupancy unless he or she excludes the others from participating. At the same time, no tenant in common is entitled to the exclusive use of any part of the land. The result is that problems arise when one cotenant wrongfully excludes the others or when it is practical for the property to be occupied by only a single tenant. Under the circumstances, in a number of states, the cotenants not in occupancy will be entitled to a fair compensation for the use of the property. Similar problems arise where a cotenant not in possession receives benefits from the property exceeding those of his or her co-owners. These types of problems can best be solved by agreement among the parties as can problems involving liability of cotenants for upkeep and improvements. When agreement cannot be reached, partition of property may be the only solution.

PARTITION

An action by which a co-owner obtains a division of property terminating any interest of other co-owners in the divided portion.

Partition is the historic method by which unwilling concurrent owners of real property may terminate the interests of fellow co-owners. Although courts traditionally ordered partition even when no statute authorized them to do so, today partition exists in some form by statute in every state. Many states make the remedy available to some holders of future interests. Under the law of almost all states, co-owners of personal property enjoy the right to partition to the same degree as co-owners of realty.

Partition may be voluntary or compulsory. Voluntary partitions are the result of agreement among the co-owners to end the relationship. They are usually carried out by deeds in which each co-owner is allocated a described portion of the realty by all the other part owners. It is also possible for all the co-owners to convey to a third party, the third party in turn conveying to each former co-owner his or her agreed-upon parcel. Although a few states recognize oral voluntary partitions, a written instrument is usually required, primarily to permit recording in the title history. Voluntary partition requires not only the consent of all the parties to the act but also agreement as to the division of the estate. Compulsory partition by judicial action is necessary when one or more of the multiple owners desire to terminate the relationship and agreement cannot be reached for dividing the property.

The right to partition appears to be absolute unless the parties themselves have agreed they will not use the remedy. A co-owner may demand partition without regard to the size of his or her share. The fact that the interest of a co-owner is subject to a mortgage or other lien, though it is a complicating factor, will not defeat the right. So extensive is the right to partition that state condominium statutes must specifically prohibit the right of condominium owners to seek partition of the condominium elements that are owned in common.

Partition is accomplished in one of three ways. The preferred method is by a physical division of the property. The court orders the property divided, allocating to each co-owner a share that is equivalent to his or her interest. Often, however, physical division is not practicable or desirable, and in these cases the property will be sold and the proceeds divided among the co-owners in relation to their interests. The third method involves physical division of the property into shares that are as nearly as possible equivalent in value to the interests of the individual owners. The court then orders monetary payment to those co-owners whose physical shares were not equivalent to their interest.

TENANCY BY THE ENTIRETY

Co-ownership of property by husband and wife; upon the death of either, the survivor remains as sole owner.

Nearly half the states recognize tenancy by the entirety, a type of co-ownership existing only between husband and wife. This type of co-ownership is based upon an ancient legal fiction by which the common law regarded husband and wife as a single legal person. One result was that, if the two acquired equal interests in real estate by the same instrument, the property was considered owned as an indivisible legal unit. Upon the death of either, the survivor remained as the parcel's sole owner. This result has long been accepted by modern law. Today a right of survivorship similar to that existing for the joint tenancy exists for the tenancy by entirety. In a small estate this right benefits the surviving spouse as it avoids the necessity and cost of probate proceedings.

CASE EXAMPLE

Jim Seaver and his wife Helen purchased an apartment building and took title in both their names. Jim died without making a will, and children by a former marriage claimed that a part interest in the property vested in them. They argued that Jim and Helen were tenants in common. The court held that Helen was the absolute owner because, when a husband and wife take title in both their names, a tenancy by the entirety is created unless otherwise indicated.

The result would not be the same in all states that recognize a tenancy by the entirety. Some of the states that accept this type of tenancy do so only if it is expressly stated in the granting instrument.

Termination of the Tenancy by the Entirety

A tenancy by the entirety is a more stable type of co-ownership than the joint tenancy. Because the marital partners are considered a single unit, neither husband nor wife can sever the tenancy without the other's consent. Unlike the joint tenancy, a sale by either the husband or the wife does not terminate the tenancy or end the right of survivorship.

In many jurisdictions, a tenancy by the entirety cannot be terminated by the forced sale of the husband's or wife's interest. This means that if either spouse individually incurs debts and then refuses to pay them, the creditor cannot *execute upon*—that is, judicially seize—the property. This rule has been criticized because it permits the debtor to escape responsibility while owning an interest in a valuable asset. In a few states, creditors of the husband, but not the wife, may reach the income, profits and title of the property. Whatever interest these creditors acquire is lost if the wife survives. Other states permit the separate creditors of either spouse to levy upon and sell the share of the debtor, whether husband or wife. If the opposite spouse survives, the creditor is deprived of his or her interest. If the creditor holds a joint judgment against both spouses, resulting from an obligation both incurred, the creditor can attach the estate held by the entirety.

Tenancies by the entireties are terminated by divorce because the marital relationship is essential to this form of co-ownership. Upon divorce the parties become tenants in common.

The common law allowed the husband almost complete control of all of his wife's property. This included her individual share in a tenancy by the entirety. The husband, thus, was entitled to all the income from the estate, and he had sole discretion as to occupancy and use. In fact, the husband could even sell the real estate, although sale was subject to the wife's right of survivorship.

A husband's absolute power over his wife's property was terminated by the passage of a number of married women's acts during the past century. These statutes entitle the wife to control and benefit from her property. Today, in most states that recognize tenancy by the entireties the wife has the same rights in the property as her husband.

ESTATE TAX PROBLEMS OF JOINT INTERESTS

Co-ownership often is the source of complicated problems involving both estate and gift taxes. Most of these are beyond the scope of this book, but one common misconception needs clarification at this point. As we know, in both the joint tenancy and the tenancy by the entirety, the share of a deceased co-owner automatically passes to the survivor or survivors. Because of this, people sometimes assume that the estate of a deceased co-owner is not subject to federal estate tax on the jointly owned property.

It is true that for the tenancy by the entirety probate is unnecessary. State taxes on the decedent's estate may be avoided on the interest of the first spouse to die, but the estate is responsible for any federal estate tax.

The Internal Revenue Code requires the legal representative of the deceased spouse to include in the decedent's estate the entire value of any real property held as a co-owner with the right of survivorship. The estate may exclude any part of that value that it can show was purchased with funds supplied by the surviving co-owner(s).

CASE EXAMPLE

Martin and Harold Chang purchased a small building for $60,000. They took title as joint tenants with the right of survivorship. Each furnished 50 percent of the purchase price. Over several years, the building appreciated in value to $80,000. When Martin died, $40,000 would be included in his gross estate for federal estate tax purposes.

If Martin had contributed the entire purchase price, the entire $80,000 value of the property could be included in his gross estate. If the joint tenancy was a gift to the Changs, then only a share proportionate to the number of joint tenants would be included. Again, if Martin had contributed nothing, the entire price being paid by Harold, nothing would be included in Martin's taxable estate. Appropriate gift taxes would have to be paid on Martin's share.

The Internal Revenue Code treats joint tenants and tenants by the entirety in a similar manner. Some limited concessions are made if the joint tenants are husband and wife. If the joint owners are husband and wife and the tenancy was created after December 31, 1976, only one-half the value of the property need be included in the gross estate of the decedent's spouse, no matter which spouse furnished the consideration. But the donor must elect to treat the joint tenancy as a gift at the time of its creation. This limited right might be advantageous if the parties intend to terminate the tenancy prior to death. In this instance, a gift tax is paid on the purchase price, not on the appreciated value of the half interest given.

TENANCY IN PARTNERSHIP

A form of co-ownership in which each partner owns partnership property together with the other partners; each partner's share is treated as personal property; partnership property of a deceased partner passes to the surviving partners.

The common law did not recognize the partnership as a legal entity. As a result, property could not be held in the partnership name. This not only caused confusion but also frequently led to complex legal problems when a partner died or experienced financial difficulty. Creditors of an individual partner could then attach specific partnership assets; upon the death of a partner, his or her share in specific partnership property passed to that person's estate, and an individual partner could terminate the relationship by selling his or her interest in a particular property.

CASE EXAMPLE

Kane and Waldron entered into a partnership agreement to operate a creamery. Partnership funds were used to purchase real estate to operate the business. Title was taken in both Kane's and Waldron's names. A short time later, Kane died. At common law, his interest in the real estate would pass to his heirs, not to the surviving partner.

Most states have now adopted the Uniform Partnership Act, which creates the tenancy in partnership. Specifically, the Uniform Partnership Act permits the firm to buy, hold and sell real estate in the partnership name. Individual partners share ownership in particular property only as members of the firm. Spouses, heirs and creditors of individual partners have no rights in partnership property.

Individual partners may not assign partnership property unless the assignment involves the rights of all partners. Although an individual partner can transfer partnership real property, any such transfer is made only as an agent for other partners of the firm.

Upon the death of any partner, his or her share passes to the surviving partners. In the previous example, Waldron, as the surviving partner, acquires Kane's share. Waldron, however, possesses this property only for the purpose of liquidation inasmuch as Kane's death terminates the partnership. During liquidation, Waldron can operate the business without interference from Kane's legal representatives.

Kane and his heirs—in fact any partner—all have a valuable interest in the partnership. The interest stems from the individual's right to share in the profits and surplus of the firm. The interest is not in specific firm property. Under the Uniform Partnership Act, this interest is regarded as *personalty*, not real property. The partner's interest is unlike the interest of a joint tenant or a tenant in common. If the partner's interest is sold separately, the partnership is destroyed and the interest is not subject to partition.

COMMUNITY PROPERTY

A form of co-ownership between husband and wife in which each has a one-half interest in property acquired through the labor of either during the marriage.

Several jurisdictions in the United States apply the doctrine of community property to real estate owned by a husband or wife. Generally, the community property states are those located in the Southwest; the law of these states was influenced by the laws of France and Spain, countries that have traditionally used the concept of community property in determining property rights of married persons. The states in which community property is an integral part of the legal system are Arizona, California, Idaho, Louisiana, Nevada, New Mexico, Texas and Washington. Other states have from time to time adopted some of the community property ideas. Since community property ownership is statutory, each state varies the characteristics of the system to fit its own needs. It is therefore difficult to generalize about a community property doctrine. When decisions are to be made, legal advice should be obtained in the particular state involved.

Community property is based upon the marital relationship. In community property jurisdictions, the husband and wife are regarded as partners. Each spouse becomes a co-owner with the other in all property acquired through the labor or skill of either or both while the two are married. This fact applies even if title to the property is held individually by the husband or wife.

CASE EXAMPLE

Tanya and Bob Kane, residents of California, were married in 1949. Tanya, following the traditional role of homemaker, managed the domestic establishment and cared for the family. Bob successfully practiced his profession as a doctor. From 1959 until 1977, Bob's practice prospered, and he earned a great deal of money. Some of this was invested in real estate, which was held in Bob's name. When Bob died in 1977, one-half of this real estate, which was community property, belonged to his wife; the other half would be in Bob's estate.

Community property is at odds with the law in other states, which recognize that property held in the name of one of the spouses is solely the property of that person, although the other spouse usually has some rights in relation to the property upon the death of the owner and in some instances upon the termination of the marriage by divorce.

Separate Property

Property owned by the husband or wife prior to marriage and property acquired during marriage by gift, inheritance or will.

Not all property owned by husband and wife in the community property states is community property. The parties retain separate title to property they owned separately before marriage and to property each acquired by gift or inheritance during marriage.

CASE EXAMPLE

The will of John Earles, who died in 1933, gave a one-third interest in a 1,600-acre ranch to his son Jesse. The remaining two-thirds was given to Helen Earles, John's wife. Jesse was married in 1940. In 1948 Helen Earles, retaining a life interest in her two-thirds share, transferred title to her portion of the ranch to Jesse. Upon Jesse's death the ranch would pass as a part of his separate estate, not as community property.

Real property purchased with the separate property of one spouse who takes title in his or her name remains separate property. In the example involving Tanya and Bob Kane, if Bob had inherited money from his mother and invested it in real estate, the real property acquired would be separate property. In some community property states, rents and profits from separate property are considered separate property. In others, rents and profits from separate property become community property.

Control of community property in most states has been given to the husband. The rationale appears to be the traditional view that the husband is the head of the family. Both the statutes that allocate this power to the husband and numerous judicial opinions require the husband to deal with the property in good faith. Recent statutory developments in several community property states have expanded protection of the wife against abuse of the husband's power to manage and control community property.

INVESTMENT ALTERNATIVES FOR MULTIPLE OWNERS

Trust

A legal relationship in which a grantor transfers legal title to property to a trustee, who manages the property for the benefit of third parties, or beneficiaries.

The trust is a device that has been used in the United States and in England for several centuries. It has been an important instrument in law reform and the legal basis for some significant economic innovations.

CASE EXAMPLE

Elaine Morgan, a successful business executive, was married to Carl Morgan, a well-known musician. Carl had little interest in financial matters. In order to ensure that Carl had adequate income throughout his life, Elaine irrevocably transferred certain securities and real estate to Central Trust Company to be administered by the company with the income going to Carl for life. Upon Carl's death, the property was to go to the Juilliard School of Music.

Elaine has created a living or *inter vivos* trust. If she had made these provisions in a will, upon her death a *testamentary* trust would have been created. Today, trusts are used for many different purposes. They are used extensively in family estate planning of the type mentioned in the example, but they are also important in business. Trusts are frequently utilized to finance real estate ventures and to protect bondholder creditors of a corporation. Many large charities are organized as trusts; wealthy individuals convey assets to a trustee, who administers them for some designated public benefit.

The premise upon which the trust is based is the division of property interests among owners. In a trust, one person or an institution is given title to specific property that is managed for the benefit of others. The property may be real or personal. In the example, Central Trust Company legally owns the securities and real estate, but it must administer them for Carl Morgan's benefit.

With but few exceptions, trusts involving real property must be in writing. Some states permit inter vivos trusts of personal property to be created orally. All testamentary trusts—whether the property is real or personal—must be in writing and executed in the same manner as required for an effective will. Testamentary trusts that are frequently part of an estate plan often supplement a will.

Fiduciary Duty

Every trust must have a trustee to hold and manage the property. The trustee has a *fiduciary* duty, the responsibility for the utmost good faith and undivided loyalty to the beneficiary in administering the trust.

The doctrine of fiduciary responsibility applies to numerous legal relationships. Because some of these—such as the attorney-client and broker-seller relationships—are very important to real estate transactions, a brief outline of the duties common to all fiduciaries is in order. A fiduciary (1) must act for the benefit of the other party in matters within the scope of the relationship, (2) must not profit at the other party's expense and (3) must make full disclosure of all information affecting transactions with the other party. In a case involving a trustee's fiduciary duties, Justice Benjamin Cardozo once said:

> Many forms of conduct permissible in a workaday world for those acting at arm's length are forbidden to those bound by fiduciary ties. A trustee is held to something stricter than the morals of the marketplace. Not honesty alone but the punctilio of an honor the most sensitive is then the standard of behavior. As to this there has developed a tradition that is unbending and inveterate. Uncompromising rigidity has been the attitude of courts of equity when petitioned to undermine the rule of undivided loyalty by the "disintegrating erosion" of particular exceptions. Only thus has the level of conduct for fiduciaries been kept at a level higher than that trodden by the crowd. It will not consciously be lowered by any judgment of this court. *Meinhard v. Salmon, 249 N.Y. 458, 464, 164 N.E. 545 (1928).*

Under the terms of most trusts, trustees are usually granted extensive powers. Sometimes these powers are statutory, but they are also included in most well-drawn trust instruments. A trustee's powers will usually include, but not be limited to, making new investments, managing real estate, carrying on a business, selling property, borrowing money, reviewing mortgages, settling litigation, voting stock, collecting income and making distributions.

The fiduciary responsibility of the trustee protects the trust beneficiary. As a result trusts continue to be important in personal financial planning. Since World War II the trust has been one of several devices used by investors to organize real estate syndicates.

Real Estate Syndicate

A group of investors who combine funds and managerial resources to develop, manage or purchase real estate for a profit or as a tax shelter.

As a syndicate is not a form of ownership, the investors involved must organize in some legal form. To answer legal questions involving a real estate syndicate, a lawyer needs to know in what legal form the syndicate holds the realty. Probably the simplest form for the organization of a syndicate is the tenancy in common. More important forms of ownership today are the S corporation (formerly called *Subchapter S corporation*), general and limited partnerships, joint ventures and real estate investment trusts (REITs). Each of these forms will be discussed in the following pages. Chapter 27 provides additional discussion of REITs and other types of real estate investments.

Tenancy in Common

The tenancy in common has been used by real estate investors for years. This form of ownership has the advantage of allowing the investors appreciable tax flexibility. Each co-owner is free to select the most beneficial tax treatment of his or her share. When the syndicate is organized as a partnership or corporation, the participants are bound by the tax characterization of the entity.

As a vehicle for syndication, the tenancy in common suffers from several legal and practical disadvantages. Individual owners are personally liable for all obligations arising out of property ownership. If someone is injured on the property or large debts are incurred, the individual assets of the co-owner can be reached. This compares unfavorably with the liability of the owners of a corporation, in which liability of each shareholder is limited to the amount that the shareholder has invested. The second legal drawback is the potential problem of marketability of property owned as a tenancy in common. If one of the owners dies or becomes insolvent and the remaining owners wish to sell their property, they usually must establish that the title is marketable. Death or insolvency of a co-owner clouds the title, causing delay and expense in clearing it to make it marketable.

S Corporations

To remedy these problems, federal law authorizes syndicates to use a modification of the corporate form. The modification allows investors to escape double taxation—that is, taxation of earnings of both the corporation and each shareholder. The S corporation allows the syndicate to pass income through without its being taxed at the corporate level. Thus the owners are not subject to the double burden associated with the ordinary corporation. Unfortunately, S corporations are limited to 35 shareholders, and some limitations are placed upon the type of income allowed. Losses that a shareholder may take are also restricted. Because of these limitations and additional complex tax problems, S corporations are used only for relatively sophisticated syndications.

Partnership

An association of two or more persons to organize a business venture and divide the profits.

Many syndicates are organized either as general or limited partnerships. Both partnership forms also avoid double taxation—the nemesis of incorporation. A partnership is not taxed on its income; any income is taxed directly to the partners as individuals.

Investors who syndicate as a general partnership face three legal handicaps. Probably the most serious is the unlimited liability of the partners. Each partner is personally responsible for all partnership obligations, and his or her property, both real and personal, can be reached if partnership assets are not sufficient to satisfy claims against the unit. A second handicap is the power of individual partners to make agreements binding the firm. Under Section 9 of the Uniform Partnership Act, "[e]very partner is the agent of the partnership for the purpose of its business...and the act of every partner binds the partnership...." Finally, death, withdrawal or bankruptcy of one of the partners automatically terminates the partnership. The syndicate must be re-created by a new agreement. In order to facilitate securing capital for business ventures, many states have legislation that allows the creation of partnerships in which some of the members have *limited liability.* Partnerships of this kind are called *limited* or *special partnerships.* They are a popular form of organization for real estate syndicates.

Limited Partnership. State laws providing for the creation of limited partnerships are based either on the Uniform Limited Partnership Act (ULPA) or on a 1976 revision of that act, known as the Revised Uniform Limited Partnership Act (RULPA). By 1986, 30 states had adopted the revised act; however, several commercially significant states—Florida, Illinois, New York and Texas—had not done so.

Both acts define a limited partnership as a partnership having as members one or more general partners and one or more limited partners. Under most circumstances a limited partner's liability to creditors of the partnership is limited to that person's capital contribution. Under the provisions of both acts, to be considered a limited partner the individual must be designated as such in a certificate filed with a designated state official.

CASE EXAMPLE

Anna, Ben and Carla Lane formed a limited partnership to invest in real estate. Anna, the general partner, invested $10,000 and agreed to manage the property. Ben and Carla, as limited partners, contributed $25,000 each. The project failed after accumulating debts of $65,000. Individual assets of Anna could be reached to cover any claims of creditors not satisfied on liquidation. Ben's and Carla's individual assets could not be reached by the syndicate's creditors beyond the amounts of their initial investment.

If limited partners participate in the "control of the business," they lose their defense against liability to creditors. However, the ULPA does not define what constitutes "taking part in control." This has been left to the courts. Generally they have interpreted "taking part in control" in a manner that significantly restricts the limited partner's ability to participate without forfeiting limited liability. In addition, under the ULPA, if the limited partner's name appears in the partnership name, the limited partner becomes liable as a general partner. This is intended to protect creditors who extend credit to the business on the basis of the financial resources of a person who is actually only a limited partner.

The RULPA specifically allows a limited partner to act in a number of situations for the business without forfeiting limited liability. For example, the revised act permits a limited partner to be a contractor for or an agent or employee of the limited partnership. A limited partner can also consult with and advise a general partner, act as a surety for the partnership and approve or disapprove an amendment to the partnership agreement. In addition, the act permits a limited partner to vote on the following matters:

- dissolution and winding up of the business;
- sale, exchange, lease, mortgage, pledge or other transfer of all or substantially all of the assets of the limited partnership other than in the ordinary course of the business;
- incurrence of indebtedness by the limited partnership other than in the ordinary course of the business;
- change in the nature of the business;
- removal of a general partner.

More importantly, under the RULPA, a limited partner is liable only to persons who transact business with the partnership with actual knowledge of the limited partner's participation in control. If, however, the limited partner's participation is substantially the same as that of a general partner, the limited partner will be liable to any person who transacts business with the partnership.

Joint Venture
A business entity in which two or more persons have agreed to carry out a single undertaking for a profit.

A joint venture is a form of business organization very similar to the partnership. Most of the law that applies to partnerships also applies to the joint venture. Like a partnership, the joint venture is based upon agreement, and the members have a fiduciary relationship to each other. They share profits and losses; each enjoys the right to manage and direct the venture; and the venture is treated as a partnership for federal tax purposes.

The major difference between the partnership and the joint venture is that the latter is usually created to carry out a single transaction. Although some limited partnerships are created for a single purpose, most partnership operations are more extensive, carrying out a general business for a period of years. Other differences also exist between a partnership and a joint venture. In a joint venture, each participant has limited power to bind the others. However, the participants can agree that each will have this power. Death of a joint venturer does not automatically dissolve the joint venture. Finally, because a joint venture cannot be adjudicated a bankrupt, claims of creditors against the joint venture's real estate holdings are limited.

Real Estate Investment Trust (REIT)

An organization in which trustees own real estate or loans secured by real estate that they manage for beneficiaries who hold transferable shares representing their respective interests.

During the late 19th century the American economy was expanding rapidly. Large sums of money were needed for investment in many segments of the economy. Real estate was no exception. Unfortunately, the corporate form of business organization that was used to attract capital into most business activity could not be used in real estate, because most of the states prohibited ownership of real property by corporations. The business trust, or Massachusetts trust, evolved to circumvent this prohibition. The trust had many advantages of the corporation, such as limited liability, ready transferability of shares and continuous existence. Because the trust was not a corporation, it was a permissible form of enterprise for real estate investment.

With the passage of time, state prohibitions against corporate ownership of property were abolished, but the business trust continued to be important. It provided investors with a major tax advantage over the corporation. For tax purposes the trust was treated as a conduit through which income passed. Income it earned was not taxable to it as long as the income was distributed to the trust beneficiaries. Corporate income is not treated in this favorable manner but is taxable to the corporation and also to the shareholder when distributed. The tax advantage enjoyed by the business trust was eliminated in 1935 by a number of court decisions that emphasized the corporate characteristics of the trust and held these sufficient to classify the trust as an association taxable as a corporation.

These rulings had little immediate impact because of the depressed economic conditions of the 1930s and later the influence of World War II. The need for capital in the real estate market was limited. Conditions changed late in the 1940s as the postwar U.S. economic boom created a need for large sums of money to be invested in real estate. About this time, an effort was made to restore to the business trust the tax advantage that it had enjoyed until 1935. This effort was finally successful in 1960 when Congress approved legislation that allowed business trusts and investment trusts dealing in real estate under certain prescribed conditions, once again to serve as a conduit through which income passes without being taxed twice. REITs are discussed in more detail in Chapter 27.

Government Regulation of Syndicates

Many real estate syndicates are financed by the public sale of participation certificates, which are securities. The public sale of securities is regulated extensively by both state and federal law.

The term *security* is defined broadly by federal and state statute. An investment in which a person is induced to participate with others expecting to profit solely through the efforts of others is usually subject to regulation as a security. Many real estate syndications fit this description. In addition to real estate syndication, statutes regulating the sale of securities have been applied to transactions as diverse as the sale of lots in undeveloped land and the sale of resort condominiums that are to be rented with profits to be divided among condominium owners. During the past decade, enforcement of federal and state statutes regulating the marketing of investments to the public has intensified. People in the real estate industry should expect this trend to continue.

State "blue-sky" laws generally require those who sell securities to be registered in the state. Practically all states also require that the security sold be registered. Usually these state laws include standards against which the quality of the security can be measured. This permits state officials to refuse to register securities that do not qualify or are fraudulent.

Two important federal statutes also regulate the sale of most securities. They are the Securities Act of 1933 and the Securities Exchange Act of 1934. Although both statutes are discussed in more detail in Chapter 27, as they apply to many real estate syndicates, they are mentioned briefly here.

Securities Act of 1933. The 1933 act is a federal statute regulating the public sale of new securities. Generally, the act requires that before securities are offered to the public a registration statement be filed with the Securities Exchange Commission (SEC) and a prospectus be prepared and furnished to potential investors. The prospectus must contain the significant information in the registration statement. Unless a registration statement is in effect, it is unlawful to use the mails or interstate commerce in the sale or delivery of the security.

The chief purpose of the 1933 act is to require a full and fair disclosure of material facts to the prospective purchaser of a security. Terms of the act do not give the SEC power to evaluate the merits of the issue as some state commissions are empowered to do. Evaluation is the responsibility of the original investor.

Securities Exchange Act of 1934. This federal statute created the Securities Exchange Commission and to a large extent regulates the sale of securities already issued. The 1934 act requires the registration of securities listed on a national securities exchange, as well as over-the-counter securities in which there is a substantial public interest. Issuers of registered securities must file periodic reports to provide the public with current information about the company. In addition to these disclosure provisions, the 1934 act authorizes the SEC to supervise markets and persons in the securities business. The act also contains provisions designed to prevent fraud and deceptive practices in the sale of securities on the exchanges or over the counter.

SUMMARY

Several legal forms have evolved by which real property can be owned by more than one individual. Joint tenancy is one of these forms. It features the right of survivorship—that is, upon the death of one of the co-owners, that person's interest passes automatically to the remaining joint owner.

Under this form, each co-owner has an equal right to possession, or an undivided interest. Joint tenancy is based on four "unities": unity of possession, of interest, of time and of title. Lacking any one of these unities, the co-ownership becomes a tenancy in common. Joint tenancy can also be terminated if the interest of one of the parties is sold as the unity of possession no longer exists. In some states joint tenancy is not permitted; in some the right of survivorship must be expressed in order for it to be upheld legally.

In the modern U.S. economy a more usual form of co-ownership is the tenancy in common. Rights of tenants in common are similar in some respects to those of joint tenants. Each has an undivided right of possession, but none has the right of exclusive use. In a tenancy in common no right of survivorship exists.

Partition is the legal method used to sever the interests of co-owners so that they may take their separate shares. Partition would be the solution to a situation in which one co-owner wished to sell and the others do not. To be valid, an act of partition must be in writing and permanently recorded in the title history. Partition may be accomplished by physical division of the property or by sale of the property and division of the proceeds.

A third form of co-ownership, when co-owners are husband and wife, is tenancy by the entirety. In case of the death of one, the survivor becomes sole owner. It is a more stable form than joint tenancy because under the law the marital partners (owners) are considered a single unit. In some states the property is protected against attachment by a creditor of one of the owners. Termination occurs mainly by divorce, upon which the parties become tenants in common.

Tenancy in partnership, a fourth form of co-ownership, is used primarily when co-owners have a business relationship to each other. Tenants who own in partnership are regulated by the Uniform Partnership Act, and the property is protected against the interests of spouses, heirs or creditors of individual co-owners. This form has become possible in recent times because of the recognition of the partnership as a legal entity.

Community property, like tenancy by the entirety, is a concept that applies only to persons married to each other. In those states where community property is recognized, any property acquired through labor or skill by either spouse during the marriage is owned equally by both. How the property is acquired is key here, because property acquired by one spouse through gift or inheritance is classed as separate property and belongs to that spouse alone.

Property may also be held and managed by another party in a trust—a legal device that has been the basis of significant economic innovations. Trusts are frequently used to finance real estate ventures and for estate planning. The person responsible for the property is known as the *trustee*; his or her relationship to the owner or beneficiary of the trust requires the utmost good faith and undivided loyalty. This is known as the *fiduciary duty*. The fiduciary relationship is pervasive in the real estate profession and its many transactions.

For business ventures in the real estate field, syndication is an important recent development. Through a syndicate, investors of many types can pool their resources to purchase, develop or manage real estate. Syndicates take many forms, including tenancy in common, S corporations, partnerships, joint ventures and real estate investment trusts (REITs). Knowledge of these developments and their legal requirements is essential to those engaged in commercial real estate sales, management or investment.

Federal and state governments exercise considerable control over the public's participation in real estate syndicates. Federal securities statutes enacted in the 1930s are particularly stringent regarding registration, sale and advertising of securities offerings.

REVIEW AND DISCUSSION QUESTIONS

1. During the past 15 years the S corporation and the limited partnership have been used extensively in real estate syndication. What factors account for this?
2. Under what circumstances will a court order the property owned by tenants in common to be partitioned?
3. Compare and contrast a *joint tenancy*, a *tenancy by the entirety* and a *tenancy in common*.
4. Outline some of the problems that real estate sales personnel face as a result of co-ownership of real property.

CASE PROBLEMS

1. J. D. Caradine owned real property in Idaho, a community property state. Caradine had lived in Idaho for several years, separated from his wife, who lived in California. In 1964 Caradine borrowed $4,300 from the Farmers Home Administration, a federal agency, to improve his real estate. As security for the loan, Caradine gave the Farmers Home Administration a mortgage on the property. At the time he executed the mortgage, Caradine completed an affidavit swearing that he was single. Caradine defaulted on the mortgage, and the government attempted to foreclose. Caradine defended upon the grounds that the mortgage was invalid because his wife was not a party. Discuss the validity of this defense. *U.S. v. McConkey*, 430 F.2d 652 (1970).

2. Lars Olsen is a general partner and Swen Nielson a limited partner in Olsen and Sons, a limited partnership engaged in the construction and sale of bowling alleys. Nielson had been in the construction business for many years but had retired because of ill health. Olsen has been in the construction business for a short time but had served as Nielson's accountant for a number of years. Although Olsen makes all business decisions, he frequently phones Nielson for advice. When asked for advice, Nielson usually replies, "Lars, I'm not telling you how to do it, but if I were doing it, I would do it this way." Olsen generally follows Nielson's advice. (a) If the venture fails, could Nielson be held liable as a general partner? Discuss. (b) Would the result be different if the business had been run by Nielson prior to his retirement? Explain.

3. Matilda Schomas owned a small apple orchard, which was operated by her son. Matilda did not wish to write a will, but she wanted her son to succeed to the property upon her death.

Without the aid of counsel, she decided that she and her son should hold the orchard as joint tenants. Matilda then conveyed the orchard to herself and her son "as joint tenants, not as tenants in common." When she died, the son claimed the orchard by right of survivorship. Was a joint tenancy created? Explain why or why not.

4. Marie Rodesney and Fred Rowlett owned property as tenants in common. They had acquired the property for speculative purposes, each agreeing to use his or her best efforts to sell it at a profit. While they owned the property, Rowlett rented it to a Mr. Wood for a used car lot. Rentals under the agreement amounted to $5,230. Rowlett disbursed $3,511.52 for taxes and improvements, leaving a net balance of $1,178.48; however, the reasonable rental value of the property while it was owned by Rodesney and Rowlett was $15,900. Upon sale of the property, Rodesney contended that in addition to her share of the proceeds she was entitled to one-half of the reasonable rental value. Is her contention correct? Discuss. *Rodesney v. Hall*, 307 P.2d 130 (Okla. 1957).

5. United Housing Foundation (UHF), a nonprofit corporation, was organized to build low-cost cooperative housing. Under federal law, builders of low-cost housing received substantial federal and state support, but they had to operate on a nonprofit basis, leasing only to state-approved low-income tenants.

   To acquire an apartment an individual was required to purchase 18 shares of stock for each room desired at $25 per share. These shares could not be transferred to a nontenant, pledged, encumbered or bequeathed (except to a surviving spouse). The shares had no voting rights. On termination of occupancy a tenant had to offer his or her stock to the corporation at $25 per share.

   Apartment rentals were based upon a proportionate share of the expenses of managing the building and construction costs. Each occupant's monthly fees were related to the number of rooms in the unit rented.

   In 1965, before construction of the planned housing. UHF circulated an information bulletin stating that the average monthly rental charges per four-room unit would be approximately $92. However, due to increased construction costs, rental charges upon completion were set at $120. As a result, residents sued United, claiming a violation of the 1933 Securities Act. The action was based upon misleading information in the information bulletin. Defendants moved to dismiss on the grounds that the shares of stock were not securities within the meaning of the act. Discuss the validity of this defense. *United Housing Foundation, Inc. v. Forman,* 421 U.S. 837 (1975).

6. Cranston and White decided to invest in some rental real estate. Cranston was a wealthy doctor. White was his son-in-law. White had recently graduated from business school and opened up a small business. Although White was an able person, the economy in the area was depressed, and the business was barely succeeding. What legal problems might Cranston face if the two took title to the rental property as tenants in common?

6

Easements and Other Nonpossessory Rights

EASEMENT

A nonpossessory interest in real property; the right to use another's real estate for a limited purpose.

Most of the ownership interests considered in prior chapters provide the holder with a current or future right of possession. In these forms of ownership, the owner enjoys or will enjoy in the future the right to proceeds from the property and the right to occupy it to the exclusion of all others.

Some people have interests in real estate that are limited to use, not possession. These are referred to as *nonpossessory rights.* One important nonpossessory right is the easement. Easements are used extensively in real estate. For example, they are essential to the operation of utilities. They also provide a legal basis for condominium ownership, scenic and open-space protection and preservation of historic buildings. Indeed, few land developments would be successful without the extensive use of easements. Although easements are interests in real estate, the person who has an easement is never entitled to possession of the land itself, either currently or in the future.

The holder of an easement has a right to use another's land or buildings for a specified purpose. That purpose might be as simple as crossing the land to reach a beach or as complicated as using a portion of a neighbor's building to support one's own. The person who owns an easement has neither title nor estate in the land burdened by it. The easement holder's limited interest is, however, protected against interference by third parties, and the easement cannot be terminated at the will of the owner of the land that it burdens.

Frequently, easements authorize a person to perform a particular act. An example would be a right to use a neighbor's driveway to reach the back portion of a lot. These authorizing easements are called *affirmative easements*. Others, called *negative easements*, prohibit the owner of the land from doing something that ordinarily an owner would be entitled to do. Easements of this nature are not as common. A negative easement might prohibit a landowner from constructing a building taller than a designated height in order to provide adjoining land with an unobstructed view; owners of lots in a development might be restricted from painting their houses a particular color.

Easements are also classified as appurtenant or in gross.

Easement Appurtenant

The right of an owner of a specific piece of land to benefit from the use of another's land.

CASE EXAMPLE

Stump and Levit own adjoining parcels of land at Lake Feather. Stump's property borders the lakefront; Levit's does not. Stump has granted to Levit a right-of-way across the lakefront property to the beach. Stump has created an easement appurtenant.

An easement appurtenant involves two parcels of land, usually but not necessarily adjoining. The easement allows the possessor of one parcel to benefit by using the other parcel of land. The parcel that benefits is referred to as the dominant estate or *dominant tenement*. The owner of such easement is also called the *dominant tenant*. The property that is subject to the easement is known as the *servient estate*. Stump's property in the example above is the servient estate; Levit's, the dominant. An easement appurtenant cannot exist without a dominant estate.

If an easement is appurtenant, any conveyance of the dominant estate automatically includes the easement even if the easement is not mentioned in the deed. The easement is said to *run with the land*. When Levit sells his Lake Feather property to Bach, for example, Bach automatically acquires the right to cross Stump's property to get to the beach.

While the easement is automatically transferred with the dominant estate, it cannot be separated and conveyed independently. In the above examples, Levit cannot simply sell or convey to some neighboring landowner the right to cross Stump's property.

Sometimes the dominant tenement or estate is divided into

two or more parcels. In such cases, provided that there is not an unreasonable number of new parcels, the courts have held that the existing easement runs with all of the newly created parcels. If, instead of conveying his entire Lake Feather property, Levit had divided the parcel into two lots and sold one of them to Bach, both Bach's land and Levit's land would have right-of-way across Stump's property. Suppose, however, that Levit had substantially increased the burden on the servient estate by dividing the parcel into six or seven lots. In that case Stump could get a court order preventing the increased use. In some states courts have held that substantially increased use terminates an easement.

In addition to running with the land, an easement appurtenant is irrevocable. It cannot be canceled by the servient owner or terminated by a conveyance of the servient tenement. When the servient tenement is sold or otherwise conveyed, the property remains subject to the existing easement.

Party Wall

A single wall located on the boundary of neighboring properties; it simultaneously serves as a common support for buildings on each of the two parcels.

In many metropolitan areas, adjacent buildings often share a single wall in order to save space and expense. Walls of this type are referred to as *party walls*. Generally, a party wall is constructed on the boundary line between two parcels of real estate, with half of the wall on one side of the line and half on the other. In the United States, the courts uniformly have held that each landowner owns that portion of the wall on his or her land and holds an *easement appurtenant* for support in the other half. If the party wall is entirely on the property of one landowner, the wall belongs to him or her; the other landowner normally has an easement in the wall.

Party walls are commonly constructed as the result of agreement, with each party contributing half of the cost. Because party walls have created many legal problems, these agreements must be drawn carefully. Related problems often involve use of the wall for advertising or purposes other than support.

• CASE BRIEF •

Berk and Ershowsky owned adjoining buildings supported by a party wall. The building on Ershowsky's property was much taller than the building on Berk's, and Ershowsky painted a large advertising sign on that portion of the wall above the top of Berk's building. Berk sued to enjoin use of the wall for that purpose. The injunction was granted, and damages were awarded.

The court stated that defendant's use of the wall was improper because it prevented plaintiff from using it for a similar purpose. *Berk-Fink Realty Co. v. Ershowsky, 116 N.Y.S.2d 529 (1952).*

Contributions for *repairs* to party walls can generally be compelled even if the agreement does not cover the issue. The cost of improvements, however, must be borne by the owner who authorizes them. Neither owner can ordinarily remove the wall, but each may remove the remainder of the building without liability if reasonable care is taken.

Easement in Gross

An easement that exists as a personal right apart from a dominant estate.

An easement in gross is not tied to another parcel of land as is the easement appurtenant. Thus an easement in gross exists without a dominant estate. Although a servient estate does exist, the privileges given by the easement belong to an individual. Stump, for example, might give the telephone company an easement to bury its line along the road bordering his Lake Feather property.

In the past, the easement in gross granted to an individual for a noncommercial purpose was considered a personal right or privilege. Only the person to whom the easement was given could use it. The easement could not be sold, assigned or otherwise transferred, and it terminated upon the death of its holder. For this reason, if the parties wished to have the easement continue or to have any value, they had to tie it to a dominant estate. If this were done, it would be appurtenant and would run with the land.

Traditionally, the courts have treated easements in gross granted for commercial uses differently. Because of their importance to the public, they are considered freely tranferable. For example, a utility easement can be sold or assigned by one utility company to another. Although transferable, an easement given for a specific purpose, such as a sewer, cannot be used for another purpose, such as an electric line.

Inasmuch as the easement in gross is not intended to benefit a parcel of land, it is considered a personal right in another's property. Because of this, it is frequently confused with a somewhat similar personal right—a license. Licenses are discussed later in this chapter.

Profit

A nonpossessory interest in real property that permits the holder to remove part of the soil or produce of the land.

Most authorities consider the profit, correctly known as the *profit à prendre*, a type of easement. Others distinguish the profit from the easement as the profit allows the holder to take specified resources from the land, such as soil, produce, wild animals, coal or timber. A person who has an easement does not have this right. Suppose, for example, that Stump grants the Cazenovia Lumber Company the right to take "any and all standing timber" from his property at Lake Feather. Although the lumber company does not have title to the timber, it has a right to remove it from the land. This is a profit.

Few differences exist between easements and profits. Like other types of easements, a profit is an interest in land, but it is nonpossessory and limited to a particular purpose. The holder of the profit has a right of reasonable ingress and egress in order to use the right advantageously. In most states, unless specifically limited by the agreement, the owner of land does not lose the right to use the resource that is the subject of the profit. Like easements, profits may be appurtenant or in gross. The usual profit is in gross. This makes it a personal right not related to a dominant estate. Unlike the easement in gross to an individual, however, the profit in gross is freely transferable.

CREATION OF EASEMENTS

An easement is generally created in one of three ways: by deed, by implication or by prescription.

Creation of an Easement by Deed

The most effective method of creating an easement is by deed describing the land and the location of the easement. Deeds are discussed in Chapter 7. Although most courts recognize that an easement can be created by implication or prescription, they have refused to accept the idea that an easement can be created orally. The reason is that an easement is an interest in real estate, and statutes in all states require that an interest in real estate—such as an easement—be created only by a written instrument.

CASE EXAMPLE

Paul Brangs owned a lot at Lake Feather next to his home. Paul wished to sell the lot but was having difficulty because it was narrow. Paul's driveway bordered the lot. To induce Nan Crampton, a prospective purchaser, to buy, Paul agreed to grant her an easement over his driveway to reach the back portion of the property. At the closing, Paul delivered a deed passing title to the lot and a separate deed describing the easement.

The granting of an easement may be an independent transaction. Utility companies often seek easements when they need to run their lines over another's property. In many states the law gives these companies the right of eminent domain if the landowner refuses to grant the requested easement. Gas pipelines, sewers and roads are based upon easements from property owners.

Documents creating easement may do so by express grant or express reservation.

Express Grant
An easement created by an owner expressly granting a specific right to use the property to another.

CASE EXAMPLE
Morgan owns two adjoining lots at Lake Feather. She sells one to Betterman. Morgan's lot includes a private alley, and Morgan's deed to Betterman *expressly grants* Betterman the use of this alley.

Express Reservation
The owner of property conveys title to another while specifically reserving an easement for him/herself or a third party.

CASE EXAMPLE
Morgan sells Betterman the lot with the alley and keeps the other for herself. Morgan's deed includes a clause that *expressly reserves* her right to use the alley.

Provisions expressly reserving an easement are usually found in a deed; some easements are created by will, but easements may also be included in a mortgage or lease.

An easement may also be created by a *contract* between the parties. This is not a preferred method, but if the courts will enforce by specific performance or injunction an agreement in which one party promises to allow another to use land for a limited purpose, an easement has been created. A few courts have even enforced oral contracts that create a limited interest in land. Usually, these involve something like a common driveway or access road.

Creation of an Easement by Implication
Courts sometimes presume that the parties intend to create an easement because certain facts exist when real estate is conveyed. The easement supposedly reflects the intention of the parties and is called an *easement by implication*. Courts have traditionally assumed easements by implication in two situations. *In both, the easement results*

only if one or more parcels are severed from a larger tract under common ownership.

In the first situation, the effective use of one parcel (the dominant estate) depends upon continuation of a use already being made of the other (the servient parcel). As a result, the easement is sometimes referred to as an *easement implied from prior use.* The other situation occurs if the severed portion is landlocked and cannot be used without passage across the other. This type is generally referred to as an *easement by necessity.* This second example is much less common than the first.

Support for the creation of easements by implication is found in the idea that a sale of real estate includes that which is necessary to use the property beneficially. If a property owner visibly and continuously has used one part of land for the benefit of another, and this use is reasonably necessary for the fair enjoyment of the other, an easement is actually created when either part is sold separately. This is true even when neither party expressly makes any commitment creating the easement.

CASE EXAMPLE

Kane owned a small farm that had a farmhouse located some distance from the road. The only means of reaching the road was over a long driveway from the house. Kane sold the house and five acres to his friend Rogers. Kane retained all of the property that fronted on the road.

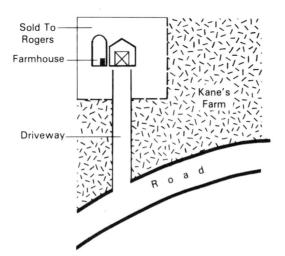

As the two were close friends, Rogers continued to use the driveway, although no written easement granted him this right. Several years later, Rogers sold the property to Dr. Gordon. Kane then blocked the driveway. Dr. Gordon contended that he had an easement by implication from prior use. Courts in most states would agree.

In addition to showing prior use, Dr. Gordon would have to show the following to establish the easement:

- The two parcels were once part of a single tract.
- The driveway was reasonably necessary for effective use of the property.
- The use had continued over a long period of time.
- The use was apparent at the time he purchased the property.

In a majority of states, an implied easement, like an express easement, may be created by reservation or grant. If the seller is trying to enforce a right to make specific use of the part that he or she has sold, the easement is implied by reservation. If the buyer claims the right to make some specific use of the parcel the seller has retained, the easement is implied by grant.

• CASE BRIEF •

Bennett and Evans owned adjoining lots. Both lots had been owned by Evans, who had built a garage in the rear. The eaves of the garage visibly extended over a fence also built by Evans. When Evans sold to Bennett, the property line was run along the fence. Evans had an implied easement by reservation in the six-inch space over Bennett's lot. If the encroachment had not been visible, the implied easement would not have existed. *Bennett v. Evans, 161 Neb. 807, 74 N.W.2d 728 (1965).*

Easement by Necessity
An easement permitting the owner of a landlocked parcel to cross a portion of land of which the easement formerly was a part.

Most courts consider the easement by necessity a form of implied easement. They reason that the parties intended that the grantee of a landlocked parcel have a means of access to his or her land. Without a right to cross the lands of the grantor, the grantee would derive no benefit from the conveyed property. A few courts have taken the position that presumed intent is not necessary. These courts feel that sound public policy dictates that no land should be inaccessible.

Whatever theory prevails, two factors *must* be established for an easement to be created by necessity:

1. Both parcels must at one time have been part of a single unit.
2. Necessity must exist—some states require absolute necessity; others only reasonable necessity.

CASE EXAMPLE

O'Mally purchased from Flynn a lot that was part of a larger parcel that abutted on Lake Feather. O'Mally did not think to get an easement to reach the lake across Flynn's remaining land. As a result, he had to drive more than five miles to use Lake Feather. If he sued to establish an easement by necessity, a court probably would reject his suit on the grounds that no real need existed.

Easements by Plats and Maps

Courts sometimes refer to an easement that arises when a document such as a deed refers to a plat or map with designated streets or areas as an easement by implication.

CASE EXAMPLE

Keene purchased several acres on the north side of Lake Feather. He subdivided the property and had prepared a map designating streets, parks and a beach area. Several of the lots were sold and described by reference to the map. Controversy arose between Keene and a number of the lot owners. Keene, as a result, attempted to restrict their use of the beach.

Courts in most states would rule that the lot owners had acquired easements, even if no easements were mentioned in their deeds. When a person buys property described by lot number on a particular map, that person acquires the right to use all common areas designated on the map. A similar rule applies when a deed describes a tract as bounded by a particular street. The purchaser acquires an easement in the street. A majority of states extend the purchaser's interest to include easements in all streets reasonably necessary for access and reasonably beneficial to the lot owner. A few states limit the easement to abutting streets.

Dedication.   The granting of real property such as a private street to a governmental unit for public use is known as *dedication*. Litigation involving public easements in streets and other parcels of land is often complicated. Complications arise because almost all states have laws dealing with dedication of land designated on plats and maps for public use. When a plat is recorded, land indicated as set aside for public use becomes public property. In many states the local government automatically acquires an easement in the land. In other states the government acquires title to the designated areas.

A completed dedication solves numerous problems for landowners because the street or area becomes public and open to all users. Complications arise when the property is abandoned by the state. Does it revert back to the former owner, or do those whose interests may be injured now have private easements in the designated parcel? A majority of courts take the position that interests for which the easement was created continue to have a right to use the street.

Creation of an Easement by Prescription

Prescription is the term used to describe the acquisition of an intangible property right such as an easement through wrongful use of another's land for a period of time. The period of time is usually specified by statute and differs markedly from state to state. Although a 20-year period exists in some states, in numerous other states prescriptive rights can be obtained in ten years or less. Several states apply a 15-year period. Basic to the creation of *the easement by prescription* is the idea that an owner who does not take some legal action against wrongful use of his or her property within a certain period of time is *estopped* or legally prohibited from asserting whatever rights he or she had. *Adverse possession*, a similar doctrine that allows actual acquisition of the real estate and all ownership rights, is discussed in Chapter 8.

At one time, the easement by prescription was justified on the presumption of a lost written document. Modern courts reject this presumption, but they continue to approve the prescriptive easement. Most courts apparently feel that land use will be stabilized and controversy reduced if the easement by prescription is recognized.

In addition to use for the designated period, two additional requirements must be met before a prescriptive easement is recognized. The use must be *adverse* to the owner's interest as well as *continuous and uninterrupted*. Over the years, both of these requirements have been the source of substantial litigation; the resulting interpretations have been both confusing and constantly changing.

A use that is adverse to the owner's interest must be open and notorious. It must be obvious enough that an owner reasonably concerned with protecting his or her property rights could readily discover it. A use is not adverse if the user has the owner's permission; no matter how long it continues, it will not ripen into an easement. If, however, the owner who has given permission revokes it, later use becomes adverse. Likewise, if the use made of the land differs from the permitted use, the use becomes adverse.

A difference of opinion exists as to the extent to which the use must be hostile to be considered adverse. In this case *hostile* refers not to ill will but to the wrongdoer's actually claiming the right to use another's property. Many courts take the position that whenever an easement has been used for the prescribed period, the user did so under a claim of right. Under these circumstances, adverse use will be presumed unless the owner introduces sufficient evidence to overcome the presumption. Adverse use has thus been found in cases where the user actually believed that he or she owned the property. A use under these circumstances is clearly hostile to the owner's interest.

In a number of situations, however, use longer than the prescribed time is not presumed to be adverse. These include use by a relative, use of land that is open and unfenced and use by many people, none of whom claim an exclusive right.

• CASE BRIEF •

Diane Poulos owned property in Lake Feather Village. For 25 to 30 years during the summer, people used the property as a shortcut to reach the beach and stores. In the spring and fall the property was used by schoolchildren as a baseball diamond or football field. Village vehicles sometimes drove over it to service water mains in neighboring streets. When Poulos built a fence around the property, Fred Dover and abutting owners sued to prevent the area from being blocked. The appellate court rejected his action, stating "evidence as to actual user was more consistent with uses by permission than by adverse user. . . . [O]ne cannot successfully contend for title by adverse user where this user is as a member of the public. . . ." *See Poulos v. Dover Boiler & Plate Fabricators, 5 N.J. 580, 76 A.2d 808 (1950).*

Creation of an easement by prescription also requires that the use by the person claiming the easement be *continuous and uninterrupted.*

• CASE BRIEF •

Dryer and Thurston owned adjoining summer properties near Lake Feather. For some time beyond the prescription period, Thurston had used a path across the Dryer property to reach the lake. In 1967, Dryer constructed a fence across his property, blocking the path. When Thurston claimed an easement, Dryer argued that, as the path was used only in the summer, its use was not continuous. The court rejected this argument. *See Dryer v. Thurston, 32 Mich. App. 341, 188 N.W.2d 633 (1971).*

Continuous use does not mean *constant use.* Use is continuous when a person uses the easement as the occasion may demand. A critical factor is that the person claiming the right does not recognize a superior claim or abandon the use during the prescriptive period. In addition, the use does not have to be a continuous use by the same person. Most states allow *tacking*—the process of adding together periods of prescriptive use by a latter user who has succeeded to the interest of earlier users.

Uninterrupted and continuous are not synonymous. *Uninterrupted* refers to the failure of the owner of the land to act. For a use to be uninterrupted, the owner must not succeed in causing a discontinuance of the use. The running of the prescriptive period is stopped when a discontinuance is effected.

Prescription and Easements for Light and Air

The energy crisis of the late 1970s has spurred interest in prescriptive easements. Owners considering installation of solar heating units in buildings need assurance of enough sunlight to operate the units effectively. Operation of these units could be hindered if the owner of the adjoining parcel were to build a structure that would block much of the incoming light. Easements for light and air over a neighbor's land are a means of dealing with this problem, but the vast majority of American jurisdictions do not recognize this type of easement except where the parties have entered into an express agreement creating it. English courts have recognized a doctrine of "ancient lights." This doctrine allows an easement for light after a prescriptive period of 27 years, but the "ancient lights" concept has been rejected consistently by American courts.

American courts have also refused to apply the concepts of implied easement or easement by necessity to create easements for light and air. The result is that the potential user of solar energy faces a substantial cost to ensure the required sunlight to operate his or her unit. The prospective user of solar energy must bargain with neighbors to prevent blocking of the necessary light. Few property owners are willing to enter into agreements restricting the height of buildings on their land because this might markedly decrease the land's value.

TERMINATION OF EASEMENTS

Although an easement is actually a nonpossessory interest, in many respects it resembles a possessory interest. Like an estate, an easement may be created for a specific period, for life or for a designated purpose. Stump, who you recall granted an easement across his property to reach Lake Feather, might have limited the easement to a designated number of years or until a road was constructed to the lake. When an easement is created for a period of time or a designated purpose, it terminates when either the time expires or the purpose is accomplished. Easements for life terminate when the measuring life ends. An easement created by necessity does not last once the necessity disappears. Most easements, however, do not expire automatically. Like the fee simple, they have the potential to last forever.

A number of methods exist for terminating easements that do not expire automatically, including release, merger, estoppel, abandonment, prescription, conveyance and eminent domain. Each of these methods is discussed below.

Release

The holder of an easement appurtenant or in gross may extinguish it by means of a written agreement to give up the right. This document is referred to as a *release*. An oral release alone is ineffective. Except for automatic termination of easements, extinguishing by release is probably the most common method.

Merger

An easement terminates by merger when the holder of either the dominant or servient estate acquires the other. An easement establishes a right to use land owned by someone else. As a result, a person cannot have an easement in his or her own land. The principle applies whether the easement is in gross or appurtenant. Either expires if ownership changes in this way.

Estoppel

A doctrine by which a person is not permitted to deny the consequences of facts that are inconsistent with his or her previous actions or statements.

Two factors must unite before the doctrine of estoppel is applied. First, a person must act in a manner that causes another to believe something. Second, the other person must rely upon the belief and stand to suffer some loss if reliance upon such belief should be barred or penalized.

An easement is extinguished by estoppel if the holder causes the servient estate owner to believe the easement will no longer be used and the servient owner relies upon this belief and suffers some damage as a result. The belief might be the result of a statement made by the easement holder or might be inferred from the person's conduct.

CASE EXAMPLE

Stump asked Bach to use another path across Stump's property to reach Lake Feather. Bach orally agreed to do so. Stump then built a tennis court that was partially on the original right-of-way. Bach found the new path inconvenient and demanded to be al-

lowed to use the old recorded right-of-way. Bach's easement
had been terminated by estoppel.

Nonuse of an easement for a substantial period of time is generally
not a sufficient basis on which to terminate an easement by estoppel.

Abandonment

Although nonuse alone does not extinguish an easement, it may indicate an intention to abandon it. For an easement to terminate by abandonment, the holder's intention to give it up must be clearly
established. This can be done if the holder discontinues use, states his
or her intention to do so or acts in a manner consistent with discon-
tinued use.

CASE EXAMPLE

Suppose Bach purchases additional land giving him frontage on
Lake Feather. He builds a fence along his line abutting on
Stump's land and clears a path across the newly acquired tract
to Lake Feather. Bach has probably abandoned his easement
across Stump's property.

Prescription

An easement may be extinguished after the owner of the servient estate acts in a manner adverse to the easement for the prescriptive period. This use must be open, notorious and uninterrupted. That is, the
servient owner must act in a manner similar to that which occurs
when an easement is created by prescription.

CASE EXAMPLE

Stump builds a garage on his property, blocking Levit's right-of-
way to Lake Feather. Levit does nothing about the garage because he has no interest in reaching Lake Feather. The
prescriptive period in the state is seven years. Levit's easement
will terminate by prescription unless he asserts his right before
the end of the period.

Conveyance

An easement is sometimes terminated when the servient estate is
sold to a person who has no knowledge of the easement's existence.
When a written easement is not recorded, or when the easement is
not visible from indications on the property, the servient estate may
become free of the easement. Easements created by necessity and by
prescription, however, are not subject to this doctrine.

Eminent Domain

The right of the state to take private property for public use applies to easements. If the state takes the servient estate for a purpose that is not consistent with the continued use of the easement, the dominant tenant loses his or her right to continue this use. This is true even if the dominant estate itself is not taken. The owner of the dominant estate is entitled to compensation for the loss in value of his or her easement right. Similarly, condemnation of the dominant estate may terminate the easement. This occurs if the condemnation and the new use destroy the usefulness of the easement.

LICENSE

A personal privilege to enter another's property for a specific purpose.

CASE EXAMPLE

Able and Baker are neighbors. Baker is having work done on his driveway, and Able gives him permission to park in Able's driveway for two weeks. Baker has a license.

Purchasing tickets to attend the theatre or a sporting event and obtaining a camping permit at a state park are other examples of licenses. Although both easements and licenses are intangible, an easement is an interest in land; a license is not. It is a right that is personal to the licensee, the party to whom it was given. Without a license, if Baker had parked in Able's driveway, Baker would be a trespasser.

Licenses may be created orally or may be in writing. Because a license is personal, the licensor may revoke it at any time. If the license was created by a contract, the revocation is a breach of the contract. Nevertheless, although the licensee can collect damages, he or she cannot require the licensor to honor the agreement by specific performance because the licensee has no interest in the realty. If Baker had paid for permission to park in Able's driveway, Able could revoke the license. Although Able would be responsible for money damages because of the revocation, Baker could not get a court order requiring Able to make space available.

Because licenses are personal, they are usually invalidated by the licensee's death and may not be transferred. An exception exists when the individual's license is coupled with an interest in the real estate. Under these circumstances the license is irrevocable. Instead of merely giving Baker permission to park in the driveway, Able sells Baker timber on Able's property. Because of his interest in the timber,

Baker has, in addition, an irrevocable privilege to enter and remove it. Baker's license to enter the land is irrevocable because of the interest in the timber. The license is said to be coupled with an interest.

• CASE BRIEF •

Durell had an oil and gas lease and was operating wells on property owned by Freese. A former owner had orally given Durell permission to place equipment on the land to aid in pumping oil. Freese removed this equipment on the grounds that all Durell had was a license that could be revoked at any time. Durell could get an injunction prohibiting Freese from removing the equipment because the license was irrevocable as it was coupled with the oil and gas lease. *Durell v. Freese, 151 Okla. 150, 3 P.2d 175 (1931).*

Licenses are sometimes the result of ineffective easements. Ordinarily, an easement must be created by a written instrument. An oral easement may be construed as a license; if held to be a license, however, the grant would be revocable. Some states suspend the right to revoke a license if the licensee has made improvements on the land.

• CASE BRIEF •

Several adjoining landowners orally agreed to erect and maintain a line of telephone poles over their lands and to contribute equally to the expense of stringing telephone wires. After phone service was in operation, Tuning changed his mind, cut the wires and removed the poles that were on his land. A court refused to grant the remaining landowners an injunction, holding that Tuning had a right to revoke the license. *Yeager v. Tuning, 79 Ohio St. 121, 86 N.E. 657 (1908).*

SUMMARY

Ownership interests described in previous chapters are those that provide owners with the right of possession—either current or future. Not all interests provide possession, however. An important example of one type that does not is the easement, which provides only a right to use the property in a limited way, such as for operation of utilities or to gain access to a roadway or beach area. This type of easement is called an *affirmative easement.* Another type—*negative easement*—prohibits an owner of land from doing something an owner would normally have the right to do.

Two other distinctions are easements appurtenant and easements in gross. The former is the right of one owner, the dominant estate, to benefit from use of the land of another, the servient estate. Characteristics of this type of easement are that it runs with the land and it is irrevocable; that is, it cannot be canceled or terminated by sale of the realty. The easement in gross is not attached to the land but is personal to the owner of the land. It cannot be sold or otherwise transferred. However, commercial easements in gross, such as those utility companies enjoy, have been treated by the courts as transferable.

Another nonpossessory interest, generally considered a type of easement, is the profit, which entitles the holder to remove something of value, such as a crop or harvest, from the land. The profit, like other easements, may be either appurtenant or in gross.

Easements may be created in three ways: by deed (express), by implication or by prescription. One type of easement best created by written agreement is the party wall—a wall shared by two neighboring buildings. Agreements relating to party walls ought to be carefully drawn by an attorney.

Easements by implication have traditionally been upheld by the courts in two kinds of situations. First, effective use of the dominant estate must depend on the continuation of the easement. In the second case, the land cannot be used at all without the easement, as, for example, in a landlocked parcel (easement by necessity). The existence of easements is a very important factor to check when selling or listing a property. Discovery of an easement would avoid complicated litigation resulting from the absence of written documents relating to the easement.

Easements may also be created by prescription over a period of time, usually specified by statute. This type of easement depends upon the continuous, open and adverse use of an easement, such as a roadway, without interruption by the owner of the servient estate.

Although easements have the potential to last forever, they may be terminated legally in a variety of ways.

A license, which grants permission only to enter another's land for a specific purpose, is sometimes confused with the profit. Licenses, which may be revoked by the grantor at any time, expire upon the grantor's death.

REVIEW AND DISCUSSION QUESTIONS

1. Compare and contrast an *easement appurtenant* and an *easement in gross*.
2. Explain the factors that must exist for an easement to be created by prescription.
3. What is a license? How does it differ from an easement?

4. What is a profit? How does it differ from an easement? In what ways is it similar?
5. Is an easement an estate? Support your answer.
6. Is an easement property? Support your answer.

CASE PROBLEMS

1. Nash conveyed property to the M & I Timber Co. The deed contained a clause reserving for Nash "the right and privilege to remove any and all timber." Nash assigned this right to the Idaho Land Co. State tax law provided that growing or standing timber be taxed separately from the land if ownership were in different persons. Would the state be entitled to levy a tax against the Idaho Land Co.? Discuss. *M & I Timber Co. v. Hope Silver-Lead Mines, Inc.*, 91 Idaho 38, 428 P.2d 955 (1967).

2. Hamilton and Tucker owned adjoining farms. For more than 40 years Mrs. Tucker, her predecessors in title, her agents and her employees had reached her farm by a roadway across the Hamilton farm.

   At one time the two farms had been a single unit, but it had been divided in 1884 by Mrs. Tucker's grandfather. He had given approximately 200 acres to each of his two sons. The Hamiltons had purchased their farm in 1972 from the widow of one of the sons.

   Upon purchasing the farm, the Hamiltons blocked the roadway to the Tucker place. Mrs. Tucker seeks an injunction to restrain this action. Will she succeed? Discuss. *McIlroy v. Hamilton*, 539 S.W.2d 669 (Mo. Ct. App. 1976).

3. Anderson owned and operated a small motel in a resort area. One of the area's principal attractions was a well-known golf course. Although it was difficult to reach the clubhouse by automobile from the motel, the clubhouse was within easy walking distance.

   In order to provide easy access to the clubhouse for his guests, Anderson acquired an easement over a neighbor's land "for use as a connecting walk by guests of the Anderson Motel." Three years later Anderson sold the motel to a national franchise, which doubled the room capacity. The neighbor attempted to stop motel guests from crossing the land, and the new owner sought an injunction prohibiting interference. Would the new owner be successful? Present arguments for both the neighbor and the new owner.

4. In 1935 Hitchins deeded to the United States a 500-foot-wide strip of land through his property. The land was to be used as part of the Colonial National Monument Parkway. This park-

way was to include a highway that would connect Yorktown, Williamsburg and Jamestown.

In the deed Hitchins reserved a 30-foot perpetual "easement...for vehicular and foot travel...which shall be located at a point to be mutually agreed upon...having due regard for the purposes and uses of each party..." The easement contained no other significant words.

Eventually a highway was constructed through the southern portion of the strip. The Hitchins easement was used until 1949. Early in the 1960s Hitchins sold his land north of the parkway to the defendants, who began to use the easement to reach the highway. In 1966 the United States attempted to end this use, contending the easement was for the sole purpose of permitting Hitchins to reach both properties and that he could turn neither left nor right on the highway. Would the United States be successful? Discuss. *United States v. Parkway Towers, Inc.*, 282 F. Supp. 341 (E.D. Va. 1968), aff'd, 405 F.2d 500 (4th Cir. 1968).

5. Soergel owned lot A. He granted Smith, who owned lot B directly to the west of lot A, a ten-foot-wide easement for installation of a sewer line. Smith sold lot B to Preston, who owned lot C directly to the west of lot B. Preston began to install a sewer line from his house on lot C across lots B and A. Soergel sought an injunction prohibiting Preston from constructing the sewer line. Was Soergel successful? Support your answer. *Soergel v. Preston*, 367 N.W.2d 366 (Mich. Ct. App. 1985).

6. Devlin leased a restaurant in a shopping center. The owner of the shopping center did not object when Devlin erected a sign in the parking lot advertising the restaurant. When the shopping center was sold, the new owner demanded that the sign be removed. (a) If Devlin refused to remove it, could the new owner do so legally? (b) Would the result be the same if Devlin had permission from the former owner to erect the sign? Discuss. *Devlin v. The Phoenix, Inc.*, 471 So.2d 93 (Fla Dist. Ct. App. 1985).

7

Title and Transfer of Title by Deed

TITLE

The totality of rights and obligations possessed by an owner; evidence of ownership.

Title is one of the elusive concepts in real property law. Thorough understanding of the concept is complicated by at least two factors. First, the term is in general use in a number of different ways, and other terms have similar meanings. Second, concepts such as *estates* and *property* are associated with title, and their meanings sometimes seem to overlap.

People often use the word *title* in the same sense as *ownership*. For example, a real estate salesperson who says that "Jane Brown has title to Lone Tree Ranch" usually means that Jane Brown is the owner of the ranch. But, sometimes *title* is used to refer to the acts and instruments by which a person becomes an owner. Title is transferred or *conveyed* primarily by an instrument called a *deed*. The deed is not ownership, however, but the means by which the owner of the land acquires ownership of the property. Finally, people in real estate also use *title* to refer to the documents, records and acts that prove ownership. Two examples are the abstract of title and the title search. An *abstract of title* is an historical summary of the publicly recorded documents that affect title. A *title search* is an examination of these public records.

CASE EXAMPLE

Martin Ziebarth agreed to purchase a home from Keith Olvic. After signing the contract, Ziebarth asked his attorney for a title opinion. The attorney reviewed the appropriate records establishing the validity of Olvic's ownership and reported his findings to Ziebarth.

Olvic asked his attorney to prepare a deed to the property. The deed, when properly executed and delivered, conveyed Olvic's title to Ziebarth.

Most titles are acquired through the voluntary acts of the parties. This fact applies whether the title is acquired by deed or by will. Title can also be acquired by operation of law. When the owner of real property dies without leaving a will, for example, statutes in each state indicate to which heirs the property shall pass. This is referred to as *intestate succession*. Titles acquired by operation of law also include those based upon adverse possession, judicial sale, accretion, escheat and eminent domain. Involuntary transfer is discussed in Chapter 8.

Historical Background

At one time in England real property was conveyed by a symbolic ceremony in which the owner delivered a twig, a stick or a handful of earth from the land to the new owner. The ceremony was known as *livery of seisin*. Ordinarily, the ceremony took place before witnesses. If the conveyance was questioned, it was their testimony that established its validity. Although no written document was required, customarily one was prepared to provide additional evidence of what had occurred. The document was known as a *deed of feoffment* and is the forerunner of the modern deed.

In 1677 the English Parliament enacted the Statute of Frauds. This statute required a person wishing to enforce certain types of agreements to produce written evidence of the agreement, signed by the person against whom enforcement was sought. If no written evidence of the agreement existed, the plaintiff could not sue successfully. One instrument that the statute required to be in writing involved the transfer of an interest in real estate. As a result of this and similar legislation, the rule requiring a written document to transfer title to real estate became embedded in English law. When the American colonies became independent, each readily adopted this element of English law. As the United States expanded, the new states passed similar legislation. Today in the United States there is no such thing as an oral conveyance of title to real estate. In every state a written document is necessary.

The use of written documents to convey title to real estate led to an increased number of fraudulent transfers. Because of the importance of land, the ancient livery of seisin ceremony with the oral conveyance received a great deal of local publicity. People living in the vicinity of a transfer knew of the change. As written documents replaced livery of seisin, secret transfer could be made more readily. To prevent fraud that might stem from a secret transfer, Parliament passed the Statute of Enrollments. This law made deeds of freehold estates void unless recorded within six months of the transfer. The Statute of Enrollments is the predecessor of the recording acts, which are so important to conveyancing in the United States today.

Each state has legislation establishing a system for recording real property conveyances and encumbrances affecting real property. Proof of title in the United States is almost always based upon these records.

The recording statutes generally provide that conveyances not recorded are void against subsequent purchasers in good faith. Thus the original purchaser's failure to record can result in superior rights to the property going to one who subsequently purchases the same property from the original seller.

CASE EXAMPLE

Frank Kramer, the owner of a parcel of land, conveys it to Ginger Shields. Shields fails to record her deed. Kramer thereafter fraudulently conveys the same parcel to Elaine Simlo, who has no knowledge of the transfer to Shields. Simlo immediately records her deed. As a result her title is superior to that of Shields. The recording laws protect Simlo, the innocent purchaser.

Although recording is important in any real estate transaction, recording is not necessary to pass title. In the previous example, Ginger Shields has title to the parcel as a result of the conveyance from Frank Kramer. As far as Frank and the rest of the world are concerned, she is the owner. If, however, Ginger does not record the deed, and Frank fraudulently conveys to another, Ginger could lose all rights in the property.

DEED

A legal instrument conveying title to real property upon delivery and acceptance by the grantee.

The deed is the primary method of transferring title to real estate. Therefore, it is one of the critical documents in the real estate transaction. Although problems involving deeds are ordinarily the concern of the attorney, the real estate professional needs to be familiar with the different types of deeds, the formal elements of a deed and the steps required for a deed to be executed properly.

The deed is a two-party instrument. One party, called the *grantor*, conveys real estate to the other party, the *grantee*. A deed does not have to follow any particular form to be valid. Any written document containing the few essential elements will be effective. Most states have adopted statutory forms for the different types of deeds. The statutory forms are almost always short, often a single page, and all the essentials are included. Although the statutory form is acceptable for all transactions, lawyers generally prepare a longer, more formal document.

States have adopted the statutory forms in order to cut the costs of recording and preserving records of deeds and other instruments affecting title to real property. Considerable expense is saved by photocopying and storing a single sheet instead of four or five pages. In some areas of the United States, especially heavily populated areas, space has become so acute a problem that recording offices are turning to microfilm or microfiche storage or similar systems to preserve the public records.

Even when a statutory form exists, lawyers often use the longer traditional forms. Custom and habit are difficult to change. The savings in individual cases are not extensive, and the legal profession and the lay public are accustomed to the traditional forms. In addition, the real estate transaction is so important to most individuals that it often seems advisable to include in the deed more than the minimal essentials needed to pass title.

Several types of deeds are common in the United States. Ordinarily, in a real estate transaction, the type of deed that the seller will use is agreed upon in the contract of sale. This is one of several reasons why each party should consult an attorney before signing the agreement. A seller is bound to furnish the type of deed stipulated by the agreement, and this is what the buyer must accept, although another type of deed might provide the buyer more protection.

Warranty Deed

A deed that conveys title and warrants that the title is good and free of liens and encumbrances.

Custom often influences what type of deed will be agreed upon in the contract. Real estate attorneys like to use the instrument in general use in a particular locality. In some areas, one type of deed is standard for residential sales, whereas a different type of deed is used to convey commercial property. Parties should remember, however, that the type of deed is subject to negotiation at the time of contracting.

CASE EXAMPLE

Olvic's contract with Ziebarth called for a general warranty deed. At the closing Olvic offered another type of deed customarily used in the area. Ziebarth was entitled to a general warranty deed.

There are two types of warranty deed—the general or full warranty deed and the special or limited warranty deed. More frequently used is the *general* or *full warranty deed*. A general warranty deed conveys the seller's title and contains warranties or guarantees respecting the title. The warranties are often referred to as *covenants*. They provide the buyer with some protection against claims that might interfere with ownership.

CASE EXAMPLE

Several months after Ziebarth acquired title to the Olvic property, the heir of a former owner claimed an interest in the land. If the heir's interest had been substantiated, Olvic would have had to compensate Ziebarth for damages resulting from the claim, since Olvic gave him a general warranty deed.

General (Full) Warranty Deed

The covenants in a general warranty deed vary from one locality to another, but five covenants are customary: covenant of seisin, covenant against encumbrances, covenant of quiet enjoyment, covenant of warranty and covenant of further assurances.

By *covenant of seisin* the seller guarantees his or her ownership of the property and the existence of a right to convey. The covenant has also been construed to mean that the seller has an estate of the quantity and quality purportedly conveyed. This covenant is sometimes referred to as the *covenant of right to convey*.

The *covenant against encumbrances* is the seller's assurance that, at the time of conveyance, the property is free of *encumbrances*. Typical encumbrances are leases, easements, mortgages and liens (to be discussed more fully in Chapter 10). The covenant does not apply to those encumbrances specifically excepted in the deed, because the buyer has agreed to accept them. In many states encumbrances that are open and visible and that benefit the land are also excluded from the covenant against encumbrances.

CASE EXAMPLE

Al Wilson purchased a lot from Bonnie McConnell. The lot and several others in the area were subject to certain building restrictions. At the time Wilson contracted he knew of these restrictions, but they were not mentioned in the contract. Wilson refused to accept a deed from McConnell on grounds that the restrictions violated the covenant against encumbrances. Because the restrictions benefited the land, however, this argument would be unsuccessful.

The *covenant of quiet enjoyment* and the *covenant of warranty* are very much alike. In both, the seller guarantees that the buyer will not be evicted by someone with a superior title. These covenants are not breached unless the buyer is actually evicted by a third party who has a better title. If this occurs, the buyer can sue the seller for damages.

In some states the general warranty deed also contains a *covenant of further assurances*. This covenant obligates the grantor to perform all acts necessary to confirm the grantee's title, including the execution of any additional conveyances or instruments that are needed.

Present covenants. The covenant of seisin or right to convey and the covenant against encumbrances are present covenants. If they are broken, it is at the time that the deed is delivered. The present covenants protect only the immediate buyer. This right is personal and cannot be used as the basis for suit by a subsequent buyer. In addition, in one-third of the states the period of time within which the buyer can sue to enforce the covenants begins to run when the deed is delivered. It is possible for that time to have expired before the buyer discovers the breach, as the statute of limitations in most of these states is less than ten years.

Future covenants. The covenant of quiet enjoyment, the covenant of warranty and the covenant of further assurances protect future purchasers as well as the immediate purchaser. They are regarded as future covenants and are said to *run with the land*. As a result their breach may be the basis for suit by a remote buyer against a previous seller who has given a warranty deed. This suit may occur many years after the particular defendant sold the property. The phrase *run with the land* is used because these covenants pass from one person to another as title is transferred.

CASE EXAMPLE

Several years after buying the property from Olvic, Ziebarth sold it to Lance Murphy. Ziebarth did not convey by a general warranty deed. Murphy's title was contested, and he was evicted from the property. Unable to sue Ziebarth, Murphy commenced an action against Olvic. Olvic defended upon the grounds that he had not sold the property to Murphy. In this litigation, a court would find for Murphy on the grounds that the covenants of quiet enjoyment and warranty run with the land and extend to future owners.

Covenants in a warranty deed do not assure the buyer that the seller has title. All they do is give the buyer a right to sue if a covenant is broken. Although they provide the buyer with some protection, that protection is limited by many factors. The seller who has made the warranties might become insolvent or leave the jurisdiction. In that case any judgment against the seller would be difficult to obtain or of little value. Many states limit the seller's liability to the original purchase price. Improvements or appreciation in value is not included as part of the buyer's losses. Not covered by the traditional warranties are invalid claims, threats of litigation or *clouds upon title*—those documents, liens or encumbrances that might impair the validity of the title. Because of the limited nature of the protection offered, a buyer should never rely only upon a warranty deed. Additional assurances, such as an attorney's opinion of title or title insurance, should be obtained.

Special (Limited) Warranty Deed

A *special* or *limited warranty* deed restricts the extent of the seller's warranties. In this type of instrument, the seller guarantees only against acts that he or she has done that might affect title. Of course the deed conveys the seller's title to the property.

CASE EXAMPLE

Ziebarth's conveyance to Lance Murphy was by a limited warranty deed. When Murphy discovered that Ziebarth's title was defective because of an undischarged mortgage given by Olvic in 1967, Murphy brought suit against Ziebarth. Because the defect arose before Ziebarth had acquired the property, the limited warranty had not been broken. As we have seen, Murphy had a good cause of action against Olvic, who had conveyed by general warranty deed.

Bargain and Sale Deed

A deed that conveys title but makes no warranties.

In common use in a number of jurisdictions is a deed that conveys title but contains no warranties, frequently referred to as a *bargain and sale deed*. Sometimes the bargain and sale deed contains covenants against the seller's acts. When this is the case, the bargain and sale deed has the same effect as the limited or special warranty deed.

An important variation of the bargain and sale deed is the fiduciary deed. A *fiduciary* is a person who has been placed by law in a position of trust regarding property that is not his or her own—for example, the administrator or executor of a decedent's estate. The fiduciary might need to convey title to the decedent's real property but would not want to make guarantees or warranties concerning the title. In that case a special form of deed similar to the bargain and sale deed will be used. In it the fiduciary guarantees only that he or she has been properly appointed and authorized to sell and convey. The deed does not make any other warranties.

Quitclaim Deed

An instrument that conveys whatever interest the grantor has.

Unlike the warranty deed and the bargain and sale deed, the quitclaim deed does not purport to convey title; it merely releases whatever interest the grantor has. If the grantor has title, the quitclaim deed conveys that title as effectively as a warranty or bargain and sale deed. A grantee who takes title by a quitclaim deed does not acquire any of the covenants that are given to a grantee accepting a warranty deed. If the contract does not mention the type of deed to be used, many states permit the seller to give a quitclaim deed.

The quitclaim deed is commonly used to clear a *defective* title. The defect could range from an incorrect description in a prior deed to an outstanding lien, a recorded easement or the release of a potential dower right.

CASE EXAMPLE

Martin Russo contracted to sell property to Elmer Hunter. At the time Russo was single, but prior to title closing he married. The marriage was secret, and only Russo signed the deed. In a state recognizing common law dower, Russo's wife has an inchoate right of dower. Upon discovering the marriage, the attorneys for both parties asked Mrs. Russo to execute a quitclaim deed releasing her right to Elmer Hunter. In executing this instrument, Mrs. Russo would surrender any interest she might have in the property.

Essential Elements of Deeds

A deed is a complicated instrument that should be drafted by an attorney. A properly drafted and executed deed is critical to any real estate sale. Errors in a deed can cause problems not only for the current owner but also for future generations of owners. Sale of the property, financing and even occupancy can be affected by errors that seem inconsequential. In order to help prevent these errors, the real estate salesperson needs some knowledge of the basic requirements of a valid deed. Since the deed should be drafted by an attorney, the salesperson's knowledge need not be extensive, but it should be sufficient to recognize potential problems. With this background the salesperson should be able to alert the drafter to issues that might lead to errors in the deed. In order to be valid, a deed must include words of conveyance, a competent grantor and grantee properly identified and a legal description. The instrument must be signed and executed correctly, and a valid delivery and acceptance must occur. The balance of this chapter discusses legal problems associated with these prerequisites, concentrating on areas of particular interest to real estate personnel.

Words of Conveyance

The heart of a deed is the granting clause. A deed must contain words of conveyance sufficient to transfer an estate from one party to another. No particular words are necessary, provided that those used express an intention to convey title. Words customarily used are *grant*, *convey*, and *bargain*. The word *grant* is used widely. In a number of states the term has been adopted as a statutory word of conveyance. A typical granting clause might read as follows: "Grantors...do by these presents grant, bargain, sell, and convey unto the said grantees forever..." The word *quitclaim* or *release* is commonly found in quitclaim deeds.

A deed without words of conveyance does not transfer title; the courts have, however, been indulgent in interpreting words in order to a give a deed effect.

• CASE BRIEF •

On September 18, 1941, Mary A. Searle conveyed land to her four children as tenants in common. On June 21, 1948, the four joined in the execution of an unartfully drawn instrument, which purported to change their rights as cotenants and to convey to others certain remainder interests.

The granting clause of this document stated, "Said premises are to be held so that as each of said parties shall die, the property shall vest in the survivors or survivor for their respective lives...." Remainders were created using as granting words "to go," "to be his," and "shall go."

In an action to establish who had title, plaintiffs argued that the operative words of grant "are to be held" and the phrases used to grant the remainder interests were insufficient and that the instrument was not a valid deed.

The court did not agree, stating "To be effective to transfer an interest in realty, a deed necessarily must contain words of present grant...But no particular verbal formula is required under our rule of construction as previously given. The quoted words express an intention to create among the original cotenants new incidents of survivorship and power of sale, and to grant remainder interests to other persons subject to defeasance upon the exercise of the power of sale. The instrument was not ineffective as a deed for lack of a sufficient granting clause."
Dennen v. Searle, 149 Conn. 126, 176 A.2d 561 (1961).

Competent Grantor

To be valid, a deed must have a competent grantor. Any natural person except a minor or a person who lacks mental capacity may convey real estate by deed. Deeds made by minors or incompetents are not void, but they are *voidable*, which means that the minor or incompetent acquires the option of either ratifying or disaffirming the deed.

The minor wishing to disaffirm his or her transfer by *deed* cannot do so until reaching the age of majority, but a minor can avoid a *contract* to buy land at any time during minority and for a reasonable time after reaching majority. The age of majority traditionally was 21. Today in many states it is 18. Once having reached majority, the minor must institute proceedings to disaffirm within a reasonable time. If this is not done, the right is lost.

CASE EXAMPLE

In November 1948, John Spencer and his sister inherited land from their father. At the time John was a minor. He attained his majority on April 5, 1949. John's sister was of full age at her father's death. In December 1948, John and his sister sold the property to Alpheas MacLoon. Shortly thereafter, MacLoon conveyed part of the property to the Lyman Falls Power Company and the residue to William Hutchins. Three years later the power company commenced substantial improvements on the land. John Spencer attempted to disaffirm. The company's attorney pleaded that Spencer had a right to disaffirm when he reached majority, but the right had been lost because he failed to assert it within a reasonable time.

To cancel a deed for lack of mental capacity, evidence of a grantor's incompetency must be clear and convincing. The test of mental capacity to make a deed is the grantor's ability to understand the nature and effect of the act at the time the conveyance is made.

• CASE BRIEF •

Florence Woodward owned a 120-acre farm near Verna, Oklahoma. When she was nearly 80, she became ill and moved to a nursing home. While a resident at the home, she conveyed the farm to a nephew. After Woodward's death, a niece contested the validity of the deed on grounds that the grantor was incompetent.

Conflicting testimony was given at the trial concerning Florence Woodward's competency. Witnesses testified that prior to her hospitalization she was often confused and vague. Her concentration was described as poor. There was testimony that her home was untidy, and she often took care of her cattle at odd hours, such as midnight. A nurse from the nursing home testified that in her opinion Woodward would not have understood the effect of signing a deed, but she always recognized her nephews and would talk about her property. Other witnesses testified that Woodward was generally alert, competent and normal.

The court held the deed valid, stating that fragmentary evidence of isolated instances of failing memory or confusion is insufficient to overcome evidence that grantor was competent. *Matter of Woodward, 549 P.2d 1207 (Okla. 1976).*

Corporate Grantor A number of special rules apply to transfers of real property by corporations. The corporate officer who executes a deed must be authorized to do so. This authorization is obtained from the board of directors, which adopts a written resolution permitting the officer to act. In most states, if the corporation sells real estate that is a substantial portion of the corporation's assets, statutes require the sale to be approved by a designated portion of the shareholders, usually two-thirds or more. Nonprofit corporations are often required by statute to obtain approval of a majority of members before selling real estate.

Grantor's Marital Status A deed by a natural person should indicate that person's marital status. In most states a surviving spouse has either a vested or an inchoate interest in a deceased's property even when the property is held separately. The extent of this interest varies from state to state, but ordinarily it will be terminated if the spouse has also signed the deed. A number of states have homestead laws, which were discussed in Chapter 4. These laws prohibit a husband from selling the family residence unless the wife agrees and executes the deed with the husband. Generally, the failure to indicate the grantor's marital status does not invalidate the deed.

Grantee

A deed does not convey title unless it names an existing identifiable grantee. Of course, few transactions exist in which the grantee does not legally exist. One example might be a deed that designated an unincorporated association as the grantee. A deed naming this group would be invalid.

Some litigation has involved transactions in which a deed has been executed with the grantee's name left blank. Although this instrument does not pass title, most courts have reasoned that the intended grantee has authority to fill in his or her name. A subsequent conveyance by this person to a bona fide purchaser creates marketable title.

Ordinarily, the determination of the proper designation of the grantee is a responsibility of the attorney or other person who drafts the deed. The real estate professional can aid this drafter by informing him or her of unusual circumstances regarding the name or marital status of the grantee or grantor. For example, during negotiations the real estate salesperson may learn of the grantee's use of another name or a variation in spelling.

Legal Description

Problems involving descriptions in deeds are, like those involving designation of the grantee, not primarily the concern of real estate personnel but of legal personnel. Sales personnel, however, are apt to be aware of boundary controversies, which may result from or indicate description problems. Legal description and controversies involving boundaries are discussed in Chapter 11.

The salesperson who is aware of a boundary or description issue should urge the seller to obtain a solution before placing property on the market. This will save time and embarrassment as well as prevent hard feelings that arise when these issues come up after agreement is reached.

Descriptions probably cause more litigation than any of the other formal requirements of the deed. Property to be conveyed must be described well enough in the deed to identify it with reasonable certainty. An imperfect description does not render a deed invalid, but the description must accurately depict the land in question. Presumably the grantor intended to convey *something*; the deed will usually be upheld unless the description is so vague or contradictory that the particular land cannot be ascertained.

Most courts interpret words of description liberally in order to uphold a conveyance. The basic rule in construction of deeds is to ascertain and carry out the real intention of the parties. To accomplish this, courts first look to the document itself, but they will accept extrinsic evidence or external proof if the description furnished a guide to identifying the property conveyed.

• CASE BRIEF •

Plaintiff and defendant owned adjoining land. A former owner of plaintiff's property had conveyed a ten-foot strip of ground to the township to be used as a drainage ditch. The ditch drained defendant's land as well as that of other landowners. The description in the deed to the township indicated a point of beginning and described the ditch as "running due south for 2,200 feet." For several years defendant had maintained the ditch, which was at the time of suit six feet wide.

In 1968 plaintiff commenced a trespass action against defendant, asking for an injunction prohibiting defendant from maintaining and using the ditch. Plaintiff argued that the deed to the township was ineffective because the description contained no boundaries. The court rejected this argument on the grounds that logically the line described was intended as the center of the ditch. The description thus furnished the means by which the property could be identified. *Franz v. Nelson, 183 Neb. 122, 158 N.W.2d 606 (1968).*

Signature

To be valid, a deed must be signed by the grantor; however, the grantee's signature is unnecessary. A few states require that a deed be subscribed, or signed at the end of the instrument. When there is no requirement of subscription, the signature does not have to be in any particular place, but the signature must clearly apply to the entire instrument. Customarily, even when not required, a deed is signed at the end. Signature may be by the grantor's mark or by any writing the grantor intends as a signature. If a grantor signs by a mark, his or her name should appear near the mark, and the act should be witnessed.

Attestation is the act of witnessing the execution of an instrument and subscribing as a witness. In general, the law does not require witnesses to a grantor's signature to establish a deed as valid. Witnessing and attestation, however, are almost universal prerequisites to recording. The attesting witness subscribes the document for the purpose of verifying and identifying it. Usually two witnesses are required.

Acknowledgment is the act by which a grantor declares before a duly authorized official that a deed is genuine and executed voluntarily. Acknowledgment, like attestation, is in most states a prerequisite to recording rather than an essential requirement of a valid deed. The purpose of acknowledgment is to prevent forgery and fraud. The official witnessing the grantor's signature is charged with determining the grantor's identity. Each state by statute prescribes the officials before whom an acknowledgment may be made and the general form the acknowledgment must follow. Attestation and acknowledgment are discussed more fully in Chapter 9, which deals with recording.

Power of Attorney.   A power of attorney is a written instrument authorizing a person, the attorney-in-fact, to act as agent on behalf of another to the extent indicated in the instrument.

A deed executed by an agent for the grantor, in the grantor's absence is invalid unless the agent has a power of attorney. In a real estate transaction, the parties should use a special limited power of attorney instead of the all-inclusive general power of attorney. Courts strictly construe the power of attorney, and thus the power must specifically authorize the attorney-in-fact to convey the real estate. A general power to sell does not grant the power to convey. In some states, *the equal dignities* rule requires that a power of attorney in a real estate conveyance be executed with the same formalities that are required to execute the deed properly. In some states, a deed executed by a person with a power of attorney cannot be recorded unless the power of attorney is also recorded.

Normally, a power of attorney may be revoked at any time. In most cases the death of either the principal or the attorney-in-fact also revokes the power of attorney. Therefore, the purchaser taking a deed signed by an attorney-in-fact should be extremely cautious. The power of attorney should not be old, and the purchaser should require evidence that the principal is living. The purchaser should also insist that the power of attorney be recorded. This provides some protection because an unrecorded revocation is ineffective against a recorded power of attorney.

Consideration

A deed does not have to state a consideration to be valid. The owner of land has the right to convey it as a gift as well as to sell it. As we have seen, the primary function of a deed is to convey title. Although the voluntary conveyance is usually based upon a contract of sale since a conveyance is not a contract, no consideration need be stated in the deed itself.

Deeds generally do identify a consideration. A deed without consideration is vulnerable against the grantor's creditors. If the deed states a consideration, it is more difficult for the grantor's creditors to assert claims against the property. If creditors can prove that the grantee gave no consideration, they may successfully levy against the property even though ownership has been transferred. Under the recording acts in all but a few states, the grantee must have given consideration in order to be protected. As will be seen in Chapter 9, most recording statutes provide protection only for bona fide purchasers for value.

CASE EXAMPLE

Elvis Carter borrowed money from Marilyn Duffy, a close personal friend. As security he gave her a mortgage on a parcel of land that he owned. Duffy did not record the mortgage. Later Carter conveyed the property to Helen Lehmen. The conveyance was a gift, and the deed stated no consideration. When Carter did not repay Duffy, she commenced a foreclosure action. Although her mortgage was not recorded, a court would direct the property be sold since Lehmen was not a purchaser for value.

Customarily, deeds will recite a nominal consideration such as "one dollar ($1.00) and other good and valuable consideration." This is done because buyers are often reluctant to have the actual purchase price shown in the public record. A recital of a nominal consideration is effective, for if the question of actual consideration arises, the courts allow the parties to prove by extrinsic evidence the amount actually involved.

Donative Intent, Delivery and Acceptance

A deed does not transfer title until delivered by the grantor and accepted by the grantee. Although manual transfer of the instrument is the common method of delivering a deed, manual transfer alone is insufficient to pass title. The grantor must *intend to pass title* and *surrender control of the instrument.* Unless these two components exist, the fact that the grantor has given up physical possession of the deed is of no consequence.

• CASE BRIEF •

Beatrice Curtiss executed a quitclaim deed to herself and to her granddaughter, Marilyn Feriss, as joint tenants. Although the deed was recorded, Mrs. Curtiss continued to occupy the property and paid all maintenance as well as insurance expenses. Both Mrs. Curtiss and other members of the family stated and acted as if Mrs. Curtiss were the sole owner. Mrs. Feriss was regarded and spoken of as "the inheritor." Mrs. Feriss never occupied the property or stayed there longer than a single night.

In litigation involving the Feriss title, the appellate court stated that "the deed in question did not operate to pass an interest in the property...to Marilyn Feriss as the grantor did not intend for it to do so." *Curtiss v. Feriss, 168 Colo. 480, 452 P.2d38 (1969).*

Conversely, even though physical transfer is the generally accepted procedure, delivery can be effective without it. Lord Coke, a noted English jurist of the 17th century, stated that "a deed may be delivered without any act of delivery."

Constructive or implied delivery, which is delivery without change of possession, is valid although rare. As with actual delivery, the essence of constructive delivery is the intention of the parties, not the manual act of transfer. If the grantor by words or acts manifests an intention to divest himself or herself of title and vest it in another, the law determines that delivery is sufficient, even if the instrument itself (but not control) remains in the hands of the grantor.

• CASE BRIEF •

On August 10, 1940, Frank and Elizabeth Agrelius, husband

and wife, executed two warranty deeds, one deed conveying 80 acres of land to Clair T. Agrelius, the other deed conveying a nearby 80 acres to Paul Kenneth Agrelius. Neither deed was recorded during the lifetime of either grantor.

On July 27, 1944, a safety deposit box was leased . . . in the names of Mr. and Mrs. Agrelius, who signed the lease at that time. Clair was also named as lessee, although he did not sign the lease contract until 1962. The deeds were placed in the safety deposit box. At some later time in 1944 . . . Mr. Agrelius told Clair of the two deeds executed in 1940 . . . At this time Mr. Agrelius handed Clair a key to the safety deposit box and said this would constitute delivery of the deed to him. After the death of Mrs. Agrelius in 1967, Clair removed the two deeds from the box and had them recorded.

The trial court held that " . . . when Frank and Elizabeth Agrelius told Clair they had executed a deed conveying one 80-acre tract to him and another deed to the other 80-acre tract to Kenneth and placed the deeds in their lock box and then handed the key to the box to Clair, such actions constituted an effective constructive delivery of the deeds, and all the circumstances showed a purpose on the part of the grantors that there should be an immediate vesting of title in Clair and Kenneth, enjoyment only being postponed until the death of the grantors. *Agrelius v. Mohesky, 280 Kan. 790, 494 P.2d 1095 (1972).*

Delivery is ineffective unless the grantor parts with legal control of the instrument during his or her lifetime. The grantor may not retain the power to recall the deed from either the grantee or a third party. Once a valid delivery has occurred, the deed may, however, remain in the grantor's custody or be returned to the grantor for safekeeping.

A deed may be effective even if it contains a provision that it is not to become operative until the grantor's death. Delivery must take place during the grantor's lifetime. The delivery can be made directly to the grantee, who holds the deed until the grantor's death. Whatever the situation, the grantor must effectively divest himself or herself of control. This does not occur if the grantor places the deeds with private papers or merely leaves the instrument in a safety deposit box, even one shared with another.

• CASE BRIEF •

Sanford and Daisy Lee Jones had two children, Alfred and Arthur. In 1981, Sanford and Daisy Lee executed a deed to certain land to Alfred and his wife, Luverne. Daisy Lee died on March 3, 1983, and Sanford died on June 13, 1983. The deed from Sanford and Daisy Lee to Alfred and Luverne was not recorded until July 29, 1983, six weeks after the father's death.

Arthur, the other son, filed suit questioning the validity of the deed. The trial court, sitting without a jury, held the deed void due to the lack of a valid delivery. On appeal, the appellate court affirmed the decision of the trial court, emphasizing the evidence at the trial that Alfred had found the deed in a trunk used by their father to store his important papers nine months after the deed's execution, that the father never divested himself of control over title to the property and could have sold it at any time and that the father retained all incidents of ownership of the property by paying taxes, collecting rent and paying for repairs until his death. *Jones v. Jones, 470 So.2d 1207 (Ala. 1985).*

A grantor may deposit a deed with a third party to satisfy the legal requirement of delivery. This is an effective delivery if the grantor has surrendered all control over the instrument and is powerless to recall it. A deed delivered to a third party is effective from that time even if the grantor dies or becomes insane before the grantee obtains possession of the instrument.

The estate created by the deed may be conditioned upon the performance of some act or occurrence of some event. Until the condition is fulfilled, the grantee's estate does not come into existence.

• CASE BRIEF •

M.A. Hinkson, while suffering from a paralytic stroke, called Hazen, an attorney, to his bedside. Acting upon Hazen's advice, Hinkson signed and acknowledged a deed naming his two daughters, Mrs. Young and Mrs. Bury, as grantees. This deed was given to Hazen with instructions not to record it but to deliver it to the grantees upon Hinkson's death. Hinkson recovered and attempted to secure possession of the deed from Hazen. Hazen refused to return it.

Later Hinkson made a will devising all his real property to Young. Upon Hinkson's death, Hazen turned the deed over to Bury. In litigation involving Young and Bury, the court held that the deed effectively conveyed title to the two daughters when delivered to Hazen. *Bury v. Young, 98 Cal. 446, 33 P. 338 (1893).*

Escrow. A means by which delivery may take place, escrow is a process by which money and/or documents are held by a third party until the terms and conditions of an escrow agreement are satisfied. In a number of localities, real estate transactions customarily close through a third party called an *escrow agent* or *holder.* This system is prevalent in some of the western states, including California. The escrow holder may be an attorney, a bank, a title insurance company or an independent escrow agent.

Buyer and seller in an escrow closing agree to submit the necessary documents and funds to the escrow holder. The escrow holder is responsible for seeing that the transaction closes upon the conditions agreed to by the parties. As stakeholder, he or she retains the funds and mortgage documents submitted by the buyer. When the seller has delivered to the escrow holder a properly executed deed to the property, and the holder is assured the seller is passing good title, the funds and mortgage documents are turned over to the seller. Completion of an escrow transaction may depend upon other conditions. The escrow holder is responsible for seeing that these are fulfilled before delivering the deed or disbursing the funds. Other facts of the escrow transaction are discussed more fully in Chapter 24.

LIMITATION OF LAND USE

In addition to passing title, a deed may be used to regulate land use. This is accomplished through a condition in the instrument or a covenant. Conditions must be included in the deed; covenants usually are, but a valid covenant may be created by an ancillary document.

Chapter 4 discussed the use of conditions to limit the use of an estate. That chapter indicated that, when a condition in a deed is fulfilled, the owner's estate is subject to termination. In some instances, depending upon the wording of the condition, termination is automatic; in others termination depends upon some action being taken by the person holding the reversionary interest.

Sometimes a purchaser of land will agree that it not be used in a particular manner. This type of commitment is called a *covenant*. Although both a covenant and a condition limit land use, the legal effects of the two differ. When a condition is fulfilled, the owner's interest is subject to termination. When a covenant is broken, the owner may be sued for damages or enjoined from breaking the contract, but the owner does not lose title to the property.

Restrictive Covenant

A provision in a deed limiting uses that may be made of the property, such as the type or location of buildings that may be erected upon it.

Restrictive covenants are an important tool used by developers to ensure consistency in land use. They are also used by persons selling a portion of their land to protect themselves from undesirable uses that the buyer might make of the property. Restrictive covenants are in effect a private type of zoning regulation. By accepting delivery, the grantee is bound by restrictions in the deed.

Typical restrictive covenants limit property to residential use, provide minimum setback and acreage requirements, prohibit certain types of buildings, limit the number of structures or set minimum cost for housing to be constructed. Because restrictive covenants limit land use, courts do not always favor them. Today, however, most restrictive covenants will be enforced if they do not violate public policy. An example of a covenant violating public policy would be one restricting ownership of the land to members of a particular racial or religious group.

Affirmative covenants are also recognized in most states. Typical affirmative covenants involve agreements to build fences, maintain party walls, provide railroad crossings and join and pay dues or an annual assessment to a homeowners' association for maintenance of roads, parks or similar facilities. In a few states affirmative covenants are not recognized as valid because courts feel that they are too difficult to enforce.

If they are to have much value, covenants must apply not only to the original parties but to future owners of land as well. In general, American courts have accepted the proposition that both restrictive and affirmative covenants run with the land if three factors exist. First, this must have been the intention of those who made the agreement. Second, knowledge of the covenant must actually exist or be readily determinable from the public record. Third, the covenant must "touch and concern" the land. This means that the covenant must benefit or burden the land in question and not be merely a personal commitment for an individual's benefit.

• CASE BRIEF •

Mary A. Schaefers conveyed land to her daughter Rosemary. The deed contained a provision that required Rosemary to provide a home for her brother William, if he requested it. Rosemary Schaefers conveyed the land to Edward Apel. William brought an action to set aside the conveyance for violating the restriction. The lower court dismissed William's action, and the appellate court affirmed.

The appellate court stated, "The covenant is not enforceable against the Apels or any subsequent grantees . . . because it does not touch the land in question. The covenant is merely a personal obligation from Rosemary to William to provide him a permanent home in some location if he requests one." *Schaefers v. Apel, 328 So.2d 274 (Ala. 1976).*

Although many covenants are part of a planned pattern of land use, they also constitute a burden on the land. Frequently buyers and sellers wish to terminate covenants because they interfere with more profitable uses of the property. A few states have legislation that provides for the elimination of stale restrictions after a fixed period of time or when the limitation no longer substantially benefits those for whom it was created. Most states, however, do not have legislation of this nature. In these states deed covenants often interfere with real estate development unless they can be eliminated.

Although several methods exist for eliminating covenants, each is either costly to accomplish or legally impractical. Covenants may be terminated by a release, by waiver or by abandonment, but these methods are usually impracticable since several people often have the right to enforce a single covenant. Other methods are by acquisition of the property subject to the covenant by the owner of the property benefiting or by litigation showing that changing conditions in the neighborhood have nullified the benefits of the covenant. Because of the difficulty of terminating covenants, a very desirable practice is to write the covenant initially to expire automatically after a period of time. Land use restrictions and covenants are discussed more fully in Chapters 12 and 13.

SUMMARY

In modern usage, *title* has many meanings. In real estate, the term refers to the totality of rights and obligations an owner possesses in the real estate, as well as the written record that is evidence of ownership. This official recording is crucial to the transfer of real estate in the United States today.

The deed is the legal instrument that conveys title when real property is bought and sold. As each sale occurs, the transfer is officially recorded, adding to the chain of title. The real estate professional needs to be familiar with state statutes concerning recording and with the various types of deeds. One type, the warranty deed, contains clauses known as *covenants* that provide the buyer with some protection against claims that might interfere with ownership. These covenants in general guarantee that the owner has the right to sell, that the property is free of liens or the claims of creditors and that the buyer will not be ousted by someone with superior title (a prior claim). If any of these covenants is broken, the buyer can recover damages from the seller. In practice, however, it is often difficult to collect such a judgment, so the buyer should instigate his or her own title search.

The bargain and sale deed, another type, does not contain warranties but may carry comparable covenants. The quitclaim deed is another type of deed; it does not convey title as such, but merely relinquishes whatever interest the grantor has. It is often used when a defective or questionable title must be cleared.

The deed is such an important instrument legally that it

should be drafted by an attorney. Errors in the written document can cause problems in the title for future generations. It is beneficial for real estate salespeople to know the elements necessary to create a valid deed. These requirements include words of conveyance that express the intention to convey title from one party (the grantor) to another (the grantee), a competent grantor and an identifiable grantee. The deed must contain a legal description of the property. It must be signed by the grantor or an authorized representative. Most deeds also state a consideration, and a deed can be challenged in court if no consideration has been given. Finally, delivery and acceptance must be demonstrated for a deed to be valid. One means for delivery to take place is by escrow; that is, the money payment and/or the document may be held by a third party until all conditions are met.

On occasion a deed is also used to limit the use to which land will be put. These restrictions or covenants usually appear in writing in the deed. If worded properly, these provisions run with the land and are difficult or impossible to terminate.

REVIEW AND DISCUSSION QUESTIONS

1. Explain the difference between (a) *general warranty deed* and a special or *limited warranty deed* and (b) *bargain and sale deed* and a *quitclaim deed.*
2. What type of deed is generally used in your area in residential real estate transactions? What are the advantages and disadvantages of this type of deed to buyers and sellers?
3. What is the result of a purchaser's failure to record a deed upon (a) the purchaser's title and (b) a subsequent purchaser who relies upon the seller's recorded title?
4. Explain the assurances provided a grantee by (a) covenant of seisin and (b) covenant of quiet enjoyment.
5. Why is it important for a purchaser to acquire additional assurances, such as title insurance, when acquiring title by warranty deed?
6. Explain the difference between *attestation* and *acknowledgment.*

CASE PROBLEMS

1. On March 7, Marlin Martin, who was very ill, executed a deed to his son Bill. Martin gave the instrument to Dr. Blaine, stating, "Take this deed and keep it. If I get well, I will call for it. If I don't, give it to Billy." On March 12, Martin died. Dr. Blaine delivered the deed as instructed. The grantee had it recorded. The grantee's sister claims the deed is ineffective. Is she correct? Discuss.
2. Dunlap owned a large farm, which he worked for many years

with his son Sam. Dunlap had a daughter, Celeste, who lived in the city. Dunlap had often told Sam, Celeste and various relatives that Sam was to inherit the farm; nevertheless, nothing was ever done to ensure that it would happen. As Dunlap aged, he became senile and difficult to live with, but in lucid moments he talked about Sam's inheriting the farm. Because Sam knew that his father had no will, Sam had a deed prepared conveying the property to himself. Dunlap signed the deed. The execution of the instrument was done properly, according to state law. Two years later Dunlap died and Sam had the deed recorded. Celeste has sued to have the deed declared invalid. Will she be successful? Discuss.

3. Stephen Takacs and his son John purchased property as tenants in common. After sharing the costs of building a house, father, son and the son's wife lived together on the premises for two years. During this period Stephen paid $40 per month for his room and board.

   While the parties were living together in the home, the three went to the office of an attorney. The attorney, at Stephen's insistence, prepared a quitclaim deed conveying Stephen's interest to John Takacs and Mabel R. Takacs, John's wife.

   At the time there was an understanding that the deed would become effective on Stephen's death and would not be recorded during his lifetime. The deed, however, was delivered to John. It was never in Stephen's possession, nor did Stephen reserve the right to recall it. Shortly thereafter, John died. Mabel Takacs recorded the conveyance and attempted to sell the property.

   Stephen sues to set aside the deed. Will he be successful? Discuss. *Takacs v. Takacs, 26 N.W.2d 712 (Mich. 1947).*

4. Ruth Halsey, a resident of New Jersey, owed money to Tom Cleaver, who lived in Colorado. Halsey wished to pay the debt and agreed to transfer a valuable piece of property to Cleaver. Halsey had her attorney prepare a deed to Cleaver. The deed was executed properly, delivered to Cleaver's attorney and recorded. Unknown to Halsey, Cleaver had died several days before Halsey executed the instrument. Is Cleaver's estate entitled to the property? Support your answer.

5. Chris Stevens, a farmer, owned 40 acres of land that he didn't use. He leased the land for three years to Orlando Baron. The lease was for farming purposes. Before the lease expired, Stevens conveyed the property by general warranty deed to Morgan Kettlewell. Kettlewell planned to subdivide the property. He had no knowledge of the lease and believed the crops on the land were Stevens's. What right, if any, does Kettlewell

have against Stevens? How could Stevens have protected himself?

6. In 1937 Joseph A. Hanns executed, dated and acknowledged a
deed to his home. The grantees were his son Santolli and his
daughter, Sylvania. The deed was discovered by another son, P.
J., in his father's safe deposit box after the father's death. P. J.
Hanns was appointed administrator of his father's estate.

For 18 years after their father's death, Santolli and Sylvania
occupied the residence. In 1956 P. J. recorded the deed. In 1962
the property was sold to Dunham Motors. A short time later P.
J. died. Suit was then brought by P. J.'s son Frank, asking the
court for a share in the proceeds of the sale. Frank claimed this
interest on grounds that the deed from Joseph A. Hanns to Santolli and Sylvania had never been delivered. As a result, his father, P. J., was entitled to an intestate share of the property.
What factors would a court have to consider to determine the
validity of Frank's claim? *Hanns v. Hanns, 262 Or. 282, 423
P.2d 499 (1967).*

8
Involuntary Transfers and Transfers Upon an Owner's Death

The conveyance of real property by deed, often called *voluntary alienation*, was discussed in Chapter 7. A conveyance by deed is generally the result of a mutually agreed-upon transaction. There are, however, several circumstances under which title to real property is transferred involuntarily. This chapter discusses some of these situations. In addition to involuntary transfers, the chapter discusses transfers of title that occur upon the death of a property owner.

INVOLUNTARY ALIENATION

The transfer of title to land against the owner's wishes.

Involuntary alienation includes forced sales resulting from liens, condemnation or adverse possession and transfer by natural forces such as accretion. Various ways in which title to real estate may be transferred against the owner's wishes are discussed below. Forced sales resulting from liens are treated in later chapters.

Adverse Possession

Acquisition of title to real property by means of wrongful occupancy for a period of time established by statute.

Adverse possession is based upon the statute of limitations. As a general rule, a person in possession of realty has good title against everyone but the true owner. The true owner has a right to bring legal

141

action to gain possession if the occupant wrongfully withholds it. The statute of limitations requires that this cause of action be brought within a certain time. The time varies from state to state but is usually 12, 15, 20 or 21 years. If the owner does not sue within the statutory term, the adverse possessor, upon meeting certain conditions, acquires title to the land.

Although the adverse possessor actually acquires title to the property, litigation is usually necessary to establish clear title before it can be sold. The reason is that the public record of land ownership shows someone other than the seller as the owner.

CASE EXAMPLE

Tom Garret was the owner of a parcel of land. In 1945, Elswood Howard entered the premises and built a residence in which he lived until 1971, when he entered a nursing home. In 1973, Garret moved into the residence, which he later sold to Bonnie Cooke. Cooke checked the records before buying and found title in Garret. Cooke had no actual notice of Howard's possession for the 26 years.

When Howard recovered from his illness, he returned to the property and found Cooke in possession. In a suit brought by Howard against Cooke, a court would probably find for Howard. However, Howard would have to prove wrongful occupancy for longer than the period required by state law and other elements necessary for adverse possession.

The Elements of Adverse Possession

A number of conditions must be met for a person to acquire title to land by adverse possession. Both case law and statutes establish requirements, although they differ from state to state and even from case to case. Some common qualifications are that such possession must be open and notorious, hostile and under claim of right and continuous and exclusive. Other adjectives sometimes used are *adverse, visible, distinct, actual, peaceable, uninterrupted, under claim of title* and *under color of title.* These requirements are expressive of judicial and legislative intention that possession must be sufficiently evident to give the owner notice of what is happening, that possession is without the owner's permission and that possession is exclusive and for the full term set by the statute.

• CASE BRIEF •

Marengo Cave Company owned land upon which the only entrance to a large cave was located. The cave was occupied exclusively by the company for the statutory term and was used as a tourist attraction. When Ross, an adjoining landowner, discovered through a survey that a portion of the cave extended under his land, he brought a quiet title suit. The court found that, even though the company's possession was widely publicized in connection with the tourist business, it was still not "open and notorious" because an ordinary observer on the land could not have readily seen that the owner's rights were being invaded. *Marengo Cave Co. v. Ross, 212 Ind. 624, 10 N.E.2d 917 (1937).*

In *Marengo Cave Company*, Ross's failure to begin litigation before the statute became effective did not prevent him from suing because he could not have known readily about the invasion of his property right. Similarly, an owner is not prevented from suing because he or she has permitted the use of land and thus does not see it as an invasion of his or her rights. A tenant, for example, cannot acquire rental property by adverse possession unless he or she clearly repudiates the permissive character of this possession, giving the owner clear notice of the invasion of property rights. The *intent* of the possessor can be crucial, especially in cases where possession is inadvertent, as in the following example.

CASE EXAMPLE

Olsen purchased a lot from Bill Kent, who told Olsen the property extended to the edge of a gravel road. Olsen built a brick wall along the road and used the land inside the wall as a garden for longer than the statutory period. Later Rogers purchased the neighboring land and had a survey done. The survey revealed that a ten-foot strip inside the wall was actually part of the tract Rogers had bought.

Most jurisdictions would resolve this case in favor of Olsen because he had exclusively possessed and claimed the land inside the wall for the required term. A few states, however, would rule that he only intended to claim what was rightfully sold to him by Kent. He may lose in these jurisdictions on the ground that his possession of the ten-foot strip was by mistake and not by a "hostile" or "adverse" claim.

The courts also require that possession be *exclusive and continuous* for the entire statutory period. This means that, if the land is abandoned or the true owner reenters either in the absence of the adverse possessor or simultaneously, the statutory term is interrupted and must start over again. A brief absence, such as a vacation, by the adverse possessor is probably not enough to defeat this requirement, however. With nonresidential property, what constitutes continual and exclusive possession may be difficult to resolve.

A related issue arises when there is a succession of adverse possessors. Most jurisdictions allow the "tacking" of one possessor's term to that of another if one acquired directly from the other, as with a sale or conveyance by will.

CASE EXAMPLE

Martin was the owner of a lot, but Boyer was in possession for five years from 1940 to 1945. Then Boyer purported to sell the lot to Lucas, who possessed it for eight years and devised it to Tenton in 1953. Tenton, however, did not enter the land. When Tenton died in 1956, his heirs took possession. They sued to quiet title in 1969.

The heirs would lose this suit in a jurisdiction with a 20-year statute, because even tacking Boyer's term to Lucas's would bring the total to only 13 years. During the three years the lot was empty (1953 to 1956), possession reverted to Martin, the true owner. Adverse possession was not exclusive and continuous for the requisite 20 years. The heirs would win in a state with a 12-year statute, however, since their own entry and possession in 1956 would start the running of the statutory term.

When Adverse Possession Does Not Apply

In addition to these elements of adverse possession, statutes and case law also often provide that in some situations statutes of limitations are prolonged or do not run at all. For example, adverse possession cannot be applied against the state or against one whose interest is not yet a possessory right, such as a holder of a future interest. It cannot be applied against those who have certain disabilities, such as infants, the mentally incompetent and the insane. For a disability to prevent the running of the statute, however, it must exist at the time a right to sue accrues, usually when the adverse possessor enters the land. An intervening disability does not bar the running of the statute. In addition, the disability is personal to the owner at the accrual of the cause of action and cannot pass to his or her successors.

The Purpose of Adverse Possession

To many, adverse possession seems like a legal way of acquiring land without compensating the owner, and some question whether, with modern legislation like the Torrens system, model title acts, recording acts and the like, society needs this ancient doctrine. Nevertheless, public policy has historically supported the doctrine. Those who defend adverse possession argue that the state has certain duties to citizens:

- It should eliminate stale claims since evidence and witnesses may be unavailable.

- It should discourage *laches*—that is, dilatory enforcement of one's rights.
- It should encourage full and efficient use of land.
- It should facilitate land transfer by providing a means to remove old title problems and thus "quiet men's estates."

It seems likely that adverse possession will continue to be an aspect of property law for the foreseeable future. The prudent owner of vacant land held for development or investment will make periodic inspections of the property to check for adverse possessors. The mere posting of "no trespassing" signs is probably not sufficient to protect the owner's interest.

Eminent Domain

The power of government to take private property for public use; state and federal constitutions require just compensation to the property owner.

The power of eminent domain is one of the major attributes of sovereignty. In the United States, both federal and state governments are sovereign and may exercise this power. No specific constitutional grant is necessary for government to have the right to take private property for public use, although several state constitutions do contain provisions allocating the power of eminent domain to the state.

Eminent domain is a power that government may delegate. The result is that eminent domain is often exercised by villages, cities and counties as well as public bodies such as school boards and sanitation districts. The power can also be delegated to private corporations such as railroads, power companies and other public utilities. Upon a proper delegation, eminent domain may be exercised by individuals and partnerships. In any case, the status of the party exercising the power is not the critical factor. For a delegation to be proper, the property must be devoted to a public use.

Public Use

A use that benefits the community.

The Fifth Amendment to the U.S. Constitution and the constitutions of the individual states require that property acquired through eminent domain be used to benefit the public and that just compensation be paid to the owners. Historically, in the United States, eminent domain has been used mostly to acquire land for public transportation systems and to satisfy government's need for space to conduct its business. As government has become increasingly involved in many aspects of life, the use of eminent domain has likewise increased. Today, government may use the power to acquire interest in land for diverse purposes such as parking lots to relieve congestion and traffic hazards, scenic beauty along highways and public recreation.

• CASE BRIEF •

Before 1967 most of the land in Hawaii that was not owned by the state or federal government was owned in fee simple by 72 private landowners. These landowners, who had acquired their titles through the descendants of Polynesian chiefs, refused to sell land. They would only lease it on long-term leases. At the termination of a lease that was not renewed, the land and improvements reverted to the landowners.

In 1967 the Hawaiian legislature, using its power of eminent domain, enacted a Land Reform Act designed to extend the fee simple ownership of Hawaiian land. The act created a mechanism for condemning residential tracts and transferring ownership to existing lessees.

The owners of the fee simple estates challenged the constitutionality of the legislative action. They argued that their property was not taken for a public use or purpose because the government itself never possessed or used the land but transferred it to individuals. The United States Supreme Court determined that the statute was constitutional. The court stated that correcting inequities in the housing market satisfied the constitutional requirement that land be taken for a public use or purpose. *Hawaii Housing Authority v. Midkeff, 467 U.S. 229 (1984).*

Although land taken by eminent domain must be used for a public purpose, different interpretations exist as to what this means. A number of jurisdictions require that the property actually be used by the public. Even in these jurisdictions, the facility does not have to be open to the public, as long as some arm of government actually supervises the operation. Thus, public use is satisfied if a utility acquires property by eminent domain even though the general public cannot use the facility. A public utility commission supervises the overall business of the company and ensures that the property is used in the public interest.

In most jurisdictions, the public use requirement is met if some benefit to the public results from the acquisition of the property. The benefit does not have to be direct, nor does all of the public have to receive some advantage. In *Midkeff,* the Supreme Court held that transferring land acquired by condemnation to individuals in order to correct inequities in the housing market satisfied the public use requirement. Courts also have allowed the state to transfer lands acquired by condemnation to a private firm to build a plant that would increase employment in the area and to a developer to eliminate a slum.

Neither actual use nor the public benefit approach is absolute in any jurisdiction. Courts have consistently looked at additional factors, such as the extensiveness of any benefits, the number of potential users, the extent to which the acquisition benefits private parties and the exclusiveness of the use.

• CASE BRIEF •

The State Highway Commission of North Carolina commenced a proceeding to acquire land to widen a 770-foot road. The road's sole purpose was to connect the property of Associated Transport, Inc., with North Carolina Highway No. 62. The road was used by some 700 employees of Associated Transport, its customers and its trucks. Thornton, who owned the land, objected to the condemnation on the ground that it was for a non-public use. The lower court agreed. Upon appeal, the lower court was reversed.

The appellate court stated that "[t]he public benefit, through the bringing into the community, or development therein, of a new source of wealth and employment is, of course, a proper consideration . . . to exercise the power of eminent domain." The court also said "that habitual use day after day by 700 people . . . by an undisclosed number of shippers and consignees and by the trucks of the carrier . . . is a use by the public of the road." *State Highway Commission v. Thornton, 271 N.C. 277, 156 S.E. 2d 248 (1967).*

Private property cannot be taken for a public purpose unless the taking is necessary. Although this would appear to limit the sovereign's power, actually it does not. In most states the courts have ruled that the legislature has broad discretion to determine what is necessary in the public interest. The legislature may delegate this extensive discretion to an administrative agency or to a public service corporation. The sovereign has not only the right to determine the necessity for a particular acquisition but also very extensive discretion to determine the location and the amount of property that will be taken. A few states require that the necessity for a taking be determined by a jury or a specially constituted body designed to make the determination. Recently Congress adopted legislation that requires those making these discretionary choices to consider formally the environmental impact of their decisions.

Just Compensation

The award the owner is entitled to when property is taken by the government under its power of eminent domain, measured by the property's fair market value.

The government and the landowner often dispute what constitutes proper compensation to the owner for taking his or her land. State constitutions and the U.S. Constitution require that such compensation be "just" or "reasonable." In each case, just or reasonable compensation must be determined by balancing the interests of the taxpaying public against those of the property owner to arrive at a result fair to both parties.

Condemnation

Legal proceeding by which government exercises the right of eminent domain, acquiring private land for a public use.

The Fourteenth Amendment to the U.S. Constitution prohibits government from taking private property without due process of law. As a result, some type of notice and some type of legal proceeding are required when a landowner is unwilling to convey to a condemning authority for the price that it has offered. Due process does not ensure any particular manner of proceeding, and federal and state law vary extensively as to the method and procedures that will be used. For example, although trial by jury is not a due process requirement in a condemnation case, many states use juries extensively in this type of action. The Federal Rules of Civil Procedure provide that in federal cases either party may have a trial by jury on the issue of compensation unless Congress by statute establishes some other method.

Even within a state, condemnation procedures may vary. A number of states have established a general procedure by statute, but this procedure may be ignored or modified by the legislature for particular situations. Constitutional protections are not violated so long as the special procedure affords the property owner reasonable notice of the proceeding and a reasonable opportunity to establish just compensation.

• CASE BRIEF •

In 1958, the Port of New York Authority, in connection with construction to add a second deck to the George Washington Bridge, attempted to acquire by condemnation lands owned by Elizabeth and John Cervieri. The Cervieris demanded a jury trial on the issue of compensation. New Jersey statute provided alternative methods for determining compensation in condemnation cases. One method was by a jury determination; the other by the court upon the recommendation of three advisory commissioners. The lower court rejected the Cervieris' motion for a jury trial because the authority had commenced the action under the statute providing for the judicial determination. Upon appeal, the higher court ruled against the Cervieris.

The court stated that "property owners are not deprived of equal protection of the law because other classes of eminent domain cases have been provided with a different method or a different tribunal for accomplishing the same result, so long as the Legislature provides a fair and equitable inquiry in which the parties interested are allowed to be heard and present evidence and are protected in their right to have just compensation. *Port of New York Authority v. Heming, 34 N.J. 144, 167 A.2d 609 (1960).*

Several states require the condemning authority to attempt to negotiate a voluntary settlement before commencing a condemnation action. Even when not a statutory requirement, this practice is followed in almost all cases. If the condemnor's offer is rejected, the most common procedure is to condemn by judicial proceeding. This action requires filing a petition in court, giving notice to the owners and others having an interest in the land. Ordinarily, the condemning authority has the burden of establishing the right to acquire the property. Once this right is established, the owner must prove the value of the property taken and any additional damages to which he or she is entitled. Upon the court's making the condemnation award, the interest necessary for the condemnor's purpose passes to the authority involved. This interest may be an estate for years, an easement or a fee simple absolute, but it may not exceed what is necessary to accomplish the public purpose for which the property was taken.

In the ordinary case, as we have seen, the condemning agency has extensive discretion to decide what property to acquire. Generally, this decision cannot be challenged successfully. Therefore, the major issue in most condemnation litigation is the amount of the award to which the owner is entitled.

Compensation should not be more extensive than the owner's loss. At the same time, the owner is entitled to be placed in the monetary position that he or she would have been in had the property not been taken.

The principal measure of the owner's loss is the *fair market value* of the property at the time. The U.S. Supreme Court has held that *market value* and *just compensation* are synonymous. Market value is normally determined by what a willing buyer would pay in cash to a willing seller in an arm's-length negotiation. The seller is entitled to have the property valued at its highest and most profitable use, even if the property is not currently being used in that manner.

• CASE BRIEF •

The United States condemned 400 acres of land for an expansion of Fort Riley. A federal court approved an award of $88,110 for the property. The owners appealed as the court had accepted the government's argument that the highest and best use for the property was a grain and livestock farm. The owners argued that the property could be used most profitably for a limestone quarry.

Although no limestone had ever been quarried, the owners had signed a contract with a local concern that quarried limestone. The owners also introduced evidence that the limestone on the property met state and federal specifications for most construction purposes. In addition, there was evidence indicating some current demand for limestone and a possibility of a future market. All of this evidence was rejected. In vacating the judgment and remanding the case to the district court, the court of appeals stated, "while the proof in no way compelled any particular valuation on the limestone, we feel it clear that the proof was such that it could not be entirely rejected in reaching a fair award of just compensation." *United States v. 1955.00 Acres of Land, 447 F.2d 673 (10th Cir. 1971).*

Market value is an elusive concept, and courts have experienced difficulty in attempting to make fair and just awards. One problem arises in compensating for the loss of business that results when property essential to a firm's operation is taken. In the United States, neither the prospective profits nor the goodwill is included in a condemnation award. Buildings, however, must be taken into account to the extent that they enhance market value. If a particular building is more valuable because it has been adapted to a specific business purpose, that increase must be included.

The most common method of determining value is to compare the property being taken with similar land recently sold. This information is generally presented to the courts through the testimony of expert witnesses. Real estate sales personnel are often expert witnesses in condemnation cases because they are familiar with the selling price of land. A good expert witness must be well prepared. He or she must be very familiar with the parcel of land involved as well as the selling price of comparable property.

Although the state usually acquires title to real property by purchase or through condemnation, title can be acquired in other ways. Sometimes people give their land to the state; more frequently, title is acquired by *escheat*, which will be discussed later in this chapter.

Accretion

With alluvion, reliction, erosion and avulsion, the bundle of rights and principles the law uses to deal with changes in the size and shape of land due to natural causes, usually the actions of bodies of water.

Accretion refers specifically to a gradual increase in riparian or littoral property as a result of deposits of sediment made by a body of water so as to create dry land where there once was only water. *Alluvion* is the term used for the land so created. *Reliction* is the word applied when water recedes and creates dry land without depositing more material. *Erosion* is simply the decrease in size of a piece of property as the result of water washing away material from the shore. Finally, *avulsion* is an abrupt and perceptible change in the size and shape of a tract as a result of unexpected events, such as a change in the course of a stream.

The general rule is that when accretion or reliction occurs the riparian or littoral landowner's boundary line and land area are extended to take in the alluvion, but when avulsion occurs it effects no change in boundary or title. One reason often given for the doctrine of accretion is that the landowner, who is subject to a diminution in the size of his or her tract through erosion, should have the corresponding benefit when the land is enlarged by natural processes. Another rationale for the rule is that the riparian or littoral owner is usually the only one in a position to use the land efficiently. A third explanation is the desirability of preserving the riparian owner's access to the water. The exclusion of avulsion from the general title-by-accretion rule is intended to mitigate the hardship that would result to abutting landowners when a river or stream abruptly changes course.

• CASE BRIEF •

Cummings owned shoreline property on the Arkansas River. Surveys from the late 1800s showed the existence of Beaver Dam Island near his property. Cummings contends that Beaver Dam Island was completely washed away in the flood of 1927, that subsequently a sandbar gradually built out into the river from his property and that by slow accretion the land now constituting Beaver Dam Island resulted. The court held against Cummings, saying: "When the formation begins with a bar or an island detached and away from the shore and by gradual filling in by deposit or by gradual recession of the water, the space between bar or island and mainland is joined together, it is not an accretion to the mainland in a legal sense and does not thereby become property of the owner of the mainland." *Cummings v. Boyles, 242 Ark. 38, 411 S.W.2d 665 (1967).*

Because of these underlying policies, one necessary element of accretion, reliction or erosion is that it be a gradual and imperceptible change. Another frequently stated requirement is that of *contiguity*; that is, that there be no separation between the riparian owner's original tract and the alluvion. It is not generally required that the alluvion be the result of natural causes alone. For example, if an upstream owner builds a levee or breakwater that affects water flow so as to increase accretion, the downstream riparian owner can still acquire title. An owner, however, cannot use the doctrine to enlarge property boundaries through his or her own acts.

Much of the case law in this area has to do with how to draw the boundaries once accretion, reliction or erosion has altered the shape of the land. Arising most often in suits for damages, declaratory judgment actions, quiet title cases or actions for ejectment, this issue is usually resolved by reliance on two general principles: that the share of each party should be proportionate in size and quality to the prior holding and that each party should have a fair share of the access to the water. The actual method of line drawing necessarily varies greatly depending on the topography in each case. The courts will strive for an equitable solution and favor compromise settlements by the parties. The law varies somewhat from state to state, and the applicable rule is that of the jurisdiction in which the accretion occurred.

TRANSFER OF PROPERTY UPON DEATH

When a person dies, title to that person's property can be transferred in one of two ways. If the decedent has made a valid "last will and testament," title to the decedent's property is transferred to the beneficiaries named in the will, subject to limitations imposed by the state. The person who has made a valid will is called a *testator* and is said to have died *testate*. A person who dies without making a valid will is said to have died *intestate*. State statutes direct to whom an intestate's property is transferred.

Intestate Succession

Distribution of property of a person who dies without leaving a will or whose will is invalid.

The general philosophy underlying the laws of intestate succession is that property should descend to those persons the intestate individual probably would want to own it. If the decedent expressed no preference by executing a will, society assumes that he or she would want the property to go to those closely related by blood or marriage. Society also benefits from this assumption because it keeps property within the family and tends to strengthen that important institution.

Laws of intestate succession are statutory. No one has a constitutional or natural right to a decedent's property. People inherit because the legislature says that they can. The law might direct that all property of an intestate decedent revert to the state, as it did in England immediately following the Norman Conquest. This system was opposed by powerful tenants of the king, however, and the English rulers were soon forced to recognize the principle of inheritance by members of the tenant's family.

In modern U.S. real estate law the concept of inheritance by family members is integral to the succession to property upon death. The idea that the state should acquire the property of an intestate is offensive to the sense of justice of almost all Americans. The state acquires title to the property only when the decedent has no close relatives. Later in this section of the chapter we will discuss this alternative (escheat) in greater detail.

Historical Background

The origin of state statutes of intestate succession is found in English law. Primarily because of the importance of land to the political and social structure of England, English law treated the transfer of real property upon the owner's death very differently from the transfer of personal property.

Until 1926 in England, when an owner died intestate, title to that person's real property passed directly to the heirs according to statutes of descent. Title to personal property went initially to an administrator. After the administrator had paid the claims against the estate, the personal property passed according to the Statute of Distribution.

For many years similar practices were followed in the United States. When a person died intestate, personal property went first to an administrator; real property passed directly to the decendent's heirs. Today laws in a few states continue to distinguish between intestate succession to real property and intestate succession to personal property.

In states where the difference is still recognized, one effect is that claims against the estate are taken first from personal property. However, in all states real property may ultimately be used to satisfy unpaid claims. Another consequence is that heirs may take immediate possession of real property, subject to the administrator's right to apply real property to estate debts.

Currently, in England and a majority of jurisdictions in the United States, the laws of intestate succession no longer distinguish between real and personal property. Statutes, commonly referred to as *statutes of descent and distribution*, treat the two types of property in the same manner.

Statutes of Descent and Distribution

**Statutes that provide for the distribution of the property
of a person who dies without a valid will.**

English law providing for the distribution of an intestate's personal
property was based upon the Statute of Distribution, which was
passed in 1670. Prior to that year, controversy had existed between
state and ecclesiastical courts as to jurisdiction over the personal property of an intestate decedent. Both claimed the right to distribute
these assets. In addition, no definite scheme of distribution existed
because each court had different rules. The 1670 statute established a
definite pattern of distribution and bolstered the power of the church
courts. A primary purpose of this pattern was to provide for the intestate's widow and children, to whom substantial shares of the intestate's personal goods were allotted.

Today in the United States the distribution of the estate of an
intestate is modeled, in a general way, upon the English Statute of
Distribution. American law also focuses primarily upon provision for
the surviving spouse and children. Both current American and English statutes provide for distribution of the entire estate—not just
personal property.

A surviving husband or wife ordinarily is entitled to a half or a
third share of the decedent's property. Many states increase this portion if the couple had no children. Some states give the surviving
spouse a specific dollar amount and a fraction of the net estate exceeding that amount. Community property states normally differentiate
between intestate distribution of separate property and that of community property.

In every state a surviving spouse and children share all of the
intestate's estate. The children take whatever remains after the
spouse's share. If there is no surviving spouse, the entire estate passes
to the children, who divide the assets equally.

Per Stirpes.   Distribution of intestate property to persons who take
the share allocated to a deceased ancestor by representing that person
is called *per stirpes distribution,* also referred to as *distribution by the
stocks.*

A difficult question of fundamental fairness arises when a child
who has children of his or her own dies before a parent. When the
grandparent dies, should the surviving grandchildren share equally
with their aunts and uncles, or are they entitled only to the share of
the deceased parent?

CASE EXAMPLE

Trent Hightower died intestate. His wife had predeceased him by
many years. They had three children: Stephanie, Joseph and

Douglas. Stephanie and Joseph survived their father, but Douglas died before him. Douglas, however, left three children of his own: Trent, Jr., Eliza and Anne. Trent Hightower's estate was divided into thirds, with one-third going to Stephanie, one-third to Joseph, and one-third to the children of Douglas. This allocation is *per stirpes* distribution.

In some states, when the only distributees are grandchildren, distribution is by modified per stirpes. In these states each grandchild takes in his or her own right as in *per capita* distribution. The decedent's estate is divided by the *number* of grandchildren.

Per Capita.   Distribution of intestate property to persons who take equal shares as members of a class, not as representatives of an ancestor, is called *per capita distribution.*

• CASE BRIEF •

Jennie E. Martin died intestate, leaving as distributees three grandchildren: Alice E. Martin, Bourke Martin and Ned Martin. Alice E. was the daughter of Earl Martin; Bourke and Ned were the sons of Charles Martin. Both Earl and Charles had died before their mother died. The court divided Jennie Martin's estate into three parts, giving one to each grandchild. Alice E. Martin argued that the distribution should have been per stirpes and that she should have received one-half.

The appellate court affirmed the lower court's action. The court stated, "those who take as a class take equally. . . . We hold that it was the intention of the legislature that grandchildren, who alone survive the ancestor, should take equally. . . ." In other words, they should take as heirs, not by representation. *In re Martin's Estate, 96 Vt. 455, 120 A. 862 (1923).*

The grandchildren of Jennie Martin were all in equal degrees of descent; they were in the same class. As a result, the court felt that the legislature intended that they share equally. Thus, they took their portions as individuals, not as representatives of their deceased parents. Had they taken as representatives, they would have taken *per stirpes.*

In the absence of children, American distribution statutes generally distribute the intestate's property to parents, subject to the share of a surviving spouse. In a few states, brothers and sisters share with parents. Issue of deceased brothers and sisters take their parents' share. In a number of states, the amount of the estate determines the relative shares of parents, brothers and sisters.

Statutes do not usually specify rights for relatives beyond the intestate's parents, brothers and sisters. Property goes to "next of kin" if no specific relatives are surviving. Most states by statute provide a method for computing next of kin. Usually the method is based upon that used in England to determine kinship under the Statute of Distribution. Details of methods used to determine kinship are not relevant to this text. Other than the surviving spouse, relatives by marriage ordinarily are not entitled to the intestate's property.

Escheat

Reversion of property to the state when a person dies intestate with no heirs or when property is abandoned.

CASE EXAMPLE

Gene DiMond, who inherited property in St. Augustine from his only brother Henri, had no immediate surviving relatives. His parents were dead, and Gene had never married. Although he had one aunt, she had died many years before, leaving no children. Upon Gene's death, the state claimed the St. Augustine property because Gene had died without leaving a will and without heirs.

As we have seen, statutes in each of the states indicate the categories of relationship of those who are a decedent's heirs. Generally, these statutes are narrowly drawn, restricting the term *heirs* to the spouse and those closely related to the decedent by blood. If the decedent dies intestate without heirs, decedent's property escheats to the state. Because most decedents have heirs or make a will, escheat is not a common method by which a state acquires title.

Escheat is an incident of state sovereignty. Because the people possess the ultimate property in land, land should revert to the state for the people's benefit when no heirs exist. State constitutions in some instances contain provisions for escheat. Ordinarily, rules governing the details of escheat are statutory, and in a number of states the only mention of escheat is in the statute.

Some type of judicial proceeding is necessary to establish the state's right to the property. In a number of jurisdictions, title vests immediately in the state when a landowner dies intestate without ascertainable heirs. In these states the judicial proceeding will be in the probate court and similar to proceedings to establish heirship. Other states require a more extensive action; in these states title to escheated property does not vest in the state until a court so orders. Escheat statutes are not favored by the courts and, as a result, are strictly construed.

Although historically the term *escheat* was applied only to real property, today the term is also applied to personal property. Many types of personal property escheat to the state when they have been unclaimed for a period of time, including bank deposits, parimutuel winnings, insurance proceeds and corporate dividends. Most legal problems that involve escheat are the result of state statutes that attempt to deal with unclaimed personal property.

Testate Succession

Transfer of property when a person dies leaving a will.

The right of an owner of property to direct to whom it should go upon death has always been subject to significant limitations. Initially the right to will one's property applied only to personal property. This right evolved in England shortly after the Norman Conquest. At that time the church won control over the disposition of a decedent's personal property but not over real property. The church encouraged people to indicate by a "last will and testament" to whom they would like their personal property to go upon death. However, the church made certain that the spouse and children as well as itself were provided for, even if the testator's will did not do so.

It was not until 300 years later, with the enactment of the Statute of Wills in 1540, that English law granted real property owners a limited right to transfer it by will. This right was curtailed substantially by dower and curtesy, discussed in Chapter 4, as well as the customs and traditions of the English landed aristocracy. Many restrictions on the disposition of real property by will also existed in the United States. During the late 19th and 20th centuries these restrictions lessened. As land became less important as a source of wealth in relation to personal property, statutes in both England and the United States provided owners with comparable rights to dispose of both real and personal property by will. Today, in both countries, a person can dispose freely of both types of property by will, subject to limitations imposed by the state to protect the family and to ensure that the debts of the decedent's estate are paid.

Will

A written instrument that permits distribution of an owner's property after death and must contain certain elements to be legally enforceable.

Our English legal heritage has had an extensive influence on requirements for making a valid will. As a result, similar requirements exist throughout the United States, although individual states deviate significantly from the common pattern. In most American jurisdictions, formality is a general characteristic of the procedure involved in executing a will. Formality is predicated upon a legislative desire to prevent fraud, undue influence, coercion or a testator's impetuousness. Legislatures apparently believe that ceremony helps to prevent rash actions. In addition, formality helps to memorialize the transaction. But even where there is formality, certain specific requirements must be met for a document to be a will.

To be legal and valid, a will must be *in writing, signed* by the testator, *witnessed* and *attested.*

Written.   All states require a will to be in writing, but a limited number of states do permit oral wills of personal property under limited circumstances. Generally, oral wills are valid if made by military personnel in actual service or under certain conditions by a person suffering a terminal illness. A will written entirely in the testator's own hand, known as a *holographic* will, is a special case.

Signed.   American courts are liberal in their interpretation of what constitutes a signature. A mark or an initial is sufficient if intended as a signature. Usually, the testator must sign personally, but someone else may if directed to do so by the testator. Usually, this must be done in the testator's presence. Generally, a signature anyplace on the document is sufficient if the intention is to validate the will. Some states require the signature to be at the end of the instrument. In those states, the entire document is invalid if the signature is in some other place.

Witnessed.   Most state laws require only two witnesses for a will to be valid. Any competent adult may ordinarily act as a witness. In some states a beneficiary under a will should not be a witness; that person's testimony is sufficient to sustain the will in court, but he or she is not entitled to take under the will.

The common practice is for the testator to sign first in the presence of the witnesses. In many states the actual signing does not have to be viewed by the witness if the testator later acknowledges the signature. In the case of the holographic will, witnesses are not always required.

Attested.   Attestation is a requirement in all jurisdictions for most wills. Attestation means that the person must intend to act as a witness and must sign for the purpose of validating the will. In a very few states the witness need not sign the instrument, but attestation is necessary even in those states. In order to validate the will, witnesses must be able to testify at a later date that the testator signed or acknowledged the signature in their presence.

In the vast majority of cases, a will includes an attestation clause. This clause appears at the end of the will following the testator's signature. Each witness signs the attestation clause, which recites the witness's observation of the formalities necessary for the proper execution of the will.

Rights of the Family

Prevailing public policy in the United States is to encourage provisions for spouse and children out of a decedent's estate. As noted earlier, if a person dies intestate, inheritance statutes in all states provide first for the decedent's immediate family. State laws also furnish some protection for the spouse, and to a lesser degree the children, of a person who fails to provide for them by will. Historically, many of these laws applied specifically to real estate. Dower, curtesy and homestead rights discussed in Chapter 4 are examples. Today, protection for a decedent's spouse in most states is accomplished by giving the spouse a right to elect a share against the will. The right of election is charged against the entire estate, both real and personal.

Elective Share

A share of a deceased spouse's estate that a surviving spouse may claim if the other by will did not provide at least this amount; called a *forced share* in some states and a *statutory share* in others.

Dower and curtesy have been replaced in many states by the right of a surviving spouse to elect a share against the decedent's will. The right of election is based on statute, and the share varies from state to state. Inasmuch as the right of election is a relatively recent trend in the law, state legislation usually reflects modern developments for this purpose, such as the elimination of distinctions between real and personal property and similar treatment of husband and wife.

The right of election is also influenced by past laws and customs. Many state legislatures regard it as a substitute for dower. Thus the survivor's elective share is often set at a fractional amount, such as one-third of the decedent's estate. In a number of states the share is less if the couple has children. However, children may be disinherited by their parents, and no state has a law that provides children an elective share.

CASE EXAMPLE

Royce and Helen Hurley were married for many years. Early in their marriage Royce made a will giving Helen a legacy of $100,000. At the time, this was the bulk of Royce's estate. Over the years Royce prospered, but he did not change his will. When Royce died in 1975, his net estate was more than $500,000. State statute gave Helen a right to take under the will or to elect to take a one-half share against the will. She elected to take the half share instead of the $100,000 legacy. The statute also provided that, after the surviving spouse had elected against the will, the balance of the net estate would be disposed of as though he or she had predeceased the testator.

One of the objections to dower was that in small estates the surviving spouse was provided for inadequately if reliance upon dower was necessary. Although a right of election ordinarily provides more for a surviving spouse because it includes personal property, the fractional share in some estates is insufficient to support the survivor adequately. In most cases a decedent eliminates this problem by will, providing the surviving spouse with adequate support.

Administration of Estates

A general term used to describe the management and settlement of a decedent's estate by a person appointed by the courts.

Many of the procedures for settling the estate of a decedent are similar for both testate and intestate decedents. A very important initial step is the appointment of a personal representative to act for the estate. The person charged with administration of the estate of an intestate decedent is called an *administrator;* the person who is appointed to administer the estate of a decedent who dies testate is an *executor.* Sometimes the person nominated in a will as an executor is unable or unwilling to serve. Under these conditions, the court appoints an administrator with the will attached. (The terms *administratrix* and *executrix* were frequently used in the past to designate a woman who served as administrator or executor. These terms, as well as the terms *executor* and *administrator,* are becoming less common. Under modern probate statutes in most jurisdictions, the term *personal representative* has been substituted.)

The administration of a decedent's estate is ordinarily supervised by a special court, frequently referred to as a *probate* or *surrogate's court.* The appointment of a personal representative is an important element in administering a decedent's estate. In the will, the testator almost always nominates a personal representative. The personal representative may be either a person or an institution, such as a trust company. The decedent's nominee is usually appointed by the court, unless that person is not qualified or refuses to serve.

Probate

Proof that an instrument is genuine and the last will and testament of the maker.

In the vast majority of cases, probate is a straightforward procedure. Ordinarily, the person nominated in the will as personal representative files a written application or petition for probate. In many jurisdictions, the probate court supplies the proper forms for this procedure. The petition alleges the testator's death and domicile at the time of death. The will is usually attached to the petition unless it has been filed previously with the court. Usually the names, relationships and residences of the heirs at law, as well as those receiving gifts under the will, must be included because they will be notified of the proceeding. Those notified are not regarded as defendants, but as possible objectors. Some states permit probate without notice to interested parties. Although the practice is legal, it can adversely affect land titles in case someone with a claim presents it later.

If a petition is unopposed, the court may order probate on the documents filed. Usually, a limited hearing is conducted in which the court takes testimony on the validity of the will. This testimony is from attesting witnesses. If they are not available, others must testify as to the authenticity of the witnesses' signatures. A number of states have developed less formal probate procedures for small estates, especially when no real property is involved.

Probate establishes that the will is valid and genuine. After the petition for probate is granted, the will can no longer be attacked on the ground of forgery, improper execution or revocation except in a proceeding to set aside probate. Probate does not establish the validity or meaning of particular provisions of the will. If the court is satisfied that the nominated personal representative is qualified to serve, this person will be furnished with *letters testamentary* as evidence of authority to settle the estate.

In more than half of the states, probate of a will may be accomplished by a process called *self-proving*. Self-proving eliminates the need for a formal probate proceeding involving a hearing. The will is self-proved while the testator is living.

For a will to be self-proved, it must first be executed, acknowledged and witnessed in the ordinary manner. Next the testator and the witnesses must declare in writing under oath that the testator was of age, the will was signed willingly and the testator was of sound mind and was under no constraint or undue influence. The sworn statement must also state that each of the witnesses signed as witnesses in the testator's presence. This sworn statement, signed by the testator, the witnesses and the officer who took their oaths, must be attached to the will.

The procedures for the appointment of an administrator differ from those for the appointment of an executor, although both procedures are carried out by the same court. State statutes prescribe the persons eligible for appointment as administrator and the order in which they must be considered. The order, based upon relationship to the decedent, parallels the order of intestate inheritance in most states. Preference is given to the surviving husband or wife. If there is no husband or wife, the relative next entitled to distribution is selected as administrator. The court selects from among those who stand in equal right the person best qualified to manage the estate. Usually, preference is given to residents of the jurisdiction, and in many states the representative must reside in the county where the estate is probated. The court grants *letters of administration* to the person appointed to administer the intestate's estate.

The personal representative, whether an executor or administrator, is authorized by the court to settle the decedent's estate. He or she is responsible for ensuring that assets are distributed in an orderly manner to those who are entitled to them. Although the personal representative has a wide variety of miscellaneous chores, four basic steps comprise the settlement of the estate:

- collection of estate assets;
- processing and payment of claims against the estate;
- management of estate assets;
- accounting and distribution of estate assets.

Acquisition of title as the result of execution and probate of a will involves procedures both standardized and formal. In some instances title to real property is acquired in a manner much less regulated. Adverse possession is an example.

Proof of Death

It is axiomatic that neither a will nor an inheritance statute is operative until a property owner dies. Ordinarily, the occurrence and time of death are easy to determine, but problems arise in at least two instances. One instance is a disaster in which several closely related people die at approximately the same time; another is a situation in which a property owner has been missing for an extensive period.

Many wills solve the problem of determining who has died first in a common disaster by including a provision in the instrument.

CASE EXAMPLE

Lance Beck and his wife, Hilda, were killed in a common disaster. Because of the nature of the accident, determining which one had died first was impossible. Lance's will left all his property to his wife if she survived him. If she did not, his estate was to go to his parents and to charity.

Lance's will contained the following provision: "In the event my wife and I shall die under such circumstances that there is insufficient evidence to determine the survivor, it shall be conclusively presumed that I survived her." As a result of this provision, the estate went to Lance's parents and the charities that he had named, not into his wife's estate.

Most states by statute make special provisions for applying distribution rules when close relatives are killed under circumstances that make it impossible to determine the survivor. More than 40 states have adopted the Uniform Simultaneous Death Act. In general, this act provides that in a common disaster each decedent's property shall be disposed of as if that decedent had survived.

States also solve by statute the problem caused by a missing owner. Generally, these statutes provide that a person whose absence is unexplained for seven years is presumed dead. The presumption, however, may be rebutted.

SUMMARY

Real property is usually conveyed voluntarily by deed; however, some transfers of land are involuntary. One procedure by which title passes involuntarily is adverse possession. The person who takes title in this way acquires it by wrongful use or occupancy (possession) for a period of time prescribed by statute. This possession must be open and notorious, hostile, continuous and exclusive. Owners who are holding vacant land for resale or for future development should make periodic inspections to guard against adverse possession.

Land may also be taken from a rightful owner by certain government bodies exercising the power of eminent domain. The right of eminent domain is exercised through the legal process of condemnation. Methods and procedures for exercising this power vary markedly from one area to another. Nevertheless, the U.S. Constitution prohibits the taking of private property without just compensation, as do most state constitutions. When an owner does not wish to give up the land for the terms offered, some type of legal proceeding is required to determine just compensation. Just compensation is based upon the fair market value of the property. The establishment of market value for a property may require testimony of an expert witness chosen from the real estate field.

Property is also transferred upon the death of the owner. *Intestate succession* is the term given to the transfer of real and personal property when a person dies without a will. Property then passes according to state statutes governing inheritance, usually referred to as *statutes of descent and distribution*. These laws differ to a degree from one state to another but generally follow similar patterns: the spouse and children have the primary right to the estate. When a person dies without a will, has no discernible heirs, or property is abandoned, the state acquires title by escheat.

When the deceased has made a valid will, both real and personal property pass as the decedent directs. All states have laws that prevent the decedent from totally disinheriting his or her spouse.

Laws in each state dictate the proper form for executing a will.

To be valid, a will must be in writing, signed, witnessed and attested. Generally, a will also names a personal representative charged with carrying out the distribution according to the decedent's wishes. This person is usually supervised by the state's probate court. Probate establishes that a will is valid and genuine and protects it from attacks by claimants.

REVIEW AND DISCUSSION QUESTIONS

1. What are the major arguments for allowing a person to acquire title by adverse possession?
2. Explain the difference between *accretion* and *avulsion*.
3. Briefly indicate some of the limitations that exist upon the transfer of real property by will.
4. Walt Smithers, a resident of the State of X, has written a will entirely in his own hand. The State of X does not recognize holographic wills. What, if anything, must Smithers do for the will to be valid?
5. Discuss the major duties of a person appointed to settle a decedent's estate.

CASE PROBLEMS

1. Kittrell owned four house trailers that were parked on the edge of his property. Unknown to Kittrell, the trailers extended a few feet over his neighbor's property. This condition was discovered by a survey after the trailers had been there several years. At the time Kittrell offered to buy the strip of land upon which the trailers encroached. The owner refused to sell but, because permanent plumbing had been installed, did not order the trailers to be moved. Several years later the property was sold and the new owner demanded that Kittrell remove the trailers. Kittrell claimed ownership of the strip by adverse possession because the trailers had encroached on the land for more than ten years, the statutory period in the state. Discuss the validity of Kittrell's claim. *Kittrell v. Scarborough*, 287 Ala. 177, 249 So.2d 814 (1971).
2. Fran, an adult, owned a tract that had been adversely possessed for 18 of the 20 years set by the statute when she died and the tract passed under the statute of descent and distribution to her infant son Jamie. Does Jamie's infancy toll the running of the statute?
3. Paul Williams and his wife, Melonie, purchased land in a remote area because they loved the unspoiled wilderness. The two invested much time and effort in building a home on the property. After living on the site for five years, they discovered

that a utility planned to run a line over a portion of the land. Paul and Melonie refused to sell the land necessary for the utility line. Discuss under what circumstances the land could be taken by eminent domain.

4. Berman owned a department store on property in a District of Columbia slum. The property was well maintained, and no building violations existed. Using the power of eminent domain, the District of Columbia Redevelopment Agency acquired Berman's property, along with that of others in the area. The purpose of the acquisition was for "the development of blighted territory." Berman argued that the taking was unconstitutional as his property was not substandard and, after redevelopment, was to be managed privately. Discuss the validity of Berman's contention. *Berman v. Parker,* 348 U.S. 26 (1954).

5. The statute of descent and distribution of the State of Y is as follows:

If a person dies intestate, his or her real and personal property, if any, shall pass:

(a) If there is no surviving spouse, to the children of the intestate or their lineal descendants, *per stirpes.*

(b) If there is a spouse and one or more children or their lineal descendants surviving, the first $30,000 to the spouse, plus one-half of the remainder to the spouse and the balance to the children equally or to their lineal descendants, *per stirpes.*

(c) If there are no children or their lineal descendants, the whole to the surviving spouse.

(d) If there is no spouse and no children or their lineal descendants surviving, to the parents of the intestate equally or to the surviving parent.

(e) If there is no spouse, no children or their lineal descendants and no parent surviving, to the brothers and sisters equally or their lineal descendants, *per stirpes.*

(f) If there is no spouse, no children or their lineal descendants, no parents and no siblings surviving, to the next of kin.

(g) If there is no next of kin, escheat to the state.

Answer the following hypothetical questions based on this statute.

(1) Graham dies, leaving a valid will that bequeaths his entire estate to his sister-in-law, Ruth. He is survived by Ruth and by his mother, his grandson and his brother. What is the result under the statute?

(2) Willis died intestate and is survived by his wealthy wife, Angela; his poverty-stricken mother, Rose; and his deserving second cousin, Ned. How will the estate be distributed?

(3) Susan died intestate, survived by her son, Jack, and by three

grandsons, Dennis, Randy and Rob. Dennis and Randy are the sons of Susan's deceased oldest son, David, and Rob is the only child of Susan's deceased daughter, Cheryl. How will the estate be divided?

(4) Rebecca died intestate, survived by her husband, Gus; her father, Bruce; her daughter, Nancy; and her grandchildren, Chuck and Jill, the children of her deceased son, Rick. The net probate estate is $50,000. Who gets it?

6. Cecily disappeared in 1970 and was not heard from for more than seven years. In 1978 Cecily's aunt died and left her a fortune in a will. Cecily's son, Tad, brought a suit to have her declared legally dead so that he would inherit the money under the statute of descent and distribution. The court-appointed personal representative of Cecily's estate defended against Tad's claim and presented evidence that several people had seen Cecily alive and well within the past year. What would be the result?

7. John and Larue Morgan were married in 1960. In 1965 Larue disappeared. Although extensive efforts were made to locate her, she was never found. In 1973 John brought a legal action to have Larue declared dead. At the hearing, Larue's brother attempted to introduce as evidence a Christmas card that he had received from her in 1967. The judge refused to accept this evidence and declared Larue dead because she had been missing for more than seven years. Was the judge correct? Discuss.

9
Recording Acts And Conveyancing

RECORDING STATUTES

Laws that require the entry into books of public record the written instruments affecting the title to real property.

Under common law, deeds and other instruments affecting the title to real property were not *recorded*, or officially entered into the public records. Problems arose for the owners when they lost or misplaced these deeds and other documents. Even more important, third parties had no way of knowing that a prior transaction had taken place. The person making a conveyance to an innocent third party may have previously conveyed to another and therefore had nothing to give to this subsequent party. These difficulties gave rise to the need for recording statutes. The primary intent of these statutes is to protect third persons by giving them notice that a prior transaction has occurred.

The recording statutes have been adopted by all states and provide a means for notifying third parties as to the ownership or other interests existing in a given parcel of land. The recording takes place when a deed, mortgage, easement or other legal instrument affecting the title to land is copied into the public record so that interested persons can discover the status of the title to the land. All entries regarding that title comprise the title history, also known as the *chain of title.*

Many centuries ago land could be transferred by a symbolic gesture, such as the giving of a handful of soil or a wild rose branch. Since England enacted the Statute of Frauds in 1677, however, a transfer of an interest in land must be in writing to attain legal recognition. The written document serves as proof of the transfer between the parties to the transaction—the buyer and the seller—and to anyone else who is aware of the writing. However, a prospective buyer unfamiliar with this transfer would have only the word of the seller as assurance that it did not take place. The buyer or the buyer's attorney can gain certainty about this transfer by referring to the public records to find the recording of the transaction. If the transaction is duly recorded, one can rely on it with relative safety. (Limitations on reliance upon the recording will be discussed later.) If the public records do not reveal the transaction, the prospective buyer would normally choose not to buy the parcel. The risk is that the seller is not telling the truth or that some other interest is outstanding in the land. To take a conveyance under these circumstances is to invite a lawsuit; under normal conditions it is too great a risk to the buyer. Thus the purpose of the recording act is to give to the prospective buyer and to the public *legal notice* of the status of a particular property.

Legal Notice

A knowledge of another's interest in real property sufficient to make the adverse interest legally binding to the prospective purchaser or any other party acquiring interest in the property.

The public recording gives legal notice to third persons as to the existence of a transaction. Under the principle of *caveat emptor,* a prospective buyer or lender is charged with the responsibility of determining whether or not the seller holds title to the property and whether or not there are any encumbrances that would adversely affect the title. If an individual has legal notice of a defect or an encumbrance before acquiring an interest, he or she takes *title subject to those prior rights.* Legal notice may take the form of actual notice, implied notice or constructive notice.

Actual Notice

Title information that is acquired personally by the interest holder.

A prospective purchaser may gain information from the seller or from other parties and from firsthand observation of the property.

CASE EXAMPLE

McCredy is negotiating an agreement to purchase Nagy's summer home. When McCredy inspects the premises, he finds several neighbors have been using a well on the property. If the neighbors have acquired and recorded an easement, that fact will appear on the record. If no easement is on the record, the users may have a prescriptive easement; that is, one imposed by law based on the extended use of his neighbors. If so, McCredy has actual notice of their easement.

An agreement between two parties gives *actual notice* to these two parties even if it is not recorded. However, unless a third party has actual notice of the parties' interests, an unrecorded deed gives no legal notice to the third party. Likewise, when a prospective purchaser is shown a house that is being occupied by someone other than the seller, the purchaser is put on notice that the occupant may have some kind of interest. The purchaser is thus obligated, under the theory of actual notice, to ascertain the status of this third party.

Implied Notice

Legal notice that is imposed by the law when conditions exist that would lead a reasonable person to inquire further into the condition of the title.

If a prospective interest holder has implied notice of a possible claim, he or she is said to have legal notice of any interest that would be discovered during the course of a reasonable inquiry into the condition of the title. *Failure to pursue such an investigation does not exempt the interest holder from notice.*

Implied notice occurs in some states when the conveyance of property by quitclaim deed is a release of rights rather than a conveyance. In such states, *use of a quitclaim deed is considered to give the purchaser implied notice that there may be defects in the title.* In states where a quitclaim deed is considered a conveyance, no legal notice of adverse claims is implied merely by the existence of that type of deed.

Constructive Notice

The knowledge of certain facts that might be discovered through a careful inspection of public records, provided that such information is within the history of title, or discovered through an inspection of the premises.

Under the concept of constructive notice, a prospective interest holder is considered to have legal notice of any information recorded within the history or chain of title, *whether or not that individual has actual notice of the existence of the document.*

Constructive notice also charges the prospective interest holder with any information contained within recorded documents. In addition, a person has constructive notice of all facts that would be revealed by an inspection of the property. For instance, constructive notice of an easement exists for a plainly visible drainage ditch that crosses the property. Notice occurs even if the person never visits the property or examines the public records, which may or may not reveal the existence of the easement.

• CASE BRIEF •

Sebastian leased land to Conley, who recorded the lease. The lease was for oil and gas exploration. Although the description in the lease was inaccurate, it did designate the land. Later Sebastian leased what he thought was adjoining land to Loeb. Part of the land leased to Loeb was the Conley parcel. Claiming that the record provided constructive notice of his interest, Conley sued to prevent Loeb from using the land. Both the lower court and an appellate court agreed that Loeb had constructive notice of Conley's interest and ordered Loeb to allow Conley access to the tract.

The appellate court stated as follows:

The constructive notice furnished by a recorded instrument, insofar as the boundary of the land and every other material fact recited therein is concerned, is equally as conclusive as would be actual notice acquired by a personal examination of the recorded instrument, or actual notice acquired by or through other means. Every person must take notice of its contents to the same extent as if he had personal knowledge of every fact that it recites. This is the very purpose of our recording law. *Loeb v. Conley, 160 Ky. 91, 169 S.W. 575 (1912).*

In addition to notice of all items contained in the public records, prospective interest holders are also considered to have constructive notice of all taxes that attach to the property.

Types of Recording Statutes

The recording statutes vary markedly from state to state, although all have a similar purpose. They are designed to give notice to parties who are considering acquiring an interest in land. Reliance upon a warranty given in the deed is inadequate. The warranty gives the buyer the right to a lawsuit for damages, but not to the land in which he or she is primarily interested. The three general types of recording statutes are pure race, race-notice and notice.

Pure Race Statutes

Statutes that provide that the first person who gives value and records an instrument prevails over all other

takers from the same source. It is not relevant that the
first recorder and prevailing party had notice of the prior
transactions.

CASE EXAMPLE

Nagy conveys Laneacre to McCredy. Later, to acquire funds for
his permanent relocation to South America, Nagy conveys
Laneacre to Brennan. Brennan knows of the prior conveyance
to McCredy, but a check of the record indicates that McCredy
has not recorded his deed. Brennan decides to take the prof-
fered conveyance and beat McCredy to the recorder's office.

Under pure race statutes, the first, Brennan or McCredy, to record his
deed will prevail. It should be noted that very few states follow the
pure race approach. Today states are just about evenly divided between
race-notice and notice statutes.

Race-Notice Statutes

**Statutes that provide that a subsequent buyer will prevail
only if he or she has no notice of the prior transaction at
the time of conveyance and he or she records first.**

Under these statutes the subsequent taker must still get to the recorder's office before the predecessor does. If the preceding example
occurred in a race-notice jurisdiction, Brennan would prevail if he recorded before McCredy *and* if he had no idea that Nagy had previously
conveyed Laneacre to McCredy.

Notice Statutes

**Statutes that provide that the subsequent buyer prevails
over all interested parties who have not recorded their
interest at the time the buyer accepts the conveyance
and pays consideration for the land without notice of the
preexisting conveyance.**

There is no *race* under these statutes. So long as the subsequent buyer
takes without notice of the previous conveyance, he or she prevails
over the previous conveyance. It is irrelevant that (1) the first deed
holder records thereafter or (2) the subsequent buyer never records.

• CASE BRIEF •

On May 9, 1860, Dignowitz executed a deed to McMillan for land
in San Antonio. The deed was signed by Dignowitz's wife, who
testified that she did not know whether it was delivered to McMillan, but she assumed that it was. This deed was not recorded
until 1889.

In 1875, several years after the death of her husband, Mrs. Dignowitz conveyed the land to the City of San Antonio. Shortly thereafter the city conveyed the parcel to the United States, to be a part of a military reservation. At the time, the mayor of San Antonio orally mentioned a possible outstanding claim; but after an exhaustive search of the record, the attorney for the United States approved the title.

In a claim against the United States for trespass brought in 1889, the U.S. Supreme Court stated, "The inevitable conclusion as a matter of law is that the United States acquired a good and valid title, as innocent purchasers for valuable consideration, and without notice of a previous conveyance to McMillan." The Supreme Court did not consider the oral mention by the mayor of an outstanding claim as actual notice of the preexisting conveyance. *Stanley v. Schwalby, 162 U.S. 255 (1896).*

It may seem unfair for the law to permit Dignowitz to make multiple conveyances of the same property. Theoretically, she no longer owns the property after the initial conveyance to McMillan and should be powerless to convey anything to San Antonio. This would be the case under the common law. Nevertheless, the impact of the recording statutes is to pry that title loose from McMillan and other nonrecording takers and to vest it in subsequent takers like the City of San Antonio.

The recording statutes are chiefly geared to protect good-faith purchasers for value. Consequently, these statutes do not afford protection to persons who acquire the land through gift or inheritance. To attain the protection of the statutes, the purchaser must give consideration, that is, a value of some sort. The value need not be equal to the fair market value of the premises, but neither can it be nominal or merely recited in the deed without actual payment. It must be a real value.

THE RECORDING PROCESS

Although the name of the specific office and official will differ, deeds are recorded at a county office created for that purpose. The recorder will be authorized under state law to record deeds, mortgages, easements, contracts for sale and, in some states, leases and any other transactions affecting the title to land. In addition, the recorder or some other county official will record notices of judgments, secured transactions, pending litigation, inheritance taxes and other dealings that may also encumber the free transfer of land. Each document either conveys a part of the owner's property rights or creates an encumbrance or lien on the parcel.

CASE EXAMPLE

George sells the western half of Laneacre to Herman. In the deed of conveyance George grants an easement to Herman to use George's driveway to get to and from the garage. To purchase the land, Herman borrows money from the bank and executes a mortgage for the western half of Laneacre to the bank in order to secure the loan. The deed conveys title to half of Laneacre and conveys an easement to Herman to use a part of the other half, and the mortgage to the bank is a lien on Herman's portion of Laneacre. Each of these documents is recorded to secure the rights of the party receiving an interest thereunder.

The early recordings under the recording statutes were handwritten, verbatim accounts of the deed or other instrument. Later these recordings were typed, and today they are in large measure photocopies of the original documents. The document presented for recording must be the original.

The recording process begins with the presentation of the instrument to the recorder, usually by the party seeking protection (for example, the buyer in a sales transaction). Upon payment of a recording fee, the recorder stamps the instrument, showing the precise time it was filed with that office. The instrument is later photocopied and entered into the deed books. These numbered books contain exact copies of all deeds ever filed in that county. Simultaneously, the names of the grantor and grantee are indexed in separate grantor and grantee index books, with a reference to the deed book number and page where a copy of the deed can be found. A similar procedure would be followed if the instrument were a mortgage, easement or other document transferring an interest in the land.

Approximately ten states use a tract index that simplifies the title searching process. In addition to the grantor and grantee indexes, the tract index lists in a single place all the transactions that have occurred affecting the parcel concerning the searcher. Once the correct page is located, all deeds, mortgages and other transactions are listed for the searcher's convenience. The title searcher can rely upon this page (or pages) as containing all the relevant transactions affecting the concerned piece of property.

The act of recording in no way legitimizes an instrument. If a deed is forged or was never delivered, recording will not remove this impediment to its validity.

Chain of Title

The recorded history of events that affect the title to a specific parcel of land, usually beginning with the original patent or grant.

Documents filed at the recorder's office are within the chain of title if they concern the parcel and are recorded during the period in which each grantee has title to the parcel of land. If the title searcher were to begin the search anew today, the chain of title would begin with the present owner's deed (who is also the last grantee of record). That deed would contain a recital stating from whom the present grantee's seller got the parcel. Continuing the example above, the last recorded deed would have as grantor, Herman, to grantee, Isaac, and something like the following: "being all of the same premises conveyed on June 16, 1968, by George to Herman and being contained in Deed Book 202 at page 1121."

Normally each deed in the chain of title contains a recital of this nature so that the searcher can trace the title back to the original patent or grant.

The attorney or other agent doing an original title search examines the grantor index from the day the present grantee got the parcel until the day the search is being done, in order to ascertain whether or not the present grantee conveyed any interest in the land to another. He or she follows the same procedure for each preceding grantee, for the period of that grantee's ownership as recited. Any conveyance in the grantor index during this time period must be checked to see whether it affects the concerned parcel. Similarly, the mortgagor index is examined to assure that no mortgage is outstanding against the parcel. The county records must also be examined to determine whether there are any unsatisfied judgments, pending litigation, mechanic's liens or secured transactions against the grantee. Each of these is an encumbrance on the land and normally must be satisfied prior to a buyer's acceptance of the deed.

If every transfer of property involved a title search going back to the original deed, title searches would be cumbersome and expensive. In many states the title is merely reviewed for transactions that have taken place since the last conveyance, inasmuch as the seller will supply his or her search for the previous title history.

Any transaction that is found within the chain of title is deemed to be constructively known by the buyer. Constructive notice is as valid a notice of the status of the parcel as that of which the buyer has personal knowledge. If a recorded transaction does not appear within the chain of title, however, the buyer is not charged with constructive notice of the facts contained therein.

CASE EXAMPLE

In 1984 George conveys to Herman, who does not record the deed. In 1985 George conveys the same parcel to Isaac, who records the deed. In 1986 Herman finally records his deed. Later that year, Isaac enters an agreement to sell the parcel to Jeremy. When Jeremy has a title search done, the deed from George to Herman is not in the chain of title. The title searcher does not examine the records for possible conveyances by George after 1985, when Isaac became the new owner. Since Jeremy is not charged with constructive notice of the deed to Herman, he takes the parcel free and clear of the prior deed to Herman. Herman has the right to sue George for damages but not for title to the land.

Some encumbrances on real estate do not appear in the chain of title, yet the buyer is charged with knowledge of them. These encumbrances include zoning laws, building restrictions, property taxes for the year of sale and subsequent years and special assessments or taxes.

If the reconstruction of the chain of title reveals a gap or a flaw in the title, then the buyer is excused from the purchase agreement because the seller cannot deliver *marketable* or *unencumbered title* for which the purchaser contracted. A *gap* occurs when the recorded documents do not indicate who owned the parcel during a given period. An example of a *flaw* in the title occurs when the buyer, in the purchase agreement, has been promised an unencumbered fee simple interest and a life estate is found outstanding in the title to the parcel. In either of these situations it is said that there is a *cloud on the title.* A cloud on the title is created whenever doubt is created as to the validity of the grantor's title. The property is unmarketable so long as a cloud on the title exists. If the seller is willing, a *quiet title action* may be brought in order to get a judicial (court) ruling that the title is marketable. The seller joins as defendants all those parties who have a potential interest in the land. The plaintiff-seller requests that the court declare his or her title valid, thereby "quieting title" to the land. The buyer can then rely on the judicial assurances of good title and consummate the deal.

Acknowledgment

A formal declaration by the person who executes an instrument that he or she is freely signing it; this signing is attested to by a public official, usually a notary public.

The recorder does not pass judgment upon the legitimacy of the instrument upon recording it, nor does the fact of recording add any degree of validity to a document that is otherwise defective or void. Most states have, however, established some prerequisites that must be satisfied before a document is acceptable for recording. The chief requirement is that the deed or other instrument be *acknowledged.*

For instance, when preparing the deed, the seller of land may sign the deed and a separate acknowledgment before a notary public. The notary public then indicates in the acknowledgment that he or she has witnessed the seller's affirmation or signature. The witnessing of the signature by a disinterested public official gives reasonable assurance that the signature on the deed is that of the seller and not an impostor. Under the statutes the deed is then acceptable for recording.

It should be noted that in most states the failure to have the deed acknowledged or to meet any other prerequisite for recording prevents the deed from serving as constructive notice to anyone. The rule seems to be overly technical and may be unfair since the subsequent purchaser has notice of the conveyance and yet because of the mistake can ignore it. As a result, some states have passed statutes to the effect that an unacknowledged or mistakenly acknowledged instrument will be notice to subsequent purchasers and to creditors.

The chief importance of the acknowledgment lies in recording, not in conveyancing itself. A deed need not be acknowledged to effectuate a conveyance because title will pass to the grantee upon delivery and acceptance of the deed, whether it is acknowledged or not.

Mistakes in Recording

Errors made by the recorder.

The rule in most states is that a person who has properly presented an instrument for recording has satisfied his or her duty; the instrument will be constructive notice to a subsequent taker. The result is that a mistake made by the recorder initially falls upon the future taker, even though that taker could not have discovered the instrument because of the mistake.

CASE EXAMPLE

Brownstein purchased a parcel of land from Peterson in 1951. In 1962 Brownstein conveyed a 20-foot drainage easement to the city. The city official presented the written easement for recording, but the recorder failed to enter Brownstein's name in the grantor index. In 1986 Brownstein conveys the parcel to Jackson. Brownstein's conveyance to the city does not appear in the chain of title for the parcel. Jackson has no legal recourse against Brownstein or the city but would be able to recover against the recorder on that official's security bond.

A mistake by the recorder is a difficult dilemma for courts to resolve because neither the party presenting the instrument for recording nor the subsequent taker is at fault. A minority of courts, recognizing that the primary concern of the recording statutes is with good-faith purchasers for value, hold that the subsequent taker does have recourse against the grantor.

CASE EXAMPLE

Brownstein purchased a parcel of land from Peterson and presented the deed for recording. The recorder misplaced the deed and it was never recorded. Brownstein later enters a purchase agreement with Jackson in which he agrees to convey "good and marketable title" to him. When doing the title search, Jackson discovers that the deed by which Brownstein took title is missing. In some states Jackson would have a legal claim against Brownstein for breach of contract.

Regardless of which rule is adopted, the injured party has recourse against the recorder on his or her security bond.

Mistakes in the Instrument

Errors made in the preparation of the instrument to be recorded.

A mistake in the instrument recorded may affect the validity of the notice given. If the mistake is minor, it will not deter the instrument from being legal notice. For example, the grantor's name listed as Franc*is* Brown rather than Franc*es* Brown in a deed would be adequate notice to a third party. However, if the nature of the mistake is such that the instrument would no longer put the third party searcher on notice to inquire further, the instrument will not be constructive notice. Thus, if the grantor's name is George Thomas but is typed in the deed Thomas George, it will be listed in the grantor index under *G* for George and not *T* for Thomas. This deed will not be notice to a subsequent purchaser.

Evidence of Title

Proof of the ownership of the parcel.

The average real estate buyer is not competent to determine on his or her own the status of the title to the parcel in question. Depending on the state, or often the local or county practice, the attorney hired by the buyer will have to provide evidence of the marketability of the title. This evidence of title may be provided by the lawyer's own research relating to the title. It is more often the case, however, that attorneys retain a title search firm or title insurance company to provide the necessary information. Specifically, evidence of title will be provided by abstract, by title insurance or by certificate.

Abstract of Title

A summary of all the recorded transactions, including deeds, mortgages, judgments and the like, that affect the title to a specific parcel of land.

The title searcher or abstractor will examine the chain of title, making a descriptive notation of all recorded transactions affecting the concerned parcel. Depending on local practice, the abstractor may be required to examine the title back to the original grant or only back to the preceding conveyance. The abstractor prepares for the party employing him or her a document—*an abstract*—that contains a description of the concerned parcel and a brief description of all the instruments affecting the land that fall within the chain of title.

CASE EXAMPLE

The abstractor will examine the grantor index for the name George Lang for conveyances between the years 1975 and 1985, the period during which George was the record owner of Laneacre. Having noted the deed book pages of all such conveyances, the abstractor will look at the deeds to see whether they affect Laneacre in any way.

The abstractor similarly examines the mortgagor index and mortgage books for outstanding mortgages. He or she examines other books in search of easements, leases, judgments, mechanic's liens, secured transactions, tax liens and pending litigation. A summary of each of these transactions is provided to the buyer or the buyer's attorney.

Attorney's Opinion. Based on professional judgment, the attorney states his or her opinion as to the condition of the title based on the facts revealed in the abstract. The abstractor makes no assertions as to the quality of the title but merely presents in the abstract the recorded events affecting the parcel. The attorney then examines the abstract and renders a professional judgment as to his or her opinion of title. The attorney does certify that all instruments pertinent to the parcel of land are included in the abstract. In large measure the buyer can be expected to rely on this attorney's opinion of title. However, forged deeds or other errors in recording may well be undetected by the abstractor or attorney, and such imperfections may leave the buyer legally unprotected. Of course, if the abstractor or the attorney is negligent, the buyer would have a right to sue either or both for damages. A judgment for damages, however, is only as good as the ability of the judgment debtor to pay. If the attorney (judgment debtor) is financially sound, the buyer may recover the financial loss resulting from the attorney's professional error. If the attorney is not solvent, however, the money judgment may be uncollectible, and the buyer will not obtain financial satisfaction.

CASE EXAMPLE

Rite hired Pierson, an attorney, to represent him when he purchased Hilltop Acres from Jack Haney. Pierson had performed the title search and provided Rite with an attorney's opinion assuring him that title was transferred to Rite. Mary Haney, Jack's sister, returned to town and asserted an ownership interest in Hilltop Acres. The facts showed that their father left Hilltop Acres "to his children" and that Jack and Mary were his two children. Pierson had negligently failed to determine that Jack Haney, Rite's grantor, was not the only child. Rite may have to buy Mary's interest to get clear title but can then sue Pierson for damages because of his negligence in performing his professional duties. Recovery on the judgment by Rite will depend upon the financial capacity of Pierson to pay.

Title Insurance

A comprehensive indemnity contract that insures the titleholder against title defects and encumbrances that may exist at the time the policy is issued.

To overcome the limitations arising from the methods just discussed, the practice of obtaining title insurance has arisen in many areas of the country. Title insurance has the advantage of insuring against loss caused by forged deeds and other undiscovered errors on the record. In the case of negligence it may also provide more financial security to the grantee-insured than would an individual attorney's opinion on the title. The title insurer pledges itself to defend—in court if necessary—the title of the grantee-insured and will pay for losses up to the maximum amount stated in the policy.

The title policy usually covers forged instruments, undisclosed heirs, misfiled documents, incorrect marital status, confusion over similarity of names, and mistaken legal interpretation of wills. Any of these defects will be defended by the title company.

Though title insurance does alleviate some of the shortcomings of the previous method, it is not a panacea. The title insurance company obtains an abstract of title for its review, and it excepts from its coverage all those defects discovered by the abstractor. In addition to discovered defects, the title policy usually excludes from coverage the rights of parties in possession, taxes and assessments not yet due or payable, zoning and other public regulations and facts that would be revealed by a survey of the parcel.

CASE EXAMPLE

Bloom purchased a title insurance policy when he obtained his parcel of land from Cedeno. Bloom can feel confident that, if a deed in his chain of title described the grantor as single but his wife has suddenly been discovered, the insurer will pay off the wife up to the maximum policy amount. However, if the description of the parcel contained in the deed is unclear as to where the property line lies or the right of a neighbor to use a "common" driveway, his title policy will exclude these discovered defects from its coverage. Prior to the conveyance of the parcel, Bloom will have to decide whether or not he can live with these discovered defects.

The single-payment title policy will benefit the titleholder and his or her heirs or devisees. Coverage will continue until the titleholder or those heirs or devisees convey the property to another party. In short, courts have held that the title insurance coverage does not run with the land but ends when the interest of the insured terminates. Thus, a seller cannot transfer title insurance to a buyer.

Certificate of Title

A statement of opinion by an attorney that describes the status of the title to a parcel.

In some sections of the country the attorney examines the title records but does not provide an abstract of title to the buyer. Instead, a certificate of title is issued that denotes the condition of the title. The attorney certifies the present title status and points out any outstanding liens and encumbrances that would impinge upon the conveyance of an unfettered title. The certificate of title is only as good as the professional competence and the financial solvency of the attorney who certifies it.

The attorney renders the opinion that the title is good, except for the restrictions noted. Should the title prove to be invalid, a legal action will exist for the client against the attorney for the damages caused by the misrepresentation of title.

Torrens Certificate

A document issued under the Torrens system, a type of land title registration.

In states where the Torrens system exists, it is not compulsory and exists along with the recording system previously described. The advantage of the system is that it eliminates the need for a title search, and the Torrens certificate shows the status of the title at any time.

The Torrens system can be used when a landowner applies in

writing to the county court to have a title registered. A current title search is made and provided to the court, which holds a type of *quiet title action.* In this action all parties who may have an interest in the parcel are notified and given a chance to be heard by the court. The purpose of the notice and hearing is to obtain assurance that all encumbrances to the title are known prior to issuance of a Torrens certificate. When the court is satisfied that the landowner is the titleholder and that all liens and encumbrances to that title have been revealed, it orders the certificate of title to the parcel to be registered.

Henceforth, the certificate of title will depict the exact state of the title. The original is filed with the recorder, and a copy goes to the owner. A party alleging to have an interest arising prior to the registration of the Torrens certificate will be precluded from attacking the present owner's or any subsequent owner's title unless his or her interest was recorded on the original certificate. To assure that the Torrens certificate is always up to date, any conveyance, mortgage, lien or other encumbrance upon the parcel will not be valid until it is entered on the original certificate. Further, title does not pass until the registration takes place. If there is a defect of title, suit is usually against the state for the loss. A limited state fund is provided for such lawsuits.

As with the normal recording system, under the Torrens system it is usually necessary to go beyond the recorder's office (or the certificate) to determine whether there are unpaid taxes or special assessments, zoning and building restrictions or federal court judgments that may affect the parcel.

For reasons not completely clear, the Torrens system has not been widely used. Perhaps the title searching apparatus already in place has successfully resisted the abolition of the title search. There is also the initial expense of having the title registered and the fact that the system is voluntary, both of which militate against its wide adoption. The Torrens system has been adopted to some degree by 15 states, but it does not seem to be spreading rapidly and is not likely to replace the present recording system in the foreseeable future.

SUMMARY

Statutes that govern the recording of transfers of real estate have been adopted by all the states. Their primary intent is to protect buyers of real estate by informing them of the status of a title to the land in question. Each successive act of recording serves as legal notice to the public of a transaction that changes the status of ownership.

Legal notice falls into three categories. When information is acquired personally by the interested party, it is called *actual notice. Implied notice,* a second type, is imposed by the law when conditions exist that would cause a reasonable person to inquire further. Finally, *constructive notice* occurs when information on record could have been uncovered in a reasonable search.

Statutes governing recording are established and enforced by the states. They can be classed in three types that relate to the priority of ownership of any claimant to the property. In the first type, pure race, the statutes provide that the first person to record has priority. The second type, race-notice statutes, provide that a subsequent buyer can claim ownership by recording first, but only if he or she had no notice of the prior transaction. Notice statutes, the third type, provide that a subsequent buyer takes precedence over an earlier one if the prior transaction was not on record at the time of sale.

Deeds are recorded in numbered books at an office designated for that purpose in the county in which the property lies. Also recorded are liens, judgments or other dealings that prevent free transfer of the land. The attorney or other agent attempting to learn whether a title is marketable refers to the book in which the chain of title is recorded. If information is missing from the record or is contradictory, there is said to be a cloud on the title, and title is not marketable. A buyer finding this situation may choose to bring legal action to "quiet" the title.

The average buyer of real estate is not competent to judge the marketability of a title and should employ an attorney or perhaps a title search firm to provide evidence of title—that is, proof of ownership of the parcel. This agent may then provide an abstract, a summary of all the recorded transactions affecting the title. The buyer's attorney, after examining the abstract, gives an opinion as to whether the title appears to be marketable or whether it contains a flaw or gap. This opinion does not guarantee that the abstract is complete or accurate. To overcome this limitation, the practice of obtaining title insurance has gained popularity. This type of policy insures against losses caused by forgeries, undisclosed heirs, misfiled documents, incorrect marital status, confusion caused by similar names and mistaken legal interpretation of wills.

In some cases the attorney/title searcher provides a certificate that the title is valid instead of an abstract. If an attorney so certifies, and the title turns out to be flawed, the buyer has grounds for legal action against the attorney.

A final type of land registration is the Torrens system, under which the Torrens certificate of title status is available. When the certificate is issued and registered, it shows that a court is satisfied with the validity and marketability of the title. Although the Torrens system has been adopted in 15 states, its use is voluntary, and it does not seem likely to replace the present county recording system.

REVIEW AND DISCUSSION QUESTIONS

1. (a) Explain the purpose of recording statutes. (b) What must a plaintiff establish to be protected by this type of legislation?
2. Define *constructive notice* and explain how it might affect a person who purchases real estate.
3. What is the difference between a race-notice and a notice recording statute?
4. What is a tract index? How does it facilitate the title searching process?
5. Describe the title searching process.
6. What are the prerequisites that must be met for an instrument to be recorded?
7. Explain why title insurance is often advisable even when the grantee receives a warranty deed.
8. What are the limitations in relying upon title insurance for protection?

CASE PROBLEMS

1. On March 24, 1954, Davidson conveyed farmland to Smith by a warranty deed in which Davidson reserved a life estate for himself. The deed was not recorded until after Davidson's death in November 1962. In October 1962 Davidson leased the land to Murphree. After Davidson died, Murphree paid rent to Davidson's estate until the deed to Smith was recorded. When Smith sued for these payments, the estate defended upon grounds that Smith had no claim until the deed was officially recorded. Discuss the validity of this defense. *Murphree v. Smith*, 291 Ala. 20, 277 So.2d 327 (1973).
2. In an agreement dated March 9, 1964, Jaynes granted Lawing an option to purchase real property. The option was open for two calendar years. Before the option expired, Lawing took it up, but Jaynes refused to transfer the property. In April 1966, Lawing sued. Lawing's action was awaiting trial in March 1971 when Jaynes conveyed the property to McLean. When Lawing instituted his litigation in 1966, he filed a notice of his claim in the county registrar's office. The notice had been indexed improperly. In a suit by Lawing to have the deed from Jaynes to McLean declared void, what must McLean establish for a successful defense? *Lawing v. Jaynes*, 206 S.E.2d 162 (N.C. 1974).
3. Dowse sold land to Pender by warranty deed dated April 1, 1984. The deed was recorded on June 3, 1984. On May 29, 1984, Dowse fraudulently sold the same land to Petez. Petez recorded his deed on June 4, 1984. Petez had no actual knowledge of the deed to Pender. Between Pender and Petez, who has

the superior claim in (a) race-notice jurisdiction, (b) race jurisdiction, (c) notice jurisdiction? Explain.

4. Gagner purchased a parcel of land in 1969 after his attorney provided him with a certificate of title stating that the land was marketable and unencumbered by easements. In fact, a water district had previously been deeded a water pipe easement across the land, but the easement was not recorded until 1973. Although the easement was not in Gagner's chain of title, there were references in the chain indicating that the water district had certain rights in a larger parcel that included Gagner's land. The attorney relied on oral assurances from the seller, Crena, that these references did not affect the Gagner parcel. (a) Is the easement valid as to Gagner? (b) If it is valid, does Gagner have a remedy against the attorney? *See Gagner v. Kittery Water District*, 385 A.2d 206 (Me. 1978).

5. McDaniel discovered the existence of a utility easement along the eastern edge of his property that was not mentioned in his deed or noted in his title insurance policy. Since the title insurance policy purported to guarantee McDaniel fee simple ownership, he sued the title insurance company for the reduction in the fair market value of his land caused by the easement. The utility easement is recorded. Will McDaniel succeed? *McDaniel v. Lawyer's Title Guaranty Fund*, 328 So.2d 852 (Fla. 1976).

10
Liens Against Title

LIEN

A claim against another's property securing either payment of a debt or fulfillment of some other monetary charge or obligation.

Liens are important in all spheres of commercial law. They take many forms and are subject to extensive variations from state to state. Despite these differences, the underlying concept of all liens is much the same. The purpose is to provide security for a debt or completion of some action or obligation. A lien cannot exist in the absence of a financial claim against another person.

CASE EXAMPLE

Revisi, a contractor, obtained a long-term lease on land outside of Utica, New York, for construction of a small warehouse. Wilson Building Supply furnished all materials for the project. When Revisi did not pay his bills, amounting to $275,000, Wilson obtained a material supplier's lien (mechanic's lien) on the building.

Shortly thereafter, the state acquired Wilson's lumberyard as part of a slum clearance project. This left the company without facilities, and it demanded possession of Revisi's building on the basis of the lien.

Although courts sometimes refer to liens as property, a lien is not a property right in the thing itself. The lienholder has neither title nor the rights of a titleholder. His or her only right is to have a monetary obligation satisfied out of proceeds from the sale of the property. A lien thus differs from an estate, which is the right to possess realty, or an easement, which is the right to use realty. No court would award

185

Wilson Building Supply possession of Revisi's warehouse on the basis of the material supplier's lien, even if the lien exceeded the value of the property, because a lien does not give the holder of the lien title or the right to possession or use.

Because the fundamental nature of a lien is security, interests in real estate are frequently the subject of liens. Land and buildings provide excellent security. They are valuable, their value is relatively stable and they are difficult if not impossible to move or conceal. Further, in the United States, land is subject to a system of recording that gives constructive notice of existence of any liens against a parcel of land to anyone who deals with that parcel. For example, Wilson Building Supply, in obtaining its lien, had to follow a procedure designed to notify other creditors of Revisi of its claim against the property by filing its mechanic's lien.

Historical Background

Both personal property and real property are subject to liens. The emphasis of early English law was upon the personal property lien. As far back as the 12th century, English courts recognized the right of a landowner to seize cattle that strayed upon his land and to retain possession until the owner paid damages. This right was later applied to other situations, and possession became the basis for the common law lien against personalty. Under the common law, when a lien existed, the lienor had the right to retain possession of property until the debtor met the obligation. The debtor's title was in no way affected. If the lienor surrendered possession, the lien was lost. The original common law lien did not permit the lienor to sell the property.

Many persons were entitled to liens at common law. Those who received the most extensive protection were people who were required by law to serve the public. This group included innkeepers, warehousemen, common carriers and blacksmiths. Under the common law, people in these occupations had only limited rights to reject customers. As a result, the law helped them to collect their fees. Also protected by common law were artisans who repaired or altered personal property. They had a right to retain the property until paid.

Because the common law lien was based upon possession, it was never particularly important to real estate. The *equitable lien* was more significant in the development and use of real estate as security. As stated in Chapter 1, English law recognized two avenues for the administration of justice—law and equity. The equitable lien was originally recognized in equity, though not in law, to apply property to satisfy a specific debt or obligation. The holder of an equitable lien did not have to obtain or retain possession of the property. Unlike the common law, equity provided for enforcement of the lien by ordering the realty sold and the proceeds applied to the debt. The equitable lien is the basis for much of mortgage law as it has developed in the United States.

The common law lien in its historic form exists in few states today because, in most states, the common law lien has been embodied in statutes. Today such statutes require that personal property subject to lien be sold and the proceeds applied to satisfy the claim. In addition, statutes have modified the requirement of possession. A lien on personal property can be created if correct procedures are followed even if the lienholder does not have possession. A common example is the security agreement—a voluntary lien a buyer enters into when purchasing an automobile.

Although many statutory liens codify the common law, legislative bodies can authorize the creation of new lien rights. This power has been exercised often, and a wide variety of statutory liens exists. Statutes that create liens usually prescribe particular conditions that must be followed for the lien to be effective. These conditions specify such requirements as filing and notice. The party seeking the lien must comply strictly with these requirements. Common statutory liens such as the mechanic's lien, the judgment lien and the tax lien are very important to people in the real estate business. They are defects in the title that make it unmarketable unless a buyer contracts to accept them.

TYPES OF LIENS

Liens are either voluntary or involuntary. Voluntary liens are those the owner places against his or her land, usually to secure repayment of long-term debt. Funds are advanced to the property owner, who agrees to repay the debt and provide a lien on the property as security. In many states a real estate mortgage is regarded as a lien. Real estate mortgages are discussed extensively in Chapters 20, 21 and 22. A number of involuntary liens are also important to real estate practitioners. *Involuntary* liens, discussed in this chapter, are created by law to protect interests of persons who have valid monetary claims against the owner of real property. The claim might arise out of a judgment, sale or furnishing of a service of some kind. Involuntary liens are also created to aid government in the collection of taxes and special assessments.

Liens are also classified as *general* or *special*. Special liens apply to a specific parcel of realty only. The mechanic's lien, which is analyzed first in this chapter, is an example. Other special liens considered in the chapter are the vendor's lien and the property tax lien. A general lien, in a real estate context, is a lien against all the realty of a person in a given jurisdiction. Thus, a judgment against Jones in a lawsuit in Washington County imposes a lien against *all* of his realty in that county, not just against one or more specific parcels owned by him in Washington County. This type of general lien is known as a *judgment lien*. The federal tax lien, also discussed in the chapter, is a general lien.

Mechanic's Lien

The right of one who renders services or supplies materials in connection with the improvement of real property to seek a judicial sale of the realty to satisfy unpaid claims.

By statute in most states, contractors and suppliers who work on real estate or furnish material for such work are entitled to a lien if they are not paid. The lien provides them with a means of compelling payment because it allows the property to be sold to satisfy the claims. Generally, the lien attaches to both buildings and the land, and the work must have been done at the owner's request. The mechanic's lien, also known as a *material supplier's lien* or *contractor's lien*, is not the only action an unpaid supplier or contractor may take. By filing the lien, the supplier or contractor does not lose the right to recover on the contract.

CASE EXAMPLE

Eldon Horn and his wife purchased a lot. Shortly thereafter they contracted with Jamco Builders for the construction of a home on the lot. Jamco subcontracted some of the work to Mid-American Homes. Mid-American, as required by law, notified the Horns of its right to place a lien against the real estate. Jamco did not pay for the subcontracted work, and Mid-American filed a mechanic's lien against the property. This established its right to petition a court to have the property sold and the proceeds applied against the debt.

Valid reasons exist for granting contractors and suppliers a special lien against real property. In collecting for services and materials, they are at a disadvantage when compared with credit sellers of personal property. When not paid, the seller of personal property who has a valid security agreement can usually repossess the item. This remedy does not exist for suppliers whose materials have been incorporated into a structure. Similarly, a contractor or laborer cannot get back time and effort expended on the job. Except for the mechanic's lien, such claimants are limited to suing for the contract price. Litigation such as this is time-consuming and expensive, and the winning plaintiff may have difficulty collecting the judgment. The lien also has nuisance value in that, until the debt is paid, a purchaser takes title subject to the lien. The mechanic's lien laws thus aid many small entrepreneurs who might be reluctant or financially unable to take judicial action to collect an unpaid claim.

Mechanic's lien laws also encourage economic activity. Because a substantial amount of construction is done on credit, these laws increase security for the contractors, subcontractors and suppliers who have invested their capital. The additional security induces financial institutions to provide more credit for additional projects in the construction industry.

Mechanic's lien laws did not exist at common law. They are the result of 19th-century state legislation that was necessary to protect the contractors, laborers and suppliers who were crucial to the building of American cities.

Every state in the United States now has some type of mechanic's lien legislation. Since this legislation is often merely the ad hoc response to problems of a particular area and time, it is extremely varied and often complicated. In those jurisdictions that have a basic mechanic's lien statute, political pressures may lead to substantial amendments, which increase variability and add further complications. Any person in real estate working with transactions involving mechanic's lien laws must be particularly concerned with local statutes on the subject. These statutes are usually quite technical, and their requirements must be followed strictly for the lien to be valid.

Claimants

Mechanic's lien statutes generally include several categories of potential claimants. A typical statute might name mechanics, material suppliers, contractors, subcontractors, lessors of equipment, architects, engineers, surveyors and teamsters. In addition, a statute usually includes a catchall provision that allows anyone to claim a mechanic's lien who has performed labor upon or supplied materials to improve property. Courts, too, have interpreted such statutes in a manner that extends the classes of persons who may claim mechanic's liens for making improvements to realty.

CASE EXAMPLE

Reet Development was constructing a large office building. It hired Francis Trucking Company to deliver materials to the site and Payne to serve as watchman. When Francis and Payne were not paid, they filed mechanic's liens. Reet argued that they were not entitled to liens as their labor did not improve the premises. Although courts in numerous states would disagree, it is reasonable to hold that the services improved the premises as they were necessary for ultimate completion of the job. These services could thus be the basis for a mechanic's lien.

Ownership Interest

Mechanic's lien laws apply to various ownership interests in real property. Absolute ownership is not required, but the lien ordinarily attaches only to the interest of the party ordering the work. Usually when the term *owner* is used in a statute, that term has been defined broadly. In addition to persons having fee simple title, among others owners include those who have life estates, persons with a remainder and tenants under lease. As the following case example illustrates, in some situations an owner's interest may be subject to a mechanic's lien even though the owner did not contract for the improvements.

CASE EXAMPLE

Balbo purchased property from Sanchez on a land installment contract. The contract was recorded. Balbo commenced to build on the property, serving as his own contractor. Balbo contracted with American Wallboard to put in the walls. American purchased the necessary wallboard from Tri-City Building. Although Balbo paid American, American did not pay Tri-City. When the wallboard was delivered, Tri-City notified Sanchez of delivery, although Sanchez had not ordered the material. Most courts would hold that this notice was sufficient to establish mechanic's lien rights against Sanchez inasmuch as Sanchez had ownership rights.

In a land installment contract (see Chapter 19), the buyer pays the purchase price on an installment basis. The owner/seller—Sanchez in the example above—retains title until the purchase price is paid.

In most states, statutes allow a noncontracting owner to block a lien against his or her interest by posting a *notice of nonresponsibility*. In general, these statutes require the owner to post a written notice indicating that he or she will not be responsible for the improvements. The notice must be in some conspicuous place on the land and be posted within a short time after the owner finds out about the work being done. Depending on the state, the time ranges from three to ten days.

Type of Work

The statutes that establish mechanic's liens use various general terms to describe the type of work for which a lien may be obtained. Frequently, the terms are defined in the statutes themselves. When they are not defined by statute, the courts as a rule have tended to interpret these general terms broadly.

• CASE BRIEF •

A state statute created a mechanic's lien in favor of all persons "bestowing skill or other necessary service on...the construction ...either in whole or in part, of any building, structure, or other work of improvement...:." In the course of supplying general engineering services to subdivide land into residential lots, Nolte located boundaries and set monuments in the ground to mark them. When Nolte was not paid, he filed a mechanic's lien. The owner argued that Nolte's lien was invalid because it was not related to any "building, structure, or other work of improvement," as the mechanic's lien statute required.

A California appellate court approved the lien. The court construed the statute to cover services bestowed upon a structure or land in any phase of the "scheme of improvements as a whole." Nolte's work was considered as essential as the work of a carpenter or an artisan whose skill was bestowed directly upon a building. *Nolte v. Smith, 189 Cal. App. 2d 140, 11 Cal. Rptr. 261 (1961).*

A number of statutes use the term *improvement* or *improvements*. This term has been defined to include demolition, erection, alterations or repairs. Some courts have refused to allow mechanic's liens for tearing down a building unless the term *demolition* is included in the statutory definition or is necessary for improvement. Terms such as *building, structure* and *appurtenance* usually have also been defined broadly when included in mechanic's lien laws. Mechanic's lien laws in a number of states use *improvements* as a synonym for *building* or *structure*, not to indicate the type of work for which a lien may be granted.

Consent

In order for property to be subject to a mechanic's lien, most states require that improvements be made with the consent and knowledge or at the request of the owner. A contract is the basis for a mechanic's lien in most states, but a contract between an owner and a person seeking a lien is not required. As a result, numerous circumstances exist in which a lien can attach even when the owner has not personally entered into a contract with the lienor.

Consent of the owner may be express or implied. One example of implied consent is when a lease provision requires a tenant to make alterations or specific improvements. If a lease contains this type of provision, the lessor's interest is subject to a lien in most jurisdictions even if the modifications are made at the tenant's expense. On the other hand, a lease that contains the usual covenant that the tenant maintain or repair the premises and nothing more does not establish implied consent. In addition, except in states that have implied consent based on knowledge, mere knowledge by a lessor that improvements are being made is not sufficient to establish a lien against the lessor's interest.

Consent of the owner may be given by an agent. Some states have by legislation established classes of persons as statutory agents for the owner. These people have the implied authority to consent in the owner's behalf. The statutory agents are contractors, subcontractors, architects, builders and any others who are in charge of work. An artisan or material supplier dealing with one of these persons is entitled to a lien, although a supplier is ordinarily not considered an agent of the owner for the purpose of passing on lien rights.

CASE EXAMPLE

Manner Electric Company entered into a contract to supply all electrical equipment for a new building. Manner then contracted with Ace Wire to furnish the necessary wire. Ace delivered the wire as per the agreement. When Manner became bankrupt without paying Ace's bill, Ace filed for a material supplier's lien. In most states Ace would not be able to acquire a lien.

Permanency

The concept that work or materials to be lienable must result in a *permanent benefit* underlies most mechanic's lien laws. *Permanent* refers to material and labor that become part of the premises. Permanent labor and materials are distinguished from those that are part of the contractor's plant or equipment in the project, which are not lienable.

CASE EXAMPLE

ABC Plumbing had a contract to furnish plumbing fixtures to a developer. The contract required delivery of fixtures to the individual units. In order to protect its delivery truck and to store fixtures, the company built a small storage shed at the site. When the company was not paid, it filed a notice of lien that included $1,500, the cost of the structure. A court would probably hold that this amount did not become a lien against the premises since the benefit was not permanent.

Permanent is construed broadly to last as long as the item remains part of the premises. As a result, many improvements of short duration as well as items detached from the structure may be the basis for a mechanic's lien. This includes work done to protect a permanent installation or even a structure not intended to be permanent but designed to be removed at a future time. Electrical signs, telephones and telephone equipment have been the basis for mechanic's liens. Items such as tables and benches have been considered permanent when necessary to the normal use of a structure and furnished for this use. Services such as mowing, trimming and spraying plants as well as weeding and raking lawns are not permanent improvements.

Perfection

The performance of those steps required by statute to sell real property under mechanic's lien laws.

The time periods and procedures involved in and required for perfecting a mechanic's lien vary appreciably from state to state. They also frequently vary within the same state for different categories of claimants as well as for different types of benefits conferred. For example, in a number of states the steps that a subcontractor must take to perfect a lien differ from those the prime contractor must follow. Material suppliers usually have to follow procedures different from those required of the artisan supplying labor. Despite these and other differences, two almost universal requirements for perfecting a mechanic's lien are: notice to the owner and the filing of a mechanic's lien claim in the county or city land records.

Notice. Statutes generally require a lien claimant to notify the owner before filing a lien. In most states a defective notice or failure to provide the owner with notice invalidates a lien. The purpose of this requirement is to warn the owner not to pay a contractor against whom outstanding claims exist in favor of laborers, subcontractors or material suppliers. Knowing of the existence of these claims, the owner may protect himself or herself against paying twice by retaining funds due to the contractor until the lien claimant is paid.

Notice to the owner ordinarily includes the following information: the name and address of the lienor, the name of the person with whom the lienor contracted if not the owner, the labor performed or material furnished, dates when the work was started and completed, the balance due and a description of the property and the owner's interest. Most states require the notice to be in writing; some require an affidavit as to the amounts due. Usually the statute gives the potential lienor a limited time period of 20, 30 or sometimes 60 days after the work is completed to notify the owner of the claim.

Some categories of claimants are excused by statute from giving a preliminary notice. An example would be a laborer working for a daily wage. The reason for this exception is to protect these people from losing the lien right because of a technicality of which they might not be aware. In a number of states preliminary notice is necessary only if the lien claimant did not deal directly with the owner. In jurisdictions following this rule a prime contractor would not be required to give notice, but a subcontractor would. A few states permit notice to the owner after the lien has been filed.

Filing.   A second critical point in perfecting a lien is filing for record. Doing the work or furnishing the materials merely gives the claimant a right to acquire a lien. In some states this right is referred to as an *inchoate lien*. Usually the statute requires that the claimant file a verified statement of the claim. This statement ordinarily includes a brief explanation of the contract, the balance due and a description of the property as well as the names and addresses of the parties.

A filed lien, like a recorded deed or mortgage, is part of the public record. The act of recording ensures that third parties dealing with the property will have knowledge of claims against it if they search the record. In a number of jurisdictions filing is unnecessary if the mechanic sues for the sum owed. These states reason that the suit provides sufficient notice of claims against the property.

Most jurisdictions require that the verified statement, sometime referred to as the *lien claim* or *affidavit*, be filed within a specified time after work is completed. This period varies, but 30, 60 and 90 days are common.

• CASE BRIEF •

Tabet Lumber Company supplied materials for a house being constructed for Richard and Jan Baughman. The Baughmans paid the contractor in full and moved into the house on October 25, 1965. On January 15, 1966, the contractor hung two mirrors in the bathrooms, installed handrails on the stairs and weather-stripped two basement doors. These items were included in the original agreement.

The contractor did not pay for all of the materials, and on April 15, 1966, Tabet filed a lien claim for the unpaid portion. The Baughmans argued that this filing was invalid, as the mechanic's lien statute required filing within 90 days of completion. Their view was that substantial completion was sufficient and the 90-day period started running in October. This contention was accepted by an appellate court, which stated, "a building is substantially completed when all essentials necessary to the full accomplishment of the purpose for which the building has been constructed are performed." *Tabet Lumber Co. v. Baughman, 79 N.M. 57, 430 P.2d 706 (1968).*

Some states attempt to solve the problem of determining when completion has occurred by allowing the owner to file a notice of completion. This notice is the equivalent of completion and begins the time period within which the lien claim must be filed.

When a premature notice of completion is filed, the time period for filing commences from the date of actual completion. If the parties disagree as to whether there was actually "substantial completion" when the notice of completion was filed, litigation similar to that in the previous case is the only means of settling the dispute.

Although proper filing of a lien is necessary for its validity, the lien is often effective from an earlier date. In many states the properly filed lien reverts back to the time construction began. In these states the lienholder's claim thus acquires priority over claims against the premises recorded or filed before the lien claim was filed but after the work was begun.

CASE EXAMPLE

Scarlet and Grey Construction Company contracted to build a stable for Perry. Work began on November 10. On December 5, before the job was completed, Perry executed a mortgage on the property in favor of Betz. The stable was finished on December 12, but a portion of the contract price was not paid. Scarlet and Grey filed a lien against the property on January 3. In many states this lien would have priority over Betz's mortgage because the lien reverts back to November 10, the day work began.

In a few states the lien attaches as of the time the original contract was made. In others the lien attaches from the date materials were first furnished at the site.

Termination

Mechanic's liens may be extinguished in numerous ways. Probably the most common is by payment of the obligation upon which the lien is based. Other procedures are also widely used.

Ordinarily, discharging a debt terminates existing liens securing the debt and precludes a future lien based on the same debt. In some jurisdictions, however, mechanic's lien rights of subcontractors and suppliers survive payment to a principal contractor. In these states the subcontractors may obtain liens for the full value of their respective claims *even if the principal contractor has been paid*. This practice is known as the *Pennsylvania Rule*. In states following this rule, the subcontractor's lien is considered direct, not a right that derives from the general contractor. These jurisdictions consider the contractor the owner's agent; thus, through an agent, the subcontractor is deemed to have contracted directly with the owner. When a state has a mechanic's lien statute of this type, the owner may be required to pay twice.

CASE EXAMPLE

Randolph Estates contracted with the ABC Pool Company for construction of a $28,000 pool. The pool was to serve residents

of an apartment complex being constructed by Randolph Estates. ABC subcontracted excavation and grading to Montefresco Company for $1,500. Upon completion of the pool,
Randolph paid ABC as per the contract. When ABC went bankrupt, Montefresco filed a mechanic's lien against the premises. In
states following the Pennsylvania Rule, Randolph would have to
pay the $1,500 again, this time to Montefresco, in order to extin-
guish the lien.

Probably the majority of states follow what is called the *New York
Rule*. In these jurisdictions a subcontractor's lien is limited to the
amount still owed the general contractor at the time the lien is filed.
The owner is not compelled to pay more than the contract price, inasmuch as any subcontractor's lien derives from the principal contractor. The result is that the owner may pay the principal contractor as
work progresses without fear of a subcontractor's lien for the same
work.

Many jurisdictions permit the owner to release an existing lien
not only by paying the claim it represents, but by giving a bond or paying cash into court to cover potential claims by contractors and/or
subcontractors and artisans. If the claim is disputed, this process protects both the owner and the claimant. The owner is protected because the funds are controlled by the court; the claimant is protected
because monies are available to pay any valid claim. This procedure is
also valuable to the owner since the property is not tied up during litigation by being subject to a filed mechanic's lien.

Liens may also terminate by *waiver*. The waiver may be made
before the improvement, as part of the contract, as a *"no-lien"* provision. This provision must be clear and unambiguous. Any doubts will
be resolved against the waiver. Some state courts have held that a
waiver by a principal contractor is also applicable to subcontractors
claiming through him or her. In other states a subcontractor is bound
by this type of provision only if he or she had actual knowledge of or
expressly consented to the contractor's waiver.

Mechanic's liens are also extinguished by the lienor's *failure to
foreclose* within a reasonable time. This period is often short. Six
months and a year are common, although in some states a two-year
limitation is applicable. A number of jurisdictions shorten the time
further by permitting the owner to demand that the lienholder commence an action to foreclose the lien. Failure of the lienor to begin
foreclosure proceedings within the allowed time results in forfeiture
of the lien. The purpose of these statutory provisions is to eliminate
the cloud on the title resulting from a properly filed mechanic's lien
claim.

Judgment Lien

A lien that automatically attaches to real property of a defendant when a plaintiff wins a judgment in the jurisdiction in which the property is located.

CASE EXAMPLE

Justin Lane purchased a lot for $10,000. Lane was the defendant in a tort case, and a judgment was entered against him for $8,500. Lane refused to pay the judgment as he believed it to be unfair. When Lane attempted to sell the lot, the purchaser's attorney refused to certify that the title was marketable because of a judgment lien resulting from the tort case.

Collecting a money judgment in a civil case is often almost as difficult as winning it. In most instances the losing defendant does not rush up to the winning plaintiff with check in hand, but is very reluctant to pay. If the judicial process by which the money judgments are awarded is to be respected, the law must assist plaintiffs in collecting their judgment.

The ultimate method is the forced sale of enough of defendant's property, real and personal, to cover the judgment. Although some property may be exempt by statute, the nonexempt property of a defendant may be seized and sold to satisfy the judgment. This is known as an *execution* or a *levy of execution*. It is accomplished by a writ from the court rendering the judgment. The writ authorizes a court officer, usually the sheriff, to sell the property.

A judgment lien is an involuntary lien attaching to real property when a judgment is obtained against the owner. The lien establishes the claim of the *judgment creditor* against the defendant's real estate in the jurisdiction of the court that awarded the judgment and helps to ensure that the plaintiff will eventually collect the judgment. While the lien exists, a sale or mortgage of the property is subject to the judgment creditor's interest. As a result, the defendant often pays the judgment to free the property from the judgment creditor's lien. If the judgment is not paid, the real estate can be levied against and sold. Some states use a process similar to that used to foreclose a mortgage.

A judgment creditor can also obtain a lien against a defendant's personal property. Personal property, unlike real estate, must be levied against by a court order before being subject to a lien. This type of lien is generally referred to as an *execution lien*. In most states the execution lien and judgment lien are treated in a similar manner. Ordinarily, the personal property must be used to satisfy the judgment before the real property becomes available for that purpose.

Judgment liens did not exist at common law. They are created by statute, and their existence and operation depend upon the statutory provisions establishing them. Not all states have provided the judgment creditor with this method of enforcing his or her judgment. If no judgment lien statute exists in a state, a lien against real property, like one against personal property, arises only when proper execution and levy have occurred.

A judgment lien is a general lien. It applies to all real estate owned by the defendant in the county where the judgment was rendered. The lien may be made specific by levy of execution. Most states have a simple procedure for extending the lien to other real estate owned by the defendant within the state. This is done by filing a transcript of the judgment in other counties in which the judgment debtor has real property. Federal statutes provide that a judgment of a United States district court sitting in a state having a judgment lien statute is a lien to the same extent as the judgments of a state court of general jurisdiction.

Requirements

The time at which a judgment lien attaches depends upon state statute. This time is important because it determines the conflicting claims of creditors. In a few states the lien commences when the judgment is rendered; however, most state statutes require that the judgment be made part of the public record in some manner before the lien is created. This is a reasonable requirement. Official records should be available to third parties dealing with a judgment debtor so that they have a source whereby they can determine potential problems. A common requirement for establishing general notice of the judgment is that it must be filed, docketed (officially listed) and indexed before a lien based upon it is effective. Some states require only that the judgment be filed and docketed.

In a few states legislation provides that when a judgment is indexed the lien reverts to some earlier date. Sometimes this is the first day of the court term during which the judgment was rendered; more often it is the day the judgment was rendered. The *doctrine of relation back* means that the judgment lien might be superior to interests created before the lien became part of the public record.

Not all judgments rendered create liens. Of course, it is critical that the judgment be rendered validly by a court having jurisdiction. Another basic requirement is that the judgment be final. An interlocutory judgment or one that settles some intermediate plea or motion is not final and cannot give rise to a judgment lien. In addition, the judgment must be for a specific sum of money. In most states liens are based upon the judgments of any court of record. Frequently, however, state statutes require judgments of inferior courts to be filed with the statewide court of original jurisdiction before becoming a lien.

Legal Effect

As a general rule, liens and other interests in realty rank in the order in which they are created. This is the principle of "first in time, first in right." As a result of this principle, judgment liens have important consequences for two classes of people: buyers from a judgment debtor and other creditors of the judgment debtor.

If a judgment lien has been perfected before the execution of a contract for the sale of realty, the buyer takes the real property subject to the lien. Because the real property is subject to a judgment lien, the real property may be sold by the sheriff to satisfy the judgment debt. As the lien existed at the time the buyer obtained his or her interest, the buyer will lose the real property unless the debt is paid off. On the other hand, in the absence of fraud, if a buyer and seller have contracted for the sale of land and the contract has been recorded, the buyer's interest will not be defeated by a later judgment against the seller even if the contract has not been performed.

Creditors of a judgment debtor are also affected by a judgment lien. A valid judgment lien has priority over the claims of creditors who have not established a security interest in the debtor's property prior to the judgment. The reason is that the judgment lien was created first. Prospective creditors also consider real property less valuable as security to the extent of judgment liens against it. If a loan is made and the debtor defaults, when the property is sold any judgment is satisfied out of the proceeds before the secured creditor's claim is paid.

Termination

In most instances statutes creating the judgment lien also establish the lien's duration. Usually the period is short. Periods of three to five years are common. In only a few states are judgment liens enforceable for more than ten years from their commencement. A few states extend the life of a judgment lien if the plaintiff obtains a levy of execution based on the lien.

In many states the period of time in which a suit on a judgment may be initiated is longer than the period during which a judgment lien may be enforced. If this is the case, the judgment lien terminates but the judgment remains outstanding.

Both the common law and a number of states by statute provide for the revival or renewal of expired judgment liens. In order to revive a judgment lien, the judgment itself must still be enforceable. Any liens that attach during the period in which the judgment lien was dormant and before its revival take precedence over the revived lien.

Notice of Lis Pendens

A recorded document that gives constructive notice that an action has been filed that might affect the title or possession of a specified parcel of real estate.

At common law a general principle existed that all persons were bound to take notice of suits affecting title to property. This principle was known as the doctrine of *lis pendens*, or "suit pending." A person acquiring an interest in real estate that was the subject of litigation, such as a suit to foreclose a mortgage, enforce a lien or set aside a deed, took the interest subject to any judgment that might later be rendered in the lawsuit. This doctrine was harsh because it was often difficult to determine if the property was the subject of litigation.

Because of the harshness of the common law doctrine, most states by statute provide for the filing of a notice of lis pendens in the county in which the property that is the subject of litigation is located. If the plaintiff does not file this notice, a person acquiring an interest in the real estate who has no actual knowledge of the litigation will not be subject to any judgment that might be awarded as a result of the lawsuit.

A notice of lis pendens is not a lien, but in many ways it has the effect of a lien, for once such a notice has been filed, the title to the real estate is encumbered. As a result, the title is unmarketable until litigation is settled or the notice of lis pendens vacated.

Attachment

The act of seizing a defendant's property by legal process, to be held by the court to ensure satisfaction of any judgment that might be awarded.

In some cases, after winning a judgment, the plaintiff discovers that the defendant has disposed of all assets that might be used to satisfy the judgment debt. In order to prevent the defendant from doing this, statutes in many states allow a plaintiff to seize property of the defendant by judicial order at the commencement of litigation. The property is held in the custody of the court as security for any judgment that the plaintiff might win.

The circumstances under which a plaintiff is entitled to attach defendant's property are regulated in detail by the various state statutes. Requirements for obtaining an attachment order usually are strict. In general, the statutes allow attachment only if the plaintiff is seeking money damages. In a number of states the monetary amount of the plaintiff's claim must be fixed or undisputed and only its validity contested.

A minority of states have unlimited attachment statutes. In these states the plaintiff is permitted to attach defendant's property in actions for money damages without showing special circumstances. Most states, however, require the plaintiff to show that some special reason exists to attach defendant's property. Permissible reasons are indicated by the state statute establishing the attachment remedy.

Typical state statutes allow attachment of the property of non-resident defendants. They also allow attachment of property that might easily be concealed or where facts indicate that the defendant might leave the jurisdiction. Ordinary business or pleasure trips outside of the state, openly made, are not within the contemplation of the statute as grounds for attachment. In many jurisdictions the fact that a defendant cannot be found is sufficient for the issuance of a writ of attachment. In almost all cases a defendant may obtain the release of attached property by posting sufficient bond.

Vendor's Lien

In some states, a right of a seller to a lien against land conveyed for any unpaid or unsecured portion of the purchase price.

• CASE BRIEF •

Dwayne and Beulah Blankenship contracted to exchange their ranch in Bonner's Ferry, Idaho, for one owned by Roy C. Myers and his son Ron. In addition, Roy Myers agreed to pay them $105,000 in contracts and cash.

Myers delivered the contracts and cash to his agent, Patrick, who converted $50,000 of these assets to his own use. A short time later Myers conveyed his entire interest in the Bonner's Ferry ranch to his son. Both the senior Myers and Patrick became insolvent, and the Blankenships asserted a vendor's lien against the Bonner's Ferry property.

Although a lower court refused the lien on grounds that the Blankenships were not unpaid, the Idaho appellate court reversed. The appellate court stated, "if through no fault of the seller the seller never receives such consideration or collateral from the buyer, then the seller is unpaid and unsecured and has a vendor's lien." *Blankenship v. Myers, 97 Idaho 356, 544 P.2d 314 (1975)*.

The term *vendor's lien* is used in several ways. In some situations, if the buyer does not pay the full purchase price, the seller reserves a lien in the deed. This is frequently referred to as an *express vendor's lien*. A lien of this type is very similar to a mortgage. It provides security for the unpaid seller just as a mortgage would. Like the mortgage, the express vendor's lien is the result of agreement between the parties. Although most of the states allow express vendor's liens, they are not in common use in this country. The probable reason is that a mortgage to the unpaid seller provides greater protection because the buyer also signs a note for the debt. In a few states, however, the vendor's lien is an important element in real estate sales when the seller is not fully paid at the closing.

In a number of states a vendor's lien arises by implication if the buyer does not pay the full price and the seller takes no other security. This is the type of lien involved in the Bonner's Ferry case. The implied vendor's lien exists without express agreement. It is based upon the principle that a person who has acquired another's property should not be allowed to keep it without paying for it. An unpaid seller should be allowed to satisfy the debt from the proceeds of a foreclosure sale of the property. Courts in some states also justify the vendor's lien on the theory of implied trust. These courts consider the buyer a trustee for the seller, holding legal title for the seller's benefit until the price is paid.

Courts and legislative bodies have often been critical of the implied vendor's lien. They consider the lien unfair because it is secret. They contend that third parties dealing with the buyer have no way of knowing of the lien's existence. Public records show that the buyer has legal title and no security interests exist against the property. As a result, a third party might be induced to buy the property or grant credit with the property as security. Although the public record is clear, a seller might have a lien that could be a cloud on the title or take priority over a mortgage. To eliminate this injustice, many states, by statute or judicial opinion, hold the vendor's lien unenforceable against encumbrances or purchasers in good faith who do not know of the lien's existence. For example, if Ron Myers had sold the Bonner's Ferry ranch to a bona fide purchaser prior to the Blankenships' efforts to assert a vendor's lien, the property would no longer be subject to the lien. Even so, a vendor's lien is not without value; it may be asserted against the seller, the seller's heirs or those who take from the seller knowing of the lien's existence.

Requirements

In those states in which it is recognized, the vendor's lien is created the moment the seller transfers legal title to the buyer. In order for the lien to exist, however, the seller must not have accepted some other type of security for the unpaid portion of the purchase price. For instance, if the seller takes back a mortgage, the lien is waived. Taking other land or personal property as security also waives the lien. In a number of states a seller who agrees to pass a title free of encumbrances is not entitled to a vendor's lien unless one has been expressly reserved in the deed. Retention of possession by the vendor after passing title also generally negates a vendor's lien. The vendor, however, does not waive the lien by instituting an action to recover the unpaid purchase money.

Priority

As has been noted, in many states the vendor's lien has no priority against the interest of a bona fide purchaser from the vendee or security rights in the property given to a creditor without notice. In most states the vendor's lien is also subject to a mechanic's lien for home construction, even if construction takes place after sale. The vendor's lien does have priority over the claims of unsecured creditors. These priority rules do not apply if an express vendor's lien is reserved in the deed and the deed is recorded. Under these conditions, third parties have a means of knowing that the lien exists.

In some sections of the United States the term *vendor's lien* has been applied to the interest of a person who sells real estate under a land contract. The vendor holds the legal title as security. If the vendee defaults, the vendor may foreclose the vendee's interest and apply the proceeds of the sale to the purchase price.

Tax Lien

A lien imposed against real property for payment of taxes.

The power of government to levy taxes is commonly coupled with the right to place liens on real and personal property to facilitate tax collection. Liens are encountered as part of the tax structure at all levels of government. In addition to federal and state governments, counties, cities, towns and villages as well as nonpolitical units such as school and irrigation districts are authorized to use liens as security when taxes are unpaid.

Many types of taxes, when unpaid, create liens upon property. These include both real and personal property taxes, income taxes and estate taxes, as well as local assessments for sidewalks, sewers, water distribution systems and so on. Less frequently, liens may be used to collect contributions to unemployment funds, wages that have been withheld and unpaid social security contributions.

Although tax liens may be placed against both real and personal property, liens on real property are generally more effective than those on personal property for several reasons. Personal property is easier to conceal than real property. Personal property can be moved from the taxing district or disguised with little difficulty. Real property's value is relatively stable, whereas many types of personal property deteriorate when used. As a result, personal property is often not of sufficient value to cover the defaulted tax.

Tax liens are not restricted to the property subject to taxation. In some jurisdictions taxes assessed on personal property may be the basis for a lien upon real property. A state may also collect taxes assessed against one parcel of real estate within its jurisdiction by proceeding against other parcels owned by the same person. A lien on property other than that against which the tax was assessed is limited to property owned when the taxes became collectible. Inasmuch as tax liens are statutory creations, the legislature has the authority to exempt certain types of property. Property exempt from tax liens varies considerably from state to state. Usually the statutory provision establishing lien exemption parallels statutes exempting property from taxation in general.

Priority

People who are unable to pay a particular tax generally have other financial problems. Often, many claims exist against their property. These claims may have been the basis for liens for other taxes, judgments or mortgages. The result is that litigation involving tax liens often concerns priority problems.

Legislative bodies have usually made tax liens superior to all other liens against the property, even those liens in existence before the tax lien. The rule of "first in time, first in right" does not ordinarily apply to tax liens.

CASE EXAMPLE

Graceland Savings and Loan held a mortgage on property owned by Ron Blue. The mortgage was recorded properly. Blue failed to pay his general property tax, and a lien was assessed against the property. The tax lien had priority over Graceland's mortgage.

State statutes ordinarily set forth any priorities existing between liens for different types of taxes. In the absence of a specific statute, the lien for general taxes is coequal with liens of other taxing units. Tax liens for general taxes are usually superior to liens for special assessments even if the special assessment lien was prior in time. The reason is that the claim for the necessary support of government is a higher obligation than the demand for the costs of a local improvement. Maintenance of civil government is the first and paramount necessity for social order, personal liberty and private property, and government cannot exist without revenue. Only upon specific legislative direction will the priority of the sovereign claims of the state be denied.

Foreclosure of Tax Liens

Sale of tax liens on real property is one method commonly used in the

United States to collect delinquent taxes. When taxes that are a lien against real property are in default, tax collectors in most states are authorized to sell the lien. These sales are usually by public auction. The successful bidder acquires the right to receive the overdue taxes and interest as these are paid. If there are no bidders, the taxing unit acquires the tax lien.

A successful bidder at a tax sale of the lien does not get title to the property but a lien against it. This lien is evidenced by a tax certificate. If the delinquent taxes are not paid after a period of time, the holder of the tax certificate can foreclose against the property. Usually this period of time is two or three years. During this time the property owner can redeem the property by paying the delinquent taxes, interest and any penalties.

The purchaser at the foreclosure sale obtains title to the property. In most jurisdictions the foreclosure procedure is very similar to that for a mortgage. A few jurisdictions continue to allow certain taxing units to conduct an absolute sale of real property at public auction if taxes are delinquent. The highest bidder acquires immediate title to the property on payment of the bid and delivery of the deed.

Federal Tax Lien

The federal taxing authority uses liens against real property to aid in the collection of federal income, estate and gift taxes. Federal tax liens for income taxes are not valid against a mortgagee, pledgee, mechanic's lienor, purchaser or judgment creditor until a notice of lien is filed. Liens for federal estate taxes do not require recording or filing. They come into existence against all of a decedent's taxable assets automatically upon that person's death. Relatively simple procedures have been developed to release a decedent's real property from the tax lien. These are designed to facilitate sale of the property. They ordinarily require a bond by the estate or partial payment of the tax. Federal gift taxes also attach automatically upon all gifts made. If the tax is not paid, the donee can be personally liable up to the value of the gift.

SUMMARY

A lien is a claim against property that either secures payment of a debt or binds a party to fulfill some other obligation. Although a lien does not transfer title to the lienholder, it establishes the right to have an obligation met out of proceeds from sale of the property.

Because land and buildings provide excellent security for a debt, liens occur frequently in real estate practice. Liens are classed as voluntary—those the property owner enters willingly—and involuntary—those attached by legal process to satisfy creditors. The home mortgage is an example of a voluntary lien. Involuntary liens important to the real estate professional are the mechanic's lien, the judgment lien, the vendor's lien and the tax lien.

The mechanic's lien provides contractors or suppliers who furnish labor or materials to improve buildings or land the right to seek a sale of the property to satisfy unpaid claims. The value of the improved property acts as security for the labor and supplies furnished. Usually, building supplies are sold on credit, and the additional security induces financial institutions as well as suppliers of materials to provide more credit for the construction industry.

Perfection is the term given to the legal steps necessary to establish an enforceable mechanic's lien. The steps and the time period required to perfect vary according to the type of lien. Basically, however, two steps are common to perfecting most liens: providing written notice of the claim to the owner and placing the lien in the public record. Payment of the full amount to the creditor is the principal method of terminating a lien.

Another common type of lien—the judgment lien—automatically attaches to real property when a claimant wins a money judgment in court. Forced sale of the defendant's property, usually by the sheriff, may be ordered by the court in a levy of execution to satisfy a judgment lien.

A third type is the vendor's lien. This lien establishes the right of a seller to levy against land conveyed to another for any portion of the purchase price not paid. In an express lien, this right is established in the deed. The implied vendor's lien, on the other hand, exists without express agreement. It may arise when the buyer does not pay the full price and the seller has not taken other security, such as a mortgage note or other property. The debt may then be satisfied from the proceeds of a foreclosure sale.

The tax lien is created by an owner's failure to pay taxes. It may be placed against real property by governments at all levels. Federal, state, county and municipal agencies and even school districts have this right. Generally, tax liens are superior to all other obligations, even those that are prior in time.

REVIEW AND DISCUSSION QUESTIONS

1. (a) Point out those factors that distinguish the common law lien from the equitable lien. (b) Explain why the equitable lien had a greater impact on real estate law.
2. When a contractor improves real property, the work is done on the basis of a contract with the owner. A contractor who is not paid can sue for breach of that agreement. Explain why a contractor should also be entitled to file a mechanic's lien against the property.
3. Mechanic's lien law differs appreciably from state to state. (a)

Indicate at least five of these differences. (b) What public policy concerns might explain some of these variations?

4. Judgment lien law differs appreciably from state to state. (a) Indicate at least five of these differences. (b) What public policy
concerns might explain some of these variations?

5. What is the chief criticism of the vendor's lien? Is this criticism
justified?

CASE PROBLEMS

1. Kile borrowed $15,000 from Chatfield, giving her a promissory
note to cover the debt. The note was unsecured, but Chatfield
knew that Kile owned substantial unmortgaged real property.
A short time later Hude won a judgment against Kile for
$150,000. When Kile filed as a bankrupt, both Chatfield and
Hude claimed priority in the real estate. Which of the two has
the superior claim? Explain.

2. Wood owned several hundred acres of land in Texas. In 1952 he
decided to explore for oil on the land and leased an oil-drilling
rig from Cabot. Under the terms of the lease, Cabot was responsible for moving the rig to the Wood property. As a result
Cabot hired White Heavy Haulers to transport the equipment.
White Heavy Haulers was not paid and filed a mechanic's lien
against Wood's property. (a) Is the lien valid? Discuss. (b)
Would your answer differ if under the lease the expense of
moving the rig was to be borne by Wood? Explain.

3. Dodd owned land, which he platted into lots and blocks. The
plat was recorded properly as the Woods Hills Subdivision.
Dodd then hired Dix to blacktop the streets and roads in the
subdivision. Upon completion of the work, Dix was not fully
paid; he filed a mechanic's lien against all the land, premises
and improvements described in the recorded plat.

    Gordon and Jenkins owned lots in the subdivision.
These lots were not on streets that Dix had blacktopped, although Gordon and Jenkins sometimes used these streets to
reach their lots. Would the properties of Gordon and Jenkins be
subject to the mechanic's lien if one were granted? Should any
of the properties be subject to a mechanic's lien? Support your
answer.

4. Ransonne won a judgment against Sneed for $120,000. A certi-
fied copy of the judgment was filed in the office of the county
recorder of Mesa County, a county in which Sneed owned real
property with a market value of about $80,000. A short time
later, Sneed contracted to sell this property for $82,000. Ran-
sonne immediately sued to enjoin the sale upon the basis of
her judgment lien. She contended that the property would ap-

preciate in value over the next few years and could then be sold to satisfy the judgment. Discuss the validity of her contention.

5. Jethro Construction Co., Inc. (Jethro), was the general contractor on two separate construction projects. Lasater Electric Co. (Lasater), was the electrical subcontractor on both projects. Lasater purchased its materials for their projects as well as others from Mac's Electrical Supply (Mac's). Lasater maintained an open account with Mac's. Over several projects, payments by Lasater to Mac's had been increasingly slow, and Mac's was worried about Lasater's ability to pay. What steps should Mac's take to ensure mechanic's liens against the projects if Lasater fails to pay?

11
Land Descriptions and Boundary Disputes

LEGAL DESCRIPTION

A description of a parcel of land that will be accepted by courts because it is complete enough to locate and identify the premises.

This chapter deals primarily with descriptions found in real estate instruments. Boundary disputes are also discussed as an intricate relationship exists between descriptions and boundaries. A description in a real estate instrument sets forth the physical dimensions of what is being conveyed. Boundaries are based upon this description. They establish the property on the earth's surface. Often they are imaginary lines, but sometimes they are marked by an object.

With only a few exceptions, American law requires a written instrument to transfer an interest in real estate. To be enforceable in a court of law, the written instrument must contain a valid description of the property involved. The courts will not enforce the written instrument if the description is incorrect or ambiguous. A seller or lessor who has agreed to transfer an interest in real estate is in breach of contract if the instrument executed does not properly describe the property. Even if the physical boundaries of a property are clear, no interest will pass if the property is not described properly.

The chief purpose of the description is to furnish a means for identifying a particular parcel of land. In addition, the description must describe an area that is bounded completely. In other words, the boundaries indicated by the description must close the parcel.

For a deed or other conveyance to be enforceable in a court of law, the description must make possible positive identification of the land. Courts consider this accomplished if a surveyor or other person familiar with the area can locate the property and determine its boundaries using the description in the conveyance. Courts do not consider a street address to be a legal description because the boundaries of the realty cannot be determined from it.

A technically accurate description that provides all the information necessary to locating land is preferable to one that needs clarification by other evidence. Courts, however, are exceedingly liberal in allowing outside evidence to clarify an ambiguous description. Testimony of the circumstances surrounding the transaction, the interpretation placed upon the description by the parties, statements of surveyors, neighbors and public officials as well as the physical elements of the area may be introduced. What the courts are searching for is the intent of the parties.

• CASE BRIEF •

Roger and his wife owned a large piece of land. The land included a lake in which there were several islands. Seventy acres of land jutted into the lake, forming a peninsula. When the tides were high and the wind right, this peninsula was separated from the mainland by a watercourse. Boats could traverse the watercourse at these times. At other times, only an inch or two of water was in the watercourse.

The Rogers deeded all their mainland holdings to Inches and the islands to Burgess. A dispute arose between Burgess and Inches over ownership of the 70 acres. Burgess contended that the jutting piece of land was an island and belonged to him. Inches argued that it was part of the mainland and he was the owner. A court eventually resolved this dispute in favor of Inches. In doing so, it considered the testimony of fishermen who sometimes traversed the watercourse, aerial photographs, the original government survey (which didn't show the watercourse), a motion picture of a boat navigating the watercourse and the testimony of surveyors. *Burgess v. Pine Island Corp., 215 So.2d 755 (Fla. 1968).*

The description in the deed in this transaction was general, not specific. Almost all courts will try to sustain a deed even though it contains a general description. They are reluctant to declare the instrument void. Judges reason that the parties must have intended to do something or they would not have been involved in the transaction.

One type of general description that courts have consistently upheld conveys all the grantor's land in a particular area. This is sometimes referred to as a "Mother Hubbard" description. Similarly, if a deed describes a particular plot in fairly general terms, but provides a clue to the land's location in a specific city, county or state, the description is effective if evidence indicates the grantor owned no other land in the designated area.

Although courts are liberal in accepting outside evidence, a deed conveying land will be invalid if the description does not identify the specific parcel or at least provide a key to identifying property to the exclusion of all other sites.

• CASE BRIEF •

The City of Atlanta owned land at the foot of Climax Place. Berchenko owned all the land on the north of Climax Place, a frontage of 1,035 feet. Berchenko also owned a tract on the south, which had a frontage of 195 feet. Climax Place was only 22 feet wide, and the city wished to widen it to 50 feet.

In order to accomplish this, the city obtained from Berchenko a deed to "a 28-foot strip along Climax Place." The city then demanded that Berchenko remove a building that encroached on the north of Climax Place. Berchenko refused, claiming the deed invalid because the description was uncertain and insufficient. Both the lower court and the appellate court agreed. The appellate court stated, "no surveyor, however expert, could take the description contained in the instrument just mentioned, and by the aid of any extrinsic evidence, locate the precise body of land." *See City of Atlanta v. Atlanta Trailer City Trailer Park, 213 Ga. 825, 102 S.E.2d 23 (1958).*

REFERENCE TO OTHER DOCUMENTS

As illustrated by the *Burgess v. Pine Island Corp.* case, different kinds of outside evidence may be used to clarify a description. The most effective clarification is provided by a deed's reference to a survey, map, plat or some similar document that correctly describes the land. The details of this extrinsic document become part of the description and can be used to resolve ambiguities or to locate the parcel. In fact, many deeds describe a parcel of land by reference to a master survey, plat or map. This is a common practice that saves time and provides clarity.

Because of the complicated nature of boundaries and the economic importance of real property, the art of surveying has been in use since antiquity to establish and verify boundaries. The Babylonians, Assyrians, Egyptians, Hebrews, Greeks and Romans perfected the art to a high degree. In the Americas the sedentary Indian peoples such as the Incas and Mayans were remarkable surveyors.

In the sophisticated technological world of today, surveys by trained professionals are an integral part of the real estate business. Although the basis of a real estate conveyance is what the parties agree as to the boundaries, agreement is seldom reached without the help of a survey. An agreed-upon boundary cannot be changed by a survey, but a survey is generally used to establish new boundaries. Only in rare instances would a tract be subdivided without a survey or would unplatted land be sold without being mapped. In these situations the surveyor's work is the basis for any description in a deed or other real estate instrument. Where title to land has been established either through an informal survey by the parties or by a prior professional survey, the surveyor's sole function is to help determine the boundaries of the grant. In litigation involving this type of boundary problem, the surveyor often testifies as an expert witness, giving an expert's opinion as to what the grantor's intention was. The surveyor's work is a critical factor in each of the three types of descriptions discussed in this chapter and commonly used in the United States: metes and bounds, the rectangular survey, and plats and maps.

Metes and Bounds

A method of describing land by specifying the exterior boundaries of the property using compass directions, monuments or landmarks where directions change and linear measurement of distances between these points.

As the eastern United States was settled and developed, probably the most common method of describing land was to name the parcel. For example, the property would be described as the Jacktown plantation or the Ebenezer Smith farm. Usually boundaries were indicated by naming the owners of adjoining property or by natural landmarks called *monuments.* An early 19th century deed in a trespass case described the property as follows:

> A certain tract or parcel of land, including the mill-seat and mill known as the "Jethro R. Franklin Mill," the said tract situated in the county of Gates, embracing as far as the highwater mark, and bounded as follows: on the north by the lands of Richard E. Parker, Reddick Brinkley, and others, on the east by the lands of Harrison Brinkley and others, south by the desert road, west by the lands of Josiah H. Reddick and others . . .

A description based primarily on *adjoiners* (names of owners of contiguous property, a road or something similar) and monuments is still used if the costs of a survey are out of proportion to the amount of money involved. Descriptions of this nature may cause problems if some impermanent monuments are selected.

Metes-and-bounds descriptions provide a more sophisticated method of describing real property. A metes-and-bounds description is based upon a survey that commences at a beginning point on the boundary of the tract and follows compass directions, called *courses*, and distances around the area to the point of beginning. Monuments are placed at the corners or at points where directions change. Monuments are visible objects, sometimes natural but often artificial. They can be posts, iron pipes, piles of stone, trees, streams or similar objects. By following the courses and distances, a person should be able to walk the boundaries of the property.

A typical metes-and-bounds description follows:

> Beginning at an iron pipe marked A and thence running South 8 degrees 15 minutes East 75 feet to a pipe marked B thence North 78 degrees 27 minutes East 34-3/10 feet to a pipe marked C thence North 11 degrees 28 minutes West 74-9/10 feet to a pipe marked D thence South 78 degrees 27 minutes West 30-2/10 feet to the place of beginning containing 2410.7 square feet, more or less.

In reading a metes-and-bounds description, one always says "north" or "south" first and then announces the number of degrees east or west of that north or south line. The number of degrees east or west of the north or south line cannot exceed 90. Thus, to say "North 95 degrees East" as a designation for Line A in Figure 11.1 is incorrect. The correct reading is South 85 degrees East."

Metes-and-bounds descriptions based upon a survey provide a very accurate method of designating the physical dimensions of a particular tract of land. When the land itself is supplied with permanent markers at each corner or angle, the parcel can be readily located for a long period of time. This method of describing land continues to be used extensively in the eastern United States. Metes-and-bounds descriptions are also used extensively in other areas of the country in conjunction with the rectangular survey to designate small parcels.

Call

A term used to refer to the different monuments, courses and distances that make up a metes-and-bounds description.

Metes-and-bounds descriptions are not always based upon a survey. Sometimes natural monuments used as calls are destroyed; in other instances, conflicting calls are the result of human error. To solve problems resulting from conflicting calls, courts have established a general order of preference to be given to calls when the intention of the parties is not clear. Natural monuments are preferred because they are considered more reliable than courses and distances. The general order of preference is as follows: (1) natural monuments, (2) artificial monuments, (3) courses, (4) distances and (5) quantity of acreage. Adjoining landowners (adjoiners) are also important elements in some descriptions and receive a high degree of priority. Unless the adjoiner is clearly a mistake, it ranks with monuments, prevailing over courses, distances and quantity of acreage.

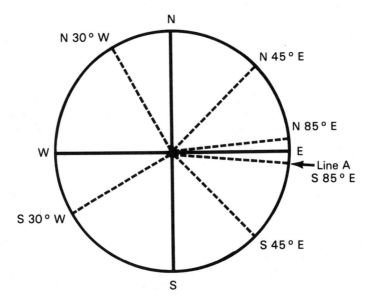

Figure 11.1

• CASE BRIEF •

Jones and Morrison purchased contiguous parcels from a common grantor. The deed to Jones described the east line of his property as being from the center of Edison Street south to a bois d'arc tree, a distance of 79 feet. Morrison's deed described his property's east line as being from the center of College Street north to a bois d'arc tree, a distance of 210 feet. Actually, the distance from the center of Edison Street to the tree was 86 feet; from the center of College Street the distance was 207 feet, as shown on the map.

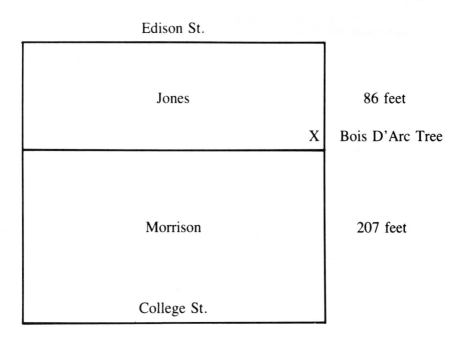

Morrison constructed a building on the property that encroached upon what Jones believed was his land. Jones sued to require the removal of the encroaching portion of the building. In finding for Jones, the court stated, "[t]his makes the case a classic example. . . for application of the rule that courses and distances must yield to natural monuments. . . ." *Morrison v. Jones, 58 Tenn. App. 333, 430 S.W.2d 668 (1968).*

Rectangular Survey System

System of land description that applies to most of the land in the United States.

After the Revolutionary War, the United States acquired a vast area of land west of Pennsylvania and north of the Ohio River. This area, known as the Northwest Territory, was acquired when states ceded their claims to the United States as a means of paying their war debts. Faced with pressures from land speculators and settlers as well as the need for revenue, Congress in 1785 passed legislation to prepare these lands for disposal.

An important element of this legislation was the establishment of a *rectangular survey system*. Although the government survey was criticized and attacked by the private land companies, it eventually became the foundation upon which vast areas of the West were surveyed and sold.

With the exception of Texas, land descriptions in all states west of the Mississippi, the five states formed from the Northwest Territory and most of Alabama, Florida and Mississippi are based upon this massive survey. Eventually, the survey covered more than two million square miles in the continental United States. It has been extended to Alaska, where hundreds of thousands of square miles remain unsurveyed. Although modified by legislation from time to time over the 200 years that the system has been used, the fundamentals of the rectangular survey have remained fairly consistent.

Initially, a large area is selected for survey and a starting point is chosen. This initial point is chosen by astronomical observation. A line called a *baseline* is run east and west through this point. A perpendicular line also runs north and south through the initial point. This is called the *principal meridian*. The survey for the entire district is based upon these two lines. Over the long history of the government survey, 32 baselines and 35 principal meridians have been established.

Principal meridians and baselines are designated in various ways. At first they were numbered, but later they were given names. The first principal meridian is the western boundary of Ohio. The 41st parallel is its accompanying baseline. All land descriptions in a particular area surveyed with reference to a principal meridian will refer to it. The basic unit of the survey is the *township*.

Township

An area of land approximately six miles square,

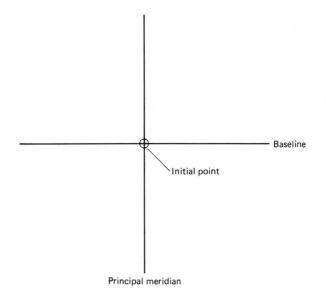

Figure 11.2: Starting point for a survey

containing as nearly as possible 23,040 acres and divided into 36 sections, each of one square mile.

Legislation guiding the surveyors required a township to be a square as nearly as possible six miles on a side. Because the lines that run parallel to the principal meridian converge toward the north, townships in the north would be smaller than the required 36 square miles. To remedy this, correction lines are run parallel to a baseline at 24-mile intervals north and south. These lines are called *standard parallels* or *correction lines*. Lines called *guide meridians* are then surveyed east and west at 24-mile intervals with a standard parallel as a base. Although the townships in the North are slightly smaller than those in the South, the constant correction kept the difference at a minimum. Some early surveys established correction lines at intervals much greater than 24 miles, leading to substantial discrepancy in township size. Continuous establishment of guide meridians and standard parallels reduced the compounding effect of surveying errors.

Each guide meridian and standard parallel, as shown in Figure 11.3, is designated by numerical order and compass direction from the appropriate principal meridian and baseline. The intersections of

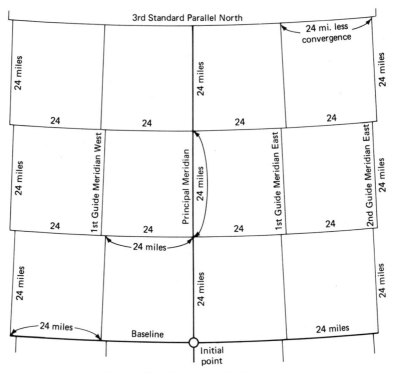

Division of Land into Tracts 24 miles square.

Figure 11.3: U.S. public land—rectangular system of subdividing

guide meridians and standard parallels create square blocks or tracts 24 miles on each side. Townships are created by dividing these 24-mile tracts at six-mile intervals. The result is 16 township units approximately six miles square in each tract.

Although these 24-mile-square blocks are not a factor in describing real estate, townships are an integral part of a land description. Over an entire area surveyed, tiers of townships are numbered north and south from the baseline. They are also numbered consecutively east and west from the principal meridian. The east-west tiers are called *ranges*. Each township as a result has two numbers and two directions. These numbers and directions thus provide a specific designation for each. Since all townships and ranges are numbered in reference to a particular principal meridian and baseline, no two have the same designation.

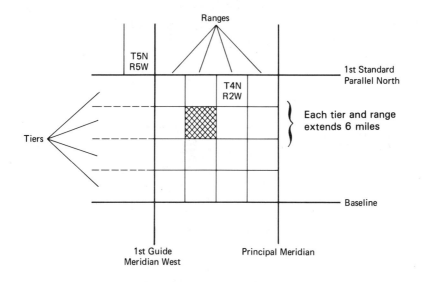

Figure 11.4: Township designations

The shaded unit in Figure 11.4 is 3 north; Range 3 west of a principal meridian. This would be indicated as T3N; R3W. Townships are not only important elements in many land descriptions, they also are often important political subdivisions.

Section

An area of land approximately one mile square, containing as nearly as possible 640 acres.

Each township of approximately six miles square is further divided into sections. A township thus contains 36 sections. The sections in a township are numbered consecutively, beginning in the northeast corner with the number 1. Six sections are numbered westerly along the far north of the township. Section 7, just south of section 6, commences a row numbered in an easterly direction (see Figure 11.5). This pattern of alternating west-east numbering is followed, with section 36 being the southeast unit in the township.

Although a different numbering system was used in some of the early surveys, most of the land surveyed has sections designated in this manner. As a result, the number of the section is also a key element in describing a particular parcel of land.

6	5	4	3	2	1
7	8	9	10	11	12
18	17	16	15	14	13
19	20	21	22	23	24
30	29	28	27	26	25
31	32	33	34	35	36

6 miles   } Township

Section {

← 6 miles →

Figure 11.5: U.S. public land survey—typical method of numbering sections.

Commercial realities of land disposal often resulted in a need to divide each section further. Half sections, quarter sections, and even smaller units were needed. This division is readily accomplished by surveying and designating smaller units by their geographic location within the section.

A half section may be described as the north one-half of section 15 and a quarter section as the northwest one-quarter of section 15. As each section consisted of 640 acres, the number of acres in each of these smaller units is easy to determine. A half section is 320 acres; a quarter section is 160. Figure 11.6 indicates additional divisions of a section that are commonly used. As each township has a numerical designation in relation to a particular baseline and each section a number, any of these smaller plots is precisely located within the square mile of which it is a part.

Governmental surveys were not made under ideal conditions. Errors often resulted because of weather, harsh terrain, hostile Indians, primitive equipment and plain ineptitude. The prevailing legal rule, however, has consistently been that, once land has been conveyed on the basis of a government survey, the conveyance will not be disturbed even if error is found in the survey.

• CASE BRIEF •

Ralph Johnson obtained title to land extending from the east shore of Water Pen Lake. His title was based upon an official government survey and map. A private survey of the lake and surrounding terrain showed a second peninsula just south of the first. The peninsula and adjacent land were sold to Wilbur Bishop.

Later it became clear that the official survey was erroneous. There was no peninsula as indicated on the official plat. The only peninsula was that indicated by the private survey. Both Bishop and Johnson claimed this area.

In litigation to quiet title, the court determined that Johnson had title. Upon appeal the appellate court agreed. The court stated, "The mere fact that a subsequent private survey shows an error by the United States Deputy Surveyor . . . is immaterial . . . It is well settled that the description of land and plats from field notes of an official survey filed in the General Land Office are conclusive . . ." *Bishop v. Johnson, 100 So.2d 817 (Fla. 1958).*

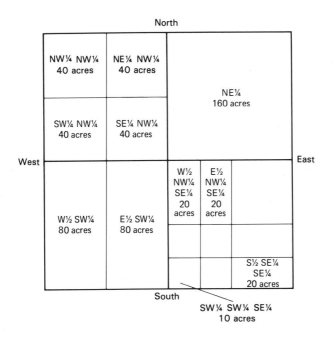

Figure 11.6: Divisions of a section

In most cases a survey does not create boundaries. Boundaries are created by the agreement of parties. The official government survey of the public land does, however, create boundaries. An original government survey, whether correct or erroneous, controls the boundaries of a section and parcels of land surveyed and platted from it. Courts feel that the parties who purchase property based upon a plat from an official survey have a right to rely on it. If the survey is confirmed by the proper officials of the Department of the Interior, attack in the courts is no longer permitted when the property is sold.

Plat

A map showing items such as natural and artificial monuments, lots, blocks and streets in a town or subdivision; generally drawn from a survey.

A third method of describing land is by reference to a recorded plat or map. This method is used frequently in metropolitan areas. Usually it is used in conjunction with the rectangular survey or a metes-and-bounds description of a larger tract that is being divided. The property to be divided is surveyed and laid out in lots that are numbered in sequence. These lots are platted and when sold are described by their designated numbers. A description of this kind might read as follows:

> All of lot 8 in block 41 in Taylors Astoria, an addition within the corporate limits of the City of Astoria, Clatsop County, State of Oregon, as said addition was laid out and recorded by the Peninsular Land & Trust Company.

Although the deed does not contain the description of the entire survey, the United States Supreme Court in an early case supported this system. The court stated:

> . . . when lands are granted according to an official plat of the survey. . ., the plat itself along with all its notes, lines, descriptions, and landmarks becomes as much a part of the grant or deed. . . as if such descriptive features were written out upon the face of the deed. . . *Cragin v. Powell, 128 U.S. 696 (1888).*

The use of maps and plats of surveys has become an important means of describing land in the United States. Plats are readily available because almost all states and many localities require a developer, when subdividing property, to have the property surveyed and a plat of it made by a competent surveyor. A typical plat is shown in Figure 11.7.

Although requirements vary, the plat generally shows the proposed streets, blocks and lots of the subdivision. The plat will also show such items as easements, rights of way and topographical de-

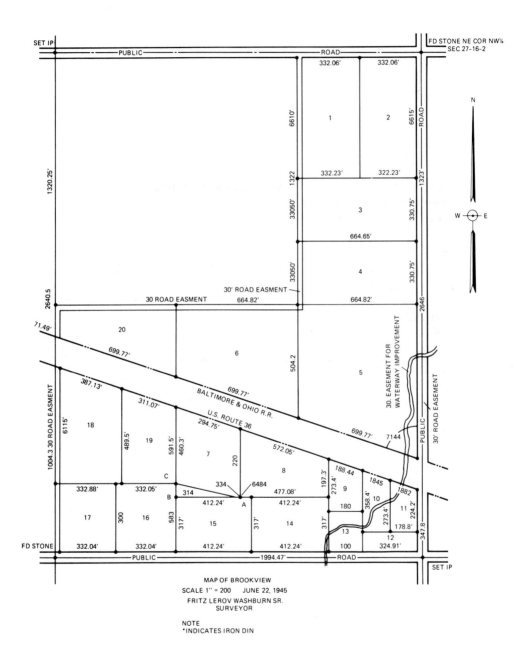

Figure 11.7: Plat adapted from *Davis v. DeVore, 16 Ill. App. 334, 306 N.E.2d 72 (1974)*

tails, such as elevations, as well as other physical features. School sites and recreational areas are indicated on plats for larger developments. Blocks and lots are designated in some manner, usually by number but sometimes by letter.

In most areas subdivision plats must be approved by some governmental body before land is sold. Usually this is a local planning commission or a designated official such as the county engineer. The approved plat is then recorded in a *plat book* as part of the public land records. The property in the subdivision is thus accurately described by reference to this record. In addition, recording of the plat serves to dedicate to public use land indicated on the plat as streets, parks and school and church sites.

In preparing land for a subdivision, the surveyor must carefully mark with permanent monuments physical boundaries of the parcels involved. The survey actually fixes the boundaries of the property, and these are reflected in the plat. If the plat and the boundaries fixed by the survey differ, the boundary as established by the physical monuments prevails.

BOUNDARY DISPUTES

Courts have adopted several rules in efforts to solve boundary disputes equitably. A fundamental principle is that the intention of the parties establishing a boundary should prevail. Although the plain meaning of the words used in a description is the best indication of intention, conflicting and ambiguous designations of boundaries must often be resolved by other rules. An example is the doctrine of "agreed boundaries."

For the doctrine of "agreed boundaries" to apply, the owners of adjoining property must be uncertain as to the true boundary. They must then agree as to what the true boundary is. This agreement does not have to be in writing. A minority of states require that there be some visible evidence of the boundary to be established. In any case, the boundary agreed upon must be definite and certain. In a few states the parties must continue to agree for a period equal to that required in cases of adverse possession. In most states acquiescence for a shorter period is sufficient; however, the period varies greatly from state to state.

• CASE BRIEF •

Rouse owned a quarter section of land. In 1932 he sold the west portion to Cooper. In 1944 Rouse sold the east portion to Huggans. At the time of the sale to Cooper, the parties did not determine the exact boundary between the two properties but described the property using an old fence as one line. When

Rouse conveyed the east parcel to Huggans in 1944, the description in the deed referred to the west boundary of the Huggans tract as the Cooper fence.

Huggans used the land up to the fence from 1944 until 1978. In 1978 the Cooper property was acquired by Weer. A survey at that time established the true property line 60 feet east of the fence. Upon acquiring the information, Weer attempted to remove the Cooper fence and Huggans petitioned the court for a temporary restraining order.

Huggans claimed that he had title to the 60-foot strip up to the fence, based upon adverse possession and the doctrine of agreed boundaries. This claim was rejected by the court because he had not met statutory requirements for adverse possession and proof of an agreed boundary was not clear and convincing. *Huggans v. Weer, 615 P.2d 922 (Mont. 1980).*

Intention in many situations is determined by what courts presume or infer the parties probably desire to occur. An example is found in the common solution to the substantial litigation involving title to a public thoroughfare. When land abutting on a public road or street is conveyed, the grantee takes title to the centerline unless the description specifically excludes this area. This rule applies even if the description designates the tract as "bounded by" or "bordering on" the particular public way. The reason is that courts consider it unlikely that a grantor conveying land on a public way had any intention of retaining title to the area dedicated to public use. Since the grantor has conveyed the abutting property, the small strip of land is of little value to him or her. It is, however, important to the grantee, who now owns the adjacent land. On the other hand, if the conveyance specifically reserves the narrow strip for the grantor, the intention of the parties will be honored.

In some boundary disputes, the intention of the parties is equated to that of the original surveyor. As a result, the actions and field notes of the original surveyor are of critical importance. If the calls indicated by the survey can be resolved logically, they will prevail. Sometimes this is not possible, and conflicts result. These conflicts are resolved by preferring those calls that minimize human error, as seen in the earlier example of *Jones v. Morrison.* Whatever method the courts use, the most important evidence is that which clearly indicates the intention of the parties.

Sales Personnel and Property Description

Property description is an important element of almost every real estate transaction. Although it is ordinarily the concern of the real estate lawyer, all real estate sales personnel should be aware of its important legal aspects. If problems involving descriptions are discovered early in the proceedings, before the deed or other document involving the property is prepared, time can be saved and trouble averted.

Sometimes real estate personnel obtain information about boundary problems when listing property or drawing up a contract. These should be carefully noted and an effort made to have the owner resolve the problems before entering serious negotiations with prospective buyers. Because boundary disputes may indicate description problems, a sales associate who becomes aware of a boundary controversy when negotiating a sale of real estate should alert the seller's attorney so that the description can be verified.

SUMMARY

In order to be enforceable, a real estate instrument must contain a legal description of the property. The description must be complete enough to locate and identify the premises. The physical boundaries are integral to this description because they locate the property on the earth's surface. The boundaries in a legal description must be complete; they must enclose the parcel. In cases where boundary disputes exist, courts hear testimony of the parties to the dispute, surveyors, neighbors and others to determine what property the parties intended to convey.

The work of a surveyor in measuring the actual parcel and translating it to a map is an integral part of real estate business. The surveyor's work is critical to the three types of land description commonly used in the United States today: metes and bounds, the rectangular survey, and plats and maps.

The first type, metes and bounds, specifies the exterior boundaries of the property, based on a survey that commences at a beginning point on the boundary and follows courses (compass directions) and distances around the area. By following the description and observing any call or monument (a tree, stream or post, for example) noted in the wording, a person should be able to walk the boundaries of the property. Over time monuments may be destroyed or obliterated. In the case of conflict courts have established an order of priority, with natural monuments taking precedence over artificial ones as well as over courses and distances. Established boundaries of other owners (adjoiners) rank along with natural monuments.

The rectangular survey is a system established by the government over 200 years ago to map a large portion of U.S. land. Based on a grid of baselines (east-west) and principal meridians (north-south), the survey for each district refers to these lines, which are either named or numbered. The basic unit, the township, is six miles square. This area is divided into 36 sections. A section is a square one mile on each side. The sections in a township are numbered consecutively. These parcels can be further divided by survey for purchase as individual lots.

Maps that are platted from official surveys are the third method of land description. They are used frequently in metropolitan areas. In most areas of the country subdivision plats, prepared by the developer from official maps and by the developer's own surveyors, mut be approved by an official agency, usually the county engineer. When approved, the map is recorded in the plat book as part of the public record.

Boundary disputes in the past have led the courts to adopt several rules or guidelines for their solution. Principal among them is that the intention of the parties should prevail. To reduce the incidence of disputes, however, real estate professionals should be aware of the need for a clearly written description as part of the legal conveyance.

REVIEW AND DISCUSSION QUESTIONS

1. Sketch an imaginary principal meridian and baseline and indicate the location of (a) Township 3 North, Range 3 East and (b) Township 1 South, Range 3 West.
2. Define the following terms and indicate their relationship to the rectangular survey system: (a) principal meridian, (b) baseline, (c) township and (d) section.
3. Using the rectangular survey system, indicate the proper designation for each of the shaded portions in the drawing below.

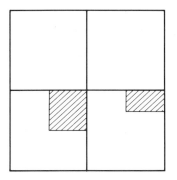

4. Locate the following tracts of land in a section and indicate the acreage of each.
(a) E1/2 SE1/4
(b) NW1/4 NW1/4 NW1/4

CASE PROBLEMS

1. A contract for sale of real estate described the property as follows:

Property of Greene D. Spillman located at Spillman, La., in Sections 48 and 49, T-1-S., R-2-W, West Feliciana Parish, La., and improvements. Bounded on the North by lands of Merrick on the South by lands of Thoms and heirs of C. H. Bickham on the East by Hwy. 967 and on the West by Mills Creek. The grounds measuring about 275 acres as per title for the sum of Sixty Thousand, Five Hundred Dollars.

Enquist signed a contract to purchase this property. A survey indicated that the farm contained only 223.64 acres. When Engquist refused to perform, the owner sued for breach of contract. (a) Would the owner be successful? Support your answer. (b) What is the meaning of the terms T-1-S, R-2-W? *Adams v. Spillman*, 290 So.2d 726 (La. 1974).

2. Sketch the following parcel.

Beginning at a point 447.18 feet East of the N.W. corner of SE1/4 SE1/4, said Sec. 21; thence North 88 degrees 57'30" East 402.00 feet; thence South 987.68 feet; thence North 89 degrees 56'West 401.93 feet; thence North 979.48 feet to the point of beginning. *LeBaron v. Crimson*, 412 P.2d 705 (Ariz. 1966).

12
Control of Land Use by Traditional Methods

The basic tenets of American property law can be traced back to feudal times in England. Between the king and the lowest serf was the great mass of landholders. The landholder was not an owner but had the right to use a parcel of land. In exchange for that right of use, certain duties were owed to the superior on the feudal scale. These duties might include providing military service or a portion of the crops grown on the land. Our system of private property has evolved from this scheme, in which each landholder owed certain obligations in exchange for the right of use, but the legal notion of private property in America took its own peculiar twist.

As in England, the landholder's *rights* gradually expanded into what we refer to as *ownership*. These rights eventually gave the owner almost absolute and unfettered control over his or her grant of land. William Blackstone, the great 18th-century authority on the common law, referred to a person's property right as "that sole and despotic dominion," thereby depicting the extensive freedom that accompanied land ownership. A person's ownership rights were never quite as absolute as Blackstone alleged, but the wide range of rights he connoted became indelibly etched in the minds of landowners in England and America.

The American difference applied not to the "rights" side of the equation but to the "duty" side. Almost from the inception of this country a landowner owed no duty to anyone except to refrain from acts on the property that would significantly interfere with another landowner's use of his or her property. Once the purchase price was paid, the buyer of land owed no additional duty to the seller. Our concept of property has always emphasized the landowner's rights over any duties arising from that ownership.

Though most Americans still cling tenaciously to the idea of absolute ownership rights in land, those rights have eroded sharply in the 20th century. The subdivider of land usually places a significant number of restrictions on use in the deed to the new homeowner. Municipal codes place an array of restraints on an owner's property rights. For instance, zoning laws limit an owner's use of the land. Other statutes or local ordinances require an owner to hook up to a sewer, to desist from playing loud music late at night, to refrain from keeping farm animals and to get a permit in order to build an addition to the house, to name only a few. This chapter will describe some of the traditional private and public restrictions on an owner's use of his or her real property.

PRIVATE RESTRICTIONS ON LAND USE

Many limitations on the use of land are the result of agreements between buyers and sellers. These limitations are often referred to as *private restrictions*. The term *private restrictions* is also used to refer to limitations on land use imposed by the common law.

Restrictive Covenants

Private agreements, usually placed in the deed by the seller when conveying land to the buyer, that restrict future use of that land.

Parties to a real estate transaction are free to enter into any legal agreement that suits their particular situation. An agreement restricting the future use of the land is called a *restrictive covenant.*

A restrictive covenant is said to run with the land if it attaches to the land and is not dependent upon the continued ownership of the parties to the original deed. The buyer's successors in title would be bound by the covenant, and the seller's successors in title would continue to benefit from the covenant.

• CASE BRIEF •

Baum, as the original grantee of a subdivided parcel, covenanted in the deed to accept and pay for a seasonal water supply provided by the original grantor. Eagle Enterprises, the successor to the original grantor, sued Gross, the successor to the grantee Baum, to enforce the restrictive covenant relating to the supplying of water. Eagle Enterprises argues that the covenant attaches, or "runs with the land," thereby binding all subsequent owners to pay for supplying the water. Gross responds that the covenant bound only Baum and did not run with the land.

The court held that a restrictive covenant will run with the land if it meets three conditions: (1) the original parties must intend that it run with the land; (2) there must be privity of estate between the parties; and (3) the covenant must touch and concern the land. Although the court found that this particular covenant was personal and did not "touch and concern" the land, any covenant that meets the threefold test will be held to run with the land. *Eagle Enterprises, Inc. v. Gross, 39 N.Y.2d 505, 349 N.E.2d816 (1976).*

Privity of estate is a phrase used to express the successive relationship of the parties to the land. For example, privity of estate exists between the grantor and grantee of an easement. The term *touch and concern the land* relates to the determination of whether the purported easement is peculiarly tied to the land itself or is rather a personal agreement between the parties involved and only incidentally concerns the land. The distinction between a personal covenant and one that touches and concerns the land is not always clear.

The restrictive covenant may carry a time limitation; for example, "This covenant shall run with the land and be in effect for 20 years from the date of the conveyance." Usually, however, no termination period is stipulated, and the covenant lasts indefinitely.

Over the years restrictive covenants have not been favored by the courts because they constituted an encroachment on the free transferability of land. Courts have never been enthusiastic about permitting land to be tied up in restrictions on use; when any doubt exists as to the meaning of the covenant, courts usually find against the party placing the restriction in the deed. Despite the clear intention of the parties in the *Eagle Enterprises* case described above, note the reluctance of the New York court to bind future parties where grounds existed for relieving the land from the restriction.

The use of restrictive covenants and the attitude of courts toward them may be shifting. Today a substantial amount of residential development takes place in the form of subdivisions. The developer usually places a broad range of restrictive covenants in the plat plan or the individual deeds of the homebuyers or both. The purpose of the restrictions is to protect other landowners in the subdivision from losing some of their property value because of the unorthodox activity of a neighbor in the subdivision. For example, a restrictive covenant might prohibit the landowners from raising pigs or other farm animals. To avoid conflicts caused by questionable land use during development or immediately after the subdivision is completed, developers are inclined to include restrictive covenants against everything not narrowly confined to normal single-family use. The developer thereby makes every subdivision owner the third-party beneficiary of the restrictive covenants in the deeds of the other homeowners in the tract. The covenants generally are part of the deed or are filed with the general plat plan for the development and then recorded, thereby giving notice to all parties having an interest in the land in the future. The covenant is now part of the chain of title and runs with the land indefinitely.

Traditionally, the person selling part of his or her land subject to restrictive covenants has the right to enforce the covenant in the courts. Similarly, any owner in the subdivision as the third-party beneficiary of the developer-homeowner contract has enforcement rights in the court. However, a modern practice is for the developer to create a group such as an architectural committee to administer the covenant procedure. The developer and some associates often comprise the committee. The committee is authorized to handle complaints and (sometimes) to permit deviations from the restriction in the covenants. For example, the restrictive covenant may bar all buildings from the land except the house and attached garage, unless approved by the architectural committee. Upon request, the committee may permit the homeowner to build a small toolshed on the property.

One problem may arise from this practice when the developer conveys all the parcels in the tract and does not provide for transfer of membership on the committee to the local subdivision residents, creating a hiatus. Theoretically, any homeowner *can* enforce the covenant. If the courts follow their traditional inclination of disfavoring restrictive covenants, however, enforcement may be impossible. It is arguable that the covenantor intended the *committee* to be the mechanism for enforcement, but the committee is now defunct.

An additional problem is that, when restrictive covenants proliferate, people tend to ignore them. County or local zoning and building codes reduce the need for restrictive covenants by controlling major use changes or construction on residential land.

CASE EXAMPLE

Rachel assembles a four- by six-foot metal shed on her property to store her lawn mower and garden tools. Although the building is prohibited (without permission) by the restrictive covenant in Rachel's deed, it is common in her subdivision to own these sheds; in other words, "everyone" ignores the covenant. The courts may not enforce the restrictive covenant upon request by a neighbor because the homeowners have acquiesced in this noncompliance.

However, there are instances where Rachel will clearly be subject to the restrictive covenant and probably to a building code. When Rachel decides to build a second house on her lot, the covenant is violated and a building permit is required. The building inspector, in order to offer some measure of protection to other residents, oversees her plans. The building code, rather than the restrictive covenant, will probably become the enforcement mechanism.

Nevertheless, the restrictive covenants still provide a mechanism for an unhappy neighbor to complain, even concerning minor alterations like the small metal storage shed.

Restrictive covenants can be terminated in several ways. *All* the concerned parties may agree in writing to the termination. This approach may prove infeasible where the number of parties to the covenant is large. The covenants can also be terminated through condemnation of the land by a public agency having the power of eminent domain.

A common method of extinguishing these covenants is through nonuse or misuse. The character of the neighborhood may change, making continuation of the restrictions meaningless.

• CASE BRIEF •

De Marco brought an action against adjacent property owners to have restrictive covenants limiting use to residential purposes declared void. Due to the construction of the Edsel Ford Freeway, replacing a two-lane country road, all surrounding land on the parties' street was in commercial use.

The court voided the restrictive covenant because the four-lane freeway had completely changed the character of the area. *DeMarco v. Pallazzo, 47 Mich. App. 444, 209 N.W.2d 540 (1973).*

The longer the covenants are ignored or violated and the greater the number of people who participate in the violations, the less likely the court is to enforce the proscriptions in the deeds.

Easement

A nonpossessory interest in real property; the right to use another's real estate for a limited purpose.

Easements were discussed in detail in Chapter 6, and that discussion will not be repeated here. Easements run with the land and are a method of encumbering free use of the parcel by a subsequent taker.

CASE EXAMPLE

In a deed to Clayton, Hurd retains a "right of ingress and egress for driveway purposes" for the benefit of the land she retains. This easement will prohibit Clayton from interfering with Hurd's driveway rights and thus from making full use of her property.

Restrictions Created by Common Law

The restrictions discussed above are the result of specific covenants inserted in the deed by the grantor. In addition to these, there are restrictions created by the common law itself. Such common law restrictions are placed on the use of one's land and imposed by the law for the benefit of surrounding landholders.

Nuisance

An unreasonable interference by one party with another's use or enjoyment of his or her land.

The notion of nuisance is an ancient creation to protect landowners from unfettered and wrongful use of land by a neighbor. It does not require a physical invasion of the complainant's land, as does trespass. Such things as noise, dust, vibration and odors may constitute a nuisance. A party who is victimized by a nuisance will be able to get compensatory damages and may be able to enjoin the nuisance. Most states, however, will grant an injunction only after balancing the equities between the parties and determining that the benefit of the injunction will outweigh the ensuing detriment to the perpetrator of the nuisance. As a result of this balancing process, injunctions are not readily available to small landowners complaining about a nuisance created by a large industrial or commercial facility. For instance, in a case entitled *Boomer v. Atlantic Cement Co.*, 26 N.Y.2d 219, 257 N.E.2d 870 (1970), New York's highest court was unwilling to enjoin the operation of the $45 million plant, though admitting that there was a substantial nuisance to several nearby landowners. Prior to this case, New York had been more liberal than most states in granting injunctions in nuisance cases.

Trespass

A wrongful, physical invasion of the property of another.

This common law remedy may be available to the landowner to put a stop to physical encroachments, whether they occur on the land's surface, in the air above or on the ground beneath.

• CASE BRIEF •

Pehrson brought an action in trespass for money damages against his neighbor, Saderup, for cutting down lilac bushes on

Pehrson's land. The court decided that Saderup had committed a trespass by cutting the lilac bushes and awarded Pehrson money damages for the trespass based upon the difference between the fair market value before the cutting of the lilacs and that value afterward. *Pehrson v. Saderup, 28 Utah 2d 77, 498 P.2d 648 (1972).*

Actual damages need not be shown in order to recover for a trespass to land, but as a practical matter the landowner is likely to get only nominal damages where he or she does not actually show loss.

PUBLIC RESTRICTIONS ON LAND USE

Compared to the recognition by law of private restrictions on land use, public restraints are of recent vintage. Comprehensive control of land use is entirely a product of the 20th century. Shortly after the turn of the century, zoning codes began to appear. After a mixed judicial reception among the lower courts, the United States Supreme Court approved the notion of zoning in 1926. The approval was based legally upon the concept of nuisance. Zoning was merely a technique for ensuring that landowners did not unreasonably interfere with each other's use.

Gradually, the emphasis has shifted away from nuisance law and toward a basis in the states' police power. Under the police power the government can regulate land use for the purpose of protecting the public health, safety and welfare. Basing land use regulations on the broad back of the police power opened the door for creative regulation for a multitude of purposes and for the use of numerous control techniques. It ushered in the decade of the 1970s, which has been widely referred to as the era of the "quiet revolution of land use." This term is indicative of the proliferation of land use controls and of the changing character of those controls. Traditional zoning remains a major technique for controlling land use, but it is no longer the only approach. A full range of nontraditional land use controls in addition to zoning will be discussed in the next chapter.

Introduction to the "Taking" Issue

The state and federal governments, along with their designees, have the power of eminent domain, as explained in Chapter 8. The federal and state constitutions state that governments may condemn land for a public use provided they give just compensation for it. In contrast, these governments also have the power to *regulate* land for a public purpose under the police power, and when regulating they need not pay the restricted landowner. Traditional zoning is an example of a sanctioned form of police power regulation. However, there is a point at which a regulation may go too far and will be treated by a reviewing court as if it were an exercise of the power of eminent domain, or a *taking*. Since this taking was accomplished without the owner's being paid just compensation, the regulation will be held to be unconstitutional. In other words, if the government wants to regulate in that fashion, it must use its powers of condemnation and pay the owner for the land.

• CASE BRIEF •

The City of Palo Alto, California, passed a zoning ordinance that zoned Eldridge's land as "permanent open space and conservation lands." This zone required a minimum of ten acres per residence and a system of trails with public access to the "foothill" lands.

The California appellate court held that an otherwise valid zoning ordinance may act in such an oppressive fashion on a landowner that it will constitute a taking without due process. *Eldridge v. City of Palo Alto, 57 Cal. App. 3d 613, 129 Cal. Rptr. 575 (1976).*

It is often said by courts that the rules for ascertaining when a taking occurs are few. Nevertheless, one rule that seems pervasive is that the regulation cannot deny owners "all reasonable use" of their land. The certainty of the rule is shaken when one ponders the word *reasonable*. What is reasonable to one person is not to another, and what is reasonable today may not be ten years from now. Use of the word *reasonable* is indicative of the shifting nature of the entire area.

For example, cases that came to the courts ten to 15 years ago attacked regulations that restricted owners of wetlands to uses that were consistent with maintaining the lands as wetlands. At that time these cases were uniformly declared to deny "all reasonable use" to the landowner. More recent cases, though not uniform, have shown a different philosophy: that one ought not to expect to use wetlands for other than wetland purposes. Different in character from upland areas, wetlands are highly valuable resources. The trend is toward declaring these regulations valid. In short, confining the landowner solely to wetland uses no longer deprives him or her of "all reasonable use."

It should be noted that, as the power of the legislature to restrict land use is broadened by its own action and by judicial approval, we move farther from Blackstone's concept of an owner having absolute dominion over his or her land. It can be said with some confidence that because of the increasing concentration of people in some areas of the country and the resultant shorter supply of available land, the support for restrictions on the use of private land has not yet reached its full force. Public regulation will continue to whittle away at the landowner's dominion. Nevertheless, the taking versus regulation issue continues to be a focal point for parties judicially attacking variations of traditional zoning or new land use control techniques.

Zoning

The regulation by the public, usually a municipality, of structures and uses of land within designated zones.

In its simplest form traditional zoning divides the municipality into districts for residential, commercial and industrial uses. Within each of these districts limitations are placed on the size and height of buildings, the siting of the buildings on the parcel, the density of development in the area, the minimum size of the parcel and perhaps the type of structure permitted on the site. The purchaser of a parcel of land must be aware not only of the restrictions revealed by a title search but also of the limitations placed upon the land by the zoning code.

The power to zone is expressly given to each locality (municipality or county) by the state through *enabling legislation*, by which that state authorizes the locality to regulate in the area of land use control. That legislation requires that the zoning code adopted by the locality be consistent with a plan for development. The zoning districts are to be placed on a map pursuant to that plan, for the purpose of maintaining property values, matching designated use to the character of the land (low-density development in unsewered areas with relatively impermeable soil, for example) and promoting the environmental, cultural and economic welfare of the area in any other way.

The courts have been lenient in approving zoning codes when the question pertains to the existence of a plan. They have not required a truly comprehensive plan in the modern sense. Often a zoning code and map drawn up by a qualified firm and adopted by the town has met with judicial approval, even when thorough review of *how* to optimize local development or nondevelopment is lacking. One reason for this judicial leniency has been that sparsely populated localities cannot reasonably afford to develop a comprehensive plan. Thus, the economic ability of the locality to generate a more comprehensive plan becomes relevant. The courts are not explicit on this point, but this economic constraint seems to underlie many decisions.

The three basic zoning classifications of residential, commercial and industrial have tended to proliferate. It is not uncommon now for localities to have 15 to 20 or more zones. The use permitted within a zone is often more narrowly confined, with separate zones for single-family houses on one acre, single-family houses on one-half acre, condominiums, garden-type apartments, double houses and so on. Separate zones are designated for shopping centers, office buildings, personal service shops (beauty parlors) and gas stations. For industry, the developer has to select the correct zone from among heavy manufacturing, light manufacturing, warehousing and the like. With this multitude of zones the locality is able to exercise tighter control over the location of development.

One intrinsic problem with zoning that is magnified by the multiplication of zones is inflexibility. Theoretically, the municipality periodically studies the needs of the locality and develops a zoning code or makes amendments to the existing codes based upon those needs. Those needs may change before the municipality undertakes to assess them, so that zones may be outdated and discourage more appropriate development.

In some areas of the country where condominiums came into vogue, there were no appropriate zones to accommodate them, and their development was therefore hindered. Other localities acted promptly to create special districts for condominiums, only to find them a passing fad and economically infeasible for the area. The result was that districts zoned for condominiums were then classified inappropriately.

A major advantage of this inflexibility is that it tends to make land values more stable. Potential uses of the land are known, and within general limits the market value of the land is known. The apparent inflexibility of traditional zoning does not tell the entire story. There are several ways in which uses are permitted to exist despite their inconsistency with the zoning code restrictions.

Nonconforming Use

A legal use that was established prior to zoning or prior to the present zoning classification and is permitted to continue despite its nonconformance with the zoning code.

Most zoning codes are superimposed on partially developed localities. There is no guarantee that all development prior to zoning took place on optimal sites, as seen by the present drafters of the zoning code. These nonconforming uses present a problem. The owners cannot be ordered to discontinue their use immediately unless they are paid full value for their land. To do otherwise would constitute an unconstitutional taking of their land. The traditional solution was to permit the nonconforming use to continue and hope that it would eventually disappear.

The law regarding nonconforming uses has not left that disappearance purely to chance, however. The nonconforming user cannot enlarge that use. Whether the use has been enlarged will be a question for the fact finder (jury or judge). Similarly, a landowner who discontinues the nonconforming use will not be able to resume it later.

• CASE BRIEF •

A prior owner maintained a trailer on his property as a nonconforming use. The trailer was abandoned for five years. The mortgagee on the trailer and property foreclosed due to nonpayment and forced a sale. The purchaser was Lawlor, who applied for a permit to continue to use the trailer on the property.

The Town of Salem denied the permit, and its decision was upheld by the court because the nonuse for five years constituted an abandonment of the nonconforming use. Without the nonconforming status the town was free to insist on conformity with the zoning ordinance and to deny the permit. *Lawlor v. Town of Salem, 116 N.H. 61, 352 A.2d 721 (1976).*

The nonconforming use is said to run with the land and not with the individual owner. The nonconforming user may convey his or her land to another, and the buyer can continue the nonconforming use. If the nonconforming building is substantially destroyed, it cannot be rebuilt in noncompliance.

Despite the precautions taken under the law to encourage the disappearance of nonconforming uses, they do not always fade away.

CASE EXAMPLE

Susan Wilson purchased a grocery store in an area subsequently zoned residential. As residential development occurs, Wilson will enjoy a virtual monopoly as a grocer because residential zoning has excluded grocery competition. Of course, Wilson will not be able to expand her store under current zoning.

Some localities have taken more direct steps to assure the discontinuance of nonconforming uses. Ordinances have been passed placing a limit on the length of time the nonconformity will be permitted. So long as the time limitation is reasonable, such ordinances will be upheld by the courts. An important factor in determining reasonableness will be the life expectancy of the nonconforming structure. However, even though there are many examples of ordinances limiting the time allowed for nonconformity of advertising signs, the authorities have been reluctant to apply similar time limitations to other structures.

Zone Change

A zoning amendment made by the legislative body that enacted the zoning code.

The apparent inflexibility of the zoning code is mythical in most localities, although the uses permitted in a given zone may be inflexible. As previously mentioned, the zoning code is created to implement a plan—master plan, comprehensive plan or some less specific plan—but none of these plans is intended or can be expected entirely to reflect the future needs of the community. The plan may soon become dated. In addition, some areas of the locality may be zoned not so much for the anticipated use but as a holding zone until more definite decisions can be made. For instance, the northern one-half of a community could be zoned A-1 for agricultural use. The reason for this zoning would not be that this part of the town would be used for agriculture indefinitely, but that since development in the area was years away, the A-1 classification would create a holding zone. This approach would permit the town to postpone its ultimate zoning decision until the time for development was closer and it could better perceive the community needs. In addition, any attempt to use the land for other than agricultural purposes would require a zone change, which would allow the town to monitor closely development in the interim.

The zone change technique employed by communities is a method for keeping their plans current and for reducing the inflexibility of the zoning code. Since the zoning code is legislation, it must be changed by the locality's lawmakers. Although a local government can initiate a zone change, generally the moving party is a landowner or developer. He or she tries to convince the legislative body that the proposed use makes more sense than the use designated in the zoning code. When granting a zone change, the legislature must be careful to establish the reasons for the change. The change must be presented as being justified by the current needs of the community. In this way the zone change is assured of being consistent with the notion that the locality is continuing to plan for its land use.

Variance

Permission obtained from the appropriate governmental authorities to deviate somewhat from the designations under the zoning code.

In contrast to a zone change, a variance is not actually a change in the law. A variance is generally a modest deviation from the requirements of the zoning code. For instance, a landowner may gain a variance to allow him to set his proposed house back only 25 feet from the street rather than the 30 feet required under the zoning law. His parcel of land would continue to be zoned R-1 as it was before the variance.

Use variances can also be granted. Since they could permit a commercial use in a residential zone, however, they are more destructive to the local plan and are less likely to be granted.

Variances are granted by an administrative body in the locality. It may be called a *zoning board of appeals,* a *board of adjustment* or some similar title. In order to obtain a variance, the applicant must prove that the failure to grant it will cause him or her unnecessary hardship. In addition, the applicant must show that the new use will not reduce the value of surrounding properties and that the granting of it is within the public interest and not contrary to the spirit of the zoning code.

• CASE BRIEF •

Banks requested a variance from the City of Bethany to allow him to use a portion of his residentially zoned property for display and storage of his merchandise. The city denied the application.

 The court upheld the city, asserting that Banks had failed to establish an unnecessary hardship to the use of his property as a result of the existing zoning. The fact that Banks would have been able to make more money had the variance been granted did not constitute unique or unnecessary hardship. *Banks v. City of Bethany, 541 P.2d 178 (Okla. 1975).*

The rule of law states that no one has a *right* to a variance, so courts will not overturn the administrator's decision to deny it unless the decision is arbitrary. This narrow scope of judicial review permits the zoning board wide latitude in approving and disapproving variances. Unless the zoning board strictly requires the applicant to meet the burden of proof mentioned above and unless it keeps foremost the goals intended to be accomplished in the zoning code, its wide latitude can lead to an undermining of the land use goals established for the locality.

Exceptions
Permitted uses provided for in the ordinance that are inconsistent with the designated zone.

Unlike variances or zone changes, exceptions are built right into the zoning ordinance. For instance, an R-1 (residential) zone may permit by exception the construction of a church, school or park within that district. The uses by exception are different from the uses allowed by the zoning code but are considered to be compatible with those uses. No special administrative permission is necessary. So long as the proposed use coincides with the exception detailed in the zoning code, the landowner will be allowed to construct the excepted use.

Special-Use Permit
A system whereby special exceptions to the zoning ordinance are granted by the land use administrator under a permit arrangement set forth in the zoning ordinance.

It has become common in zoning codes to omit certain uses from any of the zoning classifications. These uses are allowed only by getting a permit, which entails obtaining the approval of local zoning officials. Hospitals, churches, schools, recreational facilities such as golf courses, and cemeteries are handled in this fashion. Some of these uses may not be offensive in any specific zone, but the permit process retains control for community officials over their location in those situations where they may be objectionable. The special-use permit provides for flexibility in locating these uses for the applicant and maintains public control at the same time.

The special-use permit can be attacked on the basis that it is spot zoning, that is, unplanned zoning. However, this approach can be distinguished in several ways. Generally, special uses are enumerated as such in the zoning ordinance, giving rise to the notion that they may be appropriate uses in an array of zones, depending on surrounding conditions. Many of the uses are not intrinsically offensive; they are singled out for the special-use permit process so that they can be blended into the community in a planned way. This is the antithesis of spot zoning.

Even where the "permitted use" has greater potential for offending the area residents, such as a cemetery, jail or gas station, the purpose of segregating these uses in the zoning code is to ensure that they are placed on sites consistent with community needs.

Problems with Traditional Zoning

Strangely enough, the two major complaints made about the operation of traditional zoning are that it is too inflexible or unresponsive to needs and that it is too flexible. These contentions are not necessarily inconsistent.

Zoning Unresponsive to Changing Demands. The argument that zoning is inflexible comes from the increasing number of narrow designations being used to classify zones. One commercial designation may permit professional offices, while another allows only nonprofessional service offices, a third confines use to small retail stores and a fourth calls for occupation by a shopping center only. An integration of some of these uses—for example, a combination of offices and stores that falls short of being a shopping center—may be considered desirable. Yet this is not possible unless a zone change is attained, and such a change may run the risk of being labeled spot zoning, which is illegal. The detailed specificity with which the zoning classifications are made does not include the flexibility to allow new kinds of uses. For instance, suppose a developer wanted to develop a shopping district where craft-oriented small shopkeepers would sell their wares on the first floor and live on the second floor. He has sensed a growing demand for this relatively inexpensive commercial venture. Yet the local zoning code does not permit the combination of commercial and residential uses. He applies to the local governing board, which must decide whether or not to create still another zoning classification and add it to the many that already exist.

The restricted uses of traditional zoning generally prevent most types of integrated use. In fact, zoning was created to prevent harmful integration of residential, commercial and industrial uses that were considered incompatible and harmful to public health, safety and welfare. Complete lack of integration is not without its pitfalls for modern times, however. Residents of large zones that are exclusively residential often must travel miles to the nearest grocery store for a loaf of bread. This necessitates (for all but the hardiest souls) use of the family car, which is energy consumptive, in a period of high-cost energy. Other facilities such as the church, school, shopping center and doctor's office are even farther removed. These conditions are created by the zoning codes that did not hold economic or social efficiency as a goal.

One can assert that these conditions are merely the result of poor planning. Nevertheless, they have become more and more prevalent. Some flexibility seems appropriate within the zoning code to permit essential services to exist close at hand without creating the feared health and safety problems.

Zoning Too Responsive to Political Pressures. Another attack against zoning in recent years has been that it is too flexible. The zoning code itself is not overly flexible, but the administration of the code has tended to be arbitrary. When the local legislature grants zone changes without a wary eye toward consistency with the comprehensive plan, the orderly development mandated by the zoning code is lost. Local legislatures, planning boards and zoning boards have often been less concerned with orderly community development than with the additional gross tax revenues that would accrue from the proposed development. This undue concern with gross revenues is myopic. It masks the realization that net tax revenues may be less impressive or even negative. In many localities certain types of development do not pay their own way. Single-family developments on generous-sized lots tend to be more expensive for the local government than more compact developments because of the long sewer and water lines, roads and the like. Unless the local land use decision maker is aware of these added costs, he or she cannot make the best decisions for the community.

Control of Large-Scale Development

A popular method of residential development is by subdivision. Commercial and industrial property can also be subdivided as well. The developer or subdivider purchases a tract of land and prepares that land for development. Many communities have regulations governing the subdivision process. Prior to beginning the subdivision, the developer must obtain approval of the development plans from the planning board or other administrators in the community.

Subdivision Regulations

Restrictions on the division of a parcel of land into two or more units. A subdivision will require prior approval by an administrator such as a planning board.

The zoning code controls only the use and siting of construction on the land. Subdivision regulations control the size and location of streets and sidewalks, the placing of sewer and water lines and mandated drainage facilities and the location of parks and open spaces. When the subdivider presents a plat plan to the planning board, the board determines whether the streets, sewers and so forth meet the conditions necessary for maintenance of the public health, safety and welfare.

All state enabling legislation requires that land use decisions be based upon a comprehensive plan. Previously mentioned zone changes, as well as decisions made by the planning board under subdivision regulations, must be made pursuant to the notion of a comprehensive plan. Here the uniformity among the states terminates. Some states base their approval of land use action merely upon the authority's intention to promote the public health, safety and welfare, but no master plan is required. A master plan, if adopted, is merely advisory. A small but growing minority of other states require the preparation of a master plan for the community and then mandate that decisions made be consistent with that master plan. States in a third category do not require a master plan; any community that chooses to have one is selectively bound by its own (the various aspects of that) plan. In Maryland, for example, a community that opts to have a master plan is not bound to follow it when making zoning or subdivision decisions. In approving public works projects, however, the same community *is* bound by the master plan.

The master-plan discussion is relevant at this stage because one must be aware of the legal impact of a master plan in one's own state in order to determine the degree of influence it will have on the subdivision. In a majority of jurisdictions the master plan is optional and only advisory. Even so, it is likely to influence the decision. For example, a master plan calling for all developments to have municipal sewers and water supply is likely to form a ground rule for planning board decision making, even where the plan is advisory only. In all jurisdictions that have a master plan, the planning board can be expected to use it as one mechanism in an array of land use tools that help it to reach decisions.

• CASE BRIEF •

Multnomah County sued to enjoin Howell from conducting a rock quarrying operation on land in an agricultural-residential zone. The quarrying use was prohibited by the ordinance. The court held that the owners of property adjacent to the defendant's business had a right to rely upon the protection against the rock quarrying afforded by the comprehensive plan and zoning ordinance. *Multnomah County v. Howell, 9 Or. App. 374, 496 P.2d 235 (1972).*

Subdivision regulations generally take the form of standards, specifications and procedures set for street signs, streetlights, street trees, fire hydrants, storm drains, sanitary sewers, curbs, gutters and sidewalks. The regulations may require the developer to post a performance bond to ensure compliance with these rules. The final plat, or subdivision map, submitted by the developer will illustrate in detail all the improvements required under the subdivision rules.

Approval of the developer's plat plan usually coincides with the community's agreement to accept title to all streets, streetlights, sewers and so forth when completed. Herein lies the *quid pro quo,* the equal exchange that enables the community to regulate a subdivision closely. The developer agrees to comply with the various subdivision regulations and expects in return that the community will accept a *dedication,* or transfer of title, of the infrastructure facilities, including roads, sewers, hydrants and drainage structures. This transaction relieves the developer of continuing responsibility for maintaining these facilities.

A dedication that is becoming common now is that of parks or open space. The planning board may insist that the developer dedicate a percentage of its land, or money in lieu of parkland, prior to granting approval of the final plat. This type of dedication has been approved as a reasonable extension of the transaction discussed above.

• CASE BRIEF •

Aunt Hack Ridge Estates, Inc., purchased 275 acres of land in Danbury, Connecticut, and applied for approval of a proposed subdivision. The city's subdivision regulations required the dedication of not more than four percent of the total area for recreational use. The developer's plans were rejected by the city because it refused to dedicate the recreation land. The developer sued to have the regulations declared invalid because, among other things, they were an abuse of the city's police power.

The court upheld the city, stating that where the request for parkland was specifically and uniquely attributable to the subdivider's activity it was a permissible exercise of the police power. *Aunt Hack Ridge Estates, Inc. v. Planning Commission of the City of Danbury, 160 Conn. 109, 273 A.2d 880 (1970).*

States take different approaches to how closely the need for the parkland must be tied to the demand created by the residents in the developer's subdivision. In states with a more flexible rule, the planning board can exact land based upon future, as well as present, needs of the subdivision residents; that is, ten years from now 15 acres of open space per thousand people will be the standard rather than the present ten acres per thousand. The particular state rule should be investigated by interested parties.

SUMMARY

An owner has a wide range of rights connected with property. Currently, however, an increasing number of restrictions are placed on land use by both individuals and public agencies. Private restrictions on land use include many types of restrictive covenants and other legal limitations. Public restrictions on land use have developed in this century, beginning with the appearance of zoning codes. Zoning is by far the most widespread method for controlling land use. The basic zones are residential, commercial, industrial and agricultural, but often communities have as many as 15 to 20 designated zones. Several bases exist for modifying the zoning regulation even in strictly zoned communities.

Traditional zoning creates several problems. Some assert that it is too inflexible and unresponsive to changing demands. This complaint may arise when the permitted uses in an area fall into too narrow a category—for example, where homes, offices and shops are not allowed in the same downtown condominium. Other critics accuse zoning of being too flexible, stating that it is too easy for developers to obtain changes in the existing zoning regulations.

Subdivision is another popular method of controlling residential growth. Subdivision plans are designed by a builder, architect or developer and must be approved by the local planning authority. A subdivision plan should specify a percentage of land to be dedicated to parks and recreation and should allow for provision of necessary public services.

REVIEW AND DISCUSSION QUESTIONS

1. Explain the rationale used for permitting one homeowner in a

subdivision to sue a neighbor asserting a restrictive covenant in the neighbor's deed.

2. Why are courts unfavorably inclined toward restrictive covenants?

3. At this time which is the more important land use control factor—restrictive covenants or zoning? Why?

4. Distinguish between the power of eminent domain and a police power regulation.

5. Discuss the certainty with which one can predict that a police power regulation will be declared a taking.

6. In your view, which situation presents the more serious public problem: too much flexibility in zoning or too little flexibility in zoning?

7. Describe the methods intrinsic in all zoning codes for retaining flexibility in land use decision making.

8. Describe alternatives to traditional zoning districting that might prove to be more energy efficient and retain the major social benefits of zoning.

9. Discuss the statement, "Gross tax revenue increases should be the single most important criterion used in making land use decisions."

10. Contrast a zone change request with a variance request.

CASE PROBLEMS

1. P. Rose Enterprises, Inc. (PRE), purchased 20 acres of land in Cincytown. Advise them as to the proper action. (a) PRE plans to construct a warehouse on a portion of the parcel. It is zoned A-1 for agricultural use. (b) PRE plans to continue using an office building on the site for that purpose. The office building was constructed prior to adoption of the zoning code. The area is now zoned A-1 for agricultural use. (c) PRE plans to subdivide the parcel for single-family homes. The land is zoned R-1 for single-family homes, with a minimum lot size of one-half acre. According to PRE's sketch plan three of the 32 lots will be slightly under one-half acre.

2. George and Sharon Kell purchased in a subdivision called Bella Vista. All the properties in the subdivision were subject to a recorded agreement to pay periodic assessments for the upkeep of the common areas within the subdivision. The Kells failed to pay the assessment, and the Bella Vista Homeowners Association asserted a lien on the realty and foreclosed on the Kell's property. The Kells argue that the agreement does not run with the land and therefore cannot be a lien on their realty. Discuss. *Kell v. Bella Vista Property Owners Ass'n*, 258 Ark. 741, 528 S.W. 2d 651 (1975).

3. Rachel Karson's deed contained a clause that barred use of that land for purposes such as a "bar, tavern, alehouse or the like." Rachel would like to open a restaurant that serves alcoholic beverages. Will she be prohibited from doing so by the clause in her deed?

4. The Town of Preston passed a sign control ordinance. Section 8 of the ordinance stipulated that all existing signs within the town must conform to the sign ordinance within five years from the date of its enactment. Marvin Miller has a large, flashing, nonconforming sign that he does not wish to remove. What arguments should Marvin assert? Would he be successful?

5. S. Volpe & Company petitioned the board of appeals for a special permit to construct a golf course on its land. Golf courses were one of the specially permitted uses allowed under the Town of Wareham's zoning ordinance. The board denied the permit because the land included salt marshes and the golf course would destroy the ecology of the region and harm local fishing. What will be the result in court? *S. Volpe & Co. v. Board of Appeals of Wareham*, 4 Mass. App. Ct. 357, 348 N.E. 2d 807 (1976).

6. Rogers owns a large single-family house in the suburbs. She plans to move to a more expensive house in a nearby suburb. To afford the new house, Rogers wants to convert her present home into a two-family apartment. The zoning classification for her house is R-2, that is, single-family house on a minimum lot size of 20,000 square feet. Advise Rogers on how to proceed. Is she likely to be successful under your suggested procedure?

7. McCarthy earns her living by making and selling ceramics. She leases a small store in a shopping center to sell her wares and rents an apartment in a nearby residential area. McCarthy is notified that her rent will be doubled at the termination of her existing lease six months from now. She cannot afford the increased rent and will be forced out of business. A friend suggests that she purchase a house and use part of it for living space and part for her business. Discuss the legal and practical feasibility of her friend's suggestion.

8. East Neck Estates, Ltd., applied for subdivision approval for a 30-unit development along the bay. The planning board requested that the developer dedicate an 80-foot strip along the entire waterfront of its property to the municipality to satisfy the law requiring the giving of land for parks. The 80-foot strip was approximately 40 percent of the full value of the de-

veloper's land. Assuming that the ordinance was constitutional and that the 80-foot strip did not exceed the amount of land authorized for dedication under the ordinance, what argument might the developer make? *East Neck Estates, Ltd. v. Luchsinger,* 61 Misc. 2d 619, 305 N.Y.S. 922 (1969).

13
Nontraditional Land Use Controls

The shortcomings of traditional zoning have caused states and localities to experiment with some variations to cope with their land use problems. Some techniques, such as large-lot zoning, are completely consistent with traditional zoning. Others, such as planned unit developments (PUD), are moderate departures from normal zoning. All have evolved to alleviate one difficulty or another with the usual approach of traditional zoning. This chapter discusses several of the problems that arise under traditional zoning and describes techniques adopted to cope with them.

CONTROL OF URBAN SPRAWL

The post–World War II period saw rapid changes in the living habits of Americans. People abandoned the cities for the newly developed suburbs in the nearby countryside to escape noise and traffic congestion, closely clustered and aging housing and increasing crime and pollution.

As the suburbs continued to expand during the 1950s and 1960s, the urban ills people had fled the cities to avoid began to follow them into their new communities. In response, suburban communities began to adopt regulations designed to stop the decline in the quality of suburban life by limiting the rate of growth.

In this section you will read about some of the techniques used to limit growth and the reactions of the courts to them.

Large-Lot Zoning

A zoning classification that requires a minimum of one acre or more of land for each single-family house that is constructed.

The selection of one acre as the minimum size for large-lot zoning and other zoning is somewhat arbitrary. Other writers may contend that it should be slightly larger or smaller. What size lot constitutes a questionable zoning classification may depend on the location of the property. For instance, city lots tend to be small, and rural lots tend to be much larger. In any event, at some point, depending on the environment, the minimum lot size may be so large that it raises a legal question as to whether or not the size can be justified under the police power.

Advantages

In many areas of the country it is not uncommon to have zoning classifications requiring a minimum lot size of one, two or even five acres. Several legitimate public policy reasons can be given for mandatory lots of that size. Where municipal sewers and water are not available, the soil and geologic conditions may necessitate sparse development for nature to function adequately in supplying water and for cleansing wastewater. In some states where it is recognized as a salient reason for zoning, and in other states where it may be used merely as an additive reason, esthetics may be offered as a reason for large-lot zoning. Sparse development on large, generously landscaped lots is attractive to almost everyone.

Large-lot zoning, despite the language contained in the purpose clause of a local code, may have a hidden motivation. Wealthy people prefer to live on large lots, which give better assurance of privacy in tranquil surroundings. The greater the financial means of the owner, the larger the residential lot is likely to be. It is quite natural for someone who can afford it to select a dream home in suburbia. Similarly, the desire to have amenities as well as to retain the market value of their properties causes others to desire comparable high priced housing nearby.

A second purpose of this type of zoning is that sparse development on large lots tends to be less expensive in terms of the cost of public services. Though municipal sewer and water facilities, if available, may be more expensive, other community services, such as schools, fire and police, tend to be less expensive. A major share of municipal property taxes goes for schools, and taxpayers usually wish to keep these taxes down. Statistically, well-to-do people have relatively few children, and restricting developments to large lots enables residents to reduce school taxes.

Disadvantages

Hidden motivation may represent the negative side of large-lot zoning. The intent of such zoning, or at least a residual result, is discriminatory. Even when the intent of large-lot zoning is for the socially laudatory purpose of permitting people to enjoy the "fruits of their labor," one effect of such zoning is to exclude the poor and less financially advantaged.

Excluding the financially disadvantaged usually results in the exclusion of minority groups as well. A municipality that caters to the wealthy with large-lot zoning may be steering low- and middle-income housing and the resulting higher public service taxes into nearby communities. A community may feel that exclusive use of large-lot zoning will help prevent higher taxes, crime and congestion. These social ills do not go away, however; they are merely concentrated in communities that do not exclude through large-lot zoning.

Recent Judicial Responses to Large-Lot Zoning

Though not yet widespread, there is a growing tendency among state courts to reject large-lot zoning as unconstitutional. The Pennsylvania and New Jersey courts have been leaders in this movement.

• CASE BRIEF •

The zoning ordinance in the Town of Concord required a minimum lot size of one acre along existing roads and three acres on the interior. Kit-Mar Builders were denied a request to rezone their property lots smaller than mandated by the code. Kit-Mar sued Concord, contending that the large-lot zoning was an unconstitutional taking of its property.

The Pennsylvania Supreme Court held that a zoning provision of this type is unconstitutional if either its purpose or its result is exclusionary. The only exception would be where the municipality can show some extraordinary justification for requiring large lots. An extraordinary justification would be where the natural conditions of the soil, for instance, cannot handle denser population and there is no other reasonable, nonexclusionary method of resolving the problem. *In re Kit-Mar Builders, Inc., 439 Pa. 466, 268 A.2d 765 (1970).*

Most Pennsylvania communities would be hard-pressed to satisfy the judicial burden of proving extraordinary justification.

The New Jersey courts have gone a step further. The New Jersey Supreme Court, in an opinion that has implications beyond large-lot zoning, has declared that developing communities must provide for their fair share of the low- and middle-income housing needs of their region. *South Burlington County N.A.A.C.P. v. Township of Mt. Laurel*, 67 N.J. 151, 336 A.2d 713, *appeal dismissed*, 423 U.S. 808 (1975). Taking a cue from the Pennsylvania courts, the opinion permits an exception when "peculiar circumstances" can be shown. *Peculiar circumstances* sounds very much like extraordinary justification. The legal basis of the court's ruling is that under state law citizens have a right to decent shelter, and rampant large-lot zoning could effect a denial of this right.

In short, large-lot zoning will be unacceptable where the community has not otherwise provided the housing, or potential for housing, for its share of the region's less financially advantaged people. The adoption of a regional approach to land use decision making has long been espoused by scholars and planners but had not previously received broad judicial approval.

The extent to which the Pennsylvania and New Jersey constraints on large-lot zoning will spread is uncertain at this time. *See Berenson v. Town of New Castle*, 88 N.Y.2d 102, 378 N.Y.S.2d 672 (1975). If the New Jersey approach is broadly adopted, it will not sound the death knell for large-lot zoning. So long as a community is able to provide for its share of the regional housing needs elsewhere, it may continue to have large-lot zoning.

Regional Planning

Planning done along broad, physical environment lines rather than traditional political lines.

For some years now planners have maintained that the need to plan regionally makes more sense than planning according to artificial political boundaries. To optimize land use of the region, they say, land use decisions should not be made by individual municipalities divorced from other land use decision makers in the region.

Courts, too, have spoken of the sensibleness of regional planning and decision making in land use, but until very recently they have been unwilling to impose regional planning requirements on decision makers.

• CASE BRIEF •

In 1975, the Supreme Court of New Jersey struck down a municipal zoning ordinance because the town had not provided for its regional fair share of low- and moderate-income housing in a developing community. The court noted that in the future a New Jersey municipality would have to bear its share of regional land use needs unless there were "peculiar circumstances." The court made clear that the burden of showing peculiar circumstances would be onerous. The court acted out of concern for the "basic right of shelter" for people who could not obtain housing in communities that carefully manipulated their zoning codes to discourage the financially disadvantaged. In this particular New Jersey case, the town of Mt. Laurel had zoned 30 percent of its land as industrial, without any chance that that much land could be used for industrial growth. It was a method of protecting land from the threat of low-cost housing, which is expensive for a municipality to service. *Southern Burlington County N.A.A.C.P. v. Township of Mt. Laurel, 67 N.J. 151, 336 A.2d 713 (1975), cert. denied, 423 U.S. 808 (1975).*

How far the New Jersey pronouncement for a balanced community will be carried is uncertain. The states of New York and Washington have already followed New Jersey's lead. If the trend continues, economics will drive states to provide administrative vehicles for regional planning and, perhaps, regional decision making.

Growth Management Plans

Comprehensive growth plans that dictate both when and where growth will occur.

To date, growth management plans have been adopted by communities on the fringe of urban and suburban growth. These communities have felt the financial pressures of a rapidly increasing population and have seen their exurban style of life disappearing. They have reacted by trying to monitor future growth closely. These schemes can best be illustrated by describing three cases involving their use.

The town of Ramapo, New York, on the suburban edge of New York City's metropolitan growth, decided that the haphazard growth taking place under the existing zoning code could be better controlled. The town methodically went about getting the information and doing the planning to create a better community. It initiated an in-depth master plan, adopted a zoning code to implement the plan, made sewer and drainage studies to guide future growth and adopted a six-year capital budget for community services as well as a capital budget program of capital expenditure for the following 12 years. Believing that a full range of community services could not be provided adequately wherever developers happened to acquire land, the town decided that it would systematically provide those services on a section-by-section basis. Sewers, water lines, firehouses, parks, schools and drainage facilities would be provided to those sections of the community as predetermined by the town and in accordance with the capital budgeting program adopted. At the end of 18 years—the capital budget period—the town would have a complete set of community services. Obviously, some sections of the town would not receive such services until the final years of the period. A developer who wished to build in those sections of the town that had not yet acquired services could agree to provide those services. A developer who could amass 15 points on a sliding-scale arrangement for providing community services could develop the land. Unstated, but obvious in the scheme, is that the developer's cost of providing these services would probably be financially prohibitive.

It did not take long for a landowner who was not to receive community services until late in the scheme to bring a suit asserting that the arrangement was illegal. The highest court of New York upheld the Ramapo growth management plan as within the town's police power. *Golden v. Town of Ramapo*, 30 N.Y. 2d 350, 334 N.Y.S.2d 138 (1972). The court asserted that, where restrictions are necessary to promote the ultimate good of the community and are within the bounds of reason, they are within the purview of the police power. The Ramapo scheme seemed consistent with good land planning and had as its purpose the systematic development of the town.

Two major warnings have evolved from the Ramapo case and subsequent criticism of it. The Ramapo court noted that there was something "inherently suspect" about the scheme that restricted the free mobility of people, despite its professed altruistic purpose. Communities will have to balance closely the degree of public good that could ensue from a growth management plan against the level of restriction placed on the mobility of people. For instance, if the time taken by the town is longer than needed to provide the community services in a fiscally sound way, and the community is in the direct path of growth, the restraint on human mobility may be too great.

The second warning is that low- and middle-income people would be discriminated against. The Ramapo plan provided areas for low- and middle-income housing development, but there was no guarantee or community inducement for that type of development actually to take place. Since many of the state courts have become acutely interested in adequate provision for this type of housing, a community may have to take care to provide realistically for lower-cost housing to be built.

Two other communities have received notoriety after adopting a growth management plan. The City of Petaluma, California, also in the path of urban sprawl, adopted a comprehensive development plan that in essence limited growth to 500 units annually, well below anticipated unregulated growth levels. The United States Court of Appeals upheld the Petaluma Plan. *Constr. Indust. Ass'n of Sonoma County v. Petaluma*, 522 F.2d 897 (1975), *cert. denied*, 424 U.S. 934 (1976). The court noted that the plan had a rational relationship to a legitimate state interest and that was all that was required. The avowed purpose of the Petaluma Plan was to maintain the "small town character" of the city. Clearly, part of the plan was to limit, annually and ultimately, the city's growth. To this extent Petaluma is an extension of Ramapo, which overtly attempted only to regulate the pattern of growth to coincide with the temporary financial limitations of the town.

A third community was less fortunate. Boca Raton, Florida, placed a cap on population growth by limiting the number of residential units that could be constructed to 40,000. The court rejected the plan, however, because of the somewhat arbitrary way in which the number 40,000 was reached. Boca Raton did not methodically plan for the limitation, as had Ramapo and Petaluma. In fact, the court clearly stated that a population cap that *is* rationally related to sound community planning and is not unduly restrictive of private property rights *would* be within the domain of the police power. *Boca Villas Corp. v. Pence*, 45 Fla. Supp. 65 (1976).

The key tests for the notion of growth management plans have been affirmative. It would seem that the important criteria to be met are comprehensive preplanning, a rational connection between the reasonable restrictions in the plan and the public-welfare-based goal of the scheme and a provision for low-income residential units where they are needed. The ultimate goal can be to maintain the existing character of the community or even to limit ultimate community growth, although the exact interpretation of these principles will have to evolve over time. It should also be noted that only a small number of states have made any pronouncement on growth management plans; therefore, we do not have assurance of their national acceptance at this time.

In addition, due to the building slump of the early 1980s, the communities of Ramapo and Petaluma have significantly modified their growth management plans. It is likely that the economic recovery of the building industry will revive interest in growth management plans similar to those discussed above.

Judicial Conflict: Federal and State Statutory Controls

Currently, a judicial rift is growing between the federal courts and some of the state courts. Several state courts, including those of New Jersey, Pennsylvania and New York, seem intent on more closely controlling the land use regulators. Where land use regulations are likely to disfavor poor or moderate-income people, these states have abandoned their traditional hands-off policy. Traditionally, state courts have always decided that, if a public need existed and the regulation were reasonably geared to alleviate that need, the land use regulation would be approved. The heavy burden of proving a lack of reasonableness fell upon the person attacking the regulation. The tendency now is to place the burden of proof on the municipality. Where a regulation appears discriminatory on its face, it is now just as difficult for the municipality to justify it as it once was for a defendant successfully to attack a municipal ordinance.

For several decades the U. S. Supreme Court rarely heard land use cases. During the mid-1970s, however, the court became active in reviewing these cases. The tendencies of the Supreme Court and of other federal courts contrast with the views expressed by the state courts mentioned above. The view of the federal cases appears to invite municipalities to experiment with land use regulations in trying to cope with urban sprawl.

• CASE BRIEF •

The Village of Belle Terre enacted an ordinance restricting land use in the municipality to one-family dwellings. The law defined *family* as including those related by blood or marriage or any housekeeping unit, not to exceed two people, who were not so related. The village is near a state university, and the ordinance would prohibit more than two unrelated students from living together. The landlord, Dickman, and some of his tenants brought suit contending that the ordinance, among other things, was an unconstitutional restriction on a person's right to travel.

The Supreme Court upheld the zoning law with Justice Douglas speaking: "A quiet place where yards are wide, people few, and motor vehicles restricted are legitimate guidelines in a land use project addressed to family values. . . .It is ample to lay out zones where family values, youth values, and the blessings of quiet seclusion and clean air make the area a sanctuary for people." *Village of Belle Terre v. Boras, 416 U.S. 1 (1974).*

In another Supreme Court case in 1976 Justice Stevens stated that " . . .the city's interest in attempting to preserve the quality of urban life is one that must be accorded high respect. Moreover, the city must be allowed a reasonable opportunity to experiment with solutions to admittedly serious problems." *Young V. American Mini-Theatres, Inc.*, 427 U.S. 50 (1976). Justice Stevens makes the invitation to experiment clear. Often, attempts to control urban sprawl and enhance "quality of life" are the antithesis of measures that would be enacted to protect the living conditions of the financially disadvantaged.

There is no right or wrong to the conflicting attitudes of the federal courts and some of the state courts. Protecting the quality of one's living environment is critical to everyone. Equally important is an opportunity for the poor to be able to have a choice of housing or, at least, to have available a "livable" environment. The best answer is probably a balanced blending of New Jersey's regional fair share and Justice Douglas's quiet places where yards are wide.

NEW ZONING APPROACHES

Traditional zoning has been supplemented by some new methods intended to handle specific problems. Desirability of integrated uses, concern for retaining natural beauty and eagerness to minimize the negative off-site impacts of development gave rise to the approaches discussed below.

Planned Unit Development (PUD)

A concept involving a development larger than a traditional subdivision, generally permitting mixed uses within the development and attempting to provide a maximum amount of land for open space.

This definition of a PUD is necessarily vague. As it has evolved, the PUD has become many things. It is a term used to describe a development that clusters houses on undersized lots in order to provide more open space to the residents. The term is used to depict a development that permits various types of housing within the same tract, such as townhouses, apartments and single-family housing. In another community it may be flexible enough to allow mixed uses, such as residential, commercial and even light industry (such as warehouses). Some zoning maps designate areas of the community as PUD zones, while other communities adopt a *floating-zone* concept in which the PUD becomes affixed to a particular land area when an appropriate proposal for mixed use is made to the community officials. Whichever cloak PUD wears, it provides the land use decision maker with additional flexibility in planning for growth within the community.

Procedurally, the developer usually needs community approval for the total PUD at the inception of the project. This general approval both allows the PUD as such and sanctions the overall design or concept of the development presented. Since the PUD is a large development, it will be constructed in sections over several years. As the developer plans each section of the PUD, community approval will need to be obtained for the specifics of that section. A few years into the PUD construction, market conditions may change, causing the developer to seek an alteration of the general plan. For example, condominiums may not be selling in the community; the developer, seeking approval for Section 4 that was previously approved for condominiums, may seek to amend the PUD to put two-family homes in Section 4.

Since the floating PUD is more common than the fixed-zone approach, the PUD plan must obtain the approval of the planning board along with a zone change from the local legislative body. This dual clearance, added to the planning board's approval of each individual section, affords the community the opportunity for closely controlling the development. The key word is *opportunity.* The major criticism of PUDs is that this very flexibility offers too much chance for abuse by the developer. Sometimes a beautifully integrated PUD concept is undermined when the developer annually changes the proposal on the section-by-section approvals in order to take advantage of the short-run market for a given type of development. The result is a hodgepodge that gives the appearance of no planning. The antidote is a planning board, which presses the developer to retain the original plan unless there is an extraordinary reason for change or the change will enhance the overall design of the project.

The original PUD concept was intended to provide for large-scale, relatively self-sufficient development on the order of a new town. A large PUD has the potential for creating an integrated community. It provides for generous quantities of open space in exchange for an increase in density in the living areas, with total density remaining the same. Since the size of the project necessitates development over several years, it permits medium-range community planning with continuous updating through the section-by-section approvals. Where integrated multiple uses are permitted, it can provide for more proximity between residents and services and for a reduction in car miles and energy consumed. The major drawback, however, cannot be overemphasized. A PUD is only as good as the public administrators require it to be.

Zoning for Esthetics

Zoning to achieve what is considered beautiful or done in good taste.

A municipal goal to maintain beauty or esthetic quality has long been recognized as a factor upon which land use decisions can be made. A community may require use of similar external building materials or a limited density of structures to achieve a more attractive or esthetic appearance. Esthetics by itself has not usually been treated as a justification for regulation. Some triggering mechanism was necessary before esthetics could be used appropriately. For instance, a regulation based solely on esthetics would fail, but one based upon providing adequate sewage treatment (and esthetics) would be upheld. Adequate sewage treatment is accepted as a basis for regulating land use by itself. Once that basis is established, esthetics may be relevant and can be weighed by a court in determining whether there is adequate police power foundation to justify the regulation. Theoretically, when added to other land use techniques, esthetics could tip the scale in favor of the zoning regulation in the court's balancing process.

The second-class status of esthetics stems from its character. It is a fuzzy, uncertain concept that in some measure depends upon individual taste. Individual taste is highly subjective and very difficult for legislative bodies and courts to ascertain in an objective fashion. Since perceptions of esthetics are so individual in nature, it is difficult to argue that esthetics is justified within the scope of the public welfare. One person's esthetic welfare may evoke nothing but disdain in another.

Yet the analysis may overstate the case against the use of esthetics in an objective manner. Some normative attitudes can be determined. Pristine river valleys, wooded mountain slopes, tumbling waterfalls and green fields are appreciated for their beauty by most people. A carefully landscaped industrial park is more pleasing (or less offensive) to most people than one without landscaping. Although a community may split over the relative esthetic merits of lining the streets with arches of elms or flowering and crimson-berried mountain ash, most people would probably agree that either tree is better than none.

In recent years esthetics has attained a more favored reception in some courts that are making zoning decisions. In the case of *Berman v. Parker*, 348 U.S. 26 (1954), the United States Supreme Court noted that there was nothing federally unconstitutional about regulating solely on the basis of esthetics. Since that time several states have found that there is nothing improper under state law if a community chooses to regulate exclusively for esthetic purposes. *Oregon City v. Hartke*, 204 Or. 35, 400 P.2d 255 (1965); *People v. Goodman*, 31 N.Y.2d 262, 290 N.E. 139 (1972); *John Donnelly & Sons v. Outdoor Advertising Bd.*, 369 Mass. 206, 339 N.E.2d 709 (1975).

The elevated stature of esthetics is by no means universal, nor is it the majority rule in the states. However, the erosion of the old rules has begun.

• CASE BRIEF •

McCormick owned 39 acres of land on Oseetah Lake in the Adirondack Mountains. McCormick applied to the Adirondack Park Agency (APA) for a permit to develop 32 lots on the tract. The APA granted the permit subject to a restriction against placing any boat houses on the shoreline of the lake. The sole basis for the restriction was that boat houses would interfere with the rustic or esthetic quality of the area. McCormick protested the restriction in court.

The court upheld the APA decision, affirming a previous position that esthetics alone could substantiate a zoning regulation. The court noted that a "regulation in the name of esthetics must bear substantially on the economic, social and cultural patterns of the community or district." *Matter of McCormick v. Lawrence, 83 Misc.2d 64, 372 N.Y.S.2d 156 (1975).*

This latter language regarding community economic, social and cultural patterns may simply be recognition that an esthetics regulation must be supported by a public health, safety or welfare reason or an attempt to provide some criteria for reviewing the validity of this type of regulation. Regardless, esthetics as the primary reason for a zoning decision is an expansion of the limitations on traditional zoning.

Contract Zoning

Zoning in which an applicant will be granted a requested zone change only after contracting with the community to comply with certain covenants.

Contract zoning is a highly controversial concept. Under this approach the legislative body reviewing the zone change request may seek to obtain a contractual agreement from the developer that it will build in accordance with specifications more stringent than those required in the zoning code. For example, it may mandate a comprehensive landscaping plan for building and parking areas and less surface coverage by construction than allowed by the ordinance. The zoning contract provides the decision maker with needed flexibility; if not abused, it can serve the community welfare.

The controversy arises when the legislature insists that a zone change be contingent upon the meeting of certain conditions and the developer is unwilling to comply. Zoning is a legislative function, and legislative functions delegated to third parties cannot be contracted. Arguably, contract zoning is an attempt by the legislature to contract for a change in the zoning law, which would violate the exclusive grant of legislative authority in the state enabling legislation to the local legislative body.

• CASE BRIEF •

The County of Peoria rezoned five acres of farmland from agricultural to commercial, thereby permitting George Hanlon to build and operate a dance-hall tavern. A neighbor, Clarence Ziemer, sued to enjoin the rezoning, contending that it amounted to contract zoning. The county approved the zone change conditional upon Hanlon's dedicating a 50-foot strip of land along the road to the county and upon his agreeing to a restrictive convenant that would limit his commercial use to that of a dance-hall tavern and no other use that might be permitted by the commercial zone.

An appellate court held that the evidence supported the conclusion that the zone change was approved subject to the landowner's meeting the above-stated conditions. Since conditional or contract zoning is illegal, the rezoning was void. *Zeimer v. County of Peoria, 33 Ill. App. 3d 606, 338 N.E.2d 145 (1975).*

The legality of contract zoning varies from state to state. Some states have approved restrictive covenants when placed upon the developer to ensure that a community benefit evolves from the project. Other states have reached the opposite conclusion, contending that the legislature is surrendering some of its lawmaking authority and thereby making an unconstitutional delegation. Still others have sanctioned contract zoning so long as the covenants are between the developer and other private citizens. One can only be a little skeptical of the latter approach, since the zone change will not occur unless the developer agrees to the private restrictive covenants.

Performance Standards Zoning

One specialized zoning technique that is growing in popularity is performance standards zoning, which establishes certain standards that must be met by any user of land within the zone. Performance standards have been set for such things as noise, vibrations, odors, toxic wastes, signs and heat emanating from a site. For instance, a standard may provide that no odor is allowed beyond the property line. Most of these standards have been established to ensure that industrial operations do not interfere with surrounding land uses.

Performance standards are especially appropriate for multiple-use situations, such as exist in PUD developments. The concept of performance standards may also be useful for controlling adverse impacts in traditional, commercial and residential zones. For instance, they can be used to regulate impacts on drainage, visual sensitivity and traffic congestion.

CONTROLS IN SPECIAL ENVIRONMENTS

With the era of environmentalism in the early 1970s came a growing awareness of values in land that had previously gone unrecognized by most people. Certain lands become important because of their intrinsic value and not merely as items of real estate. In short, land was recognized as a resource and not solely as a commodity. Some lands became important resources because they provided habitats for wildlife and a place for storm water to collect and slowly be returned to the water cycle. Other lands became in short supply regionally, especially farmlands, and the forces of supply and demand were making these lands relatively scarce because of development pressure. Wholesale destruction of our past in the name of "progress" was no longer always seen as desirable. As an awareness of land as a resource dawned, so did the attempt to devise control mechanisms to preserve those resource values. Several of these special land environments will be discussed below.

Wetlands

Lands that have groundwater levels at or near the surface

for much of the year that are covered by aquatic vegetation.

Historically, wetlands, including treed swamps and grass-dominated marshlands, have been treated as wasteland. They were considered inaccessible areas whose major function was the breeding of pest insects. In recent years, however, we have begun to see wetlands in a different light. True, wetlands are breeding areas for mosquitoes, as is any depression that retains water, such as residential drain spouts. Nevertheless, wetlands are also an important natural resource.

Wetlands provide areas for storm waters to gather for their slow return to the groundwater and air. Therefore, they are important as flood control areas. High groundwater and storm waters do not disappear upon the development of a site or upon the laying of drainpipe. Drainpipe merely concentrates the water, shifting the wetness problem farther downstream in the watershed. Wetlands provide this retention function naturally.

In addition, wetlands provide highly productive wildlife habitats. Hunters, fishermen, bird-watchers, trappers and other recreationists find wetlands extremely important in supporting their leisure-time habits. Wetlands provide an outdoor classroom for amateur and professional scientists and are esthetically pleasant to many people. With public recognition of these resource values, and the setting aside of the traditional view of wetlands as areas to be filled and developed, legal methods for protecting these areas have evolved.

Many states have passed legislation to control development in wetland areas. The technique generally adopted has been a permitting process. Prior to filling, dredging or otherwise substantially modifying a wetland area, the landowner must get a state, regional or local permit. Permits are not issued where development will cut deeply into the resource value of the wetland area, unless there is a strong counterbalancing reason for doing so. The state wetland protection systems vary, but they generally involve the preparation of wetlands inventories and maps and the issuance of guidelines or regulations for controlling the process of issuing permits. It should be realized that a permit process does not *automatically* curtail development on all wetlands but that it *may* result in a landowner's being unable to make full economic or commodity use of his or her land.

In addition to state regulation of wetlands, the federal Clean Water Act of 1972, as amended, created a permit system administered by the U.S. Army Corps of Engineers for most dredging and filling activities in wetlands connected with navigable waters. The term *navigable waters* has been defined broadly under the statute to include any waters that have the capability of affecting interstate commerce. Prior to the issuance of any permit, the corps must prepare an environmental impact statement (EIS) that analyzes all environmental factors.

One remedy the corps has utilized against landowners who fill without a permit is to compel the removal of the fill, an undertaking that can be extremely expensive.

Some states and localities have used a zoning approach to control development in wetlands. These zones, which might be called *conservation and recreation districts*, allow only uses consistent with retaining the character of the wetland. Prior to 1970 the zoning approach, which lacked the flexibility of a permit system, was uniformly held to be an illegal taking without due process of law. The judicial rationale was that this type of zoning denied landowners all *reasonable* use of their land. Fishing, boating and hunting, which might have been allowed, were not "reasonable" uses.

Many of the states' wetland measures, as well as the federal wetland permit procedures, have been upheld under judicial scrutiny. In addition, some life has been breathed into the zoning approach for controlling wetland development.

• CASE BRIEF •

Ronald and Kathryn Just purchased 36 acres of land on the shore of Lake Noquebay. Under a county ordinance the land was defined as wetland and designated as within a "conservancy" district. All dredging or filling within a conservancy district required a permit. The Justs filled part of their land without a permit for the purpose of developing on the land. When ordered to cease filling, the Justs sued Marinette County, contending that the ordinance created an unconstitutional taking of their land.

The Wisconsin court upheld the county ordinance. The court stated that "a[n] owner of land has no absolute and unlimited right to change the essential natural character of his land so as to use it for a purpose for which it was unsuited in its natural state and which injures the rights of others." The court then used an old police power analysis by stating that the wetland zoning was an attempt to prevent a harm to the public and not to bestow a benefit upon the public by preserving a natural area. *Just v. Marinette Co., 56 Wis. 2d 7, 201 N.W.2d 761 (1973).*

Traditional analysis states that the police power can be used to prevent public harm but not to grant a public benefit. In this case, as always with this type of analysis, whether the regulation involves a harm or benefit depends on who is doing the classifying.

Another line of reasoning, which may bode well for the zoning approach, is also suggested by the *Just* case. The one constant in "takings" analyses is the rule that the landowner cannot be deprived of all reasonable use. A serious question is raised by the case as to whether or not filling for development is a reasonable use of a wetland. Also, what is reasonable in this area is a time-related notion, so yesterday's unreasonable use may become a reasonable one today.

Wetlands are being controlled as special environments in most states where they are numerous. The techniques for control vary somewhat, but judicial approval for all the approaches seems to be growing.

Floodplains

Areas near waterways that are prone to flooding.

Human beings have always tended to settle near streams, lakes and other bodies of water. The body of water provided a drinking supply, fishing and a convenient means of transportation. The first permanent settlements were made with a wary eye toward the ravages that a flood-swollen stream could cause. High, sheltered places near the water were favored over lower-lying areas that were more susceptible to flooding.

People slowly seemed to lose this sensitivity to the forces of nature. Settlements became more numerous in low-lying, flood-prone river valleys. Floods were either tolerated or, in more recent history, controlled by capital construction projects for dams, levees and dikes that alleviated the problem. In recent years it has become clear that, although dams and dikes may postpone or prevent some floods, sooner or later the dike weakens or the dam is not massive enough to handle a severe storm, and a flood ensues.

The cost of removing people from the floodplains throughout the world is prohibitive. Many people would not be willing to leave even if economic constraints did not prevail. In recent years, governments have undertaken measures to protect those living on the floodplain and to discourage others from building new structures or from repairing flood-damaged structures within the floodplain.

Some communities have used zoning as a method of controlling growth on the floodplain. A "floodplain district" would prohibit the building of new structures or filling or damming within the floodplain. It would prohibit any residential use. The purposes of this type of zoning would be to protect people who might choose to live on the floodplain unaware of the hazards of doing so, to protect those near the floodplain who would be injured by obstructions in the flow of floodwater and to protect the public at large, who must bear the cost of disaster relief when persons on the floodplains lose their property because of flooding.

The legal question raised again is whether this type of regulation, which permits very limited economic use, denies all reasonable use of the land and thereby constitutes a taking. Some courts have followed a rationale parallel to that in the *Just* case. What is a reasonable use must be looked at in the context of the land involved. Floodplain lands, with their vulnerability to massive flood destruction, are not reasonably usable for residential or other permanent types of construction. Although this line of reasoning has not been adopted uniformly to protect the floodplain, it probably represents the wave of the future.

Although this zoning trend is aimed at keeping people out of the floodplain, the federal government is involved in protecting its residents. The national Flood Insurance Program makes flood insurance available to landowners in flood-prone communities, where such insurance was previously exorbitantly expensive or simply unavailable. In essence, unless an individual in a flood-prone area has flood insurance, he or she will not be able to get a mortgage from the bank. If a community does not participate in the flood insurance program, federal aid or loans for use within the federally described flood hazard area will not be made available. An additional regulatory hook in the system is that a community must agree to establish land use controls for the flood-prone area before it is able to participate in the insurance program. In short, insurance will replace disaster relief in some measure, and new construction on the floodplain will be discouraged.

Historic Preservation

The preservation of buildings, and perhaps archaeological sites, from destruction by new development.

Just as American culture deifies youth among people, it tends to favor new structures over those that are old and obsolete. The crags and cracks of an aging building, despite its historical or architectural significance, seem to bring on a "replacement compulsion." Although some extraordinary historical sites have been preserved, the view that not enough preservation and renovation of these structures takes place has been growing. Under this view, replacement is relied upon too heavily.

Though the historical preservation concept can be applied more broadly, it is for the most part applicable to buildings in urban areas. In some regions of the country communities have designated certain areas historic districts because of their economic and cultural significance. In effect, this is a type of zoning. Within historical districts, permits have to be obtained prior to making a significant change in the facade or structure of a building. Because the historical district usually enhances the economy of the affected area, and change is only controlled by a permit system rather than prohibited, the courts have been willing to support them.

Historically significant buildings do not normally comprise an entire district but are scattered among other urban developments. Many cities have designated landmarks in the community and have established a regulatory scheme for preserving their historical significance. The landmark designation differs from an historical district in that in the former the burden falls unevenly on a limited number of landowners. Also, the benefits, of the landmark designation may accrue to the area in general and not solely to the landmark owner. In an historical district the burdens and benefits, at least theoretically, fall equally upon all landowners within the district.

One approach to landmark protection, adopted by New York City, utilizes a new concept known as *transferring development rights (TDRs)*. The TDR concept is somewhat variable and complex, so it will be oversimplified here. Each tract of land has a certain number or amount of development rights that attach to the land and are transferable. A landowner proposing to build a high-rise residential unit does not obtain enough development rights with the deed to develop to the maximum permitted by the zoning code. These rights, or TDRs, have to be purchased from other landowners—in this case, the ones who own the landmarks and are prohibited from fully utilizing the TDRs on their own property. In this fashion the economic burden of owning a landmark (or a wetland, a scenic vista or an archaeological site) does not fall solely on the shoulders of the landmark owner. Landowners simply go into a ready market to purchase or sell TDRs.

• CASE BRIEF •

New York City has an ordinance that creates a comprehensive program for landmark preservation and includes a provision allowing a landmark owner to transfer unusable development rights (TDRs) to other buildings in the area. Grand Central Station had been identified under the law's criteria as a landmark. Penn Central, the owner of the terminal, applied to the Landmarks Commission for permission to construct a 55-story office building atop the terminal building. The commission denied the request, and Penn Central sued, contending that the ordinance created a taking of its property.

The United States Supreme Court held that the refusal to permit Penn Central to maximize development atop Grand Central Station was not a taking without due process. The court noted that Penn Central could continue the present use of the building, which provided it with a reasonable return on its investment. The court did not directly decide whether the TDR provision of the ordinance was legal. It noted, however, that the TDRs may or may not have constituted "just compensation" if this had been a case of taking, but that the TDRs undoubtedly were valuable and mitigated whatever financial burden had been placed upon the landmark owner. *Penn Central Transportation Co. v. New York City, 438 U.S. 108 (1978).*

State and federal tax incentives exist to assist landmark preservation. Recent amendments to the Internal Revenue Code deny demolition expenses if an historic landmark is razed. Accelerated depreciation is also denied if new structure replaces a landmark. If the landmark is preserved, accelerated depreciation of the acquisition costs and rehabilitation is available. The entrepreneur who preserves landmarks has the option of writing off the cost of improvements over five years. Investment tax credits are also available. In addition, states and local governments often make tax rebates available to assist in preservation efforts.

Historical preservation is a relatively new concern in this country, and the law pertaining to it is evolving. Reasonably designated historical districts seem secure from judicial consternation. Landmarks legislation is legal and has found a potentially useful tool in the use of TDRs, but questions as to their legality and as to whether a convenient market arrangement will evolve for their purchase and sale create some uncertainty at this time.

Agricultural Lands

Lands that are actively being used for grazing and crop production.

Prime agricultural lands have been shrinking at an increasingly rapid rate, especially around the country's population centers. A report of the Council on Environmental Quality estimates that prime farmland is being lost at the rate of a million acres per year, or more than four square miles per day. People have become aware that regional shortages of farm crops are inevitable if farmlands continue to be lost to development and abandonment at this rapid rate.

Several factors have caused the shrinking of agricultural lands near metropolitan areas. Farmlands have been assessed for property taxes at development rates, which many farmers cannot pay out of profit from the farm operations, causing them to sell out. The inducement of high land prices has enticed many farmers to sell off their land for development. Further, the demands of farm life appeal to fewer and fewer young people as our society becomes more mobile and leisure-oriented.

Some states have undertaken measures to slow the decrease of farmland areas. They have limited the property tax assessments and acted to protect normal farm operations from the complaints of encroaching homeowners. One technique used is borrowed from zoning. Agricultural districts have been created wherein property taxes are confined to agricultural value assessments, and local governments are prohibited from enacting legislation that would constrain normal farming practices such as spreading manure or building silos.

Although farmland will probably continue to dwindle somewhat, it is expected that protective legislation now being adopted in some states will slow the loss of farms due to development pressures.

FEDERAL LEGISLATION

In the 1970s numerous pieces of federal legislation were enacted that advocated the protection of the physical environment. Other legislation came to the aid of consumers. Each law has a direct or an indirect impact on land use. All the statutes discussed below are federal, except "little NEPAs," which are state statutes patterned directly after the 1969 federal statute.

National Environmental Policy Act

Statute requiring the preparation of a document detailing environmental data and analyzing that data regarding a proposed government action.

The National Environmental Policy Act (NEPA) was enacted in 1969. It mandates that all federal agencies environmental impact statements (EISs) for all actions that could have a significant effect on the quality of the human environment. The EIS must include a discussion of the total environmental impact, the unavoidable adverse impacts, alternatives to the proposal, long-term as well as short-term effects of the action and any irretrievable commitment of resources. The EIS is supposed to gather the relevant environmental data and analyze it so that the administrator or the decision-making agency has a reasonably full understanding of the environmental consequences of the proposed action.

It should be noted that the EIS does not mandate a specific course of action. Once an adequate EIS is prepared, the administrator is required to consider the environmental information and to make the decision in a nonarbitrary manner. In short, the administrator must put environmental consequences into the decision-making calculus used, which also includes the economic, technological and perhaps social and political ramifications of that decision.

The EIS is very important to the governmental land user. It is important as well to the private applicant who needs federal approval in the form of a license, permit, loan or other federal sanction. The approving agency prepares an EIS prior to issuing the license or other form of approval. In some instances the private applicant supplies the environmental data or even the EIS itself to the agency for its approval.

More widely important to private land developers are state versions of NEPA, also known as *little NEPAs*. More than half the states have adopted some form of EIS legislation, and in some states, like California and New York, it is as comprehensive as the federal version.

It is rare that a sizable development does not require some approval from a state or local governmental agency. In many states, although the threshold that triggers the requirement is variable, these approvals may require the preparation of an EIS. The EIS and its use are similar to those provided for under the federal statute. Developers in little-NEPA states will be involved in providing the environmental information for an EIS or in the actual preparation of an EIS. This adds a new dimension to public hearings—the consideration of the environmental effects of the proposed action.

Despite the fact that the EIS does not mandate a specific outcome, the NEPA-type legislation will have a significant effect on land use decision making. Developers and government administrators at all levels will have to become conversant with environmental factors and will be required to balance these factors with the other relevant considerations in their decision-making equation.

Clean Air Act

A statute whose purpose is to cleanse, maintain, and enhance the quality of the nation's air resource.

The Clean Air Act of 1970, as amended, mandates that the Environmental Protection Agency (EPA) control pollutants that are harmful to public health and welfare. The EPA gathers together the full body of relevant information on a known harmful substance and issues what is known as a *criteria document*. Based on this document, the EPA then promulgates National Ambient Air Quality Standards for each "criteria pollutant." There are at present six criteria pollutants. Responsibility then shifts to the individual states to prepare state implementation plans (SIPs) for meeting the national standards within each designated air shed in the state. The state has three years after the approval of its SIP to meet health-related standards (primary) and a reasonable time to meet welfare-related standards (secondary). It should be noted that the 1977 amendments to the act altered this time frame for the criteria pollutants that were originally listed by the federal government.

If the air quality in a specific region exceeds or is near the national standard, the state will have to take affirmative measures in its SIP to ensure that the standard is met and maintained. In order to accomplish this goal, an array of measures is available to the state and individual source of pollution. Emission-control devices have primacy under the statute, but taller stacks or heating-stack gases are permitted to be used in a limited way under the law. The statute provides as well for the use of transportation controls in order to meet national standards.

Under the law as it is now written, new sources and major modification of sources of pollution must attain a permit prior to construction, regardless of whether or not the region of the proposed site has attained the national standards. In a clean-air area (attainment area) the statute prohibits significant deterioration of the air. Each attainment region is assigned an incremental degradation that cannot be exceeded. Through the permit system, the regional administrator is assured that the increment is not exceeded. It should also be noted that new sources within 28 categories of industry designated by the statute—the industries upon which EPA focuses for its control program—must adopt "best available control technology," regardless of the size of the increment remaining in that region.

As the increments are reached, new permits will be denied to industrial sources, thereby causing industries to locate elsewhere. Clearly this is a land use control, albeit indirect.

In nonattainment areas (nonattainment as of July 1, 1979) new sources also must obtain a permit. Although industrial pollution sources are not prevented from locating in a nonattainment area, they will have difficulty doing so. These regions must make regular annual progress toward the national standard and have met it by 1982. Thus, the total amount of new-source pollution must be offset by greater reduction of the same pollutant somewhere else in that air quality region. Unless the new source can reduce emissions from its existing sources, it is not likely to be allowed to locate in a nonattainment area. The new source will be compelled to be relatively clean, and generally to locate in attainment areas.

Clean Water Act

A statute whose purpose is to cleanse, maintain and enhance the quality of the nation's water resources.

The water pollution statute of 1972, as amended, provided that water bodies are no longer considered appropriate vehicles for getting rid of wastes. It adopted the goal of having the waters of this country clean by 1985.

The law uses effluent standards, or technology-based standards, along with water quality standards as the mechanisms for cleansing the nation's waterways from point sources of pollution. Point sources are those using a discrete conduit (a pipe) for their wastes. Industries were to adopt "best practicable technology" by 1977 and "best available technology" by 1983 as effluent standards. Some alteration of these dates has resulted from the 1977 amendments. The state will determine what use it wants to make of the stream or section of the stream (for example, trout fishing) and promulgate water quality standards for propagating that use. A point source of water pollution will have to adopt the stricter of the two standards.

The effluent standards will not have a direct effect on land use, as they only designate the technology that must be adopted by a new industrial pollution source. However, the water quality standard, which concerns itself with the quality of the ambient water, may influence the location of water pollution sources. Industrial sources will have to be relatively clean in order to locate on a stream whose use is designated for drinking water or swimming. Others will be forced to locate on streams with lower water quality requirements.

Under the statute, the federal government contributes a percentage of the cost of constructing public sewage treatment systems in order to facilitate cleaning up the water. The location of these sewage treatment facilities will have an effect on the siting of industrial, commercial and residential development because highly concentrated development will require treatment facilities. To this extent, the allocation of money for construction under the statute will direct where new development can take place.

In the past, sewage treatment works were generally underdesigned or at least reached their capacity very quickly after construction. An initial feature of the new construction grants program under the Clean Water Act is that these works were being overdesigned; that is, their capacities will be able to assimilate anticipated growth well into the future (20 years or more). From the perspective of ensuring that raw sewage is not dumped into streams, the excess capacity is a sound approach. However, the locality's share of the financing for these expensive treatment works builds into community land use decisions a bias for maximizing growth in order to spread the cost over a greater number of people. In short, the new sewage treatment works may stimulate growth in the community—growth that may or may not be desirable.

Amendments to the Clean Water Act emphasize that the municipality must adopt the most cost-effective system of wastewater treatment. The amendments encourage local governments to utilize innovative technologies and to explore alternatives to large, expensive sewage treatment plants. The changes may reduce the stimulant to growth provided under the initial statute.

Non–point sources of pollution are regulated under section 208 of the statute, which provides federal funds to the state for areawide waste treatment management plans. Non–point sources, like agricultural runoff and mining wastes, cannot be controlled simply by plugging up or filtering a pipe. Hence areawide planning and control are believed to be appropriate. One problem has been discovering and implementing control methods for non–point sources. Little progress has been made in limiting this type of pollution, although the regional approach seems to portend success in the future. Control of non–point sources, regionally or otherwise, may eventually impinge upon the location of these sources of pollution.

Other federal legislation will eventually impinge upon land use decision making. The Toxic Substances Act, the Resource Conservation and Recovery Act, the Coastal Zone Management Act and the Noise Control Act, among others, will either directly or indirectly affect some aspects of land use decision making. Similarly, state statutes, such as power plant siting laws, affect specific land use decisions. One trend among states in the early 1970s was to enact statutes that called for regional, rather than local, control of land use. The Vermont Environmental Control Law, the San Francisco Bay Conservation and Development Commission, the Adirondack Park Agency Act and many others fit this mold. This trend developed as disgruntled states took back the power over land use decisions because of the inadequacy of local controls. The trend toward regional regulation has slowed markedly during the 1980s.

Federal Interstate Land Sales Full Disclosure Act

A statute intended to protect residential land purchasers from unscrupulous sellers.

This 1969 statute was an attempt to protect the increasing number of people, many at retirement age, who decided to seek homes in warmer climates. The industry that grew up to provide lots or homes, or both, for these people, who were often thousands of miles away from their proposed homesites, was not entirely scrupulous. Beautiful brochures showed tree-lined streets, utilities in place and neatly subdivided lots, but the land often turned out to be untouched desert or wetland.

This law made it illegal for a developer to make use of any means of interstate commerce or the mails to sell or lease subdivison lots unless:

1. a *statement of record* was filed with HUD, fully disclosing information about the subdivision, and
2. a *property report* was provided to the buyer three days prior to signing the contract, which more briefly described the information in the statement of record. It is intended that the property report be read by the buyer prior to entering a contract.

The statute made it unlawful to use any scheme to defraud, to materially misrepresent pertinent information or to engage in any way in a fraudulent and deceitful transaction pertaining to this type of sale or lease.

There are numerous exemptions under the law. It excludes small subdivisions of fewer than 100 lots and subdivisions with uniformly large lots of more than 20 acres. The focus of the statute is to protect residential lot buyers who would usually purchase sight unseen, although visiting the site would not negate a buyer's rights. The buyer has several remedies, including voiding the sale and/or getting an administrative suspension of the developer's statement of record where the developer has violated the law. The administrator may seek an injunction whenever it appears that the developer is about to violate or has already violated the law. This statute has provided many potential homebuyers with protection against investing their life savings with dishonest developers.

SUMMARY

Not all land use problems have been solved by traditional zoning. Large-lot zoning, for example, requires that building lots be one acre or more for one-family residences. This policy is defended by policymakers on grounds of environmental concerns and esthetics, in addition to the reduction of costs of some public services. Criticisms relate to what may appear to be the intent of some communities—to close the door on those considered "unacceptable." For this reason, among others, some courts have ruled that large-lot zoning is unconstitutional unless a community has also made some provision for low- and middle-income housing.

Regional planning carries this task of planning beyond traditional municipal boundaries. Since the early 1970s environmental groups have been calling for preservation of various types of lands and buildings. Wetlands, floodplains, historical districts, landmark buildings, some archaeological sites, and agricultural lands have come to the attention of public-spirited citizens who point out the special value of these areas. Wholesale growth in the name of progress is no longer seen by everyone as desirable. Many people view land as a resource to be preserved with care.

Growth management plans are comprehensive schemes for growth that facilitate the budgeting of public services to meet these anticipated needs. The town of Ramapo, New York, is a case that illustrates the judicial hazards of such a plan. Two other cases, one in California and one in Florida, provide guidelines.

Traditionally, state courts and the U.S. Supreme Court have maintained a hands-off policy toward the regulation of land use by local governments when those policies were challenged by an individual. Since the mid-1970s, however, the tendency has been changing. While several eastern states have ruled against land use policies that seem to be discriminatory, the cases heard at the federal level seem to uphold a variety of departures from traditional zoning. Certainly, quality of life is a legitimate concern. It is equally important for the poor to be able to have a tolerable living environment available to them. The solution may lie in a balanced blending of the two.

A trend that effectively mixes uses in one specific land area is the PUD, or planned unit development. Larger than a typical subdivision, the PUD provided a long-term plan for economic growth in an underused or vacant space. The plan might include various types of residences, stores and banks and perhaps even light industry or warehouses. The developer needs community approval for the plan at the outset and then must seek approval as each successive section is developed. This flexibility enables the builder to react and adapt to a changing marketplace. Unfortunately, it also provides opportunity for an unscrupulous builder to sabotage the plan by changing it frequently.

Zoning solely for the purpose of maintaining a pleasing appearance—esthetic zoning—has not typically been defensible in the courts because the concept is subject to individual preference. Nevertheless, litigation concerning such zoning continues to occur, and some of the new decisions are more willing to accept zoning purely for esthetic reasons.

Contract zoning is one concept that permits controlled change in a community by requiring the builder or developer who requests a zone change to contract to build to certain standards of quality or esthetics. It is not legal in all states and is often criticized for its requirement of restrictive covenants by the builder.

Federal statutes such as the 1979 NEPA (National Environmental Policy Act) have been enacted to protect the physical environment. Specifically, NEPA requires all federal agencies to prepare environmental impact statements (EISs) when appropriate. Following this lead, many of the states are enacting their own protective statutes, which will have significant impact on land use within the states.

The Clean Air Act (1970) created the Environmental Protection Agency (EPA) to reduce the amount of pollutants released into the air by industrial sources and individuals. The laws authorize legal actions to be taken against polluters, requiring addition of emission-control devices and compliance with other controls. Air quality will be also controlled by the issuance of permits to new industries.

The Clean Water Act (1972) sets goals for achievement of cleanliness in U.S. streams and other bodies of water. Areawide planning is considered appropriate because water pollution affects areas far away from the source of the impurity.

Finally, there is now an Interstate Land Sales Full Disclosure Act (1969) to protect those purchasing land in another state, possibly sight unseen. Flagrant misuse of advertising material to misrepresent the parcels of land prompted this federal action.

REVIEW AND DISCUSSION QUESTIONS

1. Large-lot zoning, requiring one or more acres per single-family dwelling, has not been popular with poor and minority groups. Why?

2. The courts that have rejected large-lot zoning have retained an exception to their declaration of illegality. They have said that large-lot zoning is all right if there is some "extraordinary justification." What would constitute such a justification?

3. Why have courts been reluctant to approve regulations that are based solely upon esthetics?

4. What arguments can be made for regulating solely on the basis of esthetics? Is the United States Supreme Court likely to be a serious hurdle to this type of regulation?

5. If you were drafting a growth management plan for comprehensively controlling growth in your community, what provisions would you perceive as essential?

6. Since most of the planning experts have approved the idea of regional planning for years, why has this concept had so little success?

7. If the floodplains are dangerous places to live, then we should have a policy against people living there. Discuss the implications of such a policy.

8. What are TDRs (transferable development rights)? In what situations would they prove most useful as land use control measures?

9. Contrast the recent land use decisions of the U.S. Supreme Court with those of Pennsylvania and New Jersey.

10. The NEPA is a disaster. Just because a project has some environmental adversity does not mean that it isn't good for society." Discuss.

CASE PROBLEMS

1. Pursuant to a comprehensive plan, the City of Utica zoned an area "land conservation district." Within this district there were no automatically permitted uses. A special-use permit might be issued for several uses related to agriculture and recreation. Dur-Bar Realty Company sued to have the zoning ordinance declared unconstitutional. Discuss. *Dur-Bar Realty Co. v. City of Utica*, 57 A.D.2d 51, 394 N.Y.S.2d 913 (1977).

2. Backus Chemical Company operates a chemical plant along the Pristine River, an interstate stream. In order to comply with the Clean Water Act, Backus has installed Alpha technology, which meets the federal government definition of "best available technology." The attorney for Backus has assured the firm's president that meeting the effluent-based standard with Alpha technology fully satisfies the firm's responsibility under the statute. Is the attorney correct? Why.

3. Ima Nactivist, councillor for the Town of Riverview, intro-

duced legislation at the town board meeting that, if enacted, would require the removal of all structures now existing on the floodplain in Riverview. The legislation included an array of dates upon which types of structures would have to be removed, ranging from one to 15 years. Older and less valuable structures would be removed earlier, and newer and more valuable ones would be eliminated later. Cyrus Caselaw, town attorney, informed Ima that the proposed law was clearly unconstitutional. Ima retorted that Cyrus was misinformed. Discuss.

4. Bilders, Inc., brings a proposal for the Great Northern Mall to the planning board of the Town of Claymont. In compliance with the town's zoning code, and with the agreement of the state Department of Transportation, Bilders agrees to provide short highway turning lanes at all nearby intersections to alleviate congestion created by the new mall. The planning board requests that a two-mile portion of the highway adjacent to the mall be widened to three lanes. The widening is needed because of the auxiliary growth that will locate in the area after the mall is approved. Discuss the feasibility of the planning board's imposition of these requirements on Bilders.

5. Elocin, Inc., owner of 64 acres of land in Springfield Township, proposes to construct 567 high-rise apartments and 305 townhouses on the site. Zoning for the land calls for single-family detached houses only. Other areas of the township permit two-family houses and small apartment buildings, but no area permits high-rise apartments and townhouses.

Elocin is denied a zone change and sues the township, contending that it must provide zoning for high-rise apartments and townhouses under the state rule mandating that municipalities provide for their regional fair share of all types of housing. Discuss. *Appeal of Elocin, Inc.*, 501 Pa. 348, 461 A.2d 771 (1983).

14
Agency and Brokerage

AGENCY

A legal relationship in which one party, called the
***principal*, authorizes another, called the *agent*, to act in the**
principal's behalf in dealing with third parties.

Agency is a useful legal relationship in business and personal transactions. A substantial amount of business in the United States is done through agents, both by corporations and partnerships that are unable to act for themselves and by individuals, who find acting through agents convenient and efficient in their business and private affairs.

Agency and Real Estate Transactions

The agency relationship is used extensively in many phases of the real estate business. It is especially prevalent in selling and leasing residential and commercial property. Owners of these types of properties often retain agents to help them find buyers or tenants as agents usually have extensive knowledge of the market as well as contacts with potential occupants.

Agencies created to bring about the sale or lease of real estate differ in two significant ways from agencies in many other businesses. One difference is that in all states an agent appointed to sell or buy real estate must be licensed. License requirements for real estate agents will be discussed later in the chapter.

A second difference between the real estate agent and other agents is the extent to which the real estate agent has the power to contract on behalf of the principal. In many, if not most, business agencies the agent has this power. For example, if the president of a corporation that is developing land for a shopping mall signs a contract to have the land cleared, the contract is binding on the corporation. However, in most transactions that involve the sale of lease of real estate, the agent does not have the power to contract for the principal. If the owner wishes the agent to have this authority, the owner must execute a written document called a *power of attorney*. The power of attorney grants the agent, usually referred to as an *attorney-in-fact*, the authority to contract for the owner.

Creation of Agency

The usual method of creating an agency is by agreement. The principal authorizes the agent to act in the principal's behalf, and the agent agrees to do so. As a general rule, no particular formality is required to create an agency; the agreement may be oral or in writing. This rule ordinarily does not apply to transactions involving the sale or lease of real estate. To be valid, power of attorney must be in writing. In addition, almost half the states by statute require that the appointment of an agent to procure a buyer or tenant for real estate be in writing.

BROKER

An agent who for a commission or fee (1) brings parties together to negotiate or (2) conducts negotiations to complete a transaction usually involving the sale or exchange of property or the acquisition of contract rights.

A broker is an intermediary or go-between whose primary function is to facilitate a transaction. In many fields brokers play important roles in bringing business dealings to fruition. Although stockbrokers and real estate brokers are common examples, the long list of brokers includes those who arrange the sale of yachts, produce, hides and furs and, in some societies, even marriage. What brokers do and the authority they enjoy differ from one business to another, but brokers almost always represent buyers or sellers in some capacity.

Most states have statutory provisions that define real estate brokers and sales personnel for the purpose of licensing and regulation. These statutes frequently designate brokers in terms of activities relative to real estate transactions. When people engage in these activities for others and for a commission or fee, they are brokers or salespersons for regulatory purposes and must be licensed.

The statutes contain words such as *appraises, auctions, sells, offers for sale, buys, solicits prospective sellers or buyers, negotiates the sale* and *exchanges*. Similar broad terminology is used to describe activities relative to rental of real property. In some statutes, activities such as finding borrowers or lenders, negotiating or collecting loans and arranging investments secured by real estate also are included in the statutory definition of *broker*.

• CASE BRIEF •

Vivian Alligood was employed by Gulf American as a telephone solicitor. Her duties were to phone and invite people to visit the company's development in Naples, Florida. Alligood received $1.15 per hour and $3.00 for each person or "buying unit" successfully solicited. She did not quote prices or give details pertaining to the land. This was done by another employee during the prospective buyer's visit.

Florida statute required that one assisting in the procuring of prospects for real estate be licensed as a broker or salesperson. Alligood argued that she was not required to be licensed because her job had nothing to do with selling the properties. The Florida courts disagreed. They held that her activities fit the statutory definition, and a license was required. *Alligood v. Florida Real Estate Commission, 156 So.2d 705 (Fla. 1963).*

A corporation or a partnership may be a real estate broker. Members of the firm who actively engage in the brokerage business must be licensed. A few states require that anyone actively engaged in management be licensed as well. In some states one member of the firm may be designated on the license as a broker and others as associate brokers or sales personnel. License requirements will be discussed more fully later in this chapter.

The legal responsibility of a person who hires someone else to act for him or her depends upon the relationship between them. As a general rule, the more extensively the person for whom the job is being done *controls* the manner in which it is accomplished, the greater that person's responsibility. For example, an employer has appreciable control over how an employee does the job. Thus, if the employee is acting within the scope of his or her employment, the employer is legally liable for any harm the employee causes. For example, if a driver of a department store delivery van goes through a red light and injures a pedestrian while making a delivery, the department store is liable. This is known as the doctrine of *respondeat superior, i.e.,* "let the superior respond." The rationale for this doctrine is that one who carries out business activities through another whose actions he or she directs should be liable for that person's negligence in doing the job. In most real estate brokerage agreements, the seller who "hires" a broker does not direct or control the manner in which the broker performs the task. The relationship between the seller and broker is not one of employer and employee. The broker is said to be an *independent contractor.*

Independent Contractor

A person who is retained to do a job and uses his or her own judgment as to how the work will be done.

The broker is in a technical sense retained by the seller as an agent. Nevertheless, the agency agreement establishes only the broker's authority to act, not the manner in which the broker is to accomplish the result. The broker controls the hours, methods and details of the job. As the broker's actions are not controlled by the seller, the seller is not liable for negligent harm caused by the broker unless the act causing harm was authorized or within the broker's inherent powers. In addition, as the broker is not an employee but an independent contractor, the seller does not have to withhold federal or state income taxes or make contributions to social security or unemployment compensation funds in the broker's behalf.

Listing

A contract between a seller of real estate and a broker authorizing the broker to secure a buyer for the property upon specified terms in return for a fee if the broker is successful.

The listing creates the agency relationship between the seller and the broker. A number of states by statute require a listing to be in writing. In these states, if there is no written listing, the broker is not entitled to a fee. In the absence of statute requiring a writing, an oral listing is enforceable. This question should not come up, however, since both the prudent seller and the broker would insist upon a written contract clearly spelling out the rights and obligations of the parties. An appreciable portion of the litigation that centers around suits for brokers' commissions could be prevented by carefully drawn brokerage agreements. This problem as well as some others that can be alleviated by a writing will be discussed later.

In those states that recognize the oral listing, a broker may establish employment by implications arising from a property owner's actions.

• CASE BRIEF •

Frewert owned a home that he had been trying to sell. Carlson, a real estate salesperson, obtained permission to show the home to the Coopers. Carlson obtained an offer, which she presented to Frewert. In discussion the transaction, she told Frewert that she was representing him. Frewert then quoted a minimum net price that he wanted for the property and discussed possession with her. Carlson obtained a second offer from the Coopers that was slightly less than Frewert's minimum net price. Frewert rejected this offer. Two days later, he signed a contract directly with the Coopers and refused to pay a commission.

> In a successful suit against Frewert for a commission, the court stated, "[W]hile a contract of employment is necessary to create an agency relationship . . . no particular form is required. Ordinarily, all that is necessary is that the broker act with consent of his principal either by written instrument, orally, or by implication from the conduct of the parties." *Dickerson Realtors, Inc. v. Frewert, 16 Ill. App. 2d 1060, 307 N.E.2d 445 (1974).*

The listing agreement should contain all the important elements of any contract: the amount of compensation, duration of the listing, when the commission is earned and the like. The contract should also outline defects and encumbrances to which the title is subject, terms upon which the owner will sell and details as to possession. The listing should also indicate whether it is a nonexclusive, or open, listing or an exclusive one.

Open Listing

A brokerage agreement that entitles the broker to compensation only if his or her activities bring about the desired result.

The open or nonexclusive listing is common in the United States. Unless the agreement clearly indicates otherwise, courts presume that a listing is nonexclusive. A seller who enters into a nonexclusive listing agreement may list the property with any number of brokers. The broker who brings about the sale is entitled to the commission. Authority of all of the brokers is automatically revoked without notice if and when the seller enters into a contract to sell the property.

In an open listing the seller retains the right to negotiate a sale on his or her own. If the sale is effected by the seller without the aid of a broker, no commissions are due and all listings are automatically terminated. Ordinarily, an open seller listing has no time limit and the seller can withdraw at any time. The seller has no commitment until the broker has procured a buyer ready, willing and able to buy. In order to escape paying a commission, a dishonest seller suspecting that a broker is about to submit an offer, might revoke the broker's authority and attempt to deal directly with the potential buyer. A seller who revokes in bad faith under these circumstances is subject to liability if the property is sold to a buyer located by the broker. Some open listings contain provisions entitling the broker to a commission after the expiration of the listing if the property is purchased by one to whom it has been shown by the broker.

Exclusive Listing

A brokerage agreement in which the seller gives a single broker authority to procure a buyer for the property.

An exclusive listing protects the broker against appointment by the seller of any other broker. Brokers prefer this type of listing because it provides added assurance that time and money spent procuring a buyer will be rewarded. The broker does not have to fear loss of a commission if another broker arranges a prior sale of the property.

Most exclusive listings are given for a specified period of time. They terminate automatically at the end of that period unless renewed. For a broker to take an exclusive listing for an indefinite period is generally considered poor practice. In many states an indefinite exclusive listing is illegal. This protects sellers who, unaware that the exclusive listing is still in effect, list with another broker and thus find themselves liable for two commissions. If an exclusive listing is open-ended, it is subject to cancellation upon notice. A few states allow the broker a reasonable period of time to arrange the desired transaction. In any case, most courts agree that a seller may not terminate a listing where the only objective is to sell to a buyer with whom the broker has been negotiating.

There are two types of exclusive listings. The *exclusive agency* reserves for the seller a right to sell the property independent of the broker without becoming liable for a commission. In the *exclusive right to sell*, the broker is entitled to a commission regardless of who sells the property.

Courts in many states require unequivocal language in the listing agreement before accepting it as an exclusive right to sell. These courts reason that the ordinary seller should be clearly informed that even if he or she makes the sale alone the commission must be paid.

Multiple Listing

A contract among brokers who as members of a multiple-listing exchange agree to share listings with each other.

Multiple-listing is used extensively in many areas of the United States. A multiple-listing exchange is made up of brokers in an area who agree to share listings and to divide the commission received for negotiating a sale. The listing broker and the selling broker each receive a percentage of the commission negotiated by the listing broker with the seller. The percentage that each of the brokers receives is determined by the rules of the multiple-listing exchange. The division of the commission differs from one multiple-listing organization to another. Some multiple-listing organization to another. Some multiple-listing organizations allow their members to withhold certain real estate from the exchange; others require that all listings be submitted. Multiple-listing organizations also generally allow the listing broker a period of time to attempt to sell the property before registering it with the organization. Since brokers have limited rights to delegate their authority, the members of a multiple-listing exchange should be sure that their contracts with the owners permit them to submit property to multiple listing.

Authority

Term used in the law of agency denoting the agent's power to perform acts authorized by the principal.

The broker is a special agent with limited authority, usually restricted to a single transaction. In addition, although many people in real estate—and often the courts—refer to a broker's authority to sell, most listings merely authorize the broker to find a buyer, not to enter into a contract on behalf of the principal.

• CASE BRIEF •

Vance entered into an exclusive-listing agreement for three months with Management Clearing, Inc. His wife did not sign the listing, although community property was involved. Management Clearing, Inc., obtained an offer on terms identical to the listing, but Vance rejected it. Management Clearing, Inc., sued for its commission.

Vance defended on grounds that in a community property state, a husband alone cannot authorize the sale of community real estate. The court refused to accept this defense. The court stated, "[A] brokerage contract places only the duty on the broker of finding a buyer . . . It does not authorize the broker to sell the property." *Management Clearing, Inc. v. Vance, 11 Ariz. App. 386, 464 P.2d 977 (1970).*

The broker does not bargain as to terms but assists the parties in arranging terms upon which agreement can be reached. Although the seller may give the broker authority to execute a contract of sale, this authority must be clearly spelled out in the listing. Because brokers usually do not have the power to contract for a seller, a buyer should demand evidence of the broker's authority to do so if the broker signs on the seller's behalf. Brokers who are employed as property managers or rental agents often have the authority to contract for their principal.

Express Authority

Authority a principal confers upon an agent explicitly and distinctly; may be conferred orally or in writing.

An agency authorization in the listing "contract" between the broker/agent and the owner/principal is the foundation upon which the broker's authority rests. Such authorization establishes certain tasks the broker is given the power to accomplish.

Implied Authority

An agent's authority to do those things necessary and proper to accomplish the express terms of the agency.

Implied authority includes activities such as advertising, showing the property and transmitting from buyer and seller proposals relating to the sale. The broker has the implied authority to do these things as they are necessary to achieve the result sought by his or her express authority, that is, to find a ready, willing and able buyer.

The broker also has the implied authority to make certain representations about the property. A real estate broker, however, is a special agent. This means that the broker's implied authority is confined strictly to the terms of the agency, and the broker is bound by his or her obligation as an agent to obey the directions of the principal.

CASE EXAMPLE

Mustafa Ali owned a profitable bakery that he desired to sell. He listed the business and property with Dave Gould Realty, Inc., for $150,000.

Gould obtained an offer for the property, which Ali accepted; a $1,500 deposit to be held by Gould accompanied the offer. The contract provided that the *deposit* on the purchase price would be paid *to the seller* if the buyer defaulted. The buyer refused to close the sale because of alleged defects in the title. Without contacting Ali, Gould returned the $1,500. Because the contract did not close as scheduled, Ali sold the property to another. If Gould sued for a commission, the court would rule against him because he had no implied authority to modify the contract by returning the deposit to the buyer.

The extent of the broker's authority is a critical issue in determining the seller's responsibility for representations made by the broker about the property. In a majority of jurisdictions, these statements are binding upon the seller. If the statement is material and untrue, the buyer may rescind the contract and in some cases collect damages. These results follow even if the broker thought the statement was true or if the seller was unaware that the statement was being made. As a general rule, courts consider statements made by a broker within the scope of the broker's implied authority. Any loss occasioned by these statements should be borne by the seller, who selected the broker, and not by the buyer, who was misled by the false statement.

A minority of courts have concluded that a broker's representations relating to character, condition or location of the property are not binding upon the principal. These courts reason that the broker's authority is not broad enough to bind the principal. They feel that a seller who has authorized a broker to find a buyer should not be charged with the broker's deceit or error unless the seller has authorized or is connected in some manner with the broker's statements.

This line of reasoning is questionable, to say the least. A seller who has hired a broker usually has little direct contact with the buyer. Many brokers try to prevent contact between buyers and the seller as a matter of policy. Sellers, on the whole, prefer to have limited contact with buyers. As a result, the buyer must depend upon the broker for much information about the property. The sellers should be responsible for the validity of this information just as if they had furnished it themselves.

Brokers, like agents, generally are chosen for their knowledge, skill and judgment. The relationship between the broker and employer is personal, and the broker has no authority to delegate to another the tasks that he or she has been hired to perform. This rule applies, however, only to broker's actions that are discretionary, such as determining the terms of the sale.

A broker may delegate to another authority to perform acts that are ministerial or mechanical in nature. Thus the broker may assign to a salesperson the task of showing the property or finding a buyer, inasmuch as these acts do not involve the broker's discretion. When a ministerial task is accomplished by a broker through a subagent, the broker is entitled to collect a commission even if the subagent's relationship to the broker was unknown to the seller.

CASE EXAMPLE

Dave Gould Realty, Inc., was authorized to sell property that belonged to Mrs. Philbrick. Gould mentioned this to Arthur Clairmont, a fellow broker. Several day later, Clairmont obtained Gould's permission to show the property to one of Clairmont's customers. Clairmont described the property and terms to this buyer. The buyer on his own examined the property and entered into an agreement with Mrs. Philbrick, who refused to pay Gould a promised commission. Mrs. Philbrick argued that she had not authorized Clairmont to procure a buyer.

Courts would ordinarily find for Gould in this situation as Clairmont's verbal description and transmittal of terms represented a mechanical act.

Broker's Duties to Seller

A real estate broker owes his or her principal essentially the same duties that any agent owes to a principal. Like other agents, the broker is a *fiduciary.* A fiduciary is a person who acts primarily for the benefit of another in a relationship founded on trust and confidence. In selecting the broker as agent, the principal has relied upon the broker's integrity, fidelity and ability. This relationship of confidence and trust requires high standards of conduct, and the broker must exercise good faith and loyalty in all matters relating to the agency.

Good Faith and Loyalty

Good faith and loyalty require the broker to advance the principal's interest even at the expense of his or her own. A broker may not purchase the principal's property unless the principal has complete knowledge of all the facts and freely consents to the sale. This prohibition applies even if the broker can show that the transaction was beneficial to the principal and the principal was not injured in any way.

The duty of good faith and loyalty controls situations in which the broker can represent both parties. If a broker has the authority to enter into a contract for either buyer or seller, the broker violates the fiduciary duty if he or she accepts compensation from both. Courts reason that it is impossible for a broker under these circumstances to satisfy the diametrically opposed interest of both parties.

In the common brokerage agreement, however, the broker is employed merely to bring the parties together. In this situation the broker may act for both and receive a commission from each as long as this dual capacity has been fully disclosed and permitted by both buyer and seller. In the effort to bring the parties together, the broker who is to receive compensation from buyer and seller must be certain to act impartially.

Abstract terms such as *trust, good faith* and *loyalty* indicate the general scope of the broker's responsibility to his or her employer. In reality a broker must take at least three positive actions to meet these general requirements:

- The broker must fully disclose to the principal all matters relating to the agency.
- The broker must obey the principal's lawful instructions.
- The broker must account to the principal for any proceeds of the agency coming into his or her hands.

Full disclosure requires that the principal be informed of all offers, the identity of purchasers, commission-splitting arrangements with other brokers, relationships between buyer and broker, financial limitations of the purchaser and the selling price of comparable property.

• CASE BRIEF •

Neibert listed property with Alfred C. Moore, a broker. One of Moore's salespeople obtained a purchase offer for the property. The offer acknowledged receipt of $3,000 from the buyer and provided that the deposit should be "forfeited as liquidated damages" if buyer failed to close.

Unknown to Moore, the deposit was in the form of a promissory note, not cash. Moore discovered this later but failed to inform Niebert, since the buyer assured Moore that the note would be honored. When the sale did not close, Neibert demanded the deposit to cover losses incurred. The buyer refused to pay the note.

In an action affirming the real estate commission's 60-day suspension of Moore's license, the court recognized that the temptation to withhold information is "especially strong when it is only a matter of disclosing bad news which may improve. The court added that "it is an agent's duty to give his principal timely notice of every fact or circumstance which may make it necessary for him to take measures for his security." *Moore v. State Real Estate Commission, 9 Pa. Commw. Ct. 506, 309 A.2d 77 (1973.)*

Skill and Care

In addition to meeting the high standards of conduct of a fiduciary, the broker must not be negligent in carrying out the duties of the agency. A broker is negligent if he or she acts in an unreasonable or careless manner and this action is the proximate cause of loss to the principal.

• CASE BRIEF •

Ponia Towski, who could neither read nor write English, owned a house in Camden, New Jersey. There was a vacant lot on each side of the house. Between the lot on the east and the house was an alley. Towski's house was on the boundary of the west lot. Because of this, Towski wished to purchase that lot and erect a dwelling, using his west wall as a party wall.

All of this was explained to Joshua Griffiths, a real estate broker. Through Griffiths, Towski purchased what he thought was the lot on the west and built an adjoining structure with a party wall. Unfortunately, Griffiths had negotiated a sale with the owner of the eastern lot. Because Towski did not own the property on which the adjoining building was located, his tenants were forced to vacate the premises. Towski then brought a successful damage action against Griffiths. *Towski v. Griffiths, 91 N.J.L. 663, 103 A. 192 (1918).*

Although the facts of this case are unusual, in finding for Ponia Towski the court applied a test that is relatively common. It held the defendant liable because he had not used the degree of care and skill ordinarily employed by people engaged in the brokerage business.

Liability for negligence depends upon factors that vary from one case to another. As a result, it is impossible to say that a broker is negligent because of acting in a particular manner. A slight variation in the circumstances might cause a court or jury to consider a particular act careless in one instance and not in another. There are, however, a number of relatively common situations in which principals have brought successful negligence actions against their brokers or have used the broker's conduct as a defense in an action brought for commissions. Cases exist in which brokers have been found negligent because they did not use ordinary care and skill in securing an adequate purchase price, investigating encumbrances, preparing papers relative to the sale, collecting payments due the principal and filing discharges for mortgages and liens.

It has been held that a broker who fails to make a determined effort to sell, especially a broker with an exclusive agency, is liable to the principal. Other cases have held that a broker charged with renting property is liable for failure to properly investigate prospective tenants who later damage the property.

Numerous remedies are available to the principal when the broker violates these duties. The principal may:

- Sue for breach of contract;
- Bring a tort action for negligence;
- Require the broker to defend a suit against the principal;
- Discharge the broker without compensation;
- Force the broker to account;
- Recover for loss and misuse of the principal's property.

In many cases principals use the broker's violation of duty as a defense when sued for the commission.

Broker's Duty to Buyer

Business relationships between buyers and brokers arise in one of two ways. In the typical real estate sale the seller lists his or her property with the broker. The listing authorizes the broker to act as the seller's agent in procuring a buyer for the property. The buyer is a third party. In negotiations with third parties (buyers), the broker is acting in the seller's behalf and, like the seller, deals at arm's length with the buyer. In an arm's-length transaction each party acts in his or her own interest. In the past, courts have applied the principle of *caveat emptor, i.e.,* "let the buyer beware," to the relationship between the seller's broker and the buyer.

In a comparatively few cases the business relationship between a broker and a buyer arises when the broker is retained to locate a suitable property for the buyer. The broker then is generally referred to as a *finder.* In these situations the broker is the buyer's agent, not the seller's, and the broker owes to the buyer the duties that any agent owes to his or her principal. An agreement of this type between buyer and broker is usually not referred to as a listing. In negotiations between broker and seller in these transactions, the seller is the third party.

Seller's brokers are liable to buyers in some situations. Traditionally, to recover against a broker representing the seller, the buyer needed to rely on some tort theory, not on any duty the broker owed to the buyer arising out of the relationship between them. Sellers' brokers are liable to buyers for misrepresentation of material facts about the property. If the misrepresentation is intentional, the broker is liable for fraud; if the misrepresentation is made innocently, the broker is liable, but the buyer's remedies may be limited. Fraud and misrepresentation are discussed in Chapter 15.

The liability of the seller's broker to the buyer for fraud or misrepresentation has been expanded in a number of states during the last 20 years. Courts in states as far apart as Alaska, Florida, Kansas, Ohio, Illinois, California and Washington have held sellers' brokers liable to buyers for failing to disclose material facts about the property. For example, buyers have recovered against sellers' brokers who have not disclosed a termite problem, a defective sewer, a leaky basement or personal interest in the property.

Courts holding that sellers' brokers have a duty to disclose material facts to buyers justify this stance in several ways. Some have applied a theory of negligence or negligent misrepresentation. To establish a claim of negligence, the buyer must show that the broker owed the buyer a duty to conform to a certain standard. In a number of cases, to establish this standard, courts have referred to standards in ethical codes promulgated by state real estate commissions and/or the Code of Ethics of the NATIONAL ASSOCIATION OF REALTORS®. These codes impose upon the broker a duty to treat all parties fairly. In other cases courts have held sellers' brokers to a high standard of care in relations with buyers on grounds that state legislation licensing real estate brokers must be interpreted in the light of its obvious purpose of protecting the public. A broker does not stand in the same shoes as a seller. Brokers owe the buyer the same duties of integrity owed the public at large. They must be answerable at law for breaches of statutory duty to the public. In addition, courts have stated that the broker's license is a privilege conferred by the state in return for which the broker must act in the public interest.

• CASE BRIEF •

Hagar was the holder of a long-term lease granted by the Wyoming Recreation Commission. The property covered by the lease was a trailer park operated by Hagar on 18 acres of state land. In 1978 he decided to sell the business and listed the property with United Farm Agency of Wyoming (United). Hagar represented to United that the lease expired in 45 years and contained an option to renew for 25 years. In fact the lease expired in five years and had an option to renew for 30 more years. Hagar was aware of this.

United's sales associate Milton wrote to Mobley, a prospective buyer, about the business. In her letter Milton repeated the information about the lease that Hagar had provided. At that time she had not seen the lease. Later, when a copy of the lease was obtained from the Wyoming Recreation Commission, she read it briefly and told Mobley that she didn't understand it and that it was almost illegible anyway.

After inspecting the property, Mobley contracted to purchase the business. When he discovered that the lease was not as represented, he sued Hagar, United and sales agent Milton. The trial court dismissed the case against United and Milton on grounds that all Milton did was to repeat representations made by Hagar. The court stated that Milton had no independent duty to inquire into the truthfulness or accuracy of these representations. Mobley appealed.

The appellate court reversed. It concluded that the liability of United and Milton attached on the grounds of negligence. According to the court, to someone who had placed herself before the public as knowledgeable in the field, the lease was clear enough to show that the number of years remaining did not add up the way Hagar claimed. The court went on to say that a real estate broker has a statutory duty to the public to be honest, ethical and competent. This includes a duty to disclose material facts that may affect a customer's decision to purchase. *Hagar v. Mobley, 638 P.2d 127 (Wyo. 1981).*

In most states that recognize a duty on the part of the seller's broker to disclose all material facts to the buyer, the duty is limited to facts the broker actually knew or should have known. In addition, most of these states hold the broker liable only if the buyer has no reasonable opportunity to discover the information himself or herself. One intermediate appellate court in California, however, has held in a case involving residential property that the broker has not only a duty to disclose material facts but also an affirmative duty to conduct a reasonable inspection to discover all facts materially affecting the value or desirability of the property.

The Broker's Dilemma

The duty to treat all parties honestly and fairly, which includes the duty to disclose all material facts to the buyer, can create a genuine problem for the seller's broker. As agent for the seller, the broker has a duty to be loyal and to act in the seller's best interest. At some point the broker's duty to treat all parties honestly and fairly will clash with the fiduciary duties the broker owes the seller. The following case example illustrates this problem.

CASE EXAMPLE

Sanger has been transferred to a small midwestern city. He and his wife know nothing about the city. Fleming, a real estate broker, has been showing them some of her listings. The Sangers contacted her because of their interest in a home that she had advertised. The Sangers are interested in a home that Fleming has had listed for some time. She knows that the seller is desperate as he needs cash to complete the purchase of another home.

The Sangers have expressed several times a desire to live in a quiet residential neighborhood. The home that they are interested in is in this type of area. However, Fleming knows that long-range plans exist to widen a nearby road from two to six lanes. Also, a developer has purchased several acres nearby and proposes to build a large shopping mall. If Fleming fails to disclose this information has she violated her duty to the buyer?

Although the trend in the United States is to increase the broker's duty to the buyer, most courts would not hold Fleming liable for failure to disclose this information. The information is public and the Sangers could obtain it, although not necessarily easily. In a few jurisdictions, Fleming would be liable as the information is material to these buyers and, although public, not readily attainable. The case example illustrates a dilemma that often confronts a broker or sales associate. In this transaction, as in most residential sales, the broker's fiduciary duty is to the seller, but ethical codes and case law require the broker or sales associate to treat the buyer fairly.

The Broker's Commission

Disputes sometimes arise between broker and seller over whether or not the broker has earned a commission. One reason may be that terms of the parties agreement are vague, without clear provisions as to matters that later become subjects of disputes. In addition, legal misunderstandings may arise. The seller makes the agreement believing that no commission is due until the property has been paid for and plans to pay the commission out of the purchase price. On the other hand, the broker expects compensation for finding a purchaser whose offer is accepted even if title never passes. Potential problems involving payment also occur because payment is not a primary concern of the parties when the broker is hired.

When there is a problem concerning the commission, some brokers as a matter of policy refuse to litigate. They believe that a lawsuit can damage their reputation. They reason that adverse community reaction to litigation outweighs any monetary gain resulting from a successful suit. It is true that litigation is unpleasant and should be avoided, but civil suits are not publicized extensively. In fact, the word-of-mouth injury to the broker's reputation caused by a quarrel over commissions with a dissatisfied seller probably occurs even if the broker does not sue. A broker should not avoid litigation to collect a commission that has been earned, although all other solutions to the problem should be exhausted first.

Commission disputes generally involve two questions. Although they are frequently interrelated, either question may be the subject of the dispute. One common question is: Has the broker done the job he or she was hired to do? The other is: When has the broker's job been accomplished so as to entitle him or her to a commission?

In one typical scenario, the broker locates a buyer willing to purchase the property on terms agreeable to the seller. When presented with an offer, the seller refuses to accept for one reason or another, although he or she previously indicated that the terms were acceptable. In another common situation, the broker negotiates a contract between buyer and seller, but the seller cannot perform because the title is defective. Or, perhaps the owner just decides not to sell and refuses to honor the agreement. The broker cannot compel performance of the contract, and the buyer, reluctant to sue, looks for property elsewhere. The broker, feeling that he or she has performed, now seeks to recover a commission.

For the broker to be entitled to a commission, a number of threads must come together. Initially, the court needs to determine what the broker was hired to do. The broker may have been hired to sell or lease property on specific and detailed terms. If so, the broker's sole responsibility is to find a ready, willing and able buyer on these terms. Once this has been accomplished, the broker is entitled to the fee even if the parties never enter into a contract. When there is a variance between the terms authorized by the seller in the listing agreement and those tendered by the prospective buyer, the broker is not entitled to a commission if the seller refuses to contract.

• CASE BRIEF •

Ray Kuzee listed her home with Sterk & Vogel, Inc. The listing price was $38,000. The seller was willing to accept a contract on the following terms. The buyer was to pay $20,000 cash upon closing. The balance was to be paid in regular $310 monthly payments, plus five percent interest. Sterk & Vogel obtained an offer to pay $38,000 cash. This offer was rejected by Kuzee; Sterk & Vogel then sued for the commission. The lower court dismissed the complaint, and the appellate court affirmed on grounds that the cash offer was not in compliance with the listing agreement. *Sterk & Vogel, Inc. v. Kuzee, 333 Mich. 249, 54 N.W.2d 219 (1952).*

In a few states sellers have successfully avoided paying commissions by overpricing the property when listing it, rejecting initial offers below that price and negotiating a subsequent sale at less than the listing price. When the broker demands a commission, the seller defends upon grounds that the offer submitted did not meet the terms specified. If a seller accepts an offer lower than the asking price from a purchaser found by the broker, most courts protect the broker by holding that he or she is entitled to a commission. The broker, however, must remain active in the negotiations unless deliberately excluded by the seller.

In some listing agreements, the broker is merely informed of general terms that the seller would like to get for the property. Although a price is usually mentioned, specific terms are left for future determination. In this type of contract, the broker is not entitled to a commission until the buyer and the seller execute a binding contract.

• CASE BRIEF •

Caldwell listed property with Burnette, a broker, at $3,000 per acre. Burnette showed the property to several people, including Donaldson. Several months later, Caldwell listed the property with Crutchfield at $2,750 per acre. Crutchfield obtained an offer from Donaldson at this price. This offer was accepted by Caldwell. Burnette sued for a commission. The lower court awarded him 30 percent of the total commission on the grounds that according to the terms of the listing agreement Burnette had to find a purchaser ready, willing and able to buy and "also actually effect the sale or procure from his prospective purchaser a binding contract." *Leon Realty, Inc. v. Hough, 310 So.2d 767 (Fla. Dist. Ct. App. 1975).*

Procuring Cause

A broker must be the procuring cause in bringing about a "meeting of the minds" between buyer and seller. A broker is the procuring cause of a sale if he or she initiates a series of continuous events that result in a sale upon the seller's terms. Merely introducing buyer and seller will be enough if the seller takes over the negotiations and completes the transaction. If the broker is unable to obtain an offer and abandons his or her efforts, the seller is not liable for a commission if the sale is completed without the broker's aid.

Sometimes two brokers contribute to the sale. Problems may arise if the seller pays the full commission to one of the brokers, knowing that broker is under a duty to share the commission the other. The seller would be liable for half of the commission unpaid broker if the broker who has been paid the full commission refuses to share.

The best solution to this problem is to have the brokers agree as to the manner in which the commission will be divided. If no agreement is reached or if the seller does not realize that two brokers were involved, some courts insist that the full commission go to the broker who was the "primary, proximate and procuring cause of the sale." Which broker fits this definition is determined in court on the basis of whose efforts tipped the scale and induced sellers and purchasers to come to terms.

Ready, Willing and Able
Capable of present performance.

To be entitled to a commission, the broker must procure a buyer "ready, willing and able" to complete the transaction. The test of whether the buyer is ready and willing is his or her intention at the time the contract is made. Intent at the time the contract is to be consummated (closed) is not material. Most courts infer readiness and willingness if the buyer submits an offer on terms stipulated by the owner.

A buyer is said to be able if he or she has the financial ability to complete the transaction.

• CASE BRIEF •

Chester Winkelman, a real estate broker, brought suit against J. R. Allen to recover a commission. The basis of Winkelman's action was that he had procured a ready, willing and able buyer. The evidence indicated that Allen had listed his ranch with Winkelman at $350,000. The listing was open. Winkelman showed the ranch to Russell Bird and his father, Randall. Randall Bird was a prosperous rancher. Russell, age 22, had appreciable ranching experience but little capital.

The Birds and Allen discussed the sale on several occasions. On one of these, Allen was informed that only Russell, the son, was to sign the contract. After apparent agreement was reached on terms satisfactory to Allen, a written offer signed by Russell and a $1,000 deposit were submitted. Allen held the offer for several days and then sold the property to another.

> After a lower court found in Winkelman's favor, an appellate court reversed and ordered judgment for Allen. The court stated, "[W]here the only available source from which the money is to come is . . . admittedly in the possession of a third person . . . who is in no way bound . . . such a purchaser cannot be considered able to buy . . ." *Winkelman v. Allen, 214 Kan. 22, 519 P.2d 1377 (1974).*

In the *Winkelman* case the broker did not produce a ready, willing and *able* buyer. No commission was due.

In a number of states, if a seller accepts the buyer's offer, the seller waives the right to question the buyer's ability to finance the sale. The clear trend, however, if not adopted by the majority of courts in the United States, is to follow a different rule. In these states the seller's acceptance of the buyer's offer does not preclude a defense against paying a commission based upon the buyer's inability to finance the deal. In any case, the seller is not responsible for a commission if the broker has misled the seller into believing the buyer was financially able.

A buyer is considered financially ready and able to buy under any of three conditions:

- The buyer has cash on hand to complete the sale.
- The buyer has sufficient personal assets and a strong credit rating that ensures with reasonable certainty that he or she can complete the sale.
- The buyer has a binding commitment for a loan with which to finance the sale.

When Commission is Earned

In most states, the broker has procured a buyer when the broker submits a binding, enforceable offer from a buyer on the seller's terms. The result is that, as long as the buyer is financially able, the broker has earned the commission at that time. The broker and seller may, and frequently do, agree that the commission will be earned on conditions other than submission of a binding offer. Their contract may state that the commission is due on closing of title or out of the proceeds of the sale. If this is the case, the broker's commission has not been earned until that condition is met. As a general rule, if the broker procures a counteroffer that deviates in price or otherwise from the specified terms, the seller may accept or decline. If the seller accepts, the commission is due the broker for services rendered.

Recent case law in some states modifies the traditional general rule as to when the commission is earned. Courts in these states hold that the broker is not entitled to a commission if the buyer defaults on

the contract. As a result, the broker does not earn the commission until the transaction closes.

Several reasons exist for this change. For one, most sellers listing property with a broker anticipate paying the broker's commission
out of the proceeds of the sale. If the sale fails to close through no fault
of theirs, sellers feel that they should not be responsible for a commission. A second reason is that the rule obligating the seller to pay a
commission upon contracting places upon seller the burden of determining the buyer's financial ability. But the seller is the wrong person
to make this decision. Determining the prospect's financial status and
willingness should rest with the broker, for ordinarily that person has
had closer contacts with the buyer and is better able to measure financial capacity and willingness. From the point of view of paying a commission, the time when financial ability and willingness are
important is not when the agreement is signed, but at the time of
closing. If the buyer refuses or is unable financially to perform at that
time, the broker has not really done the job. If, however, failure to
complete the transaction results form the seller's wrongful act or refusal, the broker has a valid claim for the commission.

Traditionally, the broker's compensation has been based upon a
percentage of the selling price. Most brokers in the same market customarily charge a similar commission, although even informal agreement among brokers to do so is illegal. In the late 1970s and early
1980s, as competition in the real estate industry increased, some brokers adopted alternative methods for determining fees. An obvious
competitive strategy was to reduce the percentage charged to below
that being charged by other brokers in the market. Another approach
was to charge a flat fee instead of a percentage of the selling price. A
third approach was to separate or "unbundle" the services provided a
client and charge for each on an individual basis. For example, a broker might determine a separate fee for appraising the property and sug-
gesting a selling price, advertising and showing the home, conducting
negotiations or assisting at the closing. Clients could select the services desired and be billed only for these. Although discounting, flat
fees and unbundling have been resisted in the industry, they probably
will be used more frequently as real estate brokerage becomes more
competitive.

Termination of Agency

The agency relationship may be terminated in numerous ways. Probably most agencies terminate upon accomplishment of the purpose for
which the agency was created or upon expiration of the time agreed
upon for performance. The latter is important in real estate as many
exclusive listings contain a date upon which the listing will end. In
fact, regulations in many states require that a listing include a specific

termination date. Of course, the agency will continue if the parties renew the agency at that time.

By Acts of the Parties

As agency is a consensual relationship, either party has *the power* to end it at any time. However, the fact that one has the power to terminate the agency does not necessarily mean that he or she has *the right* to do so. For example, if a seller gives a broker an exclusive-right-to-sell listing for 90 days, the seller has the power to revoke the broker's authority before 90 days have passed, but if the seller revokes without justification, the broker can sue for damages.

• CASE BRIEF •

Hague owned 240 acres of farmland. He listed 80 acres with Hilgendorf, a licensed broker. Before the listing expired, Hague terminated it as he had encountered financial problems and decided to sell the entire farm. The farm was not listed with Hilgendorf.

Hilgendorf found a ready, willing and able buyer for the 80 acres. When Hague refused to accept the buyer's offer, Hilgendorf sued for his commission. Hague argued that Hilgendorf's duty of loyalty required him to give up the listing. Both the trial and appellate courts rejected this argument. The appellate court stated that "[i]n performing agency functions. . . an agent does indeed occupy a fiduciary position, and his duty requires him to place the principal's interests first. But in the contract of agency . . . neither of the parties is acting for the other; each is acting for himself."

On this basis the appellate court rejected Hague's argument and awarded damages to Hilgendorf. The court stated that, although the principal has the power to terminate an unexpired agency, the principal subjects himself to damages for doing so. *Hilgendorf v. Hague, 293 N.W.2d 272 (Iowa 1980).*

By Operation of Law

In addition to termination by the acts of the parties, the agency relationship terminates automatically by operation of law if any of the following events occur:

- death, incompetency or bankruptcy of principal or agent;
- destruction of the subject matter;
- change in law making the agent's duties illegal;
- loss of license required by either principal or agent;
- conflict of interest.

Although termination for any of the above reasons is easy to understand, a difficult termination problem arises when an unusual change in conditions related to the agency takes place. For example, if a broker is authorized to sell land at a specified price and the value of the land suddenly increases substantially, has the original authority terminated? Most courts would say so.

Agency Coupled with an Interest
An agency that cannot be revoked by the principal.

Although ordinarily an agency can be terminated at the will of either party, an agency coupled with an interest is irrevocable. In this type of agency the principal has given the agent certain powers and coupled these with a financial or security interest in the subject matter of the agency. As a result the principal does not have the right to revoke the agent's power. In addition, when an agent has authority coupled with an interest, the death, incompetency or bankruptcy of the principal does not terminate the agency.

One common example of the agency coupled with an interest is a mortgage in which the borrower gives the lender the power to have the security sold if the mortgage debt is in default (see Chapter 22 and discussion of power of sale foreclosure). A less common example would be a business arrangement in which a broker advances funds to a contractor to complete a home on speculation. In addition to agreeing to repay the loan, the contractor gives the broker an exclusive right to sell the property when the home is completed.

Real Estate Sales Associate
A person employed by a real estate broker who, under the broker's direction, lists and sells real estate.

In many real estate transactions much of the work is done by sales personnel who are not licensed brokers. Although many state licensing states use the designation *salesman* for both male and female sales personnel, the term *associate* is becoming more common. That word will be used in this chapter.

All states require real estate sales associates to be licensed. The procedures that are followed to license sales associates are similar to those for licensing brokers; however, the requirements for obtaining a sales associate's license are less demanding. For example, to obtain a broker's license a person is usually required to have experience in selling real estate, but experience is not necessary to obtain a sales associate's license. If a competency examination is required to obtain a sales associate's license, it is almost always less comprehensive than the licensing examination for brokers.

In large firms, sales associates do much of the legwork for the business. A sales associate prospects for buyers and sellers, assists the seller in determining price and completes listings and sales contract. Sometimes the sales associate helps to arrange financing and may provide assistance to lenders and attorneys with regard to title evidence and documents necessary to complete the sale of real property.

A sales associate is required by law to be associated with a broker. The broker holds the sales associate's license and directs and supervises his or her work. Commissions on each sale are collected by the broker. The sales associate receives as compensation a previously agreed-upon percentage of the commission. There is some judicial disagreement as to the relationship between broker and sales associate. A majority of courts conclude that the sales associate is an independent contractor, not an employee. Under this view the broker is not responsible for workers' compensation, unemployment insurance premiums or withholding taxes. More recent cases, however, tend to view the relationship between broker and sales associate as that of employer-employee. Where this view is taken, the broker has the same legal responsibility to the sales associate that all employers have to their employees. Actually, whether an employer-employee or independent contractor relationship exists depends upon the facts of the particular relationship.

• CASE BRIEF •

McGinnis worked exclusively for Berens on a commission basis. He was hired to obtain listings of property suitable for sale to commercial developers. McGinnis was required (a) to clear all listings with Berens, (b) to attend sales meetings, (c) to report all transactions before they were finalized and (d) to comply with requirements, standards and methods of doing business established by Berens. Berens also provided office support, advances on expenses, hospitalization and life insurance.

McGinnis was injured because of the negligence of another Berens sales associate who was driving the two in a company car to inspect real property listed by Berens. When McGinnis sued to collect damages for the injury, Berens argued that he was not liable as McGinnis was an independent contactor, not an employee. The court disagreed. It held McGinnis an employee because Berens exercised "control" over the manner in which McGinnis did his job. As the injury was caused by the negligence of another Berens employee, Berens was liable. *McGinnis v. Frederick W. Berens Sales, Inc., 308 A.2d 765 (D.C. 1973).*

Other cases have also held the real estate sales associate an employee, even though the parties themselves have agreed that the sales associate was an independent contractor. These courts looked beyond the parties' understanding of their relationship to the degree of control exercised by the broker. A sales associate can work only for a single broker who holds his or her license; state regulatory statutes require the broker to exercise supervision of the sales associate's activity; therefore, control is usually relatively simple to establish.

Licensing Laws

State laws that (1) require a person to obtain a license in order to act as a real estate broker or sales associate and (2) regulate the conduct of those who act as brokers or sales associates in real estate transactions.

Real estate licensing laws are an exercise of the police power by the state. Based upon this power, each state as sovereign may legislate to protect the general welfare of its citizens. In 1917, California became the first state to adopt a comprehensive, statewide licensing statute. Since then, all states have passed some type of legislation regulating the activities of real estate brokers and sales associates. The core of this legislation is a licensing requirement. A major goal of these laws is to ensure that only people who are honest and competent operate as brokers and sales personnel.

Most state statutes define *broker* broadly, using as a basis typical activities involved in the sale and rental of real estate. Usually these statutes exempt lawyers and others acting in special relationships under court supervision. These would include administrators, executors, trustees and receivers. All states allow an individual owner to sell his or her own property without a real estate license, although some questions arise when the owner is a corporation. The general rule appears to be that a corporation selling its own land is not required to be licensed if it operates through regular employees who have actual authority to exercise the general powers of the corporation. Ordinarily, the board of directors and corporate officers such as the president and secretary have this power. However, when a corporation hires sales personnel solely to attempt to sell corporate land, these people must be licensed.

A number of sanctions exist for engaging in brokerage activity without a license. Most states merely deny the unlicensed broker the right to collect a commission or other fee. In a few states, acting as a broker or sales associate without a license is a misdemeanor, punishable by fine and/or imprisonment. Some states allow any person who suffers a monetary loss because of the acts of an unlicensed broker or sales associate to sue for damages.

Although the license laws of the states have many differences, some relatively common elements do exist. One reason for this is that many state laws are based on a pattern of law recommended by the NATIONAL ASSOCIATION OF REALTORS®.

Licensing statutes are usually administered by an appointed real estate commission. The commissioners are usually highly regarded people active in the real estate business. The commission has the power to make rules and regulations of its own to carry out the directives of the legislature. In addition to the commission, a full-time executive director is hired by the state to perform the administrative duties of the commission. Although the primary function of the commission is to administer licensing laws, most real estate commissions have other responsibilities. These commonly include the establishment and promulgation of educational and ethical standards.

In most states the competency of applicants for brokers' and sales associates' licenses is established by written examination. Many states have added minimal educational requirements, which must be met before a person is eligible to take a broker's or sales associate's license examination. Usually, to be eligible for the broker's examination, an individual must have had some experience as a sales associate or met certain educational criteria. The examination for a broker's license is ordinarily more comprehensive than that for a license to sell. A number of states have adopted legislation requiring continuing education for brokers and sales associates. In Ohio, for example, they must complete 30 classroom hours of real estate education every three years in order to retain their licenses.

The principal sanction available against a broker or sales associate is the revocation of his or her license. Numerous actions serve as the basis for revocation or suspension. Frequently these actions are indicated by statute, but in some states the real estate commission has authority to promulgate its own rules and regulations. Misconduct punishable under statute by suspension or revocation need not involve real estate transactions or dealings with the licensee as a broker, and a broker may be punished for misconduct even when no one actually suffers a monetary loss.

Unauthorized Practice of Law

In attempting to bring buyer and seller together to complete a sale, one of the perennial problems faced by brokers is the extent to which they can give legal advice, draft legal instruments or fill in blanks on printed forms without practicing law illegally. Little agreement exists in the United States as to what the broker can do without being involved in the unauthorized practice of law. Some states allow conduct clearly prohibited in others. Nevertheless, two principles do seem commonly accepted. First, permitted activities must be incidental to a transaction in which the broker is involved. A number of states, for example, allow brokers to fill in blanks on printed forms drafted by lawyers. In any state, however, a broker who did this for someone not a client or a prospective purchaser of real estate listed with the broker would be guilty of unauthorized practice of law. Second, a broker is not entitled to charge a separate fee for any legal work that is permitted.

Some states have attempted to clarify by statute what constitutes unauthorized practice. These statutes generally prohibit someone who is not a lawyer from giving legal advice and from drafting legal instruments. A few of these states exempt real estate brokers and title insurance companies from prosecution for drafting certain types of legal instruments related to real estate. At least one state, Arizona, by a constitutional amendment adopted in 1970, specifically gives real estate brokers the right to prepare legal documents incident to their trade.

In a majority of states, by judicial decision interpreting unauthorized practice statutes, it is clear that a broker may neither give legal advice nor draft instruments relating to real estate. For the broker to do so constitutes the unauthorized practice of law. This is true even if the broker does these things only for his or her own clients, only occasionally and receives no compensation for such work. A few states do permit a broker to draft simple deeds or other real estate instruments if this is done on isolated occasions and without compensation.

Brokers in most states are permitted to fill in blanks on certain printed forms that have been prepared by attorneys. In a majority of states the forms are restricted to the contract, offer and acceptance. The rationale for this position is that these are the only forms that are incidental to the broker's business. Other states allow the broker to complete blanks on lawyer-approved instruments such as a deed or mortgage.

An additional complicating factor in a number of states is that the information that the broker is permitted to fill in must be clerical in nature. Clerical information would include items such as date, price, names, addresses, property location, date of possession and duration of offer. This position can result in confusion for brokers as it is often unclear just what information courts consider clerical.

Penalties for practicing law without a license are harsh. In most states the unauthorized practice of law is a crime. The person convicted is subject to both a fine and imprisonment. A real estate broker who engages in unauthorized legal practice can have his or her license suspended or revoked. In addition, a person who suffers a monetary loss because of a broker's erroneous legal advice can collect from the broker in a suit for malpractice.

NEW HOME CONSTRUCTION AND SALES

The examples given in this chapter have dealt with the broker's role in the sale of homes or other structures, generally with an individual owner as the principal, selling to another individual who will reside in the home or use the structure as a business.

The broker also often has a role in the sale of new homes. Frequently a broker may be engaged by a builder or developer to sell one home or many, even before the homes are completed. Because of the importance of the legal relationships of the many parties involved in such a venture—subdivider, developer, architect subcontractor—the balance of this chapter will discuss their legal and ethical responsibilities.

Like so many other areas, home construction is something done by a specialist, or more likely a group of specialists, acting in a legal relationship for the individual or group that wishes to build one home or many.

One of the most common ways to have a home constructed today is to purchase one from a subdivider. The *subdivider* may be merely a developer who divides up a parcel of land into lots and sells the lot. The subdivider or developer prepares the site for housing by dividing the acreage into lots, installing the *infrastructure*—the roads and utilities—and doing preliminary grading. When the developer has finished, the lots are ready for construction of the houses; final site grading is done as houses are completed.

The developer and the builder or contractor may be the same person, although the site is often developed by one person, and the houses are constructed by another or several others. The method chosen is of little consequence to the buyer (the individual or group) seeking to have the house built. Each has responsibilities for work performed and can be held accountable by the buyer under the contractual arrangement that is entered.

All new housing is not the product of subdividing. A person can purchase a lot and hire a general contractor to construct a house to certain specifications. Or the person can hire an architect to draw up the plans and specifications for the house and to supervise the work of a contractor, who does the actual construction. Or a well-informed person may undertake to hire and supervise construction of a house drawn to his or her specifications.

Regardless of the approach taken, there is a cast of characters with whom the owner may have to deal. The following material discusses the roles played by these people and the legal rights and duties that arise as a result of those roles.

Developer

The person or firm that subdivides a parcel of land and otherwise prepares the site for the construction of housing.

Generally, the developer takes raw land and develops it to the point where it is ready for construction of the house. Initially, the developer must acquire the land. The acquisition may be as simple as an outright purchase in fee simple from the landowner. In other instances the developer and landowner enter a joint venture arrangement, sharing in some fashion the risks, costs and profits of the development project. For example, the developer may purchase the land, with the landowner taking back a mortgage for all or a portion of the purchase price. As the developer sells each developed lot, the landowner is paid an agreed-upon percentage of the mortgage.

The developer must be reasonably careful to select land that is appropriate for the proposed construction.

• CASE BRIEF •

Several purchasers bought condominium units constructed by Salishan Properties, Inc., in a resort area in Oregon. Due to erosion from the ocean, their lots were severely damaged. The owners sued the developer/builder, contending that it had held itself out as an expert in resort-type construction and was, therefore, negligent in selecting an inappropriate site for construction of their condominium units. Salishan countered that it had no liability since it was powerless to control the erosion problem.

The court held that the developer could not be held liable for latent defects. It could, however, be held liable for negligence in site selection. Since the developer held itself out as an expert in resort construction, it was required to take reasonable precautions to assure that the lots were suitable for residential construction. *Beri, Inc. v. Salishan Properties, Inc., 282 Or. 259, 580 P.2d 173 (1978).*

Once the land is acquired, the developer undertakes to install the infrastructure for the development. The roads, sewer and water lines, power and telephone wires, gutters and sidewalks and site grading must be completed. Most of these items are installed to specifications established by federal, state, county or municipal governments.

When the infrastructure is in place, the developer, when not also the builder, undertakes to market the lots to one or more homebuilders. The lot or lots may be sold outright to the builder. When a poor market exists for housing, the developer may agree to postpone full payment for the improved lot until the house is sold by the builder.

The Developer and Government Agencies

It is the developer's responsibility to obtain governmental approval for the site and for the individual installations. The land must be zoned properly for the type of housing that will be constructed. If it is zoned inappropriately, the developer seeks to have the zone changed to dovetail with the planned development.

Once the zoning is correct, the developer must obtain subdivision approval from the municipal planning board. The board will check to see whether the developer's plans comply with its regulations. For instance, the roads must be adequate in width and depth of roadbed, sewer lines must be adequate for anticipated flow and drainage layout must prevent flooding or ponding problems.

The most extensive cost in many subdivisions is that of installing utilities (using that term to encompass the full range of items that go into site preparation). These costs may be handled in a variety of ways. Some municipalities will bond for the full cost of the utilities, recouping their money for bond retirement from the increased taxes obtained from the new homeowners in the subdivision. In other cases the locality will bond for only a fixed amount for utilities, generally on a per-lot basis. If costs exceed that amount, the developer bears the financial obligation to pay the difference between the cost and the municipal bonding limit. In still other municipalities the developer must pay the full cost of utilities without the assistance of public bonding. In the case of power and telephone lines the utilities themselves may bear the cost of installation up to a fixed maximum.

The developer is legally responsible for the construction to specification of any utility installed by it. Many times the municipality will demand that the developer provide a performance bond to guarantee that the utilities will be properly installed. The bond will be released in stages as portions of the utility installation are constructed and found to conform to public regulations.

The legal relationship lies between the municipality and the developer. The actual builder contracts for the purchase of lots with the developer, but the developer remains primarily responsible for compliance with local laws. One area where this lack of legal connection between the municipality and the builder causes trouble is final site grading. The developer grades the site pursuant to municipal specifications. Final grading on each lot, however, is usually the responsibility of the builder upon completion of construction of the house. It is the builder's contractual obligation with the developer to grade the site properly, but it is the developer that will be held accountable by the municipality.

There are various other approvals that the developer must obtain, depending on local laws. Sewer installations may need state or county health department approval. An environmental impact statement or other environmental permits may be mandated. In all of these, generally the developer has primary responsibility for compliance.

Architect

A professional person hired to prepare the plans and specifications for the construction of a house.

The subdivider or contractor uses the architect to design the model home plans that he or she will sell to buyers. Also, the architect may lay out the design or configuration of the subdivision, locating the roads, the home lots and the drainage flow. The architect may, in addition, be employed to oversee construction. For an individual home, supervision may be confined to spot-checking materials that come onto the site and labor that is being performed. In larger projects, the architect may be hired to be on the site continuously to oversee the quality of work.

In any event, the architect who is hired by the buyer, owner or subdivider in one or more of these capacities has certain authority to act and certain rights and duties that arise from that authority.

The Authority of the Architect

The architect and buyer enter a personal service contract. Selection is based on the architect's skill as well as his or her reputation for honesty and fairness in business dealings. Although the basis of the authority granted is spelled out specifically in that contract, some generalizations can be made.

When the architect is hired to design a subdivision or an individual residential unit, an *employer-employee relationship* arises between the hiring party (the buyer) and the architect. This relationship requires the architect to follow the general instructions of the buyer in drafting the design. No architect is required to comply with instructions that would make the structure unsafe or would violate the regulatory ordinances of the community.

Since the architect is hired because of particular skills and characteristics, the contract is not assignable to another architect without the hirer's consent. If a firm of architects is hired, then any architect within that firm can do the design work unless otherwise stipulated in the contract.

When the architect is hired to supervise the construction, a *principal-agent* relationship arises between the architect and the buyer.

• CASE BRIEF •

Forty-O-Four Grand Corp. hired the architectural firm of Roland A. Wilson and Associates to supervise construction of a luxury apartment building in Des Moines. A dispute arose over the performance of the architect, and the owner withheld the architect's fee.

In an action by the architect for the remainder of his fee the

court described the parties' legal relationship. When one employs an architect to supervise construction, the architect is the
agent of the one who employs him or her. The architect is bound
to use reasonable care to see that the work is done properly with
the proper materials. *Roland A. Wilson & Assoc. v. Forty-O-Four
Grand Corp., 246 N.W.2d 922 (Iowa 1976).*

The architect has no general authority to bind the buyer but has the
authority to do what is reasonably necessary to complete the job according to the plans and specifications provided.

Although the extent of the architect/agent's authority is specified in the contract, certain implied authority exists unless prohibited. The architect is impliedly authorized to make minor changes in
the plans needed to correct errors made but does not have the authority to alter the plan *materially* without the buyer's approval. In addition, the architect has the implied authority to inspect materials that
come onto the site to assure that they are of the requisite quality.

The architect has a third type of authority that does not neatly
fall into a traditional legal category. When supervising construction,
the architect has the implied authority, if not otherwise expressed, to
settle disputes that arise between the buyer and the contractor.
Though hired by the buyer and primarily responsible to that buyer,
the architect is under a duty to resolve these disputes impartially. The
architect must apply notions of equity to the dispute resolution and
lay aside any duties owed to the buyer, which may put the architect in
an uncomfortable position at times.

The Architect's Rights and Duties

The architect who designs a subdivision or residential unit has a duty
to perform in a workmanlike manner. Design work must be completed on time, or within a reasonable time if a date is not stipulated
in the contract. An architect who fails to perform in a timely fashion
will be liable in damages for that tardiness.

When the architect is the construction supervisor and therefore
an agent, the fiduciary relationship demands the duty to act in good
faith and with loyalty. The architect is prohibited from having a financial interest in the contract or in any way benefiting personally from
the contract unless there is full disclosure and consent by the buyer.

The architect does not warrant a perfect job but does assure
that the contract will be supervised with reasonable care. Failure to
use reasonable care or to be loyal will make the architect susceptible
to a suit for money damages by the buyer and to the withholding of
the fee for failure to perform adequately. In the case cited above the
court stated that "this obligation does not make the architect a guarantor of the contractor's work. Instead, it requires the architect to ex-

ercise reasonable care in supervision and inspection of the work to protect the owner against payment of money to the contractor for work not performed or materials not delivered." *Roland A. Wilson & Assoc. v. Forty-O-Four Grand Corp., 246 N.W.2d 922 (Iowa 1976).*

If the buyer fails to pay the architect for services performed, the architect has a mechanic's lien on the property. The architect can compel judicial sale of the structure if the lien is not satisfied. Lien rights are discussed in more detail in Chapter 10.

Contractor (Builder)

The person or firm that undertakes to construct a house at a given price.

The term *contractor* or *builder* can mean several different things, depending on the building arrangement that is made by the buyer. Generally, the buyer hires a general contractor to construct the building to certain plans and specifications. The general contractor is obligated to provide the materials and labor necessary to construct the planned house. Much of the work is performed by subcontractors, whom the general contractor will hire and be solely responsible for. The general contractor is neither an employer nor an agent of the buyer, like the architect, but is classified legally as an independent contractor. The independent contractor agrees to provide a house to specifications, but the buyer has no direct control while the contractor is performing the services contracted for.

The general contractor may be constructing homes in a subdivision in compliance with the model home selected by the buyer or may be hired to construct an individually designed house on a lot owned by the buyer. Also, the general contractor may be building homes on speculation, hoping to sell them during or after construction. Although these are the most common arrangements, others exist as well. The buyer may choose to act as his or her own general contractor, hiring and coordinating the subcontractors or unit contractors.

The contractor may be selected personally by the buyer or may be obtained through a bidding process. If a bidding process is used, the potential contractors will be requested to bid on plans and specifications for a specific house. The bid entered by the contractor is an *offer,* and the buyer is free to select from among the various bids unless he or she has previously agreed to accept the *lowest bid without reservation.* There is no contract until the bid is accepted by the buyer. Any attempt to alter the bid materially by the buyer will be treated as a rejection of that bid.

The contract to build entered into by the contractor and the buyer will be governed by the usual rules of contract discussed in Chapter 17. The contractor's authority is simply to provide a final product, a house that complies with the plans and specifications provided by the buyer or the architect.

The chapter on contracts provides a thorough discussion of the various legal problems surrounding contracts. Satisfactory performance, delays in performance, mutual or unilateral mistake, modification of the contract and various actions for damages are discussed there. These general contract principles apply as well to the contracts entered into by the parties discussed in this chapter and will not be covered here.

The requirement of a *building permit* from a municipal official prior to beginning construction of a house is nearly universal. Failure to obtain a building permit allows the municipality to halt construction at any time and order compliance. Prior to issuing a building permit, the municipal official examines the plans for the house to ensure that no municipal code violations will occur.

If the building permit is issued and the contractor carelessly or willfully violates the municipal code, the contractor will be required to allow a reduction of the contract price equal to the cost of remedying the defects. If payment has already been made, a suit for money damages by the buyer is the appropriate remedy.

Rights and Duties of the Contractor

One of the chief responsibilities of the contractor is to coordinate the work of the subcontractors. If the general contractor fails to coordinate the work reasonably and that failure causes injury to the buyer or to a subcontractor, the general contractor will be liable in a suit for damages.

The contractor has the duty to inspect the materials brought onto the construction site. If such materials have defects that are reasonably discoverable upon an inspection and the contractor fails to inspect them or inspects but does not reject the defective materials, the contractor will be liable for injury caused by those materials. Injury includes the final product being a less valuable house, and the contractor will be liable for money damages for the difference between the value of the house contracted for and the one actually built.

The contractor, and any commercial home seller, impliedly warrants that the house he or she constructed is habitable. If the house proves not to be habitable or otherwise does not conform to any express warranty given by the contractor, the contractor will be liable in damages for the injury caused the owner.

• CASE BRIEF •

David and Patricia Elmore purchased a new home from a builder, Robert Blume. The Elmores told Blume that they

planned on carpeting and making a recreation room in the basement. Blume assured them that the basement, which contained
standing water upon inspection, would be dry when the gutters
and windows were in place. After the Elmores took possession
of the home, it continued to have a wet basement, and they sued
for the cost of drain tiles.

The court stated that the contractor/vendor gives an implied
warranty of habitability to the vendee in the contract for the sale
of a house. Water damage caused by faulty construction would
breach that warranty. *Elmore v. Blume, 31 Ill. App. 2d 643, 334
N.E.2d 431 (1975).*

If the house is destroyed by fire, flood or other natural disaster during
the period of construction and the contract does not address this contingency, the contractor continues to be liable to provide a house completed to specifications. Once the building is finished, the contractor's
responsibility to replace the house in case of destruction not due to
the contractor's negligence terminates. If the buyer tells the contractor what lot to build on and supplies the builder with plans, the contractor is not legally responsible for soil characteristics that make the
area unsuitable for construction nor for structural weaknesses in the
house.

In general, the contractor agrees to perform in a workmanlike
manner commensurate with accepted community norms. In exchange, the buyer agrees to make payments without unreasonable delay as they come due. If there is unreasonable delay in payment, the
contractor may be justified in abandoning the job.

SUMMARY

An agency exists when one person, called a *principal*, authorizes another, called an *agent*, to act for him or her. Real estate brokers often
act as agents for sellers. Sometimes, but less often, they act as agents
for buyers. An agency is created between a seller and a broker when
the broker acquires a listing. The listing authorizes the broker to negotiate a sale of the seller's real estate. To prevent later conflict, the
listing should be written, should specify the rights and duties of the
parties and should indicate whether it is open or exclusive.

An open listing entitles the broker to compensation only if his
or her efforts bring about the desired result. The seller may list with
any number of brokers, but only that broker directly responsible for
the sale is entitled to the fee. In the exclusive listing the seller enters
an agreement with only one broker. One type of exclusive listing, the
exclusive agency, allows the seller to sell without paying the fee. Another type, the exclusive right to sell, entitles the broker to a commission even when the seller finds a buyer independently.

The multiple listing enables the broker to publicize the sale of property through a local or areawide exchange. By prior agreement, when a broker who is a member of the exchange secures a buyer, he or she is entitled to share the commission with the listing broker.

The scope of the broker's authority as agent is limited to the terms of the agreement. In fact the broker is not normally authorized to sell but merely to locate a qualified buyer. A broker's authority may be either express or implied. Express authority refers to the terms stated in the agreement; implied authority relates to activities necessary to carry out this authority.

Laws of agency define the duties of the agent to the principal as fiduciary. A fiduciary relationship require high standards of conduct, good faith and loyalty. Specifically, at least three positive duties are involved: full disclosure to the principal of all matters relating to the agency, adherence to the principal's lawful instructions and full accounting for all money exchanges relating to the agency.

Although the broker is usually not the buyer's agent, the broker has a duty to treat the buyer fairly. In general, this means that the broker cannot misrepresent the property. In several states, courts have held that the broker has a duty to disclose all material facts about the property known to him or her that a buyer could not readily discover.

Payment of commission is sometimes disputed. Litigation generally involves one of two questions: Has the broker done the specified job? Has the job been accomplished so as to earn the commission? In most listings the broker's sole duty is to locate a qualified buyer or tenant who is "ready, willing and able" to buy or rent. The job is complete when the two parties are brought together. In most states the commission is earned at the time the broker submits a binding, enforceable offer from a buyer on the owner's terms, unless the listing agreement specifically states otherwise. In some states unless the transaction closes the broker is not entitled to a commission.

The law requires that each sales associate be associated with a licensed broker who holds that person's license and supervises performance of the work. Licensing of sales associates and brokers is regulated by state laws to qualify for a license. These laws most often require acceptable performance on a written test and adherence to certain standards of conduct. Some states require continuing education to retain the license. The laws are administered by state real estate commissions. The commission is empowered to revoke a license if a sales associate or broker is found guilty of misconduct.

One problem brokers face is the charge of unauthorized practice of law. The states vary widely in their rulings as to what is unauthorized practice. In most states, however, it is clear that the broker is not permitted to give legal advice to clients or to draft legal instruments such as contracts or deeds. They are normally permitted to fill in the blanks where such forms are prepared by an attorney.

In the sale of new homes the duties of subdivider, developer, architect and builder are varied and entail certain legal responsibilities. Often the duties of the parties overlap, as when an architect owns a development company to carry out his or her own designs.

REVIEW AND DISCUSSION QUESTIONS

1. Define *independent contractor* and indicate why a real estate broker ordinarily acts in this capacity.
2. Explain why classifying a real estate sales associate as an independent contractor does not relieve the broker of responsibility for the sales associate's actions.
3. Discuss the principal duties of a real estate commission as promulgated by law in most states.
4. What are the two types of exclusive listings? Explain how they differ.
5. Compare and contrast *express authority* and *implied authority.* Provide some examples of implied authority.
6. In a short paragraph or two, indicate arguments supporting a rule holding an owner responsible for representations made by a broker.
7. In the traditional real estate transaction, what are the broker's duties to the buyer?
8. Although appreciable differences exist in the United States as to what constitutes unauthorized practice, two principles are commonly accepted. State these principles.
9. Define *procuring cause.*
10. Conflict exists in American law as to when the broker has earned his or her commission. Indicate the conflicting positions and the supporting arguments for one of them.
11. What are some of the recent developments in the methods of compensating brokers?
12. Explain how the authority of an architect supervising construction differs from the authority agents generally enjoy.
13. What authority does the architect have to bind the buyer who is having a house constructed?
14. Why has subdivision become such a popular method of single-family residential construction?
15. Compare and relate the roles of architect, contractor and developer. Which of these parties is likely to be the most involved with municipal planning officials? Why?
16. What is the warranty of habitability? Was this type of warranty of importance in another area discussed earlier in the text?

17. How can municipal officials assure themselves that the developer/builder will conform to their subdivision specifications after their approval is given to the project?

CASE PROBLEMS

1. Ed Kelly gave Dave Gould Realty an exclusive listing on property owned by Kelly. Gould showed the property to Nadine McNicols, a real estate developer. McNicols had numerous questions relating to zoning, and Gould referred her to Kelly's attorney, who answered her questions and supplied her with additional information.

   When McNicols learned that Gould was showing the property to other prospective buyers, she made an offer directly to Kelly. Kelly accepted the offer but refused to pay Gould a commission. (a) What argument could be made for Kelly? (b) For Gould? (c) Who would win if Gould sued? Why?

2. Sam Guidi, a real estate broker, learned from a friend that Arro, Inc., was interested in buying vacant land for a warehouse. Knowing that Byron Lane owned land that he was trying to sell, Guidi phoned Lane, who quoted him a price of $35,000 for the parcel. Lane knew that Guidi was a broker, but no commission or other arrangements were discussed. Guidi obtained an offer of $28,000 from Arro, which Lane rejected. Shortly thereafter Lane contacted Arro directly and entered into a contract at $33,000. In a suit by Guidi against Lane for a commission, what resulted? Why?

3. Rogers, a broker, obtained an open listing on a ranch owned by McBride. Rogers showed the property to Molander, who submitted an offer. Unknown to Rogers, earlier in the day McBride had agreed to sell the ranch to Woodard. Molander asked Rogers to notify him if McBride's contract with Woodard fell through. Rogers did nothing further, but four months later Molander and McBride executed a contract for the ranch since McBride's contract with Woodard was not consummated. If Rogers sued for a commission, would he be successful? Discuss. *Rogers v. McBride, 42 Or. App. 303, 600 P.2d 895 (1978).*

4. Ellen and Paul Neel entered into a contract to purchase real estate from Marjorie Hayes for $55,000. The contract had been negotiated by Wagner Realty, with whom Hayes had listed the property. The contract was conditioned upon the Neels' obtaining a mortgage loan of $44,000 and selling their home. The loan was obtained, but the Neels were unable to sell their home. They agreed to take title in spite of this, but

Hayes changed her mind and refused to transfer the property. She also refused to pay Wagner Realty its commission, and Wagner sued. Hayes defended on grounds that the buyers were not ready, willing and able to purchase because the contract was conditional. Will Wagner be successful? Discuss.

5. Lewis, a licensed real estate sales associate, listed residential property owned by Flavin. Flavin informed Lewis that the property was in the South West School District. Actually the property was in the Columbus School District. Flavin, however, did not know this because he had no children and had frequently received mailings from the South West schools. In addition, children who lived next door attended schools in the South West District.

   Katz and his wife were looking for a home, but they did not want to buy property in the Columbus district because children were bused substantial distances to achieve racial balance. The Katz family was interested in Flavin's home and agreed to buy it after Lewis assured them that it was in the South West District. Would the erroneous statement made by Lewis be a basis for revocation or suspension of his real estate license? Discuss.

6. Klos purchased a home constructed by Gockel. A mud slide wrecked the patio of the house, although the house itself received only minor injury. Klos sued Gockel for breach of warranty of habitability. What was the result? *Klos v. Gockel*, 554 P.2d 1349 (1976).

7. Domino Developers developed Heaven's Acre subdivision and sold many of the lots to Orion Builder. Richards contracted to purchase a house constructed by Orion on one of these lots. According to the contract, the house was to be ready for occupancy by August 1. Orion completed the house and final site grading on July 18. The building inspector for the town refused to issue a *certificate of occupancy*, which was necessary before Richards could move in, because the final grading differed substantially from the plans approved by the planning board. August 1 has now passed. Both Domino and Orion refuse to correct the situation. (a) Who is responsible for bringing the grading into compliance? (b) Against whom would Richards's legal remedy likely lie? (c) The town's remedy?

8. Sierra Pacific commissioned Carter, a licensed broker, to sell real estate for an asking price of $85,000. Sierra Pacific was to receive $80,000 and Carter $5,000. The $85,000 figure was arrived at by Sierra Pacific upon the advice of Carter, who was

familiar with property in the area. At the trial the parties agreed that it represented fair market value. Carter received several offers of less than $85,000, but all were rejected by the seller. Finally, Carter sold the property to his daughter and son-in-law for $85,000. Carter retained the $5,000 without informing Sierra Pacific of his relationship to the buyers. Upon discovering it, Sierra Pacific initiated suit against Carter for the $5,000. Will it be successful? Support your answer. *Sierra Pacific Industries v. Carter,* 163 Cal. Rptr. 764 (1980).

15
Fraud and Deceit

FRAUD

A deceptive act or statement deliberately made by one person in an attempt to gain an unfair advantage over another.

No evidence exists that misrepresentation and fraud are more prevalent in real estate than they are in other sectors of the economy. However, deceptive acts that occur in real estate transactions probably have a greater impact than they do in other areas for several reasons. First, most real estate transactions involve large sums of money; as a result, people who feel deceived are more apt to complain or take legal action to assert their rights. A second reason is that licensing laws in every state have placed substantial supervisory responsibility upon brokers for the conduct of sales associates, as was seen in Chapter 14. Unauthorized and even unintentional deception by the sales associate can subject the broker to liability, including the loss of license. Finally, in many transactions little direct contact takes place between buyer and seller. Inasmuch as information is often transmitted through a third party, misunderstanding and error can result in the buyer, seller or both feeling that they have been deceived.

Many definitions exist for fraud; however, fraud can be classified in two major categories, based upon the intent of the one who practices it. *Actual fraud*, or misrepresentation, is based upon intentional deception and is usually accomplished by misstating or concealing a material fact. Actual fraud is often called *deceit*, and the two terms are used synonymously in this chapter. *Constructive fraud*, on the other hand, is not based upon *intentional* deception. Constructive fraud often consists of a breach of duty arising out of the fiduciary relationship discussed in previous chapters.

Liability for constructive fraud may be based upon a negligent or even an innocent misrepresentation. The law reads fraud into the actor's conduct because of its tendency to deceive another or to injure the public interest.

Those who enter into an agreement because they have been deceived by a misrepresentation are entitled to some form of remedy for any injury suffered as a result. The remedy available often depends upon the extent to which the person making the misrepresentation intended to deceive. Remedies will be discussed more fully later in the chapter.

Actual Fraud

Almost any of the parties involved in a real estate transaction is potentially liable for fraud or deceit: buyer, seller, broker or sales associate. The party may be found guilty if it can be established that a statement made by that party was (1) an intentional (2) misstatement of a material fact that is (3) justifiably relied on and (4) results in damages. Although it is relatively simple to list these elements, their application in practice is much more difficult.

Intentional

An intentional, conscious misrepresentation is an essential element of actionable frauds. Courts usually refer to this as an intention to deceive. The technical term *scienter* is also used. *Scienter* exists if a person knowingly makes a false statement or asserts that something is true or false without actual knowledge of whether or not this is the case. An evil intention is not necessary, nor is it required that the speaker intend to injure the other party.

Early cases found the requisite intent only in those situations in which the speaker had actual knowledge of the falsity of the representation; the courts equated intent to deceive with knowledge of falsity. This restrictive interpretation did not long survive. Today all American jurisdictions find scienter not only when the speaker knew the representation to be false but also when the representation was made either without belief in the statement's truth or with reckless disregard of its truth or falsity. Included are statements made by a person who realizes that he or she does not have sufficient basis or information to justify them.

• CASE BRIEF •

Gertrude Hall contracted to exchange her home for one being built by Haskins. The agreement was conditioned upon rezoning her property from residential to commercial use. After the property was rezoned, Haskins asked her to sign a blank deed. Mrs. Hall questioned this and inquired of Wright, her attorney, about

the title to the Haskin property. Although Wright had never examined the title, he told her to sign the deed and that he would
see that she got an abstract showing clear title.

Hall moved into the Haskins property. Some time later, Wright
discovered that it was heavily mortgaged. Hall refused to make
the mortgage payments, and she was ousted from possession.
She then sued Wright for fraud. Wright defended on the grounds
that he had not intended to deceive her. This defense was unacceptable to the court on the grounds that Wright spoke without
knowledge. *Hall v. Wright, 261 Iowa 758, 156 N.W.2d 661 (1968)*.

A majority of courts in the United States will not award damages for
fraud if the speaker honestly believes, upon the basis of creditable evidence, that the representation is true. A substantial and growing minority do not accept this limitation when the innocent misrepresentation is made in a transaction involving the sale, rental
or exchange of real estate. In these transactions the courts allow damages but limit them to the difference in value between what the listener has parted with and the value of what has been received and
retained.

CASE EXAMPLE

Glenn, a father of two preschool children, leased a house from
Takio on a five-year term. The rental was $400 per month. Takio
had innocently represented to Glenn that a new school was to
be built in the neighborhood. Takio did not know that plans had
been canceled. When Glenn discovered the cancellation, he
sued Takio for damages, claiming deceit. Glenn was able to
prove that the rental value of the property without the new
school was $350. The court awarded damages to compensate
him for the reduced value of the property.

In all jurisdictions, even an honest misrepresentation of fact supplies
the plaintiff with grounds to *rescind* the agreement. *Rescission* is the
disaffirmation or cancellation of a transaction.

Misstatement of a Past or Present Material Fact

• CASE BRIEF •

Elfrieda A. Scantlin contracted to purchase a house being constructed by Superior Homes (Superior). In the course of the negotiations leading to the sale, an agent for Manning Real Estate,
the builder's broker, stated that Superior was "a good builder
and constructed excellent homes." After Scantlin took title, she
found several things wrong with the building. When Superior did

not repair these defects satisfactorily, she sued both Superior and Manning Real Estate. Scantlin claimed that the statement made by the agent was fraudulent. Scantlin's case against Manning was dismissed as the court held the agent's statement was merely his opinion. *Scantlin v. Superior Homes, 627 P.2d 825 (Kan. Ct. App. 1981)*.

An important premise of American contract law is that adults are competent and have the ability to make rational decisions. As a result, courts do not aid those who rely upon statements not worthy of belief. Judges reason that the rational person discounts statements that are not factual.

Although the rule that only factual statements that are misrepresented can be the basis for fraud is clear, often it is difficult to determine what statements are factual. A fact is something that is knowable, a physical object that actually exists or existed or an event that is under way or has taken place. Understanding what the law means by a statement of fact is often clarified by considering statements generally considered by courts as not factual. These include opinions and estimates (as illustrated by the previous case), predictions, guesses and promises.

Promises require a special word of caution. As will be seen in the chapter on contracts (see Chapter 17), a person who makes a promise that later is broken is subject to a suit for breach of contract. Fraud is not the basis for the injured party's action. This makes a difference in the damages that the injured party can recover. For example, in a contract action the successful plaintiff is entitled to compensatory damages only. If successful in a suit based upon fraud, however, the plaintiff can collect punishment damages as well.

Puffing.   Sellers have a natural tendency to commend the item they are selling. Such expressions as "I built it with the best," "It's the best building in town" and "You have nothing to worry about; it's a good well" are examples. Statements of opinion like this, made by a seller to induce the purchaser to buy, are often referred to as "puffing" or "dealer's talk." Such statements are not actionable as fraud, even when false, since courts treat them as expressions of opinion. A leading American jurist, Judge Learned Hand, explained why in the following language.

There are some kinds of talk which no sensible man takes seriously, and if he does he suffers from his credulity. If we were all scrupulously honest, it would not be so; but as it is, neither party usually believes what the seller says about his opinions, and each knows it. Such statements, like the claims of campaign managers before election, are rather designed to allay the suspicion which would attend their absence than to be understood as having any relation to objective truth. *Vulcan Metals Co. v. Simmons Mfg. Co., 248 F. 853 (2nd Cir. 1918).*

Although generally the law does not protect the credulous buyer who relies upon the seller's opinion, a number of situations exist in which courts allow recovery for fraud based upon nonfactual statements. Opinions expressed (1) by a person who enjoys a relationship of trust and confidence or has superior knowledge, (2) by an expert hired to give advice or (3) by a person who actually does not have this opinion are all actionable.

In the following examples, assertions that ordinarily would have been treated as opinion became the basis for fraud. In each case the court determined that the other party had a right to rely upon the representation. Courts often rule this way when there has been a pattern of deceptive conduct or the speaker has concealed something that fairness dictated should be revealed.

CASE EXAMPLE

Mel Erickson, a licensed real estate broker, specialized in investment properties. Tillitz, a wealthy rancher, wished to invest in a multifamily dwelling. Erickson showed Tillitz several properties. After inspecting one large unit, Erickson stated, "That's a fine building, and the return on your investment would be substantial." At the time, Erickson had never inspected the records and was unaware of some major problems with the heating units.

Tillitz purchased the building, lost money and sued Erickson for fraud. Because of Erickson's superior knowledge, many courts would consider the statement as the basis for fraud.

In the case that follows, a statement is clearly opinion, but the speaker is asserting an opinion that she doesn't actually have.

• CASE BRIEF •

Grover and his wife owned a house on a bluff overlooking Lake Michigan. For a number of years, the Grovers and their neighbors had been concerned with erosion along the shore and the safety of their homes. In fact, a group of people from the area, including the Grovers, had met with the Army Corps of Engineers to work out a solution to the erosion problem.

A prospective buyer of the Grover property expressed concern as to the safety of the house. Mrs. Grover responded, "The house is perfectly safe. We are living here, aren't we?" In an action to rescind the contract of sale, the Grovers defended upon the grounds that the statement was merely an expression of her opinion. This defense would not be successful, inasmuch as the Grovers did not actually have this opinion. *See Groening v. Opsota, 67 Mich. 244, 34 N.W.2d 560 (1948).*

During the past 50 or 60 years the trend has been to expand the type of statement that can serve as the basis for fraud. Courts look beyond the form of the statement and consider the circumstances in which it was made when attempting to determine whether there was deceit. One example is the manner in which most state courts treat statements of law made by a layperson. Courts traditionally considered these statements of opinion. They arbitrarily reasoned that all laypeople had comparable knowledge of the law; as a result, the person to whom that statement was made had no right to rely upon it. Today the law in most states differs. Courts generally examine the context in which such statements are made. In many instances they conclude that the circumstances are such that a reasonable person has the right to rely upon what the layperson says the law is.

• CASE BRIEF •

Florence Johnson listed her property with Mel Erickson. Erickson obtained a purchase offer from the Petersons. This offer was accepted by Mrs. Johnson. Shortly thereafter, she decided that the selling price was too low. To obtain a higher price, Erickson told the Petersons that they "would not be able to enforce the . . . agreement in court." Erickson knew that this was false because the agreement was on a form commonly used. The Petersons, as a result of Erickson's advice, signed a new contract. Later, they sued him for deceit.

The Supreme Court of Oregon recognized their right to sue on these facts. The court rejected the doctrine that misstatements of law by a layperson are mere statements of opinion. *See Peterson v. Anvel, 275 Or. 633, 552 P.2d 538 (1976).*

Both buyers and sellers of real estate have been successful in actions for fraud, even when specific words concerning particular facts were never spoken. Most actions for fraud are based upon oral or written statements, but numerous other methods are used to deceive. Actions, failure to act, concealment and silence can all be employed to mislead another.

• CASE BRIEF •

Lawson purchased land in a development called Vanderbilt Hills. He had a house constructed upon this property. After a few months, the house began to sink. Upon investigation, Lawson discovered that the developer had filled a large gully with logs, stumps and other types of debris and covered this with clay. The land apparently was level, and enough clay had been dumped into the gully so that excavation for the foundation did not disclose the fill. Lawson was successful in a suit against the developer for fraud, inasmuch as the court held that the seller had a duty to disclose what he had done because the purchaser could not discover this through a reasonable inspection. *Lawson v. Citizens So. Nat'l Bank of South Carolina, 259 S.C. 477, 193 S.E.2d 124 (1972).*

The most difficult legal questions arise in cases in which a buyer has suffered a loss because of the seller's failure to speak. In some instances the seller simply fails to disclose an element important in the transaction. In others the seller employs some trick or scheme to conceal a condition or fact that is material to the transaction.

The cases that involve concealment are much easier to decide than those that merely involve silence. Active effort to hide something usually overcomes any reluctance courts have to refuse relief on the grounds of caveat emptor.

As a general rule, a party's silence—even silence concerning a critical factor—is not actionable as a misrepresentation. American contract law does not ordinarily require an individual to disclose facts detrimental to the agreement. In a few instances, however, there is a positive obligation to disclose known facts. Courts call this a *duty to speak.* In the following situations, courts in most states have ruled with consistency that a person must speak out about relevant circumstances and facts known to him or her:

- A hidden defect exists that is likely to result in personal harm to persons using the property.
- A hidden defect exists that is likely to limit a use the seller knows the buyer intends to make of the property.
- The seller enjoys a confidential relationship with the buyer.
- The buyer has asked a question that the seller has answered truthfully, but the situation changes and the answer is now false.

Another troublesome problem exists where the seller has made an oral or written representation that is only partially true. Like silence and concealment, the "half-truth" is a misrepresentation actionable as fraud. In many cases a half-truth is more misleading than a statement that is completely false. The half-truth can more easily lull the listener into accepting other representations that are made.

• CASE BRIEF •

Franks owned property on the outskirts of town. Although sewer lines had been constructed to the area, Franks's property was not yet connected. A prospective buyer asked Franks if the property was connected to a sewer. Franks replied, "The sewer line is across the street." Later, the buyer discovered that sewage from the house was being piped to the back end of the property. She sued Franks for the cost of having the property hooked to the sewer. Franks argued that his statement was true, but the court awarded damages to the buyer. *McWilliams v. Barnes, 172 Kan. 701, 242 P.2d 1063 (1952).*

Reliance

To be successful in an action for fraud, the injured party must prove that (1) he or she acted in reliance upon the false information and (2) the reliance was justified. A person cannot have relied upon false information if the information was acquired after the person acted, nor may a person rely upon statements that investigation indicates are false.

CASE EXAMPLE

Grace Kiner was interested in purchasing a music store from Helen Little. Kiner's marketing strategy required a large volume of potential customers. Little informed Kiner that on the average 250 people came in daily. Little knew that this was false.

Upon several occasions, Kiner visited the store, remaining for appreciable periods of time. After Kiner purchased the store, it became apparent that Little's statement was false. As a result, Kiner sued to rescind. Rescission would be denied if the jury determined that Kiner had relied upon her own inspection, not Little's statement.

In spite of the previous example, the fact that a purchaser makes an independent investigation does not in itself show reliance only upon his or her own judgment. In these situations the courts must weigh the circumstances of the particular case to determine whether continued reliance upon the misrepresentation after investigation is justifiable. Critical factors are such elements as (1) the background of the person investigating, (2) the amount of time available to investigate, (3) the sources of information available and (4) the techniques needed to secure correct information.

Courts use different criteria to determine whether reliance is justifiable. Some states measure the plaintiff's conduct against that of a reasonably prudent person. If a jury decides that a reasonably prudent person, one who uses ordinary care under the circumstances, would not have relied upon the statement, the plaintiff's reliance was not justified. Most states have rejected this standard. The test that is applied is tailored to the particular individual to whom the misrepresentation has been made. Courts in these states take the position that the law should not protect positive, intentional fraud practiced upon the simpleminded or unwary. At the same time, a person who has special knowledge and competence is not justified in relying upon statements that the ordinary person might believe. Similarly, a person whose background and information are those that a normal person might have is not barred from recovery because he or she carelessly accepts a misrepresentation; but if the alleged fact is preposterous, reliance is not justified, and recovery for fraud will be denied.

Material

Not only must the misrepresentation be relied upon; it must also be material. A person is not justified in acting upon a false statement that is trivial in relation to the entire transaction. Inconsequential information of this nature is not material and thus not grounds for suit. On the other hand, some false statements that in themselves seem to be of no significance are important in particular situations. Consider the following examples, in both of which representations are false.

CASE EXAMPLES

Rex Todor is purchasing a house in Memphis, Tennessee. The sales associate states, "Elvis Presley's uncle once lived here."

Rex Todor is purchasing an inn in Memphis, Tennessee. The sales associate states, "Elvis Presley often stayed here."

In the first example, the misrepresentation would not be material. A reasonable person would not consider this a significant factor. If, however, the speaker knew that this was important to the buyer, the result would be different. Courts ordinarily will not allow a person knowingly to practice a deception, even though the supposed fact might be unimportant to most people. In the second example, the misrepresentation is material. The fact that Elvis Presley had often stayed at a particular inn would increase the property's value as an attraction for tourists.

Materiality also has a second dimension, which causes some legal problems. Frequently, a false statement is only one of several reasons that causes the person to act. A difficult factual question exists when the plaintiff has numerous bits of valid information upon which a decision could logically be reached but, in addition, has been given some information that is false. It is the view of most courts that for the false information to be material, it must have contributed substantially to the plaintiff's decision to act. If without this information the injured party would not have contracted, the false information may be the basis of an action for deceit. Whether the information is material is a question for the jury. As noted in Chapter 1, the parties may waive a jury trial. If they do so, the judge is the trier of the facts.

Remedies Available to the Injured Party

A majority of courts in the United States have taken the position that a party deceived by an innocent misrepresentation is entitled to rescind the contract but not to collect damages. A few courts have held that even an innocent misrepresentation may justify an award of both rescission and damages.

If the misrepresentation is intentional, the injured party may proceed in a number of ways. He or she may:

- Refuse to perform, using the deceit as a defense if sued for breach of contract;
- Affirm the contract and sue for damages;
- Ask a court for a decree rescinding the contract.

In a number of states, courts will not allow the party who rescinds to collect damages except for the return of any consideration that has been given up. Courts in these states reason that rescission is based upon a theory that no contract ever existed. Thus rescission is inconsistent with an award of damages for breach of contract. The trend in most states is to allow the deceived party who rescinds to collect damages notwithstanding the rescission.

CASE EXAMPLE

Mrs. Slade sold her house to Garrity. At the time that Garrity inspected the property, Slade informed him that the heating unit was new. Actually, the unit had been installed several years earlier.

In a suit for fraud based upon the deceit, Garrity would be entitled to damages. These would be related to the cost of installing a new unit. He could also, if he desired, rescind the contract and recover the expenses involved in replacing the old unit.

Although American courts generally have been solicitous of people injured by deceit, they recognize the potential harm to the defendant who is charged unjustly. Allowing recovery against a person for fraud or deceit can affect many aspects of that individual's life. His or her ability to earn a livelihood and to purchase a home or other items on credit are sorely jeopardized. As a result, the law has been reluctant to find against a defendant in a fraud action unless the plaintiff's case is sound and evidence clearly establishes all the necessary elements.

Damages

In an action for fraud and deceit, a plaintiff is not entitled to recover damages unless actual monetary loss can be proved. Ordinarily, this requirement is met easily because usually the relationship between the misrepresentation and monetary injury is clear. Few people would sue for misrepresentation unless they believed the deception caused them to lose money. The costs and trauma of litigation make it an expensive way to prove a person a liar if the plaintiff lost nothing.

Generally, the more acute legal problem involves the amount of the damages, not their existence.

CASE EXAMPLE

Sam Tremain purchased a building site in a development for $28,000. In making this purchase, Tremain relied on the developer's false representation that plans called for a community swimming pool within walking distance of the site. The sites adjacent to Tremain's sold for $27,000 and $28,500. They were comparable in size to his.

Although the seller did build a pool, it was more than three miles away. Sites near the pool sold for $40,000. In a suit against the seller for damages based on the misrepresentation, Tremain argued that he was entitled to $12,000. The developer argued that Tremain could not recover because he had suffered no damage. He contended the site Tremain purchased was worth what he paid for it.

Courts in the United States use two different rules to measure damages in this type of situation.

Benefit-of-the-Bargain Rule. Under this rule, damages are measured by the difference between the value of what the deceived party actually received and what would have been received had the misrepresentation been true. In a benefit-of-the-bargain jurisdiction, Tremain would be entitled to $12,000. Benefit-of-the-bargain damages are sometimes difficult to establish because they often depend upon subjective testimony of what something would be worth under conditions that do not actually exist. In some situations courts can simplify this problem by measuring damages as the cost of putting the property in the condition that would bring it into conformity with the value as represented.

Out-of-Pocket Rule. Under this rule, damages are measured by the difference in value between what the injured party actually gave up as compared with the value received. If a court were to follow the out-of-pocket rule, Tremain would be entitled to very little. The lot that he purchased was worth approximately what he paid for it.

In a few states courts accept both rules. In a particular case the court will apply the rule that most adequately compensates the injured party for every loss that is the natural and direct result of the fraud.

A majority of the courts in the United States use the benefit-of-the-bargain rule. Courts in these states reason that the out-of-pocket rule treats the person who commits fraud more leniently than one who honestly breaches a contract. For example, if Tremain had been promised a site close to the pool for $28,000 and the developer unintentionally breached, Tremain's damages would be $12,000. On the other hand, when falsely induced to pay $28,000 for a lot supposedly close to the pool, in an out-of-pocket jurisdiction Tremain would be entitled to almost nothing if the lot that he actually received was worth about what he paid for it.

As we have seen, rescission is also a remedy available when a misrepresentation has occurred. In many states, a person who is defrauded may rescind the transaction without showing monetary loss.

• CASE BRIEF •

Olsen wished to sell his resort property, which was listed at $15,000, but he refused to sell it to his competitor Pettibone. Pettibone induced More, a broker, to negotiate a sale naming Flatt as purchaser. More and Flatt both assured Olsen that Pettibone was not the purchaser. When Olsen discovered the deception, he sued to rescind. Pettibone argued that Olsen suffered no pecuniary loss, but the court allowed rescission as an absolute right without any allegation of injury. *Olsen v. Pettibone, 168 Minn. 414, 210 N.W. 149 (1926).*

Punitive Damages.   Punitive damages are those awarded in addition to those actually incurred by the injured party as a punishment to the wrongdoer. To recover punitive damages for the tort of fraud and deceit, plaintiff must have suffered actual damages. In most states punitive damages will not be awarded unless the action is gross, oppressive and committed with ill will. Thus a person whose misrepresentation was the result of negligence would not be responsible for punitive damages.

The purpose of punitive damages is to deter others from committing similar acts. The award of punitive damages is discretionary with the jury. Punitive damages usually include an amount sufficient to cover the injured party's attorney's fee and an amount the trier of fact considers appropriate to dissuade others. Punitive damages must have some fair relationship to the compensatory damages that have been proved. Punitive damages awards that shock the conscience of the court will not be permitted.

Negligent Misrepresentation

The rules of negligence apply to a false representation made carelessly in a business transaction. The person supplying false information because he or she failed to exercise reasonable care in obtaining or communicating it is responsible for actual loss suffered by the listener. Because there was no intent to deceive, the speaker's liability is more limited than in a case of intentional misrepresentation. In addition, the defendant may assert defenses, such as plaintiff's contributory negligence, that are not available in an action for deceit.

Waiver

Intentional surrender of a known right or privilege.

Under certain circumstances, one who has been induced to enter a contract because of fraud or deceit waives the available remedies. Generally, waiver occurs when a person discovers the fraud and then does nothing about it. American courts have generally taken the position that, once a person learns that he or she has been deceived, ordinarily he must take some action, or the contract based upon the deception will be confirmed.

In a majority of American jurisdictions, if the contract is wholly *executory*—that is, neither party has performed—the defrauded party upon discovery of the fraud must rescind. Often courts in these jurisdictions do not allow the injured party to recover damages when an executory contract is rescinded. This rule is open to criticism because it denies the injured party the benefit of any bargain that has been made. For example, in these states, if Tremain, the unfortunate purchaser of the site supposedly near the pool, were to discover the misrepresentation prior to title closing, his only remedy would be rescission. But if he had taken title to the site and it had been as represented, he would have acquired land worth $40,000 for $28,000. With rescission as his only remedy, he loses the $12,000 that was the benefit stemming from the bargain that he had been induced to enter by the misrepresentation. A few states would allow him to affirm the contract even when wholly executory and sue for the $12,000 damages.

If a contract has been substantially performed, the injured party may elect to rescind or affirm the contract and sue for damages. Some action, however, must be taken, and the position of the person defrauded must be made clear to the perpetrator of the fraud. Waiver occurs if, after discovery of the fraud, the injured party merely continues to perform. This is not to say that he need proceed with the contract. Completion of the contract and a subsequent suit for damages is an available option, but the injured party's position must be established, and within a reasonable period of time.

An injured party also waives any right to sue for deceit if, upon discovery of the fraud, he or she enters into a new arrangement concerning the subject matter of the contract. Tremain surrenders his right both to sue for damages and to rescind if, with knowledge of the developer's misrepresentation, he enters into a new contract for the same site at a reduced price. Tremain would also waive his right to sue for damages if he entered into a new contract that extended the period of time allowed to pay the purchase price or substituted another site for that agreed upon in the original agreement.

Real estate contracts sometimes contain provisions stating that the purchaser has not relied upon any representations made by the owner or broker. A modification of this is a statement that the purchaser has personally examined the property and enters the contract relying solely upon his own inspection. A typical example is a clause such as "buyers agree that they have entered into this contract relying upon their own knowledge and not upon any representations made by the seller or any other person." Clauses of this type do not waive the injured party's rights to sue for fraudulent representations made by an owner or a broker. The courts reason that to accept such clauses as defenses would provide the seller and the seller's agent with a license to commit fraud. Most buyers would neither recognize the significance of the language nor consider that it applied to outright deception. To allow its enforcement would violate the clear public policy of protecting people who act on the basis of deceptive statements.

SUMMARY

Fraud is a deceptive act or statement made in an attempt to gain an unfair advantage. It is separated into two categories based upon intent. Actual fraud, also called *deceit*, usually involves an intentional misstatement or concealment of material fact. Constructive fraud, the other type, stems from an act that violates another's trust or confidence. Intent to deceive is not required. Remedies available to defrauded parties vary, depending on the offender's intention and the extent of damages.

To establish fraud, the plaintiff must prove an intentional misrepresentation of a material fact. In addition, he or she must establish that the misrepresentation was justifiably relied upon and that it resulted in damages. Fraud may also exist if a person conceals a material fact, such as a hidden defect, or deliberately makes a statement that is only partially true.

When accusations of fraud are established in court, rescission is the normal remedy. If the injured party can show a monetary loss, damages may also be awarded. Damages are measured by two different rules. Under the benefit-of-the-bargain rule, damages are measured by the difference between what the injured party actually received and what he or she would have received if the deceitful statement had been true. Under the out-of-pocket rule, damages are measured by the amount the injured party actually gave up in relation to value received.

The right to prosecute for fraud may be lost, or waived, by the victim under certain circumstances. One example is the person who enters into a contract to buy and then finds evidence of fraud. This buyer may not be entitled to damages if he or she does not take action before accepting title. Rescission may be the only available remedy in this case.

The injured party also loses the right to sue for fraud if, knowing of the fraud, he or she enters into a new contract for the property, perhaps on new terms. In this case the party also loses the right to rescind and must perform under the new contract.

Finally, one cannot use as a legal defense against fraud a provision in the contract stating that the "buyer has not relied on any representation made by the seller...." To honor such a clause would amount to the court's giving the seller a license to defraud the public.

REVIEW AND DISCUSSION QUESTIONS

1. Explain the difference between actual and constructive fraud.
2. What is the meaning of *scienter?*
3. A limited number of situations exist in which silence can be the basis for a successful action based upon fraud. Discuss these situations.
4. (a) How does the benefit-of-the-bargain rule for measuring damages differ from the out-of-pocket rule? (b) Which is more beneficial to the injured party?
5. Under what circumstances might a court award punitive damages in a case involving fraud?
6. Many courts refuse to award damages for fraud if a contract is wholly executory. Critically evaluate this rule.

CASE PROBLEMS

1. Able hired a contractor to repair several cracks in the walls of his home. The cracks were the result of settling, but the contractor never mentioned this fact to Able. Somehow Able got the impression that the cracks were caused by green lumber. When Able later tells Baker, a prospective purchaser, about the cracks, he explains the cause as green lumber. Baker purchases the property. When additional cracks appear and Baker discovers their true cause, he sues Able for fraud. Is Able lia-

ble? Discuss. See *Schnuck v. Kriegshauser*, 371 S.W.2d 242 (Mo. 1963).

2. J. B. Williams was an experienced businessman. In 1977, he entered into a written contract to buy realty from Threlkeld and Murray for $1 million. During the negotiations, Van Hersh, who represented the sellers, stated that New York Life had made a commitment to loan $6 million to develop the property. The terms of this loan were never discussed, nor did the parties ever talk about interest rates or any possible conditions. Williams did not check with New York Life.

   When Williams discovered that the life insurance company had not made a commitment, he attempted to rescind the contract on the ground of fraud. Would he be successful? Discuss. *Williams v. Van Hersh*, 578 S.W.2d 373 (Tenn. 1978).

3. Kaye was interested in buying a large piece of land from Katzenberry, who lived nearby. Katzenberry did not want to sell the land to a buyer who would use it for commercial purposes; he asked Kaye what he planned to do with the property. Kaye told Katzenberry that he was going to build a house on part of it and probably would use the rest for a garden. This was true, but before the closing Kaye changed his mind and made plans to build a hamburger stand next to his house. Katzenberry learned of this and refused to convey the property. Kaye sued for breach of contract; defense—fraud. Would Kaye be successful? Discuss.

4. Fifty Associates (Fifty) is a firm that has been engaged in the real estate business for many years. In 1959 Fifty and the Prudential Insurance Company (Prudential) joined to finance construction of an office building on land owned by Fifty but leased to Mayer-Central Building Company. Prudential advanced $2.5 million to Mayer-Central to construct the building. Fifty's financing commitment was conditioned upon the value of the property upon completion. As a result, Fifty refused to sign necessary documents without an appraisal.

   In order to overcome this obstacle, Oaks, Prudential's officer in charge, wrote two letters to Fifty. One contained the following statement: "It is not possible for us to disclose a precise valuation of a property. We can state that upon disbursement of $3 million now and $400,000 later, the loan amount will be approximately 70 percent of valuation." Fifty knew that this statement was based upon Prudential's appraisal of the property.

   When the project failed, Fifty suffered a financial loss and sued Prudential for fraud based upon this statement. (a) What defense, if any, is available to Prudential? (b) How might Fifty argue to overcome this defense? (c) Who would win? *Fifty Associates v. Prudential Insurance Co. of America*, 450 F.2d 1007 (9th Cir. 1971).

5. Scott successfully bid $227,065 to clear land for construction. He subcontracted some of the work to Hollis for $98,000. Hollis needed financing to begin the job, and he applied to the Farmers State Bank for a line of credit. The bank extended credit after a meeting with Hollis and Scott. One reason for granting the credit was a representation made by Scott that Hollis could expect $20,000 profit on the subcontract and $20,000 on sale of timber from the site. Hollis was unable to complete the work, defaulted on repayment of funds advanced by the bank and filed as a bankrupt. The bank then sued Scott for fraud on the basis of the statements made at the meeting. Would the bank be successful? Discuss. *Scott v. Farmers State Bank*, 410 S.W.2d 717 (Ky. 1967).

16
Fair Housing Laws

FAIR HOUSING

The term used to describe a national policy against most types of discrimination in housing.

The second half of the 20th century has seen increasing involvement of government in housing in the United States. Types of housing regulations discussed elsewhere in the text include zoning and subdivision regulations, rent controls and mortgage regulations. During the same period government has exhibited an interest in assuring, through legislation, that no member of our society is refused an opportunity to obtain decent housing.

Segregation in Housing

The voluntary or enforced separation of one group from another in residential location based on religious association, ethnic background, race or a combination of these factors.

Until quite recently segregation was the American way of life. People were routinely segregated from one another on the basis of race, ethnic background and religious preference. Ethnic identity has traditionally been a source of pride among most people. This pride led to the Irish immigrants living in the Irish section of a city, the Germans in the German section and the Poles in the Polish section. Second- and third-generation descendants of these immigrants, however, began to drift away from their ethnic neighborhoods and become assimilated into the general population. The security provided by the support structure of the extended family in the ethnic community was no longer a necessity for the children and grandchildren of these immigrants. "Americanization" of language and customs along with ethnic intermarriages lessened their emotional and psychological bonds to their ethnic beginnings. Also, in most cities a parallel slow progression toward ethnic integration began in housing. Although this ethnic integration continues, it has by no means been uniformly successful for all ethnic groups.

Further, this assimilation and integration process did not occur in the area of racial segregation. Racial integration may have failed to parallel ethnic integration because of the highly visible differences among the races. Probably it also involves a host of social and cultural attitudes. Lack of integration among the races was seen in the housing market as well.

Racial segregation was institutionalized by the real estate industry. Developers, banks and realtors adopted practices that facilitated the continued separation of the races. For instance, it would not have been considered a good business practice for a realtor to negotiate the sale of a house to a black in a white neighborhood. Embittered whites would be likely to employ an embargo against the realtor because it was contended, sometimes accurately, that property values would become relatively depressed in such an integrated area. Lost business and depressed property values were negative inducements to realtors who relied on a percentage of the selling price for their commission.

"Separate but Equal" Facilities

A concept that permitted the states to enforce separation of the races so long as each race was provided with "equal" services or facilities.

In the late 19th century case of *Plessy v. Ferguson*, 163 U.S. 537 (1896), the U.S. Supreme Court affirmed the doctrine that "separate but equal" was the law of the land. This concept was used to separate the races in many sectors of American life, including public transportation, education and accommodations. In housing, some state and local governments passed laws confining blacks and whites to separate sections of cities for residential living. This practice was considered constitutional as long as both black and white sections were provided. Economic and social pressures also were factors separating the races in residential areas.

The separate-but-equal interpretation of the federal constitution prevailed until the mid–20th century. Prior to that some erosion of the doctrine began to appear, especially in cases involving housing. In *Buchanan v. Warley*, 245 U.S. 38 (1917), the Supreme Court struck down a city ordinance that prohibited blacks from moving to predominantly white streets and whites from migrating to predominantly black streets. The basis for the decision had nothing to do with the doctrine of separate but equal facilities. The legislation was held to be an undue restraint on a person's constitutionally protected right to *sell* property because it excluded an entire race from the available market.

The separate-but-equal doctrine played a more prominent role in a case decided 30 years later, in 1947.

• CASE BRIEF •

Shelley, a black man, pursuant to a contract, received a warranty deed to a parcel of land in the city of St. Louis. Unknown to Shelley, a former owner of the property had entered into an agreement with other property owners in the area restricting the sale of the property to members of the Caucasian race.

Kraemer and other property owners brought suit in the Missouri courts to prevent Shelley from occupying the premises. The lower courts in Missouri refused to enforce the agreement, but the Supreme Court of Missouri held the restrictive covenant enforceable. Shelley appealed to the United States Supreme Court.

The Supreme Court reversed the Missouri court, holding that "in granting judicial enforcement of the restrictive agreements ...the States have denied petitioners the equal protection of the laws and that, therefore, the action of the state courts cannot stand." *Shelley v. Kraemer, 334 U.S. 1 (1947).*

In *Shelley v. Kraemer,* the court did not rule that the racially based restrictive covenants were unconstitutional, but only that the states, including their courts, must refrain from enforcing racial discrimination. Obviously, the effectiveness of a restrictive covenant is markedly reduced where enforcement in the courts is not available. Unless the party restricted by the covenant voluntarily complies with the limitation based on race, it is legally unenforceable.

The *Shelley* decision was quickly followed by several other cases that made it clear that courts could no longer be used as vehicles for enforcing racially discriminatory practices in housing. In 1950, the Chicago Real Estate Board, for example, amended a relevant section of its Code of Ethics. The board rewrote a section that advised realtors never to introduce members of a race or nationality into a neighborhood where the act would be detrimental to local property values. All reference to race or nationality was deleted from the Code of Ethics.

Equal Protection

The constitutional mandate that all people be treated equally under the law.

The separate-but-equal doctrine provided equality in theory, but it has been well documented that it had little relationship to equality in fact. Black and white schools were equal neither in physical plant nor in the quality of education children obtained in them. In housing as well, the quality and locations were not equal for blacks and whites.

In 1954, beginning with the school desegregation cases, the separate-but-equal doctrine was laid aside, and equal protection became the constitutional mandate. In these cases the plaintiffs were black children who, pursuant to statutes in Kansas, South Carolina, Virginia and Delaware, attended schools segregated on the basis of race. In each of these states, with the exception of Delaware, federal district courts had denied relief to the plaintiffs, citing the separate-but-equal doctrine of *Plessy v. Ferguson*. In the Delaware case, the state supreme court adhered to the doctrine, but ordered plaintiffs admitted to the white schools because of their superiority to the black schools. Plaintiffs appealed to the U.S. Supreme Court, which rejected the language of *Plessy v. Ferguson*. In an important decision the court stated:

> We conclude that in the field of public education the doctrine of "separate but equal" has no place. Separate educational facilities are inherently unequal. Therefore, we hold that the plaintiffs and others similarly situated for whom the actions have been brought are, by reason of the segregation complained of, deprived of the equal protection of the laws guaranteed by the Fourteenth Amendment. *Brown v. Board of Education* 347 U.S. 483 (1954).

After the decision in *Brown v. Board of Education*, the country began the slow process of racially integrating society. In the late 1950s and early 1960s, several states and cities enacted fair housing laws with varying degrees of coverage. These statutes were a prelude to the entry of the federal government into the fair housing arena. Since the federal government is now the focus for regulation of discrimination in housing, the remainder of this section will concentrate on several federal legislative enactments.

FEDERAL FAIR HOUSING LEGISLATION

It was ten years after *Brown v. Board of Education* before Congress became active in the fair housing arena. It was not starting, however, with a clean legislative slate.

Civil Rights Act (1866)

Congress passed a civil rights act shortly after the conclusion of the Civil War. The act stated "[A]ll citizens of the United States shall have the same right, in every state and territory as is enjoyed by white citizens thereof to imperil, purchase, lease, sell, hold, and convey real and personal property."

The obvious intent of the statute is to prohibit discrimination based on race or color in real estate transactions. Despite the significant implications that this law would have had for elimination of racial discrimination, it lay dormant and unused until the case of *James v. Mayer*, which is discussed later in the chapter.

Civil Rights Act (1964)

The initial foray of Congress into fair housing was in Title VI of the Civil Rights Act of 1964. This law prohibited discrimination based on race, color or national origin in most programs and activities in which the federal government rendered financial assistance. As a sanction for discrimination, the agency granting the financial aid could reject an application for money or terminate assistance already granted.

The 1964 law did not cover conventional mortgages because they did not involve federal aid. In addition, most FHA and VA loans that required federal guarantees were excluded from coverage as well. One authority estimates that the statute applied to only about half of one percent of the houses purchased. Consequently, the impact of the 1964 Civil Rights Act upon racial discrimination in housing was far from dramatic.

The Civil Rights Act or The Fair Housing Act (1968)

Although a major effort was mounted in Congress in 1966 to get approval of more comprehensive fair housing legislation, the majority of the Congress was unwilling to go along. In 1968, however, Congress made its first comprehensive venture into fair housing by passing Title VIII of the Civil Rights Act of 1968, which is also called the Fair Housing Act.

The 1968 act prohibited discrimination based on race, color, religion, sex (in a later amendment) or national origin by someone either selling or leasing residential property. Residential property included any building occupied or designed for occupation, as well as any vacant land sold for the construction of a dwelling.

The act was amended in 1972 by a requirement that equal opportunity posters be displayed at brokerage houses, model home sites, mortgage lender offices and similar locations. The poster must contain the slogan "Equal Housing Opportunity" and must carry a brief equal housing opportunity statement. Failure to display such a poster will be treated as prima facie evidence of discrimination; that is, in the absence of evidence to the contrary it will be presumed that the broker discriminates in violation of the law.

Exceptions

The Fair Housing Act of 1968 does not apply to the sale or rental of commercial or industrial properties. In addition, the act creates several exceptions to the prohibited conduct stated above.

A person may discriminate in the sale or rental of a dwelling, providing he or she can meet all these criteria:

1. The person does not own more than three houses at any one time.
2. The person is living in the house or was the last person to live there. If this residency requirement is not met, then the exception applies to only one sale every 24 months.
3. In addition, the exempt person may not use a broker, an agent or a sales associate to facilitate the sale.
4. The person also must refrain from any form of discriminatory advertising.

CASE EXAMPLES

Williams owns a house in town, one at the beach and another in the mountains. She lives in each during various parts of the year. She can discriminate in the sale of the beach house (or either of the others) so long as she sells it herself (without a broker) and does not advertise that there is a discriminatory preference or limitation.

Johnson also owns the same assortment of houses. He lives in the town house only and rents the other two. In addition to the restrictions mentioned above, Johnson is permitted to sell no more than one of the rental houses every two years if he wants to discriminate against buyers.

Another exception occurs when the owner of a multiple-family dwelling with no more than four units resides in one of the units and rents out the other units.

Occupancy of dwellings owned by religious organizations may be confined to the members of that organization, provided that membership in that organization is not based upon the categories protected by the Fair Housing Act.

Despite these exceptions, coverage of the act is comprehensive. Since most single-family homes are sold through the use of a broker and most multiple-family dwellings have more than four units, the bulk of sales and rentals would be covered by the statute.

Jones v. Mayer (1968)

The Civil Rights Act of 1866 lay largely dormant until resurrected by the Supreme Court in 1968, just prior to final approval of the Fair

Housing Act of 1968. The court, in *Jones v. Mayer*, 392 U.S. 409 (1968), raised this elderly statute to the status of a major factor in fair housing control.

At issue in the case was the following legislative language: "[A]ll citizens of the United States shall have the same right, in every state and territory, as is enjoyed by white citizens thereof to inherit, purchase, lease, sell, hold, and convey real and personal property." According to the Court in *Jones v. Mayer*, the intent of Congress was to prohibit any discrimination based on race or color in real estate transactions. It should be noted that, unlike the Fair Housing Act of 1968, this law applies only to race and color and not to religion, sex and national origin, but it does prohibit *all* discrimination based on race and color. In effect, the areas of discriminatory conduct excepted from coverage in the 1968 law are prohibited by the 1866 law where race or color is involved.

Also, the coverage of the 1968 statute is not confined to the real property transfer (sale, lease and so on), as is the 1866 law, but encompasses discriminatory advertising, exaction of terms and brokerage activities. The two statutes are duplicative in some measure, but they also complement each other.

In summary, any discrimination in the transfer of real property based upon race or color is illegal. The exceptions of the 1968 statute continue to permit discrimination in limited circumstances noted above when that discrimination is based on religion, sex or national origin.

Conduct Specifically Prohibited by Federal Law

The Fair Housing Act of 1968 prohibits certain actions when based on discrimination as defined in the act. For example, to *refuse* to sell or lease or to otherwise refuse to negotiate or to make a dwelling available is illegal. More over, *variation* in the terms of the sale or lease, as in provision of services or facilities in the sale or rental of a dwelling, is also prohibited.

• CASE BRIEF •

Filippo, a broker, refused to accept from a black person a purchase offer of $22,500 the price quoted to the buyer by Filippo's sales associate. Filippo instead told the black offeree that the selling price was $26,950. Later Filippo accepted a purchase order from a white buyer at $22,500 for the same property. As a result, Filippo's license was suspended for 45 days. Filippo appealed the suspension, but his appeal was rejected. *Filippo v. Real Estate Commission of District of Columbia, 223 A.2d 268 (D.C. 1966).*

Any *statement or advertisement* for the sale or lease of a dwelling, if it indicates a discriminatory preference or limitation based upon classifications defined in the law, is illegal.

CASE EXAMPLE

Cartwright and Lindsay visited a real estate firm where they indicated to a sales associate an interest in purchasing property in a certain section of Detroit. The sales associate stated that the section was fine "if you like a busted community." When asked what was meant by "busted community," the sales associate indicated that it was one that blacks had moved into. The sales associate also stated that housing values in that community are down and will continue to go down and that, while the schools are OK, "You know what will happen eventually." The sales associate then suggested another community.

Representation that a dwelling is not available for inspection, sale or rental, when in fact it is available, is also illegal. Other illegal acts include *denying membership* or *limiting participation* in real estate brokerage firms or their multiple-listing pools, *blockbusting* and *redlining*.

Blockbusting

Inducing (for profit) the sale or rental of any dwelling by indicating that a particular class of person (for example, nonwhite) has entered or will enter the neighborhood.

• CASE BRIEF •

Bowers and a number of other real estate firms in Northwest Detroit conducted solicitation campaigns in Northwest Detroit involving fliers, telephone calls and door-to-door canvassing. As part of their campaign, fliers were allegedly delivered to "Resident." One flier contained the legend "We think you may want a friend for a neighbor . . . know your neighbors." Another mailing also addressed to "Resident" purported to carry "neighborhood news." It announced that a real estate agency had just bought a house at a specific address in the recipient's neighborhood, that the named sellers had received cash and that the recipient might receive the same service. The recipients lived in changing neighborhoods. This conduct was judged to be illegal. *Zuch v. Hussey, 394 F. Supp. 1028 (D. Mich. 1975).*

Redlining

Denial of a loan by a lending institution or the exacting of harsher terms for loans in certain parts of a city.

Although redlining is often a strictly economic decision by a lender, it has been found to be illegal in some cases because it results in discrimination.

• CASE BRIEF •

The Laufmans, a white couple, purchased a home in a predominately black neighborhood. When financing was denied by the Oakley Building and Loan Company, the Laufmans sued. They argued that the defendant had redlined areas in the community in which minority-group families were concentrated.

The defendant moved for summary judgment. The court denied the motion. In denying the motion, the court stated that "although not altogether unambiguous, we read this [Sec. 3604 and 3605 of the Civil Rights Act of 1968] as an explicit prohibition of 'redlining.'" *Laufman v. Oakley Building and Loan Co., 408 F. Supp. 489 (D. Ohio 1976).*

Permitted Discrimination

All discrimination in housing is not illegal. As mentioned within the discussion of the Fair Housing Act (1968), private individuals can continue to discriminate based upon religion, sex or national origin so long as they can comply with the terms of the statutory exemption.

All discrimination is not based upon prohibited categories. It is not uncommon to find discrimination based on age, financial reputation, marital status, number of children, position in life and the like.

CASE EXAMPLES

Polcyk has a policy of refusing to rent his apartments located in the area of a university to undergraduate students because some are notorious for loud parties and damaging the interiors of apartments. Nothing is illegal about Polcyk's discrimination.

Barton leases her garden-style apartments only to persons 55 years of age or older without children. This clearly discriminates against those under 55, against persons with children and against the children themselves. There is, however, nothing illegal about Barton's leasing practice.

There may be some sound social reasons for discriminating. Many elderly people find the continuous presence of small children in their living environment an annoyance or even an unreasonable interference with their enjoyment of their land or leased premises. This is not to say that all elderly react the same way. Although many would thrive on the presence of children, those who are annoyed should have housing available to them that provides the quiet they seek.

The Federal Fair Housing Act of 1968 states that an aggrieved party has two types of remedies: administrative and judicial. These remedies are not mutually exclusive, and the party need not exhaust the administrative remedies before turning to judicial remedies. Nor need the party choose one remedy over the other prior to satisfaction. The balance of the chapter will present these remedies.

Statutory Remedies

Under the Civil Rights Act of 1866, a person may file a suit under Section 1982 of the Federal Procedural Code in a federal district court seeking redress for harm done by discrimination based on race or color in the transfer of property. No specific remedies are provided by the law, but it was indicated in *Jones v. Mayer* that courts should frame effective equitable remedies. In practice, what the courts seem to be doing is permitting the same remedies in Section 1982 suits as are authorized by the Fair Housing Act of 1968.

The discussion of statutory remedies that follows will focus on the administrative and judicial remedies provided under the Fair Housing Act of 1968.

Administrative Remedies

Remedies provided by the agency administering the statute, in this case HUD.

A person who believes that he or she has been the victim of a discriminatory practice must file a complaint with the Department of Housing and Urban Development (HUD) within 180 days of the occurrence of the discriminatory action. HUD then has 30 days to investigate the complaint.

If the complaint is filed in a state that has a law "substantially equivalent" in provision to the 1968 Federal Fair Housing Law, HUD must notify the appropriate state authorities and turn the case over to them. Should the state undertake to act on the complaint within 30 days of its notification, HUD loses jurisdiction of the matter unless, as the statute expresses it, "justice demands" its continued interest. The "justice demands" language permits HUD to retain jurisdiction if, for instance, the state has consistently failed satisfactorily to resolve a given type of complaint. In short, it permits HUD to oversee the appropriate handling of the matter.

When HUD retains jurisdiction over the matter, it must investigate the complaint within 30 days. If HUD finds that discrimination has occurred, it can use the tools of conference, conciliation and persuasion in order to obtain satisfaction for the complainant. When HUD is pursuing the matter, it is seeking to obtain the following relief for the complaining party: (1) access to the same or similar housing, (2) compensation for out-of-pocket expenses and (3) money for the hurt or embarrassment that may have occurred. In addition, when it is appropriate, HUD will attempt to get institutional change as well by getting the real estate firm to agree actively to seek minority clients for its products. It should be noted that there is nothing that compels the party accused of discrimination to confer, conciliate or be persuaded. If HUD's efforts fail, the complainant has 30 days to file suit in federal district court or the appropriate state court where the state has a substantially equivalent statute.

Effectiveness of Administrative Remedies. Under the Fair Housing Act of 1968, HUD is confined to investigating complaints and attempting to conciliate disputes. It has no power to compel any type of conduct by use of cease-and-desist orders. Most of the complaints received by HUD allege racial discrimination, though a few claim discrimination based on sex or national origin.

According to figures released by HUD, its success rate in getting the parties to conciliate their disputes has improved markedly in recent years. In fiscal 1979 HUD received 2,833 complaints, of which 644 reached conciliation and only 342 were successfully conciliated. This means that 23 percent went to conciliation and 12 percent were conciliated. But of the 4,822 complaints filed in 1985, 1,415 reached conciliation and 1,157 were conciliated successfully. This means that 29 percent reached conciliation and 24 percent were conciliated. This higher rate of successful conciliation has been the rule since 1981. Either HUD has considerably improved its efficiency in the conciliation process or the agency changed the way it measures success after 1980.

If conciliation fails and HUD has reason to believe that the person charged with discrimination is engaged in a pattern or practice of resistance to the rights protected by the Fair Housing Act, HUD can send the case to the Department of Justice for institution of a civil suit by the U. S. Attorney General. Absent HUD's finding that there is a pattern or practice of discrimination, the complainant must pursue a judicial remedy on his or her own.

Judicial Remedies

Remedies provided by the courts.

Since a large number of the people who are the victims of discrimination are poor, most people are likely to pursue their administrative remedies within HUD. HUD does the investigating and negotiating, so there is no need for the complainant to hire a lawyer, and thus the procedure is cheaper. Also, the HUD approach involves a less formal procedure. It should be noted, however, that the Fair Housing Act does provide for the appointment of an attorney where the court deems it to be "just," enabling the victim to commence litigation without paying any fees, costs or security.

Within 30 days of HUD's failure to attain satisfaction for the complainant, or within 90 days after the discriminatory action occurred, the complainant can file a lawsuit in federal district court. The complaining party may choose to pursue both remedies simultaneously. One benefit of this dual course of action is that the court may enjoin the landlord or seller from renting or selling the premises while HUD is attempting to negotiate a settlement. Needless to say, this action by the court will place pressure upon the landlord or seller to settle on HUD's terms.

The complainant, whether before HUD or in the court, will have to prove that he or she met the objective (nondiscriminatory) requirements set out by the landlord or seller in the transaction, that the rental or sale would probably have taken place had the complainant been of a different race, religion or whatever the alleged discrimination was based on and that the offer was made in good faith and refused. Several methods can be used to establish the complainant's prima facie case.

• CASE BRIEF •

Kindt owned rental property. On September 9, Otis and Carol Smith, husband and wife, attempted to rent an apartment from him. Otis Smith is black; Carol Smith is a Caucasian. Kindt informed the Smiths that he would let them know if he would rent the apartment to them.

On September 14, Kindt showed the property to Mr. & Mrs. Robinson, a white couple. After Kindt agreed to rent the unit, Mr. Robinson left the building and returned with the Smiths and a representative from CORE. Kindt was asked to rent to the Smiths but refused to discuss the matter and left the building. A decision by the state's human rights commission that Kindt had violated the state law against discrimination was upheld by the court. *Kindt v. State Commission for Human Rights, 44 Misc. 2d 896, 254 N.Y.2d 933 (Sup. Ct. Onon. Co. (1964).*

The complainant may also use a statistical approach to satisfy the burden of proof. If he or she can show that no members of a minority group or an unexplainably small number of minority people live in the landlord's housing, a prima facie case of discrimination usually exists.

The complainant who successfully proves his or her case in court has available a full array of legal and equitable remedies. The court may grant compensatory damages and punitive damages. It may grant injunctions or issue other appropriate judicial orders.

• CASE BRIEF •

In a Pennsylvania class-action suit, the plaintiffs represented a class defined as "all low-income minority persons residing in the City of Philadelphia, who would be eligible to live in the White-man Park Townhouse Project." Defendants were the City of Phil-adelphia, various officials of that city, several federal and state housing and redevelopment agencies and a number of local community groups. Plaintiffs alleged that various actions of the defendants in an effort to prevent the construction of the project, which was in a predominantly white neighborhood, violated plaintiffs' rights under federal civil rights statutes. Evidence pre-sented at the trial indicated a background of racial segregation in the city and in the housing system of the Philadelphia Hous-ing Authority.

The federal district court ordered the project to proceed. In its opinion the court stated: "Indeed, when faced with a civil rights violation, a United States District Court has not merely the power but the duty to remedy the effects of past violations as well as bar similar violations in the future. Of course, equitable powers may be exercised only on the basis of a found violation; but once a violation is found, all reasonable methods are available to for-mulate an effective remedy to achieve the greatest possible de-gree of relief given the practicalities of the situation." *Resident Advisory Board et al. v. Frank L. Rizzo, 425 F. Supp. 987 (D. Pa. 1976).*

One of the lingering issues under the Fair Housing Act of 1968 is whether the complainant must prove that the defendant's conduct had discriminatory intent or merely discriminatory effect. About half the federal appeals courts have approved the more lenient discrimina-tory effect test, but the more stringent discriminatory intent test is fa-vored by the current administration.

SUMMARY

Fair housing is the term given to the national policy of abolishing dis-crimination in housing on the basis of race or ethnic origin. Segrega-tion of one group from another has long been a characteristic of residential patterns. The civil rights movement, begun in the latter half of this century, however, has as its goal equal opportunity for members of all races to achieve adequate housing as well as employ-ment.

Earlier in this century restrictive covenants in housing were up-held by the courts in most cases. More recently, however, those clauses forbidding sale of property to blacks have been held unenforce-able, and in 1950 the Chicago Realtors Code of Ethics was rewritten to eliminate any justification of racial or ethnic segregation.

The doctrine of equal protection under the law provided by the

Constitution started with the landmark school desegregation case of *Brown v. Board of Education* in 1954.

Ten years later Congress enacted the Civil Rights Act (1964), which refused federal assistance in the form of loans or mortgage guarantees to those who practice racial discrimination. This move had a limited impact on private housing, however. A more comprehensive venture into fair housing is found in the Fair Housing Act of 1968. This act prohibits discrimination based on race, color, religion, sex or national origin in the sale or rental of a dwelling. An earlier Civil Rights Act, passed in 1866, had been largely ignored by the courts. In 1968 the United States Supreme Court gave new life to this old statute in the case of *Jones v. Mayer.*

Certain acts, when based on discrimination, are currently prohibited by federal law. These acts include refusal to sell or lease a dwelling, variation in terms of a sale or lease from one party to another, advertising that excludes certain groups and false representation that an available dwelling is no longer available. Also prohibited are the real estate practices of blockbusting and redlining. Further, refusing membership in a multiple-listing pool on the basis of race is illegal.

Under the Fair Housing Act, the party who suffers discrimination is entitled to bring a complaint to the Department of Housing and Urban Development (HUD). The party may also file in a federal court. Judicial remedies are often more effective than the administrative remedies of HUD because that agency lacks both the enforcement mechanisms and the budget to conduct the necessary investigations.

Legal remedies available to wronged parties may include collection of damages, both compensatory and punitive, and injunctions or other judicial orders. Nevertheless, the number of cases handled by both HUD and the courts continues to be small.

REVIEW AND DISCUSSION QUESTIONS

1. Compare the theory and the reality of the policies of "separate but equal" with "equal protection."
2. Which level of government is the most prominent in enforcing fair housing?
3. Compare the coverage of the Fair Housing Act (1968) with that of the Civil Rights Act (1866).
4. Using the rationale of *Shelley v. Kraemer,* explain how Congress can justify preventing individuals from using real estate brokers in a racially discriminatory sale of a residence, which would otherwise be exempt under the Fair Housing Act (1968). Would the same rationale pertain to the prohibition against discriminatory advertising?

5. Can you suggest to Congress changes that can be made to the Fair Housing Act (1968) to improve its efficiency in accomplishing the goals of the statute?
6. How did the real estate profession play an active role in promoting racial segregation?

CASE PROBLEMS

1. D. C. Williams and his wife, a black couple, wished to purchase lots in a subdivision being developed by the Matthews Company. The subdivision was not integrated. When they made an offer to purchase, a company official informed them that lots were sold only to builders. Although generally this was the case, some lots had been sold to individuals.

   Williams and his wife approached several white builders. Each of them refused to purchase and build for the Williams family, stating that they would get no more business in that area if they built for a black. Eventually Anderson, a black builder, agreed to purchase a lot and build the house that Williams and his wife wanted. The Matthews Company informed Anderson that it would not sell him the lot because he was not on the company's approved builder list. When Anderson attempted to find out what he had to do to become approved, he was informed that only the company president could do this and he was out of the country on a trip to the Orient for two months. The company had no policy for approval of builders, but it did have an office memo indicating support for integration of the subdivision. The memo also indicated a belief that the issue was a sensitive one and should be handled at the level of company president.

   No public announcement had ever been made of the company's commitment to integration, and no black had ever acquired property in the subdivision. Has the Matthews Company violated any of the federal civil rights statutes? Discuss. *Williams v. Matthews Co.*, 499. F.2d 819 (8th Cir., 1974).

2. Defendants operated 119 buildings containing 15,484 apartments within the City of New York, with rentals ranging from $140 to $400 per month. To be eligible to rent an apartment, a family had to have weekly net income equal to 90 percent of the monthly rental, or, alternatively, the family had to obtain a cosigner of the lease who had a weekly net income equal to 110 percent of a month's rent. These financial requirements excluded a large percentage of black and Puerto Rican applicants. Suit was brought against the defendants, seeking injunctive relief on grounds that the requirements violated federal civil rights statutes. What do you think was the result? Why?

Boyd v. Lefrak Organization, 509 F.2d 1110 (2nd Cir. 1975).

3. Greenwood was a sales associate in an office visited by Bago, a prospective buyer. Bago expressed an interest in a property in a specific area of Detroit. Greenwood told Bago that she had some nice property listed outside of the city. She stated, "The school system is poor in Detroit." Later she asked, "Do you read the newspapers? Even the police are afraid to live in the area, and they are supposed to protect us." Greenwood gave Bago several listings in Detroit and a suburb and suggested that he compare prices, indicating that prices were lower in Detroit because blacks lived there. Greenwood further indicated that she would sell him any property he was interested in, wherever it was located. What, if any, violation of fair housing legislation has Greenwood committed? Support your answer.

4. Marshall and Barnett, two black men, wished to buy homes in a development called Johnson Estates. Twelve homes remained to be sold in the development. The agent for Johnson Estates told them that the company would have difficulty selling the other homes if sales were made to Barnett and Marshall. He offered to build them identical homes elsewhere. He also told them that closing costs would not be charged if they could find purchasers for some of the remaining homes but that he would sell them the homes as the law required. Commonly, white purchasers were not required to pay closing costs. What violations of fair housing legislation is the agent guilty of? *United States v. Pelzer Realty Co. Inc.*, 484 F.2d 438 (5th Cir. 1973).

5. Initially public officials in the city of Birmingham, Michigan, favored a senior citizens' housing project proposed by a church-sponsored citizens' group. The city worked with the citizens' group until it learned that a condition for obtaining state and federal funding was that one unit of low-income housing be provided for every two units of senior citizens' housing. When this condition became known to the public, there was a significant cry of opposition. The opposition complained about bringing "those people" into Birmingham and about lessening property values. The city owned the land proposed for the project and allowed an agreement for the sale of the land to lapse and refused to negotiate further with the citizens' group. Was there a violation of the Fair Housing Act (1968)? Discuss. *United States v. City of Birmingham*, 538 F. Supp. 819 (D. Mich. 1982).

6. The City of Parma, a suburb of Cleveland, had a policy rejecting any proposal for low-income housing, even if it meant losing unrelated federal funding. In addition, local ordinances

made construction of low-income housing economically infeasible. Was the Fair Housing Act violated? Note that § 3604 (a) of that act makes it unlawful "to refuse to sell or rent...or otherwise make unavailable or deny, a dwelling to any person because of race, color, religion, sex, or national origin." Discuss. *United States v. City of Parma*, 494 F. Supp. 1049 (D. Ohio 1980).

17
Basic Contract Law

CONTRACT

A promise or an agreement between two or more parties that the law will enforce.

Citizens are obliged to obey laws the government imposes upon them. No one likes to pay taxes, but failure to do so results in penalties. The obligation to pay taxes arises from a legislative act. Obligations may also arise by individual agreement. Two or more persons may come together in agreement to be bound by their own "private legislation." The law will enforce that agreement through the courts if certain ingredients are present. Such an agreement is called a *contract*.

Contracts are the essential fabric of commercial transactions. Most people enter into contracts on a daily basis, by asking for fuel at a gas station, ordering a sandwich to carry out or purchasing a paper from a newsstand. Real estate listing and purchase agreements, leasehold agreements, options and mortgages are more complex forms of contracts. Each of these agreements is governed by contract law. Every state has its own body of contract law, derived from the common law and from statutes. The general body of contract law applies to all commercial agreements, including real estate agreements.

Not every agreement entered into between parties is enforceable. The law enforces agreements arising in a commercial context, assuming that certain other ingredients discussed in this chapter are present. The law will not, however, enforce a purely social arrangement.

• CASE BRIEF •

Sam promises to buy his friend, Rhena, a steak if she agrees to meet him for dinner after work. Rhena agrees. Sam shows up,

355

but Rhena does not. Since this is merely a social arrangement, Rhena has incurred no liability as a result of her failure to show. *See Balfour v. Balfour, 2 K.B. 571 (1919).*

Social arrangements normally do not evince the type of expectation and reliance that commercial agreements do. Generally, the economic harm that could result from breaking a social promise is comparatively small. The law deems that this type of transaction is best left to the conscience of the individual.

A contract entitles each party to certain rights, as well as imposing certain duties upon them. When a legally binding contract exists, each party is assured that, should the other party or parties not perform in accordance with the terms, the court will offer a remedy to the aggrieved party. The remedy may be in the form of money damages or a court order for *specific performance*—that is, that the party perform according to the terms of the contract. A contract thus provides an incentive for each party to perform.

Preliminary negotiations normally precede an agreement. Obviously, each party desires the best possible bargain. But when negotiations ripen into an agreement, it is necessary to ensure its enforceability. The real estate purchase or sale is the largest single transaction into which many people will enter. The parties expend substantial time and expense in preparing for the closing of the real estate transaction. If the parties were not legally committed to each other by a binding contract, either the seller or the purchaser could walk away from the transaction, leaving the other party without remedy. A contract is the best legal protection against such behavior.

This chapter is designed to provide a basic introduction to Chapter 18 "Real Estate Purchase Contracts." On the following pages the general principles of contract law are examined. First, each of the elements essential to the formation of a contract—offer, acceptance, capacity, consideration and lawful purpose—is discussed. Next, the chapter covers contract interpretation, the assignment (transfer) of contracts, breach of contract and remedies available to the parties in the event one party breaks the contractual agreement. Finally, Chapter 17 discusses the circumstances under which parties are released from their contractual obligations.

ELEMENTS OF CONTRACTS

Certain essential ingredients must be present in any contract, including real estate contracts, in order for it to be enforceable. Basic to the agreement are the *offer* and *acceptance*. There also must be a genuine assent to the terms of the agreement. In addition, the parties must possess the requisite *capacity*, or state of mind, to contract. *Consideration* must be present, and the subject matter of the contract must be *legal.* These and other elements of contracts are covered in the following sections.

Offer

A proposal intended to create a contract upon acceptance by the person to whom it is made.

The offer is made by an *offeror*—one who communicates a proposal. The offer is made to an *offeree*—one to whom an offer is communicated. If Mary offers to sell her house to Martin for $70,000, Mary is the offeror and Martin is the offeree. If Martin offers to buy Mary's house for $70,000, Martin is the offeror and Mary is the offeree.

The offer must state with *specificity* what the offeror is willing to do and what is expected in return. Terms of an offer must be certain enough to be interpreted by a court. The names of the parties and a clear identification of the subject matter of the contract are essential inclusions within the offer. Indefinite or vague language such as "a price between $80,000 and $100,000 is not sufficiently definite to constitute a valid offer. However, omission of the date or place of closing or even the price does not necessarily invalidate the offer. The courts may infer a reasonable place, date and price and, when necessary, look to the usage and customs within the real estate industry to give effect to intent of the parties.

• CASE BRIEF •

Mr. and Mrs. Beadle desired to purchase three lots in San Rafael, California, and to build homes on those lots for resale. They contacted Vera Rivers, a California real estate broker. Rivers agreed to represent the Beadles regarding the purchase, without compensation, in return for which the Beadles agreed to (1) build a speculative home on each of the three lots, (2) place the lots on the market for sale as soon as the homes were complete and (3) give Vera Rivers the exclusive right to sell said houses and pay her a three percent commission on the selling price.

After the transaction the Beadles refused to build homes on the lots and maintained that the agreement was too vague. The court, in awarding $1,800 commission to Ms. Rivers, held that, within the context of the real estate industry, "the term *speculative home* means a home built with expectation of selling it for a profit. . . and that in relation to the area of said lots and the type of homes in said area, the homes, if constructed by the defendants, would have been homes that would sell for approximately $20,000." Hence, in arriving at an $1,800 damage award, the court computed three percent of $20,000 for commissions for each of the three houses. *Rivers v. Beadle, 183 Cal. App. 2d. 691, 7 Cal. Rptr. 170 (1960).*

An offer must be *communicated* in order to be effective. Communication may be actual or constructive. *Actual* communication occurs when an offeree receives and then reads or hears the offer. *Constructive* communication occurs when a reasonably prudent offeree, under the circumstances, should have read the contents of the offer, regardless of whether an actual reading occurred.

An offeror has the power to control the terms of a contract. The offeror may make a reasonable offer or an unreasonable offer. If it is to ripen into a contract, the offeree must accept the terms of the offer. Before acceptance, certain events may occur that will cause the offer to terminate.

Termination of an Offer

If unaccepted, an offer may terminate in several ways, including revocation, rejection, lapse of a reasonable time, destruction of the subject matter, death of the offeror, insanity of the offeror or illegality of the subject matter of the offer.

Revocation. An offeror may withdraw an offer any time before the offeree's acceptance. The revocation becomes effective upon actual communication to the offeree. If the offeree receives a revocation prior to acceptance, the offer is terminated. Any purported acceptance after receipt of a revocation merely operates as a new offer (counteroffer), which the original offeror may accept or reject. The revocation need not in every instance be communicated by the offeror to the offeree in order to be effective. Sometimes a revocation is implied. An implied revocation occurs when the offeree learns from a reliable source that the offeror has acted in a manner incompatible with the outstanding offer.

• CASE BRIEF •

Frank makes a valid offer in writing to Dale to sell his residence to Dale. Before Dale accepts, Dale learns from Jackie, Frank's agent, that Perry purchased Frank's property. The communication of such information to Dale results in an implied revocation of Frank's offer. *See Dickinson v. Dodds, 2 Ch. D. 463 (1876).*

Rejection. An offeree may simply reject an offer by communicating to the offeror a refusal to accept the offer. If the offeree makes a counteroffer, an implied rejection of the offer results. An offeree, who communicates a rejection of an offer and then decides to accept the offer, has actually rejected the offer. The purported acceptance merely results in a counteroffer, which the original offeror is free to accept or reject.

• CASE BRIEF •

Mr. and Mrs. Leavey owned the Hereford Ranch in Wyoming. They desired to sell the ranch. Edward Murray, a real estate broker, learned the ranch was for sale and actively looked for buyers. Verne Woods and A. Trautwein were interested in purchasing the property for $2,300,000. After negotiations, the Leaveys made an offer that was communicated by Murray to Woods and Trautwein. Woods and Trautwein signed the agreement but attached three material amendments to the instrument. The Leaveys refused to accept the agreement with the amendments because "they changed the whole deal." After learning of the Leaveys' refusal to accept the amendments, Trautwein advised Mr. Leavey that the amendments were removed and the original offer acceptable. The Leaveys refused to sell the property to Woods and Trautwein, who sued for breach of contract. The court held that the Woods-Trautwein amendments constituted a rejection of the Leaveys' offer, which terminated the offer. Consequently, the subsequent assent to remove the amendments did not result in a contract. *Trautwein v. Leavey, 472 P.2d 776 (Wyo. 1970).*

Lapse of Reasonable Time. An offeror may specify an expiration date for an offer. A purported acceptance after the specified date is ineffective. If no date is specified, then the offer lapses after a reasonable period of time. What is considered reasonable varies from case to case, depending upon the circumstances. In general, however, an offer to purchase realty will not expire as rapidly as, for example, an offer to purchase shares of stock because the price of stock normally fluctuates more rapidly than that of realty.

Destruction of the Subject Matter. Destruction of the subject matter of the offer, before acceptance, results in a termination of the offer. If a seller offers to sell land and the house on it to a prospective purchaser, the offer will automatically terminate, before acceptance, upon the destruction of the house. This would be true even if the prospective purchaser was unaware of the destruction. Nevertheless, a *contract* does not necessarily terminate because of the destruction of the subject matter. Obviously, one who willfully destroys the subject matter of the contract will not be excused from performance, but will be liable for damages. Normally, the contract specifies who bears the loss in the event the property is destroyed by accident.

Death of the Offeror. Death of the offeror results in a termination of the offer whether the offeree knows of the death or not. If the offeree accepts the offer and then the offeror dies, a contract exists. However, death will normally not excuse performance of one's contractual obligation unless the performance involves personal services. If a seller who was bound under a purchase contract to sell realty dies, the seller's representative, pursuant to probate law, may execute a good deed conveying the property to the buyer. If the buyer dies, the purchase price may be paid out of the proceeds of his or her estate, and the seller may convey the deed directly to the buyer's estate, heirs or next of kin, as the law provides.

Insanity of the Offeror. An offer terminates before acceptance in the event the offeror becomes insane. Otherwise, the offeror would be at a disadvantage because an insane person does not normally possess the faculties necessary to decide to revoke an offer. A contract for the sale of realty, however, is not affected should a party become insane after entering the contract; the guardian or other representative of the insane person is required to perform.

Illegality of the Subject Matter. A change in the law may cause an offer that was legal when made to become illegal. Such a change causes an offer to terminate. Similarly, a valid contract that later becomes illegal due to a change in law is generally unenforceable.

Acceptance

Assent to the terms of an offer.

Acceptance is the second component of the agreement. The offeree has the power to create a contract merely by communicating an acceptance. The offeree does not have the authority to modify the terms of a proposal. As mentioned earlier, should the offeree change the terms of the offer, the variation creates a *counteroffer*, which actually constitutes a rejection of the original offer. The original offeror may then reject or accept the counteroffer.

At times an offeree appears to add terms to an offer when in fact the new terms were implied within the original offer. In such a case the purported terms will not defeat the acceptance.

CASE EXAMPLE

Allen offers to sell Solid Rock to Baldoro for $70,000. Baldoro responds by saying, "I accept, provided the title is good." Since the law implies in Allen's offer that Allen will tender good title, Baldoro has added no new terms and the acceptance is valid.

The offer and the acceptance constitute the agreement. It may not always be feasible or possible to determine which party made the offer and which party accepted. In many instances, after final negotiations, the entire agreement is reduced to writing. Both parties then sign the agreement. It is only academic in such a case to break the agreement down to the offer and acceptance components. However, the party who signed first could be considered the offeror and the second signer the offeree. In reality this is not always true, since a contract may have resulted prior to the signing of the agreement. In such a case the signing is merely the evidence of the oral agreement.

Manifest Intent

Courts often articulate that no agreement exists without a "meeting of the minds." This subjective test requires an examination of the psyche of each of the parties, which is, of course, impractical and usually impossible. The more acceptable approach is the *objective test*, one that is designed to determine whether the parties manifested an *intent* to be bound. Regardless of the mind of the offeror, if a reasonable offeree believes an offer to have been communicated seriously, then an acceptance of the offer ripens into a contract. This is true even when the offer was made in excitement or jest.

• CASE BRIEF •

Bill Klein and his wife own a farm valued at $75,000. Over the years John Bloom, a friend, on various occasions at cocktail parties offered to purchase the property for $75,000. The Kleins, tired of the continued offers and not believing Bloom could come up with 75 cents, decided to call Bloom's bluff. They drew up an offer in writing to sell the property for $75,000, describing with particularity other terms of the offer. Both Kleins signed the writing and sent the offer to Bloom. Bloom accepted the offer and tendered $75,000 to the Kleins, who refused the money on the basis that they were "just kidding and had no intent to sell the property." Since the conduct and words are such that a reasonably prudent person would be led to believe the Kleins intended an offer, the acceptance results in a binding agreement and the Kleins are obligated to perform. *See Lucy v. Zehmer, 196 Va. 493, 84 S.E.2d 516 (1954).*

Transmittal of Acceptances and Revocations

An acceptance is effective upon actual communication to the offeror or the offeror's agent. The offeror may expressly name an agent, or one may be implied. The law deems that an offeror impliedly invites acceptance from the offeree by the same mode of communication the offeror used to communicate the offer. This is known as the *implied agency rule*. If an offeror communicates an offer by mail, then the mailboxes would be the offeror's implied agents. Under that circumstance the deposit of an acceptance in the mail results in a valid acceptance at the time of deposit. The offeror assumes the risk of nondelivery of the acceptance in such a case, so that even if the offeror never receives the acceptance, it is nonetheless effective at the moment of delivery to the mailbox. Of course, the offeror may eliminate this risk by expressly stating as a term of the offer that acceptance is effective only upon actual receipt by the offeror.

An offer may be revoked anytime before it is deemed accepted. Revocation is effective upon actual receipt by the offeree. The implied agency rule does not operate in the area of revocation.

CASE EXAMPLE

Jan. 3   *A* offers by mail to sell Landacre to *B* for $2,000 an acre.
Jan. 4   *B* deposits an acceptance in the mail.
Jan. 5   *A* mails a letter to *B* revoking her previous offer.
Jan. 6   *B* receives the letter of revocation.
Jan. 7   *A* receives the letter of acceptance.

A contract exists on January 4 since an effective acceptance was delivered to *A's* implied agent prior to actual receipt by *B* of *A's* letter of revocation.

The law of transmittal of acceptances and revocations is based upon fairness and establishes firm rules that a businessperson may rely upon in decision making.

Reality of Assent

There must be reality of assent to an agreement between the parties; the *appearance* of assent is not sufficient. Any nonassenting party may avoid the contract. Causes that may intervene to negate a party's assent include fraud, innocent misrepresentation, mistake, undue influence and duress.

Fraud is an intentional misrepresentation of a material fact that induces justifiable reliance to the detriment of a party. Fraud is examined in detail in Chapter 15. The defrauded party not only may seek cancellation (rescission) of the contract but also may have an action in tort to recover damages against the defrauder. *Innocent misrepresentation* is an unintentional misrepresentation of a material fact that induces justifiable reliance to the detriment of a party. Because the misrepresenter does not do so intentionally most courts permit the party relying on the material fact to rescind the contract but deny recovery for damages.

Mistake is an unintentional error. When both parties enter into a contract under a mistaken belief as to a material matter related to the contract, either party may rescind the contract. If, for example, a seller and buyer of Redacre enter into a real estate sales contract under the misimpression that the property is an historical landmark when in fact it is not, rescission is available to either party. If only one party is mistaken concerning a material fact, rescission is not generally an available remedy.

Undue influence is the exertion of dominion over another person that destroys that person's ability to exercise independent judgment. Undue influence cases giving rise to a right of rescission involve situations where one party has developed a total dependency upon another. An elderly aunt may be so mentally overpowered by a nephew that she conveys her land to him at his insistence. Or a sick patient may develop such a trust in a nurse that he loses his power to resist the nurse's plea to convey his property to her. *Duress* is coercion that overcomes a party's will. Duress results when one is coerced to enter into an agreement by force or threat of force. The threat must be of such a nature as to place a reasonable person in fear, such as the threat of bodily harm.

Capacity

The legal ability to enter into a contract.

For a legally binding agreement to exist, both parties must have *capacity* to enter into the contract. Some persons have no capacity to contract; their contracts are designated as *void*. Other persons possess limited capacity to enter into contracts; their contracts are classified as *voidable*. Examples of both categories are discussed below.

Insane Persons

An insane person, under the law, is one who lacks the requisite reason to comprehend the nature and consequences of transactions. Any contract entered into by a person who has been determined to be insane by a court—that is, one who has been *adjudicated insane*—is automatically void. Since such information is a matter of public record, all are deemed to be on notice that the person cannot enter into a valid contract and may not be held liable because the court has determined him or her to be insane. A person who is *actually insane*, but has not been adjudicated insane by a court, is deemed to possess limited capacity to enter into contracts. His or her contracts are classified as voidable. A *voidable contract* is one that may be voided or validated at the option of the party who possesses limited capacity. During the course of the insanity, up to a reasonable time after being restored to sanity, a person who is actually insane may elect to *disavow* the contract and treat it as void. In such a case the insane person must tender back the property received and is then entitled to a return of the property he or she previously conveyed. Or, after being restored to sanity, that person may *ratify* the contract and treat it as valid.

Minors

The law seeks to protect the immature as well as the insane. For that reason the law discourages adults from contracting with them. In some states those under the age of 21 are considered minors, but in most, minors are those under 18. Generally, a contract entered into with a minor is voidable by the minor. That means that the minor may choose to disaffirm the contract anytime during minority and up to a reasonable time after attaining majority. If the contract is *executory* (unperformed), then that disaffirmance releases the minor from the obligation to perform the contract. If the contract is *executed* (performed), then the disaffirming minor need only give back to the adult that which remains of what he or she received from the adult. Then the minor would be entitled to a full return of the money or property originally conveyed to the adult. In most states, however, when the transaction involves a completed sale of the minor's realty, the minor is obliged to await the age of majority before disaffirming the transaction. In these states the minor must disaffirm within a reasonable period of time after attaining majority.

• CASE BRIEF •

Clifford Spencer and his sister owned land. Clifford was a minor and did not attain majority until April 5, 1919. On November 30, 1918, MacCloon purchased the property from Clifford and his sister. MacCloon later conveyed the property to Lyman Falls Power Company and Hutchins. Thereafter Lyman Falls conveyed its interest in the property to the Public Service Company of New Hampshire. On September 8, 1936, Clifford sued to disaffirm the contract and sought to have the property reconveyed to him. The court held that, although Clifford could disaffirm upon attaining majority, "a delay of 17 years and 5 months after the plaintiff attained his majority until the bringing of this suit...was unreasonable." Consequently, Clifford's attempt to disaffirm was unsuccessful. *Spencer v. Lyman Falls Power Co., 109 Vt. 294, 196 A. 276 (1938).*

Minors are obligated to pay for the necessities of life for which they contract and receive. Although minors may still disaffirm contracts for necessities, they will nonetheless be required to pay the reasonable value of the property or services received. Normally, real estate that provides housing is not deemed to be a necessity for a minor since the minor can live with his or her parents. Generally, a minor's parents are not liable for their child's contractual obligations or debts. However, a parent may become liable by agreement. Such an agreement may involve the parents' cosigning a contract or a promissory note guaranteeing payment.

Drugged Persons

Contracts entered into by a person who is intoxicated or under the influence of drugs are voidable if the drug renders such a person unable to appreciate the nature and consequences of his or her acts. Most courts are less sympathetic to this classification of persons than to minors and will permit disaffirmance of a completed contract only if the person contracting with the drugged person can be restored to the original position, suffering no loss.

Consideration

A promise, act or forbearance bargained for and given in exchange for a promise, act or forbearance.

Consideration is a necessary element of a contract. Generally, if a defendant's promise is not supported by consideration, then it is unenforceable. In order for a promise to be supported by consideration, it must result in a benefit to the *promisor* (the one who makes a promise) *or* a detriment to the *promisee* (the one to whom a promise is made). The benefit or detriment may be in the form of a return promise, an act or a forbearance.

A *return promise* to do something that one was not otherwise obligated to do is sufficient consideration. Most real estate contracts take the form of a promise for a promise. This type of contract is designated as *bilateral*.

CASE EXAMPLE

Burnside promises to pay Yerkes $25,000 for Needleacre, and Yerkes promises to sell Needleacre to Burnside for $25,000. All the details of the contract are reduced to writing. Since there is a promise for a promise, a bilateral contract exists. Each promise is supported by consideration supplied by the other's promise.

An *act* may constitute good consideration for a promise. If the promisor is bargaining for the act, the performance of the act usually constitutes a legal benefit to the promisor as well as a legal detriment to the promisee. Such a contract is termed *unilateral* because there is only one promise.

CASE EXAMPLE

Burnside promises to convey Needleacre to Johannes if Johannes cares for Burnside's mother for her life. Johannes cares for Burnside's mother for her life. Since there is a promise for an act, the contract is unilateral. The act is sufficient consideration to support Burnside's promise since it was bargained for and results in a detriment to Johannes.

Consideration also may take the form of a *forbearance*. Such a contract is also unilateral, since there is only one promise.

• CASE BRIEF •

Burnside promises to convey Needleacre to Lasser if Lasser refrains from smoking for ten years. Lasser refrains. Since there is a promise for a forbearance, the contract is unilateral. The forbearance is sufficient consideration to support the promise since it was bargained for and results in a detriment to Lasser. *See Hamer v. Sidway, 124 N.Y. 538, 27 N.E. 256 (1891).*

In a unilateral contract, the act or forbearance constitutes both the consideration and the acceptance. If the promisor is looking for a promise and receives an act, then the act does not constitute sufficient consideration since it was not "bargained for and given in exchange." Similarly, in the event the promisor is looking for an act, a return promise is insufficient consideration.

CASE EXAMPLE

Irma Keeton promises to tender a deed to her property to Vera Stanley if Stanley produces and tenders $60,000 cash to her by July 1. Stanley promises to produce and tender the cash on July 1. There is no contract, since Keeton is bargaining for the act of payment of $60,000 and Stanley has only made a promise. If Stanley tenders $60,000 by July 1, a contract results, obligating Keeton to tender the deed to the property.

Promissory Estoppel

Promissory estoppel is a doctrine that prevents a party from denying that a promise is supported by consideration. The doctrine of promissory estoppel is applicable when no consideration exists but it is necessary to enforce a promise in order to prevent an injustice. The following elements must also be present: (1) a promise (2) calculated to induce reliance, (3) actual justified reliance by the promisee and (4) injury.

CASE EXAMPLE

Montrasor is in arrears on her mortgage payments and requests additional time from the mortgagee to permit her to pay the arrearage. The mortgagee extends the time by 90 days. There is no consideration to support the promise to extend. Thirty days thereafter Montrasor makes substantial improvements to the property in reliance on the mortgagee's promise. The mortgagee files an action in foreclosure prior to the expiration of the 90 days. Since the ingredients of promissory estoppel are present, the mortgagee's promise not to foreclose for 90 days is enforceable.

Lawful Purpose

A contract must have a legal purpose. Any contract that runs afoul of a statute or public policy is illegal and hence void. A party to an illegal bargain will not normally be assisted by the courts. Simply, the courts will leave the parties in the same position as they are found. There are, however, some exceptions to this rule.

Sometimes the parties to the contract are not deemed to be *in pari delicto*—that is, not at equal fault. A landlord who lets property to a tenant who uses the property to traffic drugs may be innocent of the illegal purpose for which the property was intended. In that instance the courts aid the innocent party in the collection of the rents. An elderly man who is tricked out of his real estate or other property will be protected in many jurisdictions regardless of the fact that he was a willing participant in an unscrupulous scheme.

When a contract involves an illegal provision, the courts may excise that portion and enforce the remainder of the contract. However, if the illegal provision is so interconnected with the whole as to render it nonseverable, the entire contract will be rendered void.

CONTRACT INTERPRETATION

All the essential terms of an agreement must be definite and certain in order for an enforceable contract to exist. Courts will not normally construct terms or fill in gaps where the instrument is deficient. It is the duty of the courts to interpret language within a contract and to give effect to the intent of the parties. If the language is ambiguous and the court cannot arrive at the intent of the parties, then it will not enforce the instrument. In a real estate purchase contract the parties and property must be identified. Essential terms left open for future negotiation may invalidate the contract.

Courts use various rules for interpreting contractual provisions, each designed to ascertain the intent of the parties. Words are assigned their plain meaning and are read in context of the entire contract. Technical language often pervades real estate contracts. Terms such as *escrow, balloon payment, wraparound mortgage, land contract* and others must be interpreted. Courts are prone to look to the real estate industry to assign meaning to these technical terms.

Sometimes there is a conflict between provisions in the contract. To resolve the conflict, specific provisions will control over general provisions. In addition, handwritten provisions will take precedence over typewritten provisions, and typewritten provisions will prevail over printed-form provisions. Once again, these rules are intended to effectuate the intent of the parties.

ASSIGNMENT

The present transfer of a property right from one person (the assignor) to another (the assignee).

The purchaser, as a party to an executory (unperformed) contract, is the equitable owner of the property; the purchaser has a right to receive title to the property from the seller in accordance with the terms of the contract. This right may be transferred to a third party. A party who transfers this right is called an *assignor*. The third party who receives the right to title is called an *assignee*. An assignee succeeds to the rights that were previously invested in the assignor. The assignee of a right to receive a deed may enforce that right against the seller.

• CASE BRIEF •

Walter and Thelma Terry entered into a contract to sell real property to William and Shirley Born, husband and wife. The Borns agreed to pay the purchase price in monthly installments over a specified period of years. A provision within the contract stated that the contract was "not assignable nor [could] the buyer convey the property without the seller's written consent." The Borns subsequently contracted to assign the contract to Rollins without the Terrys' consent. The Terrys commenced an action against the Borns seeking forfeiture of the contract. The appellate court held that the provisions prohibiting assignment were unreasonable restraints on trade unless necessary to protect the seller's security. The case was returned to the trial court to determine whether the Terrys' security would be impaired by the Borns' conveyance to Rollins. *Terry v. Born, 24 Wash. App. 652, 604 P.2d 504 (1979).*

An assignee is bound to perform the obligations the assignor promised the seller, including payment of the purchase price. Failure to perform on the part of the assignee constitutes a breach of the agreement and results in liability for damages. An assignment does not relieve the assignor from obligations under the contract. In the event that the assignee does not perform, the seller may hold the original purchaser (assignor) responsible to perform in accordance with the agreement.

The seller, as a party to an executory contract, has an equitable interest in the purchase price; the seller has a right to receive the purchase price in accordance with the terms of the contract. The seller may assign the right to receive this purchase price. The same rules that apply to the assignment of a purchaser's rights apply to the assignment of a seller's rights.

BREACH OF CONTRACT

The unexcused failure to perform an obligation under a contract.

The failure of a purchaser to tender the purchase price for the property at the appointed time is one example of a breach of contract. Another example is the seller's failure to tender title to the purchaser at the appointed time. Any nonperformance of a term within the contract may give rise to a breach of that contract. The law provides remedies in the event of breach. This serves as an incentive to both parties to live up to the terms of the agreement.

Anticipatory Breach

A breach of contract that occurs as a result of repudiating a contract before the due date for performance.

It is not always necessary to await the day designated for performance to determine that a party is in breach. Sometimes an anticipatory breach occurs. In order to constitute an anticipatory breach, the non-performing party must communicate to the other party an intention not to perform. Or, an intention not to perform may be determined from a party's behavior.

CASE EXAMPLE

R. Brower, a contractor, agreed to paint John Dooley's home for $2,500. Pursuant to the contract, the work was to begin August 1. Thereafter Brower informed Dooley that he was going out of business and asked him to find someone else to do the work. On July 15 Dooley learned from a reliable source that Brower went out of business, sold all of his equipment and had dishonored all of his existing contracts. Under such a circumstance, Dooley may treat Brower as in anticipatory breach of contract and immediately sue for damages.

Substantial Performance

The amount of compliance under the terms of a contract that discharges a party from further obligation where a party has failed to perform totally under the contract.

The law recognizes that humans, frail as they are, cannot always perform their contracts according to the exact specifications. Consequently, if the closing date is set for April 5 and the purchaser desires it to be moved to April 7, the two-day delay does not amount to a material breach, barring a provision in the contract to the contrary or exceptional circumstances. In the area of building contracts, a contractor who builds a home and incurs minor deviations from the specifications may nonetheless have substantially complied with the contractual provisions. In such a case, the contractor will be entitled to the contract price less the cost to remedy the deviations to the property. If, for example, a contractor complies with all the specifications under a $60,000 building contract but fails to paint three out of 14 window panels, the contractor is entitled to $60,000 less the cost of having the window panels painted.

• CASE BRIEF •

Thomas Haverty Company entered into a contract with Jones whereby Haverty agreed to build and install plumbing, heating and ventilation equipment in Jones's building for $27,332. The total cost of the building was $186,000. After completion Jones refused to pay a balance of $10,123 to Haverty Company. Jones maintained that Haverty's performance was defective. The company sued Jones for the balance. The trial court held that Haverty's performance deviated from the contract specifications in 12 respects, that nine could be resolved at a cost of $99, that the remaining three defects could not be remedied without a greater expenditure than was justified and that the damage to the building as a result of the three deviations amounted to $2,180. The court found that the deviations were made as a result of mistakes and misinterpretations. Finding that the contract had been substantially performed, the court awarded $7,844 ($10,123 minus $99 and $2,180) to Haverty Company. The appellate court affirmed the decision. *Thomas Haverty Co. v. Jones, 185 Cal. 285, 197 P. 105 (1921).*

There is no substantial performance if the utility of the property or its purpose is significantly affected by the contractor's deviation. If the specifications in the contract called for gas heating and the contractor installed oil heating instead, the deviation would amount to a breach, and the contractor would not be entitled to any compensation. Some courts do, however, permit the contractor to recover the reasonable value of the services rendered and goods supplied where a substantial deviation is not willful.

Remedies for Breach of Contract

Before a party is entitled to a remedy, he or she must show a readiness, willingness and ability to perform the obligations under the contract. A seller must tender (offer) the deed, and a buyer must tender the purchase price, unless it is clear from the circumstances that the tender would be rejected. The common remedies enjoyed by each party in the event the other breaches the contract are specific performance, rescission, damages and foreclosure.

Specific Performance

A court decree mandating a party to perform according to the contract.

The buyer is entitled to the deed after completion of the requirements under the contract. Should the seller refuse performance, a court may award specific performance requiring the seller to execute a deed in favor of the buyer. Refusal by the seller to comply with the decree may result in contempt of court and punishment. The court may also execute a deed in the buyer's favor, or, in the event of the seller's refusal to perform in accordance with the decree, the very court decree may be deemed to pass title to the buyer. In many jurisdictions specific performance is also available to a seller against a defaulting buyer. A decree of specific performance in such a case compels the purchaser to pay the purchase price and accept title to the property.

A court will grant specific performance only if the party seeking it has "clean hands." If one of the parties has taken advantage of the other's unsound condition, for example, or has been guilty of fraud, the court will deny this equitable relief.

Rescission

Cancellation of a contract that results in the parties being restored to the position they were in before the contract was made.

A buyer, upon a seller's default, may elect to *rescind* the contract. Under such a remedy, the seller must return to the buyer all payments received. The remedy is especially desirable for the buyer when the real estate has depreciated in value below the contract price. In the event the buyer is in breach of the contract, the seller may elect the remedy of rescission, thus restoring the parties to their original position.

Either party may seek rescission on grounds of fraud, innocent misrepresentation, mistake, duress or undue influence. In addition, a contract may be rescinded by mutual consent of the parties.

Damages

Money recoverable by one suffering a loss or injury due to breach of the contract.

A buyer may incur actual damages when the seller breaches the obligation to tender the deed. The damages may be in the nature of the loss of the bargain. Translated into monetary terms, loss of the bargain is the difference between the market value of the property at the date set for closing and the contract price. That difference represents the value of damages to which the purchaser is entitled, assuming that the market value of the property at the time of breach is greater than the contract price. In addition, damages may include the deposit made by the purchaser and actual costs incurred incidental to the contract. Incidental expenses include attorney fees for handling the purchase transaction as well as the expense related to a title search.

CASE EXAMPLE

Joe Deal, seller, refused to tender his deed to John Tiehl, purchaser, on March 13, the date set for closing. Tiehl had previously paid Deal $5,000 to be applied to the purchase price of $85,000. Tiehl additionally expended $500 for a title search of the property. The market value of the property was $90,000 on March 13. In an action by Tiehl against Deal for damages Tiehl will be entitled to $5,500, computed as follows: $90,000 (market value) – $85,000 (contract price) = $5,000 + $500 (title search). Tiehl will also be entitled to a return of the $5,000 deposit.

When the buyer breaches the contract, the seller is entitled to retain any deposit the buyer made and to keep the real property. In the event the market value of the property falls in an amount greater than the deposit forfeited, the seller may also sue for damages. Damages in such a case are computed by deducting the market price from the purchase price minus any earnest money payment forfeited to the seller.

CASE EXAMPLE

Robert Wake breaches his agreement to tender the purchase price of $75,000 to Susan Slumber on August 17. The market price of the property fell to $70,000 on that date. Wake had previously paid $5,000 as earnest money to Slumber. Slumber retained the $5,000. She is entitled to damages computed as follows: $75,000 (purchase price) – $70,000 (market value) = $5,000 – $5,000 (earnest money forfeited) = $0.

A court judgment for damages becomes a general lien on all real property a party owns until the judgment is satisfied. As a judgment creditor, a party may foreclose on the real property to satisfy the judgment. Other means of satisfying a judgment can include the attachment and sale of the debtor's personal property and garnishment of his or her wages.

Foreclosure

A legal process where a nonbreaching party can obtain possession of the real property and sell it in order to recover an amount due.

The buyer of real property has *equitable* title to the property—the right to obtain ownership upon payment of the purchase price. This right gives the buyer an equitable lien on the property securing the amount of money paid. Consequently, the buyer may foreclose on the property to recover the purchase payments in the event the seller breaches the contract.

The seller possesses a lien for the unpaid purchase price on property that has passed to the buyer. The seller may foreclose on the property to satisfy this lien in the event the buyer fails to make timely payment.

DISCHARGE

The release of contractual obligations.

Parties who complete their obligations under a contract are discharged from any further performance. Normally, total performance is required before discharge occurs. Discharge may occur, however, after substantial performance (discussed earlier in this chapter). In addition, under certain circumstances parties may be discharged from their obligation to perform by operation of the parties or by operation of law.

Operation of the Parties

Parties to a contract may mutually agree to cancel a contract. Such an agreement results in a discharge. Or, the parties may agree to substitute another person's obligation to perform. This agreement to substitute indebtedness is called a *novation*.

CASE EXAMPLE

Cary is indebted to Ponce in the amount of $5,000. Ponce is indebted to Darin in the amount of $5,000. Cary, Ponce and Darin

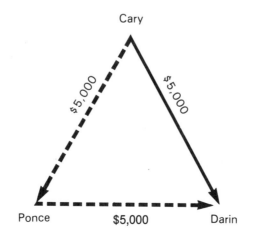

Cary

$5,000

$5,000

Ponce $5,000 Darin

may agree that Ponce will release Cary of the debt, Darin will release Ponce and Cary will pay $5,000 directly to Darin.

Finally, parties may agree to substitute a kind of performance that is different from that originally required under the contract. This agreement is called an *accord*, and the performance of the agreement is referred to as a *satisfaction*. An accord and satisfaction discharges a party from his or her original obligation.

CASE EXAMPLE

Castor Andora was indebted to Andrea Hammer, a former employer, in the amount of $2,000. Hammer made a demand for the amount. Andora was out of work and did not have the money. He offered, however, to paint Hammer's house in lieu of the $2,000. Hammer agreed, and Andora, pursuant to the agreement, painted Hammer's house. This constitutes an accord and satisfaction. Andora is discharged of any further obligation to pay Hammer $2,000.

Operation of Law

Circumstances may occur that make it impossible or impractical for a party to fulfill his or her obligation under a contract. Under these circumstances the law will excuse the party from performance. Assume, for example, that Dante and Raymond enter into an agreement whereby Dante is to purchase Hellacre. Before closing, the house on Hellacre burns down. In most jurisdictions, in absence of a provision in the contract covering this event, the parties would be excused from performance because the subject has been destroyed.

Death of a party is not ordinarily an excuse for nonperformance of a contract. In the event a party dies, the representative of the estate will be required to complete performance. However, if the contract involves personal services, the rule is different. Assume, for example, that a carpenter agrees to build a tree house. Death of the carpenter will result in a discharge of obligations under the contract because of the personal nature of carpentry services. The same rule holds regarding insanity of a party. A party to a contract who is unable to complete a personal service contract due to insanity is excused from performance.

When a contract that was legal when entered into becomes illegal, the parties are discharged from performance. Suppose, for example, that a contractor enters into a contract with a shipper to transport specified building materials from a foreign country. Should the U.S. government issue an embargo forbidding the transport of goods from that foreign country, the parties will be discharged from their contractual obligations.

Finally, the law has evolved to recognize that certain contacts cannot be performed because it is commercially impracticable to do so. Some courts have discharged parties from their obligations in these types of cases. The impetus for this rule emanates from Section 2-615 of the Uniform Commercial Code, which reads in part:

> Delay in delivery or non-delivery in whole or in part by a seller . . . is not a breach of his duty under a contract for sale if performance as agreed has been made impracticable by the occurrence of a contingency the non-occurrence of which was a basic assumption on which the contract was made. . . .

Courts have not limited this doctrine to sale of goods cases but have extended it to other cases as well.

• CASE BRIEF •

Northern Corporation entered into a contract with Chugach Electric Association. Under the contract, Northern was to install protective riprap on a dam located on Cooper Lake, Alaska, owned by Chugach. The work required Northern to transport rock to and install it on the face of the dam.

The contract was silent as to the method for transporting the rock to the dam site. Apparently the parties contemplated that it would be transported across the frozen lake during the coming winter.

Attempts to haul the rock across the ice were frustrated by the unsafe condition of the ice. On one occasion two trucks broke through the ice, resulting in the drivers' deaths.

Northern ceased performance and sought a ruling discharging it from any further obligations under the contract. Chugach countersued, seeking damages for breach of contract. In upholding the trial court's ruling in favor of Northern, the Supreme Court of Alaska said:

> Under [the doctrine of commercial impracticality], a party is discharged from his contractual obligations, even if it is technically possible to perform them, if the cost of performance would be so disproportionate to that reasonably contemplated by the parties as to make the contract totally impractical in a commercial sense. . . .
>
> . . . [The concept of commercial impracticality]—which finds expression both in case law and in other authorities—

is predicated upon the assumption that in legal contemplation something is impractical when it can only be done at
an excessive and unreasonable cost. . . .

There is ample evidence to support [the findings that]
"the ice haul method of transporting riprap. . . was within
the contemplation of the parties and was part of the basis
of the agreement which ultimately resulted in the contract
amendment," and that that method was not commercially
feasible within the financial parameters of the contract. . . .

*Northern Corporation v. Chugach Electric Association, 518 P.2d
76 (Alaska 1974).*

SUMMARY

A contract is a promise or an agreement that is enforceable by law.
Laws in each state govern contracts in general and real estate contracts
in particular. Contracts entitle the parties to certain rights but also
entail obligations. Basic to any contract are an offer, an acceptance and
consideration. Additionally, both parties must possess the capacity to
contract, and the subject matter of the contract must be legal.

In a real estate transaction an offer is a proposal to sell or purchase property. The offer may be terminated at any time before acceptance, and in such a case no contract exists. An acceptance involves an
assent to the terms of an offer. Even after acceptance, however, the
contract may be voided because of fraud, misrepresentation or other
conditions such as duress. Consideration involves a benefit to the
promisor or a detriment to the promisee, bargained for and given up in
exchange for a promise or an act. Capacity requires that both parties
be sane and of legal age to contract. Finally, persons may not contract
for an unlawful purpose.

Failure of either party to perform as promised constitutes a
breach of the contract. Remedies under the law vary from state to
state and include specific performance, rescission, damages and foreclosure. Parties may be released from their contractual obligations to
perform by agreement or by operation of law.

REVIEW AND DISCUSSION QUESTIONS

1. (a) Which agreements will a court enforce? (b) Which agreements will a court not enforce? (c) Why?
2. Name five elements of a contract and define each.
3. Explain the rationale behind the objective test of contract formation.
4. Give an example of when the doctrine of promissory estoppel
   will be applied.

5. When does a breach of contract occur? What is the consequence of a breach of contract?
6. (a) Explain the remedies available to a buyer when the seller breaches the contract for the sale of real property. (b) Explain the remedies available to the seller in the event of the buyer's breach.
7. Name ways in which parties to a contract may be discharged from their obligation to perform by operation of law.

CASE PROBLEMS

1. On November 27, 1937, Morrison, seeking to purchase a tract of land from Thoelke, executed and mailed Thoelke a contract for the sale of the property. On November 27, 1937, Thoelke signed the contract and placed it in the mails, addressed to Morrison's agent. After mailing the contract, but before Morrison's agent received it, Thoelke called the agent and repudiated the contract for the sale of the land. (a) Was Thoelke's call an effective rejection of Morrison's offer? See *Morrison v. Thoelke*, 155 So.2d 889 (Fla. Dist. Ct. App. 1963). (b) What would be the result if Thoelke died after mailing his acceptance and his executor (representative of the estate) refused to honor the agreement? (c) What if Morrison died after mailing the offer and Thoelke accepted the offer before learning of Morrison's death?

2. Hazel Miller listed her real estate for sale with a local real estate agent. Michael Normile and Wawie Kurniawan signed a written offer to purchase the property. The offer stated that "this offer must be accepted on or before 5:00 P.M. August 5, 1980." Miller signed and returned the offer with several changes, including an increase in the deposit from $100 to $500 and an increase in the down payment from $875 to $1,000. Normile and Kurniawan neither accepted nor rejected the new terms. At 12:30 A.M. on August 5 Segal signed an offer to purchase the property, which was accepted the same day at 2:00 P.M. The agent then informed Normile that Miller had revoked her counteroffer. Before 5:00 P.M. on the same day, Normile and Kurniawan accepted the counteroffer. Who owns the property and why? *Normile v. Miller*, 326 S.E.2d 11 (N.C. 1985).

3. Miss Roland, owner of a parcel of land, leased it to Mr. Kent for a term of five years. A second agreement between the parties granted Kent an option to extend the lease for another four years if Kent undertook to make about $10,000 of improvements to the property. Kent engaged and paid an architect to study the property and suggest possible improvements. Roland

died after the architect completed his sketches but before the construction of any of the contemplated improvements. Roland's executor seeks to set aside the option contract on the ground that it is a mere offer unsupported by consideration and is therefore revoked by the death of Roland. (a) Does the payment of the architect's fee qualify as good consideration? Discuss. See *Bard v. Kent*, 19 Cal. 2d 449, 122 P.2d 8 (1942). (b) Assuming that there is no consideration, what doctrine may aid Kent? Explain.

4. Plaintiff entered into an agreement with defendant whereby plaintiff agreed to construct a country house for defendant, who in return agreed to pay plaintiff for his work. A proviso of the agreement stated that Reading pipe was to be used in the plumbing system of the house. Plaintiff completed the house, yet through inattention installed Cohoes pipe, a different brand of pipe though one of substantially similar quality to Reading pipe. Defendant now refuses to pay plaintiff the balance of the contract price unless he replaces all the Cohoes pipe in the house with Reading. Defendant's demand would involve the demolition and reconstruction of a major portion of the house. (a) What doctrine, if any, can plaintiff rely on to force defendant to pay for the work "as is"? (b) Would the result be different if Reading pipe was found to be of significantly higher quality than the Cohoes pipe? Explain. See *Jacob & Youngs, Inc. v. Kent*, 230 N.Y. 239, 129 N.E.889 (1921).

5. Carmen Ruggerio contracted to sell 10.24 acres of industrial land for $38,912 to Tanners Realty. The sale was conditioned on Tanners' ability to obtain financing. The agreement provided that Ruggerio would convey good marketable title to said premises, except for utility easements. In addition to utility easements, a search of the title revealed a railroad easement on the property. (a) What remedies are available to Tanners Realty? (b) What would it have to prove in order to prevail? *Tanners Realty Corporation v. Ruggerio*, 490 N.Y.S.2d 73 (App. Div. 1985).

6. Taylor and Caldwell entered into an agreement whereby Taylor was to receive the use of Caldwell's concert hall for four days. Before Taylor had an opportunity to use the hall, it was completely destroyed by fire, rendering its use impossible. (a) Can Taylor recover against Caldwell for damages sustained as a result of being deprived of the use of the concert hall? Explain. See *Taylor v. Caldwell*, 122 Eng. Rep. 309 (1863). (b) What would the result be if Caldwell owned two halls and only one was destroyed?

18
Real Estate Purchase Contracts

The previous chapter on basic contract law provided the background necessary for a specific look at real estate purchase contracts. The purchase contract is the instrument that legally "obligates" the buyer and seller to perform. Normally, the total understanding of the parties is contained within that agreement. Consequently, the conduct of the parties will be largely dictated by its terms. For that reason careful attention to the form and substance of the real estate contract is important. This chapter details the prerequisites for a valid real estate purchase contract and the provisions customarily contained in that contract.

REAL ESTATE PURCHASE CONTRACT

An agreement whereby a seller promises to sell an interest in realty by conveying a deed to the designated estate for which a buyer promises to pay a specified purchase price.

Generally, contracts need not be in writing in order to be enforceable. Real estate purchase contracts, however, fall within a unique class of contracts that necessitate a writing. They are governed by the Statute of Frauds.

Statute of Frauds

A statute that necessitates that certain contracts, in order to be enforceable, must be supported by a written

memorandum and signed by the party against whom enforcement is sought.

The British Parliament enacted the Statute of Frauds in 1677. This statute modified the common law that enforced oral contracts for the sale of real estate. The Statute of Frauds was intended to protect against fraud and perjury. Prior to the Statute of Frauds, it was not uncommon for a person to pay witnesses to fabricate testimony to support a nonexistent oral contract for the sale of realty. Section 4 of the statute required a contract for the sale of an interest in land to be in writing, or supported by a written memorandum, and signed by the party to be charged. Nearly every state has modeled its version of a statute of frauds after the English statute. The Ohio statute, for example, reads in part:

> No lease, estate, or interest, either of freehold or term of years, in lands...shall be assigned or granted except by deed, or note in writing, signed by the party assigning or granting it, or his agent thereto lawfully authorized...

• CASE BRIEF •

A trustee of real property held a public auction to sell the property. Charles McCabe was the highest bidder. There was no written contract or memorandum of sale. On the next day, when the trustee of the property submitted a deed for delivery, McCabe refused to pay the price. The trustee sued for specific performance, and the court held for McCabe on the basis that the contract did not satisfy the Statute of Frauds. *Watson v. McCabe, 527 F.2d 286 (6th Cir. 1975).*

Memorandum

Normally, the entire agreement of the parties—the real estate purchase contract—is reduced to writing. This writing will, of course, satisfy the memorandum requirement of the Statute of Frauds. The entire agreement of the parties need not be in writing, however, to satisfy the Statute of Frauds. The statute only requires a written memorandum, which may be the "skeleton" of the contract. A memorandum must ordinarily contain:

- the names of the parties to the contract,
- a description of the property,
- the purchase price,
- other essential terms and conditions of the sale,
- the signature of the party against whom enforcement is sought (a few states also require the signature of the party seeking to enforce the transaction).

The memorandum need not be contained within one instrument. It may be gleaned from a series of related writings, such as letters and telegrams. The memorandum may be prepared anytime before suit on the contract is commenced. Loss or destruction of the memorandum does not render the contract unenforceable. In such a case, the existence of the memorandum may be proved by witnesses or other documents. In most jurisdictions the Statute of Frauds is deemed waived unless it is pleaded as a defense in court.

Party Against Whom Enforcement Is Sought

In many jurisdictions a contract for the sale of real estate may be enforced only against the party who signed the memorandum. Consequently, it is very possible that a purchaser of a parcel of real estate may not be legally able to enforce the contract against the seller, while the seller may be legally able to enforce the contract against the purchaser. The reverse is also true.

CASE EXAMPLE

Bill Barley, seller, contracts with John Harley, buyer, for the sale of Lodgeacre, with complete details of the sale contained in a writing. Barley signs the writing, but Harley neglects to sign. The contract is enforceable against Barley but not against Harley, because Harley did not sign the writing.

The best way to ensure compliance with the Statute of Frauds is to require that all parties sign the real estate purchase contract. Although the entire agreement of the parties need not be reduced to writing, as a practical matter it is best to do so. This prevents uncertainty and provides a controlling document to resolve disputes.

Part Performance

There are certain exceptions to compliance with the Statute of Frauds. The most notable exception is the doctrine of *part performance*. There are various views as to what constitutes an act of part performance sufficient to remove a contract from the Statute of Frauds so that a writing will not be required. Some courts take the position that part performance is satisfied if a purchaser takes possession pursuant to an oral contract. Other courts require both possession and payment of the purchase price to prevent the seller from raising the defense of the statute. Still others require that possession be accompanied by a substantial improvement to the property. Finally, other jurisdictions limit the scope of the doctrine of part performance by requiring payment of the purchase price, the purchaser's possession and a change of position in reliance on the contract that would result in irreparable harm unless the contract were enforced.

• CASE BRIEF •

Brown entered into an oral contract to purchase a farm from Burnside. Brown took possession of the farm, made several improvements, tore down an old farmhouse, paid taxes and made payments on the purchase price. Burnside thereafter refused to deed the farm to Brown. Brown sought specific performance of the contract. The court held for Brown on the theory that the Statute of Frauds does not apply when there has been partial or complete performance, under these circumstances. *Brown v. Burnside, 94 Idaho 363, 487 P.2d 957 (1972).*

Parol Evidence

Oral or other evidence extraneous to the written instrument.

Parol evidence is not admissible for the purpose of varying or contradicting the terms of a contract. The rule, however, does not exclude parol evidence consistent with the writings of the parties. Nor does the rule exclude parol evidence for the purpose of clarifying ambiguous terms in the contract or proving that the writing was induced by fraud, illegality, duress, undue influence or mistake. Neither does the parol evidence rule exclude evidence of a subsequent agreement that alters the previous writings.

CASE EXAMPLE

Jim Hutchins and Jerry Bolen enter into a real estate contract for the sale of Hutchins's property. Afterward they enter into a contract canceling the prior real estate contract. The introduction into evidence of the new contract containing the cancellation does not violate the parol evidence rule, since it was entered into after the purchase contract.

Brokers' Authority

Most localities use preprinted purchase contract forms that have been approved by the local attorney bar association and the board of realtors. The provisions within these form contracts are designed to reflect the practices within the locality. Normally, the broker assists the parties in filling in the blanks in such a contract, including the names of the parties, a description of the property, the price and such. A standard real estate purchase contract is shown in Figure 18.1. Sometimes it is necessary to delete certain inapplicable provisions from the form. Often lengthy additions are necessitated by the particular nature of the transaction. To what extent a broker may prepare a purchase contract without engaging in the offense of unauthorized practice of law differs from state to state. Some states prevent a broker from drafting a purchase contract because that act constitutes the practice of law. Other states permit such brokerage activity on the theory that it is normally incident to the practice of a broker's profession. Although most states permit brokers to fill in the blanks, there is often a thin line between filling in the blanks and drafting. A broker should exercise caution when rendering advice to a party or giving detailed explanation of the terms of the contract; these activities may be deemed the unauthorized practice of law.

PROVISIONS OF THE REAL ESTATE PURCHASE CONTRACT

Some of the provisions included within the real estate purchase agreement are there to satisfy the Statute of Frauds. Others are present to clarify the details of the agreement. Common real estate contract provisions include the date, the names of parties and other elements presented on the following pages.

Date

The contract should be dated. The date may appear at the beginning or the end of the contract or in both places. Failure to include the date does not render the contract unenforceable. However, the question of the date of the signing may arise in several situations. The contract may contain provisions that require the happening of events by reference to the date the contract came into existence. For example, a clause within a contract might read, "Buyer shall obtain financing within 45 days of the signing of this contract." In some instances the statute of limitations may begin to run on the date the contract was signed. The statute of limitations is the time period—for example, four years—within which one must sue or be barred from recovery. Also, certain legal ramifications attach on the date the contract comes into being. For example, the buyer becomes the equitable owner of the property. As equitable owner, the buyer may enforce the contract by specific performance in the event the seller fails to perform.

Parties

In order to satisfy the Statute of Frauds, the names of the parties must be included within the writing. Care should be taken to ensure that the names of the buyer and seller are accurate. An attorney who later draws up the deed may derive the names to insert in the deed from the contract. Accurate spelling prevents problems at a later date when a title search may otherwise uncover discrepancies.

The marital status of the seller should be included; if the seller is married, then the spouse should be named as well. A seller's spouse possesses certain legal rights that must be relinquished by signature

Real Estate Purchase Contract
Adopted by The Columbus Board of Realtors
and by The Columbus Bar Association

REALTOR®

It is recommended that all parties
be represented by legal counsel

CBA

Columbus, Ohio. _____March 30_____ , 19 88

The undersigned Buyer agrees to buy and the undersigned Seller agrees to sell, through you as Broker, upon the terms hereinafter set forth, the following real estate located in the State of Ohio, County of ____Franklin: 5293 Poplarwood Road and lot (Forest Park West).____

1. **On the following terms:** Purchase price shall be $ ____One hundred ($100,000) thousand dollars____

Buyer's obligations are contingent upon Buyer arranging, within ____10____ calendar days after acceptance hereof, a _____

first mortgage commitment in the amount of ____Eighty ($80,000) thousand dollars____

at interest not to exceed ____11____ %, repayable over not less than ____25____ years

Buyer shall purchase curtains for additional $300.00.

2. **Possession:** At closing

3. **Evidence of Title:** Seller shall furnish and pay for either an abstract of title or an owner's title insurance commitment and policy in the amount of the purchase price, with copy of subdivision plat. The title evidence shall be certified to within ten (10) days prior to closing in accordance with the standards of the Columbus Bar Association, and shall show in Seller marketable title in fee simple free and clear of all liens and encumbrances except: (a) those created by or assumed by Buyer; (b) those specifically set forth in this contract; (c) zoning ordinances; (d) legal highways; and (e) covenants, restrictions, conditions and easements of record which do not unreasonably interfere with present lawful use. If title insurance is furnished, Buyer shall pay any additional costs incurred in connection with mortgage insurance issued for the protection of Buyer's lender. If Buyer desires a survey, Buyer shall pay the cost thereof.
If title to all or part of the real estate is unmarketable, as determined by Ohio law with reference to the Ohio State Bar Association's Standards of Title Examination, or is subject to liens, encumbrances, easements, conditions, restrictions or encroachments other than those excepted in this contract, Seller shall within thirty (30) days after written notice thereof, remedy or remove any such defect, lien, encumbrance, easement, condition, restriction or encroachment or obtain title insurance without exception therefor. At closing Seller shall sign an affidavit with respect to off-record title matters in accordance with the community custom.

4. **Deed:** Seller shall convey to Buyer marketable title in fee simple by transferable and recordable general warranty deed, with release of dower, if any, or fiduciary deed, as appropriate, free and clear of all liens and encumbrances not excepted by this contract, and excepting the following:

5. **Taxes and Assessments:** At closing, Seller shall pay or credit on purchase price all delinquent taxes, including penalty and interest, all assessments which are a lien on the date of contract and all agricultural use tax recoupments for years through the year of closing. At closing Seller shall also pay or credit on the purchase price all other unpaid real estate taxes which are a lien for years prior to closing and a portion of such taxes for year of closing prorated through date of closing and based on 365 days year and, if undetermined, on most recent available tax rate and valuation, giving effect to applicable exemptions, recently voted millage, change in valuation, etc., whether or not certified.
Seller warrants that no improvements or services (site or area) have been installed or furnished, or notification received from public authority of future improvements of which any part of the cost may be assessed against the real estate, except the following: _____ (None, if nothing inserted).

6. **Rentals, Interest, Condominium Charges, Insurance, Utilities and Security Deposits:** Adjustments shall be made through date of closing for: (a) rentals; (b) interest on any mortgage assumed by Buyer; (c) condominium or other association periodic charges, and (d) transferable insurance policies, if Buyer so elects. Seller shall pay, through date of possession, all accrued utility charges and any other charges that are or may become a lien. Security deposits shall be transferred to Buyer.

7. **Damage or Destruction of Property:** Risk of loss to the real estate and appurtenances shall be borne by Seller until closing provided that if any property covered by this contract shall be substantially damaged or destroyed before this transaction is closed, the Buyer may (a) proceed with the transaction and be entitled to all insurance money, if any, payable to the Seller under all policies covering the property, or (b) rescind the contract, and thereby release all parties from liability hereunder, by giving written notice to the Seller and Broker within ten (10) days after the Buyer has written notice of such damage or destruction. Failure by the Buyer to so notify the Seller and Broker shall constitute an election to proceed with the transaction.

8. **Fixtures and Equipment:** The consideration shall include any fixtures, including but not limited to: built-in appliances; heating, central air conditioning, and humidifying equipment and their control apparatus; stationary tubs; pumps; incinerators; water softening equipment (unless leased); roof antennae; attached wall-to-wall carpeting and attached floor coverings; window shades, curtain rods and Venetian blinds; attached mirrors; light, bathroom and lavatory fixtures; storm and screen doors and windows, awnings, and blinds, whether now in or on the premises or in storage; garage door openers and controls; window air conditioners; attached fireplace equipment; all exterior plants and trees; and the following: ____All hanging curtains____

The following shall be excluded: _____

9. **Inspections:** Before closing, Seller shall furnish and pay for: (a) a report by an Ohio Certified Pest (Termite) Control Applicator stating whether based upon an inspection of the areas visible or accessible, the inspector discovered any evidence of infestation or damage by termites. Infestation and resulting damage by termites or other wood destroying insects shall be treated and repaired at Seller's expense, provided that if the cost of repair exceeds 1% of the purchase price, Seller may terminate this contract unless Buyer agrees to pay the cost of such repair in excess of 1% of the purchase price; (b) a written verification from the gas company or a licensed plumber that all gas lines, valves and appliances are free from gas leaks (gas leaks shall be corrected at Seller's expense); or Seller may provide a written guaranty or service contract for the repair of such items; and, (c) a written health department report showing in essence that any well and or on-site sewage disposal system now in use is in safe operating condition and is not a health hazard. Seller warrants, that at time of closing, water is available in sufficient quantities for ordinary household purposes.

10. **Home Maintenance Plan:** Seller, at Seller's expense, shall provide _____ (not applicable if plan name not inserted).

11. **Deposit:** Buyer has deposited with Broker the sum receipted for below, which Buyer, Seller and Broker agree shall be held in trust and disbursed as follows: (a) if this offer is not accepted within the time specified or if this offer is accepted and Seller fails or refuses to perform, or any contingency is not fulfilled, the deposit shall be returned; (b) if this offer is accepted, deposit shall be applied on purchase price when transaction is closed; (c) if this offer is accepted and Buyer fails or refuses to perform, this deposit shall be paid to Seller, which payment, or the acceptance thereof, shall not in any way prejudice the rights of Seller or Broker(s) in any action for damages or specific performance.

12. **Miscellaneous:** Buyer has examined all property involved and, in making this offer, is relying solely upon such examination with reference to the condition, character and size of land and improvements and fixtures, if any. This contract constitutes the entire agreement and there are no representations, oral or written, which have not been incorporated herein. Time is of the essence of all provisions of this contract. All provisions of this contract shall survive the closing. In compliance with fair housing laws, no party shall in any manner discriminate against any purchaser or purchasers because of race, creed, sex or national origin.

13. **Duration of Offer and Closing:** This offer shall be open for acceptance to midnight ____March 31____ , 19 88 . This contract shall be performed and this transaction closed within ____45____ days after acceptance hereof, unless the parties agree in writing to an extension.

Buyer acknowledges receipt of a copy of this contract.

Jim Darrow

The Broker acknowledges receipt of the deposit of

$____500.00____ by cash/check which shall be deposited in Broker's Trust Account upon acceptance hereof.

By ____D.R.____

(Buyer)

Address ____1836 Cedarwillow____ Phone ____885-4884____

Deed to ____Jim Darrow____
____John Todd____

Name of Buyer's Attorney _____

The undersigned agrees to and accepts the foregoing offer.

The Seller shall pay a brokerage fee of ____6½%____ of the purchase price in connection with this transaction.

Seller acknowledges receipt of a copy of this contract.

Liz Nodler

(Seller)

Address ____5293 Poplarwood Rd____ Phone ____436-7746____

Signed this ____31____ day of ____March____ , 19 88

Name of Seller's Attorney _____

© CBR and CBA 1980

Figure 18.1: Typical real estate purchase contract

Reprinted with the permission of the Columbus Bar Association and the Columbus Board of Realtors®

in order for the buyer to be assured of a good title. For this reason, the spouse must sign the contract.

There may be more than one seller or buyer. All parties should be named. If there are multiple buyers, it is essential to include a statement of the type and fraction of ownership interest each will receive.

Sometimes a party to the sale (seller or buyer) designates an agent to negotiate and/or sign the contract. This practice should be reserved for extreme cases where it is not feasible for the actual party to act. When a party designates an agent, such appointment should be evidenced by a written *power of attorney.* A copy of the power of attorney should be attached to the contract. Even here problems may occur, because no one can be sure that the power of attorney has not been revoked by subsequent act or event.

CASE EXAMPLE

Howard Moore, owner of a tract of land that is for sale, is planning a visit to Australia. To prevent his absence from the country from impeding the sale, he executes a power of attorney, giving his real estate broker power to negotiate, contract and sign the deed of conveyance. Hugh Fine, a farmer, enters into a contract for the sale of Moore's land. The broker appears at the closing and executes a deed in behalf of Moore. Fine takes possession and learns later that before the date of closing Moore was killed in Australia in a hunting accident. Since death revokes a power of attorney, Fine's title is seriously impaired.

Property Description

Property descriptions contained in the contract must sufficiently identify the property. Courts are rather liberal in upholding descriptions of real property contained within the contract. Consequently, a contract for the purchase of "all my lands" has been held sufficient to identify the subject of the sale and to comply with the Statute of Frauds. Even where the quantity of the lands to be sold is not accurate, it is enough if the terms within the description are sufficient to identify the subject property accurately.

CASE EXAMPLE

Vander Graff contracted to sell "all my lands lying on the Miami River, in the State of Ohio, 1,533$\frac{1}{3}$ acres...in my name." Should the actual quantity be above the acreage mentioned, the sale would include the excess of the quantity stated in the contract.

Parol evidence is admissible to clarify specific lands. However, parol evidence will not be admitted to reform a description to include lands not specifically referred to by the description.

CASE EXAMPLE

"December 13, 1950, received of P. H. Pilgreen ten dollars ($10.00) as binder on 20 acres of land and timber; price to be $200.00 for land and timber. Deed to be made later." Parol evidence will not be admitted in this particular case because the description as written does not allude to a definite parcel of property.

It is best to include in the real estate purchase contract a complete and accurate legal description of the property so that there is no room for any alternative interpretations. In many jurisdictions, however, it is customary to include only the street address for sales of residential property.

Method of Payment

In order to satisfy the Statute of Frauds, the amount of the purchase price must be clearly ascertainable. For example:

The total purchase price shall be $60,000 payable as follows:

1. $500 upon the signing of the contract.
2. $5,500 in cash or the equivalent to be paid at closing upon delivery of the deed.
3. The balance to be paid by assuming the existing mortgage on said property in the amount of $54,000 held by Citizens Saving & Loan Company.

In the event the purchase price is not specified, then it must be subject to ascertainment by computation. For example:

The acreage of the property is to be determined by survey, and the price is to be computed by multiplying the number of acres and any fraction thereof by $2,500.

The usual and safest form of payment is certified check or bank draft. These forms of payment prevent the buyer from stopping payment after tender, which could occur if a personal check were issued.

Contingency Clause

A provision within a contract that makes performance under the contract conditional upon the occurrence of a stated event.

A contingency clause may be inserted within a contract to benefit a purchaser or a seller. A common contingency within a purchase contract conditions performance upon the buyer's obtaining financing. The details of the acceptable financing are normally specified, for example, "The within obligations of the buyer are conditional upon buyer obtaining a 25-year loan from a financial institution in the amount of 80 percent of the purchase price at 10 percent interest; otherwise this contract to become null and void." This contingency is for the benefit of the purchaser. In the event that the purchaser could not obtain terms as favorable, he or she could elect to waive the contingency and proceed with the purchase. Other contingencies that benefit a buyer may be contained within a purchase contract—for example, making the contract conditional upon the sale of buyer's house or upon the change of a zoning regulation.

Contingencies may also be included within a contract for the seller's benefit. The seller may desire to make performance under the contract conditional upon confirmation of a job transfer by a present employer. Or perhaps other circumstances make it desirable for the seller to include other contingencies within the contract.

CASE EXAMPLE

Pete Perry owns a home in Tulsa, Oklahoma, and he is interested in selling that home and moving to Seattle, Washington. Perry enters into a valid purchase contract with Sam Sells whereby Perry is to buy Sells's residence for a stated sum. After signing the contract, Perry is not able to sell his residence in Tulsa and consequently is unable to accumulate the funds necessary to close on the Seattle property. Nonetheless, Perry is obligated to perform. A contingency clause as follows would have adequately protected Perry against such a misfortune: "The purchase of Sells's residence is contingent upon Perry selling his residence in Tulsa at market price within at least 30 days prior to the date set for closing."

Contingency clauses are often cunningly drafted in an attempt to permit a party to be relieved of obligations at the party's whim. Courts will often construe such clauses in such a way as to require good faith and honesty on the part of the party the contingency benefits.

CASE EXAMPLE

Brenda Rodgers enters into a purchase contract to buy Hedgeacre. A contingency clause within the contract reads, "Said contract contingent upon buyer obtaining a ten percent loan for 80 percent of the sales price." Brenda had a change of mind about Hedgeacre and refused to attempt to obtain financing. Brenda's

refusal would be considered a lack of good faith and would constitute a breach of contract.

Possession

The date the seller is required to surrender possession to the buyer is
usually negotiable. In many contracts the date the purchaser is entitled to possession coincides with the closing. Ordinarily, in absence of
a possession provision, the buyer is entitled to possession upon payment in full. This usually occurs at the closing. The parties can always agree to a different date of possession. It is not uncommon for
the parties to agree for the buyer to take possession upon the signing
of the contract, especially when the property is vacant. Sometimes a
purchaser is impliedly entitled to immediate possession; for example,
when the contract requires the purchaser to maintain the premises
from the date the contract is signed. There are dangers to the seller associated with the purchaser's possession before payment. The purchaser in possession may commit waste to the property and then fail
to make payment to the seller pursuant to the contract. Or the purchaser might remain on the property and refuse to close the transaction. If this occurs, the seller may have to engage in a lengthy suit
before possession is legally returned to the seller or some other favorable remedy is achieved. From the seller's viewpoint, it would be
much better for the buyer who takes possession before payment of the
purchase price to be characterized as a tenant until payment. In this
event the seller would be in a position to evict the purchaser/tenant,
an action that would normally result in a quick return of possession
to the seller.

Sometimes in residential sales the contract allows the seller to
maintain possession for a period of time after closing, such as 30 or 60
days. In such a case a danger exists that the seller will hold over or
commit waste to the premises. For protection against this possibility,
the purchaser may require a security deposit, returnable to the seller if
the premises are vacated in the condition they were in at the time of
contract, reasonable wear and tear excepted.

Evidence of Title

**A document such as an abstract or title insurance
verifying ownership of property.**

The seller is not under any affirmative obligation to prove that title to
the realty is *marketable*—that is, free of liens or other encumbrances.
If a general warranty deed is used, the seller personally warrants that
the property is free and clear of encumbrances other than those specifically excluded and that the seller will warrant and defend the title
against the lawful claims and demands of all persons. A purchaser

may maintain an action for damages against the seller under the general warranty in the event of a breach of the warranty against encumbrances. However, the warranty is only as good as the seller's net worth. When making an investment in realty, the purchaser should take extreme precaution. Toward that end, the purchaser may hire an attorney to effect a title search and render an opinion as to the marketability of the title. Or the purchaser may purchase title insurance from a reputable company. (Title search and title insurance are discussed in Chapter 9.) Still better, the purchaser may insist on a clause in the contract that the seller provide evidence of title in the form of an abstract of title or an owner's title insurance policy. The prevailing custom within the real estate industry in many localities is for the seller to provide such proof of title. The standardized real estate purchase contract within the locality normally reflects the common and approved practice within that area.

Form of Deed

The type of deed to be conveyed by the seller may be controlled by the terms of the contract. It is most desirable for the contract to specify the type of deed, whether it be a general warranty deed, bargain and sale deed, quitclaim deed or some other type. In the absence of agreement, the law within the jurisdiction governs the type of deed the seller is required to convey. Under this circumstance some jurisdictions obligate the seller to convey a general warranty deed, whereas other jurisdictions require only a quitclaim deed.

Proration

Certain expenses or income associated with the realty at the time of closing may be due but unpaid. Other expenses or income may have been prepaid. Because these expenses and income are related to the use of the premises, in part by the seller and in part by the buyer, apportionment is necessary. A clause within the contract may read:

> Taxes, insurance, utilities, assessments, and rental income shall be apportioned *pro rata* as the interests of the parties may appear at closing.

Taxes on real property, for example, may be payable annually, semiannually or otherwise. The fiscal year may not correspond to the calendar year; the tax assessment period may be, for example, July 1 to June 30. To complicate matters, some local jurisdictions run six months to a year behind in their billing so that the owner is always paying taxes due in the past. Fairness demands that an adjustment be made so that the seller is charged with accrued but unpaid taxes.

CASE EXAMPLE

Olivieri pays $260 a year for real estate property taxes on her home. The fiscal period for tax purposes is July 1 to June 30. Olivieri is billed $130 twice a year, in December and June. Each installment of $130 covers the previous six months. On March 31, 1987, Olivieri appears at a closing on her house. The contract provides for apportionment of taxes as of the date of closing. Olivieri is current in her payments of taxes and presents a paid receipt for the December installment. Olivieri will owe $65 for accrued and unpaid taxes for the period January 1 to March 31, which amount will be credited to the buyer against the selling price.

Hazard insurance policies may be transferred from the seller to the buyer. However, the transfer may necessitate an apportionment. Insurance is often payable in advance, and the unaccrued portion that was paid by the seller for a period during which the purchaser has the use of the premises must be reflected in the apportionment.

CASE EXAMPLE

On January 1, 1986 Tim Sade, the owner of residential property, pays an annual premium of $250 to cover his property for fire and other hazards for the upcoming year. On June 30 Sade appears at a closing on his house. A paragraph within the contract provides for an assignment of the hazard insurance policy and an apportionment of the insurance expense. The expense will be apportioned $125 to the seller and $125 to the purchaser.

Sometimes it is possible to notify the insurance carrier to refund the unaccrued portion to the seller and bill the purchaser for the applicable amount. Another method is for the seller to cancel the insurance policy and receive a rebate for the unused premium and for the buyer to purchase another policy.

Other expenses, such as fuel, electricity, water and other assessments, are often prorated. Usage of these utilities is not always the subject of exact computation. The parties can notify the respective companies to read the utility meters as of the date of closing and divide the bill accordingly.

Income from rentals is often apportioned as of the date of closing. Normally, rentals are paid in advance. If the closing occurs in the midst of a rental payment period, then an adjustment is required, because the seller in such an event receives from the tenant a rental payment covering a portion of the time after ownership has passed to the buyer.

CASE EXAMPLE

Jerry Rogers, seller, and Ronald Dodge, buyer, are to close July 15 on commercial property owned by Rogers. A tenant is under a leasehold agreement for such property and pays $350 per month on the first of each month. A clause within the real estate purchase contract requires apportionment of rentals as of the date of closing. On July 15 the buyer would be entitled to $175, which represents the unused portion of the rental.

Prorations are also covered in Chapter 23.

Earnest Money

A real estate purchase contract normally calls for the purchaser to deposit earnest money. Contrary to popular belief, this deposit is not necessary to validate the contract. Sufficient consideration exists in the form of mutual promises contained within the agreement.

Earnest money may be a nominal sum, such as $100, or it may be as substantial as ten percent of the purchase price or more. Normally, the real estate broker holds the deposit in an escrow account pending closing. At closing the earnest money may be returned to the purchaser or credited against the amount due to the seller.

Closing

The contract normally states the date and place of closing. The closing is discussed in detail in Chapter 23. At closing the buyer makes payment to the seller and the seller passes title by signing and conveying the deed in accordance with the terms of the contract. In the event that the time and place of closing are not specified within the contract, the law presumes that the parties intended that the closing take place within a reasonable time at a reasonable location.

Normally, time is not of the essence in real estate closings. Hence, even if a date is specified, failure to close on that date is not considered critical as long as the noncomplying party has acted in good faith and is able to close within a reasonable time thereafter. The parties, of course, may agree within the contract that time is of the essence, and under such a clause even a day's delay on the part of a party would be deemed a breach of contract.

Under certain circumstances, time is of the essence even in absence of express language in the contract to that effect. Time is of the essence in an option contract (see Chapter 19.) An option terminates after the expiration of the time provided in the option contract for exercise of the option. Also time is of the essence when parties are dealing in highly speculative land transactions that are subject to rapid fluctuations in value. In addition, when one party is made aware of particular circumstances that make the timing of the closing date critical (such as the necessity for the buyer to vacate an apartment the day of closing), time is deemed as an essential element to the contract.

When one party fails to appear at the closing, the other party must make a tender in order to declare the nonappearing party in default. A *tender* is an offer of money or property as required by the contract.

A buyer who appears at the closing unattended by the seller must be ready, willing and able to perform. The buyer must tender the purchase price by depositing it in escrow or through a show of the money to witnesses in attendance. Conversely, a seller makes tender by showing a readiness, willingness and an ability to deliver marketable title to the buyer.

Signing

A contract for the sale of real estate should be signed (executed) by both parties. A writing not executed by all parties is arguably not the agreement of any party who has failed to sign.

An agent acting in behalf of a party to the contract may bind a principal by signing the contract. Authority of the agent in some states may be oral; nevertheless, even in those states written authority is preferable. If an agent lacks proper authority, then only the agent is bound. An unauthorized act of an agent may be subsequentially ratified (approved) by a principal.

Only a few states require that a contract for the sale of realty also contain a *seal*. A vestigial remnant of the seal can be seen in some form contracts that have a mark, L.S. (for *locus siligis*), the Latin initials meaning "place of the seal."

Attestation and Acknowledgement

In most jurisdictions a contract for the sale of realty need not be witnessed (attested). The parties who sign the writing need not acknowledge their signatures as genuine before a notary public. However, some jurisdictions do not permit recording of a contract that is not witnessed and so acknowledged. A contract, however, does not have to be recorded in order to be considered binding between the parties. (Some jurisdictions require that the land installment contract, discussed in Chapter 19, be recorded.) Recording a contract would provide protection for the buyer; anyone considering purchasing the property under contract would have notice of the buyer's ownership interest in that property. The seller may, however, for good reason, object to recording because of potential problems it may cause. In the event the buyer defaults on the contract it may be costly and burdensome to remove the encumbrance that the recorded contract presents.

UNCONSCIONABLE CONTRACT

The Uniform Commercial Code (UCC), which has been enacted into law at least in part by all states, applies to the sale of goods but not to the sale of real property. Nevertheless, trends in the law of real property may be derived from an examination of certain provisions within the UCC; courts often reason by analogy from this code in reaching results in non-code-governed cases. Section 2—302(1) of the UCC recognizes that some contracts or provisions within contracts may be unconscionable:

> If the court as a matter of law finds the contract or any clause of the contract to have been unconscionable at the time it was made the court may refuse to enforce the contract, or it may enforce the remainder of the contract without the unconscionable clause, or it may so limit the application of any unconscionable clause as to avoid any unconscionable result.

In a seller's market the seller can dictate provisions on a take-it-or-leave-it basis. A buyer may be compelled to sign a contract including the provision "Buyer represents that he has examined the entirety of the property and asserts that he has not relied upon any representation made by the seller." The effect of such a clause may be to prevent the buyer from raising the defense of fraud or misrepresentation should their existence be revealed later. Some courts may relieve a buyer of this helpless position by striking the clause as unconscionable, thus treating it in a way similar to the way the UCC does when dealing with transactions involving the sale of goods.

SUMMARY

The real estate purchase contract is the instrument that legally obligates the buyer and seller to perform terms contained within it. Real estate purchase contracts are governed in all states by the Statute of Frauds. Therefore, to be enforceable the contract must be supported by a writing.

In practice, brokers normally use legal contract forms approved by local professionals. In most cases brokers or salespeople are permitted by law to assist the client by filling in the blanks of a form contract. They are not permitted to draft legal forms.

The real estate purchase contract governs the conduct of the parties. It customarily includes various provisions such as the purchase price, the type of evidence of title and deed the seller is required to tender, the various charges to be apportioned and the date the closing is to take place.

Finally, some real estate contracts are deemed unconscionable because their terms are grossly unfair. Reasoning by analogy to the

Uniform Commercial Code, courts are apt to refuse to enforce the contract or modify it to prevent an unconscionable result.

REVIEW AND DISCUSSION QUESTIONS

1. What are the elements necessary to satisfy the Statute of Frauds?
2. (a) Why does the Statute of Frauds apply to sales of interests in real estate? (b) Give an example of a case involving a real estate transfer that is excepted from the Statute of Frauds.
3. What is the purpose of the parol evidence rule?
4. What limitation may a broker confront when preparing real estate purchase contracts?
5. Describe five major provisions contained within the real estate purchase contract.
6. (a) What is a contingency clause? (b) What purpose does it serve? (c) Whom does it benefit?
7. When does the closing occur? Explain.
8. Explain how the Uniform Commercial Code influences real estate transactions.

CASE PROBLEMS

1. Shaughnessy, by oral agreement, leased a house and lot from Eidsmo for a term of one year. The agreement also gave Shaughnessy an option to purchase the property at the end of the one-year period. Shaughnessy entered into possession of the property and continued in possession throughout the one-year term, making all required rental payments. At the end of the year he informed Eidsmo of his desire to exercise his option. Shaughnessy continued in possession of the property after the expiration of the lease period and made payments toward the purchase price of the property. Eidsmo refused to honor the option, claiming that there was a failure to comply with the Statute of Frauds. (a) What is Shaughnessy's rebuttal to Eidsmo's claim? See *Shaughnessy v. Eidsmo*, 222 Minn. 141, 23 N.W.2d 362 (1946). (b) Would your answer be different if Shaughnessy, in accordance with his agreement with Eidsmo, added a new room to the dwelling?
2. The Whites entered into an agreement with the Rehns to purchase "all land west of road running south to the Rehn farmstead containing 960 acres." Nothing within the description pinpointed exactly which 960 acres was to be transferred. Immediately before the purchase agreement was to be signed, the extent of the specific parcel was explained orally to Mr. White. (a) Should the Rehns desire to back out of the sale, what argu-

ment could they make? (b) How should the Whites respond? *White v. Rehn*, 103 Idaho 1, 644 P.2d 323 (1982).

3. Ramey, a real estate broker, prepared a real estate purchase agreement on a standardized form drafted by attorneys. The purchaser, Diane Cultrum, told Ramey that she wanted to have the house inspected and be able to withdraw her offer if the inspection did not prove satisfactory to her. Ramey inserted the following contingency clause within a blank space on the contract: "This offer is contingent on a Satisfactory Structural Inspection." The inspection revealed numerous defects in the property, but none were of a structural nature. Cultrum refused to go through with the transaction and sued Ramey alleging that her draftmanship constituted an unauthorized practice of law. Is she right? Explain. *Cultrum v. Heritage House Realtors, Inc.*, 103 Wash. 2d 623, 694 P.2d 630 (1985).

4. A contract of sale required the Laddons, the buyers, to pay, as part of the purchase price, a $1,000 deposit to be held by Rhett Realty, the broker, "in escrow on behalf of seller until settlement." The contract further provided that the deposit would be forfeited to the sellers in the event the Laddons breached the contract. In such a case, under the terms of the contract, Rhett Realty would be entitled to 50 percent of the amount forfeited. The contract was contingent upon the buyers' obtaining financing, which they were unable to do. Who is entitled to the earnest money? Explain. *Laddon v. Rhett Realty, Inc.*, 63 Md. App. 562, 493 A.2d 379 (1985).

5. 805 Third Avenue Co. (Third Avenue) and M.W. Realty Associates entered into a contract whereby Third Avenue was to purchase M.W. Realty's air rights. Third Avenue needed the air rights to construct an office building. Third Avenue obtained a city permit authorizing it to commence construction, and it began to excavate and enter into contracts for the erection of the structure. M.W. Realty refused to complete its obligations under the purchase contract, insisting upon a modification of the contract on terms less favorable to Third Avenue. Knowing that any delay would result in serious injury, Third Avenue agreed to the unfavorable terms. What remedy is now available to Third Avenue? *805 Third Avenue Co. v. M.W. Realty Assoc.*, 58 N.Y.2d 447, 461 N.Y.S.2d 778 (1983).

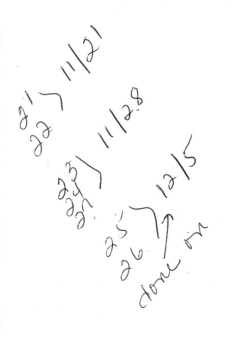

21
22 } 11/21

23
24 } 11/28
25.

25
26 } 12/5

done on

19

Land Installment Contracts and Options to Purchase

LAND INSTALLMENT CONTRACT

A legally enforceable agreement between buyer and seller whereby the buyer promises to make periodic installment payments to the seller toward the purchase price of real property and the seller promises to convey title to the property upon receipt of the last installment.

The previous chapter considered the real estate purchase agreement, the ordinary contract for the sale of real estate. This agreement defines the rights and duties of the seller and buyer in preparation for the closing of the transaction, which is discussed fully in Chapter 23. Between the signing of the purchase contract and the closing there is a short interval ranging from about one to three months. During this interval the seller is expected to prepare an abstract or secure other evidence of title and the buyer attempts to obtain financing, typically through a lending institution.

Sometimes the buyer is unable to obtain financing from a lending institution. Lacking the necessary cash, the buyer may be forced to defer purchase until his or her financial situation improves. Several alternatives are open, however, that may enable the buyer to purchase the property. If the seller is willing to extend financing to the buyer for the purchase price, one alternative is the purchase money mortgage, which will be discussed in Chapter 20. Under that method the seller transfers the deed to the property to the buyer and the buyer signs a mortgage in the seller's favor. The mortgage secures the remaining unpaid purchase price owed to the seller. The land installment contract, also known as a *land contract* or *contract for deed*, is another method of seller financing.

For the buyer, the land installment contract is a method of financing a real estate transaction through the seller; for the seller, it secures the payment of a debt. The rules that attach to ordinary contracts also apply to land installment contracts. The agreement must be supported by consideration and entered into by parties who possess the requisite capacity. Nevertheless, some obvious distinctions separate the land installment contract from the ordinary real estate purchase contract. In a real estate purchase contract the buyer's right to possession is deferred until closing or thereafter. Under a land installment contract possession is normally immediate and does not await final payment. In addition, the relationship between the parties to a real estate purchase agreement is of rather short duration, usually ceasing at the closing, when title is conveyed. The legal relationship of the parties to a land contract lasts longer. Such a contract may endure for as long as the seller is willing to extend the financing, perhaps 20 years or more, although shorter periods are more common. Often the seller extends a payment schedule based upon a 20- to 30-year payback period but requires the entire balance to be paid in full after a shorter period, for example, three to five years. The final payment is known as a *balloon payment* and normally requires the buyer to find outside financing to meet the payment. Before final payment the seller holds the deed, and thus legal title, whereas the purchaser is normally in possession of the property and enjoys *equitable title*.

Title Problems

Upon completion of all terms of the contract, including payment of the last installment, legal title passes to the buyer and the deed can be recorded in the buyer's name. Until the last installment is paid, the seller holds the deed and the property remains in the seller's name. During this interval the seller may encumber the property with mortgages or other liens. Unless the buyer is protected, he or she may pay the entire purchase price and find the property totally encumbered. By recording the land installment contract, however, the buyer can secure protection against most future encumbrances. Recording places all prospective mortgagees and lienors on notice of the buyer's interest in the property, and title problems are less likely to arise.

If the contract is unrecorded and the seller encumbers or sells the property, the installment contract buyer may be without remedy. A claim against the seller for damages will not necessarily help the buyer should the seller not be solvent. Sellers often discourage or impede the recording, since it is easier to resell the property upon the buyer's default if the contract is not recorded. However, some states by statute, require a land installment contract to be recorded.

Liens that attach before the creation of the installment contract may go unnoticed if the buyer fails to investigate the title beforehand. A certificate of title or title insurance protects the buyer's interest in the property. Normally these forms of assurance are required when a third-party lender is involved. In land installment contracts, however, there is no third-party stimulus because the seller finances the transaction. The uneducated buyer may fail to have the title examined. The prudent buyer should require proof of title in the seller as a condition of entering into the contract, should be sure the contract is immediately recorded, and should require a clause within the contract clarifying that the seller agrees to tender a deed to the property free of all liens and other encumbrances, except as specified.

After Acquired Title

In some cases the seller does not have title at the time of entering into the contract but subsequently acquires it. In this event the buyer is entitled to "after acquired title" when the time comes for the deed to be transferred to the buyer.

• CASE BRIEF •

Jim Ferguson, seller, enters into a land installment contract with Bill Hodd, buyer, whereby Ferguson is to tender a free and unencumbered deed to 20 acres of farmland designated as the Hill property, upon Hodd's completion of 60 monthly payments of $300 each. At the time the contract was entered into Ferguson possessed only a leasehold interest. Thereafter, however, he acquired the property in fee simple absolute from the lessor. Upon completing the last installment payment, Hodd is entitled to the fee under the doctrine of after acquired title. *See Bull v. Goldman 30 Md. App. 665, 353 A.2d 661 (1976).*

Nonetheless, should the buyer learn, after signing the contract, that the seller does not possess marketable title, in some jurisdictions the buyer may rescind the contract and seek return of the installment payments previously paid.

Contract Terms

Basic rules of real estate purchase contracts treated in the previous chapter also govern land installment contracts. Since a land contract involves an interest in land, it must comply with the Statute of Frauds, which requires that the contract be supported by a written memorandum. Normally, the land installment contract must be properly executed before it can be recorded. State statutes vary and should be consulted to ascertain the particular requirements for proper execution.

The parties are free to agree on the terms of the contract, and the courts will enforce those terms to the extent that they do not offend public policy. Over the years certain typical terms have emerged. Generally, the specifics of the terms reflect the relative bargaining strength of the buyer and seller. It appears that the seller has traditionally possessed the upper hand.

Price

Normally the buyer pays a modest down payment and periodic installments. The installment payments include principal and interest. The installments may be payable monthly, quarterly, annually or at any other agreed-upon interval. Unless otherwise stated, taxes and insurance are the seller's responsibility, because the seller is the legal owner of the property until the entire purchase price is paid. Neither statute nor custom prevents an allocation of taxes and insurance to the parties on the basis of their respective interests in the property. In most cases, however, the bargaining position of the seller is strong enough to require the buyer to assume the whole burden of these charges. This is not an unreasonable burden considering that the buyer receives the present beneficial use of the property and expects full ownership in the future.

From the seller's position, the method of payment may be critical. Under an Internal Revenue Code section, a seller may elect to partially defer tax treatment for gains in an installment sale transaction. A taxpayer who elects the installment method of reporting need only report as income, in a given year, the proportion of the installment payments that the gross profit bears to the total contract price.

CASE EXAMPLE

Barry Martin sells property to Sheila Cable for $40,000, payable $10,000 down with the remainder to be paid over six years at $5,000 a year. Martin had previously purchased the property for $30,000. His gross profit is $10,000 ($40,000 contract price − $30,000 original purchase price). Cable pays the $10,000 down payment. The proportion of the gross profit to the total contract price is 25 percent (10,000/40,000 = 25 percent). Martin, by electing the installment method, need report as income in the year of sale only $2,500 (25 percent of $10,000 down payment) and $1,250 in each succeeding year (25 percent of $5,000).

Waste, Removal and Inspection

The buyer is normally in possession of the premises in an installment contract. Consequently, the installment buyer is in the best position to maintain the premises and keep it in good repair. Customarily, the parties include a clause in the contract that makes the buyer responsible for the maintenance. Similarly, the installment contract may include a clause prohibiting committing waste or removal of fixtures or improvements without the consent of the seller. Failure of a buyer to comply with these clauses is a breach of the contract that gives rise to various remedies discussed later in this chapter.

The seller needs the right to inspect the premises in order to police these provisions. For that reason a clause similar to the following is often included: "Seller shall have the right to enter on and inspect the property and the buildings and improvements thereon after giving reasonable notice to do so."

Indemnification

The act of compensating another in the event of loss.

In the event that the buyer fails to keep the property in repair or causes waste, damages may result from either loss of property value or consequent injury to occupiers of the property. Mechanic's liens (discussed in Chapter 10) may also encumber the property if the purchaser fails to pay the workers or suppliers for renovations, repairs, improvements or other authorized work. An indemnification clause such as the following may be included for the seller's protection:

> Buyer shall hold seller free and harmless from any and all demands, loss, or liability resulting from the injury to or death of any person because of the negligence of the buyer or the condition of the property at any time after the date possession is delivered to the buyer. Buyer shall further indemnify seller for the amount of any and all mechanic's liens or other expenses or damages resulting from any renovations, alterations, building repairs, or other work ordered by the buyer.

Should the buyer fail to pay the tax assessments or insurance as agreed upon, the seller's security is jeopardized. The government, deprived of its taxes or assessments, may place a lien on the property and even foreclose for failure to pay. The seller's security would also be jeopardized should the property be destroyed by fire unless hazard insurance is maintained. If there is a mortgage on the property, the mortgagee may foreclose in the event taxes, assessments and/or insurance payments are in arrears. To protect the seller against these risks, a clause such as the following may be included within the installment contract:

> Should buyer fail to pay any amount pursuant to this contract for taxes, assessments, or insurance within (10) days before

that amount becomes delinquent, the seller may pay the amount and buyer agrees to repay to seller the amount paid by the seller together with interest at the rate of _____ percent per annum.

Assignment

In the absence of a provision in the contract prohibiting assignment, the buyer is free to transfer his or her interest in the land contract. Assignment does not, however, relieve the installment buyer of the obligation to continue making installment payments to the seller. The seller may desire to limit the buyer's right of assignment, being concerned that the assignee (one to whom the property is transferred) may be more likely to jeopardize the seller's interest in the property than the installment buyer. For this reason the installment contract normally includes a provision prohibiting assignment without the seller's written consent.

At any time before title passes, the seller is free to transfer the property to someone other than the installment buyer. Installment payments are then directed to the new owner. The sale is subject to the rights of the installment buyer, who still remains entitled to the property upon fulfillment of the terms of the installment contract. The seller's power to assign may be limited by agreement, but normally is not because of the purchaser's weaker bargaining position.

Mortgage

Mortgages are discussed in detail in Chapters 20 and 21. A typical clause regarding the seller's right to mortgage the property, pending the full payment of the purchase price, is often included within the land contract. A clause similar to the following is not uncommon: "The seller may mortgage the property, but in no event may such mortgage exceed the amount of the balance due on the contract."

CASE EXAMPLE

Norma Livingston sells real property to Howard Kessler on a land installment contract for $120,000, payable $20,000 down and $5,000 annually thereafter at ten percent interest for 20 years. After five years Livingston desires to borrow money and gives a mortgage in the property to the Second National Bank as security for the loan. Livingston may mortgage the property up to $75,000, the balance due on the installment contract.

In addition, the buyer may be contractually safeguarded against the consequences of a seller defaulting on a mortgage by inclusion of a clause similar to the following:

The seller shall keep any mortgage on the property in good standing, and if the seller defaults on any mortgage, seller agrees that the buyer may pay the delinquency and receive credit toward payment due under the terms of the contract.

An installment buyer who desires to borrow money from a bank or other lending institution can use as collateral the realty that is the subject of the land contract. Unless the contract expressly states otherwise, the buyer is entitled to mortgage the property to the extent that its value exceeds the amount owed on the land installment contract. A provision in the contract prohibiting assignment does not prevent the installment buyer from mortgaging his or her interest.

• CASE BRIEF •

Jaurel and Edna Fincher entered into a land contract whereby Lester Stacey and his wife agreed to purchase a one-half acre tract of land from the Finchers. The purchase price was $1,200, payable $200 down with the remainder payable in installments of $47.50 per month. Paragraph seven of the contract provided that the "Buyers may not assign their rights hereunder in whole or in part." Later the Staceys entered into an agreement with Miles Homes to purchase a precut home for erection on the tract for $6,378. The Staceys made a down payment and signed a promissory note for the balance due. The note was secured by a mortgage on the tract of land purchased. Miles Homes delivered the materials to the site in accord with the contract. The Staceys made payments to the Finchers but defaulted after the death of Mrs. Stacey. Similarly, the Staceys defaulted on their obligation to pay Miles Homes. The Finchers canceled the contract (with the consent of Mr. Stacey), reacquired possession of the land and sought a judicial order determining that the Miles Home lien was invalid. The court concluded that the prohibition against assignment did not prohibit the Staceys from entering into a valid mortgage and that the Finchers owned the property subject to the Miles Homes' lien. *Fincher v. Miles Homes, 549 S.W.2d 848 (Mo. 1977).*

If the buyer mortgages the property and then defaults on obligations under the land installment contract, a serious question arises concerning the mortgagee's rights. The seller must notify the mortgagee of the default before taking any action regarding the property. In some jurisdictions the mortgagee is entitled to acquire title to the property by paying the seller the amount due under the installment contract. In this circumstance the mortgagee may receive more value than the balance due on the mortgage loan. Other jurisdictions limit the mortgagee's recovery to the amount of the mortgagor's indebtedness due by requiring the mortgagee to invoke foreclosure, as discussed in Chapter 22. Under such an action the property is sold. The land installment seller is paid first from the proceeds an amount necessary to satisfy the amount due on the land contract. The remaining proceeds are used to satisfy the mortgagee's indebtedness, and the installment buyer receives the balance of any remaining monies. In a few states the mortgagee is obligated to pay the balance of the indebtedness owed to the seller before the foreclosure sale.

Conveyance

The buyer's ultimate objective is to receive good title to the property. Upon performance of the contractual obligations, including payment of the last installment, the seller is obligated to give a good title to the property by conveying the deed to the buyer. This requirement is normally reflected in a clause that reads as follows:

> When the buyer has paid the full purchase price with interest due and in the manner required by the terms and conditions of this contract; and, if the buyer performs all other provisions required of the buyer by the terms and conditions of this contract, seller agrees to convey the above described property to the buyer by deed of general warranty, with release of dower, if any.

Advantages to the Buyer

Most purchasers are not financially able to raise the entire purchase price in one lump sum; consequently, they must obtain financing in order to purchase the realty. A buyer, however, may not be able to secure financing from a lending institution because of an inability to meet down payment requirements or because of an unsatisfactory credit rating. Or the lender may refuse to extend credit because of the marginal value of the property. Of course, the seller may be able to extend this financing, but sellers normally do this only if protected adequately. The land contract gives the needed protection because the property remains in the name of the seller and in the event of default the seller may be able to cut off the buyer's interest quite simply.

The principal advantage that the installment contract offers to buyers is the ability to purchase the property. For little or no down payment, buyers are able to gain an interest in, and derive the benefit of, the property. The land installment contract increased in popularity as a financing tool in the early 1980s, when high interest rates decreased the borrowing power of many people. Its widespread usage continued even in face of declining interest rates.

Advantages to the Seller

The land installment contract may also benefit the seller. Such benefits may include attraction of buyers, tax advantages and continued incidents of legal ownership.

Attract Buyers

The main advantage to sellers is that the land installment contract provides a means for increasing the demand for property by attracting buyers who could otherwise not purchase the property because of an inability to secure outside financing. The ability to set the schedule of repayment so that it is affordable to the buyer often places the seller in a position to increase the purchase price above the market level and/ or charge higher interest than the seller is paying on the mortgage. Normally, however, the property is priced in accordance with the market. The attractive terms often permit the sale of otherwise unattractive property.

Tax Break

Under an installment contract, as previously noted, the seller does not receive the entire purchase price in one lump sum. Payments are extended over a period of years. Consequently, income is spread over a period of time. As a result, the seller may defer taxable income to a future time when overall income may be less. The seller consequently receives a welcome tax break.

Incidents of Legal Ownership

The land installment contract secures the payment of the buyer's indebtedness and gives the seller certain incidents of legal ownership. As discussed earlier, the seller may assign the property subject to the contract or mortgage the property up to the indebtedness. This is attractive to a seller who may reap the benefits of incidents of ownership while involved in a sale of the property.

Disadvantages to the Buyer

The land installment contract may present certain disadvantages to the buyer. These disadvantages may arise should the seller die, fail to transfer good title or neglect to record the contract or should the buyer not be afforded the right to prepay the amount due under the installment contract.

Problems Created by the Death of the Seller

Although the land contract is enforceable against the seller's heirs upon death, as a practical matter enforcement may be very costly. The buyer may be forced to hire an attorney to accomplish the transfer. The beneficiaries may be difficult to locate, and the property may be tied up in probate for years. Should there be a large number of beneficiaries, the situation becomes more laden with concurrent ownership interests and difficulties. Since minor and incompetent beneficiaries may require the appointment of a guardian, resolution may be even further complicated and delayed. Similar problems are present when the seller assigns the installment contract to another who dies.

Unwillingness or Inability to Transfer Good Title

The seller might refuse to transfer the title to the buyer after fulfillment of the contract. The buyer, who is legally entitled to the deed, may be forced to institute suit seeking specific performance. Even worse, after the buyer pays the installments in conformity with the contract, the seller may not have good title. Normally, the seller has agreed to convey title to the buyer upon receiving the final payment. By prevailing authority the seller is not required to maintain marketable title during the pendency of the contract, although a few courts have taken a contrary view. The buyer could obtain protection by insisting upon a contract provision requiring the seller to maintain marketable title or by obtaining title insurance.

Failure to Record

As stated earlier, the installment contract should be recorded to protect the buyer's interest. Sellers may try to discourage buyers from recording because in the event of default less difficulty attends to quieting title in their name if there has been no recording. In fact, some contracts may contain *in terrorem* clauses that prohibit recording at the expense of forfeiture. Although their validity is dubious, they undoubtedly discourage some buyers from recording. Some states by statute require the installment contract to be recorded.

If the installment contract is recorded, the majority of states give the buyer's contract priority over most subsequent purchasers and lienors since they are on constructive notice of the buyer's interest. Further, the land installment buyer usually has priority over subsequent purchasers and lienors who have knowledge of the buyer's interest, even if the contract is unrecorded. In many jurisdictions the fact that the buyer is in possession gives subsequent purchasers constructive knowledge of the buyer's interest, even if the contract is not publicly recorded.

Prepayment Disallowance

The installment contract buyer has no right to prepay the amount due unless provided for by agreement or statute. A buyer under such a handicap will not be able to accelerate the purchase of the property and may witness the value of the equity diminish in a declining market. Without the right to accelerate purchase and resell, the buyer is economically strapped. A court, however, might grant the installment buyer some relief.

CASE EXAMPLE

A land installment contract provides that Joe Hart is to pay $15,000 for property; the first $5,000 is to be paid to Mary Howe at the rate of $65 per month, including interest at four percent. There is no right to accelerate payments. Howe is directed, under the contract, to pay property taxes and insurance out of the $65. Payments are made for more than 15 years and the balance due on the property is more than $15,000, because of the increase in property taxes over the years. In an action by Joe Hart against Mary Howe seeking the right to pay off the entire indebtedness, a court might uphold the prohibition clause against prepayment but give Hart the right to pay the taxes and insurance separately from the $65 per month.

Disadvantages to the Seller

From the seller's viewpoint the land installment contract is often a compromise sometimes negotiated as a result of an inability to sell the property for cash. Two reasons may exist for this inability. High market interest rates may make it impractical for purchasers to obtain conventional financing, or the purchaser's financial status may prevent him or her from obtaining a loan from a lending institution. Because the land contract does often attract buyers who are otherwise not able to purchase the property because of their financial status, risk of default is high. Default may result in the buyer's forfeiture of all rights in the property. The buyer's interest may revert to the seller, in which case the seller is burdened with the property once again and must reenter the real estate market, necessitating additional brokerage costs and attorney fees. In some jurisdictions forfeiture is not an available remedy. Instead, judicial foreclosure of the property is necessary to cut off the buyer's interest. The cost of foreclosure makes it a burdensome remedy for the seller.

Seller's Remedies

A seller possesses several remedies against a buyer who fails to pay or who otherwise defaults under the terms of the installment contract, including specific performance of the contract or damages, rescission, forfeiture and foreclosure. These remedies were covered generally in the previous chapter. Forfeiture and foreclosure remedies, however, deserve special attention as seller's remedies under the land installment contract.

Forfeiture

Often included within the terms of a land contract is a forfeiture clause, which provides that in the event the buyer fails to abide by the terms of the contract the seller has the right to terminate the contract, retake possession of the property and retain all prior payments. Traditionally, these forfeiture clauses have been upheld by the courts. When enforced, the defaulting buyer loses all equity in the property, and the seller often receives a substantial windfall. The forfeiture penalty may be very severe to a defaulting buyer.

• CASE BRIEF •

In 1971 Sellmer, the seller, entered into an installment sale contract with Donaldson, the buyer, for the purchase of a summer cottage on the Ohio River. The purchase price was $16,500 at the rate of eight percent per annum for ten years. The contract called for a $2,000 down payment, and the monthly payments were $175. Donaldson, on several occasions, failed to make timely payments and failed to make three monthly installments in 1973. Donaldson failed to keep the property insured, contrary to a provision in the installment contract to do so. Additionally, Donaldson failed to keep the property in repair and left the property in an uninhabitable condition. Sellmer sued Donaldson, seeking a forfeiture and termination of the contract. The court held that because "Donaldson had wholly failed to perform his obligation to acquire adequate insurance and had allowed the property to deteriorate to such an extent that substantial repair was necessary before the house would even be habitable," forfeiture was a proper remedy. Consequently, the court ordered that more than $7,000 in payments made by Donaldson be forfeited to Sellmer and that the contract be terminated. *Donaldson v. Sellmer, 166 Ind. App. 60, 333 N.E.2d 862 (1975).*

Most states have departed from automatic approval of the forfeiture remedy, and all states have mitigated its harshness by statute or judicial decision. Some states require a "grace period," within which the buyer may cure any breach. In those jurisdictions forfeiture is permitted only after compliance with procedural technicalities. The seller must notify the buyer of the intention to invoke forfeiture and of the grace period. If the buyer fails to correct the default within the specified period the statute permits, forfeiture is proper. The lengths of these grace periods vary from 30 days to a year. Some states graduate the grace period dependent upon the portion of the contract price the buyer has paid. In the event the seller affords the requisite statutory notice and there is no response by the buyer to cure the defect, some states permit forfeiture without judicial proceedings. Others require court action. Another statutory approach ameliorating the hardship of forfeiture is the elimination of forfeiture as a remedy under certain conditions. For example, Ohio has enacted a statute that reads in part:

> If the vendee of a land installment contract has paid in accordance with the terms of the contract for a period of *five years* *or more* from the date of the first payment or has paid toward the purchase price a total sum equal to or in excess of *20 percent* thereof, the vendor may recover possession of his property only by use of a proceeding for foreclosure and judicial sale of the foreclosed property. . . . [Emphasis added.]

Another state statute eliminates forfeiture altogether by providing that the seller of a land installment contract shall be deemed to be a mortgagee and shall be subject to the same rules of foreclosure and to the same regulations, restraints and forms as are prescribed in relation to mortgages.

Even when there is no statutory modification, courts are reluctant to uphold a forfeiture clause and often employ various reasoning to relieve the defaulting buyer from a harsh result. If, for example, a seller consistently accepts late payments from the buyer and thereafter seeks forfeiture for delinquent payment, a court may hold that the seller has waived any rights under the contract for forfeiture by failing previously to object to delinquent payment. Other jurisdictions analogize a defaulting buyer in a land installment contract to a defaulting mortgagor and recognize an "equity of redemption period." In those jurisdictions courts determine the period of grace through tests of fairness and reason.

• CASE BRIEF •

In April 1967 the Allens (purchasers) entered into a land installment contract with the Ulanders (sellers) for the purchase of real estate. Under the terms of the contract, the Ulanders agreed to convey the real estate to the Allens after payment of $9,700 at the rate of $85 or more per month at seven percent interest per annum. The contract further provided for forfeiture in the event the purchasers failed to make timely payments. Over a period of 7½ years the Ulanders paid more than $7,500 in principal and interest and built up an equity of $1,583. They also made improvements to the property, adding two bedrooms, a bathroom and paneling. The Allens failed to make five payments in 1974 and 1975, and the Ulanders instituted an action in forfeiture. The court, applying equitable notions, allowed the purchasers 30 days to deposit with the court a sum equal to five months' payments to avoid forfeiture. The court held that "where a purchaser under an installment land contract has acquired a substantial equitable interest in the property, the court has discretion to utilize a remedy similar to that permitted in foreclosure actions." *Ulander v. Allen, 37 Colo. App. 279, 544 P.2d 1001 (1976).*

Still other equitable rationales may be invoked to support a refusal to recognize forfeiture. Some courts hold that, if the buyer would sustain a substantial net loss as a result of forfeiture, then forfeiture would be unconscionable; in that case the buyer is entitled to restitution. Under this view, if the seller's actual damages, based upon the fair market rental value of the property and other damages, are less than the buyer's payments, the buyer would be entitled to the difference.

CASE EXAMPLE

Mr. and Mrs. Hoyle, under an installment contract for the purchase of a motel, make total installment payments of $120,000 on a $345,000 purchase price. Additionally, they expend $30,000 on repairs and improvements to the premises. After four years the Hoyles default on their installment payments and vacate the premises. The reasonable rental value of the motel is $30,000 per year. Under an equitable approach, since the $150,000 expenditure on payments and improvements is substantial, the buyer is entitled to restitution in the amount of $30,000, computed as follows: Buyer's total expenditures are $150,000, consisting of payments in the amount of $120,000 and improvements in the amount of $30,000. The reasonable rental value of the property is $30,000 × 4 years (the period of time in which the Hoyles occupied the premises), or $120,000. The difference between the total payments and the reasonable rental value is $30,000 payable to the Hoyles.

Finally, some courts have struck down the forfeiture clause on the basis that it constitutes an unconscionable penalty.

Foreclosure

As noted, some states by statute provide for foreclosure as the proper remedy for a seller against a defaulting installment buyer. Only a few states have recognized foreclosure by judicial decision as a seller's remedy in the event of the buyer's default. Indiana is one such state. In Indiana the courts reserve the remedy of forfeiture for cases of absconding or abandoning buyers or where only a minimum amount has been paid by the buyer while the seller is making expenditures for taxes, insurance and maintenance. In all other cases in that jurisdiction and in some other jurisdictions the courts recognize judicial foreclosure as the proper remedy.

• CASE BRIEF •

Laura Virginia, seller, and Pam Osterholtz, purchaser, entered into a land contract for Whiteacre on the following terms: $10,000 down payment and $12,000 annually for five years, for a total of $70,000. Osterholtz paid $10,000 and made the first $12,000 installment but defaulted thereafter. Virginia instituted an action in forfeiture. The court held that foreclosure was the proper remedy. Under a foreclosure, if the property sold for $75,000 at a judicial sale, Virginia would receive $48,000 to satisfy the balance due on the contract and Osterholtz would receive the balance of $27,000. *See Sebastian v. Floyd, 585 S.W.2d 381 (Ky. 1979).*

Buyer's Remedies

The buyer possesses several possible remedies against a seller who fails to convey title or otherwise defaults under the terms of the contract. The remedies of specific performance, rescission, damages and foreclosure will be examined.

Specific Performance

When the installment buyer completes the requirements under the installment contract, including payment of the last installment, he or she is entitled to the deed. If the seller does not convey the deed, a court may award specific performance, mandating the seller to execute a deed in the buyer's favor. Refusal to abide by the decree may result in contempt of court and punishment. The court may also execute a deed in the seller's favor, or the very decree may act as the instrument that results in passage of title to the buyer.

Rescission

Another remedy for an installment buyer upon a seller's default is to elect rescission—that is, to have the contract terminated and the contract payments returned. In this instance fairness often requires that a value for rental of the property be deducted from the amount due the buyer. The remedy of rescission is designed to return the parties to their original position. This remedy is especially desirable for the buyer when the subject of real estate has depreciated in value below the contract price.

Damages

The installment buyer in reliance upon the contract may have spent money to improve the property. If the seller breaches under these circumstances and is unable to convey a marketable title, the buyer may prefer to sue for damages. A judgment for damages becomes a general lien on all real property the seller owns until the judgment is satisfied.

As a lienor, the buyer may foreclose on any of the seller's real property to satisfy the judgment. Other means of satisfying the judgment include attachment and sale of the seller's personal property and garnishment of the seller's wages.

Foreclosure

The installment buyer has an equitable interest in the property. As such, the buyer possesses an equitable lien on the property securing his or her interest. Consequently, the buyer may foreclose on the property in the event of the seller's default and recover the purchase payments.

OPTION

An agreement between an owner of property (optionor) and another (optionee) whereby the optionee has a right to purchase property within a specified time for a designated price.

Under an option agreement the optionor agrees not to revoke an offer to sell for a period of time. Unlike a buyer, the optionee is not under an obligation to purchase the property but may elect to do so within the time specified in the option agreement. The option confers upon the optionee the right to buy, whereas a buyer under a purchase contract or a land installment contract is under an obligation to buy.

Unless there is consideration to support the optionor's promise to keep the offer open, the optionor may revoke the offer at any time prior to acceptance. Consideration sufficient to support an optionor's promise to keep an offer open may be in the form of a payment of a sum of money. The law of consideration is discussed more fully in Chapter 17.

• CASE BRIEF •

On July 1 Jack Kelvin made an offer to Harry Hilton to sell specified property for $25,000. Kelvin agreed to keep the offer open for 30 days. On July 15 Sally Hammond offered Kelvin $30,000 for the property. On July 21 Kelvin accepted Hammond's offer. On July 23 Kelvin revoked his offer to Hilton. On July 25 Hilton accepted Kelvin's original offer. Since there was no consideration to support Kelvin's offer to Hilton, Kelvin's revocation on July 23 was effective. *See Echols v. Bloom, 485 S.W.2d 798 (Tex. Civ. App. 1972).*

Other clauses contained within the option agreement pertaining to the sale of the property are those normally found within a purchase contract. The precise manner of exercising the option should be detailed, including the time and place of delivery of the notice to exercise the option. The following is an example of a notice specification:

> Notice of exercise of this within option to purchase Cornacre shall be delivered in writing to the optionor at (his) (her) place of business at (address) on or before midnight (date).

When the optionee elects to exercise the option, the optionee becomes a buyer and both parties are bound by the terms of the sale included within the option agreement. The terms should be specific; otherwise, the agreement may be unenforceable because it is indefinite. The purchase price should be designated with provision as to whether the price paid for the option is to be applied to reduce the purchase price. The price of the option may have been as nominal as $1 or may be very substantial in the case of highly speculative property. Options are desirable from the optionee's viewpoint under several circumstances.

CASE EXAMPLE

A land developer may desire ten parcels of land. The developer wants all or none. Instead of purchasing the parcels one by one, the developer may choose to attempt to purchase options on all the parcels from the various owners. If successful, the developer, upon exercise of each, acquires all the desired parcels. If the developer cannot secure options on all the parcels, then only the price paid for the options is lost.

CASE EXAMPLE

A charitable organization desires to build a physical structure to house its operations. It locates the land but does not have the cash or the financing to purchase the land. By purchasing an option to buy the land, it may be in a better position to solicit sufficient funds from contributors to permit the exercise of the option. If the organization's efforts fail to raise the funds, then only the option price is lost.

CASE EXAMPLE

A parcel of land is located in an area that may be developed in the future and hence cause the value of the land to increase substantially. An investor may desire a long-term option to buy the land. If the area is developed and the value of the land rises, the investor may make a substantial profit by exercising or assigning the option. On the other hand, in the event the area is not developed and the value of the land is less than the price stated in the option, the investor will not exercise the option and has lost only the price paid for the option.

An option is assignable by the optionee unless assignment is prohibited expressly within the agreement. The optionee's assignee has the same rights under the option as the optionee. Upon exercise of the option by the prescribed manner, the assignee is entitled to the property subject to the terms of the option agreement.

The optionor has a right to sell the property that is under option in absence of a prohibition against sale within the option agreement. In such a case, if the sale occurs, the optionor's buyer takes subject to the option, if on notice of the option. Notice need not be actual. If the option has been recorded, then any buyer would be deemed on constructive notice.

SUMMARY

The land installment contract provides for payments to be made in periodic installments. Under this type of contract, the seller extends financing to the buyer, who does not receive full title until the final payment is made. For the duration of the contract the buyer has the right to possession, although the deed, and thus legal title, is retained by the seller. To protect the buyer, the land contract should be recorded. In addition, the buyer should examine the title to make certain it is marketable.

The land installment contract has advantages for both buyer and seller. For the buyer, paying installments to the seller may be the only way to obtain affordable financing—when interest rates are high, for example. For the seller, this type of financing widens the market for the property and attracts buyers who would not otherwise have been able to buy. In addition, there is a significant tax advantage to the seller who reports gains from the sale of the property by the installment method.

Disadvantages may sometimes outweigh the advantages. One risk to the buyer is death of the seller and unwillingness of the heirs to perform under the contract; another is failure of the seller to maintain good title for the duration of the contract. One disadvantage to the seller is the risk of default by the buyer.

Remedies are available to the seller or buyer upon breach of the installment contract. Under some circumstances, foreclosure may be the seller's only remedy. This process is both time-consuming and inconvenient because it burdens the owner with the sale of the property once again. Remedies for the buyer against a seller who fails to convey the title may include specific performance, rescission, damages and foreclosure.

An option is a kind of contract that enables a buyer to purchase property at some future time for an agreed-upon price. Options should be drawn so that they are very specific not only with regard to price and terms but also as to the time and place of delivery of notice to exercise the option.

REVIEW AND DISCUSSION QUESTIONS

1. Describe the differences between a land installment contract and an ordinary real estate purchase contract.
2. Who is helped by the doctrine of "after acquired title." In what ways?
3. What is the primary advantage to a buyer who buys property on a land installment contract? What are the advantages to a seller?
4. (a) What is the primary disadvantage to the seller who sells property on a land installment contract? (b) What are the disadvantages to the seller?
5. What are some acts that might be considered a buyer's breach of a land installment contract?
6. Describe the seller's remedy of forfeiture and explain how the states have softened the impact of that remedy.
7. Describe the buyer's remedies in the event the seller defaults on a land installment contract.
8. Under what circumstances would it be desirable for an owner of real property to extend an option to buy the property to a prospective buyer?

CASE PROBLEMS

1. Donald Reed and LaVonne McAdow entered into a land installment contract for the sale of a parcel of land owned by Reed. The contract was never recorded. Subsequently, Reed assigned his entire interest in the land to Ohio Mortgage Company, which was unaware of the contract between Reed and McAdow. The assignment was not recorded. After the assignment of the land Kagey Lumber Company obtained a judgment against Reed and is now in the process of placing a lien on the property. (a) Will Kagey's judgment become a lien on the property? Why or why not? (b) What are Kagey's rights in the property? Describe. (c) Is Ohio Mortgage Company subject to the provisions of the contract between Reed and McAdow? Discuss. See *Butcher v. Kagey Lumber Company,* 164 Ohio St. 85, 128 N.E.2d 54 (1955).
2. Moorman and Whitman signed a land installment contract for the sale of real estate owned by Moorman. The contract stated that the land consisted of three tracts totaling 460 acres. Whit-

man assigned his interest in the contract to Maxwell. The assignment, expressly authorized by the contract, contained a description of the land similar to that in the land installment contract. After three years Maxwell paid Moorman the entire balance due under the land installment contract and received the deed to the property. Maxwell then attempted to sell the property to Fentress. Before the deal was consummated, Fentress notified Maxwell that the property contained only 355.9 acres rather than 460 acres, as stated in their contract. Maxwell and Fentress agreed to a reduction in the purchase price, and the contract was signed. Maxwell then attempted to persuade Moorman to return to him approximately 23 percent of the purchase price he paid. Moorman refused. (a) Can Maxwell successfully maintain an action against Moorman for return of the disputed portion of the purchase price? Explain. (b) Does he have a cause of action against Whitman? Explain. See *Maxwell v. Moorman*, 522 S.W.2d 441 (Ky. Ct. App. 1975).

3. Newman entered into a land installment contract with Mountain Park Land Company to purchase a tract of timberland. After Newman paid approximately half of the money due to the company under the contract, the company, without the consent of Newman, cut down trees from the land and sold a substantial amount of the timber. As a result of the actions of Mountain Park, the land decreased in value. Does Newman have a cause of action against Mountain Park? If so, what is that cause of action and what are his possible remedies? See *Newman v. Mountain Park Land Co.*, 85 Ark. 208, 107 S.W. 391 (1908). (b) What if Newman harvested the trees and inflicted the damage to the property during the pendency of the installment contract? Would Mountain Park have a cause of action against Newman? Explain. See *Reynolds v. Lawrence*, 147 Ala. 216, 40 So. 576 (1906).

4. Ben Schottenstein and Jack J. Devoe entered into a land installment contract. The terms of the contract stipulated that certain property would be conveyed in fee simple absolute by Schottenstein to Devoe in return for $21,500 payable in installments over a ten year period. After signing the contract, Devoe learned that Schottenstein did not have legal title to the property at the time of the contract signing. Devoe therefore seeks to avoid the contract. (a) May he do so? Explain. (b) What is Schottenstein's counterargument? (c) What difference would it make if Devoe knew of the state of Schottenstein's title prior to signing the contract? See *Schottenstein v. Devoe*, 83 Ohio App. 193, 82 N.E.2d 552 (1948).

20
Introduction to Mortgage Law

MORTGAGE

A written instrument that uses real property to secure payment of a debt.

A mortgage is one of the two principal instruments used in a loan transaction in which real estate is the security. The other instrument, the note, is also discussed in this chapter. The purpose of the mortgage is to provide security for payment of the debt. Without the existence of a debt, a mortgage has no effect.

CASE EXAMPLE

Anders Plumbing Company, Inc., owned a valuable building. The company needed money and sold stock to Lance and Jean Billingham. In order to induce the Billinghams to purchase the stock, they were given a mortgage on the property.

Lee Sickles, a contractor, made improvements on the property. When he was not paid, Sickles attempted to enforce a mechanic's lien. The Billinghams argued that their mortgage had priority over the lien. In a suit by Sickles, the court would hold the mortgage invalid because it was not given as security for a debt.

Secured and Unsecured Debts

From the purchase of a family's modest first home to the million-dollar commercial sale, financing is the key to almost every successful real estate transaction. People and institutions lend money because lending is profitable; much of the profitability stems from the risk entailed. A lender's risk is reduced when its loan is secured by property—an automobile, real estate, a firm's inventory or some other kind of valuable asset. When a loan is secured, the lender has a right to sell the security and apply the proceeds against the debt if the borrower fails to pay or violates some other term of the loan agreement. As security, real estate has several advantages over personal property. Mortgages, therefore, increase the attractiveness of lending to individuals and firms having funds available for financing.

Not all loans are secured. Sometimes a lender will advance funds on the basis of the borrower's character and reputation. If the borrower *defaults*—that is, fails to pay according to the terms of the agreement—and the creditor wins a judgment, the creditor has a right to attach the borrower's assets. Claims of a secured creditor take priority over this type of judgment, however.

The true nature of a mortgage, no matter what its form, is to establish a security right against a debtor's interest in real property. Most often the debtor's interest will be fee simple ownership, but legally mortgages may cover almost any interest in real estate that may be sold or assigned. Mortgages may be applied to rental income, life estates, estates for years, remainders and reversions, as well as other valuable property rights. Most of these interests in real estate are seldom the subject of mortgage loans, however, since they are often of limited duration or conditioned upon something that cannot be controlled.

Mortgages are also used sometimes to secure obligations that are quite unrelated to the property mortgaged.

CASE EXAMPLE

Ray Adams wished to go into business for himself as a plumbing and heating contractor. He planned to hire one or two employees and open up a small showroom from which to sell plumbing fixtures. Although Ray had saved enough money to get started, he was advised by some of the manufacturers whose lines he wished to carry that he should have a line of credit with a local bank. Ray's bank was willing to give him a $45,000 line of credit; as security the bank asked for a mortgage against rental property that he owned.

Mortgage, Mortgagor and Mortgagee

Many common terms are not used with the precision they deserve, and the term *mortgage* is one of these. It is often confused with the underlying debt. Each month many people speak about paying "the mortgage," but what they pay is not the mortgage. They pay a debt so that a creditor will not have to turn to the mortgage, which secures the debt.

Many people, even some actually involved in real estate, are troubled by the terms *mortgagor* and *mortgagee*. This confusion arises because they ignore the true nature of the mortgage. They think of the funds the lender is advancing as the mortgage. Naturally then they have a tendency to refer to the lender as the mortgagor, but the funds are not the mortgage. The mortgage is the instrument the borrower gives to create a security right in the lender. The borrower thus is the mortgagor, just as the person who sells a home and gives a deed is the grantor. The mortgagee is the person or firm to whom the mortgage is given. Like the grantee of a deed, the mortgagee is the recipient of an interest in real estate.

Note

A written instrument signed by a borrower containing the provisions of a loan and a promise to repay according to the terms of the agreement between borrower and lender.

In addition to security aspects, mortgage transactions often involve the borrower's personal liability to pay the debt. Usually the borrower makes the commitment by signing a promise to pay or, in some states, a *bond*. The note or bond serves as evidence of the debt for which the mortgage is the security. The typical note contains the amount of the loan, the interest rate and the time and method of repayment as well as the borrower's obligation to pay. This instrument is sometimes referred to as a *promissory note* or *mortgage note*.

The existence of the note provides the lender with two remedies if the debt is not paid: to sue on the note and to obtain a personal judgment against the debtor or to have the real estate sold and the proceeds applied against the debt. If the lender wins a personal judgment on the note, the judgment may be collected by attaching other property of the debtor or by garnisheeing the debtor's wages. In addition, if the property when sold does not bring enough to pay the debt, a personal action can be brought on the note. A few states require the lender to choose either method: to sell the collateral to pay the debt or to sue on the note.

Both note and mortgage are essential to the mortgage transaction. If the mortgage is transferred, the transferee has a right to the note. If the mortgage is invalid, however, the creditor may sue on the note (or bond), since it is a promise to repay the debt.

• CASE BRIEF •

Congregation Hayushor, Inc., a New York religious corporation, executed and delivered a bond and mortgage in favor of Bernstein. Bernstein had advanced the church $20,000. New York law required a religious corporation to obtain permission of a court before mortgaging its real estate. This was not done, and as a result the mortgage was invalid. When Bernstein sued on the bond after a default, the congregation raised as a defense the invalidity of the mortgage. It asked the court to dismiss Bernstein's suit. The court refused, stating that "even though the security is voidable, the indebtedness on the bond remains unaffected and is enforceable." *Bernstein v. Friedlinder, 58 Misc. 2d 492, 296 N.Y.S. 2d 409 (1968).*

HISTORY OF MORTGAGE LAW

A brief review of the history of mortgage law will help to clarify several elements of this important instrument. Although mortgages have changed appreciably over the centuries, several aspects of modern mortgage law can be traced to the early use of the mortgage in England. A transaction quite similar to today's mortgage loan developed in that country during the 13th and 14th centuries.

At that time a borrower who mortgaged real property as security actually transferred title to the mortgagee. The mortgagee was given a deed just as if he or she had purchased the property. Often, though not always, the mortgagor/borrower also gave up possession of the real estate. As use of the mortgage expanded, courts began to require that a mortgagee in possession apply any rents and profits from the property to reduce the debt.

Because the mortgage was given as security, the title that the mortgagee acquired was not absolute. A provision in the mortgage called the *defeasance clause* provided that if the mortgagor paid the debt by the *law day*, the day it was due, the transfer of title to the mortgagee was voided. Title reverted to the mortgagor. This date was very important to the mortgagor; if the debt was unpaid at that time, the mortgagee's title became absolute. The mortgagor lost all rights in the real estate, even if it was worth far more than the debt.

The loss of all rights in the real estate for failure to pay the debt when due usually worked a severe hardship on the mortgagor. Loss of the property seemed especially unfair when payment had been missed for some justifiable reason. Faced with this injustice, mortgagors who had valid reasons for missing the law day payment began to petition the king for redress. They would ask for an additional period of time to redeem the property. Generally, the king would turn these requests over to his chancellor, who was responsible for seeing that equity (justice) was done. If the chancellor felt the mortgagor had a justifiable reason for failing to pay, the mortgagor would be given more time to meet this obligation and thus recover the property.

Over the years what initially had depended upon a review of the factors in each case became routine. By the 17th century all mortgagors had acquired the right to get back their property by paying the debt, even after default. Because the chancellor presided over a court that was called *equity*, the mortgagor's right was known as the *equity of redemption*. It is discussed in Chapter 22.

Historically, the equity of redemption placed the mortgagee in a difficult position. Although the mortgage gave the mortgagee absolute title if the mortgagor defaulted on the law day, the title could be nullified by the mortgagor's equity of redemption. This meant that the mortgagee could do little with the property inasmuch as the mortgagor could redeem it at any time. Whatever title the mortgagee had was at best uncertain. Realizing that it was equity that had created this problem, mortgagees began asking equity to set definite dates terminating the mortgagor's right to redeem. Because public policy favors certainty in title to real estate, equity as a matter of course would grant these requests. The chancellor would issue a decree giving the mortgagor a specified period of time to make the required payment. If at the end of this period the debt had not been paid, the mortgagor would be foreclosed from the property forever. This was known as *strict foreclosure*. The mortgagee then had an absolute title and could assert all ownership rights. Rents and profits no longer had to be applied against the debt; the property could be sold, mortgaged or devised. Although methods of foreclosure have changed considerably over the years, foreclosure is important in modern law. All states have statutes providing for foreclosure through judicial proceedings (*judicial foreclosure*). Judicial and other types of foreclosure are the subject of Chapter 22.

Title and Lien Theory

The historical theory that the mortgage conveys title to the mortgagee continues to be used in some states, referred to as *title theory states*. Even in these states, however, although the mortgagee acquires title, the mortgagee does not acquire the right of possession unless the mortgagor defaults.

Most states recognize that in reality a mortgage is a lien. It is a device used by debtors and creditors to secure a debt. The mortgagee is interested primarily in having the security sold and the proceeds applied to the debt if the mortgagor fails to pay or violates some other mortgage provision. States taking this position are called *lien theory states*.

In some states that consider the mortgage a lien, the mortgagee of real property has more rights than most other lienholders. Sometimes these rights are very similar to those a title holder would have. For example, in several states by statute the mortgagee is entitled to oust a defaulting mortgagor from possession. Most other types of liens permit the holder only to have the security sold and proceeds applied to the debt. Since vestiges of title theory appear in the law of lien theory states and lien theory remains in some title theory jurisdictions, few states can be classified rigidly. Writers who analyze real estate law have developed a third classification, *intermediate theory* jurisdictions. A more fruitful approach for the real estate practitioner is to recognize that, no matter what form the mortgage takes, the solution to most legal problems of mortgage law is recognition that the mortgage is a security instrument.

FORMS OF MORTGAGE

Currently the mortgage most commonly used in the United States is a two-party instrument. By its terms one of the parties, the mortgagor, creates a security interest in property for the other, the mortgagee. Because historically the mortgage was a conveyance, the mortgage often has many provisions similar to those of a deed. In some states it is called a *mortgage deed*. Legislative bodies in a few states have adopted statutory mortgage forms. Although they contain all elements essential to a valid mortgage, use of the statutory form is not required.

In general for an instrument to be effective as a mortgage, it should include at least the following information:

- names of the parties,
- description of the premises,
- language indicating that the instrument is given as security for a debt,
- statement of the debt secured, and
- terms for repaying the debt.

Additionally, the mortgage must be signed by the mortgagor and executed according to the laws of the state in which the property is located. At least between the original parties, the law treats many instruments as mortgages even without such information being contained. If the instrument is not in the proper form, however, the mortgagee often cannot assert it against other creditors, and it may not be recorded.

Most mortgages contain substantially more information than minimal requirements. Because the parties insert many provisions designed to protect their rights, mortgage instruments may tend to be lengthy. The recording process is expensive and requires a great amount of storage space. A number of states have adopted statutes that allow mortgagees to record a *master mortgage* containing the desired covenants and clauses. This practice permits execution and recording of a mortgage that incorporates by reference the provisions of the master mortgage. Stated are the recording date, file number, volume and page of the master mortgage.

Deed of Trust

**A written instrument that transfers title to real property
to a trustee as security for a debt owed by the borrower
to the lender, who is the beneficiary of the trust.**

In a number of states the typical real estate security instrument involves three parties and is based upon the law of trusts. Instead of executing a mortgage in favor of a lender, the borrower transfers title to a trustee through a deed of trust. Although we have seen that in a few states the mortgage, at least in theory, passes title, even in the title theory states the mortgage is a lien in nature. The important difference between the mortgage and the deed of trust is that in a deed of trust legal title passes to the trustee. The trustee holds this title for the benefit of both the borrower and the lender. When the debt secured by the deed of trust is repaid, the trustee must reconvey title to the borrower.

The law of trusts, which has developed over hundreds of years, requires trustees to act in utmost good faith and fairness. Like the real estate broker, the trustee is a fiduciary. In addition to this fiduciary duty, the trustee has specific obligations and powers stated in the deed of trust. A trustee who fails to meet these obligations is personally accountable.

Importantly, the trustee has the power to sell the property if the borrower fails to maintain payments on the debt or breaches some other condition of the loan agreement by failing to keep the buildings insured, by selling the property or by committing waste. The power-of-sale provision makes judicial foreclosure procedure unnecessary, although the trustee usually can elect such procedure. Because judicial foreclosure can be avoided, collection from the security is more rapid and economical than through the court procedure.

Lawyers in states where the deed of trust is common argue that the ability to sell the security efficiently is the deed of trust's major advantage over the mortgage. This advantage does not exist in all states as in some legislation requires that the trustee proceed through a judicial foreclosure. (Judicial foreclosure is discussed in Chapter 22.) Another advantage of the deed of trust is that in a number of states it avoids the borrower's right of redemption because a purchaser from the trustee acquires that party's legal title to the property. In addition, the borrower must also surrender possession to the purchaser of the trustee's legal title. There are several other reasons why lenders in many states prefer to make residential property loans under a deed of trust. For one, the statute of limitations may bar action on the note in some mortgage transactions, but not with a deed-of-trust power of sale in which the trustee has legal title. In addition, a deed of trust can be used to secure several notes. Finally, the lender may remain anonymous in a deed of trust.

Compared with the mortgage, a distinct disadvantage of the deed of trust lies in discharging the instrument. In most states a mortgage is discharged when the mortgagee executes a simple document called a *satisfaction of mortgage* or a *release of mortgage*. The deed of trust requires a reconveyance by the trustee. The trustee will refuse to reconvey the property without assurance that the underlying obligation has been paid. Otherwise the trustee would be personally liable to the lender for any amount still due. If the trustee is an individual, the problem of reconveyance can become especially acute because the person might be difficult to locate. For this reason the preferred practice is to name a corporate trustee.

Both the mortgage and deed of trust by their terms establish a security interest in real estate. In some situations, however, courts will recognize the existence of a security interest in the absence of either one of these instruments.

Equitable Mortgage

A lien arising from a transaction that shows an intention of the parties to use some particular real property as security for a debt.

• CASE BRIEF •

Esther Destro owed Lucien Pellerin $25,000. The debt was secured by a deed of trust on property in Buena Park, California. Destro wanted to sell the property and asked Pellerin if he would release it for $5,000 and a note for $20,000 secured by a deed of trust on other real property. Pellerin agreed.

Upon receipt of the $5,000, Pellerin reconveyed the Buena Park property to Destro. Destro, however, never executed the new note or deed of trust as promised. When Destro was declared a bankrupt, the trustee in bankruptcy sold the property that was to secure the $20,000 note. Pellerin claimed the proceeds, but the bankruptcy court rejected his claim. Upon appeal, the U.S. District Court reversed. The court stated that "an executory contract to execute a mortgage creates an equitable mortgage if money has been borrowed or other obligation incurred on the faith of it." *In re Destro, 675 F.2d 1037 (9th Cir. 1982).*

Where a lender advances money upon the faith of the borrower's agreement to secure the debt by a mortgage on a certain property, equity impresses a lien in favor of the creditor upon the land intended to be mortgaged. This doctrine of equitable mortgages is based upon fairness and justice. Equity considers a thing done if parties agree to do it and it ought to be done. Equitable mortgages are not limited to instruments the parties intended as mortgages. The form of an agreement by which security is given is unimportant. If the document's purpose plainly appears, equity regards the substance and gives effect to the intention.

The person who has an equitable mortgage enjoys protection, but not to the same degree as one who has recorded a mortgage. The property might be sold to a purchaser who has no knowledge of the equitable lien. Under these circumstances the rights of the bona fide purchaser are superior to those of the equitable lienholder.

Deed Absolute

An instrument in the form of a deed, which the courts construe as a mortgage.

The doctrine of deed absolute is an extension of the equitable mortgage concept. Sometimes a landowner will convey title to a creditor absolutely, although the parties recognize the conveyance as merely security for a loan. This practice should be avoided because the instrument does not indicate the true relationship between parties and may give rise to litigation.

In solving these disputes, courts in the United States have generally taken the position that if the parties intend the instrument as security the grantor is entitled to redeem the property. The courts treat the instrument as a mortgage rather than as a deed because the parties intended the instrument to create in the grantee a security interest, not title.

CASE EXAMPLE

Elmer Koch had debts of more than $5,000 that he wished to pay. He borrowed $5,000 from Jasper Wasson and gave Wasson a deed to a farm as well as possession of the property. At the time title passed, Wasson signed an agreement giving Koch an option to repurchase the farm for $5,000 plus $300 for each year Wasson was in possession. Koch was also to reimburse Wasson for improvements. The farm was worth about $12,000. When Koch attempted to exercise the option, Wasson refused to accept payment.

In litigation a question arose as to whether the instrument given by Koch was a deed or a mortgage. Although the law differs from state to state, most courts would consider the instrument a mortgage, not a deed.

In trying to determine the intent of the parties when a claim exists that an absolute deed is in reality a security instrument, courts consider several factors. Although any single factor may be determinative, the following four are usually given weight:

- adequacy of consideration,
- relationship of the parties,
- possession of the property,
- payment of taxes and improvements.

If the consideration is much less than the value of the property, as in the preceding example, the conveyance is almost always declared a mortgage. The relationship of the parties is also important. Usually a discrepancy exists in the bargaining power of the parties, and the court protects the mortgagor as the weaker party and declares the instrument a mortgage. Conversely, courts often declare a deed absolute when it is clear that the grantor was using the device to defraud creditors.

Two additional factors courts often take into account are who is in possession of the property and who pays the ordinary expenses of ownership. Allowing the grantor to retain possession is some evidence that the deed was given as security. A grantor's continued payment of taxes, insurance and maintenance is an indication that the instrument was not intended as a conveyance, but as a mortgage.

MORTGAGE FINANCING AND ECONOMIC CONDITIONS

Both the equitable mortgage doctrine and the manner in which courts construe a deed when evidence indicates that it was given as security are examples of the way the legal system responds to social needs. In the interest of justice, courts recognize the true nature of the transaction in both situations and act accordingly.

In mortgage law over the years the legal system has also responded to the economic needs of the community. Financing by mortgage is critical both to the real estate industry and to the economic system. As economic conditions change and new financing needs appear, different forms of mortgage loans develop to meet these demands. Although the process is often slow and not without strain, the courts, regulatory agencies and legislative bodies gradually develop rules and regulations to accommodate these new forms.

Money Market

Term used to designate the supply of available funds for which borrowers of all types compete.

Only limited funds are available in the money market at any one time. Borrowers wishing to obtain loans to purchase real estate must compete in the money market with those needing funds for other purposes. The availability of these funds for any one type of lending depends upon many economic factors. Sometimes economic conditions are such that funds for certain types of loans are not readily available. During the last 20 years the demand for loanable funds has been strong. Interest rates, the price that borrowers pay for funds, as a rule have tended to rise rapidly and have been subject to wide fluctuations. Other economic conditions such as inflation also have been a problem for lenders as well as borrowers. The result has been that mortgage lenders developed new types of mortgage loans to help solve these problems. Sometimes these innovative approaches to lending do not mesh easily with existing law.

The evolution of the flexible-rate mortgage during the 1970s is an example of adjustments made between traditional legal concepts and economic need. During the late 1960s and 1970s financial institutions, especially savings and loans, which carry between 35 and 40 percent of residential mortgage debt, experienced many problems because of interest rate changes. Throughout this period interest rates not only increased dramatically but also fluctuated widely. The result was that these thrift institutions frequently found themselves caught in a credit squeeze. They had extended funds for long terms at fixed rates, depending upon additional deposits to meet reserve requirements and new commitments. When they experienced difficulty in attracting and retaining deposits because competing investments offered higher interest yields, they were often forced to liquidate existing mortgages at a loss to maintain reserves and meet new commitments. Mortgage funds thus dried up, and as new home purchases and construction slowed, the entire economy felt the pinch. The flexible-rate mortgage was an attempt to lessen the strain of "interest rate risk" on lending institutions.

Flexible-Rate Mortgage

A mortgage that contains a provision permitting the mortgagee to adjust the interest rate upward or downward in a manner specified in the mortgage.

Flexible-rate mortgages tie the interest rate to an index that reflects short-term money market conditions. The index should be outside the control of the lending institution, and it should be readily verifiable by the owner. Indexes that have been used include the Federal Reserve rediscount rate, the Treasury bill rate and national mortgage loan rates compiled by the Federal Home Loan Bank Board (FHLBB) or the Federal Housing Administration. Although flexible-rate mortgages are not inherently illegal, until the late 1970s they were prohibited by statute in a number of states.

Variable-Rate Mortgage (VRM)

The first flexible-rate mortgage to win approval was called a *variable-rate mortgage*. In the late 1970s, encouraged by legislation in California that permitted financial institutions to use a variable-rate mortgage, several other states adopted statutes removing curbs on VRMs. In 1979 the FHLBB authorized federally chartered savings and loans to make this type of loan. FHLBB action provided additional impetus for financial institutions to use VRMs.

State and federal action authorizing lenders to make VRMs usually included provisions to protect the borrower. For example, regulations limited the amount that the interest could be increased over the life of the loan. These limits were referred to as *caps*. The following are some additional regulations that were designed to protect borrowers:

- Downward interest rate adjustments required on the same basis as upward;
- Interest rate adjustments only at specified times, usually semi-annually or yearly;
- Upward adjustments limited at any single period, usually to one-quarter or one-half percent;
- Borrowers entitled to prepay without penalty.

Adjustable-Rate Mortgage (ARM)

In 1981 the FHLBB authorized lenders to make adjustable-rate mortgage loans. The ARM is similar in principle to the VRM as both are tied to an index reflecting short-term interest rates. The ARM, however, places fewer limitations on the lender and is more flexible regarding the frequency and amount of interest rate adjustments. As a result the ARM has replaced the VRM as the most commonly used flexible-rate mortgage instrument.

One difference between the ARM and the VRM is that the ARM can be written with or without caps. Most ARMs are written with caps. In addition, some ARMs limit the amount that the interest rate can be adjusted at any one payment period, and some limit the amount the periodic payment can increase. As a result of these provisions, *negative amortization* is a possibility in some situations.

Negative amortization occurs when a periodic payment is not sufficient to cover all of the accrued interest on a loan. The amount of unpaid interest must be added to the principal balance that is due. The borrower pays this additional interest when the monthly payments can be increased to exceed the amount necessary to amortize the debt. Regulations limit the amount of negative amortization to 25 percent of the original principal.

CASE EXAMPLE

The Intrepid Savings and Loan granted John Bell a loan to buy a home. The loan was to be repaid over 15 years and was secured by an ARM. Monthly payments were $620. The interest rate adjustment period on the mortgage was every six months; however, the payment adjustments were made every three years. When the interest rate was increased at the end of the first year, the $620 payment did not cover all the interest that was due. The difference was added to the principal to be repaid by the increased payments beginning at the end of the third year.

The VRM and ARM are responses made by lenders to some unusual economic conditions that existed in the United States during the 1970s and the 1980s. Other types of mortgage loans that real estate personnel should be familiar with are often also the result of lenders' efforts to deal with economic problems. These mortgages—purchase money mortgage, construction mortgage, open-end mortgage, wraparound mortgage, package mortgage and rollover mortgage—will be examined in the balance of this section.

Purchase Money Mortgage

A written instrument given by a buyer to secure part of the purchase price and delivered contemporaneously with the transfer of title to the buyer.

CASE EXAMPLE

Martin Sankovich purchased a small dairy farm from his uncle for $250,000. He paid $40,000 down and assumed an existing mortgage of $ 110,000. His uncle agreed to take back a purchase money second mortgage for $100,000. At the closing, Martin executed a mortgage and note in favor of his uncle, who in turn conveyed title to him.

The purchase money mortgage provides some protection for a seller who takes back a mortgage for part of the purchase price. The principal benefit to the mortgagee is that the purchase money mortgage takes priority, or preference, over liens against the buyer that might immediately attach to the property. Suppose, for example, that Martin at the time of closing had an outstanding judgment against him for $8,000. A judgment lien would usually attach immediately to his interest in the dairy and would be superior to his uncle's mortgage. However, the law assumes that the delivery of the deed and the purchase money loan are one transaction. The result is that there is no time for an intervening lien to attach. The judgment, though prior in time, is inferior in right to the seller's mortgage. In states that recognize dower and homestead rights, the purchase money mortgage takes priority over them. If the dairy were in a state that recognized dower, Martin's wife would have an immediate inchoate right of dower when Martin acquired title to the property. Even if she did not sign the mortgage, her right would be inferior to that of the purchase money lender.

In a few states only a seller who takes back a mortgage is afforded the limited benefits of a purchase money mortgagee. Most jurisdictions, however, have extended purchase money safeguards to any lender who advances funds that are applied to the purchase price. If Martin had borrowed $210,000 from a bank to purchase the dairy, the bank would have purchase money status if the funds were advanced simultaneously with the transfer of title to Martin.

Construction Mortgage

A mortgage given to secure funds advanced to construct or improve a building.

Construction loan is a term frequently used in the real estate industry. Like many common terms, it has a variety of meanings. Sometimes people use it in a general sense when discussing sources of funds to remodel or make relatively minor improvements. More specifically, the term refers to a number of industry practices that provide substantial funding for construction or renovation. A common characteristic of these practices is that the lender agrees to advance a total sum but supplies the funds over a period of time as work progresses. The loan is secured by a construction mortgage.

For some lenders the construction mortgage does not differ materially from a regular mortgage except that funds are advanced periodically, not in a lump sum. Upon completion of the work, the lender carries the mortgage as a permanent investment or assigns it to another lender. Some financial institutions will not make short-term construction loans, either based on internal decisions or because they are prohibited from making these loans by law. If financing through one of these institutions, the property owner first must obtain a short-term loan from an interim lender. When construction is completed, permanent financing is arranged. Usually this is based upon a prior agreement made by the permanent mortgagee to provide long-term financing.

A number of states have specific statutes regulating construction lending. Generally they prohibit certain financial institutions from making construction loans and direct the manner by which others must pay out construction loan funds. The purpose of these statutes is to facilitate construction lending by providing protection for the mortgagee as well as for artisans working on the project.

Both the construction mortgagee and the mechanics look to the property as security. The periodic advances made by the lender are secured by the increased value of the property stemming from the completed work. At the same time, if those working on the structure are not paid, they have a right to a lien against the real estate. The time when the mechanic's lien attaches is critical to the rights of the parties. For example, in a number of states a mechanic's lien dates back to the start of construction. If a construction mortgage is not recorded until work commences, the mechanic's lien is superior even if perfected later. A number of states separate buildings from the land when attempting to adjust the interest of the construction mortgagee and the mechanic's lienholder. In these states the mechanic's lien has superior rights in the building even if a construction mortgage has been recorded against the property. Other states have different rules relating to time of attachment.

In order to establish the priority right of the construction mortgagee and to ensure that workers will be paid, state statutes provide the lender with a preferred position in the security if provisions for disbursing funds are followed. The construction mortgagee must be certain to follow these provisions exactly. Usually they involve two steps: obtaining detailed statements from contractors and subcontractors of the work that has been done and, when funds are disbursed, obtaining proper waivers from the parties to whom payments have been made. Not all states have statutes regulating construction loans. In those that do not, the construction mortgagee must develop procedures to ensure that the mortgage rights will be superior to the mechanic's liens.

Open-End Mortgage

A mortgage that permits the mortgagor to borrow additional funds, usually up to the original amount of the debt.

The open-end mortgage is a modern application of an old concept. In the years immediately following World War II, a number of financial institutions in the United States revitalized and expanded the mortgage to secure future advances. Probably the principal reason was to improve their competitive position, but the instrument that they developed had advantages for borrowers as well as lenders.

Traditionally, in most American jurisdictions, a mortgage to secure future advances provides the lender with priority over liens intervening between the recording of the mortgage and the future advance. This principle is especially well established when the future advance is obligatory.

CASE EXAMPLE

Midge and Tony McLaughlin, a young married couple, executed a $25,000 mortgage to United National Bank for funds advanced to purchase a small house. Midge and Tony planned to have a family and knew that additions would have to be made to the house. When they explained this to the loan officer, he suggested an open-end mortgage. A provision was included in the mortgage requiring the bank to lend them additional funds up to the original amount of the loan.

Several years later Midge and Tony requested those additional funds. During the intervening years, a judgment had been entered against Midge as a result of an automobile accident. Despite this judgment, United National advanced the money; the original mortgage provided security for the additional funds.

In most open-end mortgages the mortgagee is not required to advance the additional funds. If the mortgagee has this option, the priority of the lien over an intervening encumbrance in most states depends upon notice of the intervening claim. If the mortgagee has actual notice of an intervening lien and elects to advance the funds, any lien that results is inferior to that of the intervening claimant. In the previous example, if the mortgage was nonobligatory and United National had knowledge of the judgment against Midge, a lien resulting from any later advance would be inferior to the judgment lien.

Although the law generally agrees that actual notice of the intervening claim limits the priority of the open-end mortgage, the states are divided as to whether a recorded lien provides notice. A majority hold that the mortgagee does not have notice merely because a subsequent lien is recorded. In other states the mortgagee is charged with notice of any subsequently recorded interest. In these states the mortgagee whose instrument is nonobligatory must reexamine the record before advancing additional funds.

Benefits of the Open-End Mortgage

Open-end mortgages benefit both the borrowers and the lenders. The lender benefits because the device enables the lender to retain the business of valued customers. When a mortgagor needs additional funds, he or she will use the open-end privilege instead of going to a competitor. The general belief is that open-end mortgages also reduce the number of foreclosures. One reason for this is that borrowers can obtain needed funds without turning to short-term credit at high interest rates. The additional business is also more profitable to the lender because the costs of the loan are spread over a larger amount.

Benefits to the borrower are even more obvious. The funds are provided at the low interest rates afforded first mortgages on real estate, as compared with other more costly financing. Payments are spread over a longer period of time, and extra costs of refinancing or additional borrowing are eliminated.

Despite these advantages, the open-end mortgage has not been used extensively during recent years, primarily because of rising interest rates and inflation. Lending institutions are reluctant to lock themselves into loans that commit them to make additional funds available at the lower rates. Borrowers find the open-end privilege less attractive because of inflation. Ordinarily, they are entitled to borrow the difference between the original loan and the reduced principal. That privilege is of little value to the property owner if the difference is small compared to the cost of the item for which the loan is made.

Legal Requirements

Legal requirements for a valid open-end mortgage differ from state to state. Several states have enacted specific legislation to deal with these mortgages. The most common general requirement is that the instrument indicate clearly that it contemplates future advances. In addition, the instrument must describe the debt with enough accuracy to make identification certain. The other requirements that exist in a number of states are (1) limits on time during which a future advance position is effective and (2) limits on the amount that can be secured. Statutes in some states require that the instrument indicate at the beginning that it is an open-end mortgage.

Wraparound Mortgage

A second mortgage covering an existing debt that the lender agrees to service as well as providing the borrower with additional funds.

Wraparound financing is used in a variety of real estate transactions. This type of financing is another example of the manner in which legal and financial institutions react to economic conditions. The increase in wraparound financing during the past decade has been the result of relatively high rates of interest and tight money conditions that have prevailed during the period.

CASE EXAMPLE

Al Borne owned property appraised at $250,000. The property was encumbered by a $125,000 first mortgage at nine percent interest with 12 years until maturity. Al wished to expand his plumbing business, but he needed additional funds. A friend agreed to lend him $100,000. As security Al was to give his friend a $225,000 second mortgage on the property. Al was to pay interest on this mortgage at 13 percent. The friend agreed to service the first mortgage interest of nine percent out of the interest Al paid. Al's friend has a wraparound mortgage.

Typically, a wraparound mortgage has a higher rate of interest than the rate on the existing debt that it covers. The wraparound mortgagee collects interest exceeding that on the first mortgage, which the lender has agreed to service. This differential makes the loan attractive to the wraparound mortgagee, whose effective rate of return is increased. For example, Al's friend has advanced only $100,000, but he collects interest on $225,000. After paying the nine percent interest on the first mortgage, the friend retains the four percent difference on $125,000 as well as the 13 percent on the $100,000.

Advantages and Problems

Potentially, several factors exist that make this type of financing advantageous to Al. First, he is able to retain a substantial portion of his debt at nine percent. This is one of the reasons for the increasing popularity of wraparound financing in a market where interest rates have been increasing rapidly. Second, a good possibility exists that he will be financing at somewhat less than the market rate as the effective rate of return to the lender is increased by the wraparound. Third, the wraparound mortgage may be a potential tax-saving device because it permits installment reporting of capital gains.

Another common use of the wraparound mortgage is in selling real estate. Assume that, instead of refinancing, Al wishes to sell his property and a broker finds a prospective client who has $50,000. In order to facilitate the sale, Al might agree to accept the cash and a second mortgage for $200,000 at 14 percent. Al would be responsible for servicing the first mortgage out of the payments made by the mortgagor on the $200,000 second mortgage. Al's second mortgage has wrapped around the existing first mortgage.

Wraparound mortgages create a number of legal problems. Probably the most serious is that second mortgage loans are prohibited to many financial institutions, sometimes because of internal policy and other times because of legal prohibitions. Usury is also a question in some states; the actual rate of interest being collected might exceed the maximum rate, even though the instrument shows something less. Other problems might be caused by prohibitions in the existing first mortgage. Many first mortgages today contain clauses that limit the mortgagor's right to sell the property. Some mortgages prohibit additional financing using the same property as security. Both of these provisions would effectively limit the use of a wraparound mortgage.

Package Mortgage

A mortgage secured by both personal and real property.

Package mortgages are used today primarily in financing residential real estate, although they can also be used to finance commercial and industrial ventures. The mortgage covers not only the real property but also personal property essential to the operation of a home or business. In residential financing, a package mortgage lien attaches to real estate and to equipment needed to make the home livable. This might include a stove, refrigerator, dishwasher or freezer. In a commercial transaction the package mortgage would include items necessary to operate the business. In a mortgage covering a motel, for example, most lenders would require a lien on the furniture and other items necessary to operate the business. In the event of a foreclosure, the security would be much more valuable if it included equipment necessary for operation. Unless these items were included in the mortgage, the purchaser would have to buy them separately because the owner would have a right to remove them.

Benefits

For several reasons the package mortgage might be beneficial to the buyer/mortgagor. First, the mortgagor is able to finance appliances at the same low rate of interest provided in the real estate mortgage. This rate is considerably lower than the rate for consumer loans. Second, the purchase price of these appliances can be spread over the entire term of the mortgage, thereby reducing monthly payments. Finally, some lenders contend that a package mortgage reduces the potential for default, especially for families buying their first home. Usually these people have to purchase all their appliances in addition to the realty. With a package mortgage, they are not saddled with additional payments for appliances simultaneously with initial payments on real estate debt. The cost of all items is included in the mortgage payment. The chief argument against the package mortgage is that the buyer, in paying for the appliances over the term of the real estate mortgage, is paying for them long after their useful life has expired.

Lenders whose security includes personal property should be certain that, in addition to the real estate mortgage, a financing statement covering the personal property is completed and recorded. Although a clause in the mortgage describes both the real estate and the personalty as security, this is not sufficient notice to a bona fide purchaser of the personalty or general creditors without notice.

• CASE BRIEF •

To secure a $150,000 issue of negotiable bonds, Mt. Waldo

Granite Works purported to mortgage all real, personal and mixed property as well as all fixtures used in its business of quarrying granite. The mortgage covered air compressors, derricks, engines, cars, implements and tools and provided that these should be replaced as they wore out. This mortgage was duly recorded in the registry of deeds as required by state law. State law also required that mortgages on personal property be filed with the town clerk in the town where the property was located. This was never done.

When Mt. Waldo defaulted on the bonds, the mortgagee attempted to foreclose against all property used in operating the business. A number of firms holding chattel mortgages on air compressors, engines and tools resisted. They argued that the real property mortgage, although it supposedly covered personal property, was invalid against them because it had not been recorded properly, and the Supreme Court of Maine agreed. *Peoples Trust Co. v. Mt. Waldo Granite Works, 117 Me. 507, 105 A. 113(1918).*

Financing that uses personal property or fixtures as security is, as noted previously, governed by provisions of the Uniform Commercial Code. The UCC provisions are such that a mortgagee can protect a security interest in personal property by obtaining a security agreement and properly filing a financing statement.

Rollover Mortgage

A mortgage that must be refinanced every few years in order to adjust the interest rate up or down in response to prevailing money market conditions.

Rising interest rates create a substantial problem for financial institutions that make long-term loans. In recent years this problem has been especially acute for savings and loan institutions, which, in order to compete for funds, have to pay savers short-term rates. As interest rates increase, the return on mortgage money, invested at fixed rates often up to 30 years, lags well behind rapidly increasing short-term rates. The variable-rate mortgage (VRM) was one effort to solve this problem. The rollover, or renegotiated-rate, mortgage is another.

A rollover mortgage is written for a short term, generally three, four or five years. At the end of that period the loan is renegotiated to reflect prevailing interest rates. To protect borrowers, a maximum increase is sometimes established. In 1980, for federally chartered savings and loans this maximum was one-half percentage point per year and five percentage points over the life of the mortgage. This ceiling has since been lifted by the Federal Home Loan Bank Board. Other protections for the mortgagor include a requirement that the lender renew, formal foreclosure if the lender wants to terminate the loan and the right to pay off the loan in full with no penalty after 90 days. Many mortgagors object to rollover mortgages because they could lead to substantially higher costs if interest rates climb. On the other hand, if interest rates drop, the mortgagor will benefit when the loan has to be renegotiated.

MORTGAGE INSURANCE

Insurance provided by certain government agencies or private corporations protecting mortgage lenders against loss caused by a borrower's default.

Mortgage insurance has increased in importance since the 1940s and is today an integral part of the real estate industry. Authorities estimate that more than 25 percent of real estate mortgage loans are covered by some type of mortgage insurance. This type of insurance has numerous social benefits. Probably the most important is *liquidity*— the ease with which an asset can be converted to cash. Insured mortgage loans are much more liquid than those that are not insured. Liquidity is greater because firms initiating insured loans must follow established standards and procedures. These procedures include an approved appraisal of the structure as well as approval of the creditworthiness of the borrower. When a loan is insured, not only the lender but also the insurer must be convinced that the property value covers the loan and the borrower has the ability to repay.

Another benefit of mortgage insurance is a reduction in the number of foreclosures. When an insured loan is in default, the insurer pays the debt and takes over the property. The insurer then attempts to sell the property to cover its losses. During the 30 years following World War II, the most common type of mortgage insurance was provided by two federally supported agencies. Today, however, several private firms are gaining a substantial share of the mortgage insurance business.

FHA Insurance

Insurance provided lenders under Title II of the National Housing Act of 1934.

The National Housing Act is administered by the Department of Housing and Urban Development (HUD); the Federal Housing Administration (FHA) is an organizational unit of HUD. The FHA administers several programs providing insurance to lenders financing real estate transactions. Loans can be insured for the purchase, construction, repair and improvement of housing. Rental housing, cooperatives, condominiums, low-cost and moderate-income housing, housing for the elderly and nursing homes are among the many types of dwellings covered by FHA programs. Mortgages insured by the FHA are known as *FHA mortgages*.

The mortgage loan insurance program that resulted from Section 203 of the National Housing Act is the most important to have arisen over the years. This section authorizes insurance for loans to finance the purchase of one- to four-unit dwellings. Four common provisions of FHA insured mortgage loans are:

1. long term for repayment,
2. full amortization over the term,
3. low down payment,
4. interest rates below market.

Since a major portion of the loan is guaranteed, usually the interest rates are lower than those on conventional loans.

Applications for mortgage insurance on one- to four-family dwellings have two requirements: approval of the property based upon an appraisal and approval of the purchaser's credit. Borrowers pay a premium of one-time, 3.8 percent of the amount borrowed. From these premiums and fees, the FHA accumulates reserves to cover expenses and losses on properties acquired because of borrower default.

Veterans Administration Loan Guarantees

Guarantees provided by the Veterans Administration to lenders that finance housing construction and purchases by eligible veterans.

The loan guarantee program of the Veterans Administration provides protection to private lenders financing homes for veterans. As a result of the guarantee, veterans have been able to buy or build homes on long-term loans with no down payment. Loans may be guaranteed on one- to four-unit structures; the veteran must occupy one of the units. Most VA-guaranteed loans are for the purchase of single-family homes, mobile homes and units in condominium projects.

Although the loan may be for any amount, the guarantee covers only 60 percent of the loan or a maximum of $27,500, whichever is less. The amount of the loan that the VA guarantees is called an *entitlement*. As in the FHA insurance program, the VA guarantees a loan only upon an approved appraisal of the property. In addition, before the loan is guaranteed the Veterans Administration must be convinced that the veteran is a satisfactory credit risk.

VA-guaranteed loans have several advantages for the veteran. No down payment is required, and the loan may be paid in part or in full at any time with no penalty. If the veteran has financial problems, the VA will arrange for a modification of terms. The loan may be assumed by any buyer, veteran or nonveteran, who is an acceptable credit risk. In addition, the veteran has the benefit of VA appraisal, construction supervision and oversight of the lender's activities.

One of the basic aspects of real estate law reflected in this chapter is the idea of priority or preference between interests in real estate. Often more than one interest exists in the same property. The multiple interests might be those of owners, tenants, mortgagees or other types of lienholders. Sometimes the parties agree which of these interests is superior, but more often that decision is made by the law. Although the fundamental rule of priorities is "first in time, first in right," in numerous instances public policy considerations have led to modifications of this rule. In the chapter that follows, public policy is considered in its relationship to this and other aspects of mortgage lending.

SUMMARY

The mortgage is one of two legal instruments used when real property is utilized as security for a debt. Its purpose is to reduce the risk inherent in lending by providing the lender with collateral in case the borrower defaults. The other instrument is the note, a written promise to repay a loan according to specific terms and conditions. If the borrower defaults, the lender may collect the debt by foreclosing against the property. As an alternative remedy, the lender may bring a personal action against the borrower on the note.

In law, over half the states consider the mortgage a lien; they are known as *lien theory states*. In other states the *title theory* prevails; that is, the mortgagee retains title until the debt is paid. Laws governing other aspects of the mortgage transaction such as foreclosure and the borrower's right of redemption also vary from state to state.

Mortgage laws and procedures are influenced by economic conditions. A homebuyer wishing to borrow money to finance a purchase must compete with others for the funds available in the money market. The amount available fluctuates according to economic conditions. As demand for money increases, so does the interest rate—the amount one must pay for the use of the funds.

As a result of the relative scarcity of funds during the 1970s and 1980s, new types of mortgage financing have developed. One example is the flexible-rate mortgage. A clause in the mortgage permits the lender to adjust interest rates in response to changes in the money market. The adjustable-rate mortgage (ARM) has become the most widely used flexible-rate mortgage.

Several other types of mortgage exist. They include the purchase money mortgage, the construction mortgage, the open-end mortgage and the rollover mortgage. The appropriateness of each type varies according to economic conditions and the financial situations of both borrower and lender.

Finally, mortgage insurance has increased in importance over the past few decades. Use of insurance has reduced the number of foreclosures. Insurance is provided by private firms and by two federal agencies: the Federal Housing Administration and the Veterans Administration.

REVIEW AND DISCUSSION QUESTIONS

1. (a) Explain the differences between a mortgage and a deed of trust. (b) Compare their advantages and disadvantages as financing instruments.
2. Discuss the difference between the lien and title theories of mortgages.
3. (a) What is an equitable mortgage? (b) Indicate how the doctrines of equitable mortgage and deed absolute differ.
4. Explain how money market conditions influence the availability of funds for home financing.
5. Indicate some of the advantages and problems of wraparound financing.
6. What is a package mortgage? Why have some consumer groups objected to its use?
7. Explain how the legal rights given to a mortgagee by a mortgage differ from those given by a note.

CASE PROBLEMS

1. Rainey borrowed $12,300 from the Farmer's Home Administration (FmHA) to finance construction of a home. The debt was secured by a deed of trust that the FmHA recorded on December 30, 1969. The home was completed in February, and the Raineys obtained a homeowner's policy in the amount of $12,000. At the time $5,905 was due the Adamsville Lumber Company for materials and supplies. Before the Raineys occupied the house, it was completely destroyed by fire. The lumber company immediately perfected a mechanic's lien for the amount due. Both the FmHA and the lumber company claim the insurance proceeds. Who is entitled to them? *Adamsville Lumber Co., Inc. v. Rainey,* 348 F. Supp. 373 (W.D. Tenn. E.D. 1972).
2. In April 1985, Blankton borrowed $18,000 from his father to start a business. Blankton gave his father a promissory note to cover the loan. About $8,000 of the loan was used to purchase equipment for the business. The balance was used to help finance a building that was purchased in August 1985. In addi-

tion to the $10,000, the purchase was financed by the Hill National Bank, which took a mortgage on the property. When Blankton failed, his father claimed a lien on the property based upon the April loan. The father argued that as his loan preceded the purchase of the real estate and was used to pay part of the price he was entitled to a priority over the bank. Discuss the validity of this argument.

3. Alonzo Lane purchased a $60,000 home in a newly developed area. To finance the purchase, he executed a $50,000 note and mortgage to the Upland Bank. Shortly after Alonzo moved in, a newspaper article disclosed that much of the development was on land that had been partially filled with chemical waste. Real estate values in the area fell sharply. At about this time Alonzo accepted a job in another state, where he purchased a condominium. Unable to sell his home or keep up payments, Alonzo defaulted. The Upland Bank foreclosed. Discuss Alonzo's potential liability if the home sells at the foreclosure sale for $38,000.

4. Tom Hildebrant purchased a four-unit rental property for $175,000. River National Bank lent him $155,000 to complete the purchase. The loan was secured by a mortgage on the property. Because of a severe recession in the area caused by closing of several steel mills, Hildebrant was unable consistently to rent all of the units, and he defaulted on the debt. As a result the bank foreclosed. At the foreclosure sale, the property sold for $145,000. Does Tom have any liability on the unpaid portion of the debt? Discuss.

5. W. W. Hill executed a $2,500 demand note in favor of his son William, who had advanced him money to buy a house. A statement on the back of the note signed by W. W. Hill gave William a $2,500 interest in the property, and W. W. promised to execute a mortgage.

Title to the property was taken by W. W. and his second wife, Myrtle, as joint tenants with right of survivorship. Myrtle refused to sign the mortgage. If W.W. dies and the estate refuses to pay the $2,500 debt, may William foreclose against the property? Support your answer. *Hill v. Hill*, 185 Kan. 389, 345 P.2d 1015 (1959).

21

Mortgage Lending and Public Policy

LOAN APPLICATION AND COMMITMENT

Not too many years ago, a person who wanted to borrow on a mortgage from a bank, savings and loan or other financial institution was asked to appear before a loan committee for interrogation. Today most mortgage loans start with an application made on a printed form supplied by the lender. The information needed to complete the application is ordinarily given to a loan officer, and the form is signed by the party requesting the loan.

The application serves two purposes: it supplies the lender with information necessary to decide whether the loan should be granted and it serves as the borrower's *offer* to enter into a contract. If the lender approves the loan, it notifies the borrower and furnishes a formal commitment, often called a *loan approval*. The commitment, if it does not modify the terms in the application, is an *acceptance* of the offer. The parties have entered into a contract to make a loan with real property as security. Ordinarily, the commitment contains a clause terminating the contract if the borrower does not take advantage of the loan within a specified time.

Sometimes the lender modifies the terms in the application, in effect making a *counteroffer*. The counteroffer becomes a contract only if the borrower accepts these new terms. In practice, especially for construction lending and financing commercial real estate, the *commitment* is more important than the application. For these types of financing, the terms of the loan the lender is willing to make generally differ from those of the loan for which the borrower applied. The commitment becomes the basis for the contract; the parties are obligated by its terms if the counteroffer is accepted by the borrower.

Because the commitment is the basis of a contract between borrower and seller, all of the major loan provisions should be clearly and precisely indicated. If the contract is breached, litigation may ensue. Since neither the lender nor the borrower is entitled to specific performance, each has only damages as a remedy.

When the lender refuses to honor the contract, the borrower's damages are relatively easy to calculate. They are the increased cost of obtaining the loan from some other source. Ordinarily, the bulk of this cost would be the difference between the interest rates charged on the two loans. If the borrower does not use the funds, damages to the lender are very difficult to measure. In a number of cases the courts have held that the lender is entitled only to nominal damages. Because of problems associated with measuring the damages, many commitments for major loans contain provisions for a nonrefundable commitment fee paid by the borrower. When the fee involved is reasonable, the forfeiture of this amount has generally been accepted by courts as valid liquidated damages.

• CASE BRIEF •

In December 1956, Teachers Insurance and Annuity Association (TIAA) agreed to loan Boston Road Shopping Center (Boston Road) $1,100,000 to finance a shopping center. The commitment stated: "[W]e agree to make and you agree to accept from us, the loan hereinafter described," and further recited that TIAA agreed to make the loan "in consideration of" a $22,000 payment by Boston Road that was to be repaid if the funds were used.

Boston Road was unable to obtain the tenants necessary to set up the shopping center and abandoned the project. When TIAA refused to refund the $22,000, Boston Road sued. Boston Road argued that the $22,000 was a penalty, not liquidated damages. In finding for TIAA on appeal, the court stated, "Nothing in the public policy of New York requires the court to strike down this payment in the nature of liquidated damages for a breach of contract by plaintiff. It is entirely reasonable in relation to the nature and extent of defendant's undertaking and arrangement; no oppression or overreaching which might suggest the need for equitable intervention is demonstrated." *Boston Road Shopping Center v. Teachers Insurance and Annuity Association, 126 Misc. 380, 213 N.Y.S.2d 522 (1961).*

REGULATIONS AFFECTING MORTGAGE LOANS

Both state and federal regulations influence mortgage lending. Usually these regulations favor borrowers as legislators recognize that the borrower's bargaining position is weaker than the lender's. Usury statutes, the "Truth-in-Lending Act" and the Equal Credit Opportunity Act are examples of regulations with which lenders must contend.

Usury

The practice of charging interest on a loan in excess of a rate allowed by law.

Religious disapproval of interest resulting in usury laws has influenced relationships between borrowers and lenders for centuries. The importance of usury laws depends to a large extent upon economic conditions. When money is scarce, lenders are able to charge higher rates for loans, and usury becomes a factor that they must consider. Almost every state has laws prohibiting lenders from charging excessive interest. These statutes vary appreciably from state to state. Not only do the permissible rates differ, but major differences exist in the transactions that are covered and the penalties levied against the usurious lender. This section looks at numerous aspects of usury laws, including requirements, exemptions, penalties and criticisms. Recent state and federal modifications of usury statutes are also discussed.

Requirements

In order for a debtor to take advantage of the protection afforded by a usury statute, all three of the following elements must exist: the transaction must involve the lending of money or its equivalent, an unqualified promise by the debtor to repay and a higher rate of interest than permitted by state law. Some states also require the debtor to prove that the creditor intended to violate the law, but intent is usually presumed if the rate exceeds that permitted by statute.

Borrowing money presupposes an obligation to repay. As a result, sales on credit and leases in most states do not come within the prohibitions of usury statutes, because the buyer or lessee has no obligation to repay. Transactions in which the borrower's obligation to repay is conditional upon making a profit would also not be usurious, as the obligation is not absolute.

Exemptions

Numerous defenses and exemptions to usury statutes exist. In many states corporate borrowers are not entitled to usury protection. The justification for this is that corporations deal on equal footing with financial institutions and are not likely to need the safeguards of usury statutes. In a few states the corporation exemption does not apply when a lender requires an individual to incorporate in order to obtain a mortgage loan.

Some states exclude loans over a fixed amount from usury protection. These amounts are substantial, usually $50,000 or more. The rationale underlying this exemption is that a person borrowing a large sum is capable of protecting himself or herself from excessive interest charges. In other states all loans for business purposes are exempt. The justification for this exemption, like that for borrower of large sums, is that the businessperson is a sophisticated borrower without the need of statutory protection.

Most states have special statutes governing interest rates on small loans. Licensed small-loan lenders are permitted to charge higher rates than other lenders, but their operations are closely regulated and restricted by statute. Since small-loan companies generally cannot lend more than $5,000, their business is not pertinent to real estate financing. In a number of states, banks, savings and loan institutions and insurance companies are exempted from usury statutes. Some states also exempt FHA-insured loans. Both of these exemptions are based upon the philosophy that these loans are supervised by responsible state and federal agencies.

Penalties

In some states usury is a criminal offense if an excessively high rate is charged. Civil penalties ordinarily fit into one of three categories:

- forfeiture of all interest and the entire principal,
- forfeiture of interest, or
- forfeiture of interest exceeding the statutory rate.

Some state laws require the lender to forfeit all the interest and also allow the borrower to recover a multiple of the interest paid.

Although usury laws exist in all states but two, they have been criticized severely during last two decades. Usury laws have been criticized for ignoring the fact that market conditions determine interest rates, for having too many exemptions, for failing to protect those who actually need protection and for being difficult to enforce because of ineffective penalties.

Changes

During the 1970s and early 1980s, rapidly increasing interest rates caused serious economic problems in the United States. When market rates exceeded the interest that usury ceilings permitted lenders to charge, lenders stopped making loans to individuals. This decreased residential real estate sales, and the decrease was one of the causes for a severe recession. In order to stimulate real estate sales, a number of states adopted legislation to lessen the effects of usury statutes.

Some states simply raised the rate that could be charged. Other states adopted a floating rate as a determinant of the maximum allowable interest. Floating rates vary in relation to an economic indicator that is used as the index. A common index is the 90-day rate on commercial paper. Other indicators used are the monthly index of long-term United States bonds. Short-term money market indicators such as the Federal Reserve discount rate and the commercial bank prime rate are also used. The indicator serves as a base upon which the lender is allowed to add a fixed percentage. Depending upon the state and the index selected, the amount that can be added ranges from two to five percent.

In 1980, to provide additional stimulus to residential sales, Congress adopted legislation limiting state usury laws in some situations. The federal legislation called the Depository Institution Deregulation and Monetary Control Act (DIDMC) eliminated state interest ceilings on first mortgage loans made by financial institutions and secured by residential real estate. Individuals financing the sale of their own homes were also exempted. The DIDMC permitted states to override the federal law if they did so prior to April 1, 1983. Fourteen states elected to do so. In these states usury statutes continue to apply to residential mortgage loans as they have traditionally.

Truth-In-Lending

The popular name given to part of the Consumer Credit Protection Act of 1968, the federal statute that requires lenders to disclose the cost of consumer credit so that users can better compare terms available from different sources.

The purpose of the "Truth-in-Lending" Act is to foster the informed use of consumer credit, that is, credit extended to an individual to be used primarily for personal, family or household purposes. This legislation in no way fixes maximum or minimum charges for credit.

Real estate credit is only one of many types of credit covered by the act. To come within the scope of the act, real estate credit must be extended to a natural person and be granted to finance acquisition or initial construction of the borrower's principal dwelling. Thus, mortgage loans to corporations and to individuals for business purposes are excluded. Credit extended to the owner of a dwelling containing more than four units is also exempt.

The key to understanding "Truth-in-Lending" is *meaningful disclosure*. Provisions of both this act and of Regulation Z, the Federal Reserve Board's interpretations of the act, require that borrowers be furnished with the facts they need to make intelligent decisions on the use of credit. To accomplish this, information must be presented using terminology specified in the act and Regulation Z. This information must be clear, conspicuous and in writing. Generally, the information must cover all costs of credit, including in most cases the finance charge and the annual percentage rate.

Finance Charge

Dollar-and-cents total of all charges a borrower must pay, directly or indirectly, for obtaining credit.

Prior to "Truth-in-Lending," some lenders presented credit to borrowers in a manner that concealed or even misrepresented costs. Although institutions furnishing real estate credit were not generally as flagrant in this practice as other suppliers of consumer credit, some confusing practices did exist in the mortgage lending market. A relatively common practice was to charge a borrower for extras, loan fees, service charges or points that were not quoted with the interest rate. The 1968 act requires lenders to disclose the dollar total of *all costs* of credit. Extra charges cannot be tallied separately if they are a cost of credit but must be included in the finance charge.

Costs that a buyer would pay regardless of whether or not credit is extended need not be included in the finance charge. Items such as title examination fees, title insurance premiums, survey costs and legal fees fit into this category. These costs must be itemized and disclosed to the borrower separately if included in the total financed. One exception is a first purchase money mortgage on residential property, for which the mortgage is not required to state the total dollar finance charge.

Annual Percentage Rate

The relationship between the total finance charge and the amount to be financed in annual percentage terms.

Disclosure of the annual percentage rate (APR) allows consumers to compare finance charges on a comparable basis, making the cost of credit more understandable. Based on a time period of a year, the APR is similar to simple annual interest, a concept with which many consumers are expected to be familiar.

Credit Advertising

Regulation Z defines *credit advertising* broadly. The definition covers commercial messages that either directly or indirectly promote a credit transaction. Thus, developers or real estate brokers are subject to the act if their advertisement includes terms to be granted by a creditor. Although the definition of *advertising* includes oral as well as written communication, it does not encompass a broker or developer responding to a buyer's questions about available credit.

Of the several advertising provisions of "Truth-in-Lending," two are generally applicable to real estate transactions. A fundamental principle is that no advertisement shall contain terms that are not regularly granted by the creditor. For example, an advertisement offering new homes at "$1,000 down" violates the act if the seller does not customarily accept this amount as a down payment. A second advertising limitation that applies to real estate transactions is referred to as *triggering*. When an advertisement provides certain credit information in the message, Regulation Z mandates that additional information be supplied as well. The four triggering terms are as follows:

- amount or percentage of any down payment,
- number of payments or period or repayment,
- amount of any payment,
- amount of any finance charge.

If the advertiser supplies any of the triggering information, the following additional information must also be given.

- amount or percentage of any down payment,
- terms of repayment,
- annual percentage rate.

CASE EXAMPLE

Cullen Builders advertised the sale of homes stating that "90 percent financing was available." As this is a triggering statement, Cullen's advertisement also was required to show the down payment required, the terms of repayment and the annual percentage rate.

Equal Credit Opportunity Act

Federal statute making it unlawful for any creditor to discriminate against an applicant regarding any aspect of a credit transaction on the basis of race, color, religion, national origin, sex, marital status, age or receipt of public assistance.

The Equal Credit Opportunity Act (ECOA) prohibits a lender from refusing credit to an individual on the basis of sex, marital status or other classification protected by the act. The act also limits the type of information that can be asked on credit applications and requires the creditor to notify the applicant within 30 days of action that has been taken. If credit is refused, the creditor must furnish the reason if requested to do so by the applicant.

The purpose of ECOA is to ensure that a person who applies for credit will be considered on the basis of ability to pay. Although the act applies primarily to consumer credit, business credit when not excluded by action of the Federal Reserve Board is also covered.

Under ECOA, creditors may ask questions about a person's

spouse, marital status or age, but use of this information is permitted only for the purpose of determining creditworthiness. For example, a borrower applying for a joint account might be asked about his or her marital status if the spouse is to be permitted to use the account or the borrower is relying upon alimony, child support or separate maintenance payments to repay the credit. Information about age may be used to evaluate a borrower's length of employment or length of residence.

Creditors may not ask questions about a person's sex, race, color, religion or national origin, except in the case of a home mortgage; creditors are allowed to collect this information to show that they are complying with the law. The borrower does not have to supply answers, and failure to do so will not affect the credit application. Although a borrower can be asked to select a title such as *Ms., Miss, Mr.,* or *Mrs.,* the application must first indicate that this is optional.

An individual who is denied credit and can establish that the creditor has violated the Equal Credit Opportunity Act may recover his or her actual damages plus punititive damages up to $10,000. The plaintiff who brings a successful action under ECOA is also entitled to reimbursement for court costs and reasonable attorney fees.

RIGHTS AND OBLIGATIONS OF PARTIES

A substantial amount of mortgage litigation involves disputes concerning the rights and obligations of the mortgagor and mortgagee. The well-drafted mortgage will reduce the possibilities of litigation by incorporating provisions that clearly indicate each party's rights and obligations.

Often a mortgage instrument will be used that does not cover a problem arising between the parties. When this is the case, public policy—reflected in legislation or case law—determines what each can do. Inasmuch as questions involving possession, disposition of rents and profits and protection of the security are common, numerous rules exist to solve these problems.

Possession

The right to occupy and control real estate to the exclusion of all others.

The right to possession of mortgaged premises depends upon the theory of mortgages followed in a particular state. In title theory states the mortgagee has an immediate right to possession, but most mortgages in these states contain a provision in which the mortgagee surrenders this right. The common provision in title theory states allows the mortgagor to remain in possession and enjoy the benefits of ownership until default. Several title theory states have statutes prohibiting the mortgagee from taking possession until default.

In lien theory states, the mortgagee has no right to possession. This principle, however, is frequently modified by a provision in the mortgage allowing the mortgagee to take possession upon default. A number of lien theory states have reached a similar result by statute. Title and lien theory were discussed in Chapter 20.

As a general practice, either by statute or by mortgage terms, most mortgagors have the right to remain in possession of mortgaged premises until default. Realistically, no other result makes sense for residential real estate. For commercial property a mortgagee may find possession advantageous, especially if the property has been misman-aged. Profits from the property can be applied to the debt, and perhaps foreclosure can be prevented, an advantage to all parties. One other modification of general principles needs to be noted. In a few states with statutory right-of-redemption laws, the mortgagor is allowed to remain in possession even after a foreclosure sale. This right to posses-sion exists until the redemption period terminates unless limited by a provision in the mortgage.

The status of a mortgagor in possession differs from that of a mortgagee. Generally, the mortgagor in possession is entitled to all of the rights of ownership as long as the value of the security remains unimpaired. A mortgagee who takes possession has special, but lim-ited, rights that revolve around protecting the security and applying proceeds to pay the debt.

• CASE BRIEF •

Kansas and Missouri Bridge Company (Bridge Co.) executed a mortgage to the American Bridge Company (American) to se-cure payment on bonds issued by the mortgagor. The mortgage permitted American to take possession, manage the property and collect the rents upon default in payment of interest on the bonds. When Bridge Co. defaulted, American did not take pos-session. Later American obtained a judgment and asked that certain monies collected after default be applied to the debt. The United States Supreme Court refused this request. The court stated that "[u]pon the default which occurred, the mort-gagees had the option to take personal possession of the mort-gaged premises, or to file a bill, have a receiver appointed, and possession delivered to him. In either case, the income would thereafter have been theirs. Until one or the other was done, the mortgagor, as Lord Mansfield said in *Chinnery v. Black*, . . . was 'owner to all the world, and entitled to all the profit made.' " *American Bridge Co. v. Heidelbach, 94 U.S. 798 (1896).*

Rents and Profits

Possession is an important factor in determining who has a right to rents and profits from the property. The well-established general rule is that a mortgagor who remains in possession is entitled to these earnings. In the previous example, Bridge Co. retained the profits from the bridge even though the mortgagee had a right to possession after default—a right that it did not assert.

• CASE BRIEF •

Teal executed several mortgages to Walker on farmland and property in Portland, Oregon. The mortgages contained provisions allowing Teal to retain possession of the land but permitting Walker to take possession upon default. When Teal defaulted, Walker demanded possession of the properties. Teal refused to yield possession, collecting earnings from the property until ousted from possession by a foreclosure sale. As the proceeds of the sale fell far short of paying the debt, Walker sued for the rents collected after Teal's refusal to surrender possession. The United States Supreme Court. . . determined that the mortgagee was entitled to rents and profits only if actually in possession. *Teal v. Walker, 111 U.S. 242 (1884).*

A mortgagee who takes possession has a right to earnings from the property, but they must be applied to extinguish the debt. Amounts collected that exceed expenses are first applied to interest and then to principal.

Most mortgages that cover commercial property contain provisions in which the parties allocate rents, profits and earnings. One approach is for the mortgagor to assign the rents and profits as additional security from the date of the mortgage. A more common provision allows the mortgagee to collect the rents upon default. Until that time, rents go to the mortgagor. In both lien and title theory states, the mortgagee has a right to appoint a receiver to collect the rents and manage the property when there is a default. This right is based upon either statute or the right to protect the value of the security.

Protecting the Security

A mortgagee has a right to protect the value of the security. This right is similar to the common law action for waste, although the mortgagee in most states has a right to sue for waste only if permitted to do so by the mortgage. But even without this right it has a right to protect the security. Actions that have been held to impair the value of the security include cutting, removing and selling timber; removing machinery; removing a dwelling; failing to pay liens and failing to keep the property repaired. The mortgagee's right to protect the value of the security may be asserted against third parties as well as against the mortgagor.

Generally, the courts have held that the mortgagee's security is not impaired unless the mortgagor's actions reduce the value of the security to an extent that it will no longer cover the debt. In some title theory states, however, courts reason that the mortgagee has title and as an incident of title may sue a mortgagor in possession for waste. Whenever the parties contemplate changes in the property such as rebuilding or extensive remodeling, the mortgage should contain clauses regarding the parties' rights and duties. A mortgagee who takes possession of the property must exercise the same care and supervision over the property that prudent persons exercise over their own. Failure to do so entitles the mortgagor to collect damages or obtain an injunction.

Insurance

Although the right to maintain the value of the security is important to the mortgagee, insurance is the best protection against many risks. The law is clear that both mortgagor and mortgagee have an insurable interest in the property. With a few exceptions, the law is equally clear that neither is required to insure for the other's benefit in the absence of an agreement to do so. Commonly, in the United States, a mortgagor agrees to insure for the benefit of the mortgagee. The typical proviso not only commits the mortgagor to insure but also authorizes the mortgagee to obtain insurance if the mortgagor fails to procure it and add the premium to the debt. The mortgagee may, of course, agree to maintain insurance on the premises.

In addition to allocating responsibility for obtaining insurance, a well-drafted mortgage should contain a provision covering the application of insurance proceeds. A standard approach is a requirement that the mortgagor obtain a policy, making loss payable to himself or herself and the mortgagee "as interest may appear." The New York standard mortgage policy used extensively in the United States today also provides that the mortgagee's rights under this policy are not "invalidated by any act of neglect of the mortgagor."

When no agreement exists, each party may insure for its own benefit. In the event of loss the insured may use the proceeds as it wishes. This means that neither the mortgagor nor the mortgagee need apply the proceeds to reduce the debt. Because this rule is inherently unfair to mortgagors, courts have a tendency to find circumstances indicating that the mortgagee has insured for the mortgagor's benefit. Based upon such a determination, the mortgagee must apply the proceeds to reduce the mortgage debt.

Taxes and Assessments

Taxes and assessments are the responsibility of the mortgagor. Mortgages frequently authorize the mortgagee to pay taxes if the mortgagor does not. The mortgagee can then add these payments to the debt. Even without this provision, the mortgagee probably has the right to pay the taxes and add them to the debt. The reason is that the mortgagee has a right to protect the value of the security. A tax lien takes precedence over a mortgage. In the event of foreclosure, the mortgagee recovers only after taxes have been paid.

In the housing boom that followed World War II, numerous financial institutions adopted the practice of requiring mortgagors to pay a portion of taxes and insurance premiums each month, usually 1/12 of the estimated yearly total. These funds are held (in escrow) by the mortgagee, usually without interest. In recent years a number of consumer protection groups challenged the right of institutions to hold these funds without interest, arguing that the contract provision should be held unconscionable and thus unenforceable. On the whole, this litigation has been unsuccessful, as have been several legislative attempts to require lenders to pay interest on their tax and insurance escrow accounts.

PRIORITIES

The general principles governing priorities and recording explained in previous chapters apply to mortgages. Priority rights of purchase money and construction mortgages were discussed in Chapter 20. The balance of this section will examine priority relationships between mortgages and leases, mortgages and mechanic's liens and mortgages and tax liens.

Mortgage priority problems generally occur when a debt is in default or probability of a default exists. Under these circumstances each secured creditor attempts to ensure that its lien has first claim to the proceeds if the security must be sold. Sometimes the rank of a creditor will be determined by a provision in the security document. At other times the creditor's position is established by case law or, more often, by some statute such as the recording acts.

The fundamental principle determining priority is "first in time, first is right," but modifications of this rule affect the mortgagee's position. Remember that as a result of the recording statutes, the first in time priority generally belongs to the first party to deliver his or her instrument for recording. In a majority of states this priority is not accorded if the person recording has actual knowledge of a prior unrecorded claim. Some states do have "race to the record" statutory provisions that apply to mortgages as described in Chapter 9. Under these statutes, the first mortgage on the record has a superior right even if the mortgagee knows of a prior unrecorded mortgage.

Mortgages and Leases

In general, the "first in time" rule applies to the priority relationship between mortgages and leases. If a lease is executed before a mortgage, the lease has priority. In a foreclosure sale, the purchaser takes subject to the lease. A lease entered into after a mortgage is subordinate to the mortgage if the mortgage has been recorded. In the event of a foreclosure sale, the purchaser of the property takes it free of the lease.

In practice, most mortgages on commercial property contain agreements by the mortgagee authorizing the mortgagor to lease the premises. Under these circumstances, a lease made by the mortgagor is not subject to the mortgage lien. Unless a lease contains unfavorable terms, a mortgagee entitled to possession will often recognize a lease made after the mortgage. Although the mortgagee has a right to eject the tenant, the mortgagee will be more interested in continued rental income, which can be applied against the debt.

Mechanic's Liens and Mortgages

Litigation as to priority between mechanic's lienholders and mortgagees is widespread. Its outcome varies appreciably from state to state, even when the facts are similar. Although all state courts apply the fundamental rule of "first in time," state law differs as to when the mechanic's lien attaches, and it is time of attachment that establishes the first position. At least three different approaches are taken in the United States as to when the mechanic's lien becomes effective against other claims:

- The lien, when properly filed, reverts back to commencement of construction, no matter when the work was done or materials furnished.
- The lien, when properly filed, reverts back to the time the claimant began work or furnished materials.
- The lien attaches when the claimant files his or her claim.

CASE EXAMPLE

On April 12, 1978, Unity Bank advanced funds to Le Grand Corporation in order for the corporation to remodel facilities at its amusement park. The bank was given a mortgage as security. This mortgage was recorded on April 13. Prior to April 12, Valley Lumber Company had delivered material to the site. On April 20, Big Dig Company started excavation for an addition to the administration building. Several weeks later, when neither Big Dig nor Valley had been paid, both filed notices of mechanic's liens. When the property was sold at a foreclosure sale, questions of priority between Unity's mortgage and the mechanic's liens of Valley and Big Dig arose.

In most of the states that follow the rule that the mechanic's lien reverts back to the beginning of construction, both Valley's and Big Dig's liens would have priority. The general rule in these states is that construction begins whenever materials are delivered to the site. The result is that mechanic's liens of both Valley and Big Dig were prior in time to the bank's mortgage. In these states it is very important for a mortgagee to be sure nothing is done at the site until its mortgage is recorded. If the rule in the state is that the lien attached when work or materials were furnished, Valley would have a priority over Unity's mortgage, but Big Dig would not because it began work after the mortgage was recorded. Neither Valley nor Big Dig would have a priority in states where the lien attaches when the firm files notice of its claim.

Mortgages and Tax Liens

One type of lien to which the "first in time, first in right" principle does not generally apply is the tax lien. As a general rule, liens for unpaid real estate taxes or assessments displace prior mortgages. Although this might seem unfair, it has become acceptable as one of the risks of lending. In a number of states liens for unpaid personal property taxes also become liens against the delinquent taxpayer's real estate. Mortgages, however, do have priority over federal tax liens for nonpayment of income taxes.

Subordination Agreement

An agreement that alters priorities between parties with interests in or liens upon real property.

Subordination agreements have become increasingly important in recent years to facilitate financing of many types of real estate transaction. A common use is the situation in which a purchase money mortgagee subordinates its lien to the later lien of a construction mortgagee.

CASE EXAMPLE

Randolph Enterprises wished to purchase and develop a 200-acre parcel of land near Frederick, Maryland. The property was purchased for $400,000 from Judson Boone. Randolph Enterprises paid Boone $150,000 in cash, and Boone took back a purchase money mortgage for the balance. Both parties knew that Randolph Enterprises would have to obtain additional financing for construction. As a result, Boone agreed to a provision in his purchase money mortgage subordinating it to a subsequent mortgage to be given by Randolph Enterprises to secure funds borrowed for development of the land.

A seller such as Judson Boone is often willing to accept a junior position for a purchase money mortgage because subordination enables the seller to obtain a higher price for the property. Sellers also know that the additional funds, if used properly, will increase the property's value. The loan, though now secured by a second mortgage, continues be well protected. Because many state and federal regulations require loans of institutional lenders to be secured by first mortgages, the subordination agreement is frequently the key to selling undeveloped property.

Subordination agreements are used in a number of other transactions involving real estate. A tenant may agree that his or her lease will be junior to a mortgage or deed of trust subsequently executed by the landlord. On the other hand, it is also relatively common for a mortgagee to subordinate an existing interest to an interest arising out of a long-term lease that is created later.

• CASE BRIEF •

On August 24, 1928, Santa Monica Amusement Company (Santa Monica) leased space on a wharf to La Monica Dance Hall, Inc. (La Monica). Four years later Santa Monica mortgaged the property to Security Bank. At the time of the mortgage, La Monica executed a written agreement subordinating its lease to Security Bank's lien. When Santa Monica became bankrupt, the court found that the rights of the purchaser at the foreclosure sale were subject to the La Monica lease. This finding was reversed upon appeal. *Security National Bank v. Marxen, 28 Cal. 2d 446, 82 P.2d 727 (1938).*

The use of subordination agreements can create legal problems. Some subordination agreements are automatic, coming into existence when the interest or lien is created. Judson Boone's purchase money mortgage might be an example. The provision in Boone's mortgage could be worded to subordinate his lien as soon as Randolph Enterprises obtained its additional financing. Other types of agreements are not automatic. Such a provision might be worded to require Boone to give a subordination agreement when particular conditions are met. Enforcement of this type of subordination presents potential difficulties.

If a lender refuses to subordinate as promised, the buyer can bring an action for specific performance. In order to be successful, the buyer must prove that all conditions precedent to the lender's promise to subordinate have been met. This necessitates that the provision upon which subordination is based be clearly written. Courts will not grant specific performance unless the standard against which performance is measured is clear.

• CASE BRIEF •

Dorothy Miller executed an option in which she promised to

transfer title to certain real estate to Maximillan Roven and to take back a purchase money deed of trust. She also agreed to subordinate her deed of trust "to a First Deed of Trust. . . given to a recognized Savings and Loan. . . or bank for the purpose of securing a loan to be used for the construction of residences. . . on said property."

When Miller refused to perform, Roven sued for specific performance. Miller defended upon grounds that the subordination agreement was uncertain and specific performance should not be ordered. Both trial and appellate courts agreed with Miller. The appellate court stated that "the subordination clause . . . does not state the amount of the construction loan. . . nor any of its terms, nor when said loan would become due, nor the rate of interest it would bear. . . . These provisions are material . . . ." *Roven v. Miller, 168 Cal. 2d 391, 335 P.2d 1035 (1959).*

Terms of a subordination provision are sometimes critical in foreclosure litigation involving the subordinated and subordinating lenders. The subordinated lender will not lose its "first in time" priority if the subordinating lender advances funds upon conditions that differ from the subordination provision. In one case a seller who had taken back a mortgage agreed to subordinate to a "construction loan for the purpose of constructing on each lot a dwelling house with usual appurtenances." Partly on the basis of this provision, a construction mortgagee advanced the builder more than $2 million, but not all of the funds were used for construction. In litigation between the two lenders, the court refused the priority to the construction mortgagee because it knew the terms of subordination.

The question of priorities between different interests often raises problems for the mortgagee. Another type of security problem may occur if the mortgagor sells the premises. Although the lien of the mortgage is not affected by the sale, the mortgagee's position is weakened if the loan was approved primarily on the basis of the mortgagor's financial resources and credit reputation.

SALE OF MORTGAGED REAL ESTATE

CASE EXAMPLE

Hal Zenick owned a home encumbered with an $85,000 mortgage at nine percent interest. The mortgage was held by the Harper Hill Savings and Loan Association (Harper Hill). Hal, who had purchased the property for $98,000, had lived there for about a year when he was transferred and forced to sell. During the year interest rates had risen considerably in Hal's area, and the broker with whom he listed the property suggested that Hal

might sell his home more quickly and for a better price if the
mortgage were retained. The buyer would not have to finance at
the higher interest rates and might save in other ways.

Whether Hal lives in a title or a lien theory state, he has an interest in
the property that he can sell. He cannot, however, escape personal liability for the mortgage debt unless Harper Hill, the mortgagee, releases him. In addition, the property remains subject to Harper Hill's
lien. Nothing that Hal can do short of paying the underlying debt can
eliminate the lien so long as the mortgage is recorded properly. Hal's
right to sell his interest without discharging the mortgage may be restricted by a provision in the mortgage instrument. This is a common
clause in many residential mortgages.

Due-on-Sale Clause

**A provision found in some mortgages requiring the
mortgagor to pay off the mortgage debt if the property is
sold.**

A due-on-sale clause limits the mortgagor's right to convey the real
property without discharging the mortgage. The clause treats the sale
of mortgaged premises as a default; since almost all mortgages also
contain a clause making the entire debt due upon default, the mortgagee may call the loan when the mortgagor sells the property. Of
course a mortgagee such as Harper Hill can negotiate a modification
of the debt with the mortgagor and the grantee and not call the mortgage. In Hal's case, Harper Hill might do this if the grantee were willing to pay interest at a rate that was closer to that the association was
obtaining on new loans.

   Although some mortgagees had included due-on-sale clauses in
their mortgages for years, enforcement of these clauses was uncommon until the 1970s. In the 1970s, as interest rates increased, financial institutions wanted to eliminate from their portfolios
low-interest loans that had been made in the past. One method of doing this was to enforce due-on-sale clauses, accelerating repayment of
these loans when the property was sold.

   The use of the due-on-sale clause to accelerate repayment was
soon challenged by sellers in a number of states. Sellers argued that
enforcement of the due-on-sale clause restricted their ability to sell
and thus was a violation of public policy. A number of state courts, led
by those in California, accepted this argument and refused to let mortgagees enforce these clauses. Some states, however, held that the
clauses were legal.

   In 1976 the Federal Home Loan Bank Board adopted a rule allowing federally chartered savings and loan associations to include
due-on-sale clauses in their mortgages. The board's action was a direct

response to state curbs on the use of these clauses. The board contended that restrictions on a savings and loan's ability to accelerate repayment upon transfer of the security would adversely affect the financial stability of these institutions. In addition, the board argued that the elimination of the due-on-sale clause would impair the ability of federal associations to sell home loans in the secondary market. This would reduce the flow of new funds for residential borrowing.

The board's action precipitated a conflict between state laws and federal regulation. The board's position was that its regulation totally controlled the actions of federal savings and loan associations. It contended that Congress had given it the power to regulate the federal associations and as a result state law was preempted. The states argued that their law controlled as local real estate was involved and Congress had neither expressed an intent to preempt state law nor fully occupied the field of federal savings and loan regulation. The conflict between the board and the states ended in 1982, when the United States Supreme Court, in *Fidelity Federal Savings & Loan Ass'n. v. DeLaCuesta*, 458 U.S. 141 (1982), supported the board's position and held that the board's regulation preempted state law.

Controversy involving the due-on-sale clause is interesting as an example of a classic conflict between two basic legal principles. The law of English-speaking countries has always encouraged the free transfer or alienation of property. People like Hal should be encouraged to sell property rights for their true market value. At the same time, our law encourages freedom of contract. If Hal, as a competent adult, enters into an agreement limiting a right that he owns, the courts should enforce what he has done. At present, at least in this area of the law, the freedom-of-contract principle appears to dominate.

If Hal's mortgage does not contain a due-on-sale clause, two major approaches exist to the manner in which he may sell the property without discharging the mortgage. The property may be sold with the grantee agreeing to "assume and pay" the mortgage, or the property may be sold "subject to" the mortgage.

Assumption

A contract between a grantor-mortgagor and a grantee in which the grantee agrees to assume responsibility for the mortgage debt.

Hal's broker found a buyer who was willing to pay $100,000 for Hal's residence. The buyer had $15,000 in cash and was anxious to assume the mortgage. The purchase offer that the buyer submitted to Hal contained the following provision: "Buyer assumes and agrees to pay the obligation secured by mortgage to Harper Hill Savings and Loan Association recorded in . . . according to the terms of the mortgage and the note accompanying it." When Hal accepted this purchase offer, a contract was created, one provision of which was the buyer's promise to pay the mortgage debt. This is a typical assumption agreement. Ordinarily, agreements of this nature originate in the contract of sale, but they may be made in a separate instrument. In some states an oral assumption, if provable, is binding, although certainly oral assumptions are not a preferred practice, and several states by specific statute require assumption to be in writing. In many cases the deed also contains an assumption clause. This binds the grantee upon acceptance of the deed even when only the grantor signs the instrument.

The assumption agreement does not relieve the mortgagor/grantor of personal liability for the debt. Hal continues to be responsible to Harper Hill, but he has acquired the right to sue the buyer if the debt is not paid. This right is based upon the contract between them in which the buyer has assumed the debt. Additionally, implicit in the assumption agreement is the buyer's commitment that the seller may look to the land for reimbursement if forced to pay the debt. For Hal, additional monetary responsibility exists only if the land becomes less valuable than the debt.

The land, however, remains subject to the mortgage, and if the debt is not paid, the mortgagee may foreclose. In addition, the mortgagee without foreclosing may sue the buyer on the assumption. The mortgagee's right exists in spite of the fact that it was not a party to the assumption agreement. Its right is based upon one of two theories: third-party beneficiary or subrogation. A *third-party beneficiary* is one who is allowed to enforce a contract although not a party to the agreement. The third-party beneficiary's right is based upon the theory that the contract was made for its benefit. The following diagram illustrates the relationship among Hal, Harper Hill and the buyer. Although the contract with assumption provision is between Hal and his buyer, Harper Hill, the third-party beneficiary can sue the buyer if there is a breach.

In some states the mortgagee's right to sue the assuming buyer is based on *subrogation*. In these states the courts reason that the mortgagor/seller is a surety. He or she in effect guarantees the buyer's promise to pay the debt. The mortgagee, like any creditor, derivatively enjoys all the rights of the surety who guarantees payment. One of the mortgagor's rights is to sue the buyer if the mortgagor has to make good on its guarantee. Although the theories differ, the end result is the same. In each instance the mortgagee may enforce the buyer's promise to assume the debt.

Novation

A mutual agreement in which a creditor agrees to discharge an existing debt and to substitute a new obligation and a new debtor in its place.

ASSUMPTION

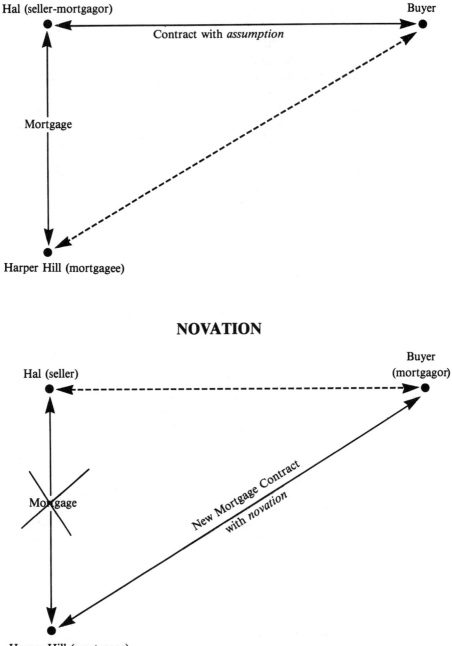

Hal (seller-mortgagor)   Buyer

Contract with *assumption*

Mortgage

Harper Hill (mortgagee)

NOVATION

Buyer
(mortgagor)

Hal (seller)

Mortgage

New Mortgage Contract
with *novation*

Harper Hill (mortgagee)

CASE EXAMPLE

Baker, a buyer located by Hal's broker, wishes to finance the purchase of Hal's home by assuming the existing mortgage debt. Hal is concerned with the proposal because he realizes that he will still have some responsibility if the original debt is not paid. Harper Hill might be asked to release Hal and substitute Baker as the debtor. If this were acceptable to Harper Hill and Baker, the parties would have entered into a contract that is called a *novation.*

A novation differs from an assumption to which the mortgagee has consented. In the assumption, the original mortgagor has a secondary liability even after the property is sold. In a novation, the original mortgagor is discharged and the old debt is extinguished. Few mortgagees will consent to a novation during periods of increasing interest rates unless the new debtor agrees to pay interest at the prevailing rate.

"Subject To"

Refers to a sale in which buyer agrees to purchase property subject to the lien of the mortgage.

Perhaps the buyer found by Hal's broker would not be willing to assume the mortgage debt. Under these circumstances, the buyer would pay Hal for his equity in the property. Any interest acquired by the buyer is "subject to" the lien of the mortgage. If there is a default, the property will be foreclosed, but the buyer has not agreed to become personally liable.

As noted, if a buyer takes property "subject to" the mortgage, he or she has no personal obligation. Both the mortgagee and the seller/mortgagor must look to the land to collect the debt in the event of default. If proceeds from a foreclosure are not sufficient, the deficiency is the seller/mortgagor's responsibility. A number of states have, however, extended the buyer's responsibility with the doctrine of *implied assumption.* In these states, the buyer is personally liable even when no promise to assume exists, when the amount of an existing mortgage is deducted from the purchase price and the buyer pays the difference.

CASE EXAMPLE

Metcalf contracted to sell property to Lay for $19,000. The property was encumbered with a $10,000 mortgage. The contract did not mention the existing mortgage because Lay anticipated financing without it. This financing did not materialize, and the salesperson for the seller suggested that Lay merely purchase the equity. Lay agreed. Lay never talked with the seller, and no express assumption was discussed. At the closing the price of the property was clearly shown as $19,000 with a $10,000 credit for the mortgage. The deed to Lay excepted the existing mortgage. When the debt was not paid, the mortgagee foreclosed. Not realizing enough from the sale to pay the debt, the mortgagee sued Metcalf, who in turn sued Lay. Lay would be held personally responsible although he had not assumed the mortgage if the court applied the doctrine of *implied assumption*.

The doctrine of implied assumption has been criticized frequently. This criticism is based upon the belief that a buyer should not be exposed to the risk of personal liability unless he or she clearly and explicitly has accepted this responsibility.

EXTENSIONS, ASSIGNMENTS AND DISCHARGE

The mortgage and note are the essential instruments used when a loan is secured by real property. After the loan has been made, other developments involving it often occur. Time for repayment may be extended, the mortgagee may transfer ownership of the mortgage and note and in most cases the debt is repaid. The real estate professional should be familiar with these transactions and the documents used to accomplish them.

Extension Agreement

An agreement by a mortgagee to extend the time when the debt is due.

Mortgagors faced with financial problems sometimes ask the mortgagee to modify the provisions of the loan. Often the request is to extend the due date of the loan. If the loan seems salvageable, mortgagees, especially financial institutions, are generally willing to extend. From the lender's standpoint, collection without foreclosure saves time and money and preserves goodwill.

One of the legal problems associated with extension agreements involves the basic contractual doctrine of *consideration*. If the mortgagee's promise to allow more time is not supported by consideration, the promise is not enforceable. Traditionally, consideration requires that the promisor, the mortgagee in this instance, receive some benefit or that there be a detriment to the promisee. If the agreement merely extends the maturity of the loan, the mortgagee does not benefit, nor is there a detriment to the mortgagor. The opposite is, in fact, the case. In a number of jurisdictions the courts allow a mortgagee who has promised to extend the time a loan is due to avoid this promise if consideration is lacking.

Some states by statute—and the more enlightened courts in others—have abandoned the need for consideration to support a promise to extend. These states substitute for consideration the doctrine of *promissory estoppel*.

CASE EXAMPLE

In 1979, Pedro Fernandez purchased an orange grove, giving the seller a note for $33,500 secured by a mortgage. The note was due on January 31, 1985. Fernandez spent substantial time and money revitalizing the grove. By 1983, the grove was profitable.

Late in 1983, Fernandez realized that he would be unable to pay the debt when due. At his request the seller extended the due date until January 1986. In reliance upon this commitment, Fernandez reinvested profits from the 1983 operation in the grove.

When the debt was not paid in 1985, the seller attempted to foreclose. He contended the extension was unenforceable since he had received no consideration. Fernandez moved to dismiss based upon the extension agreement. The courts in many states would grant the motion on the grounds that Fernandez had relied upon the promise to extend by reinvesting the 1983 profit.

For promissory estoppel to be applicable, a person such as Fernandez must be able to show three conditions: a promise was made inviting reliance, he or she relied and he or she suffered some economic loss.

In practice a mortgagee who promises to extend usually demands some concession, which will serve as consideration. Perhaps the interest rate will be increased or interest on a portion of the principal will be paid in advance. Since even a minute benefit constitutes consideration, doctrines such as promissory estoppel are unnecessary.

Another potential legal problem exists if a mortgagee extends the time of payment of the mortgage debt at the request of an assuming grantee.

CASE EXAMPLE

Ed Lane purchased commercial property from Tom Baggio. The property was encumbered with a mortgage of $148,000, which Lane agreed to assume and pay. When Lane was unable to pay the debt at maturity, Unity Bank, the mortgagee, gave him a one-year extension.

Lane defaulted, and Unity Bank sued both Baggio and Lane. Baggio asked that the action against him be dismissed because Unity had extended the due date without his consent.

Courts in most states would grant Baggio's request. They reason that the original mortgagor, remaining responsible as a guarantor after an assumption, is injured by the extension. If there had been no extension, Baggio could have paid the debt when it became due. He then would have been subrogated to Unity's claim against Lane, the assuming grantor. The year's delay is potentially harmful to him. In a minority of jurisdictions the original mortgagor would not be released by the extension agreement. In these states he is regarded even after assumption not as a guarantor but as a principal.

A comparable split of authority exists when the grantee takes title subject to a mortgage and later obtains an extension of time for payment of the mortgage debt. The prevailing view appears to be that the mortgagor is not discharged. A substantial number of states do release him from further liability, at least to the extent of the value of the land.

Assignment

The present transfer of a property right from one person (the assignor) to another (the assignee).

One of the chief incidents of ownership is the right to assign, or to transfer to another, that which is owned. This principle applies to intangible as well as tangible property.

CASE EXAMPLE

South Central Savings financed the purchase of a residence for Marlene Jefferson. As a part of the transaction, Jefferson executed the customary note and mortgage in favor of South Central. South Central wished to obtain additional funds for lending and assigned the mortgage and note as part of a package to the Britan Insurance Company. The company discounted the notes and paid funds to South Central. Jefferson would be obligated to pay the insurance company because it now owned her obligation to South Central Savings.

The example illustrates a common situation in which mortgages and notes are assigned. South Central is the assignor, and Britan Insurance Company is the *assignee*. The mortgagor, Marlene Jefferson, is referred to as the *obligor*.

In addition to mortgages and notes, rights created by contracts, leases and options also may be assigned. Sometimes, however, the document that creates the right may limit assignment unless the obligor agrees. This is unusual in a mortgage but more frequent in a contract for the sale of land. The seller might be concerned with the identity of the buyer. A mortgagor usually is not concerned with the identity of the person to whom the debt must be paid.

Understanding the mechanics of mortgage assignment is complicated by the dual nature of the mortgage transaction. Remember that a mortgage loan includes both a note, which is the borrower's personal promise to pay, and the mortgage, which is security for the debt. An assignment that is properly drafted transfers ownership of both the note and the mortgage. The assignee becomes the owner of both the obligation and the security.

Sometimes an assignment will refer only to the note or the mortgage. In these situations most courts have taken the position that the debt is of primary importance and the mortgage merely an incident of the debt. If an assignment transfers only the mortgage, courts rule that the assignee also acquires the obligation, because a mortgage without a debt is meaningless. Conversely, courts have generally ruled that any transfer of the obligation also includes the mortgage, although the mortgage is not mentioned.

Estoppel Certificate

A statement by the mortgagor that recites that the mortgagor has no defenses against paying the note or enforcing the mortgage and indicates the amount still due on the debt.

A mortgagor who executes an estoppel certificate represents that he or she has no defenses against payment. Thereafter the signer is estopped from raising any defense except one that arises after the execution of the estoppel certificate. Most mortgages will contain a clause requiring the mortgagor to complete an estoppel certificate. In some areas a statement of this nature is known as a *waiver of defenses* or *certificate of no defense*.

Another problem that sometimes arises involves situations in which the mortgagor pays the original mortgagee instead of the assignee. If the note is nonnegotiable, part payment to the original mortgagee reduces the debt, and the mortgagor is not required to pay the assignee. Because of this rule, an assignee should immediately notify the mortgagor of an assignment. Once this has been done, the mortgagor can no longer pay the original mortgagee.

When the note secured by the mortgage is negotiable, the mortgagor is not released by a payment to anyone except the holder of the note. To be discharged if payment is in full, the mortgagor must obtain possession of the instrument. If payment is partial, the mortgagor should demand that the instrument be produced and payment endorsed upon it.

Discharge

A statement releasing property from the lien of the mortgage.

Mortgages are commonly discharged by one of four methods: merger, release, running of the statute of limitations or payment of the mortgage debt.

Merger is a combination of the interest of the mortgagor and the mortgagee in the same person. It ordinarily occurs when for some reason or other the mortgagor conveys title to the mortgaged land to the mortgagee. Although a mortgage usually formally releases the land when the debt is paid, a mortgage may be released either in whole or in part under other circumstances.

• CASE BRIEF •

In order to purchase a home, Frances Green and her husband borrowed $16,500 from her uncle, A. L. Lucas. The Greens gave him a note and mortgage on the property. Although few payments were made on the note, the uncle never foreclosed. On numerous occasions before various witnesses he stated that he did not intend to collect the debt and that it was Frances's share of his estate.

When A. L. Lucas died, he left his entire estate to his mistress, Katie McLean. At his funeral, she gave the note and mortgage to Frances and her husband, stating that it was Frances's share of the estate. Later she refused to cancel the mortgage on the record and attempted to foreclose. In a suit to declare the foreclosure sale void, the court stated that "(w)hen the note was delivered prior to maturity and the express renunciation was made, the debt was discharged. . . ." *McLean & J. W. Kellum v. Green, 258 So.2d 247 (Miss. 1972).*

A blanket mortgage often contains a partial *release* provision. A provision of this nature is necessary when a mortgage covers a large tract of land that is to be divided and developed. In order to obtain financing to build or sell residences on the smaller tracts, the developer must be able to release them from the lien of the blanket mortgage.

Statutes of limitations that apply to enforcement of mortgage liens vary widely from state to state. The application of the statute of limitations to bar foreclosure actions is further complicated by the dual nature of the mortgage transaction. In general, states have adopted shorter limitation periods for debts evidenced by a note than they have for enforcement of a mortgage. This creates a problem when collection of the note is barred by a statute of limitations but the statutory period for a foreclosure action has not yet expired.

• CASE BRIEF •

On July 29, 1959, Carl Lundberg executed a promissory note payable upon demand to M. E. Tegels. The note, which was secured by a second mortgage, was for $9,100, with interest at six percent. Lundberg never paid any amount on the principal or the interest. No action was taken on the note, and by the time of Tegels's death payment was barred by the statute of limitations.

In 1971, Northwestern National Bank, trustees under Tegels's will, attempted to foreclose on the property. At this time Lundberg contended that the running of the statute of limitations on the note was a bar to the foreclosure action. Both the lower court and the Supreme Court of Minnesota disagreed. *Lundberg v. Northwestern National Bank, 299 Minn. 46, 216 N. W.2d 121 (1974).*

Although this case represents only one point of view, it is probably the majority position. Courts in a number of states have ruled that, if collection of a debt is barred by the statute of limitations, the mortgage can no longer be foreclosed.

The period established by statutes of limitations is effectively extended by various actions taken by the mortgagor or mortgagee. A mortgagor's part payment of the debt or new promise to pay starts the statute anew. His or her absence from the jurisdiction discontinues or, in legal terms, *tolls* the statute for the duration of the absence. The mortgagee may also toll the statute through a promise to extend the time for payment. As a result, the fact that a mortgage is old is not a reliable guide to its enforceability. Because of this, several states have adopted statutes that void a mortgage a specified period of time after maturity, usually 20 years. In addition, marketable title acts discussed earlier provide for the elimination of stale mortgages unless some notice of claim is filed.

Payment of the mortgage debt is the usual method of discharging a mortgage. Payment of the debt, however, does not clear the public record; this must be done by entering in the record an instrument releasing the mortgage. Various names are given to this instrument. In some places it is known as a *satisfaction piece* or *satisfaction*. In other areas it is called a *discharge* or a *release*. At one time it was a common practice merely to endorse on the margin of the recorded mortgage that it had been satisfied. A number of jurisdictions continue to follow this practice. Most states have statutes that provide for a monetary penalty if a mortgagee refuses to execute a release.

In those jurisdictions where the deed of trust is the popular form of financing instrument, the trustee who holds legal title will execute a release deed or deed of reconveyance when presented with the canceled notes indicating that the debt has been paid. Obtaining a deed of reconveyance or a satisfaction is important to the debtor. Unless these actions are taken, questions as to marketability of title may be raised.

SUMMARY

The mortgage loan starts with an application, which constitutes the borrower's offer to enter into a contract to borrow money. If the loan is approved, the lender issues a commitment which constitutes acceptance, and a contract exists. In financing commercial real estate, a lender often proposes terms that differ from the loan for which the borrower applied. The commitment thus becomes a counteroffer. No contract exists unless the borrower accepts the new terms.

Both state and federal statutes regulate the terms and conditions of the mortgage loan. Historically, each state has established a maximum interest rate that lenders can charge. Interest rates in excess of this figure are termed usurious and are illegal. In recent years, because of economic conditions, most states have increased the maximum rate. In addition, recent federal legislation eliminates state usury ceilings for certain mortgage loans.

Mortgage transactions are also affected by other federal statutes. For example, the Consumer Credit Protection Act (1968) provides for truth-in-lending, requiring lenders to disclose fully the cost of consumer credit. Another federal statute, the Equal Credit Opportunity Act, prohibits many kinds of discrimination by lending institutions.

When mortgaged property is sold, different methods of treating the loan are available to the parties. Frequently, the loan will be paid off out of the proceeds of the sale because the parties wish to do so or because of a requirement of a due-on-sale clause. Without such a clause, a potential buyer may be able to assume the existing mortgage and continue to pay according to the same terms. Or, the owner may sell the property "subject to" the existing mortgage. In either of these cases, the mortgage continues as a lien on the property; the responsibilities of the buyer and seller differ, depending on whether the buyer "assumes" or purchases "subject to" the mortgage.

Mortgage lenders, when faced with the need to raise additional funds, often assign some of their mortgage loans to another institution. Payments on the loan so assigned must still be made according to the original terms. The new holder of the mortgage—the assignee—generally requires the borrower to sign a statement that confirms the debt. This statement is known as an *estoppel certificate*.

The usual method of discharging a mortgage—that is, releasing property from the lien—is by payment of the debt. Upon payment, a notice of satisfaction is placed in the public record. Other methods of termination include merger, which is combining the interests of the mortgagor and mortgagee in the same person, release and running of the statute of limitations.

REVIEW AND DISCUSSION QUESTIONS

1. The terms *finance charge* and *annual percentage rate (APR)* are important in truth-in-lending legislation. Explain what each means.
2. Under the Equal Credit Opportunity Act a lender may ask questions about marital status and age under certain conditions. What are these conditions?
3. Outline the rights and privileges of a mortgagee who takes possession of a mortgaged premises upon the mortgagor's default.
4. (a) List the three different approaches taken in the United States as to when a mechanic's lien becomes effective. (b) In your opinion which of these is the most equitable? Why?
5. (a) What is a subordination agreement? (b) Under what conditions might a mortgagee be willing to subordinate its lien?
6. What is a due-on-sale clause? Explain why this clause has become increasingly important in recent years.
7. Compare and contrast the rights and obligations of the grantor/mortgagor with those of a grantee assuming responsibility for the mortgage debt.
8. Explain the doctrine of "implied assumption."
9. What is an estoppel certificate? Explain its importance when a mortgage is assigned.

CASE PROBLEMS

1. Oellerich and his wife sold real estate that they owned. The purchasers assumed the mortgage. The assumption agreement provided that the Oellerichs were not released from liability on the original debt if the purchasers defaulted on the note. Shortly thereafter the lender and purchasers executed a modification agreement that increased the interest on the note. The Oellerichs were not parties to this agreement. Did the modification agreement affect the rights of the parties? Explain how and why. *Oellerich v. First Fed. Sav. & Loan Assn.*, 552 F.2d 1109 (5th Cir. 1977).
2. Albert owns real property worth $35,000. He borrows $28,000 from Martin and executes a mortgage on the property in Martin's favor. The term of the mortgage is 15 years. Seven years later, Albert sells the property to Bobb for a cash amount with the mortgage remaining on the property. What difference, if any, will it make to Bobb if the deed from Albert states "subject to a mortgage indebtedness of _____," or "subject to a mortgage indebtedness of _____, which said indebtedness the grantee assumes and agrees to pay"?

3. Larson owned a commercial building that he had inherited from his mother. The original mortgage on the building had been satisfied. In January 1974, Larson leased a portion of the building to Hutchins for a five-year term. The lease was immediately recorded. In March 1975, Larson borrowed $75,000 from the Belville Bank, giving it a mortgage on the property. The mortgage was for a term of ten years. It was recorded on April 11, 1975. The $75,000 was used to renovate the property. In 1977, because the debt was not paid, the bank foreclosed.

   (a) Kane, the purchaser at the foreclosure sale, wished to use the entire building and brought an action to eject Hutchins. Would Kane be successful? Discuss.

   (b) Assume that, on March 27, Anderson began electrical work that was part of the renovation. The work was not completed until June. When Anderson was not paid, he filed a mechanic's lien. What are Anderson's rights vis-á-vis the Belville Bank? Discuss.

4. Smith agreed to purchase property from Layton. As part of the contract, Smith assumed and agreed to pay the existing mortgage. Smith immediately contracted to sell the property to Young. Layton agreed to convey directly to Young, who assumed the mortgage in the deed to him. Smith never had title to the property. The mortgage was not paid, and the foreclosure took place. There was a deficiency, and the mortgagee sued Smith. Would the mortgagee be successful? Discuss.

5. Lon Gabele is the president of Gabele Builders as well as its chief salesperson. Fredericktown Savings agrees to finance homes built by Gabele at a rate of $10^1/_2$ percent if the buyer makes a $2,500 down payment. Gabele places an advertisement in the local paper indicating that homes can be purchased at $2,500 down. The only other information in the advertisement is the offering price, Gabele's name and the location of the development.

   Prior to the advertisement's appearance, a number of buyers had visited the homes that Gabele had for sale. When asked about financing, Gabele informs them that it is available at $10^1/_2$ percent. He provides no additional information but refers them to Fredericktown Savings. Has Gabele violated the credit advertising provisions of the "Truth-in-Lending" Act? Support your answer.

6. Campbell purchased an office building. The purchase was financed by a $100,000 mortgage loan from the Irish-American Bank. Campbell leased the building to American Crafts for seven years at a yearly rental of $18,000. After two years had

elapsed on the lease, Campbell defaulted on the mortgage loan. The Irish-American Bank now demands that the rent be paid to it. It threatens to evict American Crafts if it does not do so. If nothing has been said in the mortgage pertaining to the rent, what is the result (a) in a title theory jurisdiction, (b) in a lien theory jurisdiction, (c) in a jurisdiction in which mortgagee has right of possession upon default?

22
Default and Foreclosure

FORECLOSURE

The legal procedure by which a lender who has advanced funds with real property as security recovers in the event of default.

The climax of 19th-century melodramas frequently involves a mortgage. In return for not foreclosing, the villainous mortgagee demands the mortgagor's beautiful, young daughter. In the nick of time the hero enters, back from California where he struck it rich in the gold fields. Both property and heroine are saved. The villain is foiled again.

Although in the melodrama the villain curses his luck, few real-life mortgagees are anxious to foreclose. The process is generally time-consuming, expensive and damaging to reputations. Most lending institutions turn to foreclosure as a last resort and will make every effort to prevent it. Their business is lending money, not managing property. Nevertheless, situations in which lenders must foreclose do arise. This chapter treats the different methods of foreclosure used in the United States today as well as alternative methods of realizing on the security when the debt is unpaid or a term of the mortgage breached.

In the United States foreclosure can take one of several forms. Probably the most common is foreclosure based upon a judicial decree ordering mortgaged real estate sold to pay the debt. This process is what most people have in mind when using the term *foreclosure*. The court's order is based upon the mortgage, which provides the mortgagee with a lien on the real estate as security. Another type of foreclosure is based upon a power of sale in the mortgage. This is also known as *foreclosure by advertisement*. Strict foreclosure, a third type, was discussed in Chapter 20 and will be reviewed briefly here.

Judicial foreclosure and power-of-sale foreclosure are evidence of the extent to which lien theory dominates American mortgage law. Liens require some method of eliminating the mortgagor's title and applying the security to the debt. Foreclosure and sale accomplish this. In comparison, title theory does not require that real estate be sold when the debt is in default. All that is required is a procedure to eliminate the mortgagor's equity of redemption because the mortgagee already has title. Nevertheless, foreclosure almost always leads to some type of sale even in title theory states.

DEFAULT

Nonperformance of a duty or obligation accepted by either party as part of the mortgage transaction.

The mortgagee cannot institute a foreclosure action until the mortgagor defaults. The most commonly recognized default is the failure to pay the interest or principal. Obligations other than the payment of principal and interest found in most mortgages include payment of taxes, assessments and insurance. Often these commitments are worded in such a manner that failure to carry them out constitutes a default. Some mortgage instruments merely give the mortgagee the right to make the payment if the mortgagor fails to do so. The mortgagee can then add the amount to the mortgage debt, but the mortgagee cannot foreclose since there has not been a default.

Many mortgages are worded so that the mortgagor's failure to comply with statutes, ordinances and governmental requirements affecting the premises constitutes default. Other relatively common provisions that can result in default are related to bankruptcy or the mortgagor's failure to keep the property repaired. Some mortgages provide that a mortgagor who files a voluntary petition in bankruptcy or makes an assignment for benefit of creditors is in default. Permitting waste or allowing anything to be done on the premises that weakens the security are additional prohibitions often included in mortgages. If the covenant not to permit waste is breached, the mortgagor is in default.

A mortgage provision that has become common in recent years is the due-on-sale clause discussed in Chapter 21. If the due-on-sale clause is worded in a manner that makes sale of the premises a default, an *acceleration clause* makes the entire obligation due when the property is sold.

Acceleration Clause

A provision in a mortgage giving the mortgagee the right to declare the entire debt due and payable upon default.

A critical legal question when default has occurred is the mortgagee's right to collect the entire debt. This problem arises when the mortgagor breaches a covenant that is not related to payment or when the debt is to be repaid periodically and a payment is missed. What can the mortgagee do under these circumstances to protect its investment? The solution to this problem is a clause making the entire debt payable in event of default.

CASE EXAMPLE

Lance Fazio had executed a mortgage and note in favor of West End Savings and Loan. The mortgage contained a due-on-sale and an acceleration clause. Monthly payments of $298 were due on the note.

When Fazio sold the property, West End demanded repayment of the entire debt. Fazio immediately tendered the next monthly installment, which West End refused to accept. Fazio and the new owner demanded that West End accept this amount. West End pointed out the mortgage default and that the acceleration clause entitled them to collect the entire debt.

Notice of Default

In the absence of statute, a mortgagee is not required to give notice of default before commencing a foreclosure suit. Ordinarily, the mortgagee's efforts to settle the defaulted debt will serve as notice of default to the mortgagor. Some state statutes require that the mortgagor be notified of default, and some mortgages contain provisions to the same effect.

Most acceleration clauses require the mortgagee to notify the mortgagor of an election to accelerate the debt. Commencing a foreclosure action generally is sufficient notice. A limited number of jurisdictions require a mortgagee to notify the mortgagor of acceleration before commencing suit. A mortgagee's election to accelerate is lost if the default is remedied before the mortgagee notifies the mortgagor of acceleration or foreclosures.

Waiver

The giving up or relinquishing of a known legal right.

• CASE BRIEF •

Brown owed Hewitt $8,500. The debt was evidenced by a note

and mortgage containing an acceleration clause and a ten percent penalty for collection fees. Partial payments of $90 were due on the tenth of each month. Over a period of 14 consecutive months Hewitt had accepted overdue payments. In September Brown and Hewitt quarreled. When the October payment was late, Hewitt immediately accelerated the debt, demanding full payment plus the collection fee. Since Brown could not pay the entire debt, Hewitt commenced foreclosure proceedings. Brown's suit to enjoin these proceedings was successful. The court held that Hewitt could not accelerate without notifying Brown of Hewitt's intention to depart from the usual method of dealing between the parties. *Brown v. Hewitt, 143 S.W.2d 223 (Tex. 1940).*

Ordinarily an extension of time given to a defaulting mortgagor to correct the default is not a waiver of the mortgagee's right to accelerate the debt. Similarly, a mortgagee who fails to accelerate because of one default is not precluded from accelerating upon a later default. When the mortgagee continuously accepts late payments, some courts have held acceleration is precluded if the mortgagor makes a late payment in reliance upon the previous course of conduct.

• CASE BRIEF •

Andrew J. Evans and Mary, his wife, executed a $65,626 promissory note secured by a mortgage in favor of C & B Development Company. Interest on the note was payable in installments of $3,281.32. When the Evanses missed an installment, they were given an oral extension of 30 days. The note contained an acceleration clause. When the interest was not paid after 30 days, C & B exercised its option to accelerate. The Evanses argued that, as C & B had not stated that there would be an acceleration should the interest not be paid in the allotted time, the right to accelerate had been waived. Both the trial court and the appellate court rejected this argument. *Evans v. Scottsdale Plumbing Co., 10 Ariz. App. 184, 457 P. 2d 724 (1969).*

Generally, the mortgagee's acceptance of late payments is not a waiver of the right to accelerate for defaults other than those involving the late payment. A mortgagee accepting late payments may stipulate that this action shall not negate rights arising as a result of the default. When there has been a default, a mortgagee who intends to accelerate must immediately notify the mortgagor. This initial step normally must be taken before commencing a foreclosure action.

Default in Prior Mortgage Clause

Frequently property is encumbered with more than one mortgage. If the senior mortgage is in default and foreclosure occurs, the junior lien will be eliminated. Sometimes the senior mortgage will be in default but not the junior lien. This causes a problem for the junior mortgagee as it cannot foreclose, although the debt and security are endangered. For protection a junior mortgage should contain a clause providing that a default in a prior mortgage is a default in the junior obligation. If a clause of this nature exists, the junior mortgagee may commence its own foreclosure action. Of course its lien does not become superior to the prior mortgage, but at least the junior mortgagee does not have to sit back and wait for the other to act.

Equity of Redemption

The right of the mortgagor or another person with an interest in the property to reclaim it after default but before foreclosure.

• CASE BRIEF •

Leo and Mary Blades executed six promissory notes and a second deed of trust to secure a loan of $2,000. When the Bladeses defaulted on one of the notes, the trustee advertised the premises for sale. Prior to the sale, Mr. Blades tendered full payment by cashier's check of the remaining notes. The trustee refused to accept payment, saying, "No, your property is going to be foreclosed; there is nothing I can do to stop it."

After the property was sold, Blades brought suit to redeem it. Redemption was allowed by the lower court and approved upon appeal. The appellate court stated that "[t]he fact that there was an offer to pay prior to the sale is sufficient to stop the sale from being made. . . ." *Blades v. Ossenfort, 481 S.W. 2d 531 (Mo. 1972).*

In both title and lien theory states, the mortgagor has a right to redeem the property after default. Redemption can be accomplished by paying the full amount of the debt, interest and costs. To be effective, the right of redemption must be asserted prior to foreclosure. The purpose of foreclosure is to terminate the equitable right of redemption. Once the foreclosure sale has been confirmed, the mortgagor can no longer redeem the property, except in several states in which statutes provide an additional period. This statutory right of redemption is discussed later in the chapter.

In addition to the mortgagor, other parties having an interest in the property may redeem. Junior mortgagees, tenants under a lease, judgment creditors and grantees who have acquired through the mortgagor have this right. The junior mortgagee who redeems acquires the rights of the senior mortgagee, not title to the premises. A mortgagor redeeming has a superior right. Since the debt has been paid, he or she acquires the unencumbered fee.

The right of redemption is based upon equity's recognition of the mortgage as a security instrument. Although at common law the mortgagee acquired title, equity recognized the true nature of the transaction. It was clear to the courts that the mortgagee was not purchasing the premises but securing a debt. As a result, the mortgagor is entitled to reclaim the title even after default if the debt is paid in full.

Several states have statutes that allow a mortgagor to correct a default. These statutes, like the equity of redemption, are based upon the lien nature of the mortgage. Unlike the equity of redemption, the statutes do not require payment of the entire debt to cure certain types of default. For example, a mortgagor is entitled to cure the non-payment of a partial amount due under the note or mortgage by paying the delinquent principal and interest plus costs and expenses. When this payment is made, the obligation of the mortgage is reinstated and remains in effect as if no default had occurred. The statutes also apply to default arising because of the mortgagor's failure to pay items such as taxes, assessments and insurance premiums.

Statutory Right of Redemption

The right of a debtor to redeem the property after a foreclosure sale.

Legislatures in more than half the states have provided the mortgagor with a right to redeem after foreclosure. The creation of a statutory right of redemption is generally the result of political pressure by debtors during periods of economic distress. Although the first such statute was enacted in New York, most of the legislation exists in the western states. Agricultural interests have often been behind efforts to establish this right.

The period in which the former mortgagor may redeem varies from state to state. Generally, the period is six months or a year. Laws in some states also give some classes of persons a longer period of time to redeem than others. In a number of states, instead of granting the mortgagor a right to redeem after the foreclosure sale, state laws postpone the sale to provide a longer period of time to pay a debt that is in default. Except in a few states, any attempt by the lender to have the mortgagor waive redemption rights violates public policy and is unenforceable.

JUDICIAL FORECLOSURE

A legal procedure in which a court orders real estate sold to enforce the mortgagee's rights under the mortgage.

Of the several methods of foreclosure, foreclosure by judicial action and sale is probably the most common. In a few states it is the only method allowed. Judicial foreclosure is favored because a court supervises the entire procedure. As a result the property is usually sold for close to its market value; in addition, chances for a defective foreclosure are reduced because the sale is based upon a court order. On the other hand, this type of foreclosure is expensive and time-consuming.

Most jurisdictions regulate many aspects of the foreclosure procedure by statute. These regulations, which vary from state to state, must be followed closely or the sale will be invalid. Usually an action to foreclose must be brought in the county where the mortgaged property is located. If a single mortgage covers property in several counties, the suit may be brought in any of the counties in which the property is located.

Foreclosure is an equitable action. Therefore, courts have appreciable flexibility to order remedies that will provide fair and just treatment for all parties involved. Among other things, the court's decree may determine priorities among mortgages and other liens, require a bidder to furnish a cash deposit and tell contesting creditors from which of the debtor's assets their liens will be satisfied.

• CASE BRIEF •

First Fidelity had mortgages on property owned by J. O. Brice in Haskell and McIntosh counties. The mortgages were given to secure a single note. Leonhardt Lumber Company had a materialman's lien on the Haskell County property but not on the property in McIntosh County. Both tracts were also subject to subordinate liens in favor of Vandever Investment Company. The materialman's lien of Leonhardt Lumber had priority over the investment company's lien.

When a default occurred on the note, First Fidelity foreclosed against the Haskell County property. Upon an application an appellate court held that where a first mortgagee may seek payment of its debt from either or both of two securities it may not arbitrarily select the security from which it will first seek payment. Subordinate lien claimants are entitled to have the first lien satisfied from both securities proportionately if this method ensures that each subordinate lienholder will be able to satisfy its claim. *Vandever Investment Co. v. H. E. Leonhardt Lumber Co., 503 P.2d 185 (Okla. 1972).*

Procedural Requirements

Due Process

The requirements of due process that exist for litigation generally apply to mortgage foreclosures. Mortgagors and other interested parties are entitled to notice of the action and an opportunity to defend before an impartial tribunal having jurisdiction.

Notice

If the mortgagor is within the jurisdiction, generally he or she will be served personally. Personal service is, however, unnecessary because the foreclosure action is *in rem*—that is, "against the property"—and, as such, service by publication is sufficient. Requirements for a valid service by publication vary from state to state, but generally they involve mailing a copy of the summons to the defendant and advertising the action in a general-circulation newspaper.

Parties

Few legal questions arise as to the proper party or parties to initiate a foreclosure action. Ordinarily, it would be the mortgagee or one to whom the mortgage has been transferred. If there are joint mortgagees, they must join in the litigation. Any mortgagee who refuses to join should be made a defendant. If the security instrument is a deed of trust, the trustee brings the action.

The plaintiff should join as defendants any other parties with an interest in the property. This includes anyone with a junior mortgage. In most states, if this is not done, the junior mortgagee's interest is not terminated by the foreclosure sale. This means that the junior mortgagee has the right to foreclose its mortgage or to redeem the property.

The nuisance value attributed to the continued existence of a junior mortgage is considerable. A purchaser at a foreclosure sale might have to resort to additional litigation to terminate rights established by the junior mortgage.

• CASE BRIEF •

New Miami Shores was the purchaser at a foreclosure sale of property covered by a first mortgage. Quinn Plumbing Company held a second mortgage on a small part of the encumbered land. Quinn Plumbing was not made a party to the foreclosure of the first mortgage. In order to terminate Quinn Plumbing's interest, New Miami Shores was forced to get a court order requiring Quinn to redeem the land covered or have its interest barred. *Quinn Plumbing v. New Miami Shores, 100 Fla. 413, 129 So. 690 (1930).*

Sound legal practice also dictates that a tenant under a lease executed after the mortgage be made a party to the foreclosure action. Although the tenant's rights are terminated by foreclosure, no later question can arise if the tenant is joined in the foreclosure suit. If the tenant's lease was executed prior to the mortgage, the lessee need not be joined because his or her rights are superior to the mortgage.

When the mortgagor has sold the property, the purchaser, of course, must be a party to the foreclosure. In most states it is also necessary to include the mortgagor because he or she may be liable if there is a deficiency.

Pleadings

A *complaint* or *petition* initiates a foreclosure action in the same way as it initiates other types of litigation. The document must allege facts sufficient to show that (1) the plaintiff has a cause of action and (2) the defendants are liable under the mortgage. This is accomplished by describing the debt that is secured, the mortgage and the mortgaged premises. In some jurisdictions it is necessary for the plaintiff to attach a copy of the mortgage. The plaintiff must also allege that there has been a default and indicate the relief that he or she is seeking.

The pleas available to a defendant parallel those in other types of litigation. They include (1) specific or general denial, (2) answer, (3) counterclaim or cross bill and (4) motion to dismiss or demurrer.

A common defense is the *specific* or *general denial*. These pleas are used when the defendant disagrees with the facts as alleged by the plaintiff. As foreclosure is an equitable action, factual issues are generally not determined by a jury but by the judge. Equity courts do have the power to impanel advisory juries, and sometimes this is done. A few states have statutes that require jury determinations of fact in foreclosure cases.

In an *answer*, the defendant may allege affirmative defenses such as payment, fraud, mistake or lack of consideration. Any conduct on the part of the plaintiff mortgagee that is considered unconscionable or oppressive also will operate as an affirmative defense.

• CASE BRIEF •

Eugene Ricks executed a mortgage on his home in Brooklyn, New York. The mortgage was guaranteed by the Veterans Administration. Ricks defaulted, and the mortgagee immediately commenced an action to foreclose.

In his answer Ricks alleged that the mortgagee's action violated policy of the Veterans Administration. The *VA Handbook* encouraged mortgagees "to extend all reasonable forbearance in event a borrower becomes unable to meet the terms of his loan." Another provision of the handbook stated that "it is not expected that holders. . . institute action to terminate loans, until every effort has been made to arrive at some solution." The court felt that the mortgagee's failure to follow the handbook constituted unconscionable conduct. *Federal National Mortgage Assn. v. Ricks, 83 Misc.2d 804, 372 N.Y.S.2d 485 (1975).*

A defendant may also file a *counterclaim,* called a *cross bill* or *cross complaint* in some jurisdictions, and attempt to recoup damages for losses suffered involving the property in question.

• CASE BRIEF •

Palermo, Inc., constructed a residence for Norris and Bonnie LeBleu. The major cost of the home was financed through a bank, but the LeBleus gave Palermo a note and second mortgage for a $2,000 balance. When the central heating and air-conditioning system in the home proved defective and irreparable, the LeBleus had a new system installed for $1,811.

The LeBleus refused to pay on the note, and Palermo petitioned to foreclose. The LeBleus sought an injunction preventing foreclosure and counterclaimed for $1,811. In its final order, the court ordered the $1,811 set off against Palermo's claims. *Palermo Construction Co. v. LeBleu, 272 So.2d 729 (La. 1973).*

A counterclaim is also the proper pleading when defendant asks that the mortgage be re-formed or canceled.

The *motion to dismiss* or *demurrer* is not a common plea in a foreclosure suit. When this defense is raised, the defendant is arguing that the plaintiff's complaint does not allege facts sufficient to state a cause of action.

CASE EXAMPLE

Oscar Grimm was involved in a divorce litigation. During the course of the suit, Grimm executed a $15,000 second mortgage to his partner, Leonard Arras. The mortgage was duly recorded. The purpose of the mortgage was to secure Grimm's interest in a small commercial building. Although the mortgage recited a debt of $15,000, Arras had advanced no funds to Grimm. Grimm died shortly thereafter. When the mortgage became due, Arras attempted to foreclose. A motion to dismiss made by Grimm's estate would be upheld because the mortgage was not supported by consideration.

Statute of Limitations

Legislation that limits the time within which a legal action may be commenced.

Great disparity exists in the United States for determining a limitation period in a foreclosure action. Differences in state law are further complicated by conflicting approaches that states take to the relationship between the mortgage and the underlying debt. In some states a creditor may not foreclose if suit on the debt is no longer permitted because of the statute of limitations. The limitation period for mortgages is determined by the character of the debt. The result is that the period within which a mortgage must be foreclosed differs within the state because the statute of limitations differs for various types of debt. Debts under seal or evidenced by a negotiable promissory note usually have a longer legal life than those in the form of a simple written promise.

The majority of states hold that foreclosure of a mortgage is not barred by a statute of limitations on the debt. These states recognize that the creditor has two separate remedies: one on the mortgage, the other on the debt. Since World War II, however, this majority has become smaller since a number of states have adopted statutes that apply the same limitation period to both the underlying debt and the mortgage. The tendency of these statutes is also to shorten the time period in which a foreclosure action may be commenced. Because most mortgages are documents under seal, they are subject to the same limitation periods as other sealed instruments. This ranges from five to 22 years, with ten- or 20-year periods being common.

A small number of states have adopted stale claim statutes. These generally provide that a mortgage will be barred from enforcement a certain period of years after maturity. This period ranges from eight to 20 years, depending upon the state. These statutes are not applicable if the mortgagee places an extension agreement or a memorandum of part payment on the record.

Tender of Payment as a Defense

In some states the mortgagee's refusal to accept a tender of payment after default discharges the mortgage. If the mortgagee has commenced a foreclosure action, the mortgagor may establish the unaccepted tender as a defense. This rule is followed generally in lien theory jurisdictions. Courts reason that the mortgagee loses nothing when the full amount of the debt plus interest, costs and attorney fees are paid even though they are past due.

• CASE BRIEF •

Cady purchased land that was subject to a mortgage held by Buffalo Trust. The debt that the mortgage secured was in default. Cady tendered the full amount of the past due debt, expenses and interest to Buffalo Trust. The trust company, however, refused to accept the amount, demanding an additional amount not due under the mortgage. Upon foreclosure the purchaser attempted to eject Cady, who raised the tender of payment as a defense. The New York court agreed that Buffalo Trust's refusal to accept the tender terminated the mortgage lien. The court added that, although the debt still existed, it was no longer secured by a mortgage. *Kortright v. Cady, 21 N.Y. 341 (1860).*

Some lien theory states and most title theory jurisdictions adopt a different view. In title theory states, at least technically, the mortgagee acquires title when the mortgagor defaults. Under these circumstances it can be argued that the mortgagee is not deprived of this title merely because the defaulting mortgagor now offers to pay the debt. This argument ignores reality. Even in title theory states, the characteristics of a mortgage are similar to those of a lien. The parties realize that the mortgage is security for payment of a debt; few of them are aware of the instrument's title implications. Under these circumstances the mortgagee is not injured by payment after default as long as the mortgagor also tenders interest and costs.

Foreclosure Sale

The chief purpose of a foreclosure action is to obtain a court order directing a public sale of the security. This sale terminates the right to redeem of all parties having interests in the property subject to the mortgage. The proceeds of the sale are allocated to pay expenses and the mortgage debt.

Various state laws regulate the method of conducting the sale. Usually it is carried out by the sheriff. In some states a court-appointed master or referee conducts the sale. In any case, it will be supervised closely by the court.

Most states have some type of law attempting to ensure an adequate *sale price.* One common method is to require an appraisal by a group of disinterested persons before the property is auctioned. The sale must bring at least a portion—perhaps 60 to 75 percent of the appraised value. Unless the final bid is at least that amount, the sale is not consummated. A few states allow bidding in advance. Bids made at the sale must be at least as high as the highest advance bid. If they are not, the property goes to the highest advance bidder. Finally, a court can use its equity power to refuse to confirm a sale if the amount bid is grossly inadequate. Ordinarily, however, a properly conducted sale will not be set aside merely because of an inadequate price.

• CASE BRIEF •

Marion H. MacKenzie owed the Small Business Administration (SBA) $124,000. The debt was partially secured by a mortgage on property owned by MacKenzie. Based on two appraisals, the property supposedly had a fair market value of $50,000. When MacKenzie defaulted on the debt, the SBA foreclosed. At the foreclosure sale, the SBA purchased the property for $34,000.

MacKenzie petitioned the court to invalidate the sale on grounds that the foreclosure price was inadequate. In refusing to do so, the court stated: "The difference of $16,000 between the sale price and fair market value is not so gross as to shock the conscience or overcome the inference that the price obtained represented the fair market value." *United States v. MacKenzie, 322 F. Supp. 1058 (D. Nev. 1971), aff'd, 474 F.2d 1008 (9th Cir. 1971).*

Deficiency Judgment
Money judgment awarded to the mortgagee when funds obtained as a result of a foreclosure sale are insufficient to pay the debt.

CASE EXAMPLE
Oscar Fong defaulted on a loan from Portland Trust. The loan was secured by a mortgage on real estate owned by Fong. At the time of default the outstanding indebtedness was $75,000. The mortgage was foreclosed and the property ordered sold. The selling price at the foreclosure sale was $70,000. After this amount was credited, the bank commenced a personal action against Fong to collect the additional $5,000 plus all expenses.

Most states allow the mortgagee to collect any deficiency remaining after foreclosure. Usually the right to sue for a deficiency is provided in the court decree ordering foreclosure. The theory underlying the deficiency judgment is that the creditor has a right based upon the bond or note to collect the entire amount owed. This right exists independently of the right to foreclose.

Deficiency judgments in residential foreclosures are rare, for reasons both legal and economic. Economically, situations in which sale of the property is insufficient to pay off the debt occur infrequently. Most residential loans are amortized on a monthly basis; the amount of the debt is constantly decreasing. Coupled with inflation and generally increasing property values, only in unusual cases will funds from the sale fail to cover the debt.

The law in a few states prohibits deficiency judgments. If a mortgagee elects to foreclose, that is the only remedy allowed. The reason is that the mortgagee often purchases at the foreclosure sale. If the purchase price is less than the debt, the mortgagee can thus acquire the security as well as collect the entire amount owed. This can be very unjust to the mortgagor because frequently the mortgagee acquires the property for less than its actual value. A mortgagee has an advantage as a bidder for the amount owed to it is credited against its bid. The result is that it must come up with less cash than other bidders. Other bidders are thus frozen out, and the property sells for less than its value.

POWER-OF-SALE FORECLOSURE

Foreclosure based upon terms in a mortgage, giving a mortgagee or third party the power to sell mortgaged property upon default without resorting to judicial foreclosures.

Legal complications, expense and delay associated with judicial foreclosure have encouraged alternate methods of applying the security to the debt. Many mortgages contain provisions granting a mortgagee or third party the power to sell the real estate at a public sale if the mortgagor defaults. Generally, the sale is authorized without court intervention, but a few states require judicial confirmation, and many have statutes that prescribe procedures that must be followed.

Some states by specific legislation require foreclosure by judicial action. Statutes of this type effectively prohibit the use of a power of sale. Most states, however, do allow the power-of-sale foreclosure, and it is the prevailing practice in several states.

At one time the power-of-sale foreclosure was touted as the solution to many of the problems of judicial foreclosure, but this expectation was not fulfilled. Lawyers representing potential purchasers are wary of the process because the title acquired is not based upon a judicial proceeding that establishes regularity. In addition, the purchaser's title is subject to attack because the sale does not have the official sanction of a court order. This attack can be made not only by the mortgagor but also by others who have an interest in the property.

Advocates of debtors' interests also object to extrajudicial foreclosure based upon a power of sale. In many states the terms of the power are the principal source for determining how the sale will be conducted. Because the mortgagor's bargaining position is generally weak, provisions of the power detrimental to the mortgagor's interest are often included. This is illustrated in a comparison of English and American law. English law absolutely prohibits the mortgagee from purchasing at a power-of-sale foreclosure. Generally, in the United States the rule is also that a mortgagee cannot be the purchaser when a power of sale is used, but in most states this rule can be avoided by a provision in the power allowing the mortgagee to buy. Many states also permit a deficiency judgment after a sale based upon a power. This, too, can be harmful to the mortgagor because there is no direct judicial supervision of the adequacy of the selling price.

The deed of trust, discussed in Chapter 20, is normally enforced by a nonjudicial sale. The deed empowers the trustee to sell the security when the debt is in default. Trustees ordinarily carry out the terms of the trust without going to court, inasmuch as neither court authority nor direction is needed. The trustee's power is thus similar to the power enjoyed by a mortgagee under a mortgage containing a power of sale.

Trustees are subject to the same basic statutory regulations that must be observed by a mortgagee in carrying out a power-of-sale provision. In addition, the trustee must conform to the extensive body of law that regulates fiduciaries in general. Because the trustee is a fiduciary as to both debtor and creditor, a trustee's exercise of a power of sale has been accepted more readily by the legal community than similar action taken by a mortgagee.

Statutes in many states and case law in others provide some protection for the mortgagor whose real property is subject to a power of sale. These statutes generally require notice, usually by advertisement, and a sale that is conducted fairly in order to produce a good price. A sale will not be valid if factors exist that tend to stifle competition among the bidders. In conducting the sale the mortgagee is representing the mortgagor's interest as well as its own.

• CASE BRIEF •

Union Market National Bank held a $9,800 mortgage on property owned by Missak Derderian. The mortgage was in default, and the bank advertised a sale under a power included in the mortgage. The advertisement stated, in addition to a $500 cash down payment at the time of sale, "other terms to be announced at the sale."

At the sale the auctioneer announced that a $500 deposit would be required of anyone prior to that person's bid being accepted. This was a very unusual condition, and Derderian's brother, who was planning to bid, refused to comply. The auctioneer as a result refused to accept his high bid of more than $10,000 and sold the property to the mortgagee for $8,500. All parties at the sale knew that Derderian's brother was financially responsible.

When Derderian challenged the sale as improperly conducted, an appellate court agreed with him. The court stated that "[a] mortgagee with the power to select the methods of sale must act as a reasonably prudent man would to obtain a fair price. . . If the conditions announced at the sale. . . operate to prevent free bidding, it is the mortgagee's duty to change them." *Union National Bank v. Derderian, 318 Mass. 578, 62 N.E.2d 661 (1945).*

Notice

Adequate notice of the time, the place, the property to be sold and the conditions of sale are critical to the sale's validity. Usually statutes require notice by advertisement, and in some states power-of-sale foreclosure is known as *foreclosure by advertisement.* To be effective, notice must comply with directions included as part of the power or by a controlling statute. Minor variations, omissions or inaccuracies are not fatal to the sale as long as the notice is not ambiguous or misleading.

• CASE BRIEF •

Pioneer Federal Savings and Loan (Pioneer) had its only office in the City of Hopewell. The city serviced a large rural population and was the only city of consequence in the area. Pioneer initiated foreclosure proceedings under a power of sale by advertising in the *Hopewell News.* State statute required advertisement over four successive weeks.

The first notice omitted the name of the city where the sale was to be held. The omission was discovered, and the next three notices identified Hopewell as the place of sale. After the sale, heirs of the mortgagor challenged its validity on the grounds of defective notice.

In overruling this challenge, the Virginia appellate court stated: "From the language in the first advertisement one could not have been misled as to the place of sale. There was substantial compliance with the requirement...and the omission...did not invalidate the notice and sale thereunder." *Bailey v. Pioneer Federal Savings and Loan Association, 210 Va. 558, 172 S.E.2d 730 (1970).*

A number of states allow the mortgagor to waive the notice requirement. Waiver must usually be both express and in writing. A few jurisdictions, however, require personal notice.

Adequacy of Selling Price

Inadequacy of selling price alone is not grounds for overturning a foreclosure sale. This rule applies to sales that are the result of recession or some other adverse economic condition. Risks of this nature are borne by the parties as an incident of the mortgage agreement. Courts in the United States do not ordinarily protect a party to a contract from a poor bargain or one that results in hardship. The agreement that the parties make is the one the courts will try to enforce as long as the sale is conducted fairly.

• CASE BRIEF •

Roy Massey held a second mortgage on property owned by National Homeowners. His mortgage contained a power of sale. When National Homeowners defaulted, Massey advertised a foreclosure sale. The advertisement did not indicate that buyers could purchase subject to a sizable first mortgage, which was not in default.

Mrs. Massey, Roy's wife, obtained the property at the sale for $7,090. The property had an appraised value of almost $75,000. Upon a later motion to overturn the sale, a trial court held the transaction null and void. Its holding was based upon the inadequacy of the price and insufficient information published in the advertisement. *Massey v. National Homeowners Sales Serv. Corp., 225 Ga. 93, 165 S.E.2d 854 (1969).*

The "inadequacy rule" does not apply when the inadequacy is so gross that it shocks the conscience of the court. Inadequacy of selling price is also an important factor if connected with other circumstances such as fraud, misrepresentation or mistake.

STRICT FORECLOSURE

A judicial procedure that, by terminating the mortgagor's equity of redemption, gives the mortgagee absolute title to mortgaged real estate without a sale of the property.

Foreclosures by judicial action and by power of sale are identified with the lien theory of mortgages, which establishes a mortgagee's right to have the property sold following default. The proceeds of the sale are used to pay the debt and expenses of the sale. If a balance remains, it is turned over to the mortgagor. The mortgagee does not acquire title to the property unless the mortgagee is the purchaser at the foreclosure sale.

At common law the mortgagee had a more extensive right. The mortgage gave the mortgagee a conditional or defeasible title to the security. If the debt was paid when due, the mortgagor reacquired title; if the debt was not paid, the mortgagee acquired absolute title. Even at this point, however, the mortgagee's title was not quite absolute. The mortgagor retained an equitable right of redemption—the right to redeem the property by paying the debt. This right was discussed in Chapter 20.

The mortgagee had difficulty selling or leasing the property while the right of redemption existed because the property could be reacquired by the mortgagor merely by paying the outstanding debt. In order to perfect the title so that he or she could make good use of the property, the mortgagee had to eliminate the equitable right of redemption. This was done by asking the court to foreclose the mortgagor's right to redeem in an action known as *strict foreclosure.*

Strict foreclosure is no longer common in the United States except in two or three states; a majority of states prohibit its use. A few states expressly prohibit it by statute; others accomplish the prohibition by requiring that the security be sold to compensate the creditor. The principal reason for this decline is that often strict foreclosure severely penalizes the mortgagor. At the same time, the mortgagee has the potential for windfall profit, as indicated by the following example.

CASE EXAMPLE

Jason Bolder executed a mortgage in favor of Marcia Letski on property with a market value of $55,000. The mortgage was to secure Letski's advance of $25,000, which Bolder used to finance a travel agency. The agency prospered at first, and the debt was reduced to $22,000.

When a general recession occurred, Bolder's business suffered, and he defaulted on the debt. Were strict foreclosure available, Letski could obtain title to the property. Assuming the market value was still $55,000, she would now have property worth $33,000 more than the debt.

Strict foreclosure is illogical in lien theory jurisdictions because the mortgagee never had title that was subject to an equitable right of redemption. Although mortgagors in these states often do have a statutory right to redeem after a foreclosure sale, these rights are created by statute and are terminated automatically after a statutory period. Strict foreclosure has been used in some lien theory states to eliminate the interest of a party omitted in a foreclosure action. In these cases the purchaser at the foreclosure sale has acquired title. Upon discovery of a junior claim unintentionally omitted, the purchaser may petition the court to eliminate the claimant's right to redeem.

Foreclosure by Entry and Possession

Foreclosure that terminates the mortgagor's equity of redemption through the mortgagee's peacefully obtaining possession of the security and occupying it for a stated period.

A variation of strict foreclosure exists in the New England states of Maine, Massachusetts, New Hampshire and Rhode Island. In these states the mortgagee may institute foreclosure by taking possession of the security upon default. When the mortgagee takes possession under the proper conditions, the mortgagor is allowed a specific period of time to redeem the property. If the mortgagor does not redeem, title is vested in the mortgagee. Like strict foreclosure, foreclosure by entry and possession does not require a sale of the property. The objective of the procedure is to clear the mortgagee's title by giving the mortgagor an opportunity to assert his or her equity of redemption. If the mortgagor does not take this opportunity, the equity terminates.

Foreclosure by entry and possession is a statutory remedy and varies to some extent in each of the states that use it. Four general requirements are that the mortgagee obtain possession peacefully, possession be for the purpose of foreclosure, notice of the mortgagee's intent be publicized and the mortgagee remain in possession for the statutory period, which varies from one to three years.

Appropriate methods of obtaining peaceful possession include:

- Writ of possession based upon a judgment
- Consent of the mortgagor
- Entry witnessed by two disinterested parties who confirm actual possession.

Publication of possession can be by advertising or by recording the time of obtaining possession with the appropriate local authority such as the register of deeds. Actual notice to the mortgagor or junior lienholders is not required. The purpose of requiring publication is to alert junior lienholders of the action so that they may protect their interests.

OTHER REMEDIES

Judicial and power-of-sale foreclosures are not the only methods of realizing upon the security. Other steps can be taken when a loan is in default. Sometimes the mortgagee will accept a deed instead of foreclosing. When the property is income-producing, a receiver may be appointed.

Deed in Lieu of Foreclosure

A procedure in which the mortgagor conveys the mortgaged real estate to the mortgagee, who promises in return not to foreclose or sue on the underlying debt.

CASE EXAMPLE

As security for a $50,000 loan, Naomi Tilson executed a mortgage to the Pike County National Bank. After making two payments on the loan, she defaulted. At the time of her default the market value of the property was slightly in excess of $50,000. Because Naomi and her family were valued customers, the bank offered to accept a deed to the property instead of foreclosing. After discussing the consequences of this action with her attorney, Naomi agreed to convey the property to the bank.

The use of a deed in lieu of foreclosure is a common practice in the United States. In conveying to the mortgagee, the mortgagor surrenders any rights to a foreclosure sale and to redeem the property. In return, the mortgagee cancels the underlying debt and becomes the owner of the real estate.

Potentially, the transaction can benefit the mortgagor in a number of ways. For example, Naomi Tilson's credit rating would be protected. The conveyance would be carried out in the same manner as any sale, and adverse publicity that might accompany foreclosure would not exist. Economically, she could anticipate three important benefits. First, any obligation for taxes and assessments would terminate. Foreclosure costs would also be saved. Probably most important of all, she would not be responsible for any deficiency.

The deed in lieu of foreclosure is also advantageous to the mortgagee. Long delays usually associated with foreclosure by judicial sale are avoided. In addition, the mortgagee escapes the poor public relations that are often the result of resorting to a judicial sale. On the other hand, the mortgagee faces the problem of disposing of the security. Until the property is sold, the mortgagee has to maintain it, and expenses of the sale must be borne by the mortgagee because it now owns the real estate.

A number of legal problems associated with the practice are of special concern to the mortgagee. First, the mortgagee must completely cancel the debt. If it does not, the courts treat the deed in lieu of foreclosure as a substitute for the original mortgage. The mortgagor under these conditions retains any redemption rights that exist. On the other hand, once the debt is canceled, the mortgagee loses the right to a deficiency judgment. If the market value of the property in the previous example were to be less than $50,000, the mortgagee would suffer the loss.

A second important legal consideration involves junior liens on the property. The purchaser at a foreclosure sale takes title free of such liens, but a mortgagee who acquires title to real estate by deed in lieu of foreclosure is subject to these interests. If Naomi Tilson had not paid for improvements on the property and a mechanic's lien existed, the Pike County National Bank's deed would be subject to that lien. A deed in lieu of foreclosure is also subject to attack under the Bankruptcy Act. Were Naomi to file for bankruptcy within a period of, say, 90 days after delivery of the deed to the bank, the bank could be treated as a preferred creditor. The deed would be set aside as a preferential transfer.

Another legal problem exists in some states where the courts have regarded the deed in lieu of foreclosure with suspicion. As a consequence, courts have had a tendency to consider the deed not as a conveyance but as additional security unless the transaction is clearly free from coercion. In other states the courts require proof of the absence of fraud when the value of the property exceeds the debt.

Successful legal challenges sometimes have been launched against a mortgagee on grounds that it supplied no consideration for the mortgagor's conveyance of its redemption right. The rationale underlying this claim is that the mortgagee taking a deed in lieu of foreclosure supplies nothing additional to the mortgagor. The question of consideration, however, is probably not a major concern to the mortgagee as long as no gross disparity exists between the amount of the debt and the value of the security. If the debt is small and the property valuable, the mortagee's action might be challenged as unfair.

Receivership

The appointment by a court of a disinterested party to manage or operate mortgaged property during foreclosure.

CASE EXAMPLE

In addition to borrowing from the Pike County National Bank, Naomi Tilson had borrowed $90,000 from her uncle. She used the funds to purchase a six-unit rental property. As security Naomi executed a mortgage in her uncle's favor. When Naomi defaulted on the loan, her uncle applied to the court for a receiver to manage the property and collect the rents.

The action taken by Naomi's uncle was not unusual. Most jurisdictions recognize the right of a mortgagee to have a receiver appointed when the mortgagor has defaulted. In many instances the receiver is appointed to take charge of the property for the purpose of collecting rents. Receivers are, in addition, frequently appointed to carry on a business conducted on the mortgaged premises. The purpose of a receivership is to apply the rents and profits to payment of the debt and to preserve the security while foreclosure is pending.

The mortgagee's right to request a receiver is inherent in a foreclosure. This right stems from the nature of the mortgage. Both title and lien theory states recognize the mortgagor's right to possession until default. On the other hand, the parties have agreed that once in default the security may be foreclosed to pay the debt. The problem is that foreclosure takes time. During this time courts accept as just the idea that income from the property should be available to pay the debt if needed. If the security is adequate, the mortgagee does not need this additional protection. In such a case the court will deny a motion to appoint a receiver. This does not prohibit the mortgagee from taking possession based upon some other right; it only means that the court considers a judicially supervised receiver unnecessary. Receivership then is an interim measure, not an end in itself, and is not available in all foreclosures.

A few states are critical of the concept of receivership. In these states receiverships are allowed only in extraordinary cases. Courts in some lien theory states have accepted the argument that a receivership is inconsistent with the mortgage as a lien. They rationalize that the mortgagor has the right to possession until the foreclosure sale. In a limited number of title theory states, courts have exhibited a similar reluctance to appoint receivers. In these states the argument is exactly the opposite of that used in the lien theory states. Title theory courts consider that the mortgagee has title and as a result the right to take possession of the security upon default. Because of this, the mortgagee does not need a court-appointed third party to protect its interests. In spite of this reluctance, the courts in these states—as in all others —will generally appoint a receiver (1) when the security is inadequate (some also require the mortgagor to be insolvent) and (2) when waste is being committed.

CASE EXAMPLE

Naomi Tilson answered her uncle's application for appointment of a receiver by showing the following facts:

1. The apartment had a market value of $180,000.
2. She had invested $90,000 of her own funds in the acquisition.
3. The apartment was being run profitably.
4. The default was the result of a judgment against her in a personal injury action. Settlement of this judgment had tied up her funds.

The court would probably refuse to appoint the receiver because the uncle's security was adequate.

The duties of a receiver are complex and its powers extensive. A receiver may incur tort liability for personal injury or property damage in operating mortgaged premises. The receiver may be unable to operate the property profitably. If a deficit occurs, the receiver may become personally liable for the deficit unless the court and mortgagee are kept aware of economic problems. A receiver has the power to disaffirm all leases made after the mortgage. The tenant, however, cannot escape liability because a receiver is appointed since the lease is enforceable unless the receiver elects to terminate. In addition, the receiver has the option of evicting the tenant unless the tenant will sign a more favorable lease. A receiver is entitled to all rents and profits whether the lease was made prior to the mortgage or after. If the mortgage is junior to the lease, the lease cannot be terminated. It is effective against the receiver just as it would be against a purchaser at a foreclosure sale. A receiver is required to account for all funds that come into its possession, is entitled to compensation as set by court in some states or by statute in others, and must faithfully perform its duties as would any fiduciary.

SUMMARY

Foreclosure is the legal means by which a lender recovers property when a borrower fails to make payments on a mortgage loan. The most commonly used form is judicial foreclosure, ordered by the court. Another type is based on a power of sale granted in the mortgage. Strict foreclosure is the third type.

A buyer who fails to pay according to the terms of the mortgage agreement or who fails to pay taxes or live up to other obligations of the agreement is said to be in default. In addition, a popular provision of recent mortgages is the due-on-sale clause, which defines sale of the premises as a default.

An important legal concept in foreclosure is the equity of redemption—the defaulting buyer's right to redeem property before foreclosure. In addition, some states provide the right to redeem after foreclosure. Statutes governing these rights vary from state to state.

In judicial foreclosure the court orders real estate sold to enforce the mortgagee's contractual rights. It is the most common type of foreclosure. One reason for this is that the procedure is closely regulated by the court. Because the requirements of due process apply to foreclosures, all parties must be notified and must have an opportunity to defend. As foreclosure actions are governed by state law, disparities exist in the statutes of limitations (the time period during which foreclosure action may be taken), in the defenses that are allowed and in the methods by which the property can be sold. In the event that the sale price is too low to cover the mortgage debt, most states allow the mortgagee to collect the balance due from the mortgagor by a deficiency judgment.

Some states allow foreclosures based on a power of sale granted in the mortgage document. In this form the mortgagor has the right to sell the property without resorting to judicial foreclosure. The practice is common in only about one-third of the states. Because it is not court-supervised, it is not as acceptable to many people as is judicial foreclosure. For one thing, the purchaser's title may be subject to attack. For another, the bargaining power of the mortgagor is weak, and the price of the property in this forced sale may be inadequate. Nevertheless, statutes in some states do protect the mortgagor's interest by requiring that adequate notice be given and by providing remedies in case of an obviously low sale price.

Strict foreclosure is used in only a few states. In this procedure the mortgagor's equity of redemption is terminated; the mortgagee acquires absolute title to the property in case of default. The primary reason for the decline of this method is the imbalance that exists for the parties; that is, the mortgagor is severely penalized, whereas the mortgagee has the opportunity for windfall profits.

Other procedures and remedies for foreclosure are used throughout the states; the real estate professional should be aware of local laws and practices.

REVIEW AND DISCUSSION QUESTIONS

1. Explain why having an acceleration clause in a mortgage is important to the mortgagee.
2. Indicate how each of the following protects the mortgagor: (a) equity of redemption, (b) statutory right of redemption, (c) statute of limitations.
3. Compare and contrast power of sale and judicial foreclosure.
4. (a) What is strict foreclosure? (b) Why have most states eliminated it?
5. Under what circumstances might both mortgagor and mortgagee benefit from a deed in lieu of foreclosure?
6. Describe the conditions that might induce a court to appoint a receiver when a mortgage debt is in default.
7. What is a deficiency judgment?

CASE PROBLEMS

1. Drombeck held a first mortgage on property owned by Union Wrecking Company (Union). The mortgage was recorded. When Union defaulted in June 1961, Drombeck commenced foreclosure proceedings. In October 1961 National Acceptance lent money to Union and took back a mortgage, which was immediately recorded. In September 1963 the Drombecks purchased the property at a judicial sale pursuant to a decree in a foreclosure action. National Acceptance was not joined as a party to that action, although Drombeck knew of its mortgage. What rights, if any, does National have in the real estate? Discuss. *National Acceptance Co. of America v. Mardigian*, 259 F. Supp. 612 (E.D. Mich. S.D. 1966).
2. Lakeview Savings and Loan held a mortgage on property owned by Fisher. The mortgage secured a note of $40,000. Fisher defaulted and offered Lakeview a deed in lieu of foreclosure. Lakeview took the deed and shortly thereafter sold the property

for $38,000. Lakeview then sued Fisher for $2,000. Would Lakeview be successful? Discuss.

3. Olaska purchased property at a foreclosure sale for $108,000. Shortly before the sale a large corporation had decided to build a plant in the area. This was not known to Olaska or to the public. Within a few days of Olaska's purchase, the company purchased the property from her for $200,000. The former owner sued to set the sale aside on grounds that the foreclosure price was inadequate. Would the owner be successful? Discuss.

4. Rifai sold a parcel of real estate to Morton. Morton paid part of the purchase price in cash, assumed an existing mortgage and executed a promissory note for the balance of the price. The promissory note was secured by a second mortgage. Thereafter experiencing financial difficulties, Morton reconveyed the property to Rifai. The parties made no agreement as to the effect of the reconveyance. A short time later Rifai conveyed the property to a third party in return for an assumption of the mortgage. Rifai then sued Morton for the balance owed on the note. Would Rifai be successful? Discuss. *Morton v. Rifai*, 339 So.2d 707 (Fla. 1976).

5. Hemmerle borrowed money to build houses on several lots that he owned. To guarantee payment of the loan, he signed several notes and executed mortgages on each lot in favor of First Federal Savings. The mortgages required First Federal to advance funds as construction progressed.

   Before the homes were completed and all funds advanced, Hemmerle defaulted. First Federal brought an action to foreclose. The court ordered a foreclosure sale with Hemmerle's debt being the full amount of the notes. Hemmerle argued that the judgment against him should be only for the amount disbursed. (a) What argument can you make for Hemmerle? (b) What argument can you make for the bank? (c) Who would win? *Hemmmerle v. First Federal Savings*, 338 So.2d 82 (Fla. 1976).

23
Closing the Real Estate Transaction

CLOSING OR SETTLEMENT

The final stage of the real estate purchase transaction, when the deed and the purchase money are exchanged.

After the buyer and the seller sign a real estate purchase contract, they need time to prepare for the closing. The buyer ordinarily must search for financing, while the seller needs time to prepare evidence of title. Other documents need preparation as directed by the purchase contract, laws and local customs. There is a deed to be drawn, inspection certificates to be obtained, expenses and income to be apportioned, and other preparatory matters to be completed. The interval between the signing and the closing date is intended to provide the necessary time to accomplish these matters.

The date of closing is normally specified in the contract. The date may be as early as two weeks from the date of the contract or as long as two months and occasionally even longer. One difficulty with a long interval is that lending institutions normally do not extend a loan commitment for more than 30 days without some additional cost to the borrower.

A postponement of the closing date does not result in a breach of the purchase contract as long as the adjournment is reasonable. On the other hand, if the contract specifies that "time is of the essence," even a one-day postponement could be considered a breach for which the law would afford a remedy to the innocent party.

When the contract does not provide for a closing date, a reasonable time is implied. Since the purpose of the interval is to provide the necessary time to accomplish certain aims, a reasonable time would be a period within which these aims could reasonably be accomplished.

The rights and obligations of the parties are defined by the contract. To a large extent the contract governs the closing format. Local custom, to the extent that it does not contradict contractual provisions, also shapes the closing. Some localities, for example, customarily use the *escrow closing*, wherein the deed and purchase price are delivered to a third party, who is directed to close the transaction outside the presence of the parties. The escrow closing is the subject of the next chapter. In other jurisdictions the parties meet each other face to face at the closing. This conference type of closing is the subject of this chapter.

The object of the closing is to complete the transaction so that the purchaser is vested with title to the realty and the seller receives the purchase price. Various persons who may be responsible for the closing proceedings (other than the buyer and seller) include the real estate broker, attorney and settlement clerk.

Broker

The broker has an economic interest in the closing; at this stage the real estate commission is paid by the broker's principal, who is normally the seller. For that reason the broker usually participates in the closing preparation and is present at the closing. State law varies concerning the broker's permissible role in the closing. Some states permit the broker actually to draw up legal documents, whereas other states relegate the broker to a more passive role. Often the broker facilitates the closing by communicating with the lending institution, the purchaser, seller and/or their representatives on last-minute details. The broker may hand-deliver closing documents to the parties or their legal representatives to minimize the risk of a breakdown in the critical last hours before closing. The broker may be responsible for reminding the parties what documents they need to bring to the closing. To the extent permitted by local law, the broker may even assist in the computation of prorations and the preparation of closing statements. In absence of an attorney representing the seller, the broker will explain to the seller the closing process as it unravels, thus reducing anxiety and confusion at the closing.

Attorney

The attorney's role at the closing varies, depending upon state law, the type of closing and local custom. Although not every real estate closing involves attorney representation, when it does occur, purchasers are more apt to be represented than sellers. Perhaps this is because it is legally more difficult to ascertain whether a purchaser has received good marketable title to the real estate than whether the seller has received the full purchase price prescribed by the contract. In other words, the lay seller is in a better position to ensure receipt of the full purchase price than the lay buyer is to ensure receipt of marketable title to the real estate.

At the ordinary closing the attorney's role is routine, being confined to explaining the various documents to the client. Most of the attorney's preparation for the closing—examination of documents such as the deed, abstract or title insurance policy, mortgage, mortgage note and closing statements—has occurred in advance. If the attorney has properly prepared in advance, the routine closing is normally smooth and may seem anticlimactic. An attorney has a more important role, however, in the rare closing where a difficult legal problem arises. Since no one can determine beforehand whether the closing will present an extraordinary problem, it is best for all parties to be represented by counsel. When parties are represented by attorneys, closings are likely to be smoother and less confusing because each party generally has confidence in his or her legal representative.

The seller is responsible for delivering a deed in conformity with the contract. For this reason the seller must hire an attorney for the preparation of the deed or permit the lending institution's attorney to prepare it, in which event the fee will be charged to the seller. The purchaser's attorney will examine the deed to ensure that the description of the property is accurate and that compliance with the necessary formalities for execution of the deed has occurred. The seller may be responsible, pursuant to the terms of the contract, for producing an abstract showing the history of the transactions that relate to the title of the property. An abstract may be prepared by the seller's attorney; in some jurisdictions professional abstractors who are not attorneys may perform this service. Based upon the abstract, the buyer's attorney may be called upon to provide a certificate or letter of opinion regarding the marketability of the title. An attorney who negligently renders a wrong opinion to the buyer will be liable for damages. Of course the buyer's attorney will not be liable for the inaccurate compilation of an abstract prepared by another attorney or abstractor. The attorney or abstractor who prepared the abstract is responsible to any damaged party for negligent preparation.

Settlement Clerk

The person who is designated to coordinate the exchange of documents at the closing.

The settlement clerk is responsible for ensuring that all documents are properly signed and delivered to the appropriate party. The settlement clerk may be an attorney, real estate broker, employee of the lending institution or title insurance company or any other designated person. The deed and other documents may require acknowledgment before a notary. Hence, it is advisable that the settlement clerk be a notary public. Otherwise, a notary public should be present.

At the closing, a lot of paper changes hands. The closing is routine for the settlement clerk, who has undoubtedly performed numerous closings; for the buyers and sellers, however, it may be bewildering. Unless the settlement clerk is sensitive to that fact, the closing may be less than successful. Each document and transaction should be explained to the parties, either by the clerk or by the attorney representing the client. Most problems that emerge at the closing can be remedied by thoughtfulness and a calm spirit.

PREPARATION FOR CLOSING

Preparation is the key to a successful real estate closing. Both the buyer and the seller need to take care of certain items preliminary to the closing. Failure to do so may result in a breakdown at the closing. The laws and customs that govern the buyer's and seller's conduct in preparation for closing do not vary greatly from state to state.

Buyer's Preparation

The buyer's preparation involves obtaining financing, examining the title and leases, securing hazard insurance, calculating the amount needed at closing, inspecting the premises and securing corporate documentation, when necessary.

Obtaining Financing

The buyer ordinarily lacks the available cash to pay for the property and must therefore search for a loan. The prudent purchaser selects a lending institution on the basis of the best buy available, comparing interest rates and other charges. A difference of a half of a percentage interest rate may be very substantial over the life of the loan. The real estate contract is usually contingent upon the buyer obtaining a loan. If, after exercising good faith, the buyer is unable to obtain the necessary financing, then the parties are discharged from any further obligations under the contract. A lending institution requires an application, a credit check and an appraisal before it will approve a loan. Various federal laws related to the loan, discussed later in this chapter, place certain obligations upon the lender.

The lending institution that loans money to the buyer will require the buyer to sign a note promising repayment, plus a mortgage of the property, which secures repayment by giving the lender an interest in the property. At the closing the lending institution will make sure that these instruments are signed by the buyer before disbursing the proceeds from the loan.

Examining Title

The contract usually calls for the seller to provide evidence of title in the form of an abstract, certificate of title or title insurance. The buyer should insist on the evidence of title prior to closing so that an attorney can scrutinize the documents to ensure their reliability. An abstract should be up to date and contain no gaps in the chain of title. A certificate of title should be signed by a reputable attorney. Title insurance policies should be checked to ascertain what encumbrances, if any, are excluded from protection. These exclusions may draw attention to title problems.

The purchaser is entitled to a *marketable title* in absence of a provision in the contract to the contrary. Marketable title is one for which a reasonable, prudent purchaser would be willing to accept and pay fair value. A marketable title is free from objections or encumbrances that would significantly interrupt the owner's peaceful enjoyment and control of the land or impair its economic value. In order to be marketable, it is not necessary that the title be free from every possible encumbrance or suspicion of encumbrance. It need only be free of a reasonable possibility of contentious litigation. Nobody wants to purchase a lawsuit, and, indeed, the law will not require a person to do so.

A defect that renders a title unmarketable may be in the chain of title (see Chapter 7). It may be discovered, for example, in tracing the title of a parcel of land, that the spouse of a grantor failed to sign the deed releasing dower or other spousal rights. Or probate records may reveal that a previous grantor was incompetent at the time of transfer. A break in the chain of title may result from an inability to find a record of a previous owner ever having conveyed the property to a grantee.

The title may be rendered unmarketable because of an encumbrance on the property. An encumbrance is a charge upon realty that impairs the use of the land, depreciates its value or impedes its transfer. Liens, mortgages, easements, leases, tenancies, covenants, significant encroachments and building restrictions are examples of encumbrances. Slight encumbrances that do not interfere with the use and enjoyment of the premises do not render a title unmarketable. A two-inch encroachment over a setback line is an example of a slight encroachment. Zoning and building code regulations do not render a title unmarketable. Nevertheless, a *violation* of either is deemed an encumbrance that renders the title unmarketable.

When the evidence of title is examined by the purchaser before closing, objections may be raised with the seller to be remedied before closing. If no time limitation is stated within the contract, then the seller is entitled to a reasonable time to cure any defect. In some contracts the buyer possesses the specific right to cure the title and charge the cost to the seller. Under such a provision the buyer may cure a defect out of the proceeds of the purchase price. If the defects cannot be remedied, or are not remedied, the purchaser may refuse title and sue the seller for breach of the contract.

Purchase contracts commonly provide that the seller will convey a title free of all encumbrances except "deed restrictions and easements of record." The purchaser should not sign such a contract until he or she knows what restrictions and easements, if any, are of record and is satisfied that they are immaterial. Otherwise the purchaser may find out too late that the encumbrances excepted are of such a nature as to render the property valueless.

If the contract does not require the seller to provide evidence of title, the purchaser will undoubtedly desire to obtain such evidence. Obtaining that assurance before the closing is always better than winding up in a costly suit because of title defects discovered later.

Examining Leases

The contract may provide that the purchaser takes the property subject to tenants' rights: tenants are living on the premises, and the purchaser is required to honor their leases. Of course, the purchaser sould examine the leases prior to signing the contract or require that the details of the leases be specified in the contract.

The purchaser should make sure that the seller prepares an assignment of the leases in the purchaser's favor and a letter notifying the tenants of the new ownership. At closing the seller can sign the assignment and the tenants' letter, which can be delivered to the tenants along with a notice of where to send future rental payments.

Securing Hazard Insurance

It is important for the purchaser to secure hazard coverage on the property to take effect on the day of closing. In fact, the mortgagee requires proof of coverage at the closing and will specify what type of evidence of coverage the purchaser needs to supply. Some mortgagees desire a copy of the policy; others require only a letter or binder evidencing coverage. Most mortgage instruments include a clause requiring the mortgagor to keep the premises insured at an amount at least equal to the balance due on the mortgage. Failure to do so constitutes a default. This failure is usually discovered when the insurance carrier notifies the mortgagee of a discontinuance of insurance coverage.

Calculating Amount Needed at Closing

The seller is entitled to the purchase price at closing, plus or minus any appropriate adjustments for apportionment of taxes, insurance and other apportionable expenses. The purchaser usually pays closing costs, which include the loan origination fee, appraisal charges, the credit report fee and other charges connected with the loan. Other miscellaneous fees for surveys, preparation of documents, conveyance taxes and recording costs may be payable by the purchaser at closing. In addition, the lending institution may require the purchaser to deposit an amount for taxes and insurance into an escrow account. Normally, the lending institution collects one check from the purchaser and then writes its own checks for payments to the seller, seller's mortgagee, seller's broker and any other parties entitled to funds. Determining the amount that the purchaser needs to bring to the closing necessitates a calculation that takes all these factors into consideration. This calculation is considered later in this chapter. The lender should determine the amount in advance and communicate it to the purchaser so he or she may have time to obtain the money needed. If a lending institution is not involved, either the real estate agent or the attorney for the purchaser can calculate the amount. In any event, the purchaser needs to review the amounts and calculations and be satisfied that they are accurate.

The purchaser needs to know what type of payment is acceptable; cashier's check, certified check or money order is the customary form of payment. When the purchaser is a trusted customer of the financial institution handling the closing, the institution will often accept a personal check drawn on that institution and then issue its own check to the seller.

Inspecting Premises

The real estate contract may afford the purchaser the right to inspect the premises prior to the closing. If so, the purchaser should arrange for an inspection to ensure that the condition of the premises is as stated in the contract and that the seller has made all repairs agreed upon. In addition, the premises should be searched for zoning and building code violations, potential mechanic's liens or any other encumbrances. Most buyers prefer the inspection to be near the closing date. If an inspection that is too near the closing date reveals objectionable defects, however, there may not be sufficient time before closing for the seller to remedy the problems. In absence of specific language in the contract granting the buyer the right to inspect, the buyer enjoys no such right. However, as a practical matter, the seller would not normally deny the buyer a preclosing inspection.

The purchaser may desire a survey, or the contract may call for it. A surveyor or an engineer must be contracted to perform the task. Sometimes surveys raise questions concerning encumbrances.

Securing Corporate Documentation

Corporations that purchase real estate must obtain authority to purchase from their board of directors or shareholders, depending on state law and the corporation's charter. At the closing the corporate purchaser should be prepared to present the corporate charter and the proper minutes or resolution authorizing the purchase. In addition, if the corporation is borrowing money to make the purchase, the mortgagee requires similar evidence of authorization to extend the loan.

Seller's Preparation

The seller's preparation involves obtaining evidence of title, preparing the deed, removing encumbrances, gathering utility bills and tax receipts, bringing sundry certificates and securing corporate documentation, when necessary.

Obtaining Evidence of Title

The contract may require the seller to supply the buyer with the evidence of title in the form of an abstract or title insurance. The seller may have received an abstract on the property from the previous seller. In such event the seller must call upon an attorney or abstractor to update it. If the contract calls for title insurance, then the seller must select a title insurance company from which to purchase a policy.

Preparing Deed

In most states the preparation of the deed is the seller's obligation. Even if the seller is not represented by an attorney at the closing, the seller must hire an attorney or authorize someone else to employ an attorney to draw the deed. The basic content of the deed is prescribed by the purchase contract, state law and local custom. Normally, the deed is signed at the closing. In the event the seller or anyone else who must sign the deed cannot be present at the closing, it must be properly executed beforehand.

Removing Encumbrances

The title search or inspection of the premises may reveal objectionable liens or other encumbrances not excepted in the contract, such as unrecorded easements, encroachments or building code violations. Unless these encumbrances are removed, the closing is in danger of breaking down. The seller will have an opportunity to remove any encumbrances brought to his or her attention. In the event the seller removes an encumbrance prior to closing, evidence of this removal should be produced at closing. The seller should obtain satisfaction of judgments, affidavits evidencing payment to laborers or any other appropriate documents evidencing removal of the encumbance. Sometimes the encumbrance is removed at closing when the seller deposits an amount of money necessary to discharge the encumbrance or authorizes a deduction for that purpose from the proceeds of the sale.

• CASE BRIEF •

Lone Star Development Corporation entered into a contract with Michael Miller and David Cross to sell certain realty in Pueblo County, Colorado, for $588,000. One thousand dollars was paid at the time of the agreement, and the remaining amount was to be paid at the closing on September 16, at which time Lone Star was to deliver a warranty deed and furnish a marketable title. There was an unpaid lien on the property in the amount of $479,756.71, of which all parties were aware. Lone Star intended to satisfy the lien out of the proceeds of the purchase price. Miller and Cross refused to tender the purchase price, maintaining that the unsatisfied lien rendered the title to the property unmarketable. Lone Star sued Miller and Cross for damages for breach of contract. The court held in favor of Lone Star and said that "a lien on real property which is going to be paid off from the proceeds of the sale of the property is not to be regarded as failure or inability to furnish a marketable title." *Lone Star Development Corp. v. Miller, 564 F.2d 921 (10th Cir. 1977).*

The property may be encumbered by an existing mortgage, which fact will be revealed by a search of the title. The exact amount due on the mortgage as of the date of closing must be ascertained so that it can be satisfied out of the purchase price at closing. The seller should secure a statement from the mortgagee listing the outstanding balance due as of that date and the daily interest, in the event the payment is received later than the closing date. The lending institution handling the closing often takes care of securing this statement. The statement is produced at closing; the appropriate amount is deducted from the purchase price and sent to the seller's mortgagee.

Sometimes objections to title may be cured by the use of a quitclaim deed. A quitclaim deed has the effect of conveying to the grantee any interest the grantor has in the property. For example, a title search may reveal that a prior conveyance in the seller's chain of title was the subject of an incorrect legal description, which created a title defect. The defect can be cured by the previous grantor's signing a quitclaim deed in favor of the seller with the correct description.

A purchaser may question the seller's competency to deliver a deed at closing on the basis of age or mental capacity. Sometimes the purchaser desires additional assurance that the seller is not married or that no work has been performed or supplies have been furnished on the property that might become the subject of a mechanic's lien. Sworn statements verifying facts that satisfy the objections, as in the affidavit shown in Figure 23.1, are normally sufficient.

Gathering Utility Bills

The seller should gather and bring to the closing if requested, unpaid water, sewage and other utility bills and receipts. Water and sewage charges are usually minimal, but they often cause the biggest problem and concern. Water companies read the water meter at intervals, and the exact amount owing at date of closing may be difficult to ascertain. Some homeowners elect to pay a standard monthly charge that is adjusted at the end of the year, making it difficult to determine the accrued charges or credits.

Some jurisdictions permit the imposition of a lien upon property for unpaid water or sewer charges. Others treat them as a personal debt that does not run with the property, in which case judgment against the debtor would not encumber the property. Nonetheless, water companies do have the power to cut off one of life's necessities, and no new homeowner wants to litigate this issue.

Normally, the water companies are cooperative, and the seller can arrange for a meter reading at or near closing. Based upon an experience factor, the parties may agree to an amount at closing. In such a case the seller should produce prior bills so that an experience factor may be derived. If all else fails, a sufficient amount to cover the seller's water bill for the interval may be escrowed at closing. The same principles hold for gas, electric and phone service. The seller should coordinate the turnoff date for the utilities.

Providing Real Estate Tax Receipts

The contract usually calls for an apportionment of taxes as of the date of the closing. Some real property taxes are due twice a year. If the closing occurs on any date other than the dates taxes are payable, or if tax payments are for previous time periods, it is necessary to compute the portions of the tax chargeable to the seller and to the buyer. The seller should be prepared at the closing to produce any unpaid bills and receipts evidencing payment of taxes.

Bringing Sundry Certificates

The real estate purchase contract may require the seller to produce at closing a termite inspection certificate signed by a termite control inspector and certifying that the premises are free from wood-destroying insects and damage from those insects. The contract may additionally

State of Ohio
County of Hamilton

Rod Ross, being first duly sworn, on May 1, 1987, deposes and says that:

1.   He resides at 6415 Stover Avenue, in the City of Cincinnati, County of Hamilton, State of Ohio, and has resided at such place for approximately 10 years; he is a citizen of the United States, over the age of 18 years; he is the seller named in the contract of sale dated March 10, 1987, with Bert Haas as purchaser, and is the owner of the real property therein described.

2.   He has been such owner since on or about July, 1978, having acquired the same from Harry Blythe by deed; ever since his acquisition affiant has been in peaceable and undisturbed possession of such real property and neither his possession nor his title thereto has been disputed or denied by anyone.

3.   Affiant's predecessor in interest was in peaceful and undisturbed ownership and possession of the same real property for approximately 8 years prior to conveyance to affiant.

4.   No use, tenancy exchange or occupancy of such real property or any part thereof has been such as to give rise to any claim of title or interest by adverse possession.

5.   All taxes and assessments levied against the property have been paid when due, and such property is free and clear of any tax lien except for current taxes not yet due or delinquent.

6.   The real property is free of any encumbrance by mortgage, deed of trust, or otherwise except restrictive covenants specified in the deed.

7.   Plaintiff has not suffered any judgment or decree in any court and no judgment lien has ever attached against such property during affiant's ownership thereof, or during the ownership of affiant's predecessor in interest, to the best of affiant's knowledge and belief.

8.   No lien for unpaid income taxes has been filed or is outstanding against the property.

9.   No laborer has worked on the premises, nor has anyone supplied materials used on the premises who remains unpaid.

10.   Affiant is not married.

11.   In acquiring title to the real property described in the contract of sale, and in all subsequent transactions relating to the property, affiant has been designated and described only by the name subscribed hereto.

12.   The reason for making this affidavit is to induce the purchaser named in the contract of sale to accept title to the real property therein described and pay the agreed purchase price therefor; the affidavit is made with the intent and understanding that each statement contained herein shall be relied on.

Witness   Rod Ross
                                                 Seller

Affirmed to before me this 1st day of May, 1987

                                                 Notary Public

Figure 23.1: Affidavit of title

call for a certificate from a gas company stating that the gas lines are free from leakage. Heating, plumbing, electrical, sewage or any other system may be the subject of required certificates showing the systems to be in good working order and free from defects. The seller should be prepared to produce the appropriate certificates at closing.

Securing Corporate Documentation

The requirements of a corporate seller are similar to those imposed upon a corporate purchaser. The corporate seller may be required to show proof of authority to sell the property. This may necessitate producing the corporate charter, bylaws, minutes or appropriate resolutions.

ACTION AT THE CLOSING

The place of the closing is controlled by local custom. Commonly, the closing is conducted at the office of the lending institution where the purchaser has obtained financing to purchase the property. Other possible places of closing include an attorney's office or the office of the real estate broker, title insurance company or seller's mortgagee.

Both buyer and seller have responsibilities at the closing. These are discussed below.

Seller's Actions

At the closing the seller tenders the deed, provides evidence of title, if required, and delivers any necessary assignment of leases.

Tendering the Deed

The seller is obligated to tender the deed to the buyer or to the settlement clerk for delivery to the buyer. The buyer should carefully check the deed to make sure its specifications are in accord with the contract. The deed should be of the type the grantor agreed to give. Any encumbrances that are excepted in the deed should be compared to the contract to ascertain whether they are found there. The description should be double-checked against the description contained in the prior deed of conveyance or another reliable source. The names of the grantor(s) and grantee(s) should be checked for accuracy. Even a minor misspelling of a name may cause future problems that will take time and money to remedy. Particular attention should be directed to the form of the execution to ensure conformity with state law. If the state law requires, for example, that the grantor subscribe the deed by signing an alphabetical signature, then a mark of the grantor should not be accepted. If the state law requires that two witnesses sign in the presence of each other, a deed otherwise witnessed is unacceptable. If the state law requires acknowledgment before a notary, the notary seal and notary commission expiration date should be examined for authenticity.

Evidencing Title

The seller may be required to provide evidence of title in the form of an abstract or attorney's opinion, sometimes called a *certificate of title*. Judgments or other encumbrances can intervene between the date of the abstract or attorney's opinion and the date of closing. For that reason, it is most advisable for the purchaser to make a final search of the title down to the moment of closing. Such a search is not always practical. One way to protect the buyer who is unable to conduct the final search is to close in escrow, which is the subject of the next chapter. Under this closing procedure, the settlement clerk or other escrow agent holds the executed deed and the purchase price pending a final check of the title. Upon notification by the buyer or buyer's attorney that the title is in order, the deed is transferred to the buyer and the purchase price to the seller. Sometimes the seller will be required to give the buyer an affidavit of title (as shown earlier in Figure 23.1), which covers objections that might not appear in the title search.

Assigning Leases

In the event the property is sold subject to a lease, the seller should deliver a proper assignment of the lease to the buyer. In addition, the seller should deliver to the buyer any security deposited by the tenants along with letters to tenants notifying them of the sale and advising them to pay future rentals to the purchaser.

Purchaser's Actions

The buyer's responsibilities at the closing include tendering the purchase price and closing the loan extended by the lender.

Tendering Purchase Price

The purchaser is obligated to tender the purchase price to the seller. Normally, in absence of an excusal by the seller, the purchase price must be produced and offered to the seller. It is normally not a sufficient tender for the purchaser to appear at the closing and maintain that he or she has access to the purchase money elsewhere. The purchaser must actually make a show of the money with the intent to deliver it to the seller. Of course, this is not necesary if the tender would be futile—for example, should the seller not appear at the closing.

Payment is usually made by some form of check—usually a cashier's or certified check. However, whatever medium the contract calls for must be honored.

• CASE BRIEF •

Benjamin Chertok entered into a contract to purchase realty from Aroosiag Kassabian. Chertok made a deposit and agreed to pay the remainder in cash at the closing. At closing Chertok tendered a third person's certified check to Kassabian. Kassabian requested that he cash the check, and Chertok refused. After Kassabian refused to tender the deed, Chertok sought a return of his deposit. The court held that Chertok's tender was not the equivalent of payment in cash, and consequently he was in breach and not entitled to a return of his deposit. *Chertok v. Kassabian, 255 Mass. 265, 151 N.E. 108 (1926).*

Customarily, the seller gives the buyer a receipt for the purchase money. Even if the payment is in the form of a check (which ordinarily serves as a receipt upon cancellation), it is nonetheless a good practice for the buyer to be extra cautious by requiring a written receipt from the seller at the time the purchase price is tendered.

Mortgaging the Property

Lending institutions charge closing costs, normally computed as a percentage of the amount borrowed. Closing costs are charged by the lending institution to cover the cost of services performed in connection with the loan and for servicing the loan. Closing costs vary among lending institutions.

If the buyer is financing the purchase through a new loan, the lender supplies a mortgage and a note for the borrower to sign at closing. Any existing mortgage on the property will be satisfied out of the purchase price, and a satisfaction of mortgage signed by the seller's lender will be given to the settlement clerk for recording.

In reality, most closings involve two distinct but related transactions. First, the sale of the property is closed between the seller and the buyer, with the seller receiving the purchase price and the buyer the deed. Second, the loan extended by the lending institution is closed between the lender and the borrower (buyer), with the borrower receiving the proceeds of the loan (which are used to pay the seller) and the lender receiving a note and mortgage from the borrower securing repayment of the loan. After the closing the seller pays off the old mortgage and the seller's lending institution cancels the old mortgage. These transactions are illustrated in Figure 23.2.

REAL ESTATE SETTLEMENT PROCEDURES ACT (RESPA)

A federal law that requires lending institutions to disclose certain information to purchasers of residential real estate and prohibits those institutions from engaging in specified activities.

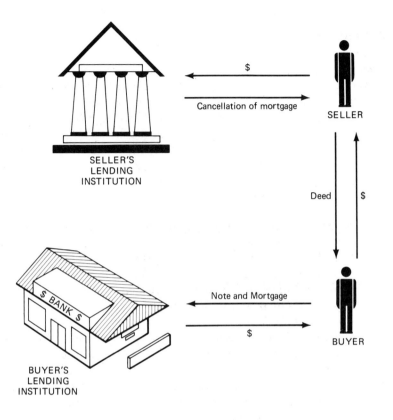

Figure 23.2: Transactions involved in a real estate closing

A borrower who seeks a mortgage loan needs full information from lending institutions in order to select a lender prudently. RESPA requires the lending institution to make certain disclosures designed to help the borrower make informed judgments. Generally, RESPA is applicable to first mortgage loans made for the purchase of residential real estate. Residential real estate includes one-family to four-family properties. Cooperatives, condominiums and mobile home lots can qualify as residential real estate. The act applies only to purchases where a lender (other than the seller) takes a purchase money mortgage to secure the loan. A purchase money mortgage in which the seller takes a mortgage back to secure the unpaid purchase price is not covered by RESPA. The requirements of RESPA are applicable only to lenders involved in a "federally related mortgage loan." The definition of *federally related* is very broad and includes any lending institution whose deposits are federally insured or regulated.

Settlement Costs Booklet

RESPA is administered by the Department of Housing and Urban Development (HUD). HUD has prepared a settlement costs booklet. Every lender is required to provide an applicant for a mortgage loan with the contents of this booklet on the day of the loan application or, failing that, to deposit it in the mail to the applicant within three business days of the application. The booklet contains informtion about the real estate purchase process, including negotiating a sales contract and home loan financing. Under the heading "Selecting the Lender," the booklet suggests certain inquiries a borrower should make in order to compare lenders. For example:

- Am I required to carry life or disability insurance? Must I obtain it from a particular company?
- Is there a late payment charge? How much? How late may the payment be before the charge is imposed?
- If I wish to pay off the loan in advance of maturity, must I pay a prepayment penalty? How much? If so, for how long a period will it apply?
- Will the lender release me from personal liability if my loan is assumed by someone else when I sell my house?
- If I sell the house and the buyer assumes the loan, will the lender have the right to charge an assumption fee, raise the rate of interest or require payment in full of the mortgage?
- Will I be required to pay monies into a special reserve account to cover taxes or insurance? If so, how large a deposit will be required at the closing of the sale?

In addition, the booklet contains informtion regarding homebuyers' rights and obligations, settlement services and escrow accounts, as well as a sample work sheet to calculate the settlement costs.

Good-Faith Estimate

Another RESPA requirement is that the lender must provide the borrower with a good-faith estimate of settlement charges at the time of the application. These charges may be expressed as a range. A lender who fails to provide the required information on the date must deposit the information in the mail within three business days of the application. The good-faith estimates include the breakdown of the costs of settlement charges rendered by the mortgagee—for example, loan origination fee, credit report fee, appraiser's fees, title search charges, attorney fees, surveys and document preparation. The complete schedule of all settlement charges is contained in Section L of the Uniform Settlement Statement, discussed later in this chapter. The good-faith estimate does not have to include prepaid hazard insurance premiums or reserves deposited with the lender such as escrow for taxes and insurance (information not usually available to lenders at the application stage). Although the estimates must be made in good faith, they are subject to change as the market alters the costs of the various settlement charges.

Inspection of Uniform Settlement Statement

A closing or settlement statement is normally prepared by the settlement clerk handling the closing. The settlement statement consists of a summary of the buyer's (borrower's) and the seller's transactions, broken down into various categories. For some items it may be necessary to apportion income and expenses between the parties. For example, assume that the seller has paid the real estate taxes for six months in advance. Credit should be given to the seller for the portion paid that covers any period after closing. Apportionment of the taxes ensures that each person bears the expense only for the months that person had use of the premises. Other expenses often apportioned include water and sewer assessments, fuel and insurance. Rental income may also be adjusted for unearned rentals received by the seller in advance.

RESPA requires that a lender permit the borrower a right to inspect the Uniform Settlement Statement (USS) one day before closing. The USS is a form settlement statement that contains a summary of the borrower's and seller's transactions and an itemization of the settlement charges as allocated to the borrower and seller. In the event that this information is unavailable the day before closing, the lender is relieved of the responsibility. In this case the completed statement must be given to the buyer no later than the closing. This requirement may be waived by the buyer, but in the event of such waiver the USS must be mailed at the earliest practical date. Where there is a closing without an appearance of the buyer or the buyer's agent, the lender need only mail the statement to the buyer as soon as practical after the closing. The lender need not provide a USS to the buyer when there are no settlement charges to the buyer or when the settlement charges are a fixed amount communicated to the borrower at the time of the loan application. However, here the lender must provide the borrower with an itemized list of services provided within three days after closing.

In all transactions covered by RESPA the USS must be used. Otherwise, a statement resembling that form is normally used.

A Uniform Settlement Statement Example

A comprehensive example of a typical residential closing is reflected in the settlement statement in Figure 23.3. Amounts in the statement are based upon the following information.

Jim Darrow has obtained an 11 percent 30-year loan commitment from the Poplar Savings and Loan for $80,000 to purchase Liz Nodler's home at 1836 Cedarwillow, Columbus, Ohio. The sales price, pursuant to the contract previously entered into by the parties, is $100,000. The closing is to take place at the offices of the Poplar Savings and Loan on May 15. In addition to the purchase price of the house, Darrow has arranged to purchase the curtains for $300. County taxes on the property are $1,200 per year, payable semiannually. The county is six months behind on billing and collecting taxes; Liz's last payment was made January 15, 1987. The seller prepaid $200 on January 1 for hazard insurance, which covers the calendar year. The house is heated by oil; 50 gallons of home heating oil costing $1.50 per gallon remain in the tank on the day of closing. Seller's tenant has paid $400 advance rent for the month of May.

Darrow is paying $20,000 down payment, which will be paid at the closing. The payoff by the seller of the first mortgage on the home, as of the date of closing, is $37,120.

Water and sewer assessments are payable quarterly at an even billing of $45 per quarter at the end of March, June, September and December. Nodler made the March 31 payment. Every six months a reading is taken to determine the actual usage for the six-month period; and adjustments are made at the end of the year. Average adjustments for the last five years have resulted in an additional assessment of $40 at the end of the year.

A listing agreement with Decade Today Realtors requires the seller to pay $6^{1}/_{2}$ percent commission. The loan origination fee was two percent. Seller, pursuant to the terms of the contract, was to pay two mortgage discount points (two percent). The appraisal fee of $100 and $15 for a credit report was paid by Darrow at the time of the loan application. The survey fee of $150 to Survey Plat, Inc., is payable by the buyer at closing. Assume that simple interest based on a 360-day calendar year is to be paid at closing for the 17-day period encompassing May 15 to May 31. Darrow will be required to deposit two months' taxes at closing into escrow. Attorney fees for preparation of the deed to be borne by the seller, are $35. The buyer's attorney fees for services connected with the closing are $350, payable to Lincoln, Todd and Harrison Law Firm at closing. The seller obtained a joint title insurance policy, as required per contract, to fully cover the lender and the owner. The cost to the seller, to be disbursed at closing to ABC Title, Inc., is $650. The buyer's charge for recording fees for the deed and the mortgage amounts to $5 for each document. The seller must pay the recording fee for the release of the existing mortgage.

Additionally, a 0.1 percent county transfer conveyance fee is assessed against the seller. Seller, pursuant to the contract, agreed to pay for termite and gas line inspection costs. She employed Exterm Pest Control to do the termite inspection; the charge was $40 for the inspection and $210 for repair work. The seller employed the city to do the gas line inspection at a cost of $75.

Summary of Borrower's Transaction

Schedule J on the closing statement is a summary of the borrower's transactions. The total of amounts paid by the borrower is subtracted from the total of the amounts due from the borrower. From this calculation we derive the net amount the borrower needs to bring to the closing.

Line 101	The contract sales price of $100,000 is inserted on this line.
Line 102	The cost of curtains, which is $300, is inserted on this line.
Line 103	The settlement charges derived from Schedule L (explained later) are inserted on this line.
Line 109	The insurance is apportioned as of the date of closing. Nodler has paid $200 in advance on January 1 for the entire calendar year. She should get a credit for the amounts prepaid that extend beyond the closing. This amounts to $125 ($7\frac{1}{2}$ mos. × $16.66 month).
Line 110	The seller should receive credit for the unused heating oil remaining in the tank on the day of closing. Since 50 gallons remain the amount of $75.00 should be inserted on this line (50 × $1.50 per gallon).
Line 120	The total due from the borrower amounts to the sum total of lines 101–112, which is $103,225.48.
Line 202	The amount of the loan, $80,000, should be inserted on this line.
Line 211	The county taxes are apportioned as of the date of closing. The taxes are $100 per month ($1,200 ÷ 12). Nodler's last payment was on January 15, 1987. Since the county is six months behind on collecting tax, Nodler owes taxes from July 15, 1987, through January 15, 1988. In addition, she owes taxes from January 15 to May 15, the date of closing (10 × $100/month = $1,000).

LENDER COPY

U.S. DEPARTMENT OF HOUSING AND URBAN DEVELOPMENT **DISCLOSURE/SETTLEMENT STATEMENT**	**B. TYPE OF LOAN**

Poplar Savings and Loan
5000 Cleveland Avenue
Columbus, Ohio 43229

1. ☐ FHA	2. ☐ FMHA	3. ☐ CONV. UNINS.
4. ☐ VA	5. ☒ CONV. INS.	

C. NOTE: This form is furnished to give you a statement of actual settlement costs. Amounts paid to and by the settlement agent are shown. Items marked "(p.o.c.)" were paid outside of closing; they are shown here for informational purposes and are not included in the totals.

6. FILE NUMBER:
238
8. MORT. INS. CASE NO.:
51003-7

D. NAME OF BORROWER:

Jim Darrow

E. NAME OF SELLER:

Liz Nodler

F. NAME OF LENDER:

Poplar Savings and Loan

G. PROPERTY LOCATION:

1836 Cedarwillow
Columbus, Ohio 43229

H. SETTLEMENT AGENT:

Poplar Savings and Loan

PLACE OF SETTLEMENT:
5000 Cleveland Avenue
Columbus, Ohio 43229

I. SETTLEMENT DATE:

May 15, 1988

J. SUMMARY OF BORROWER'S TRANSACTION:		**K. SUMMARY OF SELLER'S TRANSACTION:**	
100. GROSS AMOUNT DUE FROM BORROWER		**400. GROSS AMOUNT DUE TO SELLER**	
101. Contract sales price	100,000.00	401. Contract sales price	100,000.00
102. Personal property	300.00	402. Personal property	300.00
103. Settlement charges to borrower (line 1400)	2,725.48	403.	
104.		404.	
105.		405.	
Adjustments for items paid by seller in advance		Adjustments for items paid by seller in advance	
106. City/town taxes to		406. City/town taxes to	
107. County taxes to		407. County taxes to	
108. Assessments to		408. Assessments to	
109. Insurance 5-15 to 12-31	125.00	409. Insurance 5-15 to 12-31	125.00
110. Heating Oil 50 gal. @ $1.50	75.00	410. Heating Oil 50 gal. @ $1.50	75.00
111.		411.	
112.		412.	
120. GROSS AMOUNT DUE FROM BORROWER	103,225.48	**420. GROSS AMOUNT DUE TO SELLER**	100,500.00
200. AMOUNTS PAID BY OR IN BEHALF OF BORROWER		**500. REDUCTIONS IN AMOUNT DUE TO SELLER**	
201. Deposit or earnest money		501. Excess deposit (see instructions)	
202. Principal amount of new loan(s)	80,000.00	502. Settlement charges to seller (line 1400)	9,215.00
203. Existing loan(s) taken subject to		503. Existing loan(s) taken subject to	
204.		504. Payoff / first mortgage loan	37,120.00
205.		505. Payoff / second mortgage loan	
206.		506.	
207.		507.	
208.		508.	
209.		509.	
Credits for items unpaid by seller		Credits for items unpaid by seller	
210. City/town taxes to		510. City/town taxes to	
211. County taxes 7-15-87 to 5-15-88	1,000.00	511. County taxes to 5-15	1,000.00
212. Assessments 4-1 to 5-15	37.50	512. Assessments 4-1 to 5-15	37.50
213. Rentals 5-15 5-31	200.00	513. Rentals 5-15 5-31	200.00
214.		514.	
215.		515.	
216.		516.	
217.		517.	
218.		518.	
219.		519.	
220. TOTAL PAID BY/FOR BORROWER	81,237.50	**520. TOTAL REDUCTION AMOUNT DUE SELLER**	47,572.50
300. CASH AT SETTLEMENT FROM/TO BORROWER		**600. CASH AT SETTLEMENT TO/FROM SELLER**	
301. Gross amount due from borrower (line 120)	103,225.48	601. Gross amount due to seller (line 420)	100,500.00
302. Less amounts paid by/for borrower (line 220)	(81,237.50)	602. Less reduction amount due seller (line 520)	(47,572.50)
303. CASH (☐ FROM) (☐ TO) BORROWER	21,987.98	**603. CASH (☐ TO) (☐ FROM) SELLER**	52,927.50

Page 1 of 2 Documents   HUD-1 Rev. 5/76

LENDER COPY

<table>
<tr><td colspan="4">L. SETTLEMENT CHARGES</td><td colspan="2">Page 2 of 2 Documents</td></tr>
<tr><td>700.</td><td>SALES/BROKER'S COMMISSION
based on sale price</td><td>$ 100,000</td><td>@ 6½ %6,500.00</td><td>PAID FROM BORROWER'S FUNDS AT SETTLEMENT</td><td>PAID FROM SELLER'S FUNDS AT SETTLEMENT</td></tr>
<tr><td colspan="4">Division of Commission (line 700) as follows:</td><td></td><td></td></tr>
<tr><td colspan="2">701. $ 6,500.00   To</td><td colspan="2">Decade Today Realtors</td><td></td><td></td></tr>
<tr><td colspan="2">702. $ To</td><td colspan="2"></td><td></td><td></td></tr>
<tr><td colspan="4">703. Commission Paid at Settlement</td><td></td><td>6,500.00</td></tr>
<tr><td colspan="2">704. $ To</td><td colspan="2"></td><td></td><td></td></tr>
<tr><td colspan="6">800. ITEMS PAYABLE IN CONNECTION WITH LOAN</td></tr>
<tr><td colspan="4">801. Loan Origination Fee   2 %</td><td>1,600.00</td><td></td></tr>
<tr><td colspan="4">802. Loan Discount   2%</td><td></td><td>1,600.00</td></tr>
<tr><td colspan="4">803. Appraisal Fee</td><td></td><td></td></tr>
<tr><td colspan="4">804. Credit Report</td><td></td><td></td></tr>
<tr><td colspan="4">805. Lender's Inspection Fee</td><td></td><td></td></tr>
<tr><td colspan="4">806. Mortgage Insurance Application Fee to</td><td></td><td></td></tr>
<tr><td colspan="4">807. Assumption Fee</td><td></td><td></td></tr>
<tr><td colspan="4">808.</td><td></td><td></td></tr>
<tr><td colspan="4">809.</td><td></td><td></td></tr>
<tr><td colspan="4">810.</td><td></td><td></td></tr>
<tr><td colspan="4">811.</td><td></td><td></td></tr>
<tr><td colspan="6">900. ITEMS REQUIRED BY LENDER TO BE PAID IN ADVANCE</td></tr>
<tr><td colspan="4">901. Interest from   5-15 to   5-31   @ $ 24.44 /day</td><td>415.48</td><td></td></tr>
<tr><td colspan="4">902. Mortgage Insurance Premium for   months to</td><td></td><td></td></tr>
<tr><td colspan="4">903. Hazard Insurance Premium for   years to</td><td></td><td></td></tr>
<tr><td colspan="4">904. Flood Insurance   years to</td><td></td><td></td></tr>
<tr><td colspan="4">905.</td><td></td><td></td></tr>
<tr><td colspan="6">1000. RESERVES DEPOSITED WITH LENDER</td></tr>
<tr><td colspan="4">1001. Hazard Insurance   months @ $ per month</td><td></td><td></td></tr>
<tr><td colspan="4">1002. Mortgage Insurance   months @ $ per month</td><td></td><td></td></tr>
<tr><td colspan="4">1003. City property taxes   months @ $ per month</td><td></td><td></td></tr>
<tr><td colspan="4">1004. County property taxes   2 months @ $ 100.00 per month</td><td>200.00</td><td></td></tr>
<tr><td colspan="4">1005. Annual Assessments   months @ $ per month</td><td></td><td></td></tr>
<tr><td colspan="4">1006. Flood Insurance   months @ $ per month</td><td></td><td></td></tr>
<tr><td colspan="4">1007.   months @ $ per month</td><td></td><td></td></tr>
<tr><td colspan="4">1008.   months @ $ per month</td><td></td><td></td></tr>
<tr><td colspan="4">1009.   months @ $ per month</td><td></td><td></td></tr>
<tr><td colspan="4">1010.   months @ $ per month</td><td></td><td></td></tr>
<tr><td colspan="6">1100. TITLE CHARGES</td></tr>
<tr><td colspan="4">1101. Settlement or closing fee to</td><td></td><td></td></tr>
<tr><td colspan="4">1102. Abstract or title search to</td><td></td><td></td></tr>
<tr><td colspan="4">1103. Title examination to</td><td></td><td></td></tr>
<tr><td colspan="4">1104. Title insurance binder to</td><td></td><td></td></tr>
<tr><td colspan="4">1105. Document preparation to   Seller's Attorney</td><td></td><td>35.00</td></tr>
<tr><td colspan="4">1106. Notary fees to</td><td></td><td></td></tr>
<tr><td colspan="4">1107. Attorney's fees to   Lincoln Todd & Harrison</td><td>350.00</td><td></td></tr>
<tr><td colspan="4">(includes above items numbers;)</td><td></td><td></td></tr>
<tr><td colspan="4">1108. Title insurance to   ABC Title, Inc.</td><td></td><td>650.00</td></tr>
<tr><td colspan="4">(includes above items numbers;)</td><td></td><td></td></tr>
<tr><td colspan="4">1109. Lender's coverage $ 80,000</td><td></td><td></td></tr>
<tr><td colspan="4">1110. Owner's coverage $ 100,000</td><td></td><td></td></tr>
<tr><td colspan="4">1111.</td><td></td><td></td></tr>
<tr><td colspan="4">1112.</td><td></td><td></td></tr>
<tr><td colspan="4">1113.</td><td></td><td></td></tr>
<tr><td colspan="6">1200. GOVERNMENT RECORDING AND TRANSFER CHARGES</td></tr>
<tr><td colspan="4">1201. Recording fees: Deed $ 5.00   ;Mortgage $ 5.00   Releases $ 5.00</td><td>10.00</td><td>5.00</td></tr>
<tr><td colspan="4">1202. City/county tax/stamps; Deed $;Mortgage $</td><td></td><td>100.00</td></tr>
<tr><td colspan="4">1203. State tax/stamps; Deed $;Mortgage $</td><td></td><td></td></tr>
<tr><td colspan="4">1204.</td><td></td><td></td></tr>
<tr><td colspan="4">1205.</td><td></td><td></td></tr>
<tr><td colspan="6">1300. ADDITIONAL SETTLEMENT CHARGES</td></tr>
<tr><td colspan="4">1301. Survey to   Survey Plat, Inc.</td><td>150.00</td><td></td></tr>
<tr><td colspan="4">1302. Pest inspection to   Exterm Pest</td><td></td><td>250.00</td></tr>
<tr><td colspan="4">1303. Gas Line to City</td><td></td><td>75.00</td></tr>
<tr><td colspan="4">1304.</td><td></td><td></td></tr>
<tr><td colspan="4">1305.</td><td></td><td></td></tr>
<tr><td colspan="4">1400. TOTAL SETTLEMENT CHARGES (Enter on Lines 103, Section J and 503, Section K)</td><td>2,725.48</td><td>9,215.00</td></tr>
</table>

Buyer or Agent _Jim Darrow_   Seller or Agent _Lez Nodler_

Buyer or Agent _____   Seller or Agent _____

We have examined page 1 and page 2 of this statement, find it correct and approve the disbursements as shown thereon for our use and benefit. We hereby acknowledge receipt of this statement.

HUD-11 Rev. 9/79

Line 212	The water and sewer assessments need to be adjusted since Nodler has paid only through March. The buyer should be given a credit for the amounts unpaid from March 31 through May 15, or for $1\frac{1}{2}$ months. This amounts to $22.50 ($\frac{1}{2}$ × $45.00). Additionally, the average adjustments at the end of the year must be added to the figure or $15.00 ($1\frac{1}{2}$ quarters × $10). The total adjustment benefiting the borrower amounts to $37.50 ($22.50 + $15.00).
Line 213	The seller's tenant has paid $400 for rent covering the entire month of May. This amount must be apportioned as of May 15, the date of closing. Darrow should be given a credit for the period from May 15 through May 31. This amounts to $200 ($\frac{1}{2}$ month × $400).
Line 220	The total paid by the borrower amounts to the sum total of lines 201–219 or $81,237.50.
Line 301	The total amount due from the borrower as derived from Line 120 is inserted on this line.
Line 302	The total amount paid by the borrower as derived from Line 220 is inserted on this line.
Line 303	The cash from the borrower at closing, amounting to $21,987.98, is derived by subtracting Line 302 from Line 301. In the event the amount of Line 302 is greater than the amount on Line 301, the borrower receives cash at the closing.

Summary of Seller's Transaction

Schedule K on the closing statement is a summary of the seller's transactions. The total of the seller's reductions is subtracted from the total of the amounts due to the seller. From this calculation we derive the net amount the seller is to receive at closing.

Line 401	See explanation of Line 101.
Line 402	See explanation of Line 102.
Line 409	See explanation of Line 109.
Line 410	See explanation of Line 110.
Line 420	The total due to the seller amounts to the total of Lines 401–412, which is $100,500.
Line 502	The settlement charges derived from Schedule L (explained later) are inserted on this line.
Line 504	The amount needed to pay off seller's mortgage, which is $37,120, is inserted on this line.
Line 511	See explanation of Line 211.

Line 512   See explanation of Line 212.

Line 513   See explanation of Line 213.

Line 520   The total reduction from the seller amounts to the total of Lines 501–519 or $47,572.50.

Line 601   The total amount due to seller as derived from Line 420 is inserted on this line.

Line 602   The total reduction due seller as derived from Line 520 is inserted on this line.

Line 603   The cash to the seller at closing, amounting to $52,927.50, is derived by subtracting Line 602 from Line 601. In the event the amount on Line 602 is greater than the amount on Line 601, the seller owes cash at the closing.

Summary of Settlement Charges

Schedule L on the closing statement is a summary of the settlement charges that are paid from the borrower's funds and of those paid from the seller's funds at the settlement.

Paid from Borrower's Funds:

Line 801   The loan origination fee is $2,600 (2% of $80,000) and is payable to the mortgagee at settlement.

Line 901   The borrower is required to pay the interest on the loan for the 17-day period from May 15 through May 31. Assuming simple interest on the $80,000 loan, the daily rate amounts to $24.44/day (11% of $80,000 = $1,600 ÷ 360 = $24.44/day.) For 17 days, the interest payable by the borrower amounts to $415.48 ($24.44 × 17 days).

Line 1003   The borrower is required to deposit two months of taxes in escrow, which amounts to $200.00 ($1,200 ÷ 12 × 2 = $200.00).

Line 1107   The borrower is required to pay attorney fees to Lincoln, Todd, and Harrison in the amount of $350.

Line 1201   The borrower is required to pay the recording fees for the deed and the new mortgage, which amounts to $10.

Line 1301   The borrower is required to pay $150 to Survey Plat, Inc., for the survey.

Line 1400   The sum of the settlement charges to the seller, amounting to $2,725.48 is placed on this line and is also inserted at Section J on Line 103.

Paid from Seller's Funds:

Line 700	The total sales/broker's commission is $6,500 (6¹/₂% of $100,000).
Line 701	The $6,500 is payable at the settlement to Decade Today Realtors.
Line 703	The $6,500 commission is listed on this line on the seller's side.
Line 802	The seller is required to pay mortgage loan discount points equal to $1,600 (2% × $80,000).
Line 1105	The seller is required to pay the attorney's fee for preparing the deed, which amounts to $35.
Line 1108	The cost of the title insurance payable to ABC Title, Inc., appears on this line on the seller's side.
Line 1201	The cost of filing the release or satisfaction of mortgage in the amount of $5 is assessable against the seller.
Line 1202	The county transfer conveyance fee of $100 (0.001 × $100,000) is payable by the seller.
Line 1302	The seller is obligated to pay Exterm Pest $250 for the inspection and repair work.
Line 1303	The seller is obligated to pay the city $75 for the gas inspection.
Line 1400	The sum of the settlement charges to the seller, amounting to $9,215.00, is placed on this line and is also inserted at Section K on Line 502.

Abusive Practices

One reason Congress passed RESPA was because certain abusive practices resulted in to inflated closing costs. "Kickbacks" are one such practice expressly prohibited by RESPA. Kickbacks occur, for example, when a person or an entity gives a fee to another for business referrals.

CASE EXAMPLE

ABC Savings and Loan has an agreement with Alfred Hillman, attorney, whereby for every person ABC refers to Hillman for legal services in connection with real estate transactions, Hillman pays ABC ten percent of the fees generated. This is an illegal kickback under RESPA. In addition, Hillman would be violating the attorney's code of ethics and would be subject to disciplinary measures.

There are similar prohibitions against the payment of a "phantom" charge, a fee that is given where no service has been performed. Both kickbacks and phantom fees may result in a violation for which criminal penalties may attach. Also an aggrieved party may sue to recover three times the amount of the kickback or the phantom fee.

POSTCLOSING PROCEDURES

After the closing, the purchaser is the titleholder of the property as evidenced by the deed. The deed must now be recorded to give constructive notice to the world of the new ownership and thus protect the buyer against rival claimants. The purchaser, purchaser's attorney or, in some instances, the mortgagee presents the deed for recording in the proper office in the county courthouse. After receiving the appropriate fees the clerk photocopies and records the deed and then returns the original deed to the purchaser. Satisfaction (cancellation) of the preexisting mortgage should also be recorded. The new mortgage instrument that secures repayment of the loan is recorded by the mortgagee, the institution extending the loan to the purchaser. After the recording of these documents, the title insurer issues the title insurance policy in the name of the new owner and the mortgagee, if title insurance was purchased. In the event an abstract is given as evidence of title, the search of the title should be updated or brought down to the moment of recording.

At the closing, a problem may have been remedied by setting up an escrow and charging an escrow agent with the obligation of holding a portion of the purchase price necessary to assure the resolution of the problem.

CASE EXAMPLE

At closing Fred Thomas, seller, is unable to produce any paid receipts for water bills for the last year. Frank Hander, purchaser, is wary of closing without an assurance that any unpaid bills will be borne by the seller. An escrow account is set up with $150 funded from the purchase price, an amount everyone agrees would be more than enough to pay any unpaid water bills for a year. After closing, the contact with the water company reveals an unpaid water bill of $31. The escrow agent will pay the amount out of the escrow funds and send the remaining $119 to the seller.

In the event the property was sold subject to an existing lease, the purchaser should secure a "tenant's letter" from the seller notifying the tenants of the sale and directing them to pay rent in the future to the purchaser. After closing the purchaser should deliver that letter to the tenants.

SUMMARY

The closing, also called the settlement, is the final stage of a real estate purchase transaction. At the closing the deed and the purchase money are exchanged by the seller and buyer according to the terms of the contract.

In most cases the broker may participate in the preparation for the closing by helping the buyer arrange financing, assisting in the preparation of the closing statement and coordinating various other details that will facilitate closing. Both buyer and seller may also be represented by an attorney at the closing. The date of the closing is normally specified in the contract. All preliminary work should be completed in advance.

Between the signing of the contract and the settlement date, the buyer must normally obtain financing, secure hazard insurance and should inspect the premises, examine the title and any existing leases on the property. The seller also needs this interval to prepare by obtaining evidence of title, preparing a deed and satisfying any liens or other encumbrances.

The closing may take place at the lending institution that has supplied financing or at the office of an attorney, a real estate broker or the seller's mortgagee. A settlement officer, usually an employee of the "host" office, is responsible for coordinating the paperwork. To aid in following the flow of funds at the closing, a settlement statement is prepared. The statement includes breakdowns for taxes, utilities, rents and any other payments that must be prorated. The settlement procedures are regulated by contract, local custom, state law and a federal statute known as RESPA (Real Estate Settlement Procedures Act).

After closing, the deed should be recorded to protect the purchaser. The old mortgage should be cancelled and any new mortgage recorded.

REVIEW AND DISCUSSION QUESTIONS

1. What is the role of a broker in a real estate closing?
2. What is the purpose for the interval between the signing of the real estate contract and the closing?
3. (a) What is the role of the settlement clerk at closing? (b) Who should act as a settlement clerk?
4. (a) Name five things the buyer normally must accomplish in anticipation of the closing and describe why each is important. (b) Name five things that the seller normally must accomplish in anticipation of the closing and describe why each is important.
5. What is the purpose of the Affidavit of Title?

6. List three documents that are normally signed at the closing and describe each.
7. (a) Upon whom does RESPA impose requirements? (b) What are those requirements?
8. Why is it important for the deed to be recorded after the closing?

CASE PROBLEMS

1. Grace Zeigler and Harriet Milton entered into a contract for the sale of a parcel of land owned by Zeigler. The terms of the contract were established through negotiations between the parties. The contract did not make any provision for Zeigler to deliver an abstract of title. Zeigler neglected to furnish an abstract at the closing. Milton refused to pay the purchase price at the closing because Zeigler did not supply an abstract. (a) Is Milton's position sound? (b) Where should Milton look to determine whether Zeigler is bound to provide an abstract? (c) What can Milton do to ensure that she receives a clear title? See *Applebaum v. Zeigler*, 246 Ala. 281, 20 So.2d 510 (1945).

2. The Maple Ridge Construction Company and Kasten entered into an agreement for the purchase of lots in a subdivision owned by Kasten. Maple Ridge encountered problems in obtaining financing and requested postponement of the settlement date. Kasten agreed to an extension of four months. Maple Ridge continued to try to obtain a suitable financing arrangement without success. Repeated requests for additional extensions were turned down by Kasten. The settlement date passed with neither party performing or demanding performance from the other. Five days after the expiration of the settlement date Maple Ridge informed Kasten that it was ready to perform. Kasten refused Maple Ridge's tender, claiming that the contract had expired. Maple Ridge commenced an action in specific performance against Kasten in an attempt to force Kasten to comply with the terms of their contract. Who wins? Discuss. See *Kasten Construction Co. Inc. v. Maple Ridge Construction Co. Inc.*, 245 Md. 373, 226 A.2d 341 (Ct. App. 1976).

3. Stephanie Andrew, seller, and John and Joan Lynch, purchasers, entered into a real estate purchase agreement that included the following mortgage financing contingency clause: "Buyer shall apply to a conventional bank or other mortgage loan institution for a loan of [$155,000] payable in not less than thirty . . .

years at prevailing interest rates." The Lynchs made one application to Bay Bank for a loan of $130,000. Bay Bank indicated that it was ready to lend the money to the Lynchs if they would show where the remainder of the purchase money ($98,600) was coming from. The Lynchs responded by informing the bank that the proceeds from the sale of their house would provide the balance. There was no agreement to sell their house at that date. The bank sought to accommodate the Lynchs by offering them an additional loan for the $98,600 to be secured by a mortgage on the Lynchs' existing house. The Lynchs refused. The bank thereafter, pursuant to John Lynch's request, sent a letter rejecting the Lynchs' application. Maintaining that the contingency was unfulfilled, the Lynches refused to close on the sale of Andrew's house. Is their refusal justified? Explain. *Lynch v. Andrew*, 481 N.E.2d 1383 (Mass. App. 1985).

4. Carolista Fletcher, purchaser, and Burton Jones, seller, entered into a contract for the sale of certain real property for $45,000. The contract provided for a closing date of January 9, 1981, and contained a clause stating: "Contract is subject to seller obtaining absolute divorce from present spouse." The condition was not met prior to the date set for closing. On January 29 the parties agreed in writing to extend the closing to March 19, 1981. The condition was not met by that date. However, on August 4, 1981, Jones's attorney informed Fletcher's attorney that the divorce was final and that he was ready to close. (a) Is Fletcher obligated to close? Explain. (b) What if Jones sells the property to someone else? Can Fletcher successfully sue Jones for breach of contract? Explain. *Fletcher v. Jones*, 333 S.E.2d 731 (N.C. 1985).

5. Vega applied for and received a conventional mortgage loan from First Federal to finance the purchase of his residence. First Federal's deposits are insured by the Federal Savings and Loan Insurance Corporation (FSLIC). (a) Which federal statute should First Federal pay close attention to before completing its loan agreement with Vega? What obligations are imposed upon First Federal by this statute? See *Vega v. First Federal Savings and Loan Association*, 433 F.Supp. 624 (D. Mich. 1977). (b) How would First Federal's obligations be affected if Vega sought to borrow money for the purchase of a commercial lot?

6. Mr. LaFond negotiated a contract with Ms. Frame whereby Ms. Frame agreed to sell to Mr. LaFond a parcel of land free from all encumbrances. The date for the conveyance of the deed and the possession of the land was set for one year from the date the contract was signed. The contract was silent regarding the payment of taxes on the property during the pendency of the con-

tract. On the date set for conveyance, taxes assessed for the prior year were unpaid. (a) Who has the duty to pay these taxes? Why? (b) How could the parties have eliminated any uncertainty on this point? See *LaFond v. Frame*, 327 Mss. 364, 99 N.E.2d 51 (1951).

24
Escrow

REAL ESTATE ESCROW

A deed delivered by a grantor to an escrow agent, who is directed to deliver the deed to a grantee when a specified condition occurs.

In the previous chapter we examined a conventional closing, where buyer and seller come face to face to exchange the deed for the purchase price. The real estate escrow closing is a modification of this procedure that is practiced in some localities. Instead of the buyer and seller coming face to face, a third party acts as an intermediary. The third party, commonly called an *escrow agent*, is charged with certain responsibilities designed ultimately to invest the seller with the full purchase price and the buyer with a good deed to the property.

The subject of the escrow transaction is a written instrument. The written instrument in the normal real estate escrow transaction involves a deed. Technically, the term *escrow* characterizes the instrument—the deed itself—while it is held by the third party. This strict terminology has been relaxed in modern parlance, however, and it is common to refer to "depositing a deed into escrow." In this regard the escrow is the receptacle of the instrument rather than the instrument itself. Courts refer to escrows in both senses, and either reference is acceptable.

Escrow Closing Distinguished

The escrow closing should not be confused with the escrow account. Many mortgages include a clause requiring the mortgagee to set up an escrow account to be used to disburse payments for real estate taxes and/or hazard insurance. The particulars of this escrow account vary from jurisdiction to jurisdiction. Generally, the mortgagor pays into the escrow account monthly an amount equal to $1/12$ of the amount of the yearly property tax and hazard insurance. This constitutes an additional amount above the normal mortgage payment. The mortgagee then makes payments directly from the escrow account as the taxes and insurance become due. This type of escrow procedure is required for FHA-insured loans and for most conventional loans; it is suggested for VA-guaranteed loans.

The escrowed funds are normally placed in non-interest-bearing accounts; depositors are not paid for the use of the funds. There is, however, a trend in recent years for buyers, particularly in commercial transactions, to require the escrowed money to be deposited in an interest-bearing account in favor of the buyer. Often such buyers will deposit interest-bearing instruments as escrow funds.

The Escrow Transaction

In the most elementary real estate escrow transaction a seller and a buyer enter into a contract for the purchase of specified real property. They agree to close the transaction in escrow, and they appoint a bank or other escrow agent to be responsible for handling the closing. As part of the agreement between the parties, the seller then deposits a fully executed deed with the escrow agent. The escrow agent is instructed to deliver the deed to the purchaser after receipt of the purchase price. When the purchase price is deposited by the purchaser, the escrow agent delivers the deed to the purchaser and the purchase price to the seller. At this point the escrow closing is complete (see Figure 24.1).

Another typical example of the real estate escrow transaction involves conditions relating to title. In this arrangement the seller deposits the deed, and the purchaser deposits the purchase price with the escrow agent. When the purchaser's attorney approves the title to the property, the escrow agent is bound by the purchase contract or other agreement to deliver the deed to the purchaser and money to the seller. The escrow agent may be instructed to record the deed in favor of the purchaser as soon as the purchaser deposits the money, even before the title to the property is approved. Then, in the event the title cannot be approved, the purchaser is entitled to a return of the purchase money upon reconveying the deed to the seller. A variation of this procedure requires the purchaser to execute a quitclaim deed in favor of the seller and deposit it with the escrow agent at the time the purchase money is deposited and the deed is recorded in favor of the purchaser. In the event that title cannot be approved, the escrow agent is required to record the quitclaim deed and return the purchase money to the purchaser, thus returning the parties to their previous position.

The real estate escrow device is not confined to money transac-

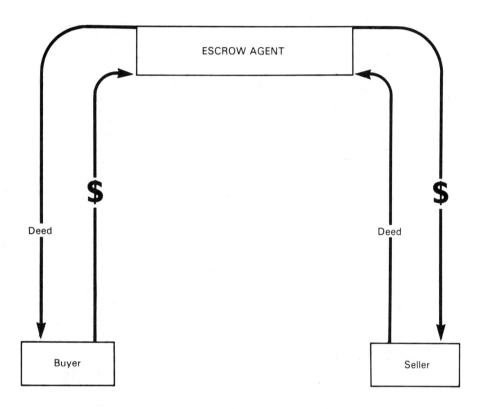

Figure 24.1: Escrow transactions

tions but may also be used when the seller and purchaser are merely interested in exchanging deeds to real estate.

• CASE BRIEF •

Rocky Hayes owns a five-acre tract of land in Florida and is interested in selling his land and moving to Colorado. Johnny Ruskin owns a five-acre tract of land in Colorado and is interested in moving to Florida. A real estate broker brings the two together, and an even exchange of property is agreed upon. Hayes deposits his deed to the Florida property with Jerry Bloom, a third party, on condition that the Florida deed be delivered to Ruskin upon receipt of the deed to the Colorado property. When Ruskin deposits the deed to the Colorado property, Bloom will deliver it to Hayes and deliver the deed to the Florida property to Ruskin, thus completing the escrow transaction. *See Morris v. Davis, 334 Mo. 411, 66 S.W.2d 883 (1933).*

ADVANTAGES OF ESCROW

The objective of the escrow transaction is to ensure that the buyer is invested with clear title to the property and the seller receives the purchase price. The use of the escrow device in closing sales of real estate enjoys the advantages of convenience and protection against a party's change of mind.

Convenience

Sometimes it is simply inconvenient for parties to be present at a closing. The escrow method of closing enjoys the advantage of facilitating interstate transactions or other closings where it is not feasible for the parties to appear at the closing.

CASE EXAMPLE

Junior Wells, a resident of California, owns farmland in Kentucky that he desires to sell. Senior Mills, a resident of Kentucky, desires to buy the farmland. The cost of Junior Wells's appearance at a closing in Kentucky is prohibitive. The parties enter into a purchase contract for the sale of the farmland and agree to close in escrow. Wells mails a fully executed deed for his Kentucky farm to Kentucky Loan & Trust Co., which is instructed to deliver the deed to Mills upon receipt of the purchase price. When Mills delivers the purchase price, Kentucky Loan & Trust, as previously instructed, delivers the deed to Mills.

Protection Against a Party's Change of Mind

With the use of the escrow device the closing is less likely to fail because an independent third party is charged with carrying out mechanical details of the transaction. Both buyer and seller are to some extent protected from the other's change of mind. For example, in a conventional closing a seller who has "second thoughts" may refuse to appear at the closing and sign the deed. In an escrow closing, however, even if the seller desires to back out of the transaction, the escrow agent, who is in control of the deed previously deposited, is instruction-bound to deliver it to the purchaser upon the happening of a specified condition. This course may not be altered at the seller's whim.

The escrow device, while avoiding face-to-face contact between parties, also often avoids a confrontation of conflicting interests and personalities. The sale and the purchase of a home in most cases is an emotionally charged transaction. As such it may create a volatile atmosphere for the parties. The slightest innuendo can often trigger a dispute and present unnecessary problems. Since the escrow closing avoids a face-to-face encounter, it prevents this potential problem from arising.

REQUIREMENTS OF AN ESCROW

In order for a valid real estate escrow to exist, the following ingredients are necessary: valid deed, enforceable contract, delivery, escrow agent, escrow agreement and condition.

Valid Deed

A deed that is the subject of an escrow must be executed properly in accordance with the state law that is applicable to the transaction. A deed lacking the essentials of valid execution cannot be the subject of a valid escrow transaction, and the escrow agent holding such a deed is under an obligation to surrender it to the grantor upon request.

• CASE BRIEF •

John Hines signs a deed and delivers it into escrow. The deed is not witnessed at the time of delivery. State law requires the grantor to "acknowledge the signing of a deed to be his or her voluntary act before two witnesses." The deposit of the deed will not operate as an escrow because it lacks the appropriate attestation. The deed is subject to recall by Hines. *See Collins v. Kares, 52 S.D. 143, 216 N.W. 880 (1927).*

Omission of the grantee's name in the deed does not invalidate the escrow so long as the grantor authorizes the escrow agent to insert the grantee's name. Likewise, failure to include a legal description of the real estate within the deed does not invalidate the escrow if the grantor authorizes the depositary to insert the designated description.

Enforceable Contract

In order for an instrument to operate as a real estate escrow, there must be an enforceable contract between the parties concerning the property. In absence of a valid purchase contract, the deposit of a deed with an escrow agent cannot be the subject of a valid escrow. Consequently, the deed is subject to recall at the grantor's request. This is true even if the deed is signed properly and is in conformity with all the requirements of execution. Since a contract for the sale of real estate is within the Statute of Frauds, there must be a written memorandum to support the contract. An oral contract to sell real estate cannot be the basis of an escrow.

• CASE BRIEF •

Anna Skibosh entered into a land contract with Auto Acceptance for the sale of her premises. Two days later Auto Acceptance assigned its interest in the land contract to Interstate. Interstate then executed a quitclaim deed in favor of Joseph Sorce and delivered it to Auto Acceptance with an attached letter stating that the deed would be held in trust by Auto Acceptance until Sorce paid off certain debts owed to Auto Acceptance.

The land contract was fulfilled, and Skibosh conveyed the property to Auto Acceptance, which conveyed it to Interstate. Sorce's creditors claimed that Sorce was the owner of the property. The court disagreed and stated as part of its rationale that the escrow of a deed to real estate must be accompanied by an agreement that satisfies the Statute of Frauds and that the letter attached to the deed was insufficient for that purpose. *West Federal Savings & Loan Association v. Interstate Investment, Inc.,* 57 Wis.2d 690, 205 N.W.2d 361 (1973).

The deed itself does not ordinarily satisfy the Statute of Frauds, because the essential terms of sale such as price are not normally included in the deed. To insert the required terms in the deed would be a cumbersome departure from acceptable deed drafting. The most common practice is for the seller and the buyer to execute a writing that, independent of the deed itself, satisfies the Statute of Frauds. This is usually the purchase contract.

Delivery

Surrender of possession and control of a document to the third party depositary.

The deed must be delivered to the escrow agent by the grantor or grantor's agent with the intent to surrender possession of the instrument. This surrender is known as the *first delivery.* The grantor must absolutely relinquish control over the deed. In the event the deed is subject to recall by the grantor, delivery has not been accomplished. Accordingly, delivery does not occur until the instrument is beyond the legal power of the grantor to retrieve.

• CASE BRIEF •

Kevin Armstrong, who is afflicted with a serious kidney disorder, deposits a deed with an escrow agent before entering the hospital for surgery. Kevin instructs the depositary to deliver the deed to his sister "in the event I do not survive the operation; otherwise I will pick it up after I am released from the hospital." Since Kevin did not relinquish total control over the document, there was no legal delivery to the escrow agent. *See Gilmer v. Anderson, 34 Mich. App. 6, 190 N.W.2d 708 (1971).*

Escrow Agent

The third party who is the depositary in an escrow transaction.

The deed is delivered to an escrow agent. The escrow agent, designated as an escrowee or escrow holder, represents the interests of both the buyer and the seller. In that sense the escrowee is a double agent who owes a duty to both to act in good faith. The escrow agent has no authority other than that derived by agreement of the parties and is strictly confined to acting in accordance with that agreement. The escrow agent is a conduit bound by the terms of the escrow agreement.

Generally, neither the buyer nor seller should act in the capacity of an escrow agent since the objectivity of either is suspect. Moreover, an escrow held by the grantor violates the principle that control over the instrument must be surrendered. Delivery of an escrow to the grantee raises the question of whether delivery is absolute. As a rule, however, the intention of the grantor governs. If the grantor delivers a deed intended as an escrow to the grantee for purposes of transporting it to a third-party depositary, the grantee is deemed the grantor's special agent for that purpose and delivery to the grantee is incomplete. Nevertheless, most authorities agree that a deed fully executed and delivered as an escrow to the grantee immediately invests title absolutely in the grantee regardless of any stated preconditions. There is some contrary authority that the intent of the grantor would control even here.

The traditional rule was that attorneys or agents of either party could not act as an escrow agent because to do so could create a conflict of interest. The trend, however, is to permit agents of the parties or their attorneys to be escrow agents as long as their capacity as such is not antagonistic to their principal's interest. Although some states expressly permit a real estate broker or salesperson to be an escrow agent, customarily real estate agents avoid this potentially conflicting office.

The escrow agent may not act contrary to the escrow instructions. Any deviation constitutes a breach of the relationship of trust. In such a case the escrow agent would be liable for any resulting damages.

• CASE BRIEF •

Lon Luebel, escrow agent, delivers a deed to Mike Lerman, grantee, prior to the deposit of the purchase price, a precondition of the instructed delivery. The purchase price is $70,000. Lon is liable to Kim Sipe, the grantor, for damages because he acted contrary to the escrow instructions. *See Allen v. Allen Title Co., 77 N.M. 796, 427 P.2d 673 (1967).*

Sometimes an escrow agent is charged with delivering the deed to the grantee and the purchase price to the grantor when a title check proves that the title is free and unencumbered. If a title check shows that the title is not free and clear, the escrow agent must return the deed and purchase money to the respective parties. If the escrow agent instead tenders the purchase money to the grantor, the escrow agent will be liable to the grantee for the purchase price.

In an escrow transaction property comes into the hands of an escrow agent who is in a relationship of trust to the parties involved in the sale. If the escrow agent unauthorizedly converts the property to personal use, by most state standards the escrow agent is guilty of embezzlement.

An escrow agent should open up an escrow account to receive funds related to the escrow transaction. Commingling of escrow funds with personal funds of the escrow agent may result in liability. However, sometimes an escrow agent is authorized to maintain the delivered funds in a personal bank account. In that case it is extremely important for the escrow agent to keep an account balance at least equal to the amount of the escrow funds. Otherwise the escrow agent is deemed to have converted the monies to personal use and is guilty of a crime.

When an escrow agent embezzles escrow funds, either the buyer or the seller bears the loss. The rule of law is that the party who was entitled to the funds at the moment of conversion is the one who must bear the loss. If the condition under which the purchase money was to be held in escrow was performed, then the loss falls upon the seller since the seller was entitled to the money. Until the happening of the condition, the loss falls upon the buyer since the legal right to receive the funds has not passed to the seller.

• CASE BRIEF •

The following condition was contained within an escrow agreement: "When Ms. Elswick, the seller, furnishes an abstract showing a marketable title, the escrow agent, the First National Bank, shall deliver the deed to Walter Foster and the purchase price to Ms. Elswick." When the abstract was furnished, Foster refused to accept it on account of alleged defects and demanded a return of the purchase price. While Ms. Elswick was attempting to cure the alleged defects, the First National Bank was found to have commingled the escrow funds with other accounts, and the money was lost. The loss fell upon Foster, the purchaser, since the condition upon which the escrow was predicated had not been met. *Foster v. Elswick, 176 Ark. 974, 4 S.W.2d 946 (1928).*

Of course an escrow agent who embezzles or otherwise misappropriates funds is liable to the person upon whom the loss falls. As a practical matter, however, it is very difficult to collect against an absconding or incarcerated escrow agent.

Escrow Agreement

An agreement that directs the escrow agent regarding terms and conditions under which the deed or other instruments are to be delivered to the parties and the disposition of the deed or other instruments on default.

The escrow agreement need not be reduced to writing. Even so, in retrospect many buyers and sellers regret their failure to do so. Some lawyers who draft escrow agreements include the terms of the escrow agreement in the purchase contract; others include them in an entirely separate instrument. The escrow agreement should be sufficiently detailed in writing to express the intent of the parties and to cover various contingencies. Some of the terms commonly included within an escrow agreement are:

- Names and addresses of seller, buyer and escrow agent;
- Description of the property that is the subject of the escrow;
- Obligations of buyer and seller regarding the deposit of instruments and money into escrow;
- Directions to escrow agent regarding the recording of the deed and disbursement of the purchase money;
- The specific condition upon which title is to pass;

- Directions to the escrow agent regarding procedure in the event the condition is not met;
- Payment of escrow brokerage and attorney fees, recording charges and other costs;
- Signatures of the seller, buyer and escrow agent.

The escrow agent is bound by the terms of the escrow agreement and may not deviate from it in any respect. Where a conflict exists between the terms of the purchase contract and the escrow agreement, the agent is bound to follow the instructions contained in the escrow agreement. The escrow agent may not follow oral instructions that contradict the terms of the written agreement. A typical escrow agreement is shown in Figure 24.2.

When the condition upon which title is to pass occurs, the escrow agent must deliver the deed to the grantee. If the condition does not occur, under the terms of the agreement the escrow agent is normally charged with returning the purchase money to the purchaser and redelivering the deed to the grantor.

An escrow agreement is a contract; it is not revocable by any party without the consent of all the parties to the agreement. In the event that one of the parties attempts to revoke and demands the return of the deposit, the escrow agent must ignore the demand. When conflict or doubt as to interpretation of the agreement arises, a judicial declaration should be sought.

Under the Federal Rules of Civil Procedure as well as many state laws whose civil rules are patterned after the federal rules, an escrow agent who is faced with conflicting claims of liability or ownership may secure a judicial declaration by *interpleading* the claimants. The practical result of this procedure is to force the parties to litigate their rival claims in one court action. The escrow agent becomes a stakeholder who holds the contested property pending the outcome of the lawsuit. The interpleader device is not available to an escrow agent who is guilty of misconduct in the escrow transaction.

Condition

Before an instrument can be considered an escrow, its deposit with the escrow agent must be coupled with the depositor's intention that it not take effect until the happening of a specified condition. This condition is essential in order to suspend passage of the instrument to the buyer. If there is no specified condition, then delivery of a fully executed deed to the escrow agent immediately vests title in the purchaser.

The escrow may be used to require any number of conditions to attach before the deed and purchase money pass to the respective parties. Buyers' conditions may include, for example, conditioning the

ESCROW AGREEMENT

This agreement is made by and between _____
_____, (hereafter referred to as Seller) and
_____, (hereafter referred to as Buyer).
Whereas, the Seller and Buyer have entered into a contract dated
_____, 19__, of which a true copy is attached, for the sale of the
premises described as follows: _____
_____
_____

Now, therefore, it is mutually agreed:

That _____ is hereby appointed escrow
agent and empowered to carry said contract and this agreement into
effect;

That the Seller will deposit with said escrow agent a deed of said
premises to the Buyer with general warranty that the title is good and
unencumbered except use restrictions and easements of record, if any,
and taxes and assessments for the year ____ and thereafter;

That the Buyer will deposit with said escrow agent the sum of
_____, being the balance of the purchase price of _____;

That said escrow agent is directed to file said deed for record and
make disbursements when the terms of said contract can be complied
with, and provided he can furnish to the Buyer a certificate of title
showing record title to said premises to be good and unencumbered in
the Buyer;

That the escrow agent shall return any deposit if all deposits and requirements necessary to closing are not made within _____days
from this date;

That Seller will pay for preparation of deed, [other items may be in-
serted];

That Buyer will pay for _____;

That taxes and assessments, prepaid insurance premiums, and rents
will be prorated as of the date of closing, and no adjustments are to be
made by the escrow agent for water and other utilities.

Dated at _____, ____, this _____ day of _____, 19__.

_____
                                    Seller

_____   _____
Escrow Agent   Buyer

Figure 24.2: Escrow agreement

passage of title on the buyer's obtaining financing, making payment of the purchase price, selling a house or securing a zoning change. Sellers' conditions may include, for example, providing evidence of title, proof that the property is free from wood-destroying insect infestation or proof that the electrical system in the house is free from defects. Before the grantee is entitled to delivery of the deed, the specified condition must occur. Until such occurrence, the legal title to the deed remains with the seller. In the event the depositary delivers the deed over to a grantee prior to the happening of the condition, no title actually passes since the delivery is unauthorized.

TITLE PASSAGE

In a completed escrow transaction there are two deliveries. The first delivery is accomplished when the grantor surrenders control over the deed and delivers it to the escrow agent. The second delivery occurs when the escrow agent surrenders the deed to the purchaser after the occurrence of the condition. As soon as the condition occurs upon which the escrow is predicated, the grantee is entitled to delivery of the escrow. The trend in authority is that title actually passes to the grantee when, pursuant to the escrow agreement, the grantee is entitled to the delivery.

Relation Back

A legal doctrine whereby the title acquired by a deed relates back to the moment of the first delivery to an escrow agent.

In some instances the *second delivery* of the deed is accounted as taking effect as of the time of the first delivery to the agent. This doctrine of relation back is applied when an event that would otherwise thwart the intent of the parties or cause a manifest injustice intervenes between the first and second deliveries.

Death and Disability

The doctrine of relation back avoids complications that might normally arise where death or insanity of the grantor intervenes between the first and second deliveries. The death of the grantor whose deed is held in escrow does not invalidate the escrow. Upon the happening of the escrow condition the grantee is entitled to delivery. The delivery relates back in time to the original moment of transfer to the escrow agent. Under this doctrine of relation back, title passage is deemed to have occurred while the grantor was living. Similarly, if after the delivery of a deed in escrow the grantee dies, the grantee's representative will be entitled to delivery upon the happening of the condition. Under the doctrine of relation back, the passage of title is deemed to have occurred at the time of the first delivery, during the life of the grantee. This fiction accomplishes a just result.

• CASE BRIEF •

Birdie H. Fuqua executed a contract for the sale of a 50-acre tract of property to Selected Lands Corporation (SLC). Shortly thereafter she signed a deed and placed it in escrow. Under the terms of the agreement the escrow agent was to deliver the deed to SLC when SLC's attorney approved the closing papers. Before the approval Birdie died. Thereafter the attorney approved the papers. The court held that the death of the grantor did not invalidate the instrument and that upon the occurrence of the condition the grantee was entitled to the deed. Under the doctrine of relation back, title would be deemed to pass as of the date of the first delivery. *Fuqua v. Fuqua, 528 S.W.2d 896 (Tex. Civ. App. 1975)*.

The doctrine of relation back is similarly applicable to a case where the grantor becomes insane or otherwise incompetent to effect a transfer after delivering the deed to the escrow agent but before delivery to the purchaser. Under the doctrine, upon the happening of the condition the grantee is entitled to passage of title, which is deemed to have occurred on the date of the first delivery, thus avoiding frustration of the intent of the parties.

Dower

The doctrine of relation back may protect the purchaser from dower claims in the seller's wife where the wife of a deceased seller had no dower expectancy at the time the deed was deposited into escrow. This may occur as a result of a marriage by the seller after delivery of the deed into escrow but before the second delivery to the purchaser. In such a case, upon the happening of the condition the title passage relates back to the date of the first delivery; consequently, the seller's wife has no dower interest.

CASE EXAMPLE

Seth Nathan, unmarried, executes a deed and deposits it in escrow. The escrow agent is directed to deliver the deed to the buyer when the buyer secures financing and deposits the purchase price. Before the deposit of the purchase price Seth marries; thereafter the buyer deposits the purchase price. Seth's wife refuses to release dower interests in the property. Regardless, the escrow agent is charged with conveying the deed to the grantee, who takes free of spousal interests pursuant to the doctrine of relation back.

Intervening Liens

Application of the doctrine of relation back may avoid problems caused by liens, encumbrances and judgments that attach between the time of the first and second deliveries. When a seller conveys title by deed to a third party who has knowledge that the deed is the subject of an escrow, the doctrine of relation back normally protects the original purchaser. Under this doctrine the purchaser is deemed to have taken title at the first delivery; consequently, the seller was without power to convey good title to the third party. If the third party is a bona fide purchaser for value without notice that the instrument is the subject of an escrow, however, the courts are less likely to apply the doctrine to defeat the third party's title. The same rules apply where the grantor creates an encumbrance on the property during escrow. If the lienholder is without knowledge of the escrow, the lienholder has priority. Otherwise the doctrine of relation back will protect the grantee since the grantor's title is deemed cut off at the time of the first delivery.

OTHER USES OF ESCROW

Two other uses of escrow are notable. They include the long-term escrow and the mortgage escrow.

Long-term Escrow

The long-term escrow is a tool for financing a real estate transaction. A long-term escrow may range in duration from a year to 30 or more years. It is actually a combination of the land installment contract and the escrow. A buyer may not be in a position to borrow funds. Nonetheless, a seller may desire to sell the land to such a purchaser by requiring installment payments. To secure the payment of the purchase price, the seller may withhold the deed from the buyer until the final installment is paid. Under such an arrangement the seller delivers into escrow a fully executed deed with instructions to the escrow agent to deliver the deed to the buyer upon full payment of the purchase price.

• CASE BRIEF •

Jake Rubin owns 50 acres of farmland that has been on the market for two years, listed at $100,000. Lance Lane desires to buy the land but is unable to obtain financing from a lending institution. Rubin and Lane enter into a land installment contract whereby Lane pays $10,000 down and agrees to pay the remaining $90,000 over nine years at 15¼ percent interest. Rubin executes the deed in favor of Lane and deposits it with Fidelity Trust Co., an escrow agent that is directed by the terms of the escrow agreement to deliver the deed to Lane upon receiving receipts evidencing that the purchase price has been paid in full. Rubin does not have control over the deed as long as Lane does not default on the terms of the installment contract. After nine years of timely payments, Lane is entitled to the deed. *See Beren Corp. v. Spader, 198 Neb. 677, 255 N.W.2d 247 (1977).*

If a purchaser fails to make the timely payments, the escrow agent is normally charged with returning the deed to the seller pursuant to the escrow agreement.

One major disadvantage of the long-term escrow is risk; the buyer takes a chance that the seller will convey the property by deed to another or mortgage the land in an amount that would interfere with the buyer's equity in the property. Since the seller remains the titleholder of record, a bona fide purchaser for value without notice of the contract may take from the seller and defeat the buyer's interest. However, if the installment buyer is in possession, then the purchaser has constructive notice of the buyer's interest and would not take good title. The installment buyer may also be protected by recording the land installment contract. This would be sufficient to give notice to subsequent grantees or mortgagees and thus protect the contract buyer. In fact, many states require a land installment contract to be recorded.

Mortgage Escrow

A mortgagee may desire to set up an escrow in order to be protected. In this event the money to be lent to the mortgagor is deposited in escrow, awaiting proof that there are no outstanding liens on the property. Upon such assurance the mortgage can be recorded and the funds released to the mortgagor as directed; the mortgagee is secure as a first lienor. The surrender of the money into escrow is deemed to be the creation of a debt, which is necessary for a mortgage to be a valid lien on property.

SUMMARY

The escrow is a deed delivered by a third party, or escrow agent, when a specified condition is met. Real estate escrow is an alternative means for transferring title to property. In an escrow transaction the buyer and seller do not meet face to face at the closing. The escrow closing is distinguished from the escrow account, also common in real estate practice, in which the mortgagor pays a monthly amount to the mortgagee to cover property taxes.

Escrow may be chosen as a transfer device for reasons of convenience or to assure that neither party backs out of a transaction. Six ingredients must be present for a valid escrow to exist: a valid deed, an enforceable contract, delivery, an escrow agent, an escrow agreement and one or more conditions. The escrow agent has a fiduciary duty to the buyer and seller and must not act contrary to specific instructions. For example, an agent who converts funds or property to his or her own use without authorization is guilty of embezzlement. It is very difficult to collect against an agent who has absconded even when embezzlement can be proven. For this reason the attorney or other party who is to act as escrow agent must be chosen with care. Further, it is good practice to express an escrow agreement in writing, with all terms and conditions clearly stated.

The legal doctrine of relation back applies in real estate escrow transactions. It states that the title acquired by a deed relates back to the moment of the first delivery to an escrow agent. Therefore, the death of the seller before the purchase price is paid by the buyer does not invalidate the deed. The doctrine also applies if the seller becomes insane or otherwise loses legal capacity to contract.

Another use of the escrow device is the long-term escrow, which resembles a land installment contract; the deed is held by an escrow agent until the final installment is paid. Finally, the mortgage escrow, another variation, may be used to protect the mortgagee.

REVIEW AND DISCUSSION QUESTIONS

1. Name the parties to an escrow transaction and describe the flow of documents.
2. What are the advantages of an escrow transaction?
3. Name the six requirements of an escrow and briefly describe each.
4. What are the responsibilities of an escrow agent?
5. Name some conditions upon which an escrow may be predicated.
6. When does the loss due to embezzlement of funds held by an escrow agent fall upon the seller?
7. Describe the doctrine of relation back and give some examples as to how it affects the buyer.
8. What is a long-term escrow and when is it used?

CASE PROBLEMS

1. Mary Jackson executed a deed in the name of her son Clarence. She placed the deed in escrow and instructed the escrow agent to deliver the deed to Clarence after the latter paid a specified sum to each of his siblings. Mary died, and Clarence tried to make the specified payments. His siblings refused to accept payment and claimed that the deed was ineffectual since the escrow condition was not met before Mary's death. (a) Why do

you think that Clarence's siblings refused to accept the payment? (b) What doctrine can Clarence rely upon in his attempt to establish the existence of a valid contract? (c) What is the theory behind this doctrine and how will it help Clarence? *See Jackson v. Jackson*, 67 Or. 44, 135 P. 201 (1913).

2. Tillie Ganser entered into a contract with her four children whereby Tillie agreed to convey a specified tract of land to each child upon the payment by each child of a specified sum. It was agreed that an escrow account would be used to handle the transaction. Tillie deposited four valid deeds with the escrow agent, but before any of the children paid the agent the amount due under the contract, Tillie died. Tillie's executor seeks to set aside the land sales as mere offers revoked by Tillie's death. (a) Will the executor be able to set aside the contracts for the sale of the land? Explain. *See Ganser v. Zimmerman*, 80 N.W.2d 828 (N.D. 1956). (b) Would the following fact pattern present a different result? Tillie deposited four valid deeds, executed in the names of each of her four children, with her attorney, accompanied by instructions to convey the deeds to her children when all contracts for the sale of the property were negotiated. Before any contracts could be negotiated, Tillie died. *See Merry v. County Bd. of Educ.*, 264 Ala. 411, 87 So.2d 821 (1956).

3. Jeff Daily, seller, deposits a deed into escrow, and Ron Williams deposits the purchase price. The escrow agent is instructed to record the deed immediately and to pass the purchase money to Daily when a certificate of title is produced showing good and marketable title in Daily, free from all liens and encumbrances. The deed is immediately recorded pursuant to instructions. Thereafter, Dr. Joel Mark obtains a judgment against Daily for $500. Shortly afterwards, the certificate of title is produced. Does the Mark judgment result in an encumbrance upon the property? Explain. *See Hall v. Harris*, 40 N.C. 295 (1848).

4. Ellen Love deposits a fully executed deed in escrow. Pursuant to a purchase contract and escrow instructions, the deed is to be delivered to Sarah Gibson when the zoning of the property is changed from residential to commercial. After the zoning change occurs, but before the escrow agent delivers the deed to Gibson, a judgment creditor of Gibson seeks to levy on the property. Will the judgment creditor be successful? Explain. *See Sturgill v. Industrial Painting Corp.*, 82 Nev. 61, 410 P.2d 759 (1966).

5. Robert O'Neal agreed to sell to Thomas Ryan a parcel of land.

The parties agreed to handle the transfer through an escrow agent. According to the escrow agreement, O'Neal was to deposit a valid deed executed in Ryan's name with the escrow agent. The agent was to deliver the deed to Ryan when Ryan deposited $12,000 with the escrow agent. Before Ryan or O'Neal performed his obligations under the agreement, O'Neal informed the escrow agent that the property was worth much more than $12,000 and that O'Neal would not deliver the deed unless Ryan paid $13,000. (a) Since neither party has performed his contractual duties, can O'Neal alter the terms of the escrow agreement? Why or why not? (b) What if Ryan agrees to the additional amount? Does that change the result? *See Gelber v. Cappeller*, 161 Cal. App. 2d. 113, 326 P.2d 521 (1958).

6. Maxum and Nelson reached a tentative agreement for the exchange of a parcel of land owned by Nelson for a parcel owned by Maxum. Maxum had not seen the Nelson property, located in a distant state, and so planned to visit the site before consummating the deal. Before leaving, Maxum deposited a valid deed to his property with Wallace. Maxum instructed Wallace that if he found the property suitable he would write to Wallace and direct him to deliver the deed to Nelson. The delivery of Maxum's deed was contingent on Nelson's delivering the deed to his land to Wallace. Nelson delivered his deed to Wallace. Maxum, after examining the property, found it unsatisfactory and promptly wrote to Wallace, instructing him not to deliver the deed to Nelson. Nelson objected to Maxum's action. Nelson claims that a valid escrow agreement was formed and, upon the tender of his deed to Wallace, Wallace was bound to deliver the Maxum deed to Nelson. Is Nelson correct? Discuss. *See Nelson v. Davis*, 102 Wash. 313, 172 P. 1178 (1918).

7. Mr. Konopka and Mr. Zaremba negotiated a contract for the sale of Konopka's residence to Zaremba. The parties agreed to establish an escrow account with Ms. Wourms, Konopka's real estate agent. The escrow agreement required that Zaremba immediately deposit a down payment of $2,500 with Wourms, which he did. The ultimate sale of the residence was contingent on Zaremba's obtaining a mortgage loan of $20,500. Zaremba obtained the loan, at which time Konopka requested delivery of the down payment from Wourms. Wourms admitted that she was unable to deliver the money because she had used the money to pay her business creditors. Konopka refuses to close the deal until Zaremba pays the contract price to him.

Zaremba contends that he owes the contract price less the $2,500 he has already paid to Wourms. (a) Who is right? Upon whom will the loss of the money fall? Why? (b) Is it relevant that Wourms was employed by Konopka to act as his real estate agent? Explain. *See Zaremba v. Konopka*, 91 N.J. Super. 300, 228 A.2d 91 (1967).

25

The Leasehold Estate and the Lease

LEASEHOLD ESTATE

An estate created when the owner of property, known as the *lessor* or *landlord,* conveys a possessory interest in the real property to another, known as the *lessee* or *tenant,* for a specific period of time in exchange for the tenant's payment of rent.

An unusual aspect of a lease is that it is rooted firmly in two distinct areas of law: contract law and real property law. As a contract, the lease must contain the essential elements of any contract—offer, acceptance and consideration—in order to be enforceable. Since it relates to real property, the lease involves a conveyance of an estate in land, or a leasehold estate. The landlord surrenders his or her possessory rights to the premises for the duration of the lease. The tenant must pay for that possession during the term of the lease. Because the tenant is getting an estate in land, he or she is required by law to pay the rent even if there is no specific agreement regarding rent. Possession is exchanged for rent.

The granting of a leasehold estate gives to a tenant the *exclusive posssession* of the premises for an agreed-upon term with a reversion at the end of the term to possession by the landlord. This exclusive right of possession deprives the owner of the premises during the lease. Even where tenants fail to comply with the leasehold bargain, landlords can remove them from the premises only by bringing formal eviction proceedings.

Four different kinds of leasehold estates can be created. They

551

are: term tenancy, periodic tenancy, tenancy at will and tenancy at sufferance.

Term Tenancy

An estate for a specified period of time that has a specific beginning date and a specific ending date. When the ending date arrives, the estate is terminated without notice by either party.

This tenancy, also known as an *estate for years*, terminates without any action by either party upon expiration of the term stated in the agreement. It should be noted that if the parties' lease stipulates notice or other conditions for termination of the tenancy, as written leases often do, then these conditions must be met. In the absence of a statute or an agreement to the contrary, the term tenancy is considered personal property and will pass as such to those entitled to take personal property from the estate of the deceased tenant.

If the parties fail to stipulate the amount of rent due, a reasonable rent is required. A reasonable rent is based on prevailing rental rates in the vicinity. Under the common law, however, the rent is not due until the end of the tenancy. By way of contrast, most modern leases require the rent to be prepaid since landlords are understandably unwilling to wait until the end of the term to receive payment of rent.

Periodic Tenancy

An estate from period to period, continuing from period to period until terminated by proper notice from one of the parties.

The periodic tenancy is normally from year to year or month to month but can be for any period up to a year. It can be created in several different ways. One way is by express agreement. If *A* leases her property to *B* "from month to month beginning April 1, 1980," a periodic tenancy is created. This estate or tenancy may also arise by implication.

• CASE BRIEF •

Rhodes leased farmlands from Sigler. The agreement was oral, and the parties did not discuss the duration of the lease, although rent was to be paid yearly. After the first year, Sigler refused to allow Rhodes to work the land. Sigler sued for the right to farm the property on the grounds that Rhodes had given him no termination notice as required by Illinois law for a periodic tenancy. Rhodes argued that the tenancy was for a fixed term of one year and no notice was necessary.

In affirming a lower court judgment for Sigler, the appellate court stated, "Where one is given possession under a parol [oral] agreement for an indefinite term with annual reservation of rent, as appears here, then a tenancy from year to year is created." *Rhodes v. Sigler, 27 Ill. App. 3d 1, 325 N.E.2d 381 (1975).*

This type of estate can also evolve from a term tenancy when the tenant remains, or "holds over," after the expiration of the term tenancy. The holdover tenancy will be discussed in more detail later in this section.

The periodic tenancy can be terminated by either party upon giving adequate notice. The parties may contractually agree on what will constitute adequate notice. Absent such an agreement, adequate notice wil be one period's notice up to six months.

CASE EXAMPLE

Karen Kaiser leases Greenacre to Franks "from year to year beginning April 1, 1981." She leases Brownacre to Martin "from month to month beginning April 1, 1981." To terminate the lease to Greenacre, either Kaiser or Franks would have to give six months' notice unless they had an agreement to the contrary. The Brownacre lease could be ended by either party with one month's notice of termination, absent a contrary agreement.

These common law notice periods have been altered by statutes in many states. For example, the Uniform Residential Landlord and Tenant Act has been adopted in part in several states. This act provides that a week-to-week tenancy requires a written notice of ten days. A month-to-month tenancy requires a notice of at least 60 days. Year-to-year tenancies are not mentioned in the act because they almost inevitably apply only to agricultural lands and not to residential premises.

Notice given by the terminating party must reach the other party a full period early. The general rule is that the notice must be given one calendar period in advance, although some cases have held to the contrary.

• CASE BRIEF •

Molter rented an apartment to Spencer on a month-to-month basis. Rent was due on the 25th of each month. On February 25, Spencer was served with notice to quit the premises as of March 25. When Spencer refused to move, Molter sued to evict him. After a judgment for Molter, Spencer appealed.

In reversing the judgment, the appellate court stated as follows:

In 1919 there were 28 days in the calendar month of February, the month in which the notice was given. Excluding February 25, the day on which the notice was served, and including March 24, the last day of the rent-paying month, the tenant had but 27 days' notice. Therefore the notice lacked one day of being a one month's notice within the meaning of the statute, as construed by this court.

Molter v. Spencer, 108 Wis. 38, 180 N.W. 261 (1920).

Where there is uncertainty as to the period of the tenancy, a good indicator is the rent payments. If the rent is paid yearly or monthly, it is a good indication that the parties have a year-to-year or month-to-month periodic tenancy. An exception occurs when the yearly rent is stated in the lease but the payment is due monthly. This would be treated as a year-to-year period.

• CASE BRIEF •

Cleveland Wrecking needed vacant land on a temporary basis to store material from buildings that it was demolishing. The company entered into an agreement with Aetna Oil Company. The agreement stipulated that "the tenant will pay to the landlord, in equal monthly installments of One Hundred Fifty Dollars ($150.00) payable in advance on the 12th day of each month, an annual rental of Eighteen Hundred Dollars ($1,800.00)."

The oil company needed the land and gave the wrecking company notice to vacate as required for a month-to-month tenancy. The wrecking company argued that the tenancy was year to year and it was entitled to remain on the premises for several more months. This contention was accepted by the appellate court, which indicated that as the rental was stated on a yearly basis, a tenancy from year to year was created. *Cleveland Wrecking Co. v. Aetna Oil Co., 287 Ky. 542, 154 S.W.2d 31 (1941).*

Tenancy at Will

A tenancy that exists until either party chooses to terminate it.

This type of estate may arise by express agreement. For example, a lease may state "to Franks at the will of Kaiser." This wording creates a tenancy at will. Despite this restrictive language, tenancies at will can be terminated by either party.

A tenancy at will is more likely to arise by implication.

• CASE BRIEF •

Rickey L. Hitchcock was a tenant in an apartment, having

signed a one-year lease. The lease had been executed on behalf of the landlord, Mayfield, by a renting agent. The lease contained a provision absolving Mayfield of any loss resulting from his negligence. Unknown to the parties, the lease was not executed properly. State law required the renting agency's authority to be in writing, and no such written authority existed.

When a fire, probably due to Mayfield's negligence, caused Hitchcock $7,325 damages, he sued. Mayfield defended using the waiver-of-liability provision. After a lower court dismissed Hitchcock's claim because of this provision, an appellate court reversed. The appellate court took the position that, because the lease was executed improperly, it was not effective. As a result Hitchcock was by implication a tenant at will and not subject to the waiver provision in the lease. The appellate court remanded the case to the lower court for it to determine whether Mayfield had been negligent. *Hitchcock v. Mayfield 133 Ga. App. 546, 211 S.E. 2d 612 (1974).*

Under the common law no notice was required to end a tenancy at will. Many states now have statutes that require a minimum notice period, thereby softening the harshness of the common law rule. Although the estate exists wholly by permission, all the rights and duties of the landlord-tenant relationship exist. Unlike the previously mentioned leasehold estates, however, a tenancy at will is terminated by the death of either party or by the sale of the property to a third party.

Tenancy at Sufferance

Created when a person is wrongfully in possession of another's land without a valid lease.

The tenant at sufferance is similar to a trespasser. The major difference is that the tenant at sufferance entered the property legally. Usually he or she is the holdover tenant from a term tenancy. The landlord owes this tenant no duties, and the tenant can be evicted at any time. The classification of a person as a tenant at sufferance, not as a trespasser, actually works to the tenant's disadvantage. The tenant is unable to possess the property adversely against the landlord and eventually gain an ownership interest, although a trespasser could.

Holdover Tenant

One who failed to vacate or surrender possession of the premises on the ending date of a term tenancy.

The term *holdover tenant* is sometimes used in relation to a periodic tenancy, where the tenant stays on despite the landlord's adequate notice to vacate. Under these circumstances, a landlord who permits the tenant to remain has technically waived the notice and allowed the continuation of the periodic tenancy.

The term tenant who holds over after the expiration date of a lease temporarily becomes a tenant at sufferance. All options shift into the landlord's hands when the tenant holds over. The landlord has the option of evicting the tenant or of holding him or her for another term.

CASE EXAMPLE

Anton leases a house and lot to Glenn and Sarah Williams. The terms of the agreement stipulate that the lease commences on July 1, 1982, and terminates on June 30, 1983. On July 1, 1983, the couple is still living in the house. Anton has the option of beginning eviction proceedings against the Williamses, who are now tenants at sufferance, or of unilaterally extending their lease until June 30, 1984.

Once the landlord exercises the option to hold the tenant for an additional period, the estate becomes a periodic tenancy. The maximum length of the period will be one year, or more accurately year to year, even where the term tenancy was for a longer period. If the original term tenancy was for less than one year, the holdover tenant will be held to a periodic tenancy for that particular period, such as week to week or month to month.

The terms of the holdover tenant's new lease will be the same as those of the original lease except as to length of time, as noted above. One exception arises when the landlord notifies the tenant before the expiration of the lease that he or she is changing the terms (for example, raising the rent). The tenant is usually held to the altered terms.

If the holdover is involuntary and for a short period of time, courts will not hold the tenant for an additional term. For instance, if the holdover is caused by a tornado, a snowstorm, a death in the family or a one-day delay of the moving van, the court is not likely to hold the tenant for an additional period.

LEASE

A contract, either written or oral, that transfers the right of possession of the premises to the lessee or tenant.

The relationship of landlord and tenant usually arises from an express contract on the part of the parties called a *lease*. As previously stated, the lease is firmly rooted in the law of contracts. The lease or contract normally includes terms giving the tenant the right to possession and entitling the landlord to a certain amount of rent. To this extent these contractual components overlap the possession-rent aspects that arise inherently from the real property notion of a conveyance of an estate in land. The lease-contract is likely to specify the terms of the possession and the amount of the rent, as well as many other factors that together compose the essence of the landlord and tenant's agreement.

Essential Elements of the Lease

The purpose of the lease is to detail the rights and duties of each of the parties in the contract. It is incumbent upon the parties to take great care in drafting the lease, especially if the terms of the agreement are complex or the duration of the lease is long. To do otherwise is to invite a lawsuit.

A Valid Contract

Since a lease is a contract, it must contain the essential elements of a contract. There must be a mutual consent to enter the agreement, and the agreement must be supported by consideration (rent in exchange for possession). The lease agreement will not require the use of any particular prescribed words. Essentially, it must be shown that it was mutually intended for the tenant to have possession and that the landlord retained a *reversionary* interest in the land (that is, the right to have the property back when the lease expired).

The consideration that supports the lease contract is usually the rent. Nevertheless, the periodic payment of rent is not necessary to have a valid contract. The requirement is merely that consideration, or something of value, be given at some time to the landlord.

The other elements of a valid contract, such as the capacity of the parties (both must be sane and of legal age) and legality of purpose, must be met as well.

Statute of Frauds

Prior to 1677, under the common law originally operating in England, leases did not have to be in writing. With the adoption of the Statute of Frauds, however, leases for a term in excess of three years had to be in writing to be enforceable beyond those three years. A few states have adopted the English version of the Statute of Frauds and require writings for leases in excess of three years. In most states, however, the Statute of Frauds provision necessitates a writing if the lease exceeds one year.

The intent of this requirement is to reduce fraud in the area of leases. It should be made clear that the statutory minimum, usually one year, does not indicate that leases for one year or less should not be in writing. The careful landlord and tenant will benefit if all terms of their agreement are reduced to writing in order to minimize the opportunity for misunderstanding or outright fraud.

It should be emphasized that an oral lease within the maximum term of the Statute of Frauds is every bit as valid as a written lease. If a dispute arises over an oral lease, however, the proof may be more difficult to derive. If a dispute arises over a lease that has gone beyond the allowable period under the Statute of Frauds, the estate is treated as a tenancy at will.

Parties

The lease must identify the parties as lessor and lessee, and both parties should sign the document. The signature of the lessor, the owner of the property, is normally mandatory. Under the Statute of Frauds, the signature of the party against whom the lease will be enforced is required.

The spouse of the lessor should sign the lease as well, if he or she has an outstanding interest or potential interest in the property. For example, if a married couple owns the premises jointly, both parties must sign the lease since the spouse is a concurrent owner. The wife should also sign the lease where the state recognizes a dower interest, inasmuch as her potential interest may come into effect during the term of the lease.

Under some contracts a lessee may have the power to sublease or to assign the property to a third party; the person signing as lessor of the property may not be the actual owner of the premises. For this reason a lessee should make certain that the nonowner lessor has the authority to sublet and convey all or part of the interest to another. Subleasing will be discussed in more detail in the following chapter.

If the lessor is an individual, he or she must have the *capacity* to contract—that is, be mentally competent and of legal age. If the lessor is a fiduciary, entering the lease for another as guardian, executor or trustee, for example, the lessee must be assured that the authority to lease is within the fiduciary's powers. Similarly, if the lessor is a corporation that is not in the business of leasing real estate, the lessee must verify the authorization of the corporation's board of directors to be assured that it is entitled to lease the premises.

Description of the Premises

In order to avoid a future dispute, the premises should be described clearly. If the landlord's entire conveyed premises are being leased, then the description as contained in the deed or deeds is satisfactory. A lot number or block number used for assessment purposes may be used if it is complete and accurate. A street number may not be adequate in itself because it relates only to the building and not to the land that is probably part of the leasehold as well.

When the lessor is leasing something less than all that he or she has, the lease should state clearly and exactly what is to be leased.

In the absence of an agreement to the contrary, the lease of a building will be construed to include the use of everything reasonably necessary for the enjoyment of the land. It is up to the lessor expressly to exclude a use, or exclusive possession may pass to the lessee.

CASE EXAMPLE

Arthur leases one-half of an apartment house to Melanie, who has three small children. Unless the lease specifically excludes use of the fenced-in backyard, Melanie can use it for ingress and egress and as a play area for the children.

It is also to the lessee's benefit to have the precise nature of his or her use or possession spelled out in the lease, rather than to rely on the uncertain notion that he or she is entitled to certain unstated uses.

Statement of a Lease Term

The term of the lease should be stipulated clearly. Stating the beginning and ending dates as well as the length of the term will reduce doubt as to date of entry and the like. The lease should state, for example, "for one year beginning January 1, 1983, and terminating December 31, 1983." Where the beginning date is not spelled out, some doubt may exist as to whether the tenant began the term on the date the lease was signed, the first of the following month or some other date. If the beginning date is not stated, the commencement of the lease should be related to some event or ascertainable time so that the beginning of the lease is clear.

CASE EXAMPLE

Sanchez leased to Williams for one year beginning upon the surrender of possession by the present tenant or April 1, 1981, whichever comes first.

The courts do not favor leases of unlimited duration. If the time of termination is not fixed, the courts may interpret the agreement to be a tenancy at will, which is probably not what the parties intended. In a periodic tenancy, of course, the time of termination is fixed, although the tenancy is subject to automatic renewal upon the existence of certain conditions, such as failure to give notice of termination.

Some courts have been inclined to hold that leases that are too long—for instance, 100 years or more—are barred by statute. The theory behind the term limitation is that when the lease gets to be too long it defies the temporary aspect, or right of reversion, inherent in a leasehold estate. The result of these statutes and judicial rulings has been to popularize the 99-year lease. Similarly, in a few states, there is a restriction on the length of leases for agricultural lands.

There is a correlation between the length of the lease and the care with which the lease must be drawn. If the lease is as long as 75 years, the likelihood increases that the structures will need to be replaced. Some agreement should be reached to cover contingencies of this sort that will occur during the long period of the lease.

Rent

The compensation paid by the lessee for the possession of the leased property.

Normally, rent takes the form of a money payment. It could, however, take the form of a percentage of the crops harvested from the land or of relief for the lessor of an obligation owed to the lessee. A statement of the amount of rent is one of the essential terms of a lease; nevertheless, where it has been omitted, courts have declared that the landlord is entitled to a "reasonable rent," based on the area's prevailing rental rates.

The usual practice is to state in the lease that the rent will be paid in advance. If such a statement is lacking, the rent is due at the end of the period. The rationale behind this rule is that the lessee is paying for the possession that he or she has enjoyed, and nothing is due until he or she has had the enjoyment.

In addition to how much and when, the lease should indicate where the rent is to be paid. Absent such an indication, it is payable at the leasehold premises.

Unless stipulated to the contrary, the total rent is due on the date set for payment. The usual practice is to require in the lease monthly, quarterly or annual payments.

CASE EXAMPLE

Karen leases Greenacre to Frank for a rent of $2,400 annually, payable in advance and on the first of each month in installments of "$200, and presented at the residence of the lessor."

This wording covers each of the above considerations.

For short-term residential leases it is most common to have a straight rental fee, such as $200 per month. In commercial leases, however, a variety of methods are used for determining the rent. The net lease, percentage lease and ground lease will be discussed later. Another technique is to assess rent on a *graduated* basis. A lease might stipulate a rent of $2,400 the first year, $3,600 per year for the following two years and $4,800 per year for the last two years. If the lessee is operating a new business, under the graduated rental the amount of rent is smallest in the start-up period and increases as the business (theoretically) grows.

Other techniques include basing the rent on the consumer

price index or on some other criterion that is particularly relevant to the parties, to the business or to the lease itself. In short, the days of the straight or flat rental fee as the sole method for calculating rent, especially in business leases, have long since passed.

Legal Use of the Premises

If the lease gives no indication as to the uses that can be made of the premises, the general rule is that the lessee can make any legal use of the land he or she wants. Some courts, however, would limit the lessee to "reasonable uses" where the agreement is silent on the matter. The question of reasonable use is a factual question that the court will examine in light of the type of premises involved and the prior uses of the property. If the building was constructed and has been used as a residence from its inception, for example, it would be unreasonable to use it now as a cheese factory.

Although it is appropriate for the lessor to limit the lessee's use by the agreement, careful drafting is warranted.

• CASE BRIEF •

Sanitary District leased vacant land to H.K.F. Development Corp. (H.K.F.). The lease contained a provision prohibiting the "dumping" of "waste." An amendment to the lease permitted the "storage of dry and liquid material." H.K.F. brought in air-dried sludge, which it intended to use in manufacturing fertilizer. The Sanitary District argued that this was a violation of the lease provision. This use was approved, however, by the court. *H.K.F. Development Corp. v. Metropolitan S.D.O.G.C., 97 Ill. App. 2d 225, 240 N.E.2d 214 (1968).*

If the lessor limits the use to a clearly designated purpose, courts will uphold that limitation. If the lessor indicates a *specific* purpose to which the premises can be put—for example, ". . . can be used for a beauty shop"—and nothing more, however, this wording will not prohibit the lessee from making other uses of the land than as a beauty shop. The rationale behind these rules is that the law favors unrestricted use of the land conveyed. In short, ambiguities will be construed against the lessor and toward maximizing the lessee's use. If the lessor's limitations on permitted uses are not designated clearly, the lease will be construed to favor the lessee. If the lessor by permitting use as a beauty shop has not clearly shown an intent to limit use to that purpose alone, the lessee will be able to make any other use as well. The careful drafter would have stated, ". . . for use as a beauty shop only."

Where the lessee's use of the property has been made illegal by a change in the law, the lease is not usually invalidated. If the lease permits other legal uses, the lessee can change the type of use. If, however, the lease limits the lessee to the now illegal use, the change in the law will invalidate the lease. The fact that the lessee's business has become unprofitable or that the property no longer suits him or her for a residence will not excuse performance under the lease contract.

A tenant who leases only part of a building for commercial purposes should be careful to reach some agreement with the lessor regarding the leasing of other parts of the building to competitors and use by the lessor as a competitor with the lessee. Without such an agreement, the lessor is free to put the remainder of the property to a competitive use.

Besides the terms of the lease, the tenant should also be careful to check the public regulation restrictions on his or her use. The zoning code may well prohibit uses that the lessor has not prohibited.

Right of Possession

In all jurisdictions the right of possession implicitly resides in the tenant; that is, no one will have possessory rights inconsistent with those granted to the tenant.

In a majority of jurisdictions the landlord covenants to give the right of possession and nothing more. If there is a wrongdoer in possession at the time the tenant's lease commences, the landlord has not violated his or her implied promise of giving the *right to possession*. The fact that the tenant may have to bring a lawsuit to obtain possession is an excellent reason why the tenant should be careful to see to it that the lease contains a provision ensuring that the landlord will give *possession* of the premises, not merely the right to possession. The possibility of the landlord's being unable to deliver actual possession is not terribly remote. Holding over by former tenants is not a rare incident.

In some jurisdictions the landlord implicitly covenants to deliver the possession of the premises. The onus then falls on the landlord to take necessary action (for example, eviction proceedings) to recover possession for the tenant.

It should be remembered that normally the tenant's possession is exclusive. Even the landlord, who may be the owner of the premises in fee simple, is not permitted to invade that exclusive possession without authorization. The landlord would be a trespasser, and the tenant could bring the appropriate legal action against him or her.

Recording the Lease

The practice of recording leases is permitted in most states since a lease is a conveyance of an interest in land. It is uncommon to record residential and other short-term leases, however, because actual possession by the tenant is notice to everyone of the tenant's interest in the land. Upon finding a tenant in possession, a potential taker of an interest in the land would have actual notice of the possession and would have the duty to inquire as to the possessor's right to be there. Failing to inspect the premises, he or she would still have constructive notice of the possession.

There is, however, more of an inclination to record leases that are for a longer period (three years or more). In about one-third of the states the rule holding that possession is constructive notice has been abolished where the lease exceeds a given period of time (usually either one year or three years). In these states it is very important that the tenant record the lease for his or her own protection.

Types of Leases

It was indicated earlier that several types of leases exist. Four of these will be discussed in more detail here. Most are used primarily in commercial applications.

Gross Lease

A lease in which a flat or fixed amount of rent is paid by the tenant.

Generally, under a gross lease the tenant pays the rent and the landlord is responsible for expenses incurred in operating the premises. The landlord pays the taxes, insurance, special assessments and the like. Responsibility for ordinary repairs may be bargained for separately. In residential leases the gross rental fee may or may not include heat and other utilities. It would seem to be to the benefit of both parties, and society as a whole, to exclude heat and utilities from the fixed rent in order to encourage the tenant to minimize the costs by reducing the consumption of energy.

Where long-term leases are desired, gross leases have gradually fallen from favor because of inflation and the fluctuation in the value of the dollar. Unless there is some provision in the lease to compensate the lessor for the gradually diminishing value of the periodic rent check, rental property becomes a questionable investment.

Net Lease

As contrasted with the gross lease, a type of lease in which the tenant agrees to pay the taxes, insurance, repairs and other operating expenses of the premises.

This type of lease assures the lessor of a steady income from the property and relieves him or her of the responsibility of overseeing the operations on the property. In short, the lessor has a real estate investment without most of the problems that usually accompany this type of investment.

Like the gross lease, the net lease does not necessarily take into account the loss of purchasing power due to inflation. Net leases can be drawn up that tie the amount of periodic rent that is payable to some recognized indicator, such as the consumer price index. In this way the lessor will have the same purchasing power at the end of a long-term lease that existed at the beginning.

Ground Lease

A specialized type of net lease in which the lessor leases a piece of vacant land to the lessee, usually with the stipulation that the lessee at his or her own expense will construct a building thereon.

The ground lease is a type of net lease in that the lessee agrees to assume the operating expense of the property. Once the building is constructed, it becomes part of the realty and title passes to the lessor. Therefore, several elements are common to the lease agreements in ground lease situations. The term of the lease is either for the life expectancy of the building or, at least, for a long period. When the term of the lease is not tied to the building's life expectancy, provisions must be made for the building at the expiration of the lease. The parties may agree that the lessor will have to pay the lessee the appraised value of the building at the time the lease expires. Of course the parties can write any agreement that suits them on this matter.

The rent agreement can be for a fixed rate but is often tied to the appraised value of the land. In this way the lessor retains the benefit of the land's appreciating value.

In most such leases the lessee needs financing to construct the building. If this is the case, provisions must be made to accommodate the mortgagee as well as the parties to the lease. The lessor will have to agree to permit the building to be mortgaged while excluding himself or herself from liability on that mortgage. Likewise, the mortgagee will insist upon the untrammeled right to sell the property in the case of a foreclosure. In addition, the mortgagee will usually insist that the term of the ground lease extend significantly beyond the duration of the mortgage so that the tenant does not lose the incentive to make mortgage payments during the latter years of the obligation.

Percentage Lease

A lease whose rental is based in part on the gross sales made by the tenant on the premises.

The lessee in such a lease is required to pay a fixed periodic rental, the amount of the rent to be less than the property's full rental value. In addition, the lessor is entitled to a percentage of the gross sales made by the lessee.

A common practice is to charge a flat minimum rent (perhaps $200 per month) plus a percentage of the gross sales over a stipulated figure (for example, $200 per month plus two percent of the gross sales over $30,000). If the lease has a long term, the percentage lease provides some hedge against inflation. As inflation grows, theoretically so do gross sales; once sales exceed $30,000, the rent increases proportionately. Since the flat minimum rent is usually lower than the maximum amount the landlord would expect, the percentage lease is a hedge for the commercial lessee against bad times.

Percentage leases have become very popular in the leasing of commercial property. The percentage may be very low (one or two percent) in the case of a supermarket or very high (70 to 80 percent) where a parking lot is involved. Regardless of the type of business or the percentage agreed upon, it is critical that the parties carefully draft their agreement. The lease should make clear exactly what is encompassed within the term *gross sales* and should establish the right of the lessor to examine records of the business. From the lessor's perspective, in addition to the protection of a carefully drafted lease, the lessee should be selected carefully to ensure a sound credit rating and good business history.

Other Types of Leases

Leases are as variable as the parties are creative. Some types of leases, such as the variety that relates rent to the consumer price index or some other index, may come into vogue temporarily as a reaction to unstable economic conditions. Others, such as the graduated lease, are tailored to meet the needs of a new business. Here the rent rises over time as the anticipated growth of the business takes place. Still others, such as the sale and leaseback arrangement, are attractive for large firms, which sell their real estate and lease it back from the new owner in order to release investment capital for future expansion. Partners under this type of lease are investors who have capital to invest in order to ensure an agreeable rate of return from the rents on the leased-back property. These examples represent only a few types of leases that have been adapted to the special needs of the parties.

Lease Renewal

Depending on the type of leasehold estate that was conveyed by the landlord, or upon the terms of the parties' agreement, the lease will terminate on its own or upon appropriate notice by either party. It is not unusual, however, to include in the lease a term that provides for the renewal of the lease. The renewal provision may be one that requires the tenant to give notice of renewal by a specified period of time prior to the termination of the lease. Alternatively, the renewal may be automatic, absent notice of nonrenewal by either party.

A renewal is a new lease. Unless otherwise stated, the renewal is under the same terms and conditions as the original lease. The par-

ties may agree that the rent will be altered to reflect the present value
of the land. For instance, each renewal may require a reappraisal of the
land and a rent adjustment to reflect a specified percentage of the appraised value. Except where the agreement is for an automatic renewal
of the lease, the parties should indicate whether the renewal clause
will be operative in the second lease and in succeeding renewed
leases.

Another method of renewal is by holding over. The legal implications for the holdover tenant were discussed in a preceding section.

SUMMARY

A lease is both a contract and a conveyance. As a conveyance a lease
creates a possessory interest in real property for a specified period of
time. The owner of the real property conveys this estate to the tenant
in exchange for rent. The tenant receives exclusive possession for the
duration of the lease. As a lease is also contractual, it must contain
the essential elements of any contract.

Four different types of leasehold estates may be created. They
are the term tenancy, periodic tenancy, tenancy at will and tenancy at
sufferance. The term tenancy and the periodic tenancy are the most
common. They differ mainly in the manner in which they are terminated. A term tenancy ends automatically at the date specified in the
lease. A tenant who fails to vacate upon termination of a term tenancy
is a holdover tenant; this person may be held for an additional term. In
a periodic tenancy, the party terminating the lease must notify the
other party. The time of notification may be established in the lease. If
no time is stated, the notice period is established by law.

Although an oral lease for a short term is valid, the Statute of
Frauds requires leases for longer periods to be in writing. In most
states a written lease is required if the term exceeds one year. In a few
states only leases with terms exceeding three years must be in writing. Regardless, parties should insist that the lease be in writing, especially if the terms are complex or the value of the leasehold estate is
high.

A lease should identify the parties as lessor and lessee, clearly
describe the premises and stipulate the term of the lease and the rent,
including how much is to be paid, when it is to be paid and where. Absent any stipulations provided in the agreement, the lessee may make
any desired legal use of the premises. Though the right of possession
implicitly resides in the tenant, tenants would be wise to make sure
that the lease provides that the landlord will give not merely the right
to possession but possession itself. For leases of three years or more, it
is becoming common to record the lease.

Four kinds of leases are common for commercial use. In the
gross lease a fixed amount of rent is paid periodically. The landlord is

responsible for taxes, insurance and utilities. Often, payment of extraordinary expenses is negotiable between landlord and tenant. This type is not popular for long-term leases. In the net lease the tenant pays many of the operating expenses of the property such as taxes, utilities and insurance. The advantage to the landlord is obvious. The ground lease, another form, is a specialized type in which the lessee pays rent on vacant land, usually with the intent of constructing a building. This type of agreement can be very complex and is often of long duration. Finally, the percentage lease is another type widely used commercially. In a percentage lease rental is based in part on the tenant's gross sales. Like all leases, the agreement should clearly stipulate the terms; it should also establish the lessor's rights to examine the tenant's accounting records.

Provisions for renewal of leases are sometimes included in the original agreement. Nevertheless, a renewal constitutes a new lease and should conform to contractual requirements.

REVIEW AND DISCUSSION QUESTIONS

1. Name and describe the application of the two areas of law relevant to a discussion of leases.
2. Match the following:
   (a) Tenancy at sufferance
   (b) Term tenancy
   (c) Tenancy at will
   (d) Periodic tenancy

   (1) has a specific beginning and ending date.
   (2) exists as long as neither party chooses to terminate it.
   (3) continues from period to period until terminated by one of the parties giving proper notice.
   (4) exists when a person is wrongfully in possession of another's land without a valid lease.
3. Name two ways in which a periodic tenancy can be created.
4. Define the term *holdover tenant.*
5. List and briefly describe four terms that should be specified in a lease contract.
6. What risks are involved in entering an oral lease?
7. Why should the lessee insist on having the precise nature of his or her use or possession of the property explained in the lease contract?
8. Distinguish between "the landlord gives possession of the premises" and "the landlord gives the right of possession of the premises."

9. Match the following:
   (a) net lease   (1) The rent is based in part on the
   (b) gross lease   gross sales made by the lessee.
   (c) percentage lease   (2) The lessor leases a piece of vacant
   (d) ground lease   land to the lessee, usually with the
                                  stipulation that the lessee at his or
                                  her own expense will construct a
                                  building.
                              (3) The tenant agrees to pay taxes, in-
                                  surance, repairs and other operating
                                  expenses of the premises.
                              (4) The rent is a fixed or flat amount.
10. Describe and discuss those rules of landlord-tenant law that
    no longer seem appropriate given present-day expectations of
    lay parties.
11. Describe the practical business situations in which the fol-
    lowing types of leases would best satisfy the needs of the
    commercial lessor and lessee: (a) gross lease, (b) net lease, (c)
    percentage lease.

CASE PROBLEMS

1. China Doll Restaurant, Inc., leased premises from Schweiger.
   China Doll agreed to pay a base rent of $600 per month and an
   amount equal to five percent of the restaurant's first $288,000
   of gross sales. The owners of China Doll had considerable experience in operating a Chinese restaurant.
      The lease also contained a provision in which lessee agreed
   to use the premises "for conducting and operating a restaurant
   business." Before the expiration of the lease, China Doll moved
   to new and larger premises. At this time they stated that they
   intended to open a Mexican restaurant at the former China
   Doll location. Little was done to accomplish this, but they
   continued to pay the base rental of $600 per month. During
   this period the premises were unoccupied. Has China Doll violated the terms of the lease? *China Doll Restaurant, Inc. v.
   Schweiger*, 19 Ariz. 315, 580 P.2d 776 (1978).
2. Chapman rented farmland to Walker on a year-to-year basis beginning each year on January 1. Chapman sold the property to
   Gregory with a stipulation that Gregory was to have possession as of January 1, 1963. On July 1, 1962, Chapman gave
   Walker notice to vacate at the end of the year. Is this notice sufficient in a state following the traditional common law rule?
   Gregory v. Walker, 239 Ark. 415, 389 S.W.2d 892 (1965).
3. Lonergan leased commercial property to Connecticut Food
   Store, Inc. The lease was a five-year term tenancy at a rent of

$175 per month. The lessee held over after the expiration of the lease and continued to send payments of $175 per month. The lessor sued to recover possession and for damages. What is the legal status of the lessee after the expiration of the five-year term tenancy? Who won the suit? *Lonergan v. Connecticut Food Store, Inc.*, 168 Conn. 122, 357 A.2d 910 (1975).

4. Doyle owed Byrne $5,000 for services performed in rewiring Doyle's house. After six months Doyle had paid nothing on the $5,000 bill and, upon being confronted by Byrne, admitted that it was unlikely that he could pay the bill in the near future. Byrne suggested that he would take a lease for a year on Doyle's camp on the lake. Doyle said "fine," and the conversation ended. In the spring Byrne moved into Doyle's camp and occupied it without incident until mid-July. At that time Doyle arrived at the camp and ordered Byrne to evacuate. Byrne refused, claiming that he had a one-year lease. Doyle retorted that there was nothing in writing, that no rent was stipulated and that the services for electrical work could not be used in lieu of cash payments for rent. Discuss the validity of Doyle's arguments.

26
The Landlord-Tenant Relationship

The signing of a lease creates obligations on the part of both the lessor and the lessee. Failure by either party to comply with obligations imposed either by contract or by law gives rise to the availability of certain legal remedies. The remedies available depend upon the nature of the obligation breached and upon the present circumstances of the parties. For example, did the lessee remain in possession, or were the premises abandoned? Some problems result from actions taken by one of the parties to the transaction—the lessee may have sublet the premises, for example—or actions involving not the parties but other persons, as when a visitor falls down the stairs of the leased premises. These occurrences lead to legal responsibilities on the part of the parties to the lease. Obligations imposed by the lease contract, by the relationship itself and by the law are the topics of this chapter.

LESSOR'S SECURITY

Several techniques have evolved over time to protect landlords from tenants who mistreat the leased premises.

Landlord's Lien

Under common law, the lien known as the right of distress provided the landlord with a lien on the personal property of the tenant where there was a failure to pay rent.

This common law rule, which arose in feudal England, has not been

571

viewed with favor by American courts because of the potential for abuse by the landlord. Under the right of distress the landlord can hold or even sell the personal property of the nonpaying tenant. The right, where it exists today, is limited to the personal property of the tenant that is on the leased premises. For the most part, states have statutorily eliminated the self-help notion of distress. It has been replaced with remedies such as actions for rent or the reclaiming of the premises for the landlord by public officials. Remedies currently available to the landlord, including eviction, are discussed later in this chapter.

Rent Paid in Advance

A normal requirement for modern leases is that rent payments are due prior to the beginning of the lease period.

Under common law where it is not otherwise specified, rent is due at the end of the rental period. The modern practice of requiring advance payment of the rent in the lease gives the landlord some additional assurance of stability. Where the rent is not forthcoming from the tenant by the first day of the rental period, the landlord is given some lead time in pursuing remedies for nonpayment. If the rent were not due until the end of the rental period, the landlord would lose additional time pursuing the remedies.

Security Deposit

Money deposited by the tenant for the security of the landlord, usually at the inception of the lease, over and above the advance payment of rent.

The security deposit is usually equivalent to one month's rent or more. Its purpose is to secure the landlord against damage done to the premises by the tenant or to clean or repair the premises, over and above normal wear and tear, when the tenant vacates. It may also provide a wider margin of security against a tenant who wrongfully abandons the premises. It has the practical effect of inducing the tenant who wants the security deposit returned to maintain the premises carefully during occupancy and to clean the premises thoroughly upon leaving.

The security deposit is held by the landlord in trust for the tenant. The parties may agree that interest will be paid on this money. In at least one state, New York, it is mandatory that the landlord of multiple-unit housing pay interest on any security deposit.

Because the security deposit is not a form of liquidated damages, the landlord can retain only as much as is necessary to pay for the damage done by the tenant. If the payment is a security deposit and not an advance rental, the tenant cannot use it in lieu of payment of rent for the last month. Whichever it is should be stipulated clearly by the parties.

Some states have adopted parts of the Uniform Residential Landlord and Tenant Act, which is geared toward promoting uniformity in landlord-tenant law. The act provides strict regulation of the security deposit. It would limit the amount deposited to one month's rent, require a written explanation of the purpose for and handling of the funds as well as an indication of the reasons for retaining any of the deposit and provide for the return of any unneeded funds to the tenant within 14 days after the termination of the lease. It also provides for penalties in case the landlord mishandles any of the security deposit funds. Most of the states have tailored these provisions to fit their needs.

Third-Person Guaranty of Rent

The landlord who has doubts about the capacity or reliability of the tenant in meeting the conditions of the lease may require a third person to guarantee performance.

In a commercial or industrial lease where the tenant is thinly capitalized, a personal guaranty by the individuals actually running the business under the corporate veil may be required. Also, where the tenant has a poor credit rating, the landlord may insist on the assurance of a more reliable third person. The guaranty would have to be in writing and signed by the guarantor. The guaranty agreement may be a part of the lease or a separate agreement usually appended to the lease.

Cognovit

A confession of judgment that permits the landlord, upon default by the tenant, to obtain a judgment against the tenant without the need for formal legal proceedings.

When this clause is present, the tenant has agreed in the lease that in case of his or her default the landlord can obtain a confession of judgment without the necessity of going to court to obtain the decree. Usually, the cognovit is executed by the landlord's attorney, who files an affidavit stating that the default occurred. Such a judgment, like any other, constitutes a lien on any real property in the jurisdiction of the leased premises.

The effect of a cognovit is to expedite the landlord's collection process after a default. It creates a situation ripe for abuse by the landlord, and in some states it is illegal for a tenant to execute such an agreement until after the default has taken place.

LESSOR'S OBLIGATIONS

The landlord is bound by any promises made to the tenant in the lease. In addition, certain obligations have been imposed on the landlord by the law over and above the contractual understanding. The following covenants and warrants are the major ones with which the parties must be concerned.

Covenant of Quiet Enjoyment

A warrant by the landlord that the tenant will have the premises free from interference by the landlord or anyone claiming better right to the premises than the landlord.

There is no general guarantee by the landlord against wrongful intrusion by third persons. Should such an intrusion take place, the tenant will have satisfactory legal avenues through which to redress the interference. For centuries, however, the general common law rule has been that the tenant is protected from a wrongful intrusion by the landlord or someone claiming better rights than the landlord or tenant.

The covenant of quiet enjoyment is breached only upon eviction by the landlord or by a third person, either actual or constructive. Actual eviction consists of a physical removal of the tenant from the premises. Constructive eviction could occur when there is a substantial interference with the tenant's enjoyment of the premises.

• CASE BRIEF •

Munic Meat Company (Munic) leased on a long term a portion of a building from Gartenberg. U.S. Department of Agriculture rules required the entire building in which a meat packer did business to obtain an MID number. After occupying the premises for several years, Munic received notice that the building's MID number was being conditionally withdrawn due to certain substandard conditions. These conditions were not the fault of Munic. The company immediately vacated the building and occupied new premises. It then sued Gartenberg for damages, arguing that it had been constructively evicted. Both the trial court and the appellate court agreed. *John Munic Meat Co. v. H. Gartenberg & Co., 9 Ill. 360, 366 N.E.2d 617 (1977).*

Generally, in the case of either an actual or a constructive eviction the tenant must have vacated the premises before asserting a breach of the covenant of quiet enjoyment.

Covenant to Deliver Possession

The landlord promises to deliver the right of possession to the tenant at the time the lease is scheduled to start.

This covenant is quite limited. It does not warrant against a wrong-doer being in possession of the premises at the time the lease commences, but only that the tenant will have the *right to possession*.

• CASE BRIEF •

Reichman leased premises from Emery for a term of five years. The lease was to commence on July 1. At the time the lease was executed the property was occupied by Drake, whose term expired on June 9. Drake, however, refused to vacate, and Reichman commenced an action to evict her. Several months later this suit was successful. After Drake was evicted, Reichman commenced a damage action against her as he had been unable to occupy the premises during the eviction proceeding. Drake argued that she had no liability to Reichman as she had no contractual relationship with him. An appellate court concluded that Drake's action violated Reichman's property rights and awarded damages. *Reichman v. Drake, 89 Ohio App. 222, 100 N.E.2d 533 (1951).*

Should a wrongdoer be in possession, the tenant has the obligation to evict him or her. A few jurisdictions have adopted the so-called English Rule, which requires the landlord to deliver *possession*, not merely the *right* to it. This interpretation is consistent with the usual expectancy of the parties upon entering the contract.

One aspect of this covenant that is sometimes misunderstood by residential landlords is that the tenant's right to possession is exclusive. This excludes the landlord as well as others.

• CASE BRIEF •

Lum's leased a portion of a building from Davis. The lease also gave Lum's the right to use the entire parking area that surrounded the building. Due to congestion in this area, Lum's leased a parcel of adjoining land to facilitate the flow of traffic. Davis, however, objected to this action and had a fence constructed between the two properties.

In a suit by Lum's to force the removal of this fence, the court stated that the action by Davis was a trespass and ordered the removal of the fence. The reason was that the fence interfered with the tenant's possession of the parking lot. *Davis v. Lum's Inc., 223 Ga. 790, 158 S.E.2d 410 (1967).*

Covenant of Fitness of the Premises
An assurance that the premises are fit for habitation.

The common law rule is that the landlord does not implicitly warrant that the premises are fit for habitation. Some jurisdictions still follow the dictate of this rule, but even in these a few exceptions have been created. Where the lease is for a furnished apartment or is intended for a short duration (a few days, weeks or months), there is an implied warranty that the premises are habitable upon entry. Similarly, when the landlord knew of latent defects—that is, defects that were unknown and not reasonably discoverable by the tenant—there is a breach of an implied covenant of fitness.

The general rule makes sense when placed in the context of the time of its creation. It arose during a period in which land was the predominant concern in a lease, and the tenant could readily discover what he or she needed to know about the land. In modern times the building is usually the chief concern of the parties, and often the building is to be used as a residence. The notion of *caveat emptor*—"let the buyer beware"—seems ill suited to a situation where the landlord is in a far superior position to know the condition of the premises and understands that the tenant wants to use it as a residence.

Implied Warranty of Habitability

A warranty imposed by law on the landlord by which he or she warrants that a residential property is safe and sanitary and fit for living at the time the tenant enters and during the period of tenancy.

In an effort to bring landlord-tenant law into modern times, many courts and legislatures have imposed an implied warranty of habitability. The reasons usually cited for changing the law is the inequality of bargaining position between the landlord and the tenant. Normally, the landlord drafts the terms of the lease and the tenant can accept them or look elsewhere for living accommodations. In addition, legislative action by state and municipal governments that created housing codes exhibited a concern for protecting tenants; these actions stiffened the backbone of the courts in finding the warranty of habitability.

Apparently the determination of what constitutes a breach of this warranty will be a question of fact. One court has noted that what constitutes a breach depends upon the nature of the deficiency, its effect on habitability, the length of time it persisted, the age of the structure, the amount of the rent, the area in which the premises are located and whether the tenant waived the defects or caused them through abnormal use of the premises. See *Kline v. Burns*, 111 N.H. 87, 276 A.2d 248 (1971). An apartment leased for an amount substantially below local standards, for instance, may not have to be in as good a condition as other leased properties in the area. At least, rent will be one factor considered by the court in deciding whether the warranty of habitability has been breached.

In effect, this warranty imposes a duty upon the landlord to keep the premises in repair during the lease period. This would be true despite his or her failure to agree to perform repairs and contrary to the long-standing common law rule freeing either party of the duty to repair unless agreed to.

More than 50 percent of the states have adopted the theory of implied warranty of habitability for residential tenancies. However, the theory has rarely been applied to nonresidential situations. The Uniform Residential Landlord and Tenant Act makes void any provision in the lease waivering or otherwise negating the warranty of habitability.

Duty to Repair

Absent the existence of an implied warranty of habitability in a state, the landlord has no duty to repair the premises.

In addition to not covenanting that the premises are habitable upon entry, the common law rule does not *require* the landlord to repair during the habitation. However, where the landlord retains control over parts of the premises, he or she will be responsible for repairing those areas.

• CASE BRIEF •

Derman Rug Company leased the first floor and basement of a building from Ruderman. The lease contained a provision requiring the tenant to keep the premises in as good order and repair as they were at the beginning of the lease. A steam pipe embedded in the basement floor leaked and was repaired by the landlord, who sued the tenant for the cost of repairs.

The landlord's claim was rejected by the court. Two reasons were given for rejecting this suit. First, the court determined that pipes embedded in floors are within the landlord's exclusive control and as such are the landlord's sole responsibility. Second, the court was convinced that the tenant's duty to repair did not extend to the basement in a building in which upper floors were leased to other tenants, because the land under the building is not part of the leased premises. *Derman Rug Co. Inc. v. Ruderman, 4 Mass. App. Ct. 437, 350 N.E.2d 727 (1976).*

Because of the uncertainty in the law created by the spreading adoption of the warranty of habitability, the parties to a lease should be cautious and thorough in declaring their respective rights in relation to repairs.

In a significant number of states, statutes have been passed imposing a duty on the landlord to perform repairs. The parties should be careful, given the variability of the rules regarding repairs, to make the terms of their agreement clear. When the landlord has the duty to repair and fails to do so, the tenant may sue the landlord for damages or make the needed repairs and deduct the cost from the rent.

If the landlord agrees in the lease to perform repairs, there is a split of authority over the responsibility for rebuilding a structure destroyed by a fire or other catastrophe. Some courts hold that the obligation to repair includes rebuilding; others claim that "repairing" is narrower than "rebuilding." Under the latter rule, once the building is substantially destroyed, it would not be encompassed within the obligation to repair.

If the landlord has agreed to rebuild, whether expressly or by implication in consenting to repair, the failure to rebuild would terminate the tenant's obligation to pay rent, at least where the building is the major concern of the lease.

Duty to Pay Taxes

Absent a contrary agreement, the landlord has the duty to pay the property taxes.

As the owner of the fee interest in the premises, the landlord is responsible for paying the taxes. If the property is sold at a tax sale for nonpayment, the sale is subject to the existing lease. Where the tenant makes improvements to the property that cause the taxes to rise, the tenant will probably be liable to pay for the increase.

Building Code Compliance

Most cities have adopted building codes for the purpose of protecting the public health, safety and welfare by regulating building and construction standards.

Through the requirement of obtaining a building permit or a certificate of occupancy for new construction or substantial alteration of an existing structure, city officials inspect structures for violations of the building code. The code is usually divided into special areas, such as plumbing code, electrical code and fire code. As a result of the division, there may be several inspectors and a multitude of permits. Failure to comply with the building code may result in the landlord's being fined.

The codes are applicable to existing buildings as well, and the code process usually comes into play when there is a tenant complaint about a violation. Often the result of these complaints is that the tenant receives a notice to vacate the premises at the earliest legal opportunity. Naturally, this discourages tenant complaints. Due to this landlord reaction, a few jurisdictions have created the affirmative defense of retaliatory eviction. Under this defense a tenant cannot be evicted for complaining, at least until a legislated period (sometimes 90 days) has lapsed after the complaint has been remedied. This provides only temporary protection to the tenant, and the landlord is free to terminate the tenancy after the time stated in the statute.

LESSOR'S REMEDIES

If the lease agreement is not complied with by one of the parties, the other party will have an array of potential remedies. The chief remedies of the landlord will be discussed here.

Eviction By the Landlord

The term usually associated with the legal procedure by which a landlord has the tenant removed from the premises because the tenant has breached the lease agreement.

Under the common law the covenants of a lease were mutually exclusive, and therefore the breach of a covenant by the tenant would not entitle the landlord to dispossess the tenant. The landlord would have a cause of action for damages resulting from the breach.

In the modern landlord-tenant situation, generally there is a provision in the lease, or the right may be provided by state statute, that the landlord can sue to regain possession of the premises in case of the tenant's failure to comply with the covenants in the lease. Though the agreement or the statute may not provide for dispossession in the case of *any* breach of a covenant, it normally applies to the failure to pay rent, the violation of the use provisions of the lease, the unlawful use of the premises or the violation of state and local health codes.

The eviction process will be used to dispossess a tenant who has received legal notice to vacate the premises and has failed to do so. Where the basis for the eviction is nonpayment of rent, the landlord will be required to notify the tenant of the possibility of eviction and make a demand for the rent prior to beginning the eviction proceedings.

The eviction of the tenant terminates the obligation to pay future rents. However, many business leases contain "survival clauses" under which the obligation to pay rent continues despite the eviction of the wrongdoing tenant. When it is a long-term lease, however, the right to sue accrues only at the termination of the lease, unless a clause in the lease indicates otherwise. It may be impractical to delay the suit for ten or more years until the lease period ends.

The term *eviction* is used to describe the wrongful dispossession of the tenant by the landlord as well as the legal action of the landlord described above. Wrongful eviction will be discussed under the lessee's remedies below.

Wrongful Abandonment

The tenant's vacating of the premises without justification and with the intention of no longer performing under the terms of the lease.

When the tenant wrongfully abandons the premises, the landlord has two options: either to do nothing until the lease period ends and then to bring an action for nonpayment of rent or to reenter the premises and reassert possessory rights.

The common law rule is that the landlord is free to do nothing and recover the full amount of unpaid rent at the termination of the lease. In some states, however, a duty arises to mitigate damages, thereby compelling the landlord to reenter and attempt to relet the premises. In all states the landlord can secure the right of reentry by including in the lease a survival clause permitting the entry but reserving the right to collect rent from the tenant. With this clause the landlord can minimize the damages by reletting the property while continuing to have the original tenant as a hedge against any losses caused by the wrongful abandonment.

When the landlord reenters after a wrongful abandonment and without the protection of a survival clause, he or she is said to accept the surrender of the premises. Upon acceptance of the surrender, the tenant's obligation to pay rent ends. In essence, by the force of the landlord's action of reentry, he or she has impliedly acquiesced to the abandonment of the tenant.

Action for Rent or Damages

The landlord may permit, or be required to permit, the wrongdoing tenant to retain possession of the property and seek money damages for the landlord's injury.

The usual action by the landlord for damages involves the recovery of unpaid rent. If no agreement exists to the contrary, the landlord will have to wait until the end of the lease to begin action for unpaid rent. However, most leases provide terms permitting an action for rent prior to termination, though these generally include the right to evict and are discussed above.

Should the tenant cause damage to the premises or otherwise violate the covenants of the lease over and above the value of the rent, the landlord has the right to sue for damages.

LESSEE'S OBLIGATIONS

Obligations arise both from the lease contract and from modern real estate law.

Duty to Repair

The tenant's obligation to use the premises in a reasonable fashion and to deliver possession at the end of the lease in about the same condition as when received, reasonable wear and tear excluded.

Absent an agreement to the contrary, the tenant has no law-imposed duty to make substantial repairs to the premises. However, the tenant is obligated to maintain the property so as to protect it from the weather. This obligation is referred to as the tenant's responsibility to avoid waste.

Waste

Damage caused by the tenant including failure to protect the premises from decay and ruin caused by the natural elements.

The notion of waste can take two different forms. Voluntary waste results from the positive actions of the tenant, such as willfully breaking the windows or destroying the landscaping. Permissive waste results from an act of omission such as the failure to repair an accidentally broken window, thereby permitting injury to the premises from the weather.

The tenant may agree to perform repairs, just as the landlord might. Similarly, as previously noted under the landlord's obligations, there is a difference of opinion among jurisdictions as to whether the tenant is liable to rebuild the premises in the case of fire or other catastrophe where that tenant has agreed to repair. Since the parties would not normally intend the requirement of repairing to encompass rebuilding, they should expressly exclude this contingency from their agreement.

Whether or not the tenant agrees to repair, he or she will be liable in damages to the landlord for any injury, beyond normal wear and tear, caused to the premises.

Duty to Insure

Neither the tenant nor the landlord has an obligation to insure the premises against loss. However, the failure of the tenant to insure his or her interest may result in an obligation to pay rent without enjoying the benefit of the property whose improvements have been destroyed by fire. Where the tenant leases both land and improvements, he or she is not relieved of the duty to pay rent despite the destruction of the premises. If the tenant leases only the improvements (such as an apartment in a multiple-family building), the obligation to pay rent will terminate when the improvements are substantially destroyed. If the destruction is only partial and the premises are still tenable, however, the tenant must continue to pay rent.

Where the tenant rents both land and buildings, the common law rule requiring the payment of rent after the buildings' destruction seems unduly harsh. In a few states the rule has been altered to provide for termination of the obligation to pay rent where the improvements have been substantially destroyed or become untenable through no fault of the tenant. The change in the rule seems equitable, given the fact that buildings are often the critical concern in modern leases.

Fixtures

Any personal property permanently affixed to the realty by the tenant; they become the property of the landlord at the termination of the lease.

The tenant can provide in the lease for removal of fixtures at the culmination of the tenancy; absent such an agreement, however, he or she will lose the right to those items attached to the realty that would otherwise be classified as fixtures. The common law created a harsh situation for the tenant.

This doctrine has been altered in some measure. To the extent that the tenant attaches items to the realty that enable him or her to carry on a commercial enterprise, for example, under the doctrine of trade fixtures the tenant will be able to remove the items up to the termination date of the lease.

CASE EXAMPLE

Lubin leases commercial shop space to Murphy. In order to sell her cards and gifts, Murphy installs shelves that are attached to brackets and the brackets affixed to the wall. Prior to the end of the lease Murphy can remove the shelves and brackets as long as the removal does not significantly or materially injure the shop.

The exception to the general rule is based upon the idea that it was the presumed intent of the parties to permit removal, and public policy supports rules that will encourage trade through flexibility.

Several things should be noted about trade fixtures. First, the question of whether an item is a trade fixture may be treated as one of fact and left up to the trier of fact (the jury). More certainty can be obtained by stipulating in the lease how these fixtures will be handled. Second, removal can be executed only where serious injury will not result to the premises. Finally, removal is not permitted after the termination of the lease. Upon termination of the lease, trade fixtures become the permanent property of the landlord.

LESSEE'S REMEDIES

The lessee has several remedies available when the lessor violates the conditions of the lease.

Wrongful Eviction

An act that occurs when the landlord without justification deprives the tenant of possession of the premises.

A tenant who has been wrongfully evicted (also referred to as an *actual eviction*) can sue for recovery of possession of the premises or for damages caused by the breach of covenant of quiet enjoyment. In a somewhat punitive aspect of this area of law, if the landlord wrongfully evicts the tenant from only part of the premises, the tenant may retain the remainder of the property but will have no obligation to pay any rent until the partial wrongful eviction ceases.

A wrongful eviction and breach of the covenant of quiet enjoyment will exist also where the tenant is ousted because a third person has proved rights superior to those of the landlord. In such a case the tenant will have an action for money damages.

Constructive Eviction

An occurrence that results when the actions of the landlord so materially interfere with the tenant's enjoyment as to make the premises untenable.

Theoretically at least, the right to assert a constructive eviction occurs when the tenant is forced by the condition of the premises to vacate. The tenant must notify the landlord of the conditions, where appropriate, and give the landlord a reasonable time to remedy the situation. Finally, the tenant must actually vacate the premises to be able to allege constructive eviction.

• CASE BRIEF •

Cooper rented a portion of the ground floor in a commercial office building from Reste Realty. The lease contained a provision indicating that the lessee had examined the premises and accepted them in their present condition. Due to improper drainage from an adjacent driveway, the ground floor was subject to flooding after a heavy rain. The water, however, was immediately removed by the building manager.

After occupying the premises for a year, Cooper renewed her lease, obtaining a promise that the driveway would be regraded. This regrading was done, but flooding still occurred, and Cooper vacated the property. The lessor sued for rental payments, argu-

ing that Cooper had waived her right to vacate by remaining on
the premises for an unreasonable time after discovering the condition and by renewing her lease. The New Jersey court did not
accept this argument. No waiver was found because Cooper remained an occupant only while the lessor tried to correct the
problem. *Reste Realty Corp. v. Cooper, 53 N.J. 444, 251 A.2d
268 (1969).*

The concept of constructive eviction is a judicial construction. It is
used to offset the fact that the landlord normally inserts in the lease a
provision permitting the eviction of the tenant for failure to comply
with the terms of the lease. Leases do not normally provide for comparable rights for the tenant.

Damages, Reformation and Rescission

**Actions a tenant may bring where an implied warranty of
habitability exists and the landlord has failed to maintain
the premises in a tenable condition.**

The remedies made available to the tenant when the implied warranty of habitability is breached are of a complementary nature. That
is, the tenant is afforded relief short of vacating the premises or withholding rent, both of which may be risky remedies.

    The tenant may sue for damages measured by expenses in-
curred as a result of the landlord's refusal to perform the covenants in
the lease. The tenant may seek reformation of the contract due to the
conduct of the landlord in refusing to perform repairs. The reformation could take the form of reducing the amount of rent due in order
to conform to the lessened value of the unrepaired premises. If the
breach of covenant has reduced the value of the lease to the tenant significantly, prior to the tenant's entry he or she may seek to have a
court rescind or negate the entire agreement.

CASE EXAMPLE

Laferty, the landlord, has agreed to provide repairs in his lease
with Manne. The roof leaks into a small bedroom. Despite requests by Manne to Laferty to repair the roof prior to Manne's
moving in, the roof remains unrepaired. Manne *needs* the bedroom for a child and seeks rescission of the lease. The tenant's
attorney chooses this as a safer, albeit more time-consuming,
remedy for the tenant than vacating after entry and contending
constructive eviction. Under constructive eviction Manne would
run the risk of the court's disagreeing with his contention that the
premises are "untenable" and charging him for unpaid rent.

Rent Withholding

The practice, allowed in a few states under limited circumstances, in which the tenant withholds rent as an inducement to force the landlord to perform repairs.

It should be remembered that at common law the obligation to pay rent arises from the possession of the land and from the covenant to pay in the lease. Each covenant in the lease is independent. Therefore, the tenant normally has the duty to pay the rent despite the landlord's failure to perform some aspect of his or her obligation.

In a few states, including New York, Illinois, Connecticut and Michigan, tenants are legislatively authorized to withhold rent in cases where the landlord has failed to obtain a certificate of occupancy as required by the municipal housing code. Similarly, welfare agencies are authorized to withhold rent payments that they normally make directly to the landlord for the welfare tenant. The rent strikes of the mid-1960s encouraged the State of New York to adopt legislation authorizing rent withholding for serious deficiencies in living conditions in multiple-family units. The statute establishes the conditions for rent withholding and the procedures for utilizing the right. It affords protection to the tenant from being evicted.

It should be noted that rent withholding is not a broadly applicable remedy, and local and state law will have to be checked carefully to determine whether the right exists and to what extent.

THIRD-PARTY-RELATED TRANSACTIONS

On occasion a person other than the landlord or tenant becomes involved with the leasehold agreement. Because of a job change, for example, a tenant may seek a substitute to complete the tenancy. Or a person visiting the tenant may fall down the hall stairway in the apartment due to poor lighting or a faulty railing. These and other third-party incidents affecting the lease are discussed next.

Sublease

A transfer of part of the leasehold interest of the tenant, with the tenant retaining a reversionary interest.

CASE EXAMPLE

Granville leases Hilltop Acres to Tomas under a term lease beginning January 1 and ending December 31 of the same year. On March 1, Tomas transfers her interest in Hilltop Acres to Nantes until November 30. This agreement is a sublease, since Tomas has retained a one-month reversionary interest.

Impact of a Sublease

When the tenant creates a sublease by conveying less than the entire interest in the land to a sublessee, there is no privity of estate or contract between the landlord and the sublessee. In short, the sublease does not alter in any respect the original landlord-tenant agreement. The sublessee will have an obligation to pay rent to the tenant, and the tenant will continue to have the obligation to pay rent to the landlord. Likewise, any restriction on limitations included in the original landlord-tenant agreement will pertain to the tenant-sublessee contract as well, since the tenant cannot give greater rights than he or she has. The tenant, despite not being in possession, will still have all the obligations arising from the initial landlord-tenant contract.

Assignment

A transfer in which the tenant gives the entire interest in the leasehold estate without retaining a reversionary interest.

Using the example above, if Tomas had transferred her interest until December 31, the agreement would have been an assignment; Tomas transferred her entire interest in the land. Unless otherwise agreed, the tenant is free either to sublet or to assign the premises. Often, however, the lease agreement includes wording that limits the tenant's right to sublet or assign. The permission of the landlord is the normal precondition to the transfer.

It is possible for a tenant to assign only *part of the premises.* The tenant can assign the second floor to an assignee, for example, retaining the first floor. This transfer would be treated as an assignment so long as the tenant gave the entire interest in the second floor to the assignee.

The distinction between assignment and sublease is not always simple. If the tenant transfers all that he or she has but retains the right to reenter the property in the case of nonpayment of the rent, the majority of courts hold that an assignment still exists. Several states, however, disagree. Courts in these states contend that the reservation of a right of reentry constitutes a reversion in the tenant/assigner, thereby making the transaction a sublease.

To create the proper interpretive environment, it should be noted that courts do not favor restrictions on a party's right to transfer real property. The landlord must be careful in drafting the limitation in the lease on the tenant's right to sublease or assign, or a court may undermine it. The courts' attitude is framed by their general objection to any restraint on the freedom to alienate or transfer property. This attitude has resulted in decisions that a landlord's prohibition against subleasing did not prohibit the tenant from assigning. Similarly, once the landlord consents to an assignment despite a prohibition in the lease, the leasehold is freely assignable thereafter. Even so, a single waiver of the limitation on subleasing does not allow the tenant to sublease later without the landlord's approval.

Impact of an Assignment

At the beginning of the preceding chapter some care was taken to describe a lease as a conveyance of an estate in land as well as a contractual obligation. In the area of assignment the dichotomy is important. Upon taking a transfer by lease, the tenant enters into a dual relationship. Under the estate-in-land aspect of the agreement, the landlord and the tenant are said to have *privity of estate*. Under the contractual side of the agreement, the parties have created *privity of contract*. As explained earlier, privity connotes the mutuality that binds parties to their agreement.

A tenant who assigns the lease to a third person surrenders possession and transfers the *privity of estate* to the assignee. The assignee literally stands in the legal shoes of the tenant, since he or she received all that the tenant has, and privity of estate now exists between the landlord and the assignee. The assignee's right to possession makes him or her liable directly to the landlord for payment of rent. Possession automatically gives rise to the obligation to pay rent.

By way of contrast, there is no *privity of contract* between the landlord and the assignee. There is no contract, or mutual agreement to be bound, created by the assignment. An outgrowth of this is that the tenant/assigner continues to be bound by the terms of the lease-contract to the landlord.

As the result of privity of estate existing between the landlord and the assignee, the landlord can sue the assignee for nonpayment of rent. If, when the assignment takes place, the assignee agrees to assume the obligations of the lease and to be bound to the lessor for rent, he or she will have privity of contract with the lessor as well as the privity of estate previously discussed.

Sale of the Leased Premises

The landlord is free to convey the leased premises at any time. The buyer takes subject to the leasehold interest of the tenant. The buyer has the right to collect all subsequent rents once the tenant has been notified of the sale.

The buyer is the successor in title to the lessor's land; the tenant has an obligation, arising out of the notion of a conveyance of real property, to pay the rent to the new owner. It would not, therefore, be necessary to have an assignment of the lease, or the lessor's contract rights to the buyer, in order to collect the rent. However, unless the lease or contract provides otherwise, the lessor would continue to be liable for covenants he or she made to the lessee in the lease.

Mortgage of the Leasehold

Absent an agreement to the contrary, the tenant can mortgage the leasehold interest. The tenant can subject only the interest that he or she has (for example, a lease for five years) to the mortgage. There may be a greater than usual risk for the mortgagee because the tenant may fail to make rent payments, thereby defaulting on the lease and causing the landlord to retake the premises. When a forfeiture takes place, the mortgage is terminated.

To avoid this consequence, the mortgagee may covenant with the lessor that notice be given to the mortgagee prior to any forfeiture, thereby preserving the mortgage and permitting the pursuit of remedies against the lessee/mortgagor.

In most jurisdictions the mortgage of a leasehold estate is subject to the recording statutes. Thus, the mortgagee will record the mortgage to protect his or her priority rights in the land from being depleted by future conveyances of the tenant.

Landlord's Mortgage of the Premises

The landlord is free to mortgage the premises that are the subject of a leasehold estate at any time. The mortgagee's rights will be subject to the rights of the existing lessee. The mortgagee will be able to foreclose on the mortgage upon the lessor's default, but a subsequent sale, whether to the mortgagee or to a third party, of the leasehold premises will be subject to the possessory rights of the lessee.

Parties' Tort Liability

In general, the person who has possession and control of the premises owes a duty to third parties to maintain the premises in a reasonably safe condition.

The leased premises are normally in the possession and under the control of the tenant, and the tenant must use reasonable care in maintaining those premises in a safe condition. As a consequence of this rule, and the rule that does not require the landlord to repair or make the property habitable, generally the landlord owes no duty to the tenant or to third parties when they are injured as the result of a defective condition of the premises. However, the general rule is under siege where jurisdictions have adopted a warranty of habitability. It should be kept in mind, however, that technically warranty is a contract theory and the extent of damages recoverable in case of a breach may be limited to contract damages (the cost of repair, not personal injury).

Even without the modern warranty of habitability, there are exceptions to the rule holding that the landlord owes no duty in tort. When the landlord retains control over portions of the premises, such as stairways and halls, he or she will owe a duty to use reasonable care to maintain safe conditions. This is consistent with the general rule, since the landlord retains control of these areas.

In addition, where the landlord is aware of latent defects on the premises and fails to notify the unknowing tenant, he or she will owe a duty to the tenant and other third parties. Also, where the lease is for a furnished apartment and the tenant has no opportunity to inspect, the landlord will be liable in tort. Likewise, the landlord will be liable where he or she carelessly performs repairs.

Measure of Damages

Since the duty of the landlord to perform repairs grows out of the contractual understanding (the lease) or from a law-imposed contractual theory of warranty of habitability, it may be construed that the measure of damages owed is the cost of the repair; however, the trend is to permit recovery for personal injury and property damages as well.

To hold that the injured tenant or third party can recover only for the cost of repairing the premises seems a bit conservative in this day and age. Nevertheless, the conclusion is consistent with the contract principle of permitting recovery to the extent of mending the breach but not for the ensuing personal injury. Much of the area of landlord-tenant law is in flux, and this measure of damages is no exception.

Some courts speak of warranty as being a tort remedy as well as a contract action. Other courts reject the utility of the concept of privity (one must be a party to a contract to allow recovery against the landlord) in a modern world of broader expectations. It is no surprise then that there is a distinct trend toward permitting the recovery of tort damages when the landlord fails to repair the premises. Under tort damages the tenant or third party can recover for the personal injury and property damage resulting from the landlord's wrongful conduct, along with the cost of repairing the premises. This trend is consistent with the broader movement toward protection of the tenant.

Exculpatory Clauses

A lease clause by which the landlord attempts to excuse himself or herself from liability for negligence in maintaining the leasehold premises.

Under the premise that the parties can reach any agreement they choose, landlords often include an exculpatory clause relieving themselves of liability for their negligence. At the present time there is a sharp split among the courts as to the enforceability of these clauses. Some courts permit the enforcement of the clause because of the notion that the parties have the right to contract freely. The incongruity in this conclusion is the erroneous assumption that the usual leasehold agreement involves equality of bargaining position. At least in residential leasing, the tenant seldom has the freedom to negotiate the terms of the lease.

Conversely, other courts have held that the position of the landlord in exculpating himself or herself from liability for negligence, in a typically unbargained-for lease, defies sound public policy. Sanctioning of these clauses would also lead to the demise of the warranty of habitability, since all form leases would incorporate a waiver clause. The trend in the courts is to prohibit the landlord from exculpating himself or herself from responsibility.

SUMMARY

A lease creates obligations for both parties. These obligations arise both from the contract itself and from the law. Legal remedies vary according to the obligation breached and the relationships of the parties.

The landlord's lien is an early example of a legal means for providing security for the landlord in case of a tenant's nonpayment of rent. This device is not used widely today. The modern landlord almost always acquires the right to demand payment of rent in advance by a provision in the lease. Another widely used protective device is the security deposit, usually an amount equivalent to one month's rent. It is normally returned to the tenant at the end of the lease term, but it may be used by the landlord to defray the cost of repairing damages caused by the tenant or as security against any rent owed by a vacating tenant. Laws in a number of states penalize a landlord who mishandles security deposit funds.

Among the obligations the landlord owes the tenant are the covenant to deliver possession (that is, to make the right of possession available to the tenant at the start of the lease period), the covenant of quiet enjoyment (protection from intrusion by someone claiming better rights than the landlord) and the covenant of fitness of the premises supplemented by the warranty of habitability. All of these obligations vary from state to state.

If the tenant fails to meet the contractual terms of the lease, the landlord has several remedies. Eviction of the tenant, one example, is the legal procedure whereby the tenant is forced to vacate the leased premises. The landlord may also seek damages for unpaid rent or injury to the property.

Along with the duty to pay rent, the tenant's obligations include the duty to keep the premises in good repair, essentially as they were at the start of the lease, without causing waste. Although neither party is required to insure the premises, a tenant's failure to insure may result in an obligation to pay rent even after the leased space has been destroyed by fire or flood.

If the landlord violates the provisions of the lease, several remedies are available to the tenant. The tenant has recourse to the law when he or she is wrongfully evicted—that is, put out by the landlord without justification. On the other hand, a tenant may claim constructive eviction and thus be released from the lease if forced to vacate because of the condition of the property. Since this remedy, as well as withholding of the rent, may be risky and inconvenient for the tenant, other legal actions are available whereby the tenant may sue for correction of conditions.

The addition of a third party, either by a sublease arrangement or through an accident resulting in injury for a guest, further complicates the landlord-tenant relationship. Unless prohibited by the lease, a tenant may arrange to transfer all or part of his or her possessory rights to another party through sublease or assignment. Moreover, the premises may be sold to a new owner, in which case the tenant owes rent and other obligations to the new owner, who is legally bound by the terms of the lease. Finally, a tenant or guest can be injured on the premises. The extent of the landlord's financial responsibility depends upon many factors, including whether negligence can be proved, the laws and the attitudes of the courts in that state and the nature and extent of the injury.

REVIEW AND DISCUSSION QUESTIONS

1. List and briefly describe four techniques implemented to protect landlords from tenants who mistreat leased premises.
2. State the purpose of the Uniform Residential Landlord and Tenant Act.
3. The covenant of quiet enjoyment is breached upon actual eviction or constructive eviction by the landlord. Define the terms *actual eviction* and *constructive eviction*.
4. (a) What is the *warranty of habitability*? (b) What environmental change has caused this warranty to come into vogue?
5. Discuss the extent of the landlord's duty to repair when a building is destroyed by a catastrophe.
6. Define the affirmative defense of retaliatory eviction.
7. List and briefly describe three tenant's obligations arising either from his or her lease contract or by law.
8. When a lease agreement is not fulfilled by either of the parties, the injured party can seek several remedies. List the remedies that can be sought by (a) the landlord and (b) the tenant.

Explain the situations that would prescribe the use of these various legal remedies.

9. Discuss the reasons why restricting an injured third person to contract damages may be impractical.

10. What is an exculpatory clause?

11. "The parties should be left to the bargain they made." Discuss the appropriateness of this position in lease situations.

12. As they relate to the area of assignment of leases, define *privity of estate* and *privity of contract*.

CASE PROBLEMS

1. Prazma leased an old building from Scott. The lease provided that lessee was to surrender premises "in as good condition and repair as he took them, reasonable wear and tear and damages by elements alone expected." The lessee was under no obligation to make repairs. After Prazma occupied the building for about two years, an inspector found numerous violations, which he ordered brought into compliance with building codes and safety regulations. Neither Scott nor Prazma was willing to make the repairs, and Prazma moved out. Scott sued for the balance of the rent. Would Scott be successful? Explain. *Scott v. Prazma*, 555 P.2d 571 (Wyo. 1976).

2. Stefanik fails to vacate premises at the end of a term lease, holding over into a subsequent month. The owner has leased the property to Nunez. In the majority of American jurisdictions, would the owner or Nunez be obligated to remove Stefanik? Discuss.

3. Lubin owns an apartment in a college town. Many units in the building are rented to college students. Lubin retains keys to these apartments. From time to time she visits the tenants. Although she always phones first, if the tenants are not available she will use her duplicate key to enter. The main purpose of Lubin's visit is to ensure that the utilities, appliances and plumbing are functioning properly. If she does not interfere with the tenants' occupancy, is Lubin's conduct legally proper? Discuss.

4. Lubin leases two separate apartments on the second floor to Stearns and Forrest. The apartments are reached by a common stairway and hall. The plumbing in Forrest's apartment becomes inoperative, and a riser on the stair splits. Who is responsible for these repairs?

5. Stankiewicz was a tenant in an apartment rented to her by Hawkes. She was forced to vacate the apartment because its physical condition was a health hazard. Many items were left

behind when she moved. Hawkes entered the apartment and concluded that the items were abandoned. He instructed his workers to put them in a pile in the yard. As a result, the items were seriously damaged. Would the landlord's argument that the property had been abandoned be successful? *Stankiewicz v. Hawkes.* 4 Mass. App. Ct. 437, 350 N.E.2d 727 (1974).

6. Addison leased a unit in an apartment building from Seikely. He tripped over a loose board on an exterior stairway and was injured. He sued Seikely, claiming negligent maintenance of the common stairway. Seikely offers as a defense that a clause in the lease excuses him from liability for any injury incurred on the premises. Discuss the validity of Seikely's defense.

7. Dimmick, a tenant, failed to get satisfactory heat during the winter despite notifying the landlord, Cornell, of the problem. Believing that the furnace was faulty, Dimmick notified city code enforcement officials that she suspected code violations existed on the premises. Code officials inspected the property, found several code violations and notified Cornell that she would have to remedy the violations promptly. Shortly thereafter, Cornell gave Dimmick 30 days' notice that she was terminating the lease. The lease was an oral, month-to-month arrangement. What defense is available to Dimmick? *Cornell v. Dimmick*, 342 N.Y.S.2d 275 (1974).

27

Condominiums, Cooperatives, Real Estate Investments and Bulk Sales

The condominium and the cooperative afford techniques for obtaining an ownership interest in a dwelling or office. They are in many ways similar, but they also have marked differences. This chapter will focus initially on the condominium and will then describe and contrast the cooperative.

The chapter also discusses various types of real estate securities as well as the special form of real estate sales known as *bulk transfers*.

CONDOMINIUM

The fee simple ownership of one unit in a multiple-unit structure, combined with an ownership of an undivided interest in the land and all other parts of the structure held in common with the owners of the other individual units in the structure.

The concept of condominium ownership has blossomed in the United States since the mid-1960s. The notion of fee ownership, coupled with a release from the repair and maintenance chores of home ownership, made condominiums attractive to many people, especially to the elderly and to single-person households.

Condominiums did not present any fundamental legal problem. The common law had long recognized separate ownership of individual rooms or floors in a structure, which in essence is the nature of a condominium. Common or joint ownership of land and building was equally well established. Condominium ownership as a specific form, however, not only was new but also was a complex form of residential ownership. Describing the co-ownership, joint management, cross-easements and enforcement of individual responsibilities was part of the complexity. To provide some clarity and uniformity for this new area, states quickly began to adopt permissive condominium legislation. By 1968 all the states had adopted some form of condominium law. Although the terminology differs, there is a great deal of similarity in the statutes adopted by the various states.

This chapter discusses condominium ownership as it applies to residential units. The condominium form is also being used in commercial and some industrial property. The legal principles are the same, regardless of the use to which the condominium unit is put.

Formation of a Condominium

The developer may purchase an existing multiple-family rental unit for conversion into a condominium. Alternatively, he or she may purchase land and obtain a construction mortgage for erecting the condominium structure. The completed condominium units are then sold to individuals. The individual purchasing the condominium unit attains a fee simple interest in the apartment unit. In addition, the individual becomes a tenant in common with the other unit owners of the land and all structures outside the walls of the individual apartments. These are known as the *common elements*.

The apartment owner, if necessary, obtains a mortgage on his or her individual unit. Payment at the time of purchase is made to the condominium developer, who in turn pays off the construction mortgage as it pertains to that individual unit and its appropriate share of the common elements and has them released from the lien of the construction mortgage.

CASE EXAMPLE

Greg and Helene Burnside purchase a condominium unit from Condo Developers Inc. for $28,000. They obtain a mortgage on the unit for $21,000 from Security Bank, provide $7,000 of their own cash and deliver a check for $28,000 to Condo in exchange for a deed to the unit. Condo pays its mortgagee an amount sufficient to obtain a release for the Burnsides' unit and for one percent of the common elements. (There are 100 units of equal value in the development.)

Condominium Declaration

A document required by state law, which must accompany and be recorded with the master deed for the condominium development.

The declaration, one of three documents commonly mandated by state law, contains a description of the property, restrictions on use and the detailed legal requirements that attach to ownership of a condominium unit. The other two documents are the bylaws and the deed to each individual unit.

The declaration precisely describes the entire development, including land and buildings. It separately describes each individual condominium unit and details the common elements, or shared areas, of the development. It assigns a specific share of the common elements to each individual unit; it restricts the owners from severing their unit ownership from that of the common elements. Provisions are made for the creation of an association to administer the condominium and to levy assessments on the unit owners to pay for the operation and maintenance of the development. Enforcement mechanisms for delinquent assessments are also included.

Certain restrictions in the declaration are relatively common. For instance, a *right of first refusal* is generally provided to the association so that it can screen potential buyers of condominium units. When the existing owner of a unit has a willing buyer, the association is given a limited time in which to determine whether the prospective owner is satisfactory to the association. If not, the association can purchase the unit under the same terms offered by the buyer.

In addition, provisions are made for the contingency that the buildings might be substantially destroyed by fire or some other disaster. The declaration usually provides for its own amendment by a majority of the unit owners.

Condominium Bylaws

The rules governing the internal operation of the condominium development.

The bylaws of a condominium development are not unlike the bylaws of any organization. They provide for the selection of the board of directors of the association, meetings, regulations for the common elements, rights and responsibilities of unit owners, assessment and collection of monthly charges and other relevant matters.

Some state statutes require that the bylaws be recorded. One problem with mandating recording of the bylaws is that each amendment to them would necessitate further recording. The cost and inconvenience of recording may discourage amendments.

Condominium Individual Unit Deed

The deed for each individual condominium unit in the development.

Since the interior of each condominium apartment, along with a share of the common element, is owned in fee simple by the unit owner, the deed must be recorded to protect the unit owner from a fraudulent conveyance by the seller. In addition, it provides a chain of title that can be relied upon by a subsequent purchaser to ensure the marketability of the title. Each individual unit owner is entitled to apply for a mortgage in order to help finance the purchase.

Condominium Common Elements

The parts of the development property that are necessary or convenient for the residents of the condominium and are owned in common by all the condominium residents.

Each condominium unit owner has a tenancy in common in the land and buildings and other structures not constituting the interior of his or her individual condominium unit. This ownership interest is undivided; that is, all unit owners have an equal right to all the common elements.

The common elements generally include hallways, elevators, recreational facilities, land, stairways, exterior of the buildings and so on. Most state statutes specifically designate what items are included in the common elements. Where not so provided, they should be described carefully in the declaration.

The percentage of the common elements ascribed to each apartment unit may be equal where the units are quite similar. Where significant differences exist among the units, however, the percentage may be based upon the differing values of the individual units. In any event, the amount attributable to each unit is designated in the declaration.

The high-rise condominium has caused a distinction to be created between two kinds of common elements. *General common elements* are those previously described, in which all the unit owners share. In a condominium made up of townhouses all the common elements are usually general. *Limited common elements* that are shared by more than one unit owner but less than all of them may include stairways, balconies and elevators in divided sections of a high-rise condominium.

The state statutes generally provide that the expenses of administering, maintaining, repairing and replacing the common elements be paid for by an assessment of the unit owners made by the board of directors of the association. The board of directors is then responsible for repairing and operating the common elements. Unit owners are bound by the terms of the declaration to pay their shares of the assessment. Payment of the expenses cannot be avoided by waiving the right to use certain parts of the common elements. For example, a nonswimmer cannot reduce the monthly assessment by deducting an amount that would cover maintenance of the swimming pool.

If the association that administers the common elements is unincorporated, the individual unit owners are liable as principals for all authorized and apparently authorized acts of the association. Incorporation of the association, however, limits the unit owners' liability to the assets of the corporation.

Condominium Association

The organization stipulated by statute to administer the operation of the common elements of the condominium.

The association, and its board of directors on a day-to-day operational level, carries out the business of caring for the condominium. Members of the board of directors are the representatives of the unit owners and bear a fiduciary relationship to those owners. Their responsibility to the unit owners is multifaceted. For instance, their fiduciary duty to the unit owners requires that the board deal fairly and carefully with the business interests of the unit owners. It must avoid participation in decisions that present conflicts of interest for individuals. In short, board members can be held legally liable for mismanagement or for secretly profiting from that management. Board members are not relieved of liability merely because they are "volunteer" or unpaid.

Since the association is generally mandated by state law, it is quasigovernmental in nature. Its actions will probably be treated as "state action" and thus subject to the proscriptions in the constitution. For instance, when a unit owner is subjected to sanctions provided in the declaration for nonpayment of an assessment, the unit owner is entitled to due process (notice and hearing). Similarly, the right of first refusal cannot be utilized by the association to exclude prospective purchasers on the basis of race, creed, color, sex or national origin. Although the boundaries of constitutional responsibility of associations are unclear at this time, it appears certain that some restrictions such as those mentioned above will be imposed.

Condominium Assessments

The regular monthly payments for upkeep of the common elements, as well as payments required for

special expenses or improvements to those common elements.

State legislation generally provides that the bylaws establish the rules for regular and special assessments. The association's board of directors, or a project manager appointed by the board, normally collects the assessments and uses them in maintaining the condominium property. The original setting of the amount of the regular assessment, the changing of that amount and the imposition of a special assessment are determined by the terms of the bylaws. The bylaws are likely to place responsibility for establishing these assessments with the association or its board of directors.

• CASE BRIEF •

The newly elected board of directors of a high-rise condominium discovered that the building had serious structural defects and that the association was in debt. The board of the Tower West Condominium discussed the woes at length and then levied a $100,000 special assessment to be paid proportionately by the unit owners. Papalexion and several other unit owners refused to pay the assessment contending that according to the bylaws a vote of the full association was necessary unless there was "an extreme emergency." They argued that this was not such an emergency.

The court held that the unit owners had to pay the assessment. Based upon the structural problem and the poor financial condition of the condominium association, the board acted reasonably in concluding that this was an extreme emergency as intended under the bylaws. *Papalexion v. Tower West Condominium, 167 N.J. Super. 516, 401 A.2d 280 (1979).*

When a unit owner refuses or is unable to pay an assessment, he or she is subject to enforcement procedures that are usually stated in the bylaws. In at least two states the statute permits the association to cut off utilities ten days after notice of delinquency is given. The normal route, however, makes any unpaid assessment a lien on the property with priority over all other liens except those designated in the statute. Generally, the liens designated in the statute are the most common forms: tax liens, prior mortgages, mechanic's liens and the like.

The procedure for foreclosing on this lien is the same as followed under the state's mortgage foreclosure law, unless otherwise stated. At the foreclosure sale the association is permitted to purchase the delinquent unit unless the practice is proscribed by the declaration. The main disadvantage of the foreclosure procedure is that the other unit owners must bear the expense of the delinquency during what may be a protracted foreclosure action.

The association also has the option of bringing an action for money damages, and this action does not preclude the subsequent lien foreclosure action described above. If delinquency is caused by a unit owner's shortage of funds, generally an action for money damages is not advisable.

In states that have homestead laws, seizure of the place of residence may be prohibited. Often the residential condominium qualifies as the homestead. A second lien method that circumvents these laws is the trust and lien upon sale technique. This technique permits recovery of the delinquent amount from the proceeds at the time the delinquent unit is sold. Because the proceeds are considered to be in trust, the assessment lien must be satisfied prior to any distribution to the seller of the condominium unit. The legal implications for the buyer are unclear. A cause of action may lie against the buyer who obtains the proceeds prior to a satisfaction of the assessment lien.

Again, this technique may force the other unit owners to bear the burden of the delinquency for an extended period of time. However, it should circumvent the difficulty under the homestead laws existing for the previously described lien technique.

COOPERATIVE

A form of ownership in which the land and buildings are (usually) owned by a corporation; individual unit residents own stock in the corporation and have a proprietary lease in a specific unit or apartment.

Unlike the condominium unit owner, the cooperative owner or tenant does not have a fee simple interest in the apartment. Instead, the owner has shares of stock in the corporation that owns the land and building, along with a long-term *proprietary lease.* Occasionally, the cooperative ownership is in a trust or partnership form rather than a corporate form.

The notion of a proprietary lease connotes that, unlike typical tenants, the cooperative tenants participate in the running of the cooperative through their stock interest in the corporation. The participation may be direct, when an individual is elected as a member of the board of directors, or indirect, when voting for directors or giving opinions to the elected directors. Despite the proprietary nature of the lease, however, it continues to be a lease and is governed by landlord-tenant law.

• CASE BRIEF •

Sun Terrace Manor, a corporation owning a cooperative, sued in municipal court to have several tenants removed for failure to comply with the bylaws and regulations governing the cooperative. Sally Gonzalez, one of the defendant/tenants, was accused of subletting her dwelling without permission and of harassing other tenants. The municipal court denied that it had jurisdiction because this was a suit between a corporation and its shareholders and not a case of dispossessing a tenant.

The court of appeals reversed the lower court's decision, holding that the shareholder/tenant of a cooperative was a "tenant" for purposes of application of the state's landlord-tenant law. *Sun Terrace Manor v. Municipal Court, 33 Cal. App.3d 739, 108 Cal. Rptr. 307 (1973)*

Financing a Cooperative

In a typical situation an investor purchases a multiple-unit dwelling to convert it into a cooperative. To finance the construction, the investor takes out a mortgage with a bank for 80 percent of the dwelling's value. The remaining 20 percent is paid initially by the investor but is recouped through the issuance of stock in the cooperative corporation to the future tenants. Future tenants pay their share of the 20 percent by purchasing stock when they enter the cooperative. In addition, each makes monthly payments that cover his or her share of the mortgage payment as well as operating expenses.

In addition to the mortgage share, each tenant as part of the monthly rent will pay a share of any other debt, taxes and operating expenses. As in a condominium, the share of these expenses may be on a per-unit basis or may vary with the relative value of the apartment. The amount of the annual or monthly assessment is determined by the board of directors of the corporation.

DIFFERENCES BETWEEN CONDOMINIUMS AND COOPERATIVES

One difference between a cooperative and a condominium is the type of mortgage obtained. In the condominium each unit owner arranges for his or her own mortgage; in the cooperative there is a *blanket mortgage* for the entire unit. The blanket mortgage may be more difficult to obtain.

In the cooperative there are restrictions on the ability of the tenants to sell their interest. Generally, the tenant needs the approval of the board of directors for the proposed new tenant. This procedure is a little more stringent than the right of first refusal used in the condominium area. These restrictions on the cooperative go beyond the outright sale and may prevent a tenant from assigning or subletting his or her share of the premises. The purpose behind these restrictions is to assure that a compatible group of tenants is assembled in the cooperative.

The cooperative form of ownership has advantages for the tenant compared to the usual landlord-tenant situation. The tenant is not subjected to annual rent increases and does not risk having the lease terminated arbitrarily. The cooperative tenant has a long-term lease and participates in any decision to raise the rent.

Like the condominium owner, the cooperative owner or tenant is subject to an extensive set of rules and regulations governing the cooperative. Failure to comply with the terms of the regulations may permit the board of directors to cancel the tenant's lease or to take some other action provided in the rules for redressing the violation.

Upon the death of the tenant, any successor—an heir under the tenant's will or by law—must clear the screening of the board of directors. There is no automatic right on the part of successors to be able to continue the cooperative lease. This differs from a condominium, where the unit is owned in fee and can freely be passed on to successors.

There are some distinct advantages to fee simple ownership, of which the condominium owner is the beneficiary. The notion of fee ownership itself carries a certain feeling of security and psychological confidence that is not matched by the lease of the cooperative arrangement. Many of these advantages are tangible and specific.

The condominium owner is responsible for his or her own mortgage and is not as vulnerable to default as the cooperative owner, who shares a blanket mortgage with everyone else in the cooperative. The condominium owner can directly take advantage of certain tax benefits, such as property tax deduction, interest deductions, casualty loss deductions and depreciation allowance if the unit is rented, that are not available individually to the cooperative owners, although residential cooperatives may be able to take advantage of some federal tax benefits, such as property tax and interest deductions, if the cooperative is formed properly. Under Section 528 of the Internal Revenue Code, however, a condominium owner is permitted to make a tax-free contribution to the association for capital expenses, maintenance and operating expenses provided the association meets the requirements of Section 528. Thus, a condominium owner can make a tax-free payment to the association for a new roof or for the pool lifeguard. A payment for similar expenses to a cooperative would not qualify.

Upon the sale of a condominium unit, the owner can sell at market value and pay the reduced capital gains rate on his or her gain. The cooperative owner generally must sell the stock back to the cooperative at a stipulated price. Often the stipulated price is the original price.

Cooperatives can be troublesome during difficult economic times. Initially, it may be more difficult to get a blanket mortgage loan than to get a mortgage loan on an individual condominium unit.

Given the nature of the interdependence created by the blanket mortgage, the default of one or several cooperative owners can cause a default on the mortgage. Upon default all cooperative owners stand to lose their investments, even those who can afford to keep up their share of expenses. In a condominium, on the other hand, the default on an individual mortgage does not affect the other condominium owners. Nevertheless, the financial straits that caused the mortgage default are likely to prevent payment of condominium assessments; in this respect, delinquencies can place a financial strain on the other condominium owners.

One advantage the cooperative has over the condominium is that it is relatively easy to get rid of an incompatible tenant. A tenant who refuses to comply with the rules of the cooperative can be evicted in summary proceedings in most instances. Although a condominium owner who is in default on assessments can be ousted through a lien foreclosure, the procedure is likely to be more prolonged and expensive.

REAL ESTATE SECURITIES

Any arrangement whereby a person invests money in a common enterprise involving real estate with the expectation of attaining profits from the efforts of a promoter or some other third party.

A normal transaction for the sale or lease of real property is not a security within the context of federal and state security laws. When a person or promoter offers an interest in the arrangement to the public, however, it may become a security. On other occasions, a person will sell a business, and the assets include real property. Real estate securities and business opportunity sales have separate and distinct control schemes from the usual real estate transactions.

If the transaction constitutes the issuance of a security, unless exempted, the promoter must comply with federal and (probably) state regulations.

CASE EXAMPLE

Fafner offers a group of his friends and neighbors an opportunity to be investors with him in a piece of mountaintop property he is about to acquire. The property has multiple-unit housing on it, and the investors will share in the profits. This purchase is a real estate security and must be registered as described later in this section.

One of the chief federal regulations in the area of securities is the 1933 Securities Act. The language of Section 2 of the act covers any investment contract or profit-sharing arrangement and is therefore broad enough to encompass almost any real estate syndication. The key factors are that transactions be a common enterprise and that there be management of the investment by a third party for the benefit of a passive investor. When an agency or court makes the decision as to whether or not a transaction involves a security, the emphasis is on the substance and economic reality rather than on the form the transaction takes. In defining what is a security, or any other regulation hereinafter discussed, the investor must take care to research the provisions of the state "blue-sky" laws, which regulate security transactions as well.

Condominiums as Securities

The offering of a condominium unit is not normally treated as a security, but as a sale of real estate. Thus, the sale is not subject to the regulation of the Securities and Exchange Commission (SEC) or to similar state laws.

• CASE BRIEF •

Joyce entered a purchase agreement for a condominium unit, which he planned to use for his personal residence. Joyce sued the condominium project owner, contending that his contract was an "investment contract" and subject to federal securities laws. The security had not been registered, nor had Joyce received a prospectus as required by federal securities law.

The federal district court held that a condominium purchase does not fall within the definition of an investment contract. An investment contract presumes that the investor hopes to realize a profit from the investment due to the activity of a third party. This is not the case where a typical condominium is purchased as a personal residence. *Joyce v. Ritchie Tower Properties, 417 F. Supp. 53 (D. Ill. 1976).*

Nevertheless, several states have extensive regulations of condominiums as securities. In California, for example, all condominium sales are regulated as securities because the common areas are not under direct control of the unit owner. It is clear, however, that in any state if condominium advertisements or other documents make any reference to providing rental services for the buyer for the period the buyer is not using the condominium, the purchase will be treated as an investment contract and the above-mentioned security regulations will apply. For more detail, SEC Release No. 33-5347 (January 4, 1973) provides guidelines for determining when condominium offerings are securities.

If the security regulations apply, registration of the entire offering must be made with the SEC. About half the states follow the disclosure rule: the prospect must be fully informed so that an intelligent decision can be made. In the other states full disclosure as well as minimum standards of "fairness" apply to the condominium offering when treated as an investment contract.

Exemptions

Transactions that would otherwise meet the definition of a security but that have been statutorily excused from the law's restrictions.

Exemptions from registration are made in the case of two types of transactions: intrastate sales and private offerings.

Intrastate Offerings

This exemption is provided in Section 3(a)(11) of the statute and applies to offerings that are made *solely* to residents of the state where the offerer or issuer is a resident and doing business. A key word in this exemption is *solely*. If one sale is made to a single nonresident of the relevant state, or if the issue is not wholly owned by residents up to nine months after the distribution of the issue is complete, the exemption will not apply.

CASE EXAMPLE

Referring back to the earlier example, Fafner, using the intrastate offering exemption, sells a share in his mountaintop venture to Thorsen. It takes six months to sell the full interest in the investment. If Thorsen, prior to completion of the sale, sells her share to her brother-in-law who lives out of state, Fafner's offering would no longer qualify under the intrastate offering exemption.

To use this exemption, therefore, the promoter must have assurances that the purchasers do not intend to resell. The burden of proving this exemption is upon the promoter. For a sizable issuance it is very risky to rely on this exemption in light of its restrictive character. Note that, despite its exemption under the federal statute, the issue may have to comply with the state law regarding securities. An array of remedies is available against an issuer who has relied on the intrastate exemption but who has failed to meet all the requirements of the exemption. Recovery of damages for the price paid for the security, plus interest, is among those remedies. For further clarification of the meaning of this exemption, see SEC Rule 147.

Private Offering

This exemption applies to offerings that are made to knowledgeable investors who have adequate information to evaluate fully the risks entailed in the transaction. It is the intent of this exemption that the offering be made to investors who are adequately informed so that they do not need the protective umbrella of the SEC disclosure rules. The purpose behind the exemption is to exclude such issues from expensive and time-consuming regulations.

• CASE BRIEF •

When the SEC challenged an offering made to employees under the private offering exemption by Ralston Purina Company, the Supreme Court adopted a several-fold test in determining the availability of the exemption.

The court stated that these questions should be asked: Were the offerees the type of persons who could fend for themselves? Did the offerees have access to the same type of information that would appear in a registration statement? Were the securities purchased for the investor's own account? *Securities and Exchange Commission v. Ralston Purina Co., 346 U.S. 119 (1953).*

The determination of whether or not an offering is private is based on numerous factors, including the number of offerees, the sophistication of the offerees, the number of units in the issue and their denomination and the manner of the offering, that is, personal contact or public advertising. There are no hard and fast rules, but the SEC will weigh the above factors in deciding whether or not the issue is a private one.

The SEC has adopted a rule creating a "safe harbor" for those seeking to take advantage of the private offering exemption. Assurance of safety is based upon meeting three conditions. First, the offering is limited to 35 persons who do not purchase for resale. Second, all the offerees or their representatives must have the capacity to evaluate the merits and risks of the offering. Third, if a representative is used, the offeree must be financially capable of bearing the economic risk of the proposed investment. These are the major limitations, but the rule should be checked to assure compliance and the protection of the "safe harbor."

Registration of Securities

The listing of an issuance that meets the definition of a security—and is not otherwise exempted—with the SEC and (perhaps) with state officials.

Prior to making any offering of a nonexempt security, the promoter must register the issuance with the SEC. No sales can take place before the SEC declares the *registration statement* to be effective. During the period between the filing with SEC and its approval, the

promoter can make oral offers or even written offers by way of a preliminary prospectus, but no investor can be bound and no sale concluded until the registration is declared effective by the SEC.

CASE EXAMPLE

MacLeish has filed a prospectus and supporting documents
with the SEC. While waiting approval, he begins to contact potential investors, providing them with a copy of the preliminary
prospectus explaining the benefits of the investment. MacLeish
asks for no commitments from these prospects. There would be
nothing illegal about MacLeish's conduct.

If the promoter makes any sale prior to SEC approval, all investors
have the right to rescind the transaction and get their money back,
plus interest.

Prospectus

**A written document containing all the information
necessary for an investor to make an independent and
intelligent decision regarding a securities offering.**

The prospectus must be filed with the SEC registration and must be
provided to prospective investors. The registration also will include
the financial statements for the promoter's operation and the operating statements for the property (for example, statements indicating
the income received from the property for the past five years). Any
publicity regarding the offering should be avoided prior to filing with
the SEC.

The SEC, in examining the proposed registration, compares
the annual earnings history to the yearly cash distributions proposed
by the issuer. The SEC attempts to see that the information alleged in
the prospectus is complete and accurate; it does not pass upon the
merits of the issue.

For example, the SEC examiner explores the registration documents to determine whether the six percent annual return in investment asserted in the prospectus is realistic in light of past
performance. The examiner does not comment on the fact that a six
percent return, given existing market conditions, is a poor investment.

Under federal law the offeror is required to give full and fair disclosure and is not permitted to give advice on the wisdom of the investment opportunity. In some states the state regulatory agency also
evaluates the merits of the offering.

Forms of Ownership

The modes of ownership or ways of setting up a real estate syndication are varied. A simple vehicle such as concurrent ownership (tenancy in common), discussed in Chapter 5, can be used. Traditional forms of doing business—partnerships, limited partnerships and corporations —are utilized. Less common techniques such as trusts, particularly the real estate investment trust (REIT), have gained popularity.

Each method of ownership has its intrinsic advantages and disadvantages. Tenants in common retain direct individual control over their investment fates, but the death of a tenant can suddenly propel an heir into the ownership picture as an unwanted tenant. Partners can retain control over decision making, but, as with tenants in common, operational rules must be clearly provided or chaos may ensue. Partners avoid the dual taxation that exists in a corporate form but do not enjoy the limited liability of corporate shareholders. Limited partners enjoy some of the best of both the partnership world and the corporate world since they generally avoid dual taxation and have limited liability. Nevertheless, tax risks exist in the limited partnership technique in the form of income tax recapture penalties that may be imposed on the investor above the loss of the initial investment capital. Because of the additional risks, the limited partnership form has been confined largely to sophisticated investors by choice of both the promoters and the investors.

Each of these techniques is used broadly within and outside the real estate investment area. A complete explanation of them would require an entire textbook; they are usually covered in a separate course of study. It may be useful, however, to discuss in more detail the trust device and the real estate investment trust in particular.

Trust

**A legal relationship in which a grantor transfers legal
title to property to a trustee who manages the property
for the benefit of third parties, or beneficiaries.**

By creating a trust, the grantor in essence splits the title to the property into legal title and equitable title. The trustee holds legal title to the real property that forms the corpus of the trust, and the beneficiaries are the possessors of the equitable ownership of the corpus. The grantor may become a beneficiary.

CASE EXAMPLE

The five McKuen brothers have received a devise of a mountain resort property from their recently deceased uncle. Having no desire to manage the property or acumen for doing so, they create a trust by conveying the property to a trustee, a successful resort owner and person of high integrity, to manage the resort for their benefit. The brothers remain as beneficial owners of the resort property.

The trustee should be selected carefully and be a highly trustworthy individual. The trustee owes a fiduciary duty to the beneficiaries of the trust and so may not have a personal financial interest in the trust. The trustee must use a high degree of skill and care in activity for the beneficiaries and cannot treat them as arm's-length business adversaries. Despite the availability of legal remedies against a bad trustee, careful selection in the first place can prevent substantial grief and financial loss in the future. Trustees are confined to individuals and banks, since other corporations are generally prohibited from serving as trustees.

The duties, powers and other responsibilities should be spelled out carefully in the trust agreement. Because of the trustee's high level of responsibility, he or she will probably have to be well paid. But there are some distinct advantages to the trust arrangement. For instance, the trustee owns the land "as trustee" and, as such, can convey as trustee when necessary. This avoids having all the beneficiaries, who could number in the hundreds, sign the deed. Additionally the trustee is the "front person," the one known to the public, whereas the beneficiaries are not generally known. This may be advantageous in some situations.

For tax purposes a trust is treated like a separate entity. As in a corporation, the trust income may be subject to dual taxation, first as income to the trust and again as income to the beneficiaries. To avoid this extra tax bite the trust can be structured so as to pay out all income to the beneficiaries. In this way the trust is treated like a partnership for tax purposes, and the tax falls solely on the beneficiaries.

Real Estate Investment Trust (REIT)

A tax shelter that exempts certain qualified real estate investment syndications from corporate taxes where 95 percent or more of the ordinary income is distributed annually to the beneficiaries or investors.

The Real Estate Investment Trust Act was passed by Congress in 1960. The rules governing these statutory trusts are very complex and must be strictly adhered to by those attempting to take advantage of the form. The real estate investment trust can exist only where it is permissible under state law.

The REIT is a conduit for getting income to certificate holders while avoiding the taxation of the trust as a corporation that would normally occur. For example, a group of friends invest some funds by purchasing certificates in a REIT. The trustee of the REIT uses their money to purchase an apartment complex for the purpose of attaining a return on that investment through rental income from the units. The net profits from the rentals are distributed to the group of friends (and any fellow investor in the REIT). These profits are taxed as ordinary income to all the investors, but the trust does not pay tax on the distributed profits.

The four major conditions for creating a REIT are:

1. There must be 100 or more certificate holders.
2. A substantial portion of the REIT's income cannot be obtained from the purchase and sale of real property, but the major source of its income must be from passive investments, such as rents and mortgage interest.
3. The trustees must have centralized managerial authority over the trust.
4. At least 95 percent of the earned taxable income from the trust business must be distributed to the certificate holders.

There are some distinct advantages to using the REIT form, in addition to the avoidance of dual corporate taxation. Other factors include centralized management, limited liability to the investors and the availability of real estate experts to do the investing. Nevertheless, the investments are limited to rentals and mortgage interest and the like, and these may not provide the highest return on the investment dollar. Because of the size of trust distribution (100 or more certificate holders), the trust must generally register with the SEC, which is an expensive procedure.

Due to the complexity of the REIT qualifications, this simplified description of the procedure should not be relied upon by anyone interested in forming this type of trust.

BUSINESS OPPORTUNITY SALE

A bulk transfer of a major portion of a business's materials, inventories or supplies that also includes real estate.

In any transfer of property classed as a business opportunity sale, both buyer and seller should be aware that the rules of law applicable to the real property portion of the sale may differ from those that apply to personal property. The rule applies no matter how small the proportion of the total realty amounts to. Under the Uniform Commercial Code (UCC), sales of goods need be in writing only when the contract involves $500 or more. Under the Statute of Frauds, however, any sale of real estate must be in writing.

Generally, under state law any attempt to negotiate the sale of realty by other than the seller must be done by a licensed broker. A broker should be able to advise the party represented on the requirements that pertain to that sale of realty. It is unlikely that the same real estate broker will be equally skilled at giving advice on the bulk sale of personalty. The advice of an attorney is probably necessary.

Bulk transfers pertain to a sale of a major part of the materials, inventories or supplies of a business. These transfers are regulated by

Article 6 of the UCC. The real estate portion of a bulk transfer is not controlled by the UCC. This statute does mandate, however, that the buyer require of the seller a schedule of all property to be sold, a list of the creditors on any of this property and notice to those creditors of the forthcoming sale. The purpose behind these regulations is to prevent bulk transferors from selling out and not paying the creditors. Without this law the creditors would have no recourse in a situation where the buyer was unaware of the fraud and the seller has left for parts unknown. Under the protective umbrella of Article 6, the failure of the parties to the sale to comply with the requirements listed above will make the sale ineffective as to the business's creditors.

Strict compliance with Article 6 of the UCC assures that the personalty part of the sale will be effective. The real estate portion will have to comply with the usual prerequisites noted throughout this text.

SUMMARY

The condominium and the cooperative are devices by which owners acquire rights in individual units of a multiunit residential or office building. Many factors have combined to make the condominium popular, although until fairly recently condominium ownership was unusual in the United States. As a result of this new popularity the states have had to develop new laws and procedures for purchase of condos and for the protection of owners. For example, the declaration, a document now required by law in most states, must accompany the master deed for condominium development and must be officially recorded with it. The law also requires condominium bylaws and individual deeds to condominium owners.

The declaration contains the legal description and lists restrictions on uses and legal requirements for each unit. The bylaws are the rules governing the internal operation of the condominium development. The deed to each unit is similar to the deed to any real property.

Each owner, in addition to fee simple ownership of a unit, has part ownership in the common elements of the structure. These include areas such as hallways, staircases, lobby and grounds. To administer these common elements, the condominium association is formed. Each owner is assessed a prorated amount of the total expense for operation of the common elements. Methods for measuring and collecting these assessments are established in the bylaws. Remedies in case of nonpayment are stipulated by state statutes.

Another form of joint ownership is the cooperative. Individual owners in this form do not own their respective units; each owns a portion of stock in a corporation that owns the land and buildings. Instead of the fee simple interest enjoyed by condominium owners, the cooperative owner has a long-term proprietary lease, which is governed by landlord-tenant law.

A major difference between the condominium and cooperative is the type of mortgage obtained: each owner in a condominium obtains his or her own mortgage, while the cooperative usually carries a blanket mortgage on the entire complex. Taxation and liquidity benefits vary accordingly.

Some real estate transactions are subject to securities regulation. To qualify as a security, the real estate investment must involve a common enterprise and the expectation of profits through the efforts of a third party. The federal agency that regulates these sales is the Securities and Exchange Commission (SEC), created by legislation in 1934. Unless exempt, all sales that qualify as securities under the law must be registered with the SEC. Each investor must be furnished a written prospectus that contains all the information needed to make an independent decision.

Several types of ownership are available to the real estate investor who wishes to pool resources with others. A popular form is the real estate investment trust (REIT). This trust has tax benefits as well as other business advantages.

Business opportunity sales or bulk transfers are a special form of real estate sales covered by state law. Parties to such a sale are usually assisted by a licensed broker and normally should also have the advice of an attorney to assure compliance under the Uniform Commercial Code.

REVIEW AND DISCUSSION QUESTIONS

1. Match the following terms with their correct definitions:

   (a) declaration   (1) document prepared for each individual condominium unit in the development

   (b) bylaws   (2) document, required by state law, that must accompany and be recorded with the master deed for condominium development

   (c) individual unit deed   (3) document outlining the rules governing the internal operation of a condominium development.

2. What are the common elements in a condominium arrangement? Distinguish between general common elements and limited common elements.

3. A condominium unit owner surrenders in writing her right to use the swimming pool, one of the common elements. Does

that action relieve her of the responsibility of sharing the cost of maintaining the pool?

4. Describe the usual decision-making arrangements made for the operation of condominium units.

5. Compare and contrast condominiums with cooperatives.

6. Contrast a blanket mortgage with an individual mortgage and explain the use of each.

7. What conditions must exist before a condominium can be treated as an investment contract?

8. Roberta Geist is undertaking to promote a shopping center construction project. To obtain the necessary capital, Geist is considering offering shares in the venture to 20 business associates and friends.

    (a)   Geist and all the offerees live in Nebraska. Discuss with Geist the pros and cons of not registering with the SEC and utilizing the intrastate offerings exemption.

    (b)   All of Geist's proposed offerees are experienced businesspersons. Would you advise her to take advantage of the private offerings exemption? Why?

9. What advantages accrue to investors entering a joint real estate venture who use the real estate investment trust form?

CASE PROBLEMS

1. Roger Van Horn owns a retail card and gift shop. Van Horn enters a contract to sell the entire business to Joan Tost. On advice of counsel, Van Horn has prepared a list of the inventory, supplies and materials included with the sale and a list of creditors and has sent notice to those creditors of the impending sale. (a) If the land on which the shop is located is part of the sale, would Van Horn have to list the real estate as well? (b) Is your answer consistent with the purpose of Article 6 of the UCC?

2. Lynne Voyant inherited $50,000 upon the death of her rich uncle. Voyant is exploring investment possibilities and is considering investing in a real estate venture promoted by a friend, Percy Shifter. Shifter has assured Voyant that the investment is an excellent opportunity to make her money grow since the offering is registered with the SEC. Voyant has a premonition that there is more to consider than this. Clarify the situation for her.

3. Jon Chai sued Support, Inc., the corporate owner of the cooperative in which he was a resident and stockholder. Chai contended that issuance of the stock was a security within the definition of federal security laws. What would be the result?

result? Why? See *United Housing Foundation v. Forman*, 421 U.S. 837 (1974).

4. Enterprise, Inc., purchased an existing shopping center and converted the commercial rentals into commercial condominium units. Jack Jackson, owner and operator of Jackson's Drug Store, tenant in the shopping center, sues to enjoin the conversion, contending that (1) condominium formulation is illegal for commercial units; (2) the conversion requires the issuance of a prospectus; and (3) it is illegal to deny him a vote since the day-to-day operation of the common elements will be done by the board of directors and not all the members of the condominium association. Is Jackson correct? Why?

5. The original officers and directors of Avila S. Condominium Association contracted with Kappa Corp. to provide the association with recreational facilities. These officers and directors were also officers and directors of Kappa Corp. Other members of the condominium association sued the original officers and directors, contending that they were unjustly enriched as a result of their involvement with the Kappa Corp. Discuss. *Avila S. Condominium Ass'n. v. Kappa Corp.*, 347 So.2d 599 (Fla. 1977).

6. Northern Terminals, Inc., leased a combination gas station–retail grocery store to Leno. In the lease Northern Terminals agreed to install a "walk-in" cooler and a "modern island marketer" to be financed by an additional monthly rental payment and a small royalty on the gasoline sold. Subsequently, Leno failed to comply with the terms of the lease, and Northern Terminals sued for breach of the lease. Leno countered that the lease agreement was an unregistered investment security due to Northern Terminals' agreement to provide the cooler and marketer. Discuss. *Northern Terminals, Inc. v. Leno*, 136 Vt. 369, 392 A.2d 419 (1978).

Glossary

Abstract of Title A summary of all the recorded transactions, including deeds, mortgages, judgments and the like, that affect the title to a specific parcel of land.

Acceleration Clause A provision in a mortgage giving the mortgagee the right to declare the entire debt due and payable upon default.

Acceptance Assent to the terms of an offer.

Accord An agreement to substitute a different kind of performance for that originally contracted for.

Accretion Gradual increase in riparian or littoral property as a result of deposits of sediment made by a body of water.

Acknowledgment In conveyancing, the act by which a person who has executed an instrument goes before an authorized officer, usually a notary public, and declares that the instrument is genuine and executed voluntarily.

Action for Rent or Damages The landlord may permit, or be required to permit, the wrongdoing tenant to retain possession of the property and seek money damages for the landlord's injury.

Actual Notice Title information that is acquired personally by the interest holder.

Adjudicated Insane Has been declared insane by a court.

Adjustable-rate Mortgage A type of flexible-rate mortgage.

Administrative Remedies Remedies provided by the administrative agencies based on power granted in enabling act.

Administrator A person charged with administering the estate of an intestate decedent.

Adverse Possession Acquisition of title to real estate by means of wrongful occupancy for a period of time established by statute.

Affidavit of Title A sworn statement verifying facts that satisfy certain objections to title.

After Acquired Title   Title acquired by a grantor after the grantor attempts to convey good title.

Agency   A legal relationship in which one party, called the *principal*, authorizes another, called the *agent*, to act in the principal's behalf.

Alienation   Transferring ownership, title or interest in real estate from one person to another.

Alluvion   Land created by sediment left by a body of water.

Amortization   Repayment of a debt in periodic installments of interest and principal over a period of time.

Annual Percentage Rate (APR)   As defined in the "Truth-in-Lending" Act, the percentage that the total finance charge calculated on an annual basis bears to the amount of the loan or credit.

Anticipatory Breach   A breach of contract that occurs as a result of repudiating a contract before the date due for performance.

Appeal   Process in which a higher court reviews alleged legal errors made by a lower court or an administrative agency.

Assignee   A party to whom a right is transferred.

Assignment   Transfer of property right from one person (the assignor) to another (the assignee).

Assignor   A party who transfers a right.

Assumption   A contract between a grantor/mortgagor and a grantee in which the grantee agrees to assume responsibility for the mortgage debt.

Attachment   The act of seizing a defendant's property by legal process to be held by a court to ensure satisfaction of a judgment that might be awarded.

Attestation   The act of witnessing the execution of an instrument and subscribing as a witness.

Authority   Term used in the law of agency denoting the agent's power to perform acts authorized by the principal. (See also Express Authority and Implied Authority.)

Balloon Payment   The final payment under a contract, which is substantially larger than the previous installment payments.

Bargain and Sale Deed   A deed that conveys title but makes no warranties.

Bilateral Contract   A contract involving a promise in exchange for a promise.

Blockbusting   Inducing (for profit) the sale or rental of any dwelling by indicating that a particular class of person (for example, nonwhite) has entered or will enter the neighborhood.

Breach of Contract   The unexcused failure to perform an obligation under a contract.

Business Opportunity Sale   A bulk transfer of a major portion of a business's materials, inventories or supplies that also includes real estate.

Call   Term used to refer to the different monuments, courses and distances that make up a metes-and-bounds description.

Capacity   The legal ability to enter into a contract.

Caveat Emptor   Let the buyer beware.

Caveat Venditor   Let the seller beware.

Certificate of Title   A statement of opinion by an attorney that describes the status of the title to a parcel.

Certiorari, Writ of   A legal document in which a higher court orders a lower court to supply the record of a case that the higher court wishes to review.

Chain of Title   The recorded history of events that affect the title to a specific parcel of land, usually beginning with the original patent or grant.

Clean Air Act   A statute whose purpose is to cleanse, maintain and enhance the quality of the nation's air resource.

Clean Water Act (formerly Federal Water Pollution Control Act)   A statute whose purpose is to cleanse, maintain, and enhance the quality of the nation's water resources.

Closing   The final state of the real estate purchase transaction, when the deed and the purchase money are exchanged.

Codification   Collection and organization of judge-made law into a code or statute.

Cognovit   A confession of judgment that permits the landlord, upon default by the tenant, to obtain a judgment against the tenant without the need for formal legal proceedings.

Commitment   Used in mortgage financing to designate the lender's promise to loan a specified amount of money at an agreed-upon rate of interest.

Common Law   (1) law based upon written opinions of appellate courts (see Judge-made Law); (2) the traditional nonstatutory law of England and the United States.

Community Property   A form of co-ownership between husband and wife in which each has a one-half interest in property acquired through the labor of either during marriage.

Comprehensive Plan   A prerequisite for regulating land use. Its contents can range from a thorough master plan to a zoning code and map.

Condemnation   Legal action by which government acquires private property for a public use. Based upon the right of eminent domain.

Condominium   The fee simple ownership of one unit in a multiple-unit structure, combined with an ownership of an undivided interest in the land and all other parts of the structure held in common with the owners of the other individual units in the structure.

Condominium Assessments   The regular monthly payments for upkeep of the common elements, as well as payments required for special expenses or improvements to those common elements.

Condominium Association   The organization stipulated by statute to administer the operation of the common elements of the condominium.

Condominium Bylaws   The rules governing the internal operation of the condominium development.

Condominium Common Elements   The parts of the development property that are necessary or convenient for the residents of the condominium and are owned in common by all the condominium residents.

Condominium Declaration   A document required by state law, which must accompany and be recorded with the master deed for the condominium development.

Condominium Individual Unit Deed   The deed for each individual condominium unit in the development.

Consideration   A promise, act or forbearance bargained for and given in exchange for a promise, act or forbearance.

Constructive Eviction   An occurrence that results when the actions of the landlord so materially interfere with the tenant's enjoyment as to make the premises untenable.

Constructive Notice   The knowledge of certain facts that might be discovered by a careful inspection of public records, provided that such information is within the history of title, or discovered by an inspection of the premises.

Contingency Clause   A provision within a contract that makes performance under the contract conditional upon the occurrence of a stated event.

Contract   A promise or an agreement that the law will enforce.

Contract for a Deed   See Land Installment Contract.

Contract Zoning   Zoning in which an applicant will be granted a requested zone change only after contracting with the community to comply with certain covenants.

Cooperative   A form of ownership in which the land and buildings are (usually) owned by a corporation; individual unit residents own stock in the corporation and have a proprietary lease in a specific unit or apartment.

Co-ownership   Ownership of real estate in which two or more people have undivided interests.

Correlative Right, Doctrine of   A legal doctrine that prohibits depletion of a common pool of oil or gas. Sometimes applied to water.

Co-tenancy   See Co-ownership.

Counteroffer   A new offer made as a response to a person who has made an offer.

Covenant of Fitness of the Premises   An assurance that the premises are fit for habitation.

Covenant of Quiet Enjoyment   A warrant by the landlord that the tenant will have the premises free from interference by the landlord or anyone claiming better right to the premises than the landlord.

Covenant to Deliver Possession   The landlord promises to deliver the right of possession to the tenant at the time the lease is scheduled to start.

Curtesy   A common law estate that provided a husband with a life interest in all his wife's real property at the time a child was born of the marriage.

Damages   Money recoverable by one suffering a loss or injury due to breach of the contract.

Decisional Law   Law that evolves from published opinions of appellate courts (see Judge-made Law).

Dedication   The grant of real property such as a public street to a governmental unit for public use.

Deed   A legal instrument that conveys title to real property upon delivery and acceptance by the grantee.

Deed Absolute   An instrument in the form of a deed that the courts construe as a mortgage.

Deed in Lieu of Foreclosure   A deed in which a mortgagor conveys mortgaged real estate to the mortgagee, who promises in return not to foreclose on the mortgage debt, which is in default.

Deed of Trust   A legal instrument in which a borrower transfers real property to a trustee as security for a debt. The lender is the beneficiary of the trust.

Defeasance Clause   A provision in a mortgage that terminates it when the debt that the mortgage secures is repaid.

Defeasible Fee   See Fee Simple Defeasible.

Deficiency Judgment   A money judgment awarded to the mortgagee when funds obtained as a result of a foreclosure sale are insufficient to pay the debt.

Delivery   Surrender of possession and control of a document to a third party.

Disavow   Avoid a contract.

Discharge   The release of contractual obligations.

Diversity Jurisdiction   Power of federal courts to hear cases involving citizens of different states.

Dominant Estate   The parcel of land that benefits from an easement appurtenant; also called *dominant tenement*.

Dower   Life estate of a widow in one-third of any real estate to which her husband had legal title during marriage. (See also Inchoate Dower.)

Due-on-Sale Clause   A provision found in some mortgages requiring the mortgagor to pay off the mortgage debt if he or she sells the property.

Earnest Money   A cash deposit evidencing a good-faith intention to complete a transaction.

Easement   A nonpossessory interest in real property; the right to use another's real property for a particular purpose.

Easement Appurtenant   The right of an owner of a specific piece of land to benefit from the use of another's land. (See also Dominent Estate and Servient Estate.)

Easement by Necessity An easement that permits the owner of a landlocked parcel to cross a parcel of land of which the landlocked parcel formerly was a part.

Easement in Gross An easement that exists as a personal right apart from a dominant estate.

Ejectment A legal action to recover possession of real property.

Elective Share The share of a deceased spouse's property that the surviving spouse may claim if the decedent left no will or the surviving spouse did not receive the minimum specified by law.

Eminent Domain Right of the state to take private property for public use. Just compensation must be paid to the owner.

Enabling Legislation State statutory authorization granting a local government the right to regulate in a specific area.

Environmental Impact Statement (EIS) A statement describing and analyzing the environmental impacts of a proposed action.

Equal Protection The constitutional mandate that all people be treated equally under the law.

Equitable Mortgage A lien arising from a transaction that shows an intention of the parties to use some particular real estate as security for a debt.

Equitable Title The buyer's right to obtain ownership of real property upon payment of the purchase price.

Equity of Redemption The right of a mortgagor or another person with an interest in real estate to reclaim it after default but before foreclosure.

Escheat Reversion to the state of title to property of a person dying without heirs or leaving a will.

Escrow A process by which money and/or documents are held by a third party until the terms and conditions of an agreement are satisfied.

Escrow Agent The third party who is the depository in an escrow transaction.

Escrow Agreement An agreement that directs the escrow agent regarding terms and conditions under which the deed or other instruments are to be delivered to the parties and the disposition of the deed or other instruments on default.

Estate The extent and character of a person's ownership interest in real property. (See also Future Estate and Life Estate.)

Estoppel A doctrine that prevents a person from denying the consequences of facts or actions that lead another person to rely on them and suffer loss.

Estoppel Certificate A statement by a mortgagor that he or she has no defense against paying the mortgage debt; also indicates the amount that remains unpaid.

Eviction by the Landlord The term usually associated with the legal procedure by which a landlord has the tenant removed from the premises because the tenant had breached the lease agreement.

Exceptions in Zoning   Permitted uses provided for in the ordinance that are inconsistent with the designated zone.

Exclusive Listing   A brokerage agreement in which the seller gives a single broker authority to procure a buyer for the property.

Exculpatory Clauses   A lease clause by which the landlord attempts to excuse himself or herself from liability for negligence in maintaining the leasehold premises.

Executed   A promise that has been performed.

Executor   Person appointed to administer the estate of a decedent who died testate.

Executory   An unperformed promise.

Exemptions   Transactions that would otherwise meet the definition of a security but that have been statutorily excused from the law's restrictions.

Express Authority   Authority a principal confers upon an agent explicitly and distinctly. May be conferred orally or in writing.

Extension Agreement   Agreement by a mortgagee to extend the time that a debt is due.

Fair Housing   The term used to express a national policy against most types of discrimination in housing.

Federal Interstate Land Sales Full Disclosure Act   A statute intended to protect residential land purchasers from unscrupulous sellers.

Federal Question   A legal dispute that involves the U.S. Constitution, a treaty, or a federal statute. Federal question cases are heard by federal courts.

Fee Simple   The most extensive estate in real property that an owner can possess.

Fee Simple Defeasible   A fee simple estate that terminates upon the occurrence of a specified condition; also called a *qualified fee.*

Fee Simple Determinable   A defeasible fee that terminates automatically if a stated act or event occurs.

Fee Tail   An interest in real property that can last forever but ceases if no lineal descendents of the creator remain alive.

Fiduciary   A person who acts primarily for another in a relationship based on trust and confidence. A fiduciary is held to a high standard of conduct.

Finance Charge   Defined in the "Truth-in-Lending" Act as the monetary total of all charges a borrower must pay the lender for credit or a loan.

Fixture   An item that was personal property but has been permanently affixed to real property.

Flexible-rate Mortgage   A mortgage that contains a provision permitting the mortgagee to adjust the interest rate upward or downward in a manner specified in the mortgage.

Floodplains   Areas near waterways that are prone to flooding.

Foreclosure   A procedure in which property used as security for a debt is

sold in the event of default to satisfy the debt. (See also Judicial Foreclosure and Power-of-Sale Foreclosure.)

Forefeiture   The loss of the right to a down payment or real estate as a result
of a breach of contract.

Freehold Estate   An interest in real property created to last for an uncertain
period of time.

Future Estate   An interest in real property that will become possessory in
the future.

General Lien   A lien that applies to all property that a person owns.

Grantee   Person who acquires title to real property by deed.

Grantor   Person who transfers title to real property by deed.

Gross Lease   A lease in which a flat or fixed amount of rent is paid by the
tenant.

Ground Lease   A specialized type of net lease in which the lessor leases a
piece of vacant land to the lessee, usually with the stipulation that
the lessee at his or her own expense will construct a building thereon.

Growth Management Plans   Comprehensive growth plans that dictate both
when and where growth will occur.

Historic Preservation   The preservation of buildings, and perhaps archaeological sites, from destruction by new development.

Holdover Tenant   One who failed to vacate or surrender possession of the
premises on the ending date of a term tenancy.

Implied Authority   An agent's authority to do those acts necessary and
proper to accomplish the express terms of the agency.

Implied Notice   Legal notice that is imposed by the law when conditions
exist that would lead a reasonable person to inquire further into the
condition of the title.

Implied Warranty of Habitability   A warranty imposed by law on the landlord by which he or she warrants that a residential property is safe and
sanitary and fit for living at the time the tenant enters and during the
period of tenancy.

In Pari Delicto   At equal fault.

In Terrorem Clause   A clause in an installment contract that prohibits recording at the expense of forfeiture.

Inchoate Dower   The expectant interest of a wife to dower.

Indemnification   The act of compensating another in the event of loss.

Independent Contractor   A person who is retained to do a job, using his or
her own judgment as to how the work will be done.

Innocent Misrepresentation   An unintentional misstatement of a material
fact that induces justifiable reliance to the detriment of a party.

Inter Vivos Trust   A trust that takes effect during the life of the creator.

Interpleader   A legal procedure whereby a party deposits money into court
so that the court can distribute it to the rightful owner.

Intestate   A person who dies without leaving a will.

Intrastate Offering   An exemption from registration under federal securities law where the offering is made solely to residents of the state by a resident offeror doing business in the same state.

Joint Tenancy   Co-ownership in which the entire estate passes to the survivor upon the death of the other joint tenant or tenants.

Joint Venture   A business entity in which two or more persons agree to carry out a single undertaking for profit.

Judge-made Law   Law based upon the written opinions of appellate courts, called *precedent*.

Judgment Creditor   A plaintiff who has won a monetary judgment that has not yet been paid.

Judgment Lien   A lien that attaches to real property of a defendant when a plaintiff wins a judgment in the jurisdiction in which the property is located.

Judicial Foreclosure   A foreclosure ordered by a court.

Judicial Remedies   Remedies provided by the courts.

Jurisdiction   The power of a court to hear a case.

Land Installment Contract   A contract in which the buyer pays the purchase price on an installment basis. The seller/owner retains title until the purchase price is paid; also called *contract for a deed*.

Landlord's Lien   Under common law, the lien known as the right of distress provided the landlord with a lien on the personal property of the tenant where there was a failure to pay rent.

Large-Lot Zoning   A zoning classification that requires a minimum of one acre or more of land for each single-family house that is constructed.

Lease   A contract, either written or oral, that transfers the right of possession of the premises to the lessee or tenant.

Leasehold Estate   An estate created when the owner of property, known as the *lessor* or *landlord*, conveys a possessory interest in the real property to another, known as the *lessee* or *tenant*, for a specific period of time in exchange for the tenant's payment of rent.

Legal Notice   A knowledge of another's interest in real property sufficient to make the adverse interest legally binding to the prospective purchaser or any other party acquiring interest in the property.

License   A personal privilege to enter another's property for a specific purpose.

Lien   A claim against another's property securing either payment of a debt or fulfillment of some other monetary charge or obligation. (See also General Lien and Special Lien.)

Life Estate   An ownership interest in real property created to last for a person's life.

Limited Partnership   A partnership formed according to the provisions of a state limited partnership act. The liability of a limited partner is limited to the amount he or she has invested.

Limited Warranty Deed A deed in which the seller warrants against acts that he or she has done that might affect title; also called *special warranty deed.*

Lis Pendens, Notice of A notice filed for the purpose of warning people that legal action has been taken that might affect title or possession of specified real property.

Listing A contract between a seller and a broker authorizing the broker to find a buyer for real property upon specified terms in return for a fee if the broker is successful. (See also Exclusive Listing and Open Listing.)

Littoral Lands Lands that border on an ocean, a sea or a lake.

Long-term Escrow A financing device that combines the land installment contract and the escrow.

Marketable Title Title that is free of liens or other encumbrances that interfere with the peaceful enjoyment of the property.

Mechanic's Lien The right of one who renders services or supplies materials in connection with improvements to real property to seek a judicial sale of the realty to satisfy unpaid claims.

Metes and Bounds A method of describing land using compass directions, monuments or landmarks, and linear measurements.

Mistake Unintentional error.

Mortgage A document that uses real property to secure payment of a debt.

Mortgagee A lender who acquires an interest in a borrower's real property as security for repayment of the loan.

Mortgagor A borrower who gives a lender an interest in the borrower's real property to secure payment of a loan.

Multiple Listing A contract among brokers who as members of a multiple-listing exchange agree to share listings with each other.

Negative Amortization When periodic payments on an amortized loan do not cover all the interest that is due, the unpaid amount is added to the principal. This is referred to as *negative amortization.*

NEPA Statute requiring the preparation of a document detailing environmental data and analyzing that data regarding a proposed government action.

Net Lease As contrasted with the gross lease, a type of lease in which the tenant agrees to pay the taxes, insurance, repairs and other operating expenses of the premises.

Nonconforming Use A legal use that was established prior to zoning or prior to the present zoning classification and is permitted to continue despite its nonconformance with the zoning code.

Note The borrower's written promise to repay a loan according to its terms.

Notice Statutes Statutes that provide that the subsequent buyer prevails over all interested parties who have not recorded their interest at the time the buyer accepts the conveyance and pays consideration for the land without notice of the preexisting conveyance.

Novation An agreement in which a creditor agrees to discharge an existing debt and to substitute a new obligation and a new debtor in its place.

Nuisance An unreasonable interference by one party with another's use or enjoyment of his or her land.

Offer A proposal intended to create a contract upon acceptance by the person to whom it is made.

Open-end Mortgage A mortgage that permits the mortgagor to borrow additional funds, usually up to the original amount of the debt.

Open Listing A brokerage agreement that entitles the broker to a fee only if his or her activities bring about the sale. The property may be listed with several brokers.

Option A contract that gives a person a designated period of time to buy or lease real property at a specified price.

Optionor One who agrees not to revoke an offer.

Optionee One who is the recipient of an option.

Package Mortgage A mortgage debt secured by both personal and real property.

Parol Evidence Oral or other evidence extraneous to a written contract.

Partition A legal action in which a co-owner obtains a division of real property, terminating any interest of other co-owners in the divided portion. Each former co-owner's share is now owned individually.

Party Wall A single wall on the boundary of adjoining properties; it serves as a common support for buildings on each of two parcels.

Per Capita Distribution of an intestate's property in equal shares to persons who have the same relationship to the decedent without reference to the share an ancestor would have taken.

Per Stirpes Distribution of an intestate's property to persons who take only the share that an ancestor would have taken.

Percentage Lease A lease whose rental is based in part on the gross sales made by the tenant on the premises.

Percolating Water Water that passes through the ground, not flowing in a clearly defined underground stream or supplied by streams flowing on the surface.

Perfection (1) Legal steps necessary to establish a valid mechanic's lien; (2) acts by which a secured party establishes priority in collateral over claims of third parties.

Performance Standards Zoning Standards set to limit the adverse off-site impact of an owner's use. For example, standards can be established for odors, noise and signs.

Periodic Tenancy An estate from period to period, continuing from period to period until terminated by proper notice from one of the parties.

Personal Property Property that is not real property; generally characterized as having substance and being movable.

Planned Unit Development (PUD) A concept involving a development larger than a traditional subdivision, generally permitting mixed uses within the development and attempting to provide a maximum amount of land for open space.

Plat A map of a subdivision indicating boundaries of individual properties. Also includes details such as lot numbers, blocks, streets, public easements and monuments.

Possibility of Reverter A possibility that an estate based upon a condition may revert to the grantor if the grantee or those who take through the grantee breach the condition.

Power of Attorney A document authorizing a person, the attorney-in-fact, to act as agent on behalf of another as indicated in the instrument.

Power-of-Sale Foreclosure Foreclosure based on terms in a mortgage giving a mortgagee or third party the power to sell the security if the borrower defaults.

Power of Termination The future interest that a grantor of an estate on condition subsequent has to terminate the estate if the condition occurs; also called *right of reentry.*

Precedent A published opinion of an appellate court that serves as authority for determining a legal question in a later case that has similar facts.

Prescription Acquisition of an easement through wrongful use of another's land for a period of time designated by statute.

Prior Appropriation Water rights doctrine giving primary rights to first users of water.

Private Offering An exemption from registration under federal securities law for offerings made to knowledgeable investors who have adequate information to evaluate fully the risks in the transaction.

Probate The legal proceeding that establishes the validity of a will.

Profit A nonpossessory interest in real property permitting the holder to remove part of the soil or produce of the land.

Promissory Estoppel A doctrine that prevents a party from denying that a promise is supported by consideration.

Property Legal rights that a person possesses with respect to a thing; rights that have economic value.

Prorate To divide or allocate proportionately.

Prospectus A written document containing all the information necessary for an investor to make an independent and intelligent decision regarding a securities offering.

Puffing Statements of opinion made by a seller to induce the purchaser to buy.

Punitive Damages Damages awarded as a punishment to the wrongdoer. Punitive damages are added to damages actually incurred.

Purchase Money Mortgage A mortgage given to a buyer to secure part of the purchase price of real property and delivered contemporaneously with the transfer of title to the buyer.

Pure Race Statutes   Statutes that provide that the first person who records an instrument prevails over all other takers from the same source. It is not relevant that the first recorder and prevailing party had notice of the prior transactions.

Quitclaim Deed   An instrument that conveys whatever title the grantor has.

Race-Notice Statutes   Statutes that provide that a subsequent buyer will prevail only if he or she has no notice of the prior transaction at the time of conveyance.

Ratify   Approve a contract.

Real Estate Investment Trust (REIT)   A tax shelter that exempts certain qualified real estate investment syndications from corporate taxes where 95 percent or more of the ordinary income is distributed annually to the beneficiaries or investors.

Real Estate Purchase Contract   An agreement whereby a seller promises to sell an interest in realty by conveying a deed to the designated estate for which a buyer promises to pay a specified purchase price.

Real Estate Securities   Any arrangement whereby a person invests money in a common enterprise involving real estate with the expectation of attaining profits from the efforts of a promoter or some other third party.

Real Estate Settlement Procedures Act (RESPA)   A federal law that requires lending institutions to disclose certain information to purchasers of residential real estate and prohibits those institutions from engaging in certain fraudulent activities.

Real Property   Land, buildings and other improvements permanently affixed to land.

Receivership   Appointment by a court of a disinterested party to manage or operate mortgaged property during foreclosure.

Recording Statutes   Laws that require the entry into books of public record the written instruments affecting the title to real property.

Redlining   Denial of a loan by a lending institution or the exacting of harsher terms for loans in certain parts of a city.

Regional Planning   Planning done along broad, physical environment lines rather than traditional political lines.

Registration of Securities   The listing of an issuance that meets the definition of a security—and is not otherwise exempted—with the SEC and (perhaps) with state officials.

Rejection   An offeree's refusal or failure to accept an offer.

Relation Back   A legal doctrine whereby the title acquired by a deed relates back to the moment of the first delivery to an escrow agent.

Release of Mortgage   See Satisfaction of Mortgage.

Reliction   Land created when water recedes.

Remainder   A future interest in real estate created when a grantor conveys less than fee simple and by the same instrument directs another estate to arise immediately upon the termination of the prior estate.

Rent Withholding   The practice, allowed in a few states under limited circumstances, in which the tenant withholds rent as an inducement to force the landlord to perform repairs.

Rescission   A cancellation of a contract that results in the parties being restored to the position they were in before the contract was made.

Respondeat Superior, Doctrine of   The legal doctrine that an employer is liable for the wrongful acts of employees done within the scope of their employment.

Restrictive Covenant   A provision in a deed limiting the uses that may be made of the property.

Reversion   A future interest in real estate created by operation of law when a grantor conveys a lesser estate than he or she possesses.

Revocation   An offeror's act of withdrawing an offer.

Right of Reentry   See Power of Termination.

Right of Possession   In all jurisdictions the right of possession implicitly resides in the tenant; that is, no one will have possessory rights inconsistent with those granted to the tenant.

Right of Survivorship   A characteristic of some forms of co-ownership by which the surviving cotenant acquires the entire estate.

Riparian Lands   Lands that border on a stream or watercourse.

Riparianism   Water rights doctrine based on the idea that all owners of riparian lands are entitled to share equally in the use of water.

Rollover Mortgage   A mortgage that must be refinanced every few years in order to adjust the interest rate up or down in response to prevailing market conditions.

Rule of Capture   A legal principle of oil and gas law allowing a land owner the right to all oil and gas from wells on his or her land, including oil and gas migrating from the land of others.

Run with the Land   Rights in real property that pass to successive owners are said to run with the land.

S Corporation   A corporation that has elected to be treated as a partnership for tax purposes.

Satisfaction   The performance of an agreement to substitute a different kind of performance for that originally contracted for.

Satisfaction of Mortgage   A written statement by the mortgagee that the debt secured by the mortgage has been paid, also called a *release of mortgage*.

Scienter   In fraud action, knowingly making a false statement or asserting that something is true without actual knowledge.

Section   An area of land approximately one mile square, containing as nearly as possible 640 acres.

Security Deposit   Money deposited by the tenant, usually at the inception of the lease, over and above the advance payment of rent for the security of the landlord.

Segregation in Housing   The voluntary or enforced separation of one group from another in residential location based on religious association, ethnic background, race or a combination of these factors.

Seisin   Ownership of real property.

"Separate but Equal" Facilities   A concept that permitted the state to enforce separation of the races so long as each race was provided with "equal" services or facilities.

Separate Property   In community property jurisdictions, property owned by either spouse prior to marriage and property acquired during marriage by gift, inheritance or will.

Servient Estate   The parcel of land that is subject to an easement appurtenant; also called *servient tenement.*

Settlement Clerk   The person who is designated to coordinate the exchange of documents at the closing.

Special Lien   A lien that applies only to a designated property.

Special-Use Permit   A system whereby special exceptions to the zoning ordinance are granted by the land use administrator under a permit arrangement.

Specific Performance   A court decree mandating a party to perform according to the contract.

Spot Zoning   A zone change permitted by the local legislature that is not in harmony with the comprehensive plan for that area.

Statute of Distribution   English law enacted in 1670 providing for the distribution of an intestate's personal property. Many state statutes providing for the distribution of an intestaste's property are patterned after this statute.

Statute of Frauds   A statute that necessitates that certain contracts, in order to be enforceable, be supported by a written memorandum and signed by the party against whom enforcement is sought.

Statutory Law   Law enacted by local and state legislative bodies and by Congress.

Statutory Right of Redemption   The right of a mortgagor to redeem the property after a foreclosure sale.

Strict Foreclosure   A judicial procedure that terminates the mortgagor's equity of redemption and establishes the mortgagee's absolute title to mortgaged real property.

Subdivision Regulations   Restrictions on the division of a parcel of land into two or more units. A subdivision will require prior approval by an administator such as a planning board.

Subject to   As used in financing the purchase of real property, a sale in which an existing mortgage on the property is not paid off. The buyer paying only for the seller's equity.

Sublease   A transfer of part of the leasehold interest of the tenant, with the tenant retaining a reversionary interest.

Subordination Agreement   As used in mortgage financing, an agreement in which a mortgage surrenders a priority lien and accepts a junior position in relationship to other liens or claims.

Substantial Performance   The amount of compliance under the terms of a contract that discharges a party from further obligation although failing to perform totally under the contract.

Taking   A regulation that deprives the owner of all reasonable use of the land constitutes a de facto taking of the property without due process of law under the Fifth and Fourteenth Amendments to the Constitution.

Tenancy at Sufferance   Created when a person is wrongfully in possession of another's land without a valid lease.

Tenancy at Will   A tenancy that exists until either party chooses to terminate it.

Tenancy by the Entirety   Co-ownership of real property by husband and wife. The right of survivorship is a characteristic of a tenancy by the entirety.

Tenancy in Common   A form of co-ownership in which each owner possesses an undivided right to the entire property. Shares of co-owners need not be equal, and no right of survivorship exists.

Tenancy in Partnership   A form of co-ownership in which each partner owns partnership property along with all other partners.

Tender   An offer of money or property as required by the contract.

Tenure   An historic system of holding lands, a characteristic of which was the possessor's subordination to some superior to whom the possessor owed certain duties.

Term Tenancy   An estate for a specified period of time that has a specific beginning date and a specific ending date. When the ending date arrives, the estate is terminated without notice by either party.

Testamentary Trust   A trust that does not take effect until the death of the creator.

Testator   A person who dies leaving a will.

Third-Party Beneficiary   A person who is allowed to enforce a contract although not a party to it.

Third-Person Guaranty of Rent   The landlord who has doubts about the capacity or reliability of the tenant in meeting the conditions of the lease may require a third person to guarantee performance.

Title   The totality of rights and obligations possessed by an owner; evidence of ownership.

Title Insurance   The comprehensive indemnity contract that insures the titleholder against title defects and encumbrances that may exist at the time the policy is issued.

Torrens Certificate   A document issued under the Torrens system, a type of land title registration.

Township   An area of land approximately six miles square, containing as nearly as possible 23,040 acres and divided into 36 sections.

Trade Fixtures   Items added to land or buildings by a tenant to be used in the tenant's trade or business.

Traditional Zoning   Zoning based on classifying land into use districts, such as residential, commercial and industrial uses.

Transferable Development Rights   A system of land controls that permits the transfer of the right to develop from sites that are desired to be preserved to sites on which maximum development is desirable.

Trespass   A wrongful, physical invasion of the property of another.

Trust   A legal relationship in which a person transfers legal title to property to a trustee who manages it for the benefit of third parties, the beneficiaries of the trust. (see also Inter Vivos Trust and Testamentary Trust.)

Unconscionable Contract   A contract that a court may render unenforceable because it is grossly unfair.

Underground Streams   Subterranean waters that flow in clearly defined channels discoverable from the earth's surface.

Undivided Interest   Interest of a co-owner that gives him or her the right to possession of the entire property along with other co-owners (see Co-ownership).

Undue Influence   The exertion of dominion over another person that destroys that person's ability to exercise independent judgment.

Uniform Partnership Act   A model act that establishes the legality of the partnership form of ownership.

Uniform Settlement Statement   A closing statement required for all federally related residential first mortgages.

Unilateral Contract   A contract involving a promise in exchange for an act.

Usury   The practice of charging interest on a loan in excess of a rate allowed by law.

Variable-Rate Mortgage   A type of flexible-rate mortgage.

Variance   Permission obtained from the appropriate governmental authorities to deviate somewhat from the designations under the zoning code.

Vendor's Lien   The right of a seller to a lien against land conveyed for any unpaid or unsecured portion of the purchase price.

Voidable   A contract that may be voided or validated at the option of a party.

Warranty Deed   A deed that conveys title and warrants that title is good and free of liens and encumbrances. (See also Limited Warranty Deed.)

Waste   Damage caused by the tenant, including failure to protect the premises from decay and ruin caused by the natural elements.

Wetlands   Lands that have groundwater levels at or near the surface for much of the year or that are covered by aquatic vegetation.

Wraparound Mortgage   A second mortgage covering an existing mortgage that the lender agrees to service.

Wrongful Abandonment   The tenant's vacating of the premises without jus-
    tification and with the intention of no longer performing under the
    terms of the lease.

Wrongful Eviction   An act that occurs when the landlord without justifica-
    tion deprives the tenant of the possession of the premises.

Zone Change   A zoning amendment made by the legislative body that cre-
    ated the zoning code.

Zoning   The regulation by the public, usually a municipality, of structures
    and uses of land within designated zones.

Alphabetical Index of Cases

Subject Index
of Cases

Index